STRAVINSKY

Igor Stravinsky with the author, Hollywood, June 1968.
(Photo by Bobby Klein)

Robert Craft

VINSKY

F A FRIENDSHIP   1948-1971

Alfred A. Knopf, New York   1972

THIS IS A BORZOI BOOK
PUBLISHED BY ALFRED A. KNOPF, INC.

Library of Congress Cataloging in Publication Data

Craft, Robert.   Stravinsky; chronicle of a friendship, 1948–1971.

1. Stravinskiĭ, Igor' Fedorovich, 1882–1971.   ML410.S932C8   780'.924 [B]
79–173776   ISBN 0–394–47612–3

FIRST EDITION

Manufactured in the United States of America

Portions of this book originally appeared in *The New York Review of Books, Harper's,*
and *Vogue.*

Grateful acknowledgment is extended to the following to reprint copyrighted material:

Harper & Row, Publishers, Faber & Faber Ltd., and Olywyn Hughes: Lines from "Face
Lift" from *Crossing the Water* by Sylvia Plath. Copyright © 1971 by Ted Hughes.

Alfred A. Knopf, Inc.: From *Themes and Episodes* by Robert Craft and Igor Stravinsky.
Copyright © 1964, 1965, 1966 by Robert Craft. Also from "From the Diaries of Robert
Craft, 1948–1968," in *Retrospectives and Conclusions* by Igor Stravinsky and Robert Craft.
Copyright © 1966, 1968, 1969 by Robert Craft.

Random House, Inc.: Lines from "Metalogue to the Magic Flute," from *Collected Shorter
Poems* by W. H. Auden. Copyright © 1955 by W. H. Auden.

I.S. and V.

They went quietly down into the roaring streets, inseparable and blessed; and as they passed along in sunshine and shade, the noisy and the eager, and the froward and the vain, fretted and chafed, and made their usual uproar.

Little Dorrit

But, O the heavy change now thou art gone.

Lycidas

A Personal Acknowledgment

Many people have read this book, or portions of it, and I am grateful to them for corrections and improvements. But I owe more to the late Herbert Weinstock than to anyone else. It is not generally known that for the last decade he was Igor Stravinsky's editor, as well as my own. But it should be known that Stravinsky respected his intelligence, and appreciated his care and his unfailingly sound advice. Shortly after reading this manuscript, Herbert Weinstock encouraged me to write a biography of the composer and convinced me to try. I shall do my best to meet his high standards, but I will miss him and miss his help.

R.C.

October 22, 1971

Contents

Illustrations

Listening to the author rehearse *Perséphone* with the New York Philharmonic, Carnegie Hall, January 1957.

Feeding cats in the Campiello "Drio la chiesa San Fantin," September 1957.

The author with W. H. Auden in the Martini Restaurant, Venice, after the première of *Threni,* September 23, 1958.

Rehearsal of *Threni* at the Metropolitan Museum of Art, New York, January 1959.

At the ruins of Pachacamac, Peru, August 18, 1960.

Stravinsky with the author, recording the *Movements* for Piano and Orchestra, 1961.

FOLLOWING PAGE 300

At Lewisohn Stadium, New York, July 11, 1962.

With Mme Furtseva, the Minister of Culture, and Mr. and Mrs. Dmitri Shostakovich; Moscow, 1962.

At a rehearsal conducted by the author, Moscow, 1962.

Applauding the author's performance of *The Rite of Spring,* Moscow, 1962.

The *dramatis personae* on the S.S. *Bremen,* April 1963.

At home, with dictionary, 1967.

On his eighty-fifth birthday, Coronado Beach.

At home, a year later.

The *dramatis personae,* two decades down, New York, September 24, 1968.

Hôtel Royale, Evian, August 1970.

The Essex House, New York, March 1971, with Mme Natasha Nabokov.

A wall in Venice, April 13, 1971.

Approaching San Michele, April 15, 1971.

Preface

This book of pericopes from a chronicle of twenty-three years represents only about a third of the whole. It is incumbent on me, therefore, to explain my principles of selection. But readableness—comparative readableness, anyway—is the only one. It is the reason that the fifties are so thinly represented, for my actual notes covering the first decade of my association with Stravinsky are more voluminous than those dealing with the second decade, but they are in no sense "written-up," and are personal in a way that this book is not. They can be used only in the different medium of the biography.

A broken chain of events, then, which I can repair only to the extent of showing the position of each link in a fuller itinerary. This skeleton schedule amazed me when I was compiling it and it continues to amaze me now. How could a man so constantly in orbit compose so much new-thought music, conduct so much, read and write so much, and accomplish so much else? I was a third of his age when I first knew him, and half of his age at the time of his last compositions, yet I could not keep pace with him even physically.

His concert tours inevitably account for the contents of the book, as well as for some of the lack of contents: the absence, for example, of any description of the concerts themselves, except in the U.S.S.R., where they revealed so much of Stravinsky the man. My excuse is simply that I was too busy conducting to write, rehearsing not only my own portions of his concerts, but his share in them as well, in the later years trying to prepare the music so that little more than a run-through would be required of him.

But the rarity and brevity of the close-ups of Stravinsky himself in the middle part of the book is a more serious fault, and, in truth, my title is a misnomer. Only the very beginning and the last two-fifths of the book focus directly on Stravinsky. It goes without saying that those are the most valuable parts, and that the reader is invited to skip between them, especially the reader uninterested in Lascaux, the Japanese theater, and other irrelevant matter which I nevertheless retain, "for the record."

"Didn't Stravinsky know any ordinary people?" one critic has asked. And though the answer is obvious, perhaps these pages do contain an overdose of poets, painters, writers, and philosophers. (They do *not* contain, in some cases do not even mention, the Stravinskys' closest friends, both because I did not wish to involve them and because some of these people, who have seen Stravinsky in a different way than I have—I was often too close to see him at all—will make their own contributions to his portrait.) However that may be, I lack the novelist's talent that can make "ordinary" people interesting, whereas the extraordinary ones take care of themselves, with little help from me. According to Coleridge, "An inquisitiveness into the minutest circumstances or casual sayings of eminent contemporaries is . . . quite natural." It is also self-destructive, for recorders of the sayings of the eminent are a hapless breed, more abused than thanked for their labors, which in any case seldom live by their own merits, or even die peacefully for lack of them, but merely hang on as pendants.

I should mention that Stravinsky himself was a sometime diarist, and Vera Stravinsky a consistent one, both during the Russian Revolution and again in the years of this book, for which reason I have checked my records with hers.

R.C.
Venice
July 20, 1971

Look, what thy memory cannot contain.

Sonnett LXXVII

STRAVINSKY

1948
1949
1950
1951
1952
1953
1954
1955
1956
1957
1958
1959
1960
1961
1962
1963
1964
1965
1966
1967
1968
1969
1970
1971

February 7: I.S.'s to San Francisco by train. **12, 14:** I.S. conducts concerts in San Francisco. **16:** I.S.'s to Los Angeles by train. **20:** I.S.'s fly to Mexico City. **27:** I.S. conducts concert in Bellas Artes. **March 2:** I.S.'s fly to Los Angeles. **18, 19:** I.S. conducts the Los Angeles Philharmonic. **28:** I.S.'s leave for Chicago on the "Chief." **30:** I.S.'s by train from Chicago to Washington. **April 4:** I.S. conducts concerts in Washington. **5:** I.S.'s to New York by train, attending Bach's *St. John Passion* in Carnegie Hall at night, and a dinner at Auden's after that. **10:** I.S., R.C., Balanchine, Kirstein interviewed on WQXR. **11:** Concert in Town Hall. **28:** I.S. conducts *Orpheus* at the City Center Ballet. **May 5:** I.S.'s by train to Los Angeles, arriving the 7th. **June 22:** Death of Lisa (Mrs. Vladimir) Sokoloff, V.S.'s closest friend in California, and co-owner with her of "La Boutique," an art gallery on La Cienega Boulevard. **July 18:** I.S.'s depart for Denver (train). **20:** R.C. arrives in Denver. **22:** We go to *Così fan tutte* in Central City. **25:** I.S.'s return to California, R.C. to Mexico. **27:** I.S.'s arrive in Hollywood. **30:** R.C. flies to Hollywood from Mexico City. **August 9:** R.C. to San Francisco and New York. V. buys an automobile from Sir Charles Mendl as a gift for the Soulima Stravinskys, lately arrived from France. **September 9:** Death of Dr. Alexis Kall, I.S.'s secretary of many years. **October 14:** The I.S.'s celebrate the eighth anniversary of their church wedding in Los Angeles (in the Russian Orthodox Church on Micheltorena Street). **November 22–24:** I.S.'s in Palm Springs. **28:** Visit from André Maurois. **December 2:** Poulenc for lunch.

MARCH 31

Washington, D.C. Arriving at the Raleigh Hotel for my first appointment with Stravinsky this morning, I find Auden pacing the lobby. "The night train from Pittsburgh was late," he says, "and the Stravs aren't receiving yet." In that case, I ask, would he care for a second breakfast? But no, he wouldn't because "There are no hard rolls in America." He fidgets and chain-smokes instead, and lay-analyzes "the old boy, in whose case, obviously, the mother figure is money." Suddenly remembering *The Rake*'s *Progress,* he delves into a battered attaché case and brings forth the type-script wrapped in *The New York Times.* Counting on only a brief wait, he opens the libretto to the final scene and hands it to me, saying, "This might interest you." Then while I read, he turns the *Times* to the obituary page, at which he registers disappointment, and to the book page, at which he emits a groan; he watches me thereafter at a tangent. I tell him that I think that the Bedlam scene contains some of the most beautiful verse ever intended for an opera, and he reacts by granting me ten additional minutes for the rest of the book, or approximately the time it would take *him* to read it. In fact, I have hardly finished Scene One when he jumps up exclaiming, "Surely the old boy must be ready by now," and fire-chases back to ring the apartment.

"The Lily Pons Suite," says the brass nameplate, but we are admitted by the tall, queenly beautiful Mrs. S., in a blue turban and white piqué housecoat. Mr. S., in a *robe de boudoir,* waits behind her, and he continues to hide behind and to depend on her throughout the meeting, like a small pet mouse with a large friendly cat. They greet me warmly, and smother Auden, whom they have not seen since the scenario-planning in Hollywood last November, with Russian-style kisses. But Auden, lovable, even kissable though he may be, is a Public School Englishman, plainly horrified by such open demonstrations of affection. He winces and quickly poses a number of deflecting questions about the S.'s health, house, lovebirds, parrots, etcetera. Then yes, too, dear me, we are forgetting the opera. And the manuscript is again delved for, but this time he hands it in like a schoolboy returning an exam. Mr. S. receives it solemnly, even superstitiously, asking Mrs. S. ("Verusha" this time, at other times "Vierotchka") to bring whiskey, which is not Auden's drink, but he takes it. Toasting the opera, we rapidly sink four toothglass tumblers-full, after which I feel less nervous, if also a little too well oiled. But why have I not been more nervous in the first place? Is it because Mr. S., from his music and from the rehearsals and concerts in which I have watched him, sometimes hitchhiking to Washington, Philadelphia, and Boston to do so, seems like someone I know very well already?

He talks about his new concerto for strings, the "Basiliensis," and his performance of it in Mexico City last month. Whereas all exchanges with Mrs. S. are in Russian (a long one in which they are probably deciding what to do about me with regard to seating strategy at luncheon), the language of this narrative is an assortment of handy French, German, and English phrases. But Mr. S.'s pursuit of verbal exactitude, and his interruptions of himself to demand English equivalents for foreign expressions, can be exasperating. At one point he seeks edification on the difference between a cad and a bounder, words encountered in a detective story on the train last night, but apart from the distinction that one of the terms applies chiefly to moral, the other chiefly to social, behavior, I do not catch Auden's would-have-been-immortal answer, being obliged at that instant to open the door for the waiter.

According to popular concepts of the changing evolutionary design of human physique, Mr. S. is something of a throwback. He is physically so extraordinary, in any case, that nothing less than a lifesize statue (not merely a head or bust), or scaled-to-lifesize drawing (the seated portrait by Picasso is misleading), could convey his uniqueness: the pygmy height, short legs, fleshlessness, football player's shoulders, large hands and wide knuckles, tiny head and recessive frontal lobes, sandy hair (black in photographs), smooth red neck, and high hairline. He is so absorbing to look at, in fact, that an effort is required to concentrate on what he says. And when that predicament has been overcome, a greater one arises in knowing how to respond. Many of his remarks are so sweeping, absolute, exclusive, as well as so exaggerated and *parti-pris,* that the listener is uncertain whether his leg is being pulled.

Add to this the difficulty that agreement is obviously expected for no matter what he says, and that the composer in person frequently seems to be saying the opposite of the composer in his autobiography, at any rate insofar as some of his colleagues are concerned. Thus, the mention of his *Symphonies of Wind Instruments*—my own forthcoming New York performance of this opus being the topic of our business today—provokes a tirade against Ansermet and his recent broadcast of it with the NBC Symphony.

Still, respond one must. I do so easily to a joke about "Hollywood composers who farm out their orchestrations and whose scores should be marked 'Coloring added,' like the labels on food cans." But I have no idea how to react to a verbal thumbsdown on the Beethoven Violin Concerto because "That D sharp in the first movement is such an ugly note"; or to a Nietzschean argument denying the Germanness in German music, "Because, you see, Bach was a Saxon, Beethoven was Flemish, Haydn was a Croat, Mozart was Austrian, Mendelssohn was a Jew." I do not quarrel with these demographic attributions or propose other candidates, but then neither does Auden, and he cannot think them less preposterous than I do.

We pair off for a moment, Mr. S. and Auden to look at the libretto, Mrs. S. and myself to talk about books. Her English is as charming as everything else about her. "I tried to but could not read *The Nak'd and the Dead,*" she says (whereas at table, later, she defends American cuisine to the extent of saying that our "ba-ked potatoes are good"). She says "here it's"—the logical reversal of "it's here"—and "fas-ten" for fasten. But her accent is more French than Russian. "Tell me, please," she says, "what means 'doctrine'?" and the word comes out so French-sounding—"doctreene"—that I answer "a female doctor." Her long cilia flutter slowly over her large blue eyes as she asks whether I agree that "Women are more appreciative of flowers than men," and that "Intellectual men hardly notice, and are rarely able to identify, any flowers except carnations and roses. Auden not only failed to sniff our bouquets, but he deposited his coat on a cluster of gardenias still lying in their box. "'Eager' loves flowers," she goes on, leaving me no time to consider the relationship between floral indifference and male intellect. "He always has flowers in his room while he works, and he cuts and waters them himself. He gardens every day, too, if he has time." But 'Eager's' delectation of the blossoms is less apparent to me than his compulsive folding up and tidy tucking away of the wrapping paper and ribbons.

Lunch is welcome not so much gustatorily as for the relief it brings from the tonnage of Mr. S.'s *tête-à-tête* attention. But we get smashed. I do, anyway, and my head begins to turn like a pinwheel halfway through the third bottle of Bordeaux, at which time Auden, intellect unbowed, begins to chat about linguistic science as a key to thought structure, and about the "British nanny as the true source of all philosophy in the Empiric Isles." He further devalues philosophy with the statement that "It can be no more than a game anyway, for St. Paul's reason that 'We are part of what we know.'" Besides this I recall only Mr. S.'s fuss about a wobble in the table, his annoyance with a butter-fingered waiter, his obsession with scraping up crumbs, and his exculpatory rubbing out of two spots on the tablecloth (what is he apologizing for?). He also makes a marvelous remark to the effect that "Music is the best means we have of digesting time." And he talks at some length about words, which involves a great deal of slow-fishing translation and of which, probably because of its nonlogicality, I retain only the information that the Russian for "ladybug" means, literally, "God's little cow." After several demi-cups of *espresso* Mr. S. retires for a catnap, as he says, though Mrs. S. predicts it will last until dinner.

1948

1948
1949
1950
1951
1952
1953
1954
1955
1956
1957
1958
1959
1960
1961
1962
1963
1964
1965
1966
1967
1968
1969
1970
1971

January 16: I.S. finishes Act I of *The Rake's Progress,* at 11 PM. **23:** The I.S.'s to Houston on the Sunset Limited, arriving the 25th (Rice Hotel). **31:** I.S. conducts the Houston Symphony. **February 1:** The I.S.'s to New York, met in Pennsylvania Station (on the 3rd, at 6:55 AM) by Auden and R.C. **6:** The I.S.'s and R.C. to Boston by train. **8:** I.S. conducts the Boston Symphony in Cambridge. **11, 12:** I.S. conducts the Boston Symphony in Boston. **15, 16:** I.S. conducts the Boston Symphony in New York. **23:** I.S. records *Orpheus* in New York. **24, 25:** I.S. records the *Mass.* **26:** I.S. conducts the *Mass* in Town Hall. **27:** The I.S.'s by train to Urbana. **March 3:** I.S. conducts in Urbana. **4:** I.S.'s to Denver, by train. **April 19:** R.C. conducts *Les Noces* in Town Hall, New York. **June 1:** R.C. flies to Los Angeles to work as musical assistant to I.S. **16:** I.S. conducts *Histoire du Soldat* in Royce Hall, U.C.L.A. **September 2:** We drive to San Diego (Grant Hotel). **4:** We go to a *corrida* in Tijuana. **6:** R.C. flies to New York. **October 22:** R.C. conducts *Renard,* Berg's *Kammerkonzert,* etc., in Town Hall. **28:** R.C. to Los Angeles. **November 6:** R.C. to New York. **21:** R.C. conducts *Zvezdoliki, Perséphone, Four Etudes, Pulcinella* (complete) in Carnegie Hall. **24:** Benjamin Britten visits I.S. **30:** I.S. attends Britten concert at U.S.C. **December 9:** I.S. attends a performance of *Albert Herring.* **10:** R.C. records *Mavra* in New York. **11:** R.C. to Los Angeles.

FEBRUARY 4

New York. Dinner with the Evelyn Waughs, who come in evening dress—for a late party at the Astors, they explain—the glaring perfection of which seems to exaggerate the crumples in our own everyday togs. Mrs. W. is fair and lovely, Mr. W. pudgy, ruddy, smooth-skinned, ramrod. He offers favorable comments on the temperature of our hotel rooms (at the Ambassador), complaining that he is obliged to keep the windows of his own rooms (at the Plaza) all the way open or suffocate, a confession that may help to account for his icy exterior no less than for his inner heat. I.S. replies in French, attempting to excuse the switch in language with a compliment on the French dialogue in *Scott-King's Modern Europe.* Mr. W. cuts in, however, disclaiming any conversational command of the tongue, and when Mrs. W. contradicts him—"That's silly, darling, your French is very good"—he reprimands her in injured, *tu-quoque* tones.

We mention Mr. W.'s lecture on *The Heart of the Matter* in Town Hall last week, the coolest performance of the sort I have ever seen, no matter how much he disparages it. Unencumbered by text or even notes, the novelist was able to study the audience (he says), and even to turn the tables on it (I say), to judge by the ruthlessly observed details in his descriptions of three people who walked out.

But Mr. W. prefers to talk about the Undertaking Industry and the ban

7

it has imposed against burying him should he, as the Industry must fervently hope, expire in the United States. He is keenly interested in our own burial plans, too, and eager to know whether we—our *beaux restes*—are destined for family vaults. But this down-to-earth talk makes I.S. uneasy.

A crisis occurs when the Waughs refuse the Stravinskys' whiskey and caviar, not because of the refusal, but because the S.'s unthinkingly exchange a few words in Russian, a pardonable recourse for them in many instances, but not now. Not taken in by V.'s pretense of referring to the cigarettes she rummages for in her handbag, the Waughs naturally, and correctly, deduce that the subject of the exchange is themselves. At long last I.S. proposes that we go to dinner, thus bringing the abstemious and uncomfortable half-hour to a close.

Mr. W.'s spirits take an upward turn during the freezing, and in his case, coatless, block-and-a-half walk to Maria's; and the sight of the Funeral Home at the corner of Lexington Avenue and Fifty-second Street so restores his *joie de vivre* that for a moment we fear he may actually take leave of us and explore the Service Entrance. Maria's, small, dark, crowded, is the wrong restaurant: the W.'s are too swank here. But the starchiness and defensive verbal sparring that the I.S.'s think of as the normal English method of making acquaintance vanish with the Valpolicella (which the temperature-sensitive Mr. W. mulls). It seems to me, too, that the novelist is succumbing to V.'s charm; he has begun to behave gallantly to her, in any case, and even some of the suspicion in the glowering glances he directs at intervals to I.S. has diminished.

Talk turns with the *fettuccine*—no apparent connection—to the Church. Here I.S. shines, showing himself to be at least as ultramonanist as Mr. W., as well read in Chesterton and Péguy, and as prone to believe in the miraculous emulsification of St. Januarius's blood. From some of the novelist's remarks, I would deduce that he supposes the composer to be one of Maritain's Jewish converts, which is a common and, so far as the Maritain influence is concerned, partly accurate supposition.

Another crisis looms when V. mentions the forthcoming New York première of her husband's *Mass* and invites the W.'s to attend. Mrs. W. handles this, regretting that they have already "booked passage home." But lest the conversation continue in this dangerous direction, her husband adds, with a bluntness that seems to show that he has been inwardly lacerated all evening by the threat of I.S.'s cacophonous art: "All music is positively painful to me." The statement can only be ignored, and V. does so, superbly, with a compliment to Mr. W. on *his* art, and a comparison between his *Decline and Fall* and Sade's *Justine*. When at length Mr. W. realizes that the S.'s have read everything he has written, a new character emerges in him as magnanimous and amusing as the old one was unbending and priggishly precise. If he does not brook the literary talk of literary types, he certainly seems to enjoy it from outsiders like (though no one is quite like) the I.S.'s and even from semi-insiders like (there are many like) me, for I admire Mr. W.'s fictions, too, and no longer object, as I once did, that chance and arbitrariness play too important a part in them. We seek to draw him out on other writers, but are rewarded with only one acidulated reference to fellow lecture-touring compatriots, and the commendation, in which the last two adjectives are wickedly emphasized, of Christopher Isherwood as "a good young American novelist."

The meal concluded, Mr. W. asks permission to smoke a cigar. Choosing one from a case in his breast pocket, he holds it under his nose (where it looks like a grenadier's mustache), circumcises the sucking end with a small blade, passes a match under the other end as if he were candling a pony of precious cognac, avidly stokes and consumes it. (Holy Smoke!)

JULY 27

Los Angeles. Aldous and Maria Huxley to dinner, she petite and eager, with large, believing eyes in a small pinched face, he even taller than anyone had warned. But one looks first at his silver-point features—especially the slightly hooked, slightly haughty nose—and rarely away from them thereafter. His right cornea is covered by a milky film like clouded glass, and it is the unflawed but rapidly nictitating left eye that he turns to us, though its powers of sight are hardly greater. His skin has a desiccated appearance—from the desert sun during his anchorite period, one would suppose, except that it is also deathly white. Everything else about the man except the big weedy brows suggests not the out-of-doors, however, but the tightly sealed edifices of intellectual respectability. What strikes me next is that he seems so absurdly out of scale in the diminutive I.S. house. He crouches under the low ceilings, ducks through the doorways, flinches past a chandelier, reaches out for tables, making us feel that it may really be unsafe for him here, that he could actually trap himself in one of I.S.'s tiny WC's and never get out.

We are more precisely aware of his visual limitations at dinner where he feels for his knife, fork, and plate with the palpations of the blind. His wife helps him to find the food, and she continues to direct him throughout the meal in almost unnoticed asides. *"Un tout petit peu à gauche, chéri,"* she whispers when his knife fails to find a purchase on the meat, and in the same voice she advises him how long to uptilt the salt shaker; but I think he would not welcome, indeed would resent, any solicitude from another source. Conversation is in French. This is partly because Mr. and Mrs. H. use that language domestically, but principally because I.S.'s ear, having been confined to my backwoods American, is not well attuned to Huxleyan English. (The word "issue," for example, a clean, sibilant "iss-u" in Mr. H.'s mouth, a gooey "ish-shoe" in mine, must confound the S.'s as it distracts me.) In any case I.S. seems to think of Mr. H. as an English-born Frenchman whose manners may be the quintessence of Englishness (very good in I.S.'s book), but who in other important respects is more civilized (French). Language apart, the two men inhibit each other. If Mr. H. is the

9

wrong size, he is also the wrong culture. That sovereignty of scientific rationalism, the very blueprint of his intellectual heredity, is a planet away from I.S.'s mystagogical view of human existence. I.S. has not followed any science or philosophy of science since his reading of Bergson a half-century ago. It is for this reason, also, that he lives in terror all evening lest Mr. H. dwell on scientific deeds and books of which he has never heard. Yet I think that Mr. H. is as self-conscious of his own limitations in being unable to stem the flow of his thoughts long enough to approach the world of the other from the other's bias. The two men watch each other like champions of two mutually incomprehensible games, but for basic toeholds rather than for gambits.

Mr. H.'s voice, a lambent, culture-saturated purr, is as memorable as his head. His stories ripple musically through pursed lips, the longer anecdotes beginning in low dove-tones, rising toward what promises to be a loudly explosive finish, but then knotting into a *Knödel* instead, or fizzling out at the climactic high note. And what a storyteller he is! As family history alone, his autobiography would contain the richest material of any living writer, while to judge from tonight's tales of Joyce, Pound, Eliot, Yeats, such a book could be one of the most entertaining for the twenties and thirties as well. Best of all, he betrays no mark of the repertory company, and good as these performances are, the most astonishing occurs when he examines I.S.'s collection of sea shells. Holding each specimen under a magnifying glass two inches from his left eye, Mr. H. casually sheds a mass of recondite conchological information about it, apologizing for his knowledge, and begging our pardon with perfect punctilio each time he drops a Latin name.

The hunching and cringing from the confines of Lilliput begin all over again on the way back to the living room, though having charted the dangers in his memory, he now moves with a more gliding, somewhat rubbery walk. We ensconce him in the largest chair, from which he seems to squirm away—parts of him anyway—like a cornered cephalopod, now stretching its peripatetic tentacles to alarming length, now cupping them in. His fingers plait and unplait, as he listens to us, or tickle the fenders of his chair; but when he talks, his arms move continuously and rapidly in large illustrative gestures so that he seems to have several pairs of them, like Vishnu. And what does he talk about? The finding of bacteria at ocean depths; the heightening of erotic sensibilities through breathing exercises; the sexual customs of the American utopias, especially the Oneida experiment of training adolescent boys on women past the menopause; Baudelaire's Latin poems, which "demonstrate wide reading in the type of poem but show complete ignorance of stress, merely duplicating the number of syllables"; problems of multiple meanings in Pali, "which, after all, is not a very subtle language but nevertheless has thirty different words for 'knowledge'"; Augustus Hare (whose taste for oddity seems to me rather like Mr. H.'s own); the possibility of flights to the moon within a decade if enough money were diverted to the project, though Mr. H.'s only interest in visiting another planet would be "to establish contact with an older civilization." This river of learning is continually nourished by tributaries of quotations—a couplet by Trumbull Stickney, a clerihew, the whole of *"Le vierge, le vivace et le bel aujourd'hui,"* which he recites as though he were reading from an oculist's chart, except for one small stumble of memory, from which he picks himself up with an air of surprise that none of us had caught him as he tripped. The listener feels confident that Mr. H. would have as much Bartlett no matter what the topic, and that every volume in the anthology automatically flicks open to the right page.

Brilliant as it is, we are a little relieved when it comes to an end; *I* am, anyway, for I have resolved a dozen times an hour to keep my Boeotian ignorance to myself, or at least not to expose it in *this* public. But he is one of the gentlest human beings I have ever seen, as well as one of the most delightfully giggly.

AUGUST 10

Lunch at the Farmers' Market with the I.S.'s, Christopher Isherwood, and the Huxleys, the latter cooing at each other today like newlyweds, or oldly-weds making up after a spat. Owing to its extensive variety of salads, seeds (Aldous eats quantities of sunflower seeds, for his eyes), nuts, health foods, exotic fruit (Milton: "The savoury pulp they chew, and in the rind"), the restaurant is a Huxleyan haunt. Most of the other tables are held down by drugstore cowboys, movie stars, Central European refugees, and—to judge by the awed glances in our direction—Aldine and Igorian disciples. All are vegetarians, for the nonce, and all nibble at their greens like pasturing cows.

Virginia Woolf likened Isherwood to a jockey, and it is easy to see what she meant. Nothing in his clothes suggests that profession, of course, and I might add that they are less conspicuously suited to Hollywood than those of Aldous or I.S. (both of them sporting much too resonant neckwear, as if their sense of the dapper had run to seed at such a remove from the more discriminating centers of haberdashery). It is a question rather of the stature, bantam weight, somewhat too short legs, and disproportionately, even simianly, long arms, a comparison forced on the attention because of their frequent employment for metrical purposes. In short, it is in the build of the man that one sees how Mrs. Woolf saw him, whether at the pari-mutuel window or the furlong post: as an ornament of the track and the turf.

His manner is casual, vagabondish, lovelorn. One does not readily imagine him in a fit of anger or behaving precipitately or enduring extended states of great commotion. At moments he might be thinking of things beyond and remote, from which the conversation brusquely summons him back to earth. But he is a listener and an observer—he has the observer's habit of staring—rather than a propounder and expatiator, and his trancelike eyes will see more deeply through, and record more essential matter about, us than this verbosity of mine is doing about him. At the same time, his sense of humor is very ready. He maintains a chronic or semi-permanent smile (a network of small creases about the mouth), supplementing it with giggles and an occasional full-throttle laugh, during which the tongue lolls. (This happens as he tells a story of why he is no longer invited to Charlie Chaplin's: "Someone told him I had peed on his sofa one night while I was plastered.") But he is not at ease in spite of the drollery. Underneath—for he is as multi-layered as a *mille* (which in practice is rarely more than a *huit* or a *dix*) *feuilles*—are fears, the uppermost of which might well be of a musical conversation or high general conversation about The Arts. But I could be miles off. Perhaps he is merely suffering from the prohibition rule of the Farmers' Market, and in this case the contents of I.S.'s thermos bottles will come as an agreeable surprise.

Isherwood brings greetings to All-deuce (as he pronounces it) from a Swami. The voice, both in pitch and volume, is somewhat too high, and the words are too deliberated. Aldous, replying, digresses to make room for a ribald story, which Isherwood follows like an eager schoolboy, exclaiming, "Oh boy!" once, and rubbing his knees in anticipation of the outcome. He also says "heck!" "swell" "by golly!" "gosh!" and "gee-whiz!"

How do the two men regard each other apart from their evident mutual affection? Isherwood cannot match the softly orating Huxleyan delivery or the Huxleyan intellectual ammunition (a stunning aside on the "haeccities of the later Persian mystics," an apt quote from the *Biathanatos,* and the most recent information about amino acids and cellular differentiation). But then, the younger man has made his name partly because of his wariness of fluency at supernal intellectual altitudes. Is he mildly baiting the sage, perhaps, gently tweaking his nose a bit by that overly credulous way of asking those further questions about the marvelous, the horrendous, and the barely believable that loom so large in the older man's talk? Or does he regard him as ever so slightly unbalanced from too much book learning? Not really deranged, of course, like Don Quixote, but a bit "off" nevertheless?

And am I wrong in sensing just the faintest tinge of doubt on the Huxley side as to the hundred per cent impregnability of his younger colleague's spiritual dedication and final severance from The World? And in detecting just the hint of a suspicion that one last unburned boat may still be hidden somewhere in the reeds? We suppose, in any case—it is the I.S.'s impression as well as my own—that the younger man is obliged to apply himself to those spiritual exercises which the older man masters merely by turning his mind to them. But while the Huxley universe is the larger of the two, the author does not sit more securely in the center of it than the author of the Isherwood books does in the center of the Isherwood universe. Partly for this reason, it is more of an encounter to meet Isherwood than to meet Aldous, though another reason is simply that most of us are little more than enchanted audiences to Aldous, not because he wills it that way, but because we have no choice. Finally, whatever the truth of these speculations, how improbable a team the two of them make to represent Vedanta in the Wild West!

I.S., as I know him, is even less comfortable than Isherwood. He dislikes being outnumbered by Englishmen speaking their language, and these particular Englishmen probably seem to him too freely, richly verbal, for in I.S.'s book the important things must never be, cannot be, said. But I.S. presents an almost exaggerated contrast in other ways as well: in, for instance, his deep diapason (versus their duet of flute-stops); in his love of concreteness (the Englishmen's talk about religion must seem abstract to him, for he believes in the physical existence of the Devil and his Infernal Regions, as at one time people believed in centaurs and mermaids); and in the autocracy and absoluteness of his views, though these can seem more extreme than they are because of his imperfect command of the flutey language's syntactic qualifying paraphernalia.

I would exchange some, if less than half, of my kingdom for a peek at the picture these two observers draw of I.S. Will they discover that the barricade of epigrams, paradoxes, *bons mots,* conceals nothing at all in their line, the line of "intellect"? Or will they conclude that the treasures are being kept to the deeps out of reticence, to be surfaced again on other, more favored days? Whatever the answer, and both conclusions would be wrong, the polite side of I.S., that Bellona's armor of will in the man and of style in the music ("Music may symbolize, but it cannot express"), is the only side anyone except V. ever sees.

Why, then, have so many people mistaken I.S. for an "intellectual"? Primarily, I think, because it was his own preferred image of himself. He is vain of his "factual knowledge," and would actually like to be regarded as a mere *summa* of erudition, the wielder of the ultimate gavel of sophisticated judgment. Nor will he tolerate such terms as "instinct" and "genius" in regard to himself, pretending instead that "brains" and "technique," meaning the mastery of means and the perfection of the ear, constitute the composer's full equipment. "Emotions," I hardly need to add, are scarcely allowed to be an ingredient. Moreover, he seems to think of the affective functions as physiologically zoned, like the separation of emotion and intelligence in Comte's *tableau cérébral.*

Little as it matters, I.S.'s intellectual world apart from music has been formed to an unusual extent by his intimates. He is in fact radically susceptible to personal influence, which I say because I can see the reactive effects that I myself have had on him. (V. has said that I am the only friend in his adult life who has disagreed with him and survived, which is a dubious distinction both as to conduct and as to consequence.) For my own part, and though it hardly requires saying, I entertain few if any fixed views capable of withstanding "rigorous intellectual investigation" (I am a "feeler" rather than a "thinker," myself), and I certainly want no responsibility for any of them, musical or otherwise, settling on such a man. But the point is I.S.'s susceptibility, not *whose* view.

13

The chief influences were Diaghilev (V. cites certain aesthetic attitudes as virtually parroted from him and she insists that "Before age and America changed Stravinsky's character, he opened his heart only to Diaghilev, and Diaghilev's criticisms were the only ones he ever heeded"); C. F. Ramuz and C. A. Cingria (a *homo faber* philosophy and the ideal of the village virtues, meaning the moral superiority of simple things; *les vins honnêtes*, for instance, which, unfortunately, often means Grade B as well); Arthur Lourié (proselytizing for Maritain); Suvchinsky (a philosophy compiled from Herzen, Rozanov, Shestov, Berdyaev). Certainly these men, and the very few others who knew I.S. intimately, must have realized that, uncanny as his artistic intelligence is, and acute and varied as are the palettes of his sense perceptions, his critical range outside of music is peculiarly limited. What he offers are judgments without trials in a no-man's-land of likes and dislikes. And at a time when no-man's-lands quickly become so much real estate crossed by so many beaten paths, the hazard to himself hardly requires spelling out. "Taste," as we grow older, is a narrowing tyranny.

I would like to have put many questions to these illustrious predecessors, of course, but must put some prior ones to myself. What, for example, of Chamfort's warning that "A philosopher attached to the train of a great man finds it necessary to conceal his true feelings"?

AUGUST 19

To the Huxleys for tea—parsley tea with crystal sugar, and a tray of molasses cookies, wheat germ, raw carrots, small wedges of nonfattening fruit cake. Architecturally the house would satisfy the taste in mansions of a retired Kenya colonial. And it is a contrast in most other ways to the I.S. house, which, like the composer himself, is small, snug, brightly lighted, not forbiddingly private, as packed as a provincial museum. The lights are off as we enter, drawn curtains notwithstanding, and the sole evidence of Edison is a lamp in Mr. H.'s study which would seem more suitable for third-degree interrogations. The walls are bare, except for a few of Mr. H.'s own watercolors (landscapes with trees and rocks, reminiscent of Cézanne), and the furniture, what there is of it, is severe. I.S. does not scintillate in such surroundings. And when Mrs. H. withdraws, taking V. with her so that the boys may have a smoking-room chat, he is not only uncomfortable but positively frightened of having to face Mr. H. without V.'s support. As I know I.S., he is whetting for a whiskey, but the display of health foods and Mrs. H.'s gingerly proffered carafe of sherry (after a slightly snickering reference to booze) intimidate him and he does not ask for it. The sepulchral lighting and raftered baronial hall dampen the conversation, too. Mr. H. is serious here, and we are reverent and hushed—though for my part I could not have contributed more than five or six twigs to the blaze of Mr. H.'s talk anyway, and I hold these back not because of the bleakness of the décor, but because of self-consciousness for my pawky verbal congestions.

Mr. H. alone and uninterrupted is not easily bettered, in any case, and

I regret that no tape recorder has preserved him today, especially his description of the culinary mortifications of St. Philip Neri. For he is more engaging to listen to than to read, the conversationalist being superior to the writer in at least two definite ways. First, the talk is wholly free of the late-Tolstoy sermonizing that has become such a heavy part of the books; second, the talker embroiders his main thematic paths with a luxury of odd links, an anastomosis of curious connections (the Huxley vocabulary is beginning to affect me!) which the writer could not—no writer could—afford to follow.

What is Mr. H. to I.S.? A kind of handy, neighborhood university, whatever more besides. I.S., like a radio quiz master, is forever wanting immediate answers to random matters of fact. He will leave the dinner table to trace some scrap of information and return thirty minutes and two cold courses later—empty-handed, more often than not, for lack of a methodology. But if Mr. H. is in town, I.S. need only pick up the telephone, as he did yesterday when he wanted a rundown on the history of scissors. I.S. is convinced that Mr. H. suffers from his encyclopedic erudition, incidentally, and that he is a prisoner of it. And I believe that this is true, and even that the Tao of his seemingly unquenchable quest is freedom through possession.

And I.S. to Mr. H.? A "genius"—or, as scientists prefer, "hopeful monster"—is the simple but, I think, complete answer: one of the sacred few invested with the divine power of creation. Not only does Mr. H. prostrate himself before the mystery of this power, but also he seems to regard it as a justification for the existence of the rest of humanity. D. H. Lawrence was Mr. H.'s genius in his early years, and whatever qualities the word represents for him now, Lawrentian or otherwise, he thirsts for them still, as others do for religious inspiration. At the same time, he would disclaim that he himself possessed even a pinch of these qualities, and allow the classification "creative writer" to be used with reference to himself only if he were attempting to explain his low income to a tax collector. He writhes when anyone so much as hints at a reference to his work, and actually groans aloud today when V. alludes to a dramatization of *Brave New World;* a direct question about a book-in-progress would doubtless dissolve him altogether. Contrast this with I.S., who beams with satisfaction at the mention of *his* tiniest opus. But, then, I.S. *is* a creator.

Mr. H. also looks to I.S. as a source of knowledge *about* music, and not only for the so-called secrets of art, but, curiously, for the plainest of lexical facts as well. His appetite for this knowledge appears to be insatiable, moreover, though he already commands a huge store of music history and a tune-humming acquaintance with the repertory which is (on that level) almost as wide as I.S.'s. He does not seem to have considered that such knowledge has little interest for, or bearing on, the mind of the composer, or that the composer's stock of prejudices might be narrow and cranky because of creative preoccupations of the moment. How long, I wonder, will it take Mr. H. to discover that I.S.'s genius is wrapped—for protection from musical data—in a vacuum?

1948
1949
1950
1951
1952
1953
1954
1955
1956
1957
1958
1959
1960
1961
1962
1963
1964
1965
1966
1967
1968
1969
1970
1971

ITINERARY

January 3: R.C. in bed with pleurisy. **19:** The I.S.'s buy a new Dodge. **27:** Eugene Berman marries Ona Munson in the I.S. house. **February 6:** We leave for New York by car, staying at El Centro, Las Cruces (7th), Del Rio (8th), Beaumont (9th), New Orleans (10th), Tallahassee (11th), Sarasota (12th), Miami (13th), Daytona (14th), Charleston (15th), Williamsburg (16th), Philadelphia (17th), New York (Lombardy Hotel, 18th). **March 1:** Auden works with I.S. on *The Rake.* **7:** We lunch with Marino Marini. **18:** I.S.'s go to Urbana. **20:** I.S.'s hear Dylan Thomas read his poems in Urbana. **21, 22:** I.S. conducts concerts in Urbana and St. Louis. **23:** The I.S.'s return to New York. **April 17:** I.S. records *Apollo* for RCA, and poses for Marino Marini. **May 17:** We arrive in Los Angeles by car via Rapid City, Yellowstone, Monterey. **28:** I.S. attends Ojai Festival concert. R.C. introduced to Lawrence Morton. **July 25:** We leave for Aspen by car, via Eureka, Portland, Olympia, Coeur d'Alene, arriving on the 31st. **August 2:** I.S. conducts in Aspen (in blue jeans, his concert clothes having been lost in a railroad strike). **3:** We drive with Babin and Vronsky to Taos. **4:** Meet Frieda Lawrence, Mabel Dodge, Miranda. **5:** Santa Fe: meet Witter Bynner. **7:** Return to Aspen. **8:** I.S. conducts second concert in Aspen. **11:** Arrive at Los Angeles. **September 7–12:** Automobile trip in Oregon and Washington. **20:** R. C. flies to New York. **December:** We drive to San Francisco, where I.S. conducts a series of concerts.

JULY 5

Hollywood. Not only angels fear to tread! After my visit to Schoenberg today, I am aware of having walked from the street to his house on the grass, instead of the gravel driveway; of tiptoeing to the door; and of waiting there in the hope of being seen and not having to ring the bell. In fact, Schoenberg's pretty daughter does see me, and she leads me to the living room, abandoning me there except for a few peeps at me from the kitchen. A photograph of Kokoschka is the only picture in the room, and the only furniture is a gravy-colored leather armchair, a sofa, and a piano crowded with the tennis trophies of Schoenberg's elder son.

The composer enters, walking slowly and with the help of his wife. Stooped and wizened, but as suntanned as an athlete, he seems thinner than last time—that pained, sensitive face, difficult to look into and impossible not to look into—and the bulging veins in his right temple are even more prominent. Probably from the same cause his ears appear to have grown larger; they *are* larger (the concha and outward antitragus) than I.S.'s, which I remark because the oversized hearing apparatus of both composers is their outstanding sculptural feature. He sits in the gravy *fauteuil,* but on the edge of the cushion and without repose; seated, he seems even smaller, as well as older than his years. Then, beginning to talk, he adjusts caster-thick eyeglasses previously dangled from his neck by a ribbon and rubber bands. The voice is soft, but as pained and sensitive as the face, and at moments almost embarrassingly intense.

He seeks to convince me to use an English translation for my forthcoming New York performance of *Pierrot lunaire,* and he recommends the version by Ingolf Dahl. In answer to my question about performing his *a cappella* male choruses, he suggests that I double each line with an instrument offstage and transmit the instruments to the singers from individual earphones. As I also plan to perform his Suite, Opus 29, he proposes that we listen to a recording of the work made in Paris at the time of the première. The fact that he conducted the performance does not stay him from censuring it briefly during nearly every turn of the page in the score, and at length during each pause to change the record side. "This is the most difficult of all my piano writings," he remarks at one point, though I am thinking that the clarinet parts are as much of a problem. He listens to the music (what can be heard of it beneath distractingly crepitant surface noise) as though he had forgotten having written it, and the rediscovery leaves him radiant. At the end, in spite of his criticisms, he entrusts the records to me, which is very like I.S., who will also play acetates of his radio broadcasts and lend them out to prospective performers.

A question of mine concerning the *Lieder,* Opus 22, seems to surprise him—agreeably, I think. He wants to know how I know them, and with total ingenuousness confesses his guilt "in using too many instruments, though orchestras of that size were not impracticable at the time the music was composed." He remarks, with no complaint in his voice, that "the songs had to wait twenty years for a performance," which makes me want to tell him that I think they are the most beautiful orchestral songs ever written, but I refrain from doing so partly because of the text of his canon for G. B. Shaw and partly because one does not gush to Schoenberg—though I regret later that I did not say it. He is still more surprised to discover that I know the score of *Von Heute auf Morgen,* and even less able to conceal his pleasure in recalling that long-buried masterpiece, the largest completed work of his mature years. But the fact of these reactions is also shocking evidence of the neglect of his music. How, in this age of? . . . But that's it, exactly.

He knows of my association with I.S., but does not allude to it, nor do I, because I have not come on I.S.'s account. I think he is curious, though, and would at least like to inquire after I.S.'s health—even though his own is so frail and though age has so suddenly crushed him. At one point when his younger son tears through the room yelping like a bloodhound, Schoenberg calls after the boy, makes a show of shrinking from the noise, and begs him not to play in the house. It seems to me that anyone observing this incident who was not already aware of the relationship must naturally suppose the composer to be the grandfather instead of the parent. As I prepare to go, he autographs my score of *Pierrot lunaire,* adding the phrase "expecting a good performance"; and he invites me to visit him again next week. My feeling of lightness outdoors is a measure of the almost unbearable intensity of the man, as well as of the strain created by the danger of crossing the circle of his pride, for though his humility is fathomless, it is plated all the way down with a hubris of stainless steel.

1950

1948
1949
1950
1951
1952
1953
1954
1955
1956
1957
1958
1959
1960
1961
1962
1963
1964
1965
1966
1967
1968
1969
1970
1971

ITINERARY

February 20: Leave for Miami by car, via Wickenburg, Demming, El Paso (Cortes Hotel), Dallas, Shreveport (here I.S. learns of the death of Gide), Natchez, Mobile, Saint Augustine, Pompano Beach (Astor Motel, February 27). **March 4, 5:** Concerts in Havana. **6:** We fly to Miami and drive to Daytona. **7:** Drive to Macon. **8:** Chattanooga and Lawrenceburg. **9:** Hot Springs, Arkansas. **10:** Webbers Falls. **11:** Santa Fe. **12:** Flagstaff. **13:** Los Angeles. **21-25:** Nicolas Nabokov is a houseguest. **April:** Deaths of Koussevitsky and Adolphe Bolm (on the 16th). **24-26:** We drive with the Huxleys to San Diego, returning via the desert. **July 13:** Death of Schoenberg, a profound effect on I.S. **19:** Dinner at Alma Mahler's, where I.S. sees Schoenberg's death mask. **21:** R.C. in Cedars of Lebanon with undiagnosed ailment. Shortly after, I.S.'s go by train to New York (Lombardy Hotel). **August 4:** R.C. flies to New York. **7:** We sail to Naples on the *Constitution.* **September:** I.S. conducts in Milan. **October:** I.S. conducts in Cologne (*Oedipus Rex*), Baden-Baden (Symphony in C), Munich (*Oedipus Rex*), Geneva. **November:** I.S. conducts in Rome and Naples. **21-22:** Fly to New York from Rome, Auden and Isherwood at New York airport. **26:** I.S.'s move from Lombardy to Gladstone Hotel. **December 29:** Train to Los Angeles.

FEBRUARY 28

Miami to Havana in a Cuban airplane, rising over ghostly gray live-oaks, covered with dangling and feathery, ropy and tentacular aerial moss. From the air, lower Florida is a brocade of swampy islands, sheened pools, and a rim of indigo sea. The colors of the Caribbean shimmer like shot silk, and the sand and coral floors sloping away from the Keys seem to be no more than a thin pane of aquamarine glass from the world of air. The line of the Keys near Key West, which resembles a fortress on an old map, is shaped like the skeleton tail of an ice-age mammoth. At the Havana airport, our stewardess, a dumb soubrette with retroussé nose, announces that "This is Cuba." I.S. to me: "It better be."

The customs officers bring us frozen daiquiris, which is nice except that our luggage is lost meanwhile. Havana is an aromatic city, preponderantly of cooking oil and coffee, the latter thick enough, it seems, to filter out of the air. We go directly to a press conference in the bar of the Hotel Nacional, where we are greeted with more daiquiris and *entusiasmo*. Lunch follows, at La Zaragosana (two lisps), in an atmosphere of Habana Habana smoke; and after lunch, a visit to Wilfredo Lam, who puts on a private exposition of his paintings, accompanying it with a great deal of talk about his gods, Stravinsky and Picasso.

The hacienda of Fifi Tarafa, where we go for dinner—a carafe of daiquiris this time—displays photographs of, and many recordings by, *her* god, Toscanini. It could be partly for this reason that I.S. elects to sit in the patio, which is paved with eighteenth-century terra-cotta beer bottles (bottoms up) and which looks toward a garden with a statue of Benjamin Franklin. I.S. confides to me that he is impatient to go home and finish *The Rake.*[1]

APRIL 17

Hollywood. An afternoon with Universal Knowledge. Aldous calls, asking me to read to him; he has overtaxed his "good" eye. I find him typing the witchcraft book, nevertheless—in the den at the end of the darkened corridor, and on a table ominously stacked with publications in Braille. He is wearing his "Chinese glasses," black cellulose goggles with perforations instead of lenses: they force the pupils to move stroboscopically, hence prevent staring; Aldous has taped a bandage over the pinholes on the right side, which means that he no longer has any sight at all in his opaline right eye.

He seems pleased to be interrupted, but is clearly less hungry for a dose of reading than for a discussion of his work—except that he refuses to talk about it as *his:* he will give himself no credit, even for the discoveries of his own research. Without any stepping-stone small talk he pulls me into the deeps of the *Malleus Maleficarum* and "the appalling materialism to which it testifies." In developing this thesis he seems to shirk no opportunity for scatological descriptions, and, of course, the torturing of witches provides an abundance of such occasions. I suspect some Swiftian compulsiveness in this, but may be wrong; it could be merely the yeast in his arguments as to the naturalness of human vileness. At one point, telling me how bellows and tongs were used to exorcise the Devil from a child's stomach, he is put in mind of a cartoon by Wilhelm Busch, and the thought of that fellow misanthrope seems to leave him gay and exhilarated. "Has anyone ever detested humanity more?" he asks, and his voice glitters mordantly and as heartlessly as the ice cubes at a cocktail party.

The thought strikes me today, as it has before, that two of Aldous's most prominent qualities are clarity and, at the same time, credulity, and that they make a very odd team. On the one side is an apparently unshakable *credo ut intelligam* (which includes logic and the analytic disciplines), and on the other, a radical susceptibility to the nostrums of quacksalvers and spiritual confidence men. The clarity side is descended by school from nineteenth-century philosophers for whom there could be no unruly ideas; and one cannot help remarking that this instrument is not quite the right one for the verbally elusive "perennial philosophy." But what of the teammate? What school is *he* from, Paracelsus High?

---

1. The Epilogue was completed on April 17. A note in my diary reminds me that we played it together, four-hands, that evening. The Prelude was composed three days later.

Where was he keeping himself at the time of *Antic Hay,* one would like to know, and what has befallen the author of the early novels that he can now look for salvation in a pill? For the man who was always hurrying to expose *les paradis artificiels* of yesterday has become the readiest exponent, even the guinea pig, for those of today. Why, as it appears, is he grasping at straws? As a so-called uncommitted liberal, he may simply feel committed to try everything, and to give every idea its due. But a profounder explanation would have to explore backwards, to Victorian roots. For it seems to me that Aldous is a shocked Victorian, even a shell-shocked one, as much as the poets of the trenches. And he is capable of being shocked by what to most people are common happenings. His hardest-worked word is "extraordinary," and the runner-up word, "absolutely," functions as its geminate. In fact, only the extraordinary and the exaggerated seem to interest him, so that at times one thinks he has ceased to believe in ordinary human beings. Only Mozarts and imbeciles inhabit his world, only extreme aspects of humanity, and these extremities continually shock him. And whereas he allows that some of the shocks, such as the creations of Mozart, are ennobling, most of them are the contrary; and it is the larger statistic that offers so much more satisfaction for the anti-meliorist in him. Irony is the surfacing trick of the shocked Victorian, but irony stales with the speed of yesterday's events, and how much of Aldous's will outlive him?

1951

The point about ordinary and "whole" people is the crux of Aldous's failure as a novelist—though "failure" is unfair because he never set out to succeed in the usual sense; and, anyway, why should he not write about extraordinary people? A readable journal is rarer than a readable novel, and its characters and records of events, being "true," are at least as likely to endure, at any rate the characters and events in a journal by Aldous Huxley. Such a journal—the unfictionalized raw material, the ideas and speculations, the thumbnail portraits, the highlights of conversations, the commentaries about books (the cross-references in his annotations of Evans-Wentz's *Tibetan Book of the Dead* draw on a whole unknown—to me—library)—this would be a treasure indeed. As far back as *Point Counter Point,* Philip Quarles's musings indicated that a journal was Aldous's own form par excellence; except that Aldous in the first person is far superior to Aldous under any guise—being surpassed, in fact, only by Aldous in person.

[**Postscript, 1971.** I cannot excuse the impudence of these arguments which I had manufactured out of some no longer remembered necessity, but I might try to improve my appearance by emphasizing that the real subject is not so much A.H. as my own growing pains. A.H. had had a considerable influence on me long before I knew him, and in my prep school and early college years the appearance of each new book by him was an exciting event bringing new notions and new bearings for old ones. I should add that in the year of my discovery of him his reputation had begun to suffer because of his pacifism—more that, I think, than his espousal of a religious philosophy which was on the way to a wartime vogue. He had recently published an *Encyclopedia of Pacifism* and a shorter tract arguing pacifism as a practical policy. The argument broke ground with the claim that "Feeling, willing, thinking are the three modes of ordinary human activity." Not action? The statement derives from Fulgentius, or Ficino and the Florentine Neoplatonists—though, as Kierkegaard says somewhere, "In Greece, philosophizing was a mode of action," and it was certainly that with Aldous himself. But the oversight was unfortunate, polemically speaking, and so was the title of his pamphlet, *What Are You Going to Do about It?*, which fairly begged for the rejoinder it soon received, C. Day Lewis's *We're Not Going to Do Nothing.*]

APRIL 28

Tonight's Russian Easter Midnight Mass is presided over by a Bishop, for which reason, probably, the crowd is greater than in other years. The little white church with the blue onion dome being filled to capacity, we join two or three hundred other latecomers who pack the grounds and spill into the street, where the service is relayed through a spluttery public-address system. "D.P.'s," with close-shaven or *en brosse* heads, ill-fitting, donated clothes, and faraway eyes, comprise the majority of this outdoor congregation. The others are the White Russian regulars, a loud clan, locally, with whom the I.S.'s have little traffic and by whom, in consequence, they are snubbed. Both factions appear to be deeply homesick tonight, the flamboyant professional exiles no less than the timid and indigent "D.P.'s"; so I judge from the soulful singing of a hymn, and not only soulful either, but drastically out of tune, like an "atonal" version of the beginning of "*1812.*" Even the mire—we have had a week of heavy rain—seems to contribute to their nostalgia by responding to their footsteps with Russian-size squelches.

Shortly before midnight all of us in the open-air congregation light tapers. Then at exactly twelve o'clock the church doors open and the clergy and congregation pour forth into our dense and now literally inflammable human chandelier. A deacon in a newly starched alb heads the procession, swinging the censer and spreading incense over us with a vengeance. Behind him, the Bishop, in scarlet, white, and gold samite, pauses on the top steps and sings *"Christos Voskreseh"* ("Christ Is Risen"), to which the whole crowd cries *"Vieestinoo Voskreseh"* ("He Is Risen Indeed")—though it does not come out like that but tumbles around the church letter by letter, like noodles in alphabet soup. Next in the procession is a priest carrying a tall cross, and after him a train of acolytes displaying icons, *haroogve* (holy banners or icons made of cloth), and the globe and scepter of Christ the King; these clerics have long, soft, Spanish-moss-like beards. Three times around the church they parade, and thrice, in tow, follow the "D.P.'s," whose attention, however, is directed more and more to their wilting and dripping candles. *"Christos Voskreseh,"* sings the Bishop as he launches each successive trip, and each time the *"Vieestinoo Voskreseh"* wobbles around the church in response. The service concludes with an orgy of congregational kissing, in the sequence left cheek, right cheek, and again left, and with everyone you know or cannot escape, Easter kisses being unrefusable.

At the I.S.'s afterward, the Lenten fast is symbolically broken—not having been physically observed—by eating *kooleetch,* the Easter bread with a paper rose; and *paskha,* the million-calorie (sugar, milk, cheese, eggs, raisins, tutti-frutti) Easter cake. After draining in its obelisk mold for almost a week, the *paskha* was taxied to church today to be blessed. The mold and a cheesecloth wrapper are now removed revealing the imprint "X.B."—"Christ Is Risen"—on the front of the decanted cake, as well as Easter flower designs on the sides.

JUNE 18

I.S.'s birthday begins, as it does each year, in a bad mood. But this seems to be owing to nothing more grave than the deprivation of breakfast until after Confession; it is characteristic of I.S. to complain of cramps at the first crinkle of hunger, and to demand food immediately, no matter where he is or in what company. On the way to church this morning, in any case, he growls from time to time like a hungry tiger; and I might add that since this is the second most sacred day in the year (next to Christmas), the growl is the only sound permitted. The birthday Confession and the Mass following it consume two hours, most of which time is knelt through on an uncushioned and rugless floor. When we enter the church, I.S. goes directly to the altar rail and prostrates himself. After a while an acolyte appears, rattling a thurible and showering us with incense. A priest enters next, half-concealing himself behind a rood screen, like an intrigant in a Restoration comedy. He signals I.S. to approach the screen, where he asks him—furtively, as if he were demanding the password in a speakeasy—the name of his patron saint. And from this point I.S. is "Igor" (correctly pronounced "Eager" only by V., who, at the same time, is the only person he will allow to pronounce it). "What, Igor, do you have on your conscience?" the confessor inquires, and whatever it is, I.S. tells him standing. For the Absolution, the priest holds a partlet over I.S.'s head, recites a prayer, and extends his pectoral cross to the penitent's lips. The church doors are opened after this, and a few stray people enter to join in the Mass and form a chorus, of sorts, in the *"Gospodi Pomilui."* A second acolyte now carries the monstrance for the priest and follows the Communion cup with a red cloth with which to wipe away pendant drops of wine. After taking the sacraments, I.S. prays with his head to the floor.

The ride from the church is silent, like the ride going, but at least the odor of sanctimony is dispelled—by the odor of whiskey and cold Russian cutlets. At home, I.S. goes directly to his studio and prays, as if to a fertility idol, before the icon that watches over him as he composes. From noon on, friends call, bringing gifts and offerings, while more than a hundred telegrams from the faithful but faraway pile up on the hall table. I.S.'s mood is unaffected, though, and he remains removed and untalkative to the end of the day.

JULY 7

I call on Schoenberg to return a tape of his Violin Concerto. Two sculptured heads of him are in the living room now, one from *ca.* 1936, the other, of recent date, shrunken to two-thirds, it seems, of the former size. He is unwell today, and unable to come downstairs, but his voice is audible from the bedroom, and from there he inscribes my scores of *Erwartung* and *Die glückliche Hand,* besides sending me a gift of the facsimile of *Dreimal Tausend Jahre.* He also sends a message inviting me to stay and listen to the Concerto (I have been doing little else all week). "He likes to hear it," Mrs. Schoenberg explains, "whatever he can hear of it, upstairs, for it is his favorite among his orchestral works, as the String Trio is of his chamber music." After we have listened twice through, she shows me Schoenberg's studio, which is as small and crowded as I.S.'s, but without I.S.'s finicky aesthetic arrangement of working paraphernalia, and without the tinsel and décor. The desk is tinted with red, yellow, and blue light from a stained-glass window which is eery, though not more so than the self-portraits, obsessive about eyes. Manuscripts and papers cover a desk, a table, and an old harmonium, and every inch of shelf space is stuffed with music (I notice orchestra scores of *Otello* and *Falstaff*) and bound sets of books (Strindberg, Ibsen, Byron). A mandolin, wistful reminder of the *Serenade* and *Pierrot,* hangs from a peg on the wall.

AUGUST 17

Naples. The balcony of I.S.'s room at the Excelsior. Soft blues of bay and sky, Sorrento and Castellmare, Vesuvio and the famous islands. But in spite of these views, our eyes are fixed on the waterfront below, which is an arena of strolling Americans and the touts who prey on them with fountain pens, black market rates of exchange, offers of the favors of their female relatives. These salesmen lean against the seawall, pretending to be absorbed in the view, then pounce around and harrow the victim at close quarters until he buys something "to get rid of the nuisance."

The shores are crowded with bathers, and the bay is white with sails. Beneath the balcony to the left are the docks of the Capri excursion boats. Here, every half-hour or so, a small steamer leaves or lands, low in the water with tourists. On the right side of the hotel is a restaurant, the Transatlantico, and the Castle of Lucullus, now a jail. Another restaurant, the Zi' Teresa, faces these incongruous buildings across a small inlet, and at night the rival names are spelled out in the brightest Neapolitan neon. Chinese lanterns festoon the façades of each dining establishment, and from each we hear the same music: guitars, violins, soulful tenors. In the morning, table laundry flutters from both their porches, and by morning, too, we hope that I.S.

will have recovered from an intestinal instability, the result of a lunch at one of them.

Dinner at the Pappagallo with Auden and Kallman. Auden—last seen sprawled on the floor of his New York apartment surrounded by open volumes of Saintsbury's prosody and the O.E.D.—looks outstandingly non-aboriginal in these surroundings. His hair is sun-hennaed, and his skin is raw with sunburn. Nor is his once-white Panama suit any help as a disguise. A gang of gamins single out and pursue him as we walk, but though he shouts *"Basta"* at them, the foreign ring of the word only increases his plight.

His right hand flaps circularly as he talks, and when his subject is serious, the movement becomes more forceful and the static between words increases. His arguments tend to be categorical: "There are actually just two points: (a) . . . and (b) . . . " Another of his characteristics is a contempt for ill-health. "Bad weather cannot exist if it is ignored," he will say, and on the strength of this philosophy eschew a coat and catch cold. Puzzle games, quizzes, quests, hypotheses, delight him. At dinner tonight he contends that "Italian and English are the languages of Heaven, 'Frog' the language of Hell." I am supposed to follow this by inventing Celestial and Infernal usages, but can think of none and, anyway, he is already developing the idea that "The 'Frogs' were expelled from Heaven in the first place because they annoyed God by calling him *cher maître*." (This is in reaction to some French visitors who have annoyed Auden by calling I.S. the same thing.) He has a prodigious repertory of unintentionally funny C. of E. hymns, and of opera prima donna anecdotes; and though he is very proper, even a Puritan, delicately indecorous stories amuse him like the one about my German friend who when ill in Paris swallowed a suppository thinking it a strange kind of French pill. His brilliant all-seeing brown eyes are set in a rumpled face (I.S.: "Soon we will have to smooth him out to see who it is"), but his actual eyesight is poor, and without spectacles he may fail to apprehend furniture; he once waded through the glass front doors of his own apartment. We drink grappa in the Galleria, but Auden is able to stay awake only long enough to swallow his sleeping pills. And he tips the table over as we leave, having forgotten its presence.

AUGUST 20

The boat to Ischia, a pocket steamer, absurdly class-segregated, is crowded and excruciatingly smelly; I am obliged to stand all the way to Casamicciola, where I finally find a seat next to a man who is reading Goldoni and evidently trying to memorize a passage he thinks extremely funny. At Forio I transfer to a scavenger-like trawler and am rowed ashore. Wystan meets me at the pier, barefoot and with the "bottoms of his trousers rolled," and he carries my bag through the toylike town to his house on the Via Santa Lucia. At street level this is an empty stable and carriage room, but the upstairs rooms are ample, bright, and immaculate, except for the burnt offerings in unemptied ashtrays, which may very well represent a protest against the sterility of American cleanliness. Americans are not responsible, in any case, but a handsome Neapolitan Ganymede with a manner like his not quite believable name, Giocondo. While Giocondo spreads the lunch, we move to a patio, the domain of a cat and a dog, Moses, for whom Wystan throws a ball, or pretends to, taking in the eager retriever again and again with the same feint, but once cuffing the poor cur for barking, which alters the quality of the noise to something resembling the voice of a screech owl.

Giocondo does not seem to understand very much of Wystan's Italian, and it must be a relief to him, as it certainly is to me, when the poet resumes the language of his muse. What, he asks, will become of I.S.'s promised Ischian visit? It can take place, I tell him, only when the doctors allow and when I.S. is prepared to brave the gauntlet of journalists standing round-the-clock guard in the hotel lobby. "Oh," says Wystan, "but the way to rid oneself of journalists in Italy is to pretend to believe in the Church. They will look at you, at that, as if you were wearing lawn sleeves, and scatter as if you had brought news of the plague." In this instant a courier arrives with another form of news, an express letter which Wystan passes to me without so much as glancing at it, and asking me for no more than a précis. It is an invitation from the intendant of La Scala to attend *The Rake* in Venice at La Scala's expense, and Wystan is unable to conceal his pleasure.

Conversation turning to *The Rake,* Wystan repeats his story about Benjamin Britten liking the opera very much, "Everything but the music" (a story I.S. did not find very amusing). But Wystan *is* worried about the score, I think because of some of the obvious resemblances, as for example between the first Bedlam aria and an aria in *Semele;* between the *fandango* in the graveyard scene and, well, a *fandango;* and between "Love that too quickly betrays," "Dear Father Truelove," the whores' chorus, and three pieces in *Così: "Un aura amorosa," "Vorrei dir,"* and *"Di scrivermi ogni giorno."* In short, what if the Great Auk (which had white spots around the eyes and was called pengwyn by the Newfoundland Indians) proves to be a dodo in the colloquial sense?

We walk to a beach in the afternoon, Wystan at high speed (he is now wearing Plimsolls) in spite of the heat, and, himself excepted, universal indolence; but the water is bathtub warm, and only Moses, still starting at every false throw, is aquatically inclined. On the return to Forio we meet Chester Kallman, just back from a visit to another part of the island. Wystan is always happier in tandem with Chester, and the best of his former good spirits now seem like doldrums in comparison. He dotes on the younger poet, in fact, listening admiringly to his talk, calling attention to jeweled bits of it, and supplying helpful interpretations for rougher gems, though as a rule if Chester appears even to be on the verge of speaking, Wystan will remain quiet. When the younger poet goes to the kitchen for a moment, Wystan says of him that "He is a very good poet and a far cleverer person than I am." Whatever the truth of these assessments, Chester most certainly *is* a very good cook. By some oversight, however, the spinach has not been washed tonight, and after what sounds like a painfully gritty bite, Wystan reports a considerable presence of sand; then lest we think him persnickety, he quickly adds that he doesn't in the least mind, and even manages to suggest that he has become quite fond of it.

His talk flows with generalizations, not all of them, at first flush, a hundred per cent self-evident. "Jews are more complex than Gentiles," he says, which seems a vulnerable thesis under the circumstances. But while his Manichean mind is almost continually engaged with polarizing moral distinctions, he goes about the sorting out of the Good and the Evil as if it were a game, and without the assumption of any rectitude on his own part. The language of it, however, is oddly diocesan and Sunday-School-like, as when, with vigorous rotary movements of his right hand and his always uptilted head held still farther back, he declares himself to be "very cross with Stalin" because the monster has been "naughty." (Stalin's icons flourish on Forio's walls side by side with those of the Virgin Madonna.)

At *passeggiata* time, we go to a café in the Piazza. There the librettists repeatedly raise their glasses to the *Rake* première—*"Prosit!"* from Wystan, whose natural foreign language even in Ischia is German. But the music the great man sings on the return to the Via Santa Lucia is from Fricka's waffling scene in *Die Walküre*. It sounds more than a little strange in this deserted—the whole town has gone to bed by ten o'clock—Mascagni scenery.

AUGUST 21

At 6 AM, Wystan, discalced in spite of the cold flagstones, escorts me to a bus which meets the Naples boat at Laccoameno; and only just meets it, for we stop at every turn to collect still more passengers and to tie still more bundles and cardboard suitcases to the roof. The boat being overcrowded as well, I debark at Pozzuoli and return to Naples by taxi. The driver is a testy type, very free with oaths, his favorites being, at high speed, *"Cretino!"* and, at low speed, *"Mezzo-culiliello!"* (half-assed). The latter is directed largely to inattentive pedestrians and to animals. Once we nearly collide with a vegetable cart hauled by a poor old Rosinante. *"Mezzo-culiliello!"*

I reach the hotel just as Dottore Musella, on his rounds, is telling I.S. that he is cured of his pneumonia, but at the same time confining him to bed for the balance of the week and forbidding the Ischia trip. (I.S., thin and aquiline, knees hunched to chin, a pack of hot compresses on his crown, looks remarkably like an eagle.) Dottore Musella, like many of I.S.'s physicians around the world, is eager to chat with his patient about the arts, but when he brings up the name of Eleonora Duse, V. does the talking, describing a performance of *A Doll's House* that she saw in Moscow as a child, and in which Duse played Nora in Italian "supported by" an otherwise Russian-speaking cast.

When the Dottore departs, V., attempting to dissuade I.S. from conducting *The Rake* even if he *has* fully recovered, attributes some of his desire to conduct it to vanity. I.S., in an access of pique, answers that he *is* a performer, and hence an actor, but not a vain one. "Acting," he continues, "is an element in my make-up. My father was renowned for his dramatic talent as much as for his voice. And besides, I *like* to perform."

After this burst of off-telling, I accompany V. to a *farmacia* to fetch I.S.'s medicines. We join a queue of American tourists, all purchasing paregoric and all looking intensely uncomfortable as V., in turn, asks for milk of magnesia.

AUGUST 26

To Milan. The train, a *rapido,* is wobbly, sooty, and two hours late. I.S.: "Italians will not believe without a certain amount of exaggeration. Thus the expression *'una cosa tremenda'* is applied to something of no great moment, and the words *'brutissimo'* and *'repellente'* are used with reference to quite minor inconveniences. As you see, too, the slowest and least punctual trains are called *'rapido,' 'accelerato,' 'direttissimo.'* "

I.S. receives a film star's reception at the Duomo Hotel, where the entire street is blocked off and the entranceway is protected by ropes.

SEPTEMBER 5

On the train from Milan to Venice: cast, chorus, and orchestra of *The Rake* in three reserved cars. We are in the restaurant car when the train stops at Verona, and an American tourist, across the aisle, says to his companion: "Hey, didn't Shakespeare live here?" Auden, interrupting: "But surely it was Bacon."

Venice. Wystan, finding his La Scala-financed accommodations at the Bauer to be bathless and viewless, flees to the I.S.'s over-upholstered and luxuriously uncomfortable Royal Suite and bursts into tears. V. calls the *"Direzione,"* explaining that Maestro Auden is not only the co-author of *"La carriera d'un libertino"* but "a kind of Guglielmo Shakespeare, who, moreover, has been received at Buckingham Palace by the King." A better room is promptly found, of course, but Wystan's tears, exposing so much frustration and wounded pride, have watered us all a bit, not because he is beyond the most appropriate age for them, but because of his vastly superior mind.

I.S.'s piano arrives. Trussed in canvas and hawsers, it is pulleyed from the canal to his second-floor room like a mule up the side of a ship. Faint sounds escape through his door thereafter, the same notes over and over, like piano tuning. (I.S.: "My brothers used to call me the 'piano tuner,' because I would repeat a note that I liked.") Later, V. remarks that the hotel staff seems much relieved. They have evidently expected him to compose as Liszt and Chopin have been made to do in films, i.e., with cascades of sound and stormy "passages."

The Piazza. Pigeon love. The male treads and turns, blinks, treads again, chases. I.S. says that the bands playing on either side of the Piazza "sound together like Milhaud."

A *Rake* rehearsal at La Fenice this evening. No syllable of the Scala chorus sounds English. And a midnight gondola ride to the Zanipolo with Auden, drunk and full of song—*Die Walküre.* I.S. says that Colette once sang Wagner to him when they were drunk together on the Paris–Nice train. A large rat runs along the molding of a wall two feet from our boat. "The D.T.'s," says Auden.

SEPTEMBER 11

The première. A damp day. Auden, very out of patience, threatens to change the line "A scene like this is better than a sale" to "A scene like this is slower than a snail." I.S.: "Auden is as nervous as an expectant aunt." But the opera survives its performance, including a dozen disastrous entrances, and is very moving in spite of all the mistakes. Each loge is crowned with a bouquet of roses, and the audience is the *ne plus ultra* of elegance. At the Taverna, afterward, we play a tune-detection game of citing resemblances to other operas. V. thinks the Mourning Chorus begins like the *Volga Boat Song.* Auden says the beginning of Act III, and especially the woodwind trill with the *fermata,* reminds him of the dance of the apprentices in *Die Meistersinger,* and he adds that "They are rebuked" in Bedlam is "an unexpected venture into Richard Strauss. The Terzetto," he goes on, "is Tchaikovskyan, and the Epilogue is modeled on *Don Giovanni.*" But here I.S., who neither recognizes nor admits any of the attributions, objects. "The Epilogue is a vaudeville or pasquinade, of which opera's greatest examples are in the *Seraglio* and *L'Heure espagnole.* In fact, some of *The Rake* is close to Broadway, Baba's music especially."

SEPTEMBER 14

We go to Chioggia in the afternoon, a two-hour ride even in our fast motorboat. South of the "island of the mad," San Servelo (*sans cervelles?*), our propeller is strangled in seaweed and we are obliged to ask for help from a passing barge—in return for which the crew asks to (and does) shake hands with I.S. North of Chioggia, near the passageway to the open sea, sails swarm over the lagoon, some of them red, yellow, and blue, some framing St. Christophers and other saints and madonnas—including a Madonna of the Kettledrums—who grow fat or lean according to the Adriatic wind.

We park in the canal of San Domenico, mooring to the outermost of several fishing boats and scrambling over them to a cobblestone street. A crowd applauds I.S. and follows him over canal bridges and past rundown Venetian palazzi with flowerpot chimneys—Chioggia is the *very* poor man's Venice—to the center of the city. V.'s golden sandals are objects of universal fascination, but, then, all the children and many of the men are barefoot; the women wear clogs.

The whole city stinks of fish, an overpowering odor because of which we stop at a café on the main street and drink Fernet Brancas. A moment later an ancient automobile bleats its way through the crowd and to our table. This dilapidated vehicle is Chioggia's unique taxi—so its driver claims, though just then two other ancient jalopies come rattling and racing each other in our direction. Not knowing which to choose—the early bird might not be the hungriest, and the chirping and flapping of the other birds can hardly be ignored—we hire all three and set out on a brief tour, each of us in his own car. Mine has a wooden bench for a seat and a hole in the floor as large as the windows, where hands reach in displaying lottery tickets, toy gondolas, religious medals.

We leave our taxis—exchanging innumerable *addio*s only at the *pescheria,* where fishermen are putting their boats to bed under tarpaulins, and we walk from there to San Domenica. This otherwise rather bare church has two treasures, Carpaccio's "St. Paul," invisibly high on the south wall, and a large wooden crucifix, "miraculously" discovered in the canal like a piece of driftwood. We apply to the sacristan, a small boy, for permission to see it, and follow him behind the altar, where he unlocks two tall doors, draws a velvet curtain, and swings the cross out so that it can be viewed from all angles. The Christ is a gaunt, larger-than-life figure—ropes of veins stand out even at thirty feet—yet strangely alive. To judge by the rococo curls in the beard and hair it dates from the eighteenth century; and to judge by the carving, it is probably the work of a Tyrolean peasant—in spite of the stylized hair and the routine halo and crown of thorns. But the source of its power is that half of it remains a wild tree trunk. And whereas the head, slumped to the side, is fully formed, the torso and legs are dispro-portionately elongated and the arms, which are still the limbs of a tree, are unnaturally thin. Its maker must have had an apparition, coming on the tree in the woods, an apparition that survives even in this sunny Italian church—the ghost in the closet, the *"Ecce Homo"* behind the altar's sweet-faced Christ and Mary dolls.

The lagoon is hazy on the way back to Venice, and full of mirages; and from time to time birds rest on our prow. It is after dark when we reach the Grand Canal. The black gondolas gliding by might be coffins bearing victims of a plague to the islands for secret burial.

1948
1949
1950
1951
1952
1953
1954
1955
1956
1957
1958
1959
1960
1961
1962
1963
1964
1965
1966
1967
1968
1969
1970
1971

ITINERARY

January 1: Arrive at Pasadena. **4:** Dinner at the Huxleys. **12:** Maria Huxley's first operation. Aldous for lunch, after which R.C. taxis him to the hospital. **13:** Aldous for lunch. **15:** I.S. conducts concert in Royce Hall, U.C.L.A., and attends a reception at Alma Mahler's. **20:** Aldous for tea. **27:** Dinner with Aldous and Frieda Lawrence. **February 23:** R.C. drives Aldous to the Turner Show at the Huntington Museum in Pasadena. **24:** R.C. conducts Schoenberg's Suite, Opus 29, at U.S.C. **28:** Dinner with Frieda Lawrence. **March 22:** I.S. flies to Mexico with his son-in-law for concerts (Hotel Del Prado). **30:** I.S. flies to Los Angeles. **April 23:** We fly to New York, and, on the 28th, to Paris. **29:** We fly to Geneva, where I.S. attends an evening rehearsal of *The Rake.* **May 2:** *The Rake* in Geneva. **3:** We fly to Paris (Plaza-Athénée), and go to *Wozzeck.* **4:** Monteux conducts *Le Sacre du printemps* in the Théâtre des Champs-Elysées, an ovation for I.S. **14:** *Orpheus* danced by the New York City Ballet. **19:** I.S. conducts *Oedipus Rex,* with Cocteau narrating. **22:** I.S. conducts a concert at the Théâtre des Champs-Elysées. **23:** We go by train to Brussels, where I.S. conducts (29th). **June 1:** We drive to The Hague via Ghent, Bruges, Vlissingen. **9–10:** We fly from Amsterdam to New York. **15:** Fly to Detroit with Alexei Haieff. **16:** The I.S.'s buy a Buick at Flint. **18:** I.S.'s birthday; lunch in Duluth. Drive to Los Angeles via Minot, Kalispell, Calgary, Banff, Spokane, San Francisco, arriving in Los Angeles on the 29th. **July:** I.S. begins the *Septet.* **25:** Maria Huxley is again hospitalized. Aldous for dinner. **October–November:** R.C. conducts four concerts in memory of Schoenberg. **November:** I.S. conducts première of his *Cantata* at Royce Hall. **13:** V. has a thyroid operation. **December 21:** I.S. conducts *Cantata* in Town Hall, New York, for the New Friends of Music. **22:** I.S. records his *Cantata.*

FEBRUARY 23

I witness and sign Aldous's Last Will and Testament, in token for which I receive a volume of risqué French verse, an inducement to improve my "command" of the language, he says, adding that the book had been given to him in his youth for the same purpose.

He has just returned from a trip in the desert, and, as always after a spell in depopulated regions, is refreshed and in high spirits. He has brought back a garland of rare-blossoming—once-in-a-decade—lilies, but he himself is a far rarer and more spectacular burgeoning. "Cacti," he says, "grow no more than an inch in five years, hence the large ones are among the world's most venerable plants." But he is more excited by his discovery that "desert 'poorwills' hibernate. They are genetically related to hummingbirds, you remember, and heretofore hummingbirds were the only species known to hibernate. The early Hindu philosophers called them 'sleeping birds.'" He then digresses for a fascinating quarter of an hour on the Trochilidea family, "what the onomatopoeic Mayans called the Dzunuum . . . "

I drive him later to the summit of Doheny Hill, the start of one of his favorite rambles. (But *not* one of mine; though scarcely five minutes from the center of Beverly Hills, it has a reputation for rattlesnakes.) We follow rutted tracks into a wilderness, the daddy-long-legs easily ahead. But the intellectual pace is even faster, and here, without trying, he keeps a good sprint in front, which makes me feel mentally pigeon-toed in pursuit, and I am trying very hard. He drops dendrological information along the way, as if we were on a botanical tutorial, and I learn and forget all sorts of things about flora to right and left of the path, from the tallest pedunculates to the tiniest sessile organisms—though one wonders how he, purblind as he is, can tell.

Not until the return trek does he switch to a subject I am able to follow, "the lit'ry cult of dirt, Auden's 'Nor make love to those who wash too much.'" According to Aldous, Ford Madox Ford was probably the least frequently washed of modern novelists. My own unique contribution to all this is a quote from the dirt-specialist historian Lecky, though after quoting it I suddenly realize I have mistakenly attributed the remark to J. B. Bury, whose name I mispronounce, as though it had to do with graveyards. Aldous is greatly taken aback by his ignorance of this author until dawn breaks and he discovers that "You mean Professor Bewry." His most interesting remarks of the afternoon, however, are about "Tom Eliot," whose criticism he compares to "A great operation that is never performed: powerful lights are brought into focus, anaesthetists and assistants are posted, instruments are prepared. Finally the surgeon arrives and opens his bag—but closes it again and goes off." He says that "The marriage in *The Cocktail Party* was inspired—if that is the word—by Tom's own marriage. His wife, Vivienne, was an ether addict. Her face was mottled, like ecchymotic spots, and the house smelled like a hospital. All that dust and despair in Eliot's poetry can be traced back to this fact. Then, too, of course, *The Family Reunion* is a play about murdering one's wife."

After the walk we drive to an ice-cream parlor in Beverly Hills and, at Aldous's suggestion, eat banana splits. "Cerebrotonics should eat bananas every day," he says.

MAY 3

Paris. *Wozzeck* at the Théâtre des Champs-Elysées, and after it a dinner with Albert Camus at the Café Relais (Plaza-Athénée). Camus is uncommunicative at first, annoyed, I think, by our talk about the music. At one point he attempts to turn the conversation to Melville, saying that he plans to devote an essay to this "greatest American writer, an infinitely more important writer than the pederast voyeur Henry James." No one takes the bait, however, and the Büchner-Berg talk continues. But if the opera made little impression on Camus—in comparison with the permanent dent in myself—he is attentive to whatever is said about the play. I.S. suggests that "Gogol is the only contemporary of Büchner with whom he might be compared. He lacks Gogol's sense of humor, but his vision was more radical, and he threw off the social blinkers of his time with more power of poetry. I am thinking of Wozzeck's: 'People like us, if we ever did get into Heaven, they'd put us to work on the thunder.'" I.S. contends that the last orchestral interlude is a mistake. "Until this point the composer stays behind his constructions; but here he comes up front to tell us exactly how he feels about it all and how we should feel, as if there had ever been any doubt about how anyone felt. Berg should have avoided this apotheosis and ended with the Doktor's *'Jetzt ganz still'* or the Hauptmann's *'Kommen Sie schnell.'*"

1952

Camus says that "Like Caliban, Wozzeck sees and hears with an animal being, a radar apparatus which reaches into Nature itself. That he is under the spell of an enchanted Nature is established already in the foraging scene, where he sees a strange fire while his companion sees only a man having visions. And again in the scene with the Doktor, this Nature that Wozzeck seeks to understand is hardly ever absent. 'If only one could read the lines and figures in the toadstools,' he says, which reminds me of De Quincey's "great alphabet of Nature,"[1] but the medical materialist forbids the thought, telling him that *his* Nature is the merest superstition. At times, too, Wozzeck might be describing the effects of a hallucinatory drug: 'The world gets dark, and you have to feel around with your hands and everything keeps slipping, like a spider's web.' The Fool is also subject to visions, incidentally, and though he is something of a stock character, his visions put him, briefly, on the same wavelength as Wozzeck."

At this point I.S. interrupts, saying that the great feat of the Fool's scene is in the music. "Berg really does succeed in creating the impression that the concertina, the band, the soldiers' chorus have all been improvised then and there for a one and only performance. And this may be the greatest achievement of the opera as a whole: the audience's sense of a totally spontaneous expressive freedom from a score compounded of formal devices."

Camus goes on to say that "Wozzeck's isolation is defined less than a minute after the curtain goes up. He talks to the Captain and the Captain to him, but without communicating. And in the next three scenes it is the same between Wozzeck and his comrade, Wozzeck and his wife, Wozzeck and the man of science, that proto-Nazi doctor who is the most astonishing creation of all—though Büchner's doctor is not quite the same as the Nazi scientists who treated men as objects of experiment, because he still has to tell himself not to 'let a mere man upset you.' The catechism of the Doktor scene is a no less amazing anticipation, incidentally, and the way

1. And today (1971) of Michel Foucault's "The madman sees nothing but resemblances everywhere; for him all signs resemble one another, and all resemblances have the value of signs."

33

the name of Marie comes to Wozzeck's lips is a stroke of genius. So is the fact that the scientific-materialist Doktor fails to perceive this 'Freudian slip' and the further fact that when the man of true human nature—'the dumb soul of humanity,' as Rilke described Wozzeck—is delivered to his tormentor, it is the tormentor who is destroyed, who disintegrates as a human being as his indifference to suffering progresses. Thus the Doktor in this scene and the Captain at the end of the play, when he says, 'Come away, it is not good to listen.' That statement stands as the antithesis to all those questions in which Wozzeck seeks to discover the meaning of Nature."

MAY 10

The people with whom we dine at noon devote the greater part of their conversation to gossip about the people with whom we dine in the evening, and vice versa. This is uncomfortable because, as I.S. says, "People who talk this way *to* you will talk the same way *about* you. 'The Judgment of Paris' is not a pretty picture, but you can learn from it that hate and greed make the world go round."

In the evening we go to the Deux Magots with Balthus, who is slim, pale, handsome, bittersweet, dandyish, and femininely conscious of his clothes, which are evidently meant to identify him as a Hebridean laird or, at any rate, to conceal that his profession could have anything to do with paint. But whereas he will say nothing about art, except to vent some scorn on "the latest daubs of Chagall," it is difficult to steer him away from music, Schubert's above all. Otherwise the conversation centers on the Reverend James McLane, pioneer Balthus collector and Los Angeles friend of I.S.; in fact, I.S. is soon performing missionary and ambassadorial roles for artist and buyer alike, the painter being as curious about his clergyman admirer as the reverse; but the first question in the minds of both undoubtedly concerns the erotic sensibilities of the other, and that question Balthus approaches only very indirectly.

And what about Balthus's portrait of Eros? Do his open-legged, mirror-fixated pubescent girls represent joyful innocence, as Camus and Artaud think? Or do they project a Lesbian appetite (a storm behind the dyke), as I think, for it seems to me that the girls openly dream of being fingered by an older woman—which actually happens in "The Guitar Lesson"—while all of them are either flushed with desire or pale with satisfaction (or is it the other way around?). They are definitely not the little girls to gratify little boys, in any case, or for that matter big ones: those barely budding bosoms and itchily self-conscious pudenda, those girl bodies with acromegalic boys' heads, those stubby legs—edematous calves, puppy-fat ankles, teeny feet— are at any rate a long way from *my* visions of the voluptuous.

But I also fail to glean any insight from the man concerning the other oddities of his artistic eidos. Why, for example, indisputable master of his technique that he is, does he seem at times hardly to know how to draw? And why, apart from the juvenile would-be-delinquents, is his work in no

34

way concerned with the contemporary? In fact, a list of influences would read like a catalogue of loans from the Louvre: Piero, Carpaccio, Caravaggio, Velázquez (the dwarfs, duennas, cats, mirrors, goldfish bowls), the French seventeenth century, Courbet, Corot, David, Ingres, Seurat, Cézanne. Whatever the answers, Balthus is peerless among living portraitists—his "Miró" and his "Derain"—and the same could be said, in their genre, of his landscapes, especially those with trees somewhat in the manner of the early Mondrian. And he stands no less alone in another dimension, the representation of Evil. I am thinking of *"La Chambre,"* in which, surely, the sexually ambivalent Satanic dwarf-witch cannot be ignored, the picture meaning more than, as I.S. would have it, spatial architecture and chiaroscuro.

MAY 14

We reach wild and holy Rocamadour in mid-afternoon, and immediately begin the ascent of the great crag, at first via 143 stairs, worn and grooved by the knees of a millennium of expiators, including Thomas à Becket's assassin, Henry II. A chapel, containing the bones of St. Amadour and the shrine of a Black Virgin, clings to the precipice like a clematis. The Virgin is a worm-perforated doll with crown and streaming tulle, but a hypnotizing totem, too, its eyes abjuring the world and fixing to a point beyond, and its smile radiating a higher, gnostic wisdom. The attribution of miraculous powers to the carving would not have been surprising a few centuries ago and, in fact, not very surprising now, as a party of pilgrims, some prostrate, some piously telling their beads, attests.

The cliff can be scaled by another route as well, a Stations of the Cross, and it is by this path, leaving the chapel, that we continue the climb. Each Station is equipped with a stone bench in which we discover wavy trilobite imprints—and wonder whether the medieval masons chose the stones because of the fossil patterns, and if so, what did they suppose them to be? (Xenophanes, after all, predicated his cyclical theory of geological history on fossil imprints of fish in the marble quarries at Syracuse.)

The view from the summit is worth the exertion in obtaining it and in staving off the souvenir touters. We return to Rocamadour village on an automobile road leading to the principal, twelfth-century gate. Now in late afternoon, the cliff is in shadow, and some of the chimneys of the windowless and tomblike stone dwellings are emitting smoke—a macabre effect, in the absence of other signs of life. The claim of the *Guide Bleu* that these edifices have never been restored is too obviously true; it is more difficult to believe that people still inhabit them.

Our hotel, the Notre-Dame de Rocamadour, has not been disturbed by post-medieval developments in plumbing, but the restaurant is reasonably recent in date, as well as highly recommended for truffles. We dine on the terrace, not wishing to disappoint a waiter who has taken great pains to attach a Chinese lantern to our table. This looks over the Alzou River, on whose banks the townswomen are spreading laundry; the smack of wet clothes on stone flip-flaps through the valley long after dark.

MAY 15

1952

Cave entrances, some of them wholly or partly boarded up, are in view from time to time during the forty-mile ride to Lascaux, and many of the names on the route signs, Les Eyzies for one, and Les Combarelles, and Font-de-Gaume, are renowned in archeology, the last-mentioned for its paintings of mastodons. (I might add that the road itself competes in kind with these main attractions of the region by plunging our 1932 Studebaker, the best rentable automobile in Souillac, to its fenders in holes.) But the name Lascaux does not appear until Montignac-sur-Vézère, the town nearest to that most celebrated of the Magdalenian painted caves. A mile or two up a hill beyond Montignac, we come to a clearing and a footpath leading through pine woods to the entrance. There, posted to a tree, is a hospital-type notice of visiting days and hours, and as there are few enough of either, we are left wondering why this possibly ruinous information was not available in Paris, and at our luck in coinciding with one of the rare times of admission.

The guide is one of the cave's discoverers, one of the former schoolboys who stumbled on it twelve years ago searching for a ball that had disappeared in a golf-sized hole; probing with sticks, and eventually digging their way in, these youths were the first to see the buried Sistine Chapel of Stone Age art. The true entrance has never been found, however, probably having been closed as a result of volcanic faulting, and the one we use, an airlock with double sets of iron doors, was only recently installed.

Seepage from overhead rocks has flooded the ground beyond as well as before the first door, but on choice I prefer the clamminess and the creepy-crawlies to the twinges of claustrophobia with which I am afflicted when we pass from the airlock propylaea to the cave proper. But those sensations are dispelled or forgotten as soon as our eyes accustom to the dim, eery glow of a dozen feeble footlights—eery because they suggest the troglodyte artists' grease lamps—and, with the supplement of the guide's electric torch, begin to distinguish brilliant red-and-yellow patches and glistening black lines on the walls and ceilings ahead and overhead.

When my eyes form a system of these lines and colors into a bull, I suspect an ocular trick. Then the beauty and power of the animal, and the rhythm of it on the rough surface, inspire an awe in me such as no terranean temple ever has, the stronger, no doubt, because Stone Age Man, when I have tried to imagine him at all, has heretofore provoked only a vague loathing. But I think that no one could fail to be humbled before the spectacle of so much resplendent life—after that instant of incredulity attributable to the incomprehensible gulf of so many thousands of years.

The cave is toothlike, not only in that the two principal chambers branch from the main rotunda like dental roots, but also because the right root contains a cavity that bores into the earthen gums to a depth of about eight feet. The cave's unique representation of a human being is in this cavity, and our visit there is a turning point, our experience before having been primarily aesthetic, while after it we are concerned with meaning. The human figure is schematically scratched, like a stick man. It is bird-headed, as well, and its other most conspicuous feature is its semi-tumescent and distended—with a horim?—sex. Whatever this picture represents—shaman, hunter, god—the contrast between the crudeness of it and the naturalistically perfect depictions of animals implies a complex relationship of human being and beast which involves, in turn, a system of natural gods and divine attributes (zoomorphism) and a system of sympathetic magic, for a matching bird-headed wand is etched near the birdman, along with a club and an arrow. In short, we are confronted with symbols and the symbol-making power, hence with evidence for the existence of a dualistic belief system some two to three hundred centuries ago.

Still, this discovery of a metaphysical cave man is not more impressive than the discovery of his refinement of artistic technique and delicacy of artistic feeling. He must have lived very like the beasts he killed, after all, yet his art is the least primitive imaginable even by academic standards. The purity of the artist's emotion, partly owing to which the animals are as real as yesterday and almost breathingly alive, is matched by a mastery of proportion, a power of line, an intelligence in abbreviation, all as canny, it seems to me, as in the greatest pictorial creations of any historical period.

To acquaint us with the astonishing profusion of paintings at the start of the tour, the guide plays his torch panoramically over all of the decorated surfaces of the oval-shaped main room. The superimposition of animal on animal, presumably by successive generations of artists, is bewildering at first, yet the form of whatever individual outline the eye seeks to trace stands out clearly. This, I think—as if I could "think" anything about the state of consciousness of a prelogical mind thirty millennia ago—is because each artist must have formed his own view of a painted area, and composed his own picture according to his own new and different scale. In every case the contours and surface qualities of the calcite walls are determining factors in the composition. Thus the line of a vertebra will run congruently with a crack in the rock; and an eye socket prove to be a natural hole or indentation, from which locus the entire animal has been designed. No animal is placed in a rectangular field, and none seems to have been composed to any sight line or beholder's eye other than the artist's, which is a reminder that in spite of all the framed squares of paint in square rooms throughout the world, neither nature nor the human eye is box-shaped.

By similar tokens, photographs and drawings are no preparation for the 3-D effects of the convexities and concavities of the surfaces. And in matters of color and scale, all the photographs I have seen are positively misleading, the sizes of the animals being so various, and the colors so vivid—for one expects to see faint, flaked lines, scarcely visible in the dark, and forms at least as faded as Uccello's Noah frescoes. In fact, the reds, yellows, and blacks glisten as if they had been newly varnished and had not yet had time to dry; the "Last Supper" is in far worse condition. This extraordinary state of preservation—part of the reason for that initial moment of disbelief—is explained to us as good geological luck. The cave must have been sealed like a jar for most of its estimated twenty to thirty thousand decorated years.

The right wall of the right root, from the main room to the crypt of the bird-headed man, is traced with engravings. Beyond that, the bulging and hollowing—and, surprisingly, never artificially smoothed or flattened— surface is covered with horses and bovids, after which the chamber coils navel-like into the earth. The left root, however, funnels away even more suddenly and deeply, and is even more richly embellished. Arrows are depicted in greater numbers here than elsewhere in the cave, too, both *in* their ungulate targets and on the ground; if it *is* the ground, for the viewer's perspective limits *him*.

Our inspection is terminated when the guide reminds us that, owing to the small ration of air, visits are limited to an hour. A longer term would corrupt the paintings, but it would also provoke visual indigestion, at any rate in me. For I attribute the brief feeling of suffocation and intoxication *outside,* in the morning sun, not so much to the cave's anemic air as to its teeming chthonian life. The silence of the cave continues to reverberate, too, and, finally, we all suffer from a kind of aerio, or, rather, tempero embolism, for want of a time decompressor or Wellsian time machine to throw us back into the present.

I climb the hill above the cave and emerge from the woods into a field of cornflowers and wild poppies. But the cave continues to haunt me there, and will continue to haunt me in some degree all my life.

1952

DECEMBER 18

Albuquerque, aboard the "Super Chief," Los Angeles to Chicago. Rain turning to feathery snow. Cattle-cars, bound for a Chicago hecatomb, are parked on a siding next to us, the animals moaning restlessly in their cold, wet cages, under which pigeons huddle, as if trying to give comfort.

In the club car, late morning, we sit opposite a man wearing a spiv suit, a glossy, unseasonal suntan, brown suede shoes, a rancher's string tie, and—this on the seat beside him—a multi-gallon Texan hat. It is impossible not to notice that he leaves a tip of the change from ten dollars minus one scotch-and-soda; and as other waiters and porters happen over-casually to pass his table—no doubt after scrambling madly through other cars to get there—the tipping is repeated on the same scale. Barmen, chefs, busboys, even the conductor: all seem to be confederates of this Maecenas, and no wonder. A gambler flush from the tables of Las Vegas buying a Christmas-time conscience, we suppose. Then I try, unsuccessfully, to put him out of mind while I work on some lines begun last night as the train crossed the desert:

In the Desert near Las Vegas

No green hope braves the brown eternity
And among the sun-worshipers no saint
(I think of the Thebaid in the third century)
Hears or heeds the body's de luxe complaint

        O where do the lions go
        to have their thorns removed?

Receding seas ebbed this startled ground
Where Saurian shapes, still struggling as they drowned
Now pillorying the eye on their weird halt
Impillar fleeing gamblers turned to salt.

        O where is the old man's cave
        the old man whom lions trust?

The snowflakes are larger by noon and they swing slowly down on the tumbleweed and piñon like parachutes. We go to the dining car, but are no sooner seated than a crackling fire breaks out at a table behind us. It is the guiltily generous tipper, of course, or, more exactly, a steak on a portable charcoal broiler on the table in front of him. Smoke and commotion fill the dining car, and the stewards flutter from table to table, reasoning with complainers and assuring them there is no "fire." A man entering the car at this point and obviously thinking the train is ablaze, recoils in panic. Then four others, coming from the other direction and evidently on the drink, stop and gawk at the private stove with the amazement of Ensor's "Celebrated Persian Physicians examining the stools of King Darius after the Battle of Arbela." But before long the lavish tipper pokes a thermometer into the meat, appears satisfied with the result, extinguishes the flame, seasons, and—amidst universal staring, less hungry but hardly less curious than that of the mob watching the King at table in Versailles—eats it. Later, a waiter tells V. that we have been in the presence of the World's Champion Steak Eater.

DECEMBER 26

New York. A Christmas dinner at Auden's. He kisses us as we enter, the prerogative being a sprig of mistletoe dangling over the barricade of book-filled crates by the door (which does not shut tightly and exposes the residence to footpads). Shuffling about in *pantoufles* (bunion-accommodating babouches, actually), he distributes a pile of fetchingly wrapped and rib-boned Christmas presents: for me a copy of *Portrait of a Whig* (his essay on Sydney Smith), and his new poem, *The Woods*.

The apartment is imaginatively decorated for the Yuletide, with empty bottles, used martini glasses, books, papers, phonograph records, all realistically strewn about to create a marvelously lifelike impression of randomness. And the decorators have achieved other, subtle touches of picturesqueness as well, such as, in lieu of frankincense, filling the flat with stale, boozy air. We compete for the most recently occupied, and hence dusted, chairs—the furniture looks as if it had been purchased with Green Stamps—then choose drinks, tipping out cigarette butts and ashes, dregs of earlier drinks and other detritus from the glasses in which they seem most likely to be served. But, shortly before dinner, the fine line between décor and reality momentarily confuses V. Visiting the lavatory and finding shaving utensils and other matter in the sink, a glass containing a set of snappers (store teeth), a mirror in which it would be impossible even to *recognize* oneself, a towel that would oblige the user to start over again, and a basin of dirty fluid on the floor, she unthinkingly empties the basin and fills it with fresh water. Not until dessert time do we discover, with mixed emotions, that she has flushed away Chester's chocolate pudding.

Wystan diverts us at dinner with stories about a mouse who shares the flat (born and brewed there, no doubt), and of whom he has become extremely fond. "There are usually scraps enough lying about for the poor dear to eat," he says, inviting speculation about the other livestock that may be boarding there. And not just lying about, either; the plates and silverware are greasy, and, such is the dishwasher's myopia, not entirely free of hardened remnants of previous meals. The dinner—smoked clams, steak, potatoes with dill—is excellent, and Wystan tucks in like Oliver Twist, which helps to account for his marsupial-like paunch; his plate soon looks as if it had been attacked by locusts. Five bottles of Pommard, from a case deposited on the floor at the end of the table, are drained as well, but whereas I am heavy-lidded in consequence, Wystan remains a searchlight of intelligence. Nor does he put on his mortarboard tonight. In fact, the Christmas merriment is intruded upon only once, by a telephone call from a female admirer, the same who followed him to Venice at the time of *The Rake,* and from whom, like Casanova but for the opposite reason, he was forever escaping, jumping into passing gondolas, and once almost taking a header into a canal.

After dinner he plays recordings of bits of *Dido, Nabucco,* and *Die Walküre.* I.S. knows he is being courted with the Wagner but is not in a compliant mood, and after twenty minutes of squirming puts it down as "improvisation." Which visibly disappoints Wystan.

DECEMBER 27

A visit from Wystan and Edith and Osbert Sitwell. "Now remember," Wystan says, briefing us on the telephone, "Edith drinks like a fish." On this recommendation V. places a standing order for double martinis and double scotches to be sent up at regular intervals. But the poetess merely sips her concoction, while her brother's hands shake uncontrollably and would be unable to hold anything: he sits on them during most of the meeting. The toping, therefore, is done entirely by I.S. and Wystan himself, who between them siphon off the contents of a full tray.

Dr. Edith's accoutrements include a Persian lamb coat, thick tubular gold bracelets, a rosewood walking stick, a strong dose of unidentified scent. But after a first glance one's attention never leaves her head. It is swathed in black silk (denying verification to Wystan's contention that she is "as bald as a coot"), which, in conjunction with her most estimable nose, evokes a likeness, in profile, to a pileated woodpecker. The spectral blanc-de-chine face might have come from a tapestry, or beneath the swirling *lettrine* of an illuminated manuscript. Yet the eyes are its most remarkable feature. They are heavily underpenciled with blue, like the woad dye of a Briton warrior, and they squint as narrowly as the eye slits in a medieval helmet.

Dr. Edith enters the room peeling long black gloves and remarking that a gorilla in the Ringling Circus at Sarasota watched her do this, then tried to do the same with his hands, failing in which he kissed hers—which homage appears neither to have surprised nor frightened her, whereas the animal's trainer, she reports, is still in hospital recuperating from the shock. And who, having met this intimidating woman, would presume to doubt the story?

Turning the talk to Hollywood, Dr. Edith asks I.S. about "the extent to which Aldous really believes in Tantra." But whatever I.S.'s estimate of Aldous's beliefs (which he undoubtedly regards as strictly Aldous's affair), his mind turns like a compass needle to the center of his own: "Sacrifice is the basis of religion," he says, "but sleeping on beds of nails and living on diets of grass are only experiments, not sacrifices." Later in the evening, nevertheless, he resolves to bone up on the Upanishads.

Shortly after the departure of this literary royalty, our upstairs neighbor, Mrs. George Orwell, tells V. she had been giving a party in her rooms at the same time as ours, but the bar service was very slow. "When I complained to the waiter, he advised me to 'Do like those Russians on the seventh floor, lady, order doubles.'"

1948
1949
1950
1951
1952
1953
1954
1955
1956
1957
1958
1959
1960
1961
1962
1963
1964
1965
1966
1967
1968
1969
1970
1971

ITINERARY

February 14, 19: *The Rake's Progress* is performed at the Metropolitan Opera. **15:** I.S. goes to Baltimore with V. and Edward James for a concert on the 18th. **26:** I.S. conducts the New York Philharmonic. **March 1, 10:** I.S. records *The Rake*. **11:** Fly to Hollywood. **31:** I.S. flies to Havana with his son-in-law, for concerts in Havana and Caracas, then to New York. **May 2:** I.S. and V. fly to Boston, where R.C. is rehearsing *The Rake*. **17, 18:** I.S. conducts *The Rake* at Boston University. **27:** We drive to New York. **29:** Drive to Hollywood via Pittsburgh, St. Louis, and, June 2, Albuquerque. **June 3:** Phoenix, Hollywood (4th). **July 24:** I.S. has a prostate operation at the Good Samaritan Hospital, by Dr. Elmer Belt (the Leonardo collector), with disastrous after-effects from the spinal anaesthetic on his sense of balance and walking. **August 2:** I.S. is released from the hospital. **September 14:** Construction is begun on a new room at the back of the I.S. house. **October 19:** Stravinsky "jazz" concert at Evenings-on-the-Roof. **November 9:** Death of Dylan Thomas. **18:** I.S. conducts the Los Angeles Philharmonic in Pasadena. **19, 20:** I.S. conducts the Los Angeles Philharmonic in Los Angeles. **27-29:** Drive to Palm Springs and La Jolla. **December 6:** I.S. receives a decoration from the Italian government, at the home of the Italian Consul in Los Angeles.

JANUARY 21

New York. Dinner at Maria's with Auden. He is whey-faced, shaken by the latest trials with his female admirer, who "finally had to be taken to the coop. She was ringing up every few minutes, hammering at the door in the middle of the night, even bribing the manager of the building to be let into my apartment; though once inside she did no more than take measurements of my old suit in order to buy me a new one. And she began to shout in public that we had had intercourse together, though Gods knows, and she herself *in petto*, I met her only once and that at the request of her psychiatrist. Still, it is unpleasant to commit someone: the ambulance, the men in white coats, the straitjacket, that sort of thing."

He talks about the Yale Younger Poets series, and his job of introducing a sheaf of poems by the winnowed final candidate. "Everyone is writing fragments now, but I continue to look for good whole lines. . . . 'Originality' and 'striking images' are the very last ingredients I could care about." He discourses on whiskey cultures *versus* wine cultures, too, dividing all Europe by this measure, as Feuerbach divided it into bean-eating cultures and potato-eating cultures. And, finally, he expatiates on the texts in I.S.'s

Cantata, explaining that "The Whinny-Muir is the gorse moor where souls are ceaselessly nettled, a familiar landscape of the time"; and that "The Brig o'dred is the narrow bridge to Purgatory from which the wicked topple into Hell." I.S. says that he had not thought of the *Lyke-Wake Dirge* as Scottish, but it seems to me that the accompaniment has a Scottish drone.

We go to *Pal Joey* after dinner, but Wystan hates it, and the bawdiness shocks him. In one number the chorus girls bump their bare bottoms audiencewards, revealing bouquets of violets fixed like tail feathers in the cleft, and at this he dashes from the theater and does not reappear.

MAY 22

Boston. The Sheraton Hotel. Dylan Thomas at about 11 AM, eyes already glassy. He is in a bad way, obviously, and nervous about meeting I.S., to boot. But I.S. himself is ill and in bed today, and he cannot dissipate Thomas's tension by joining him in a scotch, although the one he pours for the tubby poet calms *him* so effectively that the D.T.'s seem ever so slightly less imminent.

Propping himself up, I.S. explains exactly what he requires in an opera libretto. But Thomas says he has a science-fiction idea, "at least to be going on with. It is about the rediscovery of the planet after an atomic misadventure, and the re-creation of language: a person, an object, a word." He is very worried about his wife, he says, and anxious to return to England. But perhaps seeing that this isn't explanation enough for the chain-smoking and trembling hands, he adds that gout is giving him pains. "Still, the cure is worse. They shove bayonets into you." He "heard the Venice première of *The Rake* on the wireless," he says. "Auden is the most skillful of us all, of course, but I am not at all like him, you know."

1948
1949
1950
1951
1952
1953
1954
1955
1956
1957
1958
1959
1960
1961
1962
1963
1964
1965
1966
1967
1968
1969
1970
1971

ITINERARY

January 23: I.S. conducts the première of the *Septet* at Dumbarton Oaks. **February 3:** I.S. flies from New York to Hollywood. **8:** R.C.'s first Webern concert at Evenings-on-the-Roof. **24:** I.S. flies to Portland with his son-in-law for concerts there and in Seattle. **March 10:** I.S. flies to Hollywood. **16:** Auden for dinner. **25:** I.S.'s fly to New York but land in Washington owing to fog, and complete the trip by train. **April 2:** We fly to Rome. **7:** I.S. is excluded from the première of Henze's *Boulevard Solitude* at the Rome Opera, because he is not in evening dress; the story is on the front page of (tomorrow's) *New York Times.* **14:** R.C. conducts the *Septet* in the Eliseo. **17:** I.S. conducts *Oedipus Rex* at the Foro Italico. **19:** I.S. goes with his son-in-law by train to Turin. **23:** I.S. conducts his Violin Concerto and *Perséphone* in Turin. **24:** I.S. goes to Lugano for a concert (29th). **30:** Car to Stresa, train to Geneva. **May 1:** Dinner with Ansermet at Theodore Stravinsky's. R.C. to Baden-Baden to record a concert. **6:** R.C. to New York, via Frankfurt, and Hollywood. **27:** I.S. receives the Gold Medal of the Royal Philharmonic, London, at concert there. I.S. flies to Lisbon with his daughter and son-in-law, for a concert. **June 14:** I.S. returns to Hollywood. **August 19–22:** Las Vegas. **September 20:** Première of *In Memoriam: Dylan Thomas.* **October 22:** I.S. goes to Chicago for concerts, returning on the 29th. **November 27:** Auden for dinner. **December 6:** We fly to San Francisco. **7, 11:** I.S. conducts staged performances of *Petrushka.* **12:** We fly to Hollywood. **25, 31:** I.S. conducts *Petrushka* at the Shrine Auditorium.

1948
1949
1950
1951
1952
1953
1954
1955
1956
1957
1958
1959
1960
1961
1962
1963
1964
1965
1966
1967
1968
1969
1970
1971

ITINERARY

January 5: I.S. and V. fly to Portland. **10:** Concert in Portland. **11:** R.C. arrives in Portland (after conducting a Mozart concert in Phoenix). Concert in Salem. **12:** Train to Chicago. **14:** I.S.'s in Chicago. **16:** I.S.'s by train to Birmingham. **20:** I.S. conducts in Birmingham. **21:** I.S.'s fly to New York. **26:** We fly to Atlanta for a concert (31st). **February 1:** We fly to New Orleans. **2:** Train to Los Angeles, arriving on the 4th. **11:** Death of Ona Munson (Mrs. Eugene Berman). **12:** Death of Maria Huxley. **15:** I.S. records *Japanese Lyrics, Balmont Songs, Four Russian Songs* (with flute, harp, guitar). **16:** Aldous Huxley for dinner. **March 4:** I.S.'s to Pittsburgh by train, for concerts on the 11th and 13th. **14:** We fly to the Azores and, on the 15th, to Lisbon. **25:** I.S. conducts in Madrid. **27:** We fly to Rome. **April 6:** I.S. conducts in Rome. **12:** I.S. is in the hospital because of diverticulitis. V.'s vernissage at the Obelisco. **17:** Train to Venice. **18:** We spend the morning with musicians from the Fenice Orchestra testing the acoustics of the Frari and the Salute for the *Canticum Sacrum* (if it is not played in San Marco), after which I.S. goes by train to Baden-Baden. **20:** V.'s vernissage in Milan. **22:** I.S. conducts in Baden-Baden, and on the 28th, Lugano. **29:** Train to Zurich, plane to Stuttgart. **May 3:** I.S. conducts in Mannheim. **4:** Car to Frankfurt, plane to Copenhagen. **5–6:** We fly via Greenland to Los Angeles. **22:** I.S. conducts at the Ojai Festival. **August 2–5:** We drive to Carmel and Yosemite. **October 16:** We drive to Santa Barbara with Aldous Huxley for a Bach-Gesualdo concert. **November 20:** I.S. conducts concert at Royce Hall. **December 1:** Train to New Orleans, Chicago (3rd), Cleveland (4th). **8, 10:** I.S. conducts in Cleveland. **11:** Train to New York. **23:** Lunch with Auden.

MARCH 15

Lisbon. The Aviz Hotel. I.S. is asleep this morning when a reporter calls requesting an interview about the Sibelius Prize, a sum of $18,000 which, the reporter says, I.S. has won. "What will you do with the money?" the reporter asks, and I.S. answers that he hopes to sell it to Calouste Gulben-kian, the oil billionaire whose rooms are next to ours and whose low, dry cough coming through the wall makes us think of the goat in *Gerontion*. To avoid the interview, I.S. pretends he has a cold, and immediately there-after believes he is catching one.

We leave for Evora, stopping on the way to see the golden Coaches of Belém, a museum of horse carriages heavily gilt with rococo furbelows.

45

Lifting a seat cushion and discovering a privy-shaped aperture, I.S. is delighted to find that the passenger could relieve nature in transit, like the horses.

The proprietor of the Evora restaurant is absorbed in a newspaper, on the back page of which is a photograph of I.S., illustrating a story about the Sibelius Prize. Soon the paper will be turned around, there will be glances in our direction, and I.S. will be caught, one consequence of which could be the gift of a new *spécialité de la maison*—the one already before us is a soup of rancid olive oil—which we would somehow have to eat. But in the event, the proprietor merely sends for a certain professor, the most learned of the guides, in fact the only one worthy of us. By the time he arrives, however, we are dropping off like narcoleptics from the effects of the local wine, a drop of which would have cured the insomnia of the Thane of Cawdor. To make matters worse, it is clear that there will be no *Reader's Digest* version of the pertinacious professor's tour. We follow him to a charnelhouse in which we are meant to shudder (and do); to São Braz, a cathedral whose wide buttresses and knobbed finials remind me of the legs of a colossal grasshopper; and to a convent school, the walls of whose classrooms tell the story of Portugal's heroic age in bright blue *azulejos*.

Returning to Lisbon we stop at Arrabida and walk on a high road overlooking the sea. Back at the Aviz, a batch of congratulatory telegrams for the Sibelius Prize awaits I.S., some of them soliciting contributions as well, and one of them asking for a loan.

MARCH 18

To Seville, via Badajoz, where the Spanish customhouse contains too many photographs of El Caudillo and too large a contingent—are they expecting an invasion?—of his soldiers. The chief clerk ignores us until he has finished flipping through a magazine. Then, after stamping our declarations and allowing us to return to our car, he suddenly detains I.S. with a request for an autograph—not, as we suppose, in connection with the Sibelius Prize, or even because of a suspicion that I.S. might be a film producer (that fatal "Hollywood" in his passport), but for the reason, as we see after he signs and the clerk shows the name to a guard: *"Es un famoso violinista."* ("*No me gusta,*" says the guard.) The narrow Guadiana bridge is choked with purple pigs who, at the approach of the car, turn around and curdle the air with their squeals.

Reaching Seville at dusk, we go directly to the cathedral where, after groping about in the gloom for a few minutes we are startled by cries of *"Estravinsky, Estravinsky!"* *"Qu'y a-t-il, mon père?"* says I.S., when he sees that they are coming from a priest. *"Vous êtes riche, n'est-ce pas?"* the padre hopefully inquires. *"Comment?"* says I.S. *"Le prix d'Esibelius."* But I.S. dampens the enthusiasm with *"Peut-être je suis riche, mon père, mais je suis très avare."* At this point our new companion identifies himself as the organist, which could account for his having descried I.S. in the *noche oscura* of the cathedral, but does not explain why he is on the lookout for him in Seville in the first place, I.S. not having registered in a hotel. Later he tells us that he had as quickly recognized Richard Strauss and Ravel on their visits here—and no doubt surprised them as much as he did us. We follow him, enveloped in his cloud of garlic, on a tour of the paintings and the treasuries, for he is empowered to unlock doors and light lights.

MARCH 26

Madrid. We spend the morning in the Prado, but it is a dark day and the only pictures within range of electricity are the primitives. The most memorable of these are one showing a St. Vincent being fished from the sea by his nimbus; and a *retablo* of the Ascent into Heaven, a "before-and-after" advertisement in which the Holy Feet protrude below a dark cloud in one panel, but have been pulled out of sight in the other, leaving billowing clouds and a fiery wake.

At noon we go to the Escorial, in a car driven by the Infante, Prince Eugenio de las Heras, a nephew of Alfonso XIII, whom he much resembles, above all in the Hapsburg mandibles. The mountains and pine forests are still covered with snow, and in spite of our heavy coats we shiver indoors as well as out, though Prince Eugenio, wearing only a light suit, appears not to notice the cold. We follow him across freezing pavements and down drafty corridors to the icy vaults, where the rows of royal tombs begin with Charles V and end with an empty niche for the uncle of our host.

Back in Madrid, we spend the evening with Ortega y Gasset and the young Marquesa de Slauzol, who warns us in advance that Ortega is hard of hearing and helps him with bits of conversation that he fails to catch. Everything about the man is vivid, his clothes—natty blue jacket, bow tie, pearl cuff links—no less than his mind. He is resonant, too, and so, obeying the Marquesa, are we. Our chorus of deaf men's voices grows louder, moreover, as we ply each other with whiskey, two bottles of which are emptied before Ortega departs, leaving us wonderfully elated, not to say high.

From midnight until two we watch a flamenco troupe in the Zamora Club, a small room full of Americans and smoke. The performers sit on a platform in a semicircle flanking two guitarists, an old man and a boy. The men coax their songs with their hands, tracing aerial patterns as elaborate as the arabesques of the music. But whereas the male dancers affect not to notice the audience, every bump of the females, especially of one Rosa, the beauty of the troupe in spite of a blemished skin, is directed exclusively there. To liven the long limbering-up period, the audience applauds, stomps, shouts *"Olé!"* but the performances drag on according to a worst-first protocol.

1948
1949
1950
1951
1952
1953
1954
1955
1956
1957
1958
1959
1960
1961
1962
1963
1964
1965
1966
1967
1968
1969
1970
1971

ITINERARY

January 7: A party at Auden's for the birthdays of V. (New Style) and Chester Kallman. **11:** Train for Los Angeles, arriving the 14th. **February 4:** Dinner with Aldous. **19:** Dinner with Aldous. **28:** Drive with Aldous to V.'s vernissage in Santa Barbara. **March 2:** We tape fifteen minutes of music from *Petrushka* for an animated cartoon. **April 6:** Aldous and new wife to dinner, with Isherwood and Gerald Heard. **May 23-27:** Ojai. I.S. conducts *Les Noces* on the 27th. **June 16:** We leave for New York by train. **27:** The I.S.'s, R.C., and Lawrence Morton sail on the *Vulcania* for Patras. **29:** I.S. receives a cable announcing the death, in Berne, of Mina ("Madubo") Svitalski, the former nurse of his children. **July 4:** We visit Mafra, Sintra, Queluz. **6:** Dinner with Eduardo Toldrá in Barcelona. **8:** Drive to Gesualdo from Naples. **9:** We visit the Palazzina Cinese, Palermo. **19:** Fly to Istanbul. **27:** Fly to Athens. **28-30:** We sail on the *Mediterranean* to Venice. **August 12:** Drive to Villa Manin, Grado, Aquileia. **20:** To Stra and the Villa Contarini, the Barbarigo Gardens in Valsanzibio, and Petrarch's house in the Euganean Hills. **September 2:** Urbino. **13:** I.S. conducts the *Canticum Sacrum* in the Basilica of San Marco. **14:** Visit the Villa Maser. **20:** I.S. by car to Montreux, for a concert. **26:** I.S. flies from Geneva to Berlin, accompanied by Eric Winkler. **27:** Balanchine and I.S. discuss *Agon*. **October 2:** I.S. suffers a thrombosis while conducting. **3:** I.S. receives a visit from Scherchen. **4:** We fly to Munich. **9:** I.S. cancels concerts in Munich, Zürich, Winterthur, Vienna, London. **10:** I.S. enters the Rote Kreuz hospital. **November 10:** R.C. conducts Stravinsky and Webern concert for the *Domaine Musical,* Salle Gaveau, Paris. **17:** I.S. is discharged from the hospital. **18:** R.C. to Vienna. **22:** I.S.'s depart for Rome on the night train. **29:** I.S. conducts the *Canticum Sacrum* in Rome. **December 2:** Train for Paris. **3:** R.C. records *Vom Himmel Hoch* Variations and *Canticum Sacrum* in Paris. I.S. and Suvchinsky meet for the first time since 1939. We go by night train to London. **4:** Savoy Hotel. **7:** I.S. begins a phlebotomy treatment, six bleedings this week in London. **8:** I.S. lunches with Boulez and Barrault. We go to Hampton Court in the afternoon. T. S. Eliot and Stephen Spender for tea. We go to *Cymbeline* at the Old Vic in the evening. **10:** Isaiah Berlin and Nabokov for lunch with the I.S.'s. **11:** R.C. conducts a Stravinsky concert in St. Martin's-in-the-Fields. **14:** We sail for New York on the *Mauretania,* arriving the 21st.

Aboard the S.S. *Vulcania,* somewhere in the southern Adriatic. Awakened by the periodic moan of the ship's fog signals, I go to my porthole, but the sea is invisible, and the pulse of our engines is so feeble that we can hardly be moving at all. Later in the morning a trajectory of clear atmosphere exposes a wall of blue mountains, then Cephalonia and Zante appear, but still in dense vapors, like fragile objects wrapped for shipment.

At Patras we wait a mile or so offshore for a welcoming deputation. but when at last it arrives, no doubt having been difficult to convoke, hospitality proves to be a lesser article of its business than propaganda. I.S. is asked to make a statement protesting British atrocities in Cyprus, but he parries the request by condemning all atrocities everywhere and at any time. Finally stamped and ticketed for landing, we go to a sponson amidships and transfer from there to a pinnace whose leathery old Charon guides the tiller with his bare feet and acknowledges his gadfly passengers only by expectorating in their (our) direction.

Photographs of the Cyprus atrocities are displayed on the walls of the customs shed, but the point of those in which the soldiers are shown frisking priests is not always clear, clerical transvestism suggesting that the real complaint may be indecent assault. Prodigal sons home from Chicago and the Bronx evidently not being trusted in the always highly corruptible customs service, none of the officials who mill us through the turnstiles of questions, documents, inspections speaks a word of any language but Greek. Add to this confusion a declaration form that requires wildly disparate commodities to be counted under a single heading. Thus a tourist with a camera, a watch, a fur coat, and one hundred cigarettes would declare a total of 103.

We are rescued from this pandemonium by the dust-raising arrival of a taxi whose driver's cap advertises the Cecil Hotel; or, more precisely, rescued by the driver himself, whose authoritative manner in dealing with the officials, and in paying one or two of a suddenly formed regiment of porters, might otherwise have identified him as a satrap of the province, or at least the Mayor or chief of police. That this timely, mettlesome person *is* something more than he seems, we discover on reaching the Cecil. There, removing the cap and changing his jacket, he becomes, in rapid succession, the registering clerk, the waiter, the unique supplier of room service, the sole operator of a reluctant and tremulous lift. He is in fact the only staff, as we eventually learn, but now, entering a lobby crowded with other guests clamoring for one or another of his miscellaneous functions, we do not yet realize that they have probably been clamoring during the entire boat-meeting expedition.

Patras is a miserable city, a threat to preconceptions that several rounds of mastikas—Greek "redeye"—do not offset. At twilight we go to a restaurant on the Gulf shore, on a road whose other traffic consists mainly of overcrowded buses, women with head bundles, and bearded and stove-pipe-hatted priests, some of them skillfully managing bicycles in spite of their skirts. We sit at the water's edge, facing the mountains of Aetolia, with Calydon behind and Missolonghi to the west. But the view is better than the alimentation, which consists of calamari and a nonresinated though thick-as-malmsey Achaian wine; to me anyway, but in my case the very thought of calamari, like the thought of haggis and chitterlings, is enough to sustain a fast, whereas I.S. eats so many of them that he complains later of having swallowed "too many spiders."

At nightfall, lights begin to flicker like fireflies on the opposite shore, marking, as we suppose, a heretofore invisible city, until they move into the Gulf and are seen to be fishing boats. In fact, the mothlike dazzling and clubbing of susceptible fish is a method of angling described by ancient writers—"The fire-producing stone of night rowers" is Satyrius' periphrastic definition of flint—with the difference that pine torches have been replaced by electric and kerosene lanterns.

But our pleasure in this spectacle is destroyed by a parcel of tourists dumped from a bus for an *al fresco* banquet. We retreat to a café in Patras and embalm ourselves with more mastikas, though a single swallow of the fluid can make it difficult to tell whether the starry firmament is inside or out.

JULY 11

The scene from my window at 6 AM is a Chirico: a deserted square and an empty railway station, with a large new clock over the door to divide the void into hours and fractions of hours. Directly below me, men at sidewalk tables are reading newspapers, and extending their shoes to shoe polishers, while beyond the station, fishermen are tying up at the docks, the Ionian Sea already blazing with the morning sun.

Our bills paid, we pack into a "limousine." The driver, Mr. Spyrakis, is an expert chauffeur, a "nimble planner," an informal cicerone—like Mr. Eugenides, he speaks demotic French—and an able exchequer, dispensing justly proportioned perquisites, or so his manner, if not invariably that of the recipients, implies. His only evident failing appears to be a national one, the too-frequent use of his automobile's too-resonant horn.

We drive east of Patras to a ferry slip, which is the reason for our early rising: crossings are infrequent and, after the first one, unscheduled. The vessel, a war-surplus LST, does not inspire confidence, but we embark nevertheless, along with a dilapidated donkey wagon, a tribe of goats, and some pedestrian *polloi,* among whom a ragged and unshod boy attempts to peddle a tray of preposterously stale-looking cakes. The ferry plies between the castles of Morea and Roumeli, twin Venetian forts on facing promontories.

The north-shore road is obstructed near the outset by a gypsy caravan departing from a squalid roadside bivouac. While the men corral donkeys, dogs, goats, and chickens, the women, wrapped in blankets and wearing headgear like that of the peasant women in *Les Très Riches Heures du Duc de Berry,* wait by the wagons in a one-hundred-degree sun. The I.S.'s are as much impressed by this encounter as I, a one-time addict of George Borrow, am disappointed. They still half believe in gypsy kidnaping, gypsy sorcery, and other such arrant superstitions as the gypsy power to charm away warts. V.'s credulity is greater than I.S.'s, having been strengthened once by an experience in the rue Passy when a gypsy clairvoyant called to her from across the street in Russian(!), offering to tell her interesting things about her future. V. regularly consults a gypsy palmist in Los Angeles, moreover, a seer recommended by the Huxleys. And I.S. has been influenced by the prophecies of this Azucena, too, in spite of his protestations that any knowledge of the future would make the present unbearable.

Lepanto, the first city on our route, can have undergone little if any reconstruction since the battle of that name—which occurred south of Oxia, fifty miles to the west. It is a pile of crumbling fortifications, a description that includes the harbor's lobster-shaped sea walls and sea gate. After Lepanto, the road climbs steeply, and it climbs and descends sheerly and precipitously all the way to Delphi. It is narrow, bumpy, and unpaved as well, and a thick dust-cloud trails the car. Two stretches are bedded with crushed rock, but they are the most dangerous of all; we stick fast in one of them and are obliged to brave a sheepdog and apply to a herdsman for help. During the entire seven-hour drive we see no other automobile nor any vehicle other than the mules and old women who apparently transport all freight on the road.

The ground is barren in spite of the shaping and reshaping of terraces on every arable slope and the gathering and regathering of rocks into fences. We see only one remnant of an earlier culture, a thin-waisted Byzantine arc-bridge spanning a gorge. Nearby, some women are pounding stones to gravel; their faces are partly veiled, but orientally, not for protection, as their eyes are exposed to flying chips of stone. We stop in a mountain village still choked with rubble from the war, and drink *ouzo*s, chased by cold spring water, and eat *rahat loukoom.* At another table are three men dolled up in highlanders' tasseled caps, fustanella, tufted slippers, handlebar mustaches. They look like ex-brigands, in spite of the costume, and anyone seeing their grizzled faces peering through his window at home would call the police, or say a prayer, or become a teetotaler. But they take only lateral and begrudging notice of us, their interest being directed to Mr. Spyrakis's "limousine."

The road climbs again afterward to a point from which the Gulf is in view nearly as far back as Patras, crow-wise so short a distance away, compared with all the colonic miles we have come. From here to Amfissa the landscape is less bleak, and the sempiternal olive trees are relieved by eucalyptus and pepper, oleander and thistle, now in bloom. The inhabitants are less savagely aloof, at least to the extent that everyone from toothing toddlers to edentate beldams screams at us for cigarettes.

The hotel at Delphi is unfinished, and our balconies overlooking the valley of the Pleistos River have not yet been enclosed. The sun is too strong for ruin-climbing, and we venture out only at six o'clock; but the heat is still fierce then, and only the Phaedriades are in shadow. The ruins—broken columns, shattered walls, crippled temples and treasuries—are disappointing, nor does the superstitious, opportunistic, and cruel religion to which they are monuments inspire my awe. The oracle flattered the favored, told the powerful what they wanted to hear, and sold the equivalent of stock market tips to big investors.[1]

JULY 12

To Athens, via Osios Loukas, Levadia, Thebes. I.S., very grouchy because of the heat, dismisses the contents of the Delphi museum as "breakage." As the sun mounts and we descend into ever-hotter valleys, he protects his head by knotting the corners of a handkerchief and wearing it like an English housemaid's bonnet. An hour or so beyond Parnassus, where the stone huts of the shepherds have been succeeded by thatched roofs and wood, is a viewpoint of the Triodos, the intersection of the Delphi-Thebes and Daulis-Ambrysus roads. I.S. denies that he had pictured this landscape scenically while composing his *"trivium"* music, but he says he would have supposed the area to be very small. "In these wide" (and now aforested) "slopes, Laius and his unrecognized son would hardly have noticed each other, let alone contested each other's passage," he says. Suddenly a blast explosion fills the road fifty yards ahead with a fountain of rocks and earth, nearly jolting us over the unrailed ledge. When the debris has settled, a workman jumps down from a dugout in the hillside above, signaling us to stop, which we have long since done, and warning Mr. Spyrakis—so I interpret his gesturing toward the abyss—that we could have been killed. And what if our departure this morning had been slightly less unpunctual?

The road to Osios Loukas is bumpier, and the towns are more harshly destitute than any we have seen. The country is deserted, except for a few old women hoeing in the fields ("Ancient women/Gathering fuel in vacant lots"). Mr. Spyrakis explains this in a horrifying account of the wartime murder of the entire male population in retaliation for the shooting of a Gauleiter. We stop in an outdoor restaurant at Osios Loukas, but the thought of the murdered villagers has killed our appetites. As for Luke-the-Stiriote's churches, the walls and ceilings are cracked and bruised, the dome frescoes disturbingly new, spoiled by too much restoration. The monastery buildings are synthetic, compounded of segments of Roman and Byzantine walls and modern bricks and cement. Their most attractive feature, the stone-shingled roof with round, whitewashed chimney, is indigenous to practically every edifice, sacred and secular, in the region.

The Athens road descends spirally, and the countryside prospers with each

1. For an answer to this impudence, see H. W. Parke's *Greek Oracles* (London, 1968).

downward loop. But so does the heat. At Levadia, abode of the oracle of Triphonius, we dip our arms in the icy spring water until they turn blue; which makes the heat blister, afterwards. Owing to the sun we are hardly able to turn our heads in the direction of Thermopylae, Thebes, and Marathon. But the latter holds the promise of a breeze: "The mountain looks on Marathon and Marathon looks on the sea." And compared to the mountain towns, Thebes, whose ancient remains could be carted off in a few truckloads, has an almost hopeful look. Refreshed, finally, by the pine forests of Attica and the sea air at Eleusis, we enter Athens from above, Mount Lycabettus coming into view first, then the Parthenon and the dusty-white city beneath. Our hotel, formerly the Grande Bretagne, is now simply the Grande, and the statue of Byron across the street is draped with the sign: "Aren't you ashamed to be an Englishman?"

JULY 13

In a shore restaurant several miles of dowdy cottages south of Athens, we enter the bead-curtained kitchen ourselves and choose our fish from a display laid out on a morguelike slab—as if their aesthetic attractions were a clue to their culinary ones. Next to the display of dead fin-fish are tubs of living cuttlefish, and calamari—whose cousin the octopus provoked William James's "Such intensity of life, in a form so inaccessible to our sympathy."

Back in Athens, we trudge the steep paths and climb the tall steps to the Acropolis, where sunburned and perspiring Teutons (dirndls, *Lederhosen*) are photographing each other and reading aloud to each other from Baedeker. The interior of the Parthenon is whiter, less wheat-colored than I expect, having been told as a child that it is beige.

JULY 16

Mycenae. Excavations are in progress outside the walls, but except for ghosts ("This house, if it had a voice . . .") we are alone in the citadel. The ascent is arduous and the path is a cauldron, except at the summit, under Prophet Elias Mountain, which is cooled by winds from Argos, and which looks over slopes of olive and cypress to Tiryns and Arcadia. Agamemnon's tomb, below the citadel, is hive-shaped. The stonework, unseen in the time of the incumbent under bronze, gold, and jeweled lading, is as smoothly chamfered as an Inca wall. The actual tomb was in a second room, joined to the first like a Siamese twin, but without an outside entrance of its own; it is totally dark, therefore, and Mr. Spyrakis sets fire to a newspaper and thrusts it through the jointure—to expose possible reptiles, he says, adding that a woman was snakebitten here only a few days ago. However fitting as retribution for a despoiler of Agamemnon's grave, the story abruptly terminates my own explorations of the site. The bee farms and pine woods of Epidaurus are perfect relief. Moreover, the amphitheater is agreeably human-sized, after all the photographs that make it look like the Hollywood Bowl.

By the time we reach Nauplia the mountains are purple and the bay is rippling with boats. We climb Palomedes Rock, but the Lions of St. Mark on the walls there seem a glib emblem after the great Lion Gate at Mycenae. After dark the quay is a corso for the whole population, ourselves included, until some small boys ferret us out shouting "Stick-em-up!" and "Bang-bang!" followed by torrents of Greek the cowboys in our films do not know.

JULY 17

The mountains are brown and barren again this morning, as we drive to Nemea. Green and mountain-girdled, its Temple of Zeus tumbled in a deep field and its cave of Hercules-and-the-lion—a cave for Zarathustra or Jerome in other mythologies—Nemea, ever hereafter, will be my vision of the Valley of the Blest.

1956

JULY 18

Sunion. Here at last, on the windy cape, where Daedalus begat Icarus, is the Greece of my prejudices, and, which comes to the same thing, child-picturebook imagination: the Temple of Poseidon is incontestably white, comparatively intact—although the surfaces are densely scratched with visitors' names and dates, including many early Bostonians'—and it looks upon blue seas.

JULY 26

Istanbul. We join a motor-launch excursion on the Bosphorus with I.S.'s one-time patrons Mr. and Mrs. Robert Woods Bliss. Decaying villas and palaces line the shore the whole way, and only those housing the Egyptian and Soviet embassies are in trim condition. The villas are unpainted, and most of them have a large number of shuttered windows. The plainest remind V. of Sebastopol, but to me they recall the old clapboard frame houses now being razed in downtown Los Angeles. Not many *are* plain, though, the architectural motifs going as far afield as Gothic spires and Alpine roofs. Some imitate Venice, standing to their ankles in water, while others approach the water stepwise, or through Ganges-type ghats. We sail along the European shores to a cordon marking the channel to the Black Sea, then cross to Asia and return on that side as far as the pink villa of Pierre Loti. Just as we re-enter the Golden Horn, the President of Pakistan is debarking from a Turkish battleship, and I.S. notes with glee that the (*au fond*) anti-American motorcade awaiting this dignitary is a solid line of Cadillacs. Our route back to the hotel leads through a street called "Pig Alley" because of a shop that sells pork to giaours.

Kariye Djami, near the Adrianople Gate, has been severely damaged by earthquakes, and perhaps as many as a third of the frescoes have been washed away in the resulting leaks. But Muslim pargeting has preserved the others, most perfectly the Anastasis, in the parecclesion, in which the

Resurrected Christ joins hands in a dance of jubilation with Adam and Eve. The Last Judgment, in the eastern domical vault, is partly obscured by bandage-like scaffolding, but not the Paradise, which is a cool white park partitioned by small, easily fordable rivers, and abundantly stocked with birds and beasts; nor the Hell, a dark hole with a long funnel too small to receive the multitudes being driven there after their souls are found wanting on the Stimasis, a kind of grocer's scales. A young American restorer tells us that a Simeon Stylites was discovered this very morning during the cleaning of one of the frescoes.

The mosaics are even richer, above all the portraits of Christ's ancestors in the vestibule dome; the portrait of a leper with black sores; the portrait of a donor in oriental hat and costume; and a baptism scene in which a white eel is swallowed by a large fish (is this a marriage symbol?). The mosaic restorers work like dentists, and in fact use dental tools.

The Blue Mosque is actually a pearly gray, the color of the sacred pigeons in its yard. But the inside is flooded with blue light from tiles in the direct aim of the dome and side windows. I.S. is impressed by "the feeling of unity in the single large room, so different from a many-chapeled church," but he objects to the absence of iconography, adducing it as a sign of the abstractness of the religion. The legs of the Mosque are four great columns, sequoia trees in girth. Grandfather clocks, gifts from Queen Victoria, stand next to the two front trees, and odd as they seem as furniture, the fact of them, of "clock-time" (Laurence Sterne) in a place of prayer, arouses I.S.'s interest more than anything else has done in all of Istanbul. Some worshipers enter, carrying their shoes in their hands, then kneeling with their heads to the rug-covered floor. The men congregate on a dais at what would be the place of the altar in a church, while the veiled and shawled women squat in a distant corner, as far from the men as possible. When an imam enters, shouting, everybody stands, and a small boy amuses himself running over the floor in his stocking feet. Near the right wall is the hassock for the Koran reader, and in front of it the circle for the ulema—the exegetes and dis-putants—testifying, as I.S. says, to the religion's scholasticism. A pulpit-shaped paladin projects from the center wall, next to a balcony covered with gold lattice for the sultan's wives, a hen-yard on stilts. As we leave the mosque, a muezzin is chanting from one of its minarets and the faithful are washing their feet in stone troughs along the outer wall.

Hagia Sophia, in comparison, is an empty, dirty, stale-smelling turn-of-the-century railway station, except for large round plaques, green like the Prophet's robe and inscribed in gold with mottoes from the Koran, hanging like banners from the aisle columns. A guide, attaching himself to us, becomes abusive when we fail to discern the features of the Empress Theodora in the grain of one of the marble walls. Escaping him, we climb a dark ramp to the balconies. But the upstairs floors seem to weave and sway, and the columns to thrust out from the center.

Venice. An open-air *Tosca* in the Campo San Angelo. The Scarpia is a seasoned wobbler with a blubbery *crescendo* on every note, while the Tosca's tremolo spreads at times to a minor third. The better spectacle is not in front, but around, every window with a view of the Campo being a family-circle loge. I.S., talking about theaters indoors and out, says that what most impressed him in Bayreuth was "the weblike blend of the orchestra from under the stage. *Parsifal* was still a headache, but a headache with aspirin." This leads to a remark about Wagnerian singers, especially Tristans and Isoldes. "Naturally such people have to swallow philters before they can *do* anything."

1956

A windy morning. Sea-size waves beat against the Fondamenta and the sky rumbles like an empty stomach. At noon, a heavy rain turns the Grand Canal green, which makes Palladio's white faces even whiter. We spend the day in museums and churches, starting with the illuminated manuscripts in the Corner, one of which, *Marco Polo in Tartaria,* no doubt intended to inspire terror of the Turk, is opened to a scene of Christians skewered through the extremes of their digestive systems. Antonello's "Christ Lamented by the Angels," in an adjoining room, is one of the most affecting pictures in the world. The dead Christ, in the center of the composition, is surrounded by shadowy angels,[1] one of whom, directly behind, seems to have transferred his wings to Him. But the dead God is an Adonis, and His beauty—a glowing *morbidezza*—is too fleshy.

Some of the tapestries in the San Marco Museum are woven in toto with different tones of gold: gold angels threaded on faded gold backgrounds, gold lions-of-St. Mark on gold maps of Venice framed with ropes of purled gold. But to me the most striking tapestries are one composed entirely of geometric swatches, a collage of squares, arcs, circles, half-moons, all differ-ently dyed; and another, a Resurrection, woven in Arras, in which the pure white diaphanous light of the Christ dazzles the waking Roman soldiers and corrupts their motley. But the Venetian climate is unkind to color, and we remember how luminous in comparison were the tapestries in the dry cold of the Escurial.

S. Francesco della Vigna, the first church on our itinerary, is in Palladio's best First National Bank style. But whereas V. describes the façade as "pompous," I.S. thinks a more apt word would be "imposing." However that may be, the building would look better in the large open space it once commanded (*cf.* the Canaletto of 1744), for it is so encroached upon now that hardly half of it is in view from the end of the Campo. San Lorenzo,

---

1. Much of the chiaroscuro was dirt, and the now cleaned picture, whether or not it has lost any of its power, does not make the same impression (1971).

nearby, also needs wider dominion and is also rudely crowded by newer buildings, except that its façade has long since been stripped of stone and its brick underclothes have become a hanging garden of weeds. Still another neighborhood Palladian masterpiece dying of dilapidation is San Pietro di Castello, whose white, tipsy *torreloggio*—by Coducci—is, I think, the most beautiful in Venice. Yet these churches are in good condition compared with Santa Maria Maggiore, once praised by Burney for the quality of its music; the exterior is testudinarious—more even than other Venetian churches, for all of them have skin diseases—while the interior is a rat-infested ruin. The Rio di Santa Maria Maggiore leads to a prison, whence the name of the filled-in canal changes to Rio Terra of the Thinkers, but whether or not with didactic intent I do not know. Lively radio music blares over the walls, but a dark-faced guard on the parapet scowls at us when we pause to listen, and motions us on.

We visit three more churches at vesper hour: San Nicolo dei Mendicoli, where a Mary doll in a black evening frock stands in the nave, the seven swords of the Seven Sorrows piercing her silver heart; San Sebastiano, where the white stone flesh of the statue on the pediment is pierced by green, oxidized arrows; and San Anzolo Raffaele, where the antiphonal responses between a young priest and about forty old women are so lullingly mechanical that, when one of the priest's sentences is unexpectedly longer than the others, the *"Ora pro nobis"* breaks in too soon from at least half of the congregation.

AUGUST 10

An audience with the Patriarch, Cardinal Roncalli,[1] to seek his permission to perform the *Canticum Sacrum* in the Basilica of San Marco. The Cardinal's gondola fetches us at the Bauer Grunwald at noon, and ferries us to a tunnel on the Rio Palazzo, where a secretary guides us through passageways and up flights of stairs. Ushered into the presence, I follow I.S. in bowing and kissing the proffered ring hand. After that, the only problem is in adjusting to so much scarlet: the scarlet skullcap on the Cardinal; the scarlet *galero* on a *credenza* by the Cardinal's chair; the scarlet watered-silk cape; the scarlet-lined soutane with scarlet buttons; the scarlet stockings; the scarlet-bordered and scarlet-beaded slippers; the scarlet sash over the stomach—the stomach of a woman about to be rushed to a maternity hospital. The Cardinal's French is fluent, and his conversation is easygoing. His Eminence is worldly wise, which I do not expect, having imagined such a man living in seclusion. He can spring some strong surprises, too (but does not do so for that reason), as when, recalling his years as nuncio in Sophia and Istanbul, he remarks that "Orientals are more profoundly religious than we Catholics." Telling us that he officiated at vernacular Masses in these cities, he observes, clearly aiming at Rome, that "Stupidity is always stubborn,

---

1. Elevated to the tiara two years later as John XXIII.

intelligence is usually resilient." He is fascinated by I.S.'s Russian Orthodoxy, and, I think, would like to discuss the Filioque Clause with him, but I.S.'s own attitude toward both the Roman and the Russian churches is a mystery at present, possibly even to himself.

Eventually turning to the matter of the meeting, the Cardinal wishes to know why I.S. has chosen a passage from the Song of Solomon for a service in a Christian church. I try to come to I.S.'s help here by providing a quick account of Sinfoniae Sacrae in the Cardinal's own San Marco, but as I talk, His Eminence twiddles the gold cross dangling on his stomach and this epigastric play nearly distracts me from my subject. Still, the argument from precedents seems to satisfy him, for he hoists his huge croup from the chair—it is another surprise that such a figure and all of that tropical plumage moves—and, standing, vouchsafes his blessings both on the concert and on ourselves. We "exeunt," again genuflecting, again bussing the ring, then sidling and scraping *al rovescio.* But before we leave the palace the Cardinal escorts us to the throne room, site of the Doges' ambassadorial dinners, to show us an unexpected view of San Marco's plain brick back.

1956

We go to Torcello for dinner, stopping at San Michele to place a wreath on Diaghilev's grave—all except I.S., who waits in the boat, superstitiously refusing even to put his foot on the island. The church of San Michele, so white from the lagoon, is the darkest sepulcher inside.

The Laguna Morta is alive with birds and barges, the rhythm of whose boatmen as they lever their poles in the mud and walk from bow to stern is hypnotic to watch. We follow a channel marked by telephone poles and buoys but are obliged to stop from time to time to free our propeller from seaweed. The sky is a mass of Turner-like billowing movements, and at times the horizon seems to be high in the air and our boat to be sailing upward. At one point we pass a gondola whose only passenger—an Edward Lear image—is a goat.

SEPTEMBER 1

I.S. works on *Agon* all morning at the pink piano in the hotel nightclub, undeterred by ghosts of dance music and odors of half-smoked cigars. But he complains regularly of the difficulty in "composing my 'dry' music in this humidity. To live in Venice is to live in a glass of water." Emerging at two o'clock for lunch, he remarks that "A series is a facet, and serial composition a faceting, or crystallizing, way of presenting several sides of the same idea."

Venetian dialects lack the soft "j"; hence Zulian, Zuan, Zan, Anzelo, *"zorno"* (for *"giorno"*); and *"ze ne peux pas,"* this from our friend Alessandro Piovesan, whose French reminds I.S. of Manuel de Falla's substitution of "h" for "j," and of the Spanish composer's inability to begin a word with "st"; *"He ne peux pas, mon cher Estravinsky."* But the Venetian Vulgo generally softens and shortens. Thus *"figlio"* becomes *"fio,"* and *"ospitale," "ospedale."* The sharp-edged "c" is avoided, too, *"portego"* replacing *"portico,"* for instance, *"siguro"* replacing *"sicuro,"* and *"Mi digo"* (the accusative) replacing *"Io dico."* Finally, even the word *"Doge"* is softened to *"Dose,"* and the name Coducci, the architect of the church of San Michele, is written and pronounced Codussi. Double "1's" are not pronounced like Italian either, thus *"stelle"* comes out as an extremely palatal *"stey-ye."* Nor are the English "sh" and "ch" sounds natural here; thus the Marzeria (for Merceria), Gre*gh*i (for Gre*ci*), and *Petruska.* The "n" is dropped in certain positions, too, as in Fr*a*cesca da Rimini and Artur Rub*i*stein, and it is dropped altogether as a double consonant: the Venetians say "Madona," not "Madonna." But I do not know why they say *"dasseno"* instead of *"davvero."*

It is the lot of my vaporetto from the Piazzale Roma today to inherit a horde of U.S. tourists at the Ferrovia. But as the boat rams down the Grand Canal, not one of the Americans within earshot exclaims on the beauty of any of the buildings, while, instead, all of them worry aloud the whole way about flooded basements.

A regatta. Rival brass bands open up in the Piazza long before the races begin, while a concert of opera arias blasts forth simultaneously from a loudspeaker near the Bucintoro; which is Venetian antiphony, perhaps, but not in the tradition of the Gabrielis. By mid-afternoon almost every boat in Venice has gathered in the Grand Canal, from gaggles of gondolas and flotillas of smaller barks, each bearing the standards of its patron saint and *sestiere* or island, to the boats of the police and fire departments, the latter spouting a variety of fountains. A few still buoyant or baleable leviathan relics from the Arsenale Museum lead the water parade, including galleys and caravels with gold-leafed Tritons and baldachins on the poop decks trailing velvet canopies in the (filthy) water. The crews of these museum pieces carry arquebuses, halberds, culverines; and they wear tabards, doublet and hose, hauberks, piebald caps, and assorted other antique garb in which they are as encumbered as an opera chorus at a first costume fitting. But the actual races are an eternity in getting started and extremely dull when they *do* start, except for one heat of a dozen swift, pod-shaped canoes.

Venetian night sounds: the lap of waves on stone; the plash of oars; the grating of oars in tholepins; the clatter, at sundown, of the *saracinesche* (the iron shutters on shop fronts); the terrible trumpeting, high, like elephants, of the *motoscaffi;* the gondoliers' *"OEI"*—which seems louder at night because their big, black water-limousines glide by so quietly—and the loud voices of gondoliers arguing (what are they always arguing about?); the shouted numbers from a *tombola* on the Giudecca (*"tren-ta-du-e"*); the hooting of ships as they arrive and depart in the canal of the Giudecca; the soft singing of women issuing from darkened houses in the *calli,* strong and vibrant in the morning when they are spreading their laundry, but quiet and gently palpitating at night; the bells of San Trovaso, in two tones and two speeds, at nones, and the bells of San Marco at midnight. At that hour I walk to the bridge corner of the Doge's palace with the frieze of the drunken Noah. Eyes closed in semi-slumber, the old man swoons and holds the trunk of the vine for support. I count twelve birds singing in the vine.

NOVEMBER 4

Paris. A gray Sunday. It is stamp-exchange and purchase day, and the sidewalk on the Rond Point, across the street from my room, is filled with huddles of philatelists. In my room, too, I hear the applause, boos, stomps, shouts of *"Oui!"* and *"Non!"* from children watching *guignol* in the park.

Boulez comes at noon, bringing his *Marteau* recording, and we eat at the Berkeley. He is balder, shorter, stockier, more solid in the solar plexus than I remember, but as lithe and springy as a boxer. Quick, precise, and as sure of himself as if he were carrying an infallible plan of conquest in his pocket, he seems to me a mental creature primarily—this in contrast to I.S., who is a physical creature first, the rare escapee from "that violent severance from man's animal past" which bothered Nietzsche. In I.S., physical appetites and body gestures are apparent long before the mind comes out of hiding, which may be why the self-identification and the personality of the physical gestures in the music are so immediate. Or, to put it differently, with I.S., "abstract thought"—for which he has an unlimited capacity, no matter how contemptuously he regards it—is never dissociated (or prescinded) from physical instinct. Boulez's physical instincts, on the other hand, are either hidden or neuter. He is, of course, charming, even-keeled—in spite of a rapid nervous blink—witty, enviably intelligent. But the thought occurs to me—perhaps because he talks about *Un Coup de Dés* ("Writers are in a worse way than composers, Mallarmé and Joyce already having done it all")—that with an eyeshade he would look like a croupier.

We speak our own languages, the arbitrary assignation of gender to every noun in his constituting an insurmountable obstacle for me, to say nothing of such pronunciation problems as the proper palatalizing of the cacuminals. We seem about equally able to follow one another, too, except that the wines, which do not faze him, fuddle me.

His musical opinions having preceded him, we talk about my performance of his *Polyphonie X* in Los Angeles four years ago; and we talk about his background. He claims to be wholly immune from religious feeling, adding that the Church never meant anything to him even in earliest childhood; which tallies with his claim that he has always been more interested in oriental than in Latin cultures, this to the point of an aversion for most things Italian except food.

Finishing our own food, we go to a street where Cézanne lived as a young man—near the place de la Bastille—and there, in an apartment building, climb four flights of stone stairs and two of wood to Boulez's garret. Every object and utility in this tiny lair conforms to the size of his script and musical detail: the small bed, desk, salamandre, reproduction of Klee's portrait of

1956

I.S., upright piano—on which he improvises a funny Brahmsian accompaniment to the beginning of the second movement of Schoenberg's Violin Concerto. His own manuscripts are rolled like diplomas and piled on the floor like logs.

Dinner with Boulez and Suvchinsky in a restaurant two Métro stops before the Pont de Neuilly: turbot and Sancerre; gigot and Richebourg; gâteau St.-Honoré and raspberry liqueur. Suvchinsky's hair is wintry; his handshake, in which the last two fingers do not engage, is limp, and his nearly albino complexion is mottled as if from a tropical disease, with patches of marchpane and pink. But these aspects are belying, for he is big-boned and *"robuste"* (a favorite word, in fact near the top of the list after *"con"* and *"salaud"*), has a trencherman's appetite, and speaks in a powerful (a Boanerges'), though also a musical (a *viola pomposa*), voice. As if in compensation for the unhearty handshake, he crushes me with Russian bear hugs and Russian-style (double-cheeked) kisses.

Despite forty years in Paris and Parisian habits of criticism formed before that, Suvchinsky is more Russian- than French-minded. In fact, he reminds me in many ways of I.S., is in truth more like I.S. than anyone else I have ever met. This Russianness—as I have come to think of it, for of course the qualities I have in mind are personal and individual first, and Russian second, if at all—is characterized by an openness and volubility, a warmth and generosity formerly understood by the now loaded word "aristocratic."

Suvchinsky is renowned for his talent in discovering talent, and for his selfless efforts to enlist support for it, efforts entailing special difficulties in his case because he himself is poor to the point of hardship. He has been the closest friend, champion, and unsparing critic of both I.S. and Boulez, and in his conversation tonight, centering on I.S., his hand is not stayed in the sense of pulling any critical punches because of I.S.'s confinement in the Rote Kreuz Krankenhaus in Munich. I.S. and Suvchinsky, intimates before the wars, have not seen each other since 1939 because of Suvchinsky's alleged derogation of I.S.'s American-period so-called neo-classic music. When I first encountered Suvchinsky, at a performance of *Erwartung* in Paris in 1952, I.S. received my report of the meeting in silence.

Suvchinsky leads off with questions about I.S.'s children. He is sympathetic to the difficulties of "life with father" when father is a tyrant of genius, and he is aware that the ambidexterity of Theodore and Milene may be an inverted, or leftover, manifestation of their father's gifts, and even that the cerebral zones themselves might be transposed. "In all fairness," he says, "simply to know that one has *those* genes is a burden."

He then advances the theory that money is the root of all compromise in I.S.'s case. "Money was always too important to him. The lure of it led him away from composition and into conducting. And he hated to part with it, even to pay the smallest tradesman's bill.

1956

61

"But can you tell me what happened after *Les Noces?* The descent into *Mavra,* the Pergolesi *rifacimenti,* the Tchaikovsky anthology, the titivated echoes of operetta composers in *Jeu de cartes* and the other *'gaietés parisiennes'?* Surely such a *'bizarre métamorphose'* must have some other explanation besides money? Wasn't the real trouble that he did not understand—in Taine's sense—the general ideas of his time? The general ideas were Schoenberg's ideas, and it was Stravinsky who turned the younger generation against Schoenberg. Poulenc, describing the extent to which he and his group were dominated by Stravinsky, told me not long ago that the mere suggestion by any of them that Schoenberg or Berg might be worth investigating would automatically have made them traitors in Stravinsky's eyes. 'At that time Stravinsky was dismissing *Wozzeck,* which he had not heard, as *une musique boche,* and Mahler, of whom he knew nothing, as Malheur.'"

I put my oar in here and protest that if Poulenc's version is accurate, he was as much at fault as I.S. and should not try to hang the blame on the older man. And I add that as Poulenc now goes about belittling I.S. as "too old for the new hats he tries on in the *Canticum Sacrum,*" the French composer shouldn't mind being told that those new hats are part of the reason I.S. is I.S. and Poulenc only Poulenc. But my interruption does not deflect the arraignment, and Suvchinsky's engrossing analysis continues with the indictment that I.S. is "incapable of sustaining a reasoned and developed argument. He cannot go beyond doctrinaire aesthetics, *le goût, plaisanteries,* and paradoxes!" This tempts me to interject that I would have thought *Les Noces* a highly reasoned and developed argument, but Suvchinsky would agree; what he means are mere habits of verbal discourse, more cultivated among professors than among creative artists.

He goes on to say that "Olga Soudeikine's lover, Arthur Lourié, was closer to Stravinsky in the twenties and thirties than anyone else. In fact, Lourié's ascendancy between 1920 and 1926 was nearly total. But Lourié should publish his memoirs; he was a kind of *valet de chambre* to Stravinsky, after all, and no one knows more about a man than his valet,"[1] though of course the sort of person who *could* be a factotum or camerlingo, to I.S., would be unlikely to know very much about him. "Having discovered that Stravinsky was a savage of genius—*'eine wilde Musik'* was Berg's description of *Petrushka*—Lourié set out to tame him, introducing him to Philosophy in the person of Maritain, and to Literature in various other august persons; I remember seeing *Ulysses* in Stravinsky's studio in 1926, brought there, of course, by Lourié." [Not necessarily. I.S. and Joyce had many Parisian acquaintances in common, George Antheil for one, and, for another, Henrietta Hirschmann, the sister of Joyce's secretary, Paul Léon, and a friend of I.S. and V. for forty years.] "It was the old story of the man who explains

---

1. Hegel answering the Prince de Condé's "No man is a hero to his valet": "That is true not because the hero is not a hero but because the valet is a valet."

latching on to the man who *does*. Fortunately, the genius was not tamed out of existence along with the savage, but there were portents, such as *Mavra*. What I do not understand is how Lourié could have had Stravinsky's musical esteem. But he *did* have it, was in fact the first person to be shown each new work up to the time of *Perséphone*. Just how little progress was made at Lourié's *école* is another, almost unknown, matter, however, and it is one of the ironies of contemporary music that the savage of genius, the man who was all 'creative instinct' and 'natural talent,' came to be thought of as a mere arbiter of taste pontificating about the glories of Gounod."

It was Arthur Lourié, Suvchinsky might have added, who intrigued against V. before her marriage to I.S., which is the reason that the name is never mentioned in the I.S. household, and the reason I have no information to contribute myself.

"If Stravinsky had not gone to America in 1939," Suvchinsky continues, "he might have compromised himself politically. He was a frequent and welcome visitor to Blackshirt Italy during the Ethiopian and Spanish wars, after all, and he conducted at the Maggio Fiorentino as late as 1939, by which time that festival had become a loudly pro-Axis celebration. He even inscribed a copy of his *Chroniques de ma vie* for Mussolini. Was this out of pro-Fascist sentiment? Or only because Mussolini's trains ran on time? Absolutely none of the first alternative, certainly, for he was deeply afraid of fascism, but of the German rather than of the Italian kind. Still, these fears did not stop him from recording *Jeu de cartes* in Berlin in 1938, by which time the orchestra had been purged not only of its Jews but also of all good contemporary music including most of Stravinsky's; and by which time all of his colleagues with even a scrap of political, if not moral, sense, and not least among them Stravinsky himself, were protesting Nazism.

"The explanation, apart from the immediate excuse of money, lies in his even deeper dread of Stalin. The lecture in the *Poétique Musicale* on music in the U.S.S.R. convinces me that the fear of communism would eventually have driven him into the arms of the Occupier. He was a White Russian, after all, and his French friends, like T. S. Eliot's French friends, included Maurras and other former *Action française* writers, as well as Drieu la Rochelle and Lucien Daudet." (In fact, I.S. and Daudet were friends only at the time of *Petrushka*; it was Daudet who took the composer to visit the Empress Eugénie in her Riviera villa.) "The political tendency of these associations is noted in Klaus Mann's *Journal,* by the way, and Mann's good friend Gide was well aware of them too. The truth is that the friction between the authors of *Perséphone* was more political than artistic. In Stravinsky's eyes Gide was a COMMUNIST—it was the time of Gide's first infatuation with the U.S.S.R.—hence, *ni plus ni moins,* not only despicable but dangerous. Now from this alone you can see that Stravinsky was not a political animal. Actually, he did not have the remotest grasp of political facts, not the trace of a social concept. Which accounts, in part, for his turning to dogma, though of that, too, he understood precious little. 'I have no explanation of my own,' he used to say. 'Questions of that sort are for the Church to decide,' and he would quote Bossuet's 'The heretic is he who has an opinion.' And what did the Church decide to do about Hitler? To keep very quiet while he murdered Communists and Jews."

It is a passionate, if also a well-rehearsed, recital, not by any means having its maiden tryout. Clearly I am thought of as a plenipotentiary, rather than a famulus, which is more often the case—along with satellite, court jester, and gray eminence who "operates" I.S. and is responsible for shanghaiing him into the "12-tone system" (as if anyone could even lead *that* horse to water, if it didn't want to go, let alone make it drink). The wording is for my benefit, too, though this hardly surprises me, for anyone who has spent two minutes in the same room with I.S. has a theory about him, and a self-including story to put at the disposal of a potential biographer. But from even this nonimpersonating and compendious rather than complete translation, it must be apparent that Suvchinsky's recital is the result of long-pent-up pressures. I.S.'s friendship was the central event of his life. Bereft of it, he would naturally swing to a critical viewpoint in the opposite direction, the direction, as it happened, of Boulez, the *enfant terrible* of the late forties.

What of the content? Some of the daggers are rubber, it seems to me, and some are real, though I cannot comment on the Suvchinsky version of the Lourié influence but only continue to suspect from my observations of him at Tanglewood a decade ago, and from what I know of his music and writings, that the evaluation is exaggerated. (But V. says that Suvchinsky is right and I am wrong.) As for the alleged perpendicular decline of I.S.'s music after the Russian period, that is the official postwar view of it in France; nor will *Oedipus Rex* and the *Symphony of Psalms* be released from French quarantine until some extremely daring antiquarian discovers that whether or not these masterpieces are "neo-classic" is wholly beside the point.

The money issue is less easily disposed of. Leaving aside the question of his deep generosity, I.S. is oddly, aberrantly thrifty, and undoubtedly tradesmen *have* had to dun him for payment. But he can be as extravagant as a grand duke, too, and he is improvident to the extent of being regularly overdrawn at the bank. That his possessiveness is all-powerful any photograph of his workroom will show, but the possessions he most wants are people, and he has rarely succeeded in his friendships, demanding too great a sacrifice—fealty, in fact—and too exclusive a loyalty. V. blames the money drive exclusively on the trauma of the war years, when his coffers really were empty and he really was forced to grub around, but surely it is older and more anal than that. Whatever the explanation, and however formulated—for all acts, including acts of charity, are selfish, as Stirner very persuasively argued over a century ago (ours being a society in which everybody uses everybody else for his own ends)—I.S. has supported a whole welfare department of relatives for most of their lives, and for at least as long as I have known him has kept several destitute friends in funds.

64

The imputed right-wing political sentiments are a more vexed question than this account allows, however, because of prior religious questions requiring disentanglement and differentiations of a kind that I myself, understanding little of that side of I.S., am not able to undertake. I would agree that he does not understand political philosophy and does not believe in the political medium, and that his socio-political parts did not grow up to match his genius parts; but, then, it seems to me that the authoritarian mold of his mind is only spuriously related to politics. What it does relate to is the Church. And all that I can say positively about even that one aspect of his much greater religiosity is that he associates institutionalized religion with his first wife and his guilt feelings concerning her; and that the influence of the church seems to have been balanced by the more "liberal" influence of the woman around whom his life has revolved since 1921. For I.S. *is* influenced by people he loves and admires, and his capacity for change and growth is not only one of his most "striking characteristics," along with an inexhaustible intellectual curiosity, but also a phenomenon of our age.

Finally, the "no mind" diagnosis, the gravamen of the argument concerning I.S.'s supposed failure to understand Schoenberg's "general ideas," is in my opinion not even a factor; nor, for that matter, is the Schoenberg antinomy "true," which is not to go to the other extreme and claim that I.S. was among the original 12-tone commandos. The real reasons for his musical attitudes as described by Poulenc were the circumstantial ones: his musical isolation and—both the cause and the result of that—his lack of communication with other composers. But the equipment itself was and is up to any complexity of understanding, the mind of the *Sacre* and the *Psalms* being, if anything, too subtle for such measurements. Nor, in I.S.'s case, do I concede a penchant for paradox as an intellectual limitation. It is, in fact, no more than a mannerism, a device of social rather than of mental behavior. But, once again, what Suvchinsky means by mind is a rhetorical discipline, while what I mean is something similar to Eliot's description of the mind of Henry James as so fine that no "idea" could violate it.

Still, this is the testimony of a man who was as close to I.S. at one time as I am now. By extension I am able to recognize everything and confirm much in Suvchinsky's picture. But it is another I.S. So, too, the I.S. *I* know would seem greatly transformed to Suvchinsky, though doubtless he could see by looking ahead, as I am able to see by looking back, the "continuity of personality." But the differences lead me to wonder whether anyone has ever known more than one or another aspect of I.S., for even V., who can collate these views, is held apart from his deepest feelings by at least the length of each new composition.

1948
1949
1950
1951
1952
1953
1954
1955
1956
1957
1958
1959
1960
1961
1962
1963
1964
1965
1966
1967
1968
1969
1970
1971

ITINERARY

January 10, 11, 13: I.S. conducts the New York Philharmonic (*Petrushka, Perséphone*), and, on the 14th, records *Perséphone*. **15:** V.'s vernissage at the Iolas Gallery. **21:** The I.S.'s see *Godot*, and, on the 23rd, depart for Los Angeles by train. **February 19:** Visit from Peter Brook. **March 2:** Boulez for dinner. **11:** Boulez and R.C. conduct a Monday Evening Concert, Los Angeles. **June 13, 14:** I.S. is interviewed on film, at home, for the NBC "Wisdom" series. **15, 16:** Rehearsals for *Agon* and *Canticum Sacrum* at Royce Hall. **17:** A concert for I.S.'s seventy-fifth birthday at Royce Hall, première of *Agon*, address by Aldous Huxley. **18, 19:** I.S. records *Agon* (R.C. records Schoenberg's Variations, Opus 31). **28, 29, 30:** R.C. conducts Stravinsky concerts at the Boston Arts Festival, Boston Common. **July 7:** I.S.'s depart for Santa Fe (Lamy) on "Super Chief." **15:** V.'s vernissage at Santa Fe. **18, 19, 20:** *The Rake's Progress* at the Santa Fe Opera. **21:** We leave for New York by train. **August 1:** We sail on the *Liberté*. **7:** We land at Plymouth and go to Dartington. **8:** Drive to Exeter. **9:** Train to London (Dorchester Hotel). **12:** R.C. records *Dumbarton Oaks Concerto* and *Histoire du Soldat* for the BBC. Train to Newton Abbott and car to Dartington. **16:** I.S. attends a concert of Beethoven's *Grosse Fuge* and Bach's *Aus der Tiefe* in Totnes, Devon. **17:** Drive to Tintagel. **19:** With H. D. F. Kitto at Bath, also visiting Wells and Glastonbury. **21:** Drive to London via Salisbury. **24–25:** Train to Paris. **27–28:** Train to Venice. **September 10:** Mantua. **12:** Malamocco. **15:** I.S. photographed in Bologna by Mili. **22:** Asolo. **23:** Torcello. **30:** We drive to Munich (via the Grossglockner), where I.S. conducts a concert. **October:** I.S. rehearses *Agon* in Baden-Baden. **9–10:** Train to Paris. **11:** I.S. conducts *Agon* with the Sudwestfunk Orchestra in the Salle Pleyel. **13:** I.S. poses for Giacometti in the Berkeley Hotel. **15:** R.C. to Rome. **17:** I.S.'s to Zürich. **18:** I.S.'s to Donaueschingen. **19:** I.S. conducts *Agon* in Donaueschingen, then goes to Zürich by car. **20:** I.S.'s fly to Rome. **21:** R.C. conducts Italian première of *Agon* at the Teatro Eliseo. **23:** I.S. conducts in Rome. **25:** Train to Paris. **27:** Dinner with Giacometti, Suvchinsky, Boulez. **29:** Sail for New York on the *Liberté*. **November 10:** I.S. sees a Balanchine rehearsal of *Agon*. **12:** We leave for Los Angeles by train.

Venice. Lunch with Giorgio di Chirico, who looks almost photographically like one or another of his innumerable *autoritratti:* the subtle brown eyes; the quiet, well-manicured fingers; the pale, womanish skin; the soft silver hair parted as it was in the pictures of forty years ago—which, Chirico says, is when he first met I.S.[1] Later in the day Eugene Bermon, talking to us about him, says that "In his case decadence seems to have begun a few minutes after birth. He had great vision as a young man but it quickly lost its force. After that he devoted himself to technical studies. Canvas after canvas came out devoid of any idea but always displaying remarkable technical prowess. When I first knew him, thirty years ago, his notebooks were filled with drawings copied from old masters. He would copy anything that attracted him in anyone else's work, often trying to fob it off, without acknowledgment, as his own, his own imagination apparently having dried up. But another reason for this copying was his prodigious vanity. 'I can paint like Giotto or Raphael, or anyone else, even early Chirico,' he seemed to be saying. . . . I was with him in his studio in Paris one day in the thirties when 'Argyrol' Barnes dropped by to inquire if he had a painting for sale similar to one from 1911 that Barnes admired. Chirico calculated for a moment, then answered that he did just happen to have another one like it, which he could retrieve from such-and-such an exhibition in a month or so and sell to Barnes. And after Barnes left, Chirico promptly set to work copying the 1911 picture from a photograph, changing a few details, and signing and dating it 1911.

"But Chirico would be a perfect subject for a full-scale Freudian biography. Consider all those self-portraits as Apollo, Don Giovanni, King Lear, a courtier to Louis Quatorze, and so on, and consider the tragedy of a man given a few years of lucidity during which he is a great painter, and after which, being unable to live with the knowledge, he denies he has ever been the former person. Yet he is even aware of this. I remember an exhibition in Paris just before the war of his latest and most academic paintings. They were so bad that no one could find anything to say, and we all left the gallery silently shaking his hand. Chirico described this to me later, saying that 'It was as if I were dead and the visitors were mourners who came to pay their respects but knew I couldn't hear.'"

1. Chirico was Stravinsky's, but not Diaghilev's, first choice of painter for *Apollon Musagète.*

1957

1948
1949
1950
1951
1952
1953
1954
1955
1956
1957
1958
1959
1960
1961
1962
1963
1964
1965
1966
1967
1968
1969
1970
1971

ITINERARY

January 2: The I.S.'s fly to Houston. **6, 7:** I.S. conducts concerts in Houston. **8:** I.S.'s fly to Los Angeles. **February 3:** R.C. records *Le Marteau sans maître.* **26:** R.C. flies to New York to conduct a concert of I.S.'s sacred music in St. Thomas's, Fifth Avenue (March 2). **April 7:** R.C. records *Zeitmasse.* **10:** We drive to San Francisco. **18:** I.S.'s last concert in San Francisco. **19:** Drive to Los Angeles. **May 19:** I.S. has a bleeding ulcer. **June 7:** I.S. in Cedars of Lebanon for transfusions. **16:** I.S. conducts *Mavra* at Royce Hall. **19:** R.C. records Gesualdo. **20:** V.'s vernissage at the Comara Gallery. **July 2:** I.S. given radioactive phosphorus injection at Cedars of Lebanon. **20:** The "Super Chief" to New York. **23:** Arrive at the Gladstone Hotel, New York. **29:** We sail for Genoa. **August 8:** We drive to Venice, via Piacenza. **17:** We spend the afternoon at San Lazzaro of the Armenians. **25:** Mesola, Ferrara, Mirandola. **30:** R.C. to Hamburg to rehearse *Threni.* **September 16:** Opening of V.'s *mostra* at the Cavallino Gallery (Venice). **23:** I.S. conducts première of *Threni* in the Scuola di San Rocco. **24:** I.S. to Zürich by car to conduct *Threni* in Swiss cities. **October 1:** I.S. returns to Venice, R.C. to Brussels. **13:** I.S. conducts *Threni* in Hamburg. **15:** We drive to Baden-Baden. **16:** Dinner with Stockhausen, Boulez. **19:** Drive to Zürich. **21:** Train to Florence. **26, 30:** I.S. conducts concerts in Florence. **31:** I.S.'s to Venice by car, then by train to Vienna. **November 4:** We attend *Oedipus Rex* at the Vienna Opera. **7:** I.S. conducts *Apollo* in Vienna. **8:** Train to Paris. I.S. conducts an ill-prepared and ill-received *Threni* in Paris, after which he resolves never to conduct there again (and doesn't). **20:** Train to London. **26:** I.S. has an audience with Pope John. **December:** London. I.S. conducts in Festival Hall. Sail from Southampton on the *Liberté* to New York.

MAY 22

Hollywood. Ernst Krenek for dinner, more suntanned than ever; I do not know how good a Catholic he is, but he certainly practices his heliolatry. We drink two bottles of Aigle-les-Murailles, after which he becomes an engaging memoirist of Webern, Berg, Karl Kraus, Loos, and especially Busoni. Describing Busoni's Berlin *soirées* shortly after the 1914–18 war, Krenek says that the composer sat between a fortune-telling mystic, and—for

68

good luck, like Verdi's Duke of Mantua—a hunchback, and that this odd trinity was always separated from the guests by a row of empty chairs. "Busoni did all of the talking, and he was seldom less than brilliant; he had great qualities of imagination, and great visionary powers—far beyond his abilities as a composer to realize his ideas. Coffee was served regularly, but once we were given *Sekt,* which had not been paid for, and even as we were drinking it, the merchant pounded on the door asking for his money."

Krenek himself is a man of impressive intellectual qualities, some of which are displayed tonight as he explains to I.S. how the time and density controls in his *Sestina* were derived from the original twelve-note structure by multiplying and dividing the numbers of the semitones of the intervals. Nor does it really seem to matter that all this has been worked out well away from the music.

AUGUST 8

Nearing Genoa this morning, on the top deck of the *Cristoforo Colombo,* an elderly couple who have been eyeing I.S. all the way from New York are suddenly emboldened to address him. (All first-class passengers are elderly, which is part of the reason why we look longingly from our superior deck to the progressively poorer and livelier decks of the cabin and tourist classes.) The man puts me in mind of a well-groomed Afghan, apart from his rosewood walking stick and gardenia lapel, but his wife is that altogether different kind of canine, the huntress of social big game. *She* does the talking, moreover, dropping into Italian at one point and then identifying the language in case I.S. might have taken it for Swahili. When eventually they move off we overhear the Afghan barking at his bitch for "trying to catch *him.*"

The Genoa harbor is in dense fog, in and out of which small boats dart like phantoms. Gulls hover overhead as if to warn and guide us—as, long ago, other birds guided Alexander across the sands to Siwa—but they disappear when tugboats siphon us between the breakwaters and then escort us, one on each side, like a mustache, to the pier.

The storms of temperament in the hotel dining room are in radical contrast to the imperturbable routine on the boat. The hotel service is clamorous, sweaty, melodramatic. Our waiter mumbles a *"Mamma mia,"* on each return from the kitchen, and his state of nerves is such that he smites his breast and cries *mea culpa* when we so much as point out the shortage of a spoon.

The Campo Santo—*"Il più bello cimitero del mondo,"* as the souvenir hawkers claim—has become a major tourist stop, with *ciceroni* interpreting and extolling as if it were the Bargello. The monuments include sculptured family groups "taken" at the bedsides of the dying, wives and daughters with their tears in their eyes, husbands and sons with their hats in their hands. In one *tableau mourant,* the pose of a mother and child by the bedside is almost exactly that of David's "Andromache Mourning Hector." In another, a young wife draws the bedclothes over her expired husband's face. And in still another, a newly widowed mother raises her infant son to his deceased papa's cheek for a farewell *bacio*. Almost as common are resurrection scenes in which the dead are shown setting out for Heaven while traffic-policemen-angels point the way. But the *fin de siècle* is marked by a trend to the nude, and especially to *pudicità*, in the persons of Eves and Niobes holding their fig leaves to attract attention to the forbidden place as coyly as stripteasers hold their fans. And a trend to Philosophy, translated sculpturally as resignation: what horrible poses of resignation there are! Of the philosophers, Socrates (in an Inverness cape!) is a surprisingly popular saint for a Christian cemetery. But then, Christ Himself is often made to look like a kind of Hegel, a Hegel surrounded by brooding, pinions-folded, philosophy-student angels.

I.S. recalls a monument in another illustrated 3-D cemetery at Padua, "A sculptured reconstruction of the actual automobile accident in which the entombed family was killed. A careening 'lifesize' automobile was carved on the grave, with a goggled chauffeur inside and a woman screeching through her veil. It was as real as Madame Tussaud's. Surely Taste is a moral category." But of all the thousands of figures represented on these sarcophagi, none portrays any of the repose or beauty of expression of the Etruscans, so serenely smiling on their tombs.

SEPTEMBER 17

Venice. Leaving a concert at night, we collide in a side street with Auden. Wearing an open-necked shirt and espadrilles cut to accommodate his corns, he is rushing back to his hotel in a great hurry, he tells us, "Because I've just learned that Leopardi wasn't born in the south."

SEPTEMBER 19

Auden for lunch at the Bauer. He fusses obsessively about punctuality, and when I.S. is five minutes late predicts that "The Russians won't win the war because they won't be there on time. '*Dieses warten,*' as Tristan says." Auden is in a German period. He not only plans to translate one of Goethe's prose works, he says, but promises "to make him sound like a limey." Less annoyed by untidiness than by unpunctuality, he seems to suggest that the Augean cleaning was a great mistake. Then when I.S. finally does arrive, Auden is openly contemptuous of the pill bottles arranged in front of his plate, whispering to me that "The steadiest business in the world would be a pharmacy next door to Stravinsky." Auden then observes to I.S. that "True creators are always ashamed of most of their past work. Are you ashamed?" I.S.: "No. I would do many things differently but I am not ashamed." Auden asserts next that Tolstoy had a great sense of humor. "I'm sure that even in his dreary late years if you had said to him, 'Now come off that old plow,' he would have laughed." But I.S. thinks he would have died of apoplexy. Talking about "*l'esprit de con* in literature," Auden calls the work of a famous male writer "a *connerie bien élégante*," but says that certain female writers, Virginia Woolf for one, lacked this *esprit*. I.S. wants to know precisely what the "female" difference is, of course, but Auden says it is simply a *"vas deferens."* Auden confesses that one of his critical yardsticks is: "People one would like to be with at dinner. No character in Dostoievsky would have made an amusing dinner companion, I think, whereas most of Dickens's characters, including many who were evil, would have been fascinating company at table." And he proposes as a new category of literary criticism, "Great classics of boredom," nominating Dostoievsky as "a major bore. He always wants to talk about his soul. I cannot stand the Russians' total lack of reticence."

The O.E.D. missed "unkiss," a word he found in Aubrey, he says. And suddenly he shows his new poem, *Farewell to Mezzogiorno,* which explains his concern about Leopardi's birthplace. After a while, I.S. complains of intestinal unrest, saying he has swallowed so much bismuth he feels like a weir, whereupon Auden starts to sing the Methodist hymn:

. . . every bowel of our God
With soft compassion rolls.

Auden's fists are milk-white, pudgy, hairless, but the fingers are stained with nicotine, and the nails are nibbled halfway to the moons.

We attend a concert with him at the Fenice, at night. In a café, at intermission, he engages I.S. in a discussion about an opera and suggests that "One should study it." I.S.: "No, one should just steal from it." When I.S. observes that the second half of the concert will begin in two minutes, Auden replies that "Cyril [Connolly] would say, 'Just time to eat a lobster.'" Back in the theater, Auden notes that the women's chorus "looks like a bed of petunias."

OCTOBER 18

Schloss Fürstenberg, Donaueschingen. We stay in the Kaiser's suite, on the third floor, a five-minute walk from a shuddering lift, through galleries of royal portraits and an armory capable of sustaining an old-fashioned Central American revolution. The furniture includes cheval glasses, consoles, flocculent beds, dressing tables. Propped on the latter, next to the intra-Castle telephone directory (which lists 104 numbers), are seating charts for luncheon and dinner guests—Prinzen, Grafen, Barone, musicians. We follow a concierge to the dining room, which is a half-mile hike from the cruelty-to-old-machines elevator through corridors gory with battle paintings and bristling with antlers of slaughtered stags. At table, I am seated next to Messiaen, a humorless, limp, loose man, but with profound eyes. (I.S. has not seen him since May 1952, when he played Boulez's *Structures* with the composer in the Petit Théâtre des Champs-Elysées, an occasion made the more memorable by a girl whose sudden out-loud laughter, provoking a

1958

71

franc-tireur of the *avant-garde* to vault several seats and slap her, set off a fracas eventually put down by the police.) After the lunch I try to convince I.S. that a part of Messiaen's mind and emotions would be more at home in the century of Francis of Assisi, and that he is a mystic and a Holy Roller rather than a *naïf,* which is I.S.'s epithet. But I.S. really *does* dislike the sentiment (call it the Bad Taste), the repetition, the mechanical phrasing, the blockbusting volume of what he knows of Messiaen's music, besides which, and perhaps most important of all, he will never forgive the Frenchman's criticisms of *The Rake.*

DECEMBER 7

London. Dinner at Stephen Spender's with Graham Greene, who is so much taller than I.S. that a distant onlooker, not already aware of the diminutive height of the one, might take the other to be an ex-center on a basketball team. Greene says that he had been told that I.S. was in the audience at one of the New York previews of *The Potting Shed,* and regrets are exchanged that they had not met then. But conversation-making is heavy going, and lulls frequent. Greene's talk is topical, which is not unlooked-for, but the I.S.'s have never heard of the Wolfenden debate, concerning which Greene suggests that T. S. Eliot and John Hayward should be induced to address a letter to *The Times* on the respectableness of two men keeping house together.

He is more interesting on the difficulties of unblocking royalties in bamboo-curtain countries, where *The Quiet American* is immensely popular: "It looks as if I will have to spend the rest of my days in China." But he intimidates the I.S.'s. They have read all of his books, starting with, because of their fascination with Mexico, *The Power and the Glory;* and they are attracted in advance to the author of them, if not by his obsessions with pity, fear, self-destruction, failure, the need to run away, the hollowness of physical love, the problem of Pelagian moral arguments. Yet they do not know how to say *"Bonjour"* to him in a way to make him talk; and though not shy as a rule, they cannot bridge the shyness of the other along with their own. And Greene *is* shy: if he were aware of how much the I.S.'s admire him, he would freeze altogether. As it is, he lends no support to the infrequent moments of not exactly doubling-up general amusement, nor quite shows how he regards our own participation in them, for when his implacable blue eyes focus on one of us, they are transparently seeing something else. His brows knit, instead, his jowls weigh down, and his saggy face sags a little more. It is a sad, wise, fanatical face, the mask of a man who has seen a great deal and knows the worst.

DECEMBER 8

Dinner with the T. S. Eliots in their Kensington Gardens ground-floor flat. The name does not appear on the roster of tenants, but they are waiting for us in the hall when we arrive, and holding hands. Their walls are bare except for bookshelves, and these are mainly in the dining room, "which is where arguments come up," Eliot says, "and the reason that dictionaries and reference books should be kept there." As if to illustrate the remark, and in response to some speculations by I.S. concerning the word "paraclete," he fetches a well-worn Liddell and Scott from behind his own chair but offers the identical information himself before opening it. He helps again, no less impressively, when I.S. cannot recall the name of the monastic order on San Lazzaro degli Armeni; "The Mechitarist Fathers," Eliot says, and he recounts some episodes in their history. He also provides apt and exact translations of the foreign expressions that occur regularly in I.S.'s talk, at the same time disclaiming that he is a linguist: "I only pretended to be one in order to get a job in a bank." But he is a quiet man, slow in formulating his remarks, which trail off in *diminuendo;* the life in him is not in his voice, but in his clear, piercingly intelligent gray eyes. He breathes heavily and harrumphs a great deal: "Hm, Hmm, Hmmm," deepening the significance, it seems, with each lengthening "m." His long, fidgety fingers fold and unfold, too, or touch tip to tip, which suddenly makes me aware that I.S.'s hands, otherwise remarkable for the large spread between the knuckles, are the least nervous I have ever seen.

Table talk is mainly about taxes—I.S. says he feels guilty on learning that tonight's dinner is not deductible—and writers. "Cocteau was very brilliant when I saw him last," Eliot remarks, "but I had the impression he was rehearsing for a more important occasion." All of Eliot's anecdotes, otherwise, are self-effacing. One of them is about "a young woman who, during the stop at Gander, on my last flight from New York, hovered nearer and nearer, until finally I invited her for coffee, during which she asked for my recollections of Virginia Woolf." Another is about a taxi ride in New York one day with Djuna Barnes. "I noticed that the driver had become engrossed in our conversation; then after Miss Barnes left he asked whether that *woman* was a writer."

Eliot says that I.S.'s published remarks about Dylan Thomas interested him. "Thomas had the richest gift of humor of any contemporary poet," he says. "He might have written a good comedy, too, though whether he ever could have fashioned a libretto I am unable to say."

Eliot confesses that he cannot remember his own poetry, "because it was rewritten so many times I forget which version was final." We drink sherry before, claret during, whiskey after, dinner. Eliot carves and serves the meat himself, and walks around the table filling our glasses like a wine steward.

After dinner he brings a scrapbook bulging with photographs and clippings, and invites I.S. to compose something for it, saying that he writes in it himself every night.

> A time for the evening under lamplight
> (The evening with the photograph album).

During most of the evening I.S. refrains from medical talk, but once he mentions that his blood is too thick, which reminds Eliot that in 1911 a doctor in Munich told him that *his* blood was too thin.

I.S., in the car returning to Claridge's: "He is not the most exuberant man I have ever known, but he is one of the purest."

New York. Auden for dinner. He drinks martinis before, wine during, whiskey after. When I.S. tells him we hope to see *The Seven Deadly Sins*—he and Chester Kallman have composed the lyrics for the English version—he says, "Better hurry and get tickets or you will never get in. *Vanessa* is on at the 'Met' that night."

DECEMBER 29 **1958**

I.S., telephoning the G. Wittenberg Surgical Appliances Company: "This is Mr. Stravinsky, S-T-R-A . . ." He spells it loudly and deliberately, as he does dictating telegrams. "Two years ago you fitted me for a truss. I want an appointment to have it repaired." But he has dialed a wrong number, and the other party has apparently had to hear the entire speech without finding an opportunity to interrupt. I.S. ill-humoredly cradles the receiver, then carefully dials again. "This is Mr. Stravinsky. S-T . . . You made a . . . " But the same party answers, this time very annoyed. Annoyed now himself, I.S. double-checks the number in his address book, finds it correct, still believes he has misdialed, tries again. "This is Mr. . . ." But the man on the other end, doubtless supposing himself the victim of a raving lunatic, slams down the receiver. At this point V. discovers from the telephone directory that I.S. has miscopied the number. (The foregoing is a typical I.S. "scene." At least one such occurs daily.)

1948
1949
1950
1951
1952
1953
1954
1955
1956
1957
1958
1959
1960
1961
1962
1963
1964
1965
1966
1967
1968
1969
1970
1971

ITINERARY

January 4: The New York première of *Threni.* **5:** I.S. records *Threni.* **7:** A birthday party for V. and Chester Kallman at Auden's. **8:** Fly to Hollywood. **February 27:** R.C. and Gerald Heard tape a "dialogue" for television. **March 25:** We fly to Honolulu (Princess Kaiulani Hotel). **April 5:** Fly from Hong Kong over Okinawa to Tokyo. **24:** V.'s vernissage at the Matsuja Department Store, Tokyo. **May 1:** I.S. conducts a concert in Osaka. **3, 7:** I.S. conducts concerts in Tokyo. **9:** Fly to Los Angeles from Seattle. **21:** I.S.'s fly to Copenhagen to receive the Sonning Prize; they meet Isak Dinesen. **25:** I.S. conducts a concert in Copenhagen. **26:** I.S.'s fly to Los Angeles. **June 15:** I.S. conducts at Royce Hall. **29:** I.S.'s go by train to Lamy (Santa Fe). **July 12:** I.S. conducts *Threni* in Santa Fe Cathedral. **August:** I.S.'s fly to New York; I.S. talks to students at Princeton seminar, and meets Robert Oppenheimer. **September:** We fly to London. **8:** Train to Edinburgh. **13:** Train to London. **14-15:** Train to Paris. **16-17:** Train to Venice. **October:** We go to Udine and Duino. **12:** I.S. and R.C. fly to Rome, then go to Naples by car with Eugene Berman. **18:** I.S. conducts in Naples, then takes night train to Bologna. **21:** Concert in Bologna. **24-25:** Train from Milan to Paris. **25:** R.C. flies to Hamburg. **26:** I.S.'s go by train to London. **31:** R.C. flies to London. **November 9:** I.S. conducts *Oedipus Rex* with Cocteau at the Royal Festival Hall. **13:** We sail to New York on the *Liberté,* arriving 19th. **December 20:** I.S. conducts *Les Noces* in Town Hall, and records it (21st).

MARCH 28-29

Honolulu to Wake Island, nine hours of empty ocean, crossing the International Date Line in late afternoon. We scuff through pink coral dust to the shore of the shadowless island, then go to an open-air canteen. Another plane, eastbound, has landed meanwhile, and one of its passengers, a Swiss, introduces himself to me with: "I want to thank you for your Webern records." On Wake Island! One of the island's Philippine work crews gathers by the gates to watch our take-off. They are charcoal black, like figures in an underexposed negative.

75

We land again at Guam, at midnight, bathed in a large moon. A warm wind rustles the palm trees.

MARCH 30

Manila Airport, 5 AM, the I.S.'s counting their baggage—*ras, dva, tri, chetiry*—over and over, like rosary beads. The U.S. cultural attaché, a Mr. Morris, delivers us to the Manila Hotel, where a dozen eager porters pack us into our rooms. Old Manila, what we see of it on the way, is black and grim except for pretty lattices and grilles and the translucent mother-of-pearl, clamshell windows. The Bay shores are lined with hundreds of "nightclubs," actually tiny, two-customer booths and simple Coca-Cola carts. They are a squalid sight now, at daybreak, but after we have seen the clusters of orange-crate dwellings inside the old walls, they seem rather prosperous and gay.

We drive to Taytay and Lake Taal, stopping on the way at the Church of Las Piñas, to hear a bamboo organ. Built by a metal-less Spanish friar, the entire organ—keys, pedals, 714 pipes—is made of bamboo. A young monk plays Gounod's *Ave Maria* for our alms, and the sound is like a choir of recorders: sweet, weak in volume, out of tune.

The road leaving Manila crosses salt flats, and the roadside is heaped with bags marked ASIN, the dialect word for salt. Another common sign is SARI-SARI, the Chinese for "sundries"; but all directions and most billboards are in English, the eight major Philippine dialects having made no progress toward consolidation. Beyond the flats, at the edge of the jungle, a police roadblock warns of banditry in the neighborhood, but this more encourages than alarms the I.S.'s. The road is hemmed in by thick canebrakes at first, and at times is entirely canopied by liana. The only human habitations are bamboo huts on stilts in the midst of coconut and banana groves. And we see only two people on the road, men carrying red-shakoed cocks. Halfway to Taytay a carabao herd crosses the road in front of us.

Taytay is high and treeless, and the natives carry large black umbrellas against the torrid sun. We are startled by the sight of a bus, parked on the main street, with all of the passengers asleep as if they had been chloroformed or gassed, but they are merely taking their siesta. All unsleeping Taytayans clamor to be photographed and to sell us fruit. Some of them say "Happy New Year," but the only other "English" they know is "Coca-Cola," which product appears to be the economic index to the whole community, to judge by the stacks of empty cases all over the town. We eat on the terrace of the Taal View Lodge, which offers a panorama of the great volcanic lake a thousand feet below.

Dinner at the U.S. Embassy with the Bohlens, who obviously enjoy exercising their Russian, which they speak with an attractive American drawl. Afterward we look at their color slides of Russian churches, taken during the years of their incumbency in Moscow; and at slides of the Banaue

1959

76

country in northern Luzon, where a week ago two geologists were decapitated, probably, the Ambassador says, because they had asked indiscreet questions. He shows one frightening photograph of a Banaue warrior charging toward the camera brandishing a spear, though *his* intention, says Mrs. Bohlen, was not to throw but to sell it. We ask about José Rizal, the Philippine "Washington" and "Goethe," whose statues populate Manila's parks and whose biography fills its bookstores; but the Ambassador says that Rizal's *Noli Me Tangere* is "competent literature, no more." Dog meat is a delicacy in the islands, according to the Bohlens. It is served in the highest society, moreover, and markets exist where the buyer may select his canine still in the quick. So great is the native appetite, in fact, and the danger from dognapers, that the Bohlens' own poodle has been under guard ever since its arrival in the country. When at one point the Ambassador opens the screen doors for more ventilation, a large rat leaps inside and up the stairs. Nor is it found by the time we leave.

We try to sleep with the lights on, hoping they may discourage the musical geckos on the wall, and the cockroaches and other monsters on the floor, from joining us in our beds.

1959

MARCH 31

The great rice fields of Antipolo and Morong are burned out and brown, and the whole island world is waiting for the rains. In one town a draughts contest is in progress in the middle of the street, and in another a billiard contest. From time to time we overtake water carriers trotting along the road in a swinging caracole; they hold their shoulder poles with the right hand and balance themselves with the left, like football players running interference. Planting has already begun in one irrigated paddy near Morong, and nearby we come upon a circle of women pounding the rice with flails. Morong itself is draped from end to end with fishing nets, and its church, a cross-breed of pagoda and baroque, is inhabited solely by pigs.

APRIL 1

Hong Kong. A travel agent escorts us from the airport to the Kowloon ferry and, across the water, in Hong Kong itself, to the Repulse Bay Hotel. As the boat starts to move, a BBC voice warns us through a loudspeaker not to smoke. The warning, repeated in Chinese, lasts ten times as long and swoops up and down a whole xylophone of inflection. Among the foot passengers are coolies who slough their shoulder poles and baskets to the deck, and small boys who go from car to car peddling Wrigley's gum.

The Repulse Bay Hotel might have been built by the Canadian Pacific Railroad for a Chinese settlement in Saskatchewan. We sit by a stained-glass-peacock window in the restaurant, then move to a terrace with a view of the jade sea, the purple sampans, and the sugar-loaf islands. But the food is deliberately British; and the waiters are obliged to inquire three times whether we want "fiss" before we realize they mean fish ("You want eat egg first or fiss?"). I.S. remarks that the *salon de thé* orchestra "has made a Rossini overture sound like 'Chopsticks.'"

At William McGee's, in Gloucester Road, fifteen tailors take turns speaking to us through the English of one young boy who, as they measure and fit us, translates a stream of questions about life on "stateside." The McGees are Shanghai Chinese, he says, and they do not understand the Mandarin and Cantonese dialects that are more common in Hong Kong. And he adds that while few boys of his age can do brush calligraphy, older people are nonetheless contemptuous of penmanship. But, then, according to him most Hong Kong Chinese cannot write at all or remember enough characters to be able to read a newspaper. As he himself cannot pronounce "r," his English is a language of lallations. Thus he says "foul dollas" but means "four dollars," not "filthy lucre." I.S. wonders why the boy's English is so monotone. "After all, he singsongs his native tongue." When we leave, V. asks the Chinese word for "good-bye," but the boys says "Bye-bye is all we know."

We hire three rickshaws and bump alongside buses, trolleys, automobiles, pedestrians: Chinese, Indians, British civil servants, tourists, beggars, porters with yokes, women with head-loads. Our runners, who are barefoot and who carry towels in their belts to mop perspiration, deposit us at a pier where we watch a junk unloading crates marked "Made in Japan." In addition to the cargo, the small vessel carries a family of seven, and it is an ark of domestic animals as well. At sunset, Hong Kong is curtained in mist. We go to sleep with the hoot of harboring boats in our ears.

1959

At the Kowloon Resettlement Area, rows of concrete apartments housing half a million refugees, children swarm around us but turn superstitiously from V.'s camera. We are delayed by a wedding, at one place, and at another by a funeral, the former with red, the latter with white flowers. Through the large windows of the silver-plated hearse we see six men in Western-style business suits but Chinese headdress, seated around the coffin.

We eat at Shatin on a terrace overlooking the valley of the Kowloon-Canton railroad. Farther inland are walled cities, temples, pagodas, but it is Chinese All Souls' Day and the road is filled with processions. Buddhist dead are exhumed after seven years and reburied in blue urns; the first place of burial being marked by what looks like a concrete armchair, a large first-burial ground full of these armchair cenotaphs suggests an auditorium. Near Taipo our driver promises to show us a "model poetry farm," and for a moment we expect to see a group of aspiring Chinese poets, perhaps attending a lecture by Stephen Spender, until we realize that the driver was simply unable to pronounce the "l" in poultry. A little farther, at the border of the People's Republic, women come to be photographed, demanding "one Melican dolla, please" for the service. They wear loose black trousers, high-collared jackets slit at the sides, and lampshade hats, and the bicycle of one of them carries a caged pig on the handlebars. We return to Kowloon by way of Castle Peak, where black-sail junks fill the bay.

APRIL 5

Tokyo. The city is preparing for the royal wedding. Railings are being built around the moats of the Imperial Palace to keep the crowds from falling in, and, the cherry blossom season being over, celluloid and paper imitations have been fixed to street poles and trees. Throughout the city, colored balloons float messages of felicitation.[1]

On the way to a press conference this morning I.S. says he is "curious to hear what 'neo-classic' is going to sound like in Japanese." The interpreter is Hans Pringsheim, a nephew of Frau Thomas Mann. His translations are generally rapid, but occasionally a short phrase of I.S.'s—"No, I don't like it"—lasts an inexplicable minute in Japanese. Cameras grind throughout the hour-long interview, but the faces behind them betray no interest in their target, and the questions, too, are very wide of their man.

APRIL 6

Kamakura. The sea is the gray of Whistler's "Pacific" in the Frick, and the beaches are obsidian black. We eat shrimps in scrambled eggs in a Chinese restaurant, sitting cross-legged around a revolving table. This is our first meal negotiated entirely with chopsticks, but a more difficult part of it is the numbing at the knees.

The Great Buddha seems smaller at three yards than at three hundred, from which distance, moreover, the eyes appear to be closed. "It is full of electricity," says I.S. "I would be afraid to touch it." People wait in long lines to kneel before it, then pray quickly when their turn comes, and clap their hands as they rise. The crowds at the nearby toy-stalls are almost equally rapt, though some of the toys, magnetic cylinders and so forth, look to me more like mechanical aptitude tests.

On the return to Tokyo, I.S., complaining of pyloric spasms, wonders "Why no one has written a book about toilets and travel, with chapter headings on 'WC's in Greece,' 'Spain from the Bathroom Window,' etcetera. In fact, the subject is so extensive that a two-volume compendium is required. Our intestines regulate our travels, and they are the uppermost worry and anal anxiety the profoundest emotion of all those miserable crowds at Persepolis and the Parthenon. But travel literature never mentions the subject, and of the major authors only Voltaire gave due importance to 'la chaise percée.'"

---

1. Only in my erroneous imagination. The messages were business-as-usual advertisements.

Dinner at the Fukudaya, a seventeenth-century farmhouse converted to a restaurant of *chambres privées*. We exchange our shoes for slippers in what was formerly a stall for massaging steers—to distribute the fat evenly, a still widespread (no pun) practice among gourmets. Inside, we dangle our legs over a brazier deep in the floor beneath a low table, while geishas bring hot saké and kneel at our elbows to replenish our cups after each sip. Tonight's special *hors-d'oeuvre* is a spoon-size tennis racket made of fried kelp, in honor of the first meeting, which occurred on a tennis court, of the Prince and Princess-to-be. Successive courses—*tempura, unagi* (eel), and too many other seafoods to remember, let alone eat—are served in a larger room, in which we squat around an open firepit. After dinner, the geishas, accompanied by scratchy phonograph records, perform some very boring folk dances.

1959

We arrive at the Kabukiza Theater during an interval between plays, and are taken to see costume and prop rooms, the offstage music room, and the mechanism of the revolving stage, which the Japanese invented four centuries ago. An eleven-year-old actor, sword carrier to Togashi, the Keeper of the Barrier Gate in *Kanjincho,* the next play, is introduced to I.S., while behind the curtain an even younger actor is being readied for presentation to the audience in a formal initiation rite, a kind of Thespian Bar Mitzvah that proves to be as moving and theatrical as the play itself. Both children glisten with greasepaint.

Back in the foyer we buy boxes of *sushi* (rice) and *magura* (raw, red tuna) to eat during the play. This is announced by the clapping together of two wooden blocks, and we take our places just as an attendant runs across the wide stage-front, pulling the curtain open with him. The child debutant and six adult actors march onstage and kneel on mats facing the audience. One of the elders makes a speech in this position, every few words of which are punctuated by deep bows from the other five.

The *Kanjincho* performance impresses us, above all, in the unity of sound and gesture, for the actors are no less accomplished musically—in the art of *Sprechgesang*—than they are plastically, as actors and dancers. *Kanjincho* might be described as a *Sprechgesang* opera, in fact, with *Sprechgesang* arias, recitatives, dialogues, ensembles. And to us, of course, the musical element is primary: the grunts, groans, strangulated falsettos; the *glissando* on the hourglass drum; the wheezy Kabuki flute with native wood-notes "wild."

When the hero, Benkei, prevents the villain, Togashi, from seeing that the scroll from which he has pretended to be reading is blank, and when Benkei crosses his eyes—the *Mie*, as it is called—to indicate extreme tension, the audience shouts. Prolonged shouting occurs later—"Take your time"—"Do it well"—"*Olé*"—as Benkei, again escaping Togashi's suspicions, performs the series of leaps known as *Tobiroppo*.

At night I go with Kaoru K. to the Benibasha, a loud, crowded club. "Ladies and gentlemen, winter is over," the menu declares. "Spring is of most comfortable climate and every creature begins. We should be happy if you are able to smell Real Japanese Nation." This is by way of introducing some deodorized folk dances to an almost entirely American clientele. All of the announcements are more or less in American, I should add, and in fact the only non-American feature is a herd of about fifty girls standing behind a grille, an over-made-up but totally expressionless harem for hire.

Classical Japanese pornography acts antiseptically on Western sensibilities, at any rate on mine; or so I conclude from a rapid inspection of some improper prints surreptitiously shown to me today in a bookshop. For instead of voluptuous postures of idealized naked bodies, only inert people are portrayed and always fully and elaborately clothed. Furthermore, while the point of many of the illustrations is puzzling or obscure, in others the viewer is confronted with grossly exaggerated sexual organs. Like the best European erotica, this is mostly eighteenth-century.

1959

The landscape is more beautiful in the rain, and not far from Tokyo farmers still wear the straw raincoats pictured by Hokusai. But the spectacle of so many bicyclists with umbrellas is nervous-making because "acrobatic," as I.S. says. (Every Japanese owns one or more umbrellas, and an umbrella is part of the equipment of hotel rooms.) We drive to Hakone, but take refuge during a thunderstorm at a hotel in Miyanoshita. South of Kamakura, concrete fortifications, unwelcome reminders of 1945, still defend the beaches, but it seems to me that a more formidable obstacle to an invading army would be the roads; in fact, one wonders how so highly industrialized a country can afford such narrow and imperfectly paved ones. Near Hakone, a funeral procession passes us, its colored-paper wreathes wilting in the torrent.

On the return to Tokyo, we count seven major traffic accidents. "Kamikaze drivers," says "Slim"-san, *our* driver. "They even come down the wrong side of the road hoping to bluff the counter-traffic into the ditch." Motorcycles outnumber automobiles, and *their* drivers are even more reckless and aggressive. Like many pedestrians, they wear surgeons' bandages over their noses and mouths.

Cannonades at 6 AM proclaim the royal wedding day as well as startle us out of bed. Having been warned not to brave the crowds, we watch the parade on television, where the horse guards gallop almost into the screen, and the banzai-ing mobs are shown at close range. But the Prince and Princess are never seen except at a great distance.

From V.'s notebook: "Japanese eyesight is not so poor, or at any rate spectacles are not so endemic, as wartime caricatures have led us to expect. But teeth are worse." And: "Men and women belong to different races here. A cult of quintessential femininity—of shyness and modesty, high, hushed voices and doll-like make-up—is pursued in contrast to a loud and bellicose masculinity. But this exaggeration of sexual characteristics is in no sense chivalric, for the Japanese woman is the 'parfit' servant of her knight." Still other entries observe that "The Japanese say 'Yes' when they don't understand, hoping you will forget"; and that "The women giggle without apparent provocation, yet fail to react in any situation we think of as humorous." But, then, I.S. is enjoying himself here more than V., and part of the reason is his Japanese height. Whereas my knees press the wall of the WC and my head is a foot above the mirror when I shave, these utilities are exactly tailored to him. But another reason is the absence of tipping, of, as I.S. says, "The fumbling for money, the nuisance and embarrassment we suffer at arrivals and departures everywhere else in the world."

APRIL 12

The crowd on the station platform awaiting the early train to Kyoto includes young women with puffy cheeks and flat profiles, carrying babies in back-pouches; old men with white wispy beards; and old women in kerchiefs, smocks, boots, accompanied by children dressed like Eskimos. In spite of the crush, everyone queues up in an orderly manner when the train arrives. We are helped to our seats in the caboose by officials from the Osaka Festival, who say, it seems in response to no matter what *we* say or do, "Thank you very muts," and "If you pease, if you pease." All of our fellow passengers are camera fanatics who while away the journey photographing exits from tunnels. But at least this so-called observation car is equipped with a bar—"Scotch" whiskey, both Japanese and imported—and two WC's, respectively identified on the doors as "Western Style Lavatory" and "Japanese Style Lavatory"; the latter, a hole in the floor, attests to the superior strength and flexibility of Japanese knees.

Waiters canvass the train for luncheon orders hours in advance so that the meal may be served at appointed times and without delay, but at noontime the smell of *sushi* eaten out of wooden boxes in the third-class carriages makes us regret not having ordered the Japanese-style meal ourselves. In the European-style *wagon-restaurant,* the division of labor is so minute that one person sets the table with knives, another with forks, and another with spoons. *Oshibori* (hot towels) are distributed before and after each course, as they are every hour or so in the caboose.

The landscape is densely industrial as far as Atami, where we reach the sea. After that, neatly rounded rows of tea bushes cover mile after hilly mile before giving way to flat land growing rice. Photographers and publicity department geishas meet us at Kyoto. The geishas, who clack along on high wooden shoes and in full costume, may be as embarrassed as we are, but faces under so much white flour betray nothing.

APRIL 13

The temple of Sanjusangen-do is a forest of 1,001 lifesize wood-and-gold-leaf images of Kwannon, Goddess of Mercy, each with eleven faces and a prodigious number of hands; moreover, the long, straight ranks of this graven assembly occupy the largest room in Japan. The other rooms are repositories of other wood sculptures, chiefly of diabolical figures—demons, demiurges, winged Beelzebubs—but with a few ascetics and contemplatives and two gentle Sivas playing cymbals and a lute. The proliferation of the Kwannons, the literalness of the multiplication, has horrified I.S., however, and he can think of nothing else. "That repetition is arrogant," he says. "I am afraid of having one thousand and one sleepless nights."

We drive to Osaka in the afternoon, for a performance of *Figaro* by the Vienna State Opera. But the long avenue entering the city is choked by streets and alleys debouching dense and perpetual traffic; and our driver can neither make his way through it very ably nor find the Grand Hotel, our appointed meeting place with friends. He asks taxi drivers, policemen, pedestrians for directions, but it is a long time before we find anyone who seems to know. I.S.: "How did they ever manage to find Pearl Harbor?"

As for the *Figaro,* in the Osaka Festival Hall, the Japanese orchestra and chorus are good enough, if never quite in tune. But the drama is disappointing: we want more Kabuki. At intermission, a Japanese musician approaches I.S., addressing him in, so it seems, English, but I.S. says that it sounded to him "exactly like Donald Duck." We escape, before Act Two, to the nearby Alaska Restaurant. It is ten flights up, from which elevation the neon advertisements in all directions are like millions of abstract paintings. How pleasant not to be able to read them!

APRIL 14

Kyoto is rectilinear, like a Chinese city; and it is a city of black houses with black slate roofs; and a city of permanent rush-hour crowds in gray and black kimonos; and a city of black-robed monks and priests with shaved heads; and a city of swarming bicycles; and a city of bamboo television antennas; and a city of tourists, predominantly Japanese, who pour out of temples and shrines like the wind from Aeolus' bag. Kyoto is not conspicuously clean except in certain residential districts, where great piles of firewood are tidily stacked against each immaculately proper house. I.S. remarks that the survival of the city, most of whose buildings are made of wood, "must be attributed to miraculous rains and fire departments."

The lake of Ryuan-ji is girdled by red camellias, a carpet of moss, and trees that are no less holy than the temples. Never destroyed and apparently never even pruned, many of the limbs are supported by Dali-like systems of crutches. The spiky ginkgos, tied with strips of white cloth representing *ex voto* messages, look like women in curlers. We rest on the temple porch, regarding, but I am afraid not contemplating, the furrowed sand and its famous islands of rock.

The twin images of the Deva kings, under the eaves of the gate to Ishiyama-Tera, are worm-browsed and whitewashed by birds. Inside the gate, novices and lay brethren gently whisk the grass with besoms. The temple itself is half-hidden in a forest of tall cryptomerias. We enter by way of a porch hung with huge paper lanterns, just as a priest kneels before an altar piled with oranges and bread and performs some ceremonious hand flourishes, accompanying them with strangely animalian guttural noises. According to tradition, the *Tale of Genji* was written in the adytum's "Murasaki Room," for which the lady paid the rent by copying a sutra—now on display and indubitably in her hand. Two scroll portraits of her are also preserved here, "Murasaki Looking at the Moon" and "Murasaki at Her Writing Table." In the first, the great writer stands gazing out of a window, her long hair covering her shoulders and back. In the second, the hair is braided, and a magnificent pleated kimono billows behind her like a tent.

APRIL 15

The treasure of the Shugakuin Palace is a fragment of painting on the walls of the Middle Tea House, a picture of a fish escaping through a torn net. But the place is famed for its cherry trees, on which some late-season blossoms look like popped popcorn; and for its gardens, which are the tidiest imaginable, thanks to a task force of old women in white smocks and caps who tiptoe about dusting the moss. But we are dogged by a guide, whose patter, if not incomprehensible, always requires the transposition of "r's" and "l's"; only after the visit, for example, do we realize that the "pray house" was really the "play house."

We go in the afternoon to the woodland temple at Kozan-ji, the repository of the eleventh-century animal-cartoon scrolls by the priest Kakuyu. The houses in the region are moss-thatched, and the roofs appear to be held down at the gable ends by sawhorse braces. At the temple, which is at the edge of a ravine, a priest and his wife welcome us with low bows, as well as with green tea, meringues, candy butterflies, candy blades of grass; temple tea can be neither sipped nor gulped, but must be swallowed over the meringues, held in the mouth like Communion wafers, in three draughts. Our signatures in the guestbook are the first in Western script.

At the Kyoto Geisha review tonight—a caricature, not always intentional, of posturing Kabuki actors—I.S. marvels most at the instant changes of scenery. Every prop turns upside down or inside out, and the winter scene becomes the cherry blossom scene in two seconds flat. The final tableau, a sunrise over the rocky Japanese coast, is a tawdry but breathtaking spectacle that wins prolonged applause. I.S.: *"C'est très Mikado."*

We have heard too many expressions of rapture about the Katsura Detached Palace, and, partly for this reason, are disappointed. But our visit is also spoiled by showers that muddy the paths, and by the guide to whom we are leashed and who lectures us on "modular co-ordination." I.S. compares the paperbox rooms to "Mondrians in three dimensions," and he claims to like the idea—the formality—of the "Moon-Viewing Platform."

At Sambo-in, the temple walls are covered with paintings of golden clouds, bamboo and pine branches, gold-flecked chrysanthemums, willows lightly trembling in the wind—Auden: "One knows from the Japanese what a leaf must feel"—and the black hats of some horsemen winding in procession through one series of panels would alone make a Zen picture. In the last pavilion, a fat Buddha statue gazes without appetite at a tray of fresh fruit.

The gardens of Byodo-in are the red, white, and mauve of magnolias, plum blossoms, wisteria. A bell booms as we enter the temple, which is in the middle of a small lake, and which has a bronze phoenix on top, like a weathercock. The Amida-Butsu, inside, is attended by *putti* who play zithers and shepherds' pipes and who dance for joy, each on a private cloud.

We stop at a roadside restaurant in Uji, and drink saké and eat candied fish—when we can finally persuade the proprietor to leave his television set long enough to serve us. In the street, an old man is selling cinnamon cakes from a cart harnessed to three monkeys.

Nicolas Nabokov arrives from Tokyo, and we go together for a massage, an hour of steel-fingered female musculature—androphobic musculature, in fact—without a moment's pause and at a cost of only 300 yen. After dinner we walk in the paper-lantern district of the Gion, which I.S. likens to "a dainty Broadway." N.N. is whiter and shaggier since we saw him last, and he looks more and more like Turgenev—while behaving like a big lapdog, for he is constantly smooching and hugging the I.S.'s and cuddling them with animal affection. The corners of his mouth have turned down, too, for the reason, says I.S., that he has so often imitated American speech out of the sides of it, he is now beginning to talk that way naturally. But N.N.'s culture-and-sex talk is as lively as ever, and best of all, it helps the I.S.'s to forget all about Kyoto for the moment, and they need a moment of relief. N.N.'s impersonations, however, are even more brilliant, and once he has been heard in such set pieces as "The American Fulbright Student in Florence" and "Stephen Spender and the Sanskrit Poet Reciting Their Verses to Each Other," to say nothing of improvisations like the hilarious "Noh" play he puts on for us tonight, the butt of the mimicry can never again be seen in the same, pre-N.N. way.

As a result of a letter this morning from the Webers in Zürich, who have commissioned his *Movements* for piano, I.S. says, "I think I will have to add another minute or two of music." To which V.'s comment is: "So much for 'all-encompassing conceptions of form.' The artist simply makes it up as he goes along."

The rooms of Nijo Castle are peopled with lifesize mannequins, posed and costumed to illustrate scenes from the Shogun's court. (I pose V. and I.S. by the moats and great stone walls to illustrate some future book.) When trod upon, the floorboards outside the Shogun's bedroom chirp like nightingales—on purpose, it is said, to betray a would-be assassin.

The paintings at Nanzen-ji, for me the most marvelous of all, include scenes of a hunter wearing the deerskin and antlers of a decoy; a jungle full of brightly burning tigers; and a fantasy picture of a man on a crane's back, high in the sky. But a collection of percussion instruments here interests I.S. even more, above all the *mo kugyo*, a fish-shaped wood block—*"gyo"* means fish—with a flat mouth. Struck by a sponge mallet, it emits a long, low moan, like the sea.

APRIL 18

The temple of Konju-ji smells too sweetly of sandalwood, and the young Buddha in the half-lotus position on a dais strewn with lilies seems to me over-refined. But what I.S. dislikes are the "crustacean" Buddhas with several sets of arms. Our guide, a young monk, is not very happy either, being annoyed almost equally with us and with his job; and to show us that we are wasting both his and our time, he deliberately Baedekerizes in Japanese. When V. films a game of ring-around-the-rosy in front of the temple, children come running from all directions to be in the picture, bowing to her gracefully afterward.

APRIL 19

On the road to Osaka this morning we pass two Buddhist pilgrims. They are dressed in white robes, white hats, and white leggings, and they carry wooden staves.

The Osaka Noh Theater is a square room half filled by an elevated stage and a long, wide *hanamichi* (ramp). The audience faces the acting areas from two sides, but during the whole of the nearly five hours we are present, not more than half of the two hundred or so seats are occupied; and about two-thirds of the occupying half are always asleep, but in rotation, like the election system of the United States Congress. The audience eats continuously, and the knitting of chopsticks is a steady accompaniment to the plays. A few stalwarts, all elderly men, follow the texts in score books—from back to front, like rabbis reading the Bible.

The first play, whose actors are three white-faced ghosts, is a riddle (to me). A chorus of eight men in gray-blue aprons and black cassocks chants somberly for a *mauvais quart d'heure,* I have no idea what about. In the next piece, a kind of *entr'acte* called *Futari-Daimyo,* a peasant boy outwits two pompous Samurai, defeating them in duels and stripping them of their finery. It is a *Don Quixote*-type satire for the amusement of a decadent age, but the two ballets of dueling fans are comparatively so exciting that as many as half the audience wake up to watch.

In the third piece, the back row of the chorus chants while the front row dances, one performer at a time. The dancers brandish their fans from time to time as if for momentous action, but nothing happens and the play is inhumanly slow and boring. A foot is poised in the air for so long that the spectator forgets it and is startled out of his seat when the actor suddenly stomps it down with a great racket. The actors wear *tabi,* the two-compartmented white footgloves, and walk by sliding their feet and raising their toes first. The solo dancers chant, too, alone at first, then in dialogue with the chorus. Toward the end of the play, the chant rises a diminished fifth, a comparatively earthquaking effect that reminds I.S. of the Russian Church.

The next piece, *Hanagatami,* is an oriental *opera seria,* slower moving than *Parsifal.* Five instrumentalist musicians and eight choristers enter the stage like burglars, through a half-height butler's pantry window in the right rear corner. The choristers hold their fans in front of their heads during this infiltration, but conceal them in the sleeves of their surplices during the drama. The latter is concerned with a maiden who wishes to present a basket of flowers to a Prince, but who presents it improperly and is rebuked; the first two hours, at any rate, are a lesson in floral presentations to princes, though at the end of the play, when the maiden again offers her bouquet and this time it is accepted, I see no difference in her method. The Prince, a child of eight or nine, wears an orange costume with white pants, and a black *Kammurai* hat with a tail. He does not speak, and his only action is his exit; but he wiggles and looks worried, as if he had neglected to relieve his bladder.

1959

Near the beginning, an old man enters carrying a flower basket, followed by a girl dressed like Pocahontas, and carrying the same. The "girl" is a man, of course, but the mask is small, and a man's gullet wobbles beneath its chin. The "girl's" voice, furthermore, is deeper than any of the men's, besides which the mask distorts "her" words acoustically—though we hardly have cause to complain about that. During about thirty minutes the old man and the flower girl stand motionless while the chorus mumbles a low dim chant. Then Pocahontas exits, and for a hopeful moment the end seems near. But, instead, the music, a duet of wolf cries accompanied by clicks and taps from the drums, grows more dramatic until she reappears with a twin sister, for whose benefit the whole lesson is repeated.

The musical element is always paramount, from the ritual untying of the chords around the percussion instruments at the beginning to the last note of the offstage flute. A fanfare for flute and drum heralds the Prince, and this is the only time when the drummer is not almost continually licking his thumb and moistening his drum head. The vocal noises—gravel-filled gargles, slow slurs in falsetto—are as astringent as the instrumental. (Abé, the author of a classic book about Noh, had studied with Schoenberg in Berlin shortly before *Pierrot lunaire,* which at least allows for the possibility that Schoenberg had heard something concerning Japanese *Sprechgesang* from him.)

Hanagatami is followed by an offstage concert of flute and drum; and by another chant play in which each member of the chorus executes a solo dance, in effect a walk punctuated by loud stomping, except that some of the dances conclude with comparatively spectacular leaps.

The final play is named for the god of fencing, whose abode is Mount Matengu. The god himself, Kuramatengu, makes an appearance toward the end, and his entrance—with the *hanamichi* curtain raised straight out and up, like a canopy, and not, as ordinarily, rolled or drawn—is its most impressive moment. Five- and seven-syllable verse patterns are easily distinguished, owing to the higher pitch of what I take to be the first syllables; but the drum also measures the beat of the verse, and provides the play, as I.S. says, with its "pulse." The story deals with young Prince Yoshitsune's education in swordsmanship; at any rate, the first part of the drama exposes his lack of skill in that art, for which reason the old god is summoned. Kuramatengu wears a gorgeous purple, white, and gold coat, and to distinguish him as a god his mask is several times larger than the masks of humans. He moves by leapfrogging, too, to indicate the eccentricity of a god as imagined by earthly characters.

APRIL 20

Osaka. The Bunraku theater greatly surprises us at first: the puppets are so much larger than we expect, and the stage is a hundred times the size of a European marionette booth. Four puppeteers, one bare-faced and three black-hooded, like executioners or Elizabethan stage-keepers, manipulate a single doll. By some optical deception, moreover, the three black figures, whose three pairs of legs are distractingly spider-like, appear to be following, the puppets. The manipulating crews are so apparent, in fact, that a sustained effort is required to focus our attention away from them, and though we are able to disregard the controlling machinery to a somewhat greater extent as the play unfolds, we can never entirely give ourselves to the reality of the dolls. The puppeteers move in waist-deep trenches except during duels, battles, and other crowd scenes, for which they emerge full height on the open steps. With characteristic Japanese fidelity to scale, the child puppets are manipulated by children.

The musical element, the *joruri,* interests us more than the play, and the performance of the narrators, who read, sing, and ventriloquize for as long as an hour at a time, is a *tour de force.* The vocal gesticulation is far wider in range than that of Kabuki or Noh, but naturally would be, given the demand for realism. The narrative style of today's play, a talky tearjerker full of murders and kidnapings, provides a corresponding swagger and exaggerated pathos. The narrators are accompanied by a single samisen.

The audience is made up largely of old women, but it is a noisier and hungrier audience than at Kabuki or Noh, and the theater smells nauseatingly of *sushi* and hard-boiled eggs. Each act is announced by the offstage clapping of two wooden blocks—*tsuke-uchi*—and by accelerating beats of an offstage drum, while drum rolls separate the scenes, exactly as in *Petrushka.* Before the curtain parts, the musicians are swung in at stage left on a revolving shelf. They kneel rigidly behind a row of lecterns, the narrators on the audience side, the samisen players toward the stage. Before beginning to read, they hold their books to their heads, in both hands, while at the end of the play they drop their heads to the lectern, woodenly, like the puppets, and remain in this position until the musicians' platform is revolved out of sight. But, then, the audience never watches the readers, as we do most of the time.

The plot of today's play seems to glorify a peasant woman who has sacrificed her son so that the son of a nobleman may live. We follow it vaguely through three brief, action-filled scenes, but the fourth scene goes on for nearly three hours and is all narration.

1959

APRIL 21

We attend a lunch in Kobe at the home of the Muriyamas, who are the principal patrons of the Osaka Festival as well as the owners of a celebrated collection of silk-screen portraits of *haiku* poets. The meal, eaten in the garden, is barbecued American style, but served orientally, men first. Madame Muriyama listens acutely to I.S.'s every word, and at one point questions him about his use of "conservative." I.S.: "I dislike the idea of conserving, of keeping in cans. The conservative bores us, I might add, when he tries to stop new things from growing, while the radical bores us when he begins to shout, 'Look here, see how radical I am!'"

APRIL 22

Nara. The rice fields are guarded by scarecrows equipped with noisemakers that clap loudly in the wind, but the ruse is unsuccessful and flocks are feasting everywhere. Horyu-ji, the oldest temple in Japan, is being rejuvenated board by board, and by expert architectural geriatricians. But its great pagoda is also a sparrows' nest, for which reason it whistles like a colossal wooden flute. Among the most striking objects in the museum are a kind of Neptune holding a trident and riding a frog's back (Amanojako), a black horse with white glass eyes, and a portable shrine with a traveling salesman's sample case of Buddha dolls.

The forest of the Kasuga Shrine is full of overfed but still greedy deer, and the Great Buddha is not only the largest, but also one of the ugliest statues in the world. Women wait in line to touch another, smaller Buddha, for insurance against baldness.

APRIL 24

Tokyo. We go to an afternoon of Gagaku at the Imperial Palace. According to the program, the first piece, *Etenraku,* "has been source of inspiration for creation of Japanese folk songs as well as having been set for Western symphony orchestra." The choreography, for male dancers, is without event or interest, and our attention is confined strictly to the music. The dance stage looks like a boxing ring set in a gravel court, and the musicians are seated outside and behind it, between two twenty-five-foot-tall drums called the *taiko,* which are struck by men on ladders. The other instruments are mouth organs; kotos; flutes; small cymbals; deep, thudding theorbos; and the *hichiniki,* which resembles a shawm. Of these, the *hichiniki* and the mouth organs are the most curious. The latter, held like periscopes and with the pipes pointing up, sustain harmonic clusters and in most of the pieces are the first and last instruments to sound. The *hichiniki* produces a sloping, siren-like wail in which all intermediate step-wise pitch is dissolved. (I.S.: "We cannot describe sound, but neither can we forget it.") The instrument is a handspread long, and it has a large double-reed mouthpiece through which the player appears to breathe in as he blows out, as though performing a Yoga exercise. One of the dances tells the story of Ch'ang Kung of the Ch'i Dynasty, a Prince so fair of face that he was obliged to wear a grotesque mask in battle. The music is alternately monophonic and polyphonic, but no matter, it being so much more attractive as sonority than as composition. Ch'ang's mask is the head of a mythical beast.

We pay a visit to the retired diplomat Suma-san, to see his collection of Chinese art, one of the richest still privately owned. Suma-san himself greets us at his garden gate wearing a kimono and wooden shoes; which surprises us because heretofore we have seen him only in American-style business suits. Among his treasures are Wei Buddhas, Middle Chou bronzes, Han terra cottas, and innumerable steles, porcelains, jades, screen paintings, scrolls, each of which he introduces with the same phrase: "A very singular piece, don't you think?" But though this is invariably true, the most singular piece of all is Suma-san himself. He is bald, powerfully built and barrel-chested, like an ex-wrestler, or one of his Buddhas. But however imposing he is physically, it is his vaingloriousness that one remembers. It is on such a grand scale as to be almost forgivable, and in fact he can hardly finish a remark without complimenting himself: "My water colors are very attractive, very well done, don't you think?" And though his English is fluent, he regrets that the conversation is not in any of a dozen or so of his other languages. (In truth, he *has* served widely in the diplomatic corps, last and least fortunately, except for his collection, as Ambassador to China during the Japanese occupation.) The new Crown Princess is his niece, a bit of information we hardly have to pry out of him, and the royal wedding has no doubt puffed him up even more. But his account of it is interrupted by Madame Suma's summons to tea. Later, as we prepare to leave, the great connoisseur endears himself to us by collecting some twenty to thirty children and grandchildren to line up with I.S. for a photograph.

Dinner tonight, in a geisha restaurant by the Tokyo River, consists of fried bees, tentacle soup, and cold, candied, and undecapitated fish. The geishas are uncommunicative. After undressing us, and helping us into kimonos, they kneel at our elbows like guards.

In the interval of a short private concert for I.S. at University House, this afternoon, a flutist demonstrates a throat trill, and a slow *portamento,* like that of the *hichiniki,* and a kotoist, wearing clawlike picks on his right thumb and first two fingers, demonstrates the uses of his instrument in a variety of music from sixteenth-century polyphony to twentieth-century Hawaiian guitar. When our host observes that the new koto music is "at least sincere," I.S. tells him that "sincerity is no excuse." And when a young composer asks I.S. whether he would change the order of a series if he came to a place where he "heard" it in a different order, I.S. says, "Certainly not; I would find a way to 'hear' the notes in the proper order." In reply to a question about "melody," he says that the word is restricted by usage to a small, fairly recent range of music. "What is the melody in a piece of sixteenth-century koto music, or in a *virelai* by Machaut? 'Contour' may have some meaning, but not our 'melody.'"

1959

APRIL 30

I go to Yokohama tonight with Kaoru K., who suddenly complains that a large particle has blown in her eye. I escort her in a taxi to a hospital, ring the emergency night bell for some twenty minutes before a nurse appears, and, inside, wait another twenty minutes for a doctor. Cockroaches swarm over the floor—which would bother me less had we not been obliged to leave our shoes at the entrance—but the doctor, when he comes, does not seem to notice them. (He certainly *sees* them.) Without washing his hands, he lifts Kaoru's eyelid between bare thumb and finger. But no mote is found and no remedy prescribed. I pay 100 yen, and we depart, Kaoru not relieved.

MAY 8

A final, matinée visit to the Kabukiza, to see a play about an Emperor who is remembered for having treated his human subjects less kindly than his animals. It is remarkable chiefly for the acting of three "dogs" and for a ballet of demons.

We fly at night to Anchorage.

SEPTEMBER 6

London. Dinner with the Eliots at Claridge's. T.S.E. looks younger and *is* livelier than last year, but he seems to think of himself as a hoary ancient with little time left. Social obligations are the bane of his existence, he says. "I cannot accept lectures because the people who pay for them expect me to attend cocktail parties at which I am caught between someone wanting to know what I think of Existentialism and someone asking what I really meant by such-and-such a line." A critic is mentioned, whom Eliot promptly describes as a brainpicker. "I know, because he tried to get me drunk and pick mine. He is insanely jealous of all creative writers, and his own only good line either must have happened to him or been told to him by someone else. In one of his stories, a man is stroking a woman's back and exclaiming how soft it is, to which she rejoins, 'What the hell did you expect, scales?'"

Concerning Pound's new *Cantos,* Eliot notes that "There are more Chinese characters than ever. Ezra is becoming the best Chinese poet in English." Then when I.S. talks about his impressions of the Japanese theater, Eliot says he once watched a Noh dancer in a play by Yeats and was very moved by the performance. "One really could believe that the dancer had become a bird." He asks I.S. about Japanese tastes in Western theater: "Ionesco, I suppose, and Tennessee Williams?" Büchner's name comes up in this context, too, whereupon Eliot remarks that "*Wozzeck* is too simple for a play but just simple enough for an opera."

He gazes at each of us in rotation, positively beaming affection in the direction of his wife each time around. And he drinks a gin and tonic before, claret during, and whiskey after the dinner, which in his case is confined to the main course, a partridge; for while it is evident that he enjoys sniffing the platter of cheese, after some deliberation, and a final moment of indecision, he does not actually choose one. When somehow Aldous is mentioned, he says, "I don't read him, of course; I am much too fond of him for that. He was pretty pessimistic when we saw him last. Too many people in the world already, and more all the time. So there are indeed, indeed." And because one looks for hidden twists and ironies in everything Eliot says, the echoed word seems to ring with extra meaning.

To judge from his parting remarks about the weather—"Isn't it unusual? Why last year at this time . . . "—I think he would have welcomed a chat on the subject. Telling us about his plans to visit his birthplace near St. Louis, he says that the house doesn't exist any more. "If a plaque is erected, it will have to go to one of the neighbors'."

1948
1949
1950
1951
1952
1953
1954
1955
1956
1957
1958
1959
1960
1961
1962
1963
1964
1965
1966
1967
1968
1969
1970
1971

ITINERARY

January 3: I.S. conducts *The Rite of Spring* in Carnegie Hall, and records it (4th) in the ballroom of the St. George Hotel, Brooklyn. **10:** Première of the *Movements,* in Town Hall. **21:** We leave for Los Angeles, by train. **February 12, 17:** I.S. records *Petrushka.* **March 10:** We attend a lecture by Isherwood on Kipling, in East Los Angeles. **April 24:** R.C. to Toronto for a concert. Dr. Max Edel begins work sculpting I.S.'s head. **June 7:** I.S. conducts at the Los Angeles Music Festival, Royce Hall. **20:** V.'s vernissage at the Comara Gallery. **23:** A party for the completion of the I.S.'s new living room. **30:** R.C. records Mozart's Serenade for thirteen wind instruments. **July 5:** We leave for Lamy (Santa Fe) on the "Super Chief." **31:** Return to Los Angeles. **August 4, 7:** Concerts in Mexico City. **12, 13:** Concerts in Bogotá. **29:** Concert in Buenos Aires. **September 3:** Concert with the Mozarteum of Buenos Aires. **17–18:** We fly from New York to Rome and drive to Perugia. **19:** Borgo San Sepolcro, Gubbio, Venice. **27:** I.S. conducts the première of his *Monumentum* in the Palazzo Ducale. **October 15:** Venice is flooded, two feet of water in the hotel lobby; I.S. decides to call his new composition *The Flood.* **November 5:** We drive to Genoa. **13:** Concert in Genoa. **14:** Train to Rome. **24:** Concert in Rome. **25:** Train to Paris. **30:** Sail from Le Havre on the *Rotterdam* for Weehawken; *The Flood* scenario is completed during the crossing. **December 7:** Arrive in New York (St. Regis Hotel). **13:** Death of the Reverend James McLane. **16:** R.C. records the *Lulu* Suite, *Der Wein,* and the *Sieben frühe Lieder.* **21:** We go to Washington where I.S. conducts *Le Rossignol* and R.C. *Erwartung,* both works also recorded. **31:** Train to New York.

AUGUST 1

In flight to Mexico, I.S. talks about Maximilian and Juárez as an ideal subject for Verdi in his *Don Carlo* period. "Imagine the scene with Maximilian tipping the soldiers before they shoot him, and the scene of Carlotta going mad in the Vatican." But these pictures are interrupted by a stream

93

of announcements from the steward, one of which is that "Men and women may use the lavatory indistinctly."

I.S. is applauded at the airport by a committee of composers, a detachment of soldiers and several busloads of schoolchildren. We go to the hotel in a "crocodile" taxicab, so called because of a black sawtooth necklace painted around its perimeter, but the taxi's tactics are even more jagged and perilous than the emblem suggests. We contest the road against buses with long Aztec names knotted with "tl's," "tz's," and "xt's"—Ixtapalapa, Tlalnepantla, Azcapotzalco—as destinations.

AUGUST 2

At our rehearsal this morning, the Bellas Artes is half filled with students. One of them approaches I.S., saying, "We are too many to meet you, and I have been chosen to shake your hand for all." But I.S. thanks them all, from the stage, for the, as he calls it, delegated handshake. In the interval, following my read-through of excerpts from *Lulu,* he remarks that "Berg is a thematic composer, and how he loves to caress his themes, to turn them this way and that. But the vibraphone goes on urinating in the ear a little too long." I.S.'s friends the Bal y Gays are present at the rehearsal. They are refugees from Franco Spain who keep a small gallery on the Paseo de la Reforma, and who in forty years of marriage have grown as alike as twins. When introduced to them, I try to make conversation in a gabble of Italian and Spanish, and they let me go on and on before saying, in excellent English, that they do not understand a word. We laugh over this, of course, and are instant friends. Edward James, another friend of I.S., also turns up at the rehearsal. He has a mad laugh, like a hornbill in the jungle.

At Guadalupe, the two main buildings tilt so radically away from each other that from the front portal of either the toppling of the other seems imminent. When we arrive, a score or so of Indians are lurching across the wide plaza toward the church on their knees. They inch forward, in evident pain, sometimes with long waits between moves, like birds changing position on a beach. One of them, a young woman, leans on the shoulder of her son, a child, also on his knees and in turn carrying a baby in his arms. I.S. is impressed by the visit—and deeply offended later, by a mock prayer of E.J.'s: "Dear God, forgive us our outlets." He has knelt before the Image of the Virgin, touched his forehead to its glass case, and burned a candle at Her shrine.

But Guadalupe does not increase his charity at this afternoon's press conference. He dismisses a New York music critic as "a crab: he even walks sideways"; and he describes *"Les Six"* as "Six Characters in Search of an Author," while referring to an opera by one of them as *"Les Mamelles de ma tante."* His only kind words, in fact, are reserved for his late friend the Mexican poet Alfonso Reyes. "Reyes was a small man with a large wife. He resembled Burl Ives facially, but his wife looked more like the rest of Ives. In spite of their sizes, Reyes tried to follow the custom of the abduction rite and carry his bride over the doorstep. I did not see him do this, of course, but will picture him doing it as long as I think of him at all."

A "Museum of the Revolution" is under construction in Chapultepec Park, but the engineering is not very revolutionary: the workmen pass their buckets of cement hand to hand, like an eighteenth-century fire brigade. We go from Chapultepec to the astronomical pyramid at Tenayuca, except that the driver hasn't the vaguest idea how to find it; we stop every few minutes for fresh supplies of information, but always turn in a radically different direction afterwards. In Tenayuca town, women are the only creatures, including mules, actually at work, grandmothers hauling heavy bags past staglines of idling young, and great-grandmothers collecting laundry from the limbs of cactus plants. The Tenayuca pyramid is small, disproportionately so for the stone serpents, weighing several tons each, coiled in its yard. I.S. compares it to a *paskha,* the Russian Easter cake, but it is flatter than that and its lines are melted—or blurred, as if it had been under water for a long time. We scale the walls and burrow through the catacombs at the base.

But pre-Columbian cultures do not attract me. They were slave-state societies, priest-ridden and god-ridden, and the favorite gods were snakes. And they were cruel; even the greatest heroes were not immune from the possibility that their hearts might be torn out. As suicides were allowed to go directly to Heaven, it is a mystery that the civilization did not disappear by its own hand.

At our concert tonight, in the Bellas Artes, V. sits in the silk-and-feather audience, flanked by the President's wife, and Don Celestino Gorostiza, the director of the theater. The orchestra plays the *"Viva México"* for I.S. at the end, and the *"Diana,"* the salute accorded, but very rarely, to the bravest matador.

8 AM. The airport. A wrangle with an immigration official who insists that I.S.'s first name is really George. The man next to me on the plane crosses himself frantically as we speed down the runway, then sits calmly back and reads *El Universal.* Beyond Antigua we fly over volcanoes, some red-lipped and still steaming, others filled with pools or sealed with vegetation. We land at San José, where the terminal is full of progressive frescoes and reactionary guards, and we land again, two hours later, with a view of both oceans, at Panama. A gathering of Panamanian musicians is waiting as, bathed in a cloud of steam heat, we leave the plane. Their spokesman proudly introduces himself as an "electronic composer," then presents a beautifully embroidered native fabric to I.S. Cameramen appear, too, and

1960

as we make our way to the plane for Bogotá, joined by a Panamanian woman in a feather shako, this touching, humid scene is filmed.

The new plane, a jet, roars and flexes before rising like a rocket over the bay and canal and into the sudden, equatorial night. Bright orange fires—milpas, I think—are burning on the lower Andean slopes. At Bogotá, where we need heavy coats, the path to the terminal is thick with dead *cucarones*—beetles.

AUGUST 9

We awake, at the Tequendama, breathless and lightheaded, and I.S., complaining of vertigo and fluttering heart, sends for an oxygen mask, which he clasps to his nose for periodic ten-minute inhalations.

The eaves of hillside houses project over and, in some cases, almost completely cover the narrow streets. The Indian women here, all with heavy burdens on their backs, wear bowler hats and do their hair in long braids, whereas in the market place many of them carry head trays the size of card tables, loaded with pineapple. Mules, I note, do not, in most neighborhoods, distinguish between street and sidewalk.

1960

The furnishings of the Teatro Colón were brought from Europe a century ago by boat and mule train, a journey of many months. More than half of the present orchestra is European, too, and I.S., switching from Italian to French to German to Russian, is always understood by at least one faction. The theater is cold, and most of the musicians wear ponchos throughout the rehearsal. We still do not know whether our second concert is to take place the day after tomorrow or not until Saturday, but this is simply *mañana*-ism, I.S. says, and we must adjust to it.

Our driver, on a late-afternoon tour, vigorously shakes hands with us as we enter his cab and thanks us again and again for hiring him. The city is a mixture of ugly-new-international and pretty-old-local (green balconies and white walls, virtually all with *"Cuba sí, gringos no"*). For some reason the driver thinks we should visit a cemetery above the city, a desolate place with cows pasturing in the streets and buzzards banking overhead like airplanes unable to land. We then learn that his daughter, who was "killed in a hospital," is buried here. An Indian family, kneeling with lighted candles by the cemetery gate, reminds us of a Holy Family by Georges de la Tour. Leaving the taxi, back at the Tequendama, we receive not only more handshakes and innumerable *"muchas gracias,"* but untold gratitude as well.

Linguistic ambiguities add to the confusion in the Tequendama restaurant. Thus I.S. asks for a side order of ham, but receives jam, the waiter mistaking English for Spanish. A party of *"norteamericanos"* arrives next to us, the men pushing the chairs of their women to the table like lawn mowers. Compared to the Colombians, the *"norteamericanos"* talk and laugh too loudly and too much. The dinner music begins with "A Song of India," which, says I.S., makes him feel very old. "I remember the day Rimsky composed it. How surprised he would be to know that the opera is remembered by it alone!" Our dinner guest, a Bogotano, is interested in Albert Schweitzer, whom I.S. describes as he knew him in the mid-thirties. "He came to a concert of mine in Strasbourg and we dined together afterward. His clothes—the frock coat and the wing collar—were those of a provincial pastor, but he himself reminded me of Maxim Gorky. One could see that he possessed great charisma, and anyone who had talked with him would readily believe stories of the sort I heard at Aspen after his visit there, of animals coming out of the woods to him. But already then, that night in Strasbourg, the poor man was surrounded by idiotic adulators."

The collection of pre-Columbian gold cached in the basement of the Banco de la República is the richest in the world, and its gleam is so great that the room requires almost no supplementary lighting. Some of the gold is alloyed with copper and platinum, but most is pure and bright yellow. All of the Andean cultures are represented, too, though my impression is of a preponderance of Chibcha objects. These include disc-shaped diadems, doughnut-shaped earrings, heart-shaped pectorals, crescent-shaped crowns; and gold breastplates, armlets, penile ornaments, greaves, as well as goldfoil bangles, ear spools, lip pendants, and nose ornaments like epaulettes of Napoleon III. But perhaps the largest part of the trove consists of death raiments—including laminated funeral masks and burial charms and talismans—and funerary urns, the most common of which are shaped like whiskey flasks. But another large part is from the boudoir—gold tweezers for eyebrow depilation, gold hairpins and safety pins—masculine utensils all, as are all body ornaments. I remember gold canes and cane finials, too, and gold scepters, gold aspergillums, gold flutes, a gold *boca marina,* gold fishhooks, gold animal figures—alligators, sad-eyed frogs, abstract snakes

—and gold-wire Klee-like cacique figures

strung together in necklaces like paper cutouts.

The bookstores of Bogotá are well stocked, and the city's literary reputation is borne out in the people we meet, but according to our new friend Edgardo Salazar de Santa Columa, "Bogotanos read only because they have no place to go and nothing else to do." The principal newspaper, *El Espectador,* publishes book reviews of the caliber of those in *Les Arts* and *The Sunday Times* and *The Observer,* he says. One of the customers in the first bookstore we visit is a hunchback, and as soon as the I.S.'s see him they want to touch his hump for good luck. I ridicule this Russian superstition, of course, as

I have before, comparing the I.S.'s to scrofula victims seeking the royal touch, and, when that has no effect, protesting the indignity to the afflicted and stigmatized man. But they are perfectly serious, and deeply disappointed when he departs before they have time to push near him.

Today's reception for I.S. at the United States Embassy is attended by many mustached *señores* and large, bosomy *señoras*—"plump, florid viragos," V. says, remembering Hazlitt. The talk is largely about a language congress now in session in Bogotá, whose aims are the elimination of certain silent letters from written Spanish and the expunging of anti-Semitic definitions from the dictionary of the Spanish Academy.

From a visit to an emerald dealer, I learn that the valuable stones are the deep-green, perfectly homogeneous ones rather than the pale ones with gardens inside. We also visit a souvenir shop selling skins of boa constrictors, ocelots, alligators, as well as stuffed adult alligators and live, puffing, glaucous-eyed baby alligators. The proprietor says that some jungle Indians employ poisonous but tameable snakes to *protect* their youngest children, these babysitter reptiles not only being trained to guard the hearth from animals and other snakes, but also refraining, as a rule, from stinging their keepers.

From V.'s memo book on Bogotano habits: "Bogotanos drink large quantities of post-prandial coffee, then retire for long siestas; a Bogotano says *gracias* and *con mucho gusto* an average of a thousand times a day; Bogotanos are long-winded, in spite of the altitude, and the largest expenditure of air is about politics; Bogotanos commit a fair number of the nearly two hundred murders that occur in Colombia every month."

1960

AUGUST 12

I.S., or a part of him, is monumentalized. Early this morning three sculptresses come to make a cast of his left hand, which they place on a wet towel and cover with a gray pudding. This takes twenty minutes to dry, after which one of the women cracks the plaster with a hammer and piles the artifacts into a pail.

At the concert tonight, I.S. reads Simenon when not conducting. But after my performance of the Bach-Schoenberg chorale preludes he remarks that "It is *Farben* and *Dynamik* music and so rich in both that one must hear it a dozen times to hear it all. Only I regret the final harp arpeggio in *Schmücke Dich* and the last cymbal crash in *Komm Gott.*" At intermission he discovers a spider on the lavatory wall, reaches for one of his scores, says, "I will kill it with the *Firebird.*" I.S. is terrified of typhus and dysentery, but just before bed he says, "I am getting very bored brushing my teeth in ginger ale."

AUGUST 14

To the Salt Mine Cathedral at Zipaquirá, a pre-Columbian excavation now expanded and impregnated—like a ship in a bottle—with a church. During the first part of the drive, rain pulses against the car like surf, but at Chía, where a beautiful colonial-period bridge still spans the muddy Río Bogotá, all is clear. Thereafter the architecture in the villages—and the window-sill geraniums—is predominantly Swiss. It is farmers' fair day and the people along the road are unsteady on their feet due, no doubt, to too much *aguardiente.*

The tunnel into the mine envelops the car very closely, and after some confusing turns and a few hundred yards of Lascaux-like obscurity, we suffer as much from claustrophobia as from the nearly suffocating salinity. The sodium-chloride Chartres itself—or rather, a subterranean parking lot from which we trek to the eery lead-and-blue church—is about a quarter of a mile inside its mountain. Today being Sunday, the church is crowded with Indians kneeling before priests in green, Shinto-like robes. I.S.: "They might be an heretical sect—Adamites, Albigensians—but are an underground movement, in any case." The church was built for the convenience of the miners, and is regarded by them, and by Colombians generally, as the eighth wonder of the world. At the inaugural service, a few years ago, half the congregation fainted in the thin, salt-flavored air. Fearing to do the same, we hasten our departure, but the car lacks air too, stalls, and has to be pushed.

After returning to Bogotá, we continue in the opposite direction, to Tequendama Falls and the *"tierra caliente,"* a corkscrew descent of three thousand feet, at every downward coil of which the tangle of vines, flowers, and fronds is thicker and more richly tropical in color. We peel overcoats, then jackets, and eventually even shirts. Only twenty miles from Bogotá the air is forty degrees warmer.

"Twice as high as Niagara," shouts a souvenir-hawking Indian at the precipice of the falls, but the view is obscured less than halfway down by mist. In the absence of a retaining wall, a statue of the Madonna is the only deterrent to suicides, the latest of which took place only a few days ago, an Indian woman throwing herself into the cataract and pulling her screaming son with her in full view of a horrified crowd.

From the falls to Santandercito, at the edge of the jungle, the road is a narrow, fenceless shelf overlooking a two-thousand-foot drop. It is also unpaved, riddled with cavities, and in places all but sealed off by fallen rocks, so that the threat of a landslide is almost as unnerving as the threat of the abyss. We cower close to the mountain, nevertheless, and on the theory that forward movement, to no matter where, is less of a risk than a "U" turn, crawl ahead. Shrines and crosses commemorate slips over the side, but to little avail, apparently, as warnings against new ones. At one point, while I am in the throes of a swooning, Icarus-like moment, a bus named Jesús María Pizarro roars by us, wheels bulging over the brink, horn blaring contempt. (Colombian drivers pass or stop anywhere without signaling, nor can they be trusted to obey traffic lights, for which reason the Bogotá police stand on lofty daises—and under awnings of tinted glass—*au-dessus de la mêlée.*) Finally reaching the jungle level, we stop in the Hostería de los Andes, and, before starting back, eat a *fritanga* and drink a nerve-steadying herb tea.

AUGUST 15

The air route to Quito follows the Magdalena River to the Cauca River (the *tierra adentro* of the archeologists); but it also follows the ups and downs of air pockets, in which we are buffeted violently much of the way. Ecuador is a cracked, reddish crust dotted with rhomboid villages. Quito has a new terminal, newly splashed with murals, newly stocked with Indian wares, but in the street, other, nonfranchised Indians sell the same things—silver buckles, blankets, Panama hats, shrunken heads—at a tenth of the price. Taking off again, we skim adobe and red-tile houses and mountain shelves on which clouds droop like Dali watches or partly deflated balloons. At Guayaquil, a riverain city and the junction of sea, jungle, and desert, small boats cross the bay, leaving white tails of water that look like spirochetes from our height. We fly low over the excavation sites of Trujillo and Chan-Chan, where curious mounds imprint the sand like tents, higher than the waves of the sea.

At Lima, where we drop through several layers of bad weather, I.S. is received like a film star. But the night is cold and damp and so is the Country Club, a gloomy Manueline hotel whose rooms are a lonely half-mile from the lobby. We flee to the no less palatial but centrally located Gran Hotel Bolívar, which supplies within-walking-distance accommodations as well as portable heaters. For dinner, each of us tries a different fish, corvina, liza, and pejerrey, but all are delectable.

AUGUST 16

I suffer from dizziness and the "bends" this morning, partly from the loss of altitude, partly from the quantities of powerful black coffee taken to be alert for an 8 AM rehearsal. But the orchestra cannot hold a *tempo,* its tuning is vaguely Pythagorean, and the players read slowly and forget immediately. The work is wearying, too, as each direction has to be repeated three times and the Indians do not, on principle, admit to mistakes. Either the player wasn't ready, or his instrument was at fault, or he hadn't understood where we were beginning, or one of the *gringos* in the orchestra had said something to confuse him. No doubt I.S. shocks them deeply by saying, at one point, "Sorry, gentlemen, that was *my* mistake." But according to the orchestra's regular conductor, the Indians are dependable in the concerts, whereas the *gringos* are often nervous and erratic.

We spend the greater part of our time in the Museum of Anthropology and Archeology this afternoon looking at textiles, the laces from the necropolis of Paracas above all. "The life of an ancient Andean was a purgatory of weaving," I.S. says. But we also admire the Chimú ceramics of owls, turtles, monkeys, cats carrying litters, a *vicuña* giving birth. One room

1960

contains ceramic models of legless, armless, and otherwise mutilated people, as well as skeletons evidencing surgery (among them, several skulls with copper or bronze trepanning), and some two hundred pre-Columbian surgical instruments. Other exhibits include cases of *repoussé* gold masks; objects carved in nacre set with precious stones; a yard full of steles from Tiahuanaco, some of them almost as large as the sarsens of Stonehenge; a *sub rosa* collection of phallic objects (including jugs whose spouts whistle when poured through) and depictions of sexual acts, from which it would appear that sodomy was the pre-Columbian norm; and finally, as well as most unpleasantly, large numbers of mummies. Many of these are in flexed position, knees to chin, with hands and feet bound by hemp-of-byssus, and with bamboo tubes—through which the corpses were fed chicle from above ground—still in their mouths. An eternity symbol, cornucopia, or crowing rooster adorns each coffin.

We drive from the museum to a corral of llamas and alpacas. They are snooty beasts, and given to spiteful spitting.

AUGUST 18

Marmosets are for sale on the street in Lima, from cages resembling hand-organs, but, then, almost everything is available out of doors here. And in this and other respects Lima reminds us of Naples. The cafés, the street noise, the boys who clean the windshields of cars stopped at traffic signals, our favorite restaurant: all these are Neapolitan. The resemblance game breaks down, however, with the architecture, the statuary, and the thick gray sky. Driving in Lima is like driving in the Lincoln Tunnel: the visibility is about the same—the lights are phosphorescent in both cases— and the air is equally foul.

The ruins of Pachacamac are an hour's drive from Lima between the sea and pink-brown dunes of sand. But the better road, in fact as solidly paved as the Appian Way, is in the disinterred city itself, which is on a hill facing the sea and Pachacamac Island, white with guano, like a frosted cake. We walk in a stillness pierced by the cries of guano birds echoed in a moaning seaward wind. The dead city is severely geometrical, and so is the architecture of its afternoon shadows. Behind us are the Andes, vague, blue, illusory, perhaps not there at all except known to be from maps.

We return to a cocktail party by the Lima Music Club, in a home which is a museum of Cuzco primitives and colonial-period soapstone carvings. The cocktail-party language, here and elsewhere in Lima, is French, and much of the talk is about mutual acquaintances in Paris. Another subject is servants. "Peru is the only country left where servants are still inexpensive," someone informs me, as if this were my most pressing problem. But Lima is feudally class stratified. And race stratified: the only Indians at this party, or anywhere in "society," are servants.

Pizarro's cadaver, in Lima Cathedral, is a yellowish, viscous sack lying in a glass case to the right of the door. Kika, the Peruvian girl who accompanies us there, will not look at it. "That is the man who destroyed our culture," she says. After four hundred years! I go with V. to the Cemetery of the Presbyterian Master, where the dead are stacked in long rows of granite filing cabinets, and where we search unsuccessfully for the grave of her uncle, the Marquis Théodore de Bosset.

AUGUST 19

Shortly before our concert tonight we receive a visit from Manuel Prado, the President of Peru. Señora Prado tells I.S. that she saw him "conduct something or other" in Venice in 1951, when she "went over for Carlos de Beistegui's Ball." ("*Elle a du chien,*" V. says later, but I remind her that this classic expression can be translated "She's a bitch.") Unfairly, no doubt, but by the end of the interview I have formed a prejudice in favor of any form of revolution in Peru. Yet satisfaction comes sooner than I expect. The President, entering his loge, is greeted by hisses and boos from the dress circle and by still ruder noises from the upper balconies, all in the greatest possible contrast to the stomping, cheering, and bravoing a minute later for I.S.

AUGUST 20

Ascending over roofless hovels (it never rains!) and the white-rimmed, beryl-green sea, we fly to Antofagasta and Santiago. Although the Antofagasta airfield is in a featureless desert, the Chilean police warn us not to take photographs. We walk here for nearly an hour, in a warm sun and cold, dry wind. The desert from Antofagasta to Santiago is a spilled chemistry of cobalt, laterite, copper, sodium, and sulphur, and the Andes are an almond-white wall rising out of a sea of dirty cottonwool clouds. Dry riverbeds wind down from the mountains and spread into dry alluvial fans, but it is raining in Santiago, and we turn above the airport for nearly an hour before landing. At the Carrera Hotel, after a dinner of filet of *congrio,* we go early to bed.

AUGUST 21

A brass band playing the national anthem in the Plaza in front of our rooms jolts us out of bed at 7 AM. Going to our windows, we see a platoon of Germanic-uniformed and goose-stepping soldiers at a flag-raising ceremony. But above them and behind is the cordillera, white, gleaming in the sun, and higher than anything in the world.

To Las Vertientes in the afternoon, with a group of Chilean musicians. Mimosa and wild peach blossom whiten the hills, and the trees, which include pines, poplars, and willows, are, after Peru, refreshingly green and varied. The party at Las Vertientes is a feast of pies, cakes—a delicious *loukouma*—and remarks by I.S., one of which is that "Palestrina was a great bureaucrat of counterpoint." He describes Santiago, from his drive through, as a "used-car lot of statues and monuments. The smaller the national history, the larger the commemorating stones."

A light rain falls during our return to Santiago, and black ponchos appear everywhere.

AUGUST 22

Fabian Fedorov, a friend of V.'s father, comes to tell her about her father's death and burial in Santiago twenty-five years ago. Other visitors include Delia del Carril, who is the former wife of Pablo Neruda and an old friend of the I.S.'s; Juanita Guandarillas, the wife of I.S.'s Diaghilev-era friend Tony Guandarillas; the sister of Paulet Thévenaz, Cocteau's friend who painted I.S.'s portrait in Leysin in 1914; a friend of the late Eugenia Errazuriz, who owns one of the Picasso drawings of I.S.

Chatting with musicians after the rehearsal this morning, I.S. says that he has "a sense" of his material long before he begins to compose, and he believes that all composers do. Which reminds me of Hume's "It is impossible for us to think of anything which we have not antecedently felt." "But," I.S. goes on, "I am always surprised by the suddenness with which my material comes to an end. I feel like a satisfied animal then." When someone asks the inevitable question about his borrowings from the eighteenth century, he answers simply, "Let's say that I was a kind of bird, and that the eighteenth century was a kind of bird's nest in which I felt cozy laying my eggs." The no-less-inevitable question about electronic music provokes the answer that he is afraid of involuntary physical reactions to it, and he makes his meaning clear by telling how Russian peasants could induce their horses to urinate by whistling to them.

We have acquired a taste for *chirimoyas,* the sweet, white, mushy fruit with black-almond pips which is scooped out of hard avocado-like shells.

AUGUST 24

Webern's *Marcia funebre* goes more smoothly than I expect in tonight's concert at the Teatro Astor, although the orchestra has no idea of attack, phrasing, anacrusis. But in the last movement of the *Firebird,* the horn comes in on F instead of F sharp; "which," I.S. says, "is like salt when you expect sugar."

AUGUST 25

The cordillera turns to fire in the setting sun, and for a time, as our plane bumps and drops between the mountains, we are afraid of turning to the same thing. Buenos Aires, at midnight, feels like a New York January, but in spite of the cold and the hour, I.S. manages some affable remarks for television. "BIENVENIDO STRAVINSKY," reads a big banner at the airport entrance. We reach the Plaza Hotel at 1 AM and start to unpack, but at 2 AM I.S. complains about his bed, and we resettle on another floor.

The Teatro Colón is a perfect sound box, and Webern's *ponticello* whispers are clearer than I have ever heard them. The musicians are a little dour, a little unwilling to be corrected—their languages are German and Italian, and apparently no one speaks a word of French or English—but they are the quickest and ablest we have conducted on the tour. After a run-through of the *Firebird,* an elderly gentleman introduces himself to I.S. as a fellow pupil of Rimsky-Korsakov. (I.S. to me: "Not true, of course, but even if it were, what right does that give him to disturb me now?") Rimsky apart, he wishes to commission a piece "of major proportions" for the opening of a new hall. (I.S. to me: "Why doesn't he ask some Elgar specializing in that sort of thing? 'Of major proportions' simply means pompous.")

Buenos Aires is a city of beautiful trees: jacarandas, Japanese magnolias, hydra-headed ombús, aguaribays. And a city of absurd statues and monuments. I.S.: "A lifesize statue of a man in an open place is ridiculous. Size can suggest the heroic, as it does in Michelangelo's 'David,' and why bother to carve the man next door?"

The complaints of the white-collar class in Buenos Aires, from race hatreds to the plumbing, are scapegoated to Perón, but the blue-collar neighborhoods are scrawled with the slogans *"Vuelve Perón"* and *"Obra de Perón."* According to our silk-collar host at dinner tonight, the people are divided, bitter, without hope. "The true *obra de Perón* is that *nous ne sommes pas les nouveaux riches mais les nouveaux pauvres."* This conversation takes place in the La Cabaña restaurant, but the photographs of prize steers on the walls and the stuffed steer in the lobby inhibit our appetites.

1960

"Señor Stravinsky, what does South America mean to you?" a reporter asks; and I.S.'s answer could hardly be more candid: "Hotel rooms, first of all, some too old, some too new. And wildernesses, deserts and jungles, with their extremes of climate. And faces in symphony orchestras that might have come from Inca tombs. And nationalism: each country hates its neighbor. And racialism, for I saw swastikas in Santiago and have been told that they can be found here. But South America is culturally colonial to Europe; it has few ties to the United States and no vital ones, such as religion and language; from here, the Monroe Doctrine does seem a purely *yanqui* idea. Finally, you will not like this, but I will say anyway that my general impression of South America is of a *triste* continent." And they do *not* like it, of course, but I.S. was never one to withhold his mind for that reason, or to curry to the press for *any* reason, and he is chaffing today because of the 26 per cent service charge on his hotel bill.

We spend the day with Victoria and Angelica Ocampo at San Isidro, Victoria's book-filled house and garden of giant philodendrons, overlooking the Río de la Plata. Warming ourselves beside a quebracho fire, we eat *empanadas* (a beef-and-raisin *pirochki*) and flick through photograph albums of former house guests including I.S., Tagore, Count Keyserling, Isherwood, St.-John Perse. Afterwards we drive to Algarrobo, where in 1818 San Martín y Pueyrredón planned the wars of Chilean and Peruvian liberation; but Victoria is wearing slacks, and on that account is admitted only after making a terrific row. Not slacks, of course, but blue stockings are her normal garb, and though hosiery of that color rarely carries attractive connotations, Victoria is a beauty with the fresh pink complexion of a young girl. She is also very proud—the portraits of her grandparents in her living room were painted by Pueyrredón *père*—and contemptuous of her new Krupp and Thiessen neighbors, with their protective electric fences.

At teatime I.S. meets with a group of Argentine musicians. Among the questions discussed are: the problem of trying to teach both an "integrated-traditional" and a "mathematical-experimental" study of musical composition (no conclusions); and the faults of *avant-gardisme,* which are its dependence on a superficial competition—the need to outdo—and its ignorance of music in the pre-electronic era (no remedies). In the course of this chatter, something is said about the "power" of Beethoven. But I.S. jumps on the word: "I don't like it because it has acquired too much of the meaning 'use of power.' Say 'might,' rather." This exchange makes me realize how little my published colloquies with I.S. show of his cunning with words, his many-sided apprehension of them, and his sense both of their aptness and weight. I also realize that I have nowhere recorded one of his favorite and most characteristic expressions, "Who needs it?" This is employed in a variety of circumstances, but never more frequently than at concerts of modern music. He will listen quietly for a minute or so to the new string quartet by Professor Q., for example, then grow restless and start to squirm, then turn to me and stage-whisper: "But who needs it?"

In the car returning to Buenos Aires, a Russian woman diverts the I.S.'s with recitations, by heart, from *Old Possum's Book of Practical Cats.* But Argentine night traffic is even more dangerous than Argentine day traffic. The intersections on the long suburban avenue are without traffic signals, and the only law appears to be every man for himself. Headlights, moreover, are turned on only at the *suspected* approach of another vehicle.

AUGUST 30

The audience is warm to Debussy's *Martyre,* polite to Webern's *Six Pieces,* and thunderous to *Petrushka,* even though I.S. stops conducting after the beginning of the Fourth Tableau, which is played chaotically, and after a fearful pause starts it over again. "Such are the humiliations of fame," he says later. "The notes should be articulated like *petit pois,* but they come out like pease porridge, and the public applauds all the same."

Lunch with Jorge Luis Borges, who is nervous and shy as a ferret; his fingers fidget continually, folding and unfolding his napkin, realigning the silverware, tracing the creases in his trousers. Nearly blind—his lenses are as thick as piano-leg casters—he fixes each of us in turn with one eye, but says he cannot see anyway, and compares himself to the captain in *The End of the Tether*. Borges teaches a course in advanced English at the University of Buenos Aires, "for which a mere eight months were allotted formerly," he says, "but which the clever people who control the University have reduced to four." His range of reading in English and five other languages leaves us far behind, however, and we sit around a centerpiece of purple anemones listening to him—and eating *dulce de leche,* which I.S. fears later has made him ill.

SEPTEMBER 4 **1960**

6:30 AM. We fly over the long causeway and the muddy river, both shores of which are visible from the middle, and after which Montevideo is a glimpse of red rooftops, beaches, and pines. At one place in northern Uruguay or Brazil the earth looks as if it had been churned by whirlpools, but after that it is covered with dark green *fazendas*. Between São Paulo, where we put down long enough to cancel our concert, and Rio, where we circle for some time before being able to land, it splits into canyons shaped like streak lightning.

The Ouro Verde is a small Copacabana hotel with a terrace on the wave-patterned mosaic sidewalk. As we sit there before bed, drinking thimble-sized cups of blue, sugary coffee, a huge yellow moon appears, and with it an army of dark-complexioned girls in tight pants and sweaters soliciting every man on the walk.

SEPTEMBER 5

6 AM. A canine beach chase, two terriers running pell-mell to the water and back again as fast as possible. The earliest bather is a fat man exercising with a fat rubber ball. Watermelon carts appear next, and boys with condor kites, and soon after the beach is crowded—chocolate skins, *pousse-café* skins, and pale skins in about equal numbers, although an American in the bar tells us that "Integration is more apparent than real, and even apparent only on the beach."

Rio is a city of iron balconies, iron grilles, iron shutters; a city shaded by beautiful trees; a city of new buildings on stilts and old buildings *made* of stilts; a city of curvaceous wooden churches. We drive to the Paneiras Corcovado on a road canopied in places with vines, like a tunnel, and alternately washed away and blocked by landslides. But at the top, and at moonrise, Rio is indeed a *"Cidade Maravilhosa."*

We dine at the Bec Fin, but would have done better, I suspect, at one of the street stands selling fresh crabs. The beach, at midnight, is littered with lovers.

The same American in the bar says that he lives by borrowing at 6 per cent in the United States and lending at 28 per cent here, "But it's risky."

I.S., back from a stroll, says he was propositioned by one of the *poules* patrolling the hotel area. "And I was tempted, too; you could dial a telephone with her nipples."

Brasília, Port-of-Spain, New York. Our pilot for the first lap is an I.S. "fan," a fact that once cost him a job, he says, the staff psychiatrist of a U.S. airline having rejected him because in answer to "What is your favorite book and favorite piece of music?" he wrote "Nietszche's *Zarathustra* and Stravinsky's *Rite of Spring*." We stand behind him in the cockpit during take-off and an unscheduled tour of the bay. Beyond Rio are jagged mountains, cities clinging narrowly to winding dirt roads, eroded and sun-calcined plains. Beyond the agglomeration of new buildings at Belo Horizonte are clumps of jungle, dried-up water holes, coiling black rivers with sand islands—like spotted snakes. Brasília from the air is a large-scale map with future streets traced in and circular perforations for future trees. From the ground its few lonely skyscrapers suggest a partly undenticulated comb (V. says) and a bombed city (I.S. says).

We change planes here, and three hours later cross the Amazon at Santarem, where the great brown river is swollen by transfusions from large blue tributaries. From here to the Orinoco the thick green jungle mat is flecked with smokelike puffs of clouds from storm detonations.

Trinidad seems exaggeratedly British, what with the BBC accents on the loudspeaker, the pith helmets, the Bermuda shorts, and the Crown insignia of the airport employees. In the waiting room, I.S., watching a baby's unsteady walk, says, "Just like me." A whole native village, come to see someone off, forms a quilt of color as we lift into the air.

1960

Venice. A flood. The water in the hotel lobby is thirty inches deep, but barelegged porters provide a piggyback ferrying service between the stairs and an elevated plank-board highway leading to the Piazza. A parade of refugees, shoes and stockings in hand, gingerly walk this single-file bridge, although the Piazza itself is a boat basin where gondolas and drowned rats float in the garbage water of a long-needed street cleaning. A few tables are above water in one of the arcades, however, and tourists sit at them writing postcards; one of the café orchestras is bravely playing on, too, like the band on a sinking ship. On the Piazzetta side, pigeons flutter nervously overhead as booted boys wade excitedly in the mounting tide, but a cold Bora blows whitecaps on the Grand Canal and sends us back to our rooms.

DECEMBER 1

Paris. "Lunch" at the Boule d'Or with Suvchinsky and François Michel. At other tables: baby-faced North Americans, oily-faced South Americans, brewer's-bloom-faced (telangiectatic) Gauls. But the tempo of François Michel's conversation is too fast for me, and with the exception of my meager contributions to his *Encyclopédie,* I know too little of what it is about (local literary *mesquineries,* Saussure's distinction between *langue* and *parole,* and Claudel, whom I.S. describes as a *"cochon incontestable"*). His gourmet talk, however, what I manage to digest of it, contains useful knowledge on such matters as *perdreaux* basting, the wisdom of asking for the less exercised left *patte* of the *poulet,* and of choosing the Gruyère close to the *croûte*—while of course avoiding any cheese at the slightest whiff of ammonia. He complains that our first wicker-cradled bottle of wine has not been sufficiently aerated, though the glasses are like goldfish bowls. This leads to a discussion of pre-phylloxera clarets, after which everyone begins to sniff, sip, debate the merits of body and bouquet, and report the reception of the palate, as if, after a flagon of vodka, that abused organ could differentiate between Lafite-Rothschild and plonk. Yet, after all, perhaps François Michel's can.

1960

All told, we soak up, or down, two bottles of vodka, three of claret, two of Dom Perignon, several slugs of Calvados; and in consequence, of course, are stupefied. The worst of this is that we have an appointment at five with Chagall, who has come expressly for it from Rouen. Fortunately V., finding herself in conversation with the South Americans at the adjoining table, and realizing early on that she is near the brink of inebriety herself, takes no more, and is therefore able to guide her debauched and reeling menfolk back to the hotel. (As I test one leg, then the other, the thought strikes me that I might turn to stone—on the analogy that certain chemical elements convert from one to another until stability is reached, at which point they become lead.) But it is already four o'clock by the time we arrive and steer I.S. to his bed, on which, after replying to V.'s "Are you drunk?"—I.S.: "And how!"—he goes out like a light. Trying to sober me up for the meeting, Suvchinsky and V. work me over as if I were a K.O.-ed boxer, Suvchinsky holding ice-filled compresses to my forehead in spite of my protestations on behalf of my sinuses and my insistence that the real trouble is the medulla oblongata:

> They played him a sonata—let me see!
> "Medulla oblongata"—key of G.

It is after five when, I.S. being beyond communication, I venture forth alone with V. But although I go with her as far as Nicolas Nabokov's apartment, where the meeting is to take place, I am too queasy to enter and can only truckle ignominiously, as well as headswimmingly, back to the hotel.

An hour later, with the return of the valiant V., we learn that Rolf Liebermann, who had flown from Hamburg for the meeting, took the story as a great joke—"for which I will always love him," V. says, adding with a feline scratch that "Chagall couldn't have behaved more pompously, and his wife looked at me as if I were depraved, or had come from a Roman orgy. Wasn't *her* husband ever drunk? I wanted to ask. What about all those upside-down roosters?"

1960

1948
1949
1950
1951
1952
1953
1954
1955
1956
1957
1958
1959
1960

ITINERARY

1962
1963
1964
1965
1966
1967
1968
1969
1970
1971

January 9: We fly to Los Angeles. **18:** R.C. to Toronto to record the Schoenberg Concerto with Glenn Gould. **February 1, 10, 12, 13:** I.S. records. **26:** R.C. to New York by train. **March 2:** V. in hospital for a minor operation. **30:** We fly from Los Angeles to Mexico City. **April 3:** We fly from Acapulco to Mexico City. **4:** V.'s vernissage at the Diana Gallery. **7, 9:** Concerts in Mexico City, I.S.'s last performances of *Le Sacre du printemps*. **10:** Fly to Los Angeles. **26:** R.C. to New York to conduct all-Varèse concert in Town Hall. **May 3:** R.C. to Hollywood. **12:** The Huxley house is destroyed by a fire. **June 4:** I.S. records the *Symphony of Psalms* (not released). **5:** I.S. conducts his Violin Concerto and the *Symphony of Psalms* in Royce Hall. **8:** Visit from Khrennikov and other Russian composers, who extend an invitation to I.S. to visit the U.S.S.R. **29, 30:** I.S. records the Violin Concerto with Stern. **July 1:** Train to Lamy (Santa Fe), where I.S. conducts *Oedipus Rex*. **August:** Return to Los Angeles by train. **24:** Fly to New York (Hotel Pierre). **September 1:** We sail on the *Kungsholm* for Göteborg. **9:** Train to Stockholm, flying from there to Helsinki. **13:** Stockholm. **24:** Concert in Stockholm. **25:** Fly to Berlin, via Hamburg. **29:** I.S. conducts *Perséphone* in Berlin. **October 18:** I.S. conducts *Histoire du Soldat* at the Zürich Opera. **19:** We fly to London (Savoy Hotel), where I.S. conducts *Perséphone*. **December 10:** Fly from Tahiti to Los Angeles.

MARCH 31

Good Friday. Cuernavaca. The lawns at Las Mañanitas, where we dine, are a bird paradise featuring black herons with gold combs, pigeons with shuttlecock fantails and feather leggings that resemble the long-underwear tights of pugilists in the nineties, peacocks strutting like Ziegfeld Girls (but emitting a harsh cry that sounds to me like "Help!"). Heard but not seen are innumerable parrots screeching in the surrounding plumbago bushes.

At table, I.S. wanting butter but confusing Spanish with Italian, orders *"burro"* (mule); then, to apologize, says *"vergogna"* ("large lingam").

In the Plaza, at three o'clock, the Savior's death is marked by acolytes in white dalmatics shaking rattles and turning ratchet wheels. We drive to Taxco and the Borda Hotel, where our rooms look over the town.

At nightfall, the moon rises like an observation balloon. It is a signal both for the dogs on the adjacent hills to begin a nonstop barking contest and for the start of a candlelight parade that, for the next three hours, winds out of the hills and weaves through the dark town below, moving in spreads and bunches like an accordion or a worm. Virtually the whole population participates in this procession, which disbands in the streets below Santa Prisca, but reconverges at midnight at the convent of San Bernardino for the final act of the day-long Passion Play.

We go to Santa Prisca ourselves at about eleven o'clock, or, rather, are chauffeured through the almost impassable streets by Vicente, a powerfully built man who looks like Victor McLaglen and might have had a highly successful career as a bandit. The church, when we reach it—Vicente: "This is Santa Prisca, you see what I mean?"—is empty except for two boys polishing some gold altar columns (*"No tocar el dorado,"* a sign reads) that look as if they had been squeezed from tubes of gold paste; and some Indian women who scorn the benches and say their orisons to a Christ draped in purple, kneeling on the bare aisle stones. The walls are galleries of silver hearts and souls in mandorlas, and *ex voto* pictures, many of them of lost pigs and cows.

At midnight the crowd outside the convent of San Bernardino is silent and motionless. Immediately inside is an unshrouded Christ image with silver angel's wings and a black cross roped to His lacerated and bleeding back. Beyond, in the main room, a hill of Calvary has been erected in front of the altar, with three lifesize crosses. The center cross is empty, but the ladder used for the deposition still leans against it, and strips of embalming linen still hang from it like curtains; effigies of limp, dead bodies are nailed to the two other crosses. The room, otherwise, is a mass of kneeling Indians, every face, except those of children tottering on the edge of sleep, transfixed. Strange, somber music begins to wail from a remote organ, and at this a path is cleared from the door to the center cross. A teen-age boy, black-hooded and bare to the waist, with a heavy cactus cross on his back and a lighted candle tied to the wrist of each spread-eagled arm, then enters the room, and, with a great effort and in evident pain, makes his way to the empty cross. He kneels, with the help of four other boys, and as his knees touch the floor the organ stops and he himself begins a long, slow chant that is gradually taken up by the whole congregation.

One of the odder aspects of the ceremony is that no clerical vestments are seen, and, for all outward signs, the officiating priests could be plain-clothes detectives. Which makes it all the more real, for the god of this drama is no mere embodiment of virtues and ideals, and still less a projection of the wish for a higher humanity: he is simply Man, who suffers and dies, and whose death gives the death of each of us the dignity of tragedy. After the drama in the convent, a score of young Indian boys, dressed in the helmets and tunics of Roman legionaries, gather in the Plaza to stand guard over the sepulcher until dawn, when an air-raid siren screams the end of their vigil, and we go to bed under clouds that look like curdled milk.

APRIL 1

Vicente, helping us to check out of the hotel this morning: "Have you enough [*i.e.,* more] bags?" Many boulders and barns on the road to Acapulco are embellished with exhortations, in white paint, to *"Muera Apurto"* ("Kill Apurto"). "Apurto is the Governor of the province," Vicente explains. "Mexicans funny people, señor. You see what I mean?" The shoulders of the steep road *bajando,* to the hot country, are studded with crosses marking precipitations of the careless or unlucky. At one particularly dangerous turn a stone coffin stands at the place where a fence could do more good. Automobiles, fortunately, are far rarer than donkeys, which the Indians ride far back, not neckward like the *gringos.* Once we pass five small boys clinging to each other in the deeply ridged back of an old mule.

The arid cactus *barrancas* are relieved in the valleys by maize, the husks, cobs, and stalks of which are stored in trees, like giant birds' nests. Pigs and cows roam, if not freely, then attended only by vultures. And the farther *bajando,* the more fragmentary the clothing. Vicente: "It is hot, señor. You see what I mean?" Near Iguala, Indians along the road are selling ceramics, baskets, guavas, chicle, lovebirds, and pulque, swinging pots of the latter toward our passing car like priests with censers. We stop at a stand here, and, surrounded by dark-eyed children, drink coconut milk spiked with gin, a combination that, back on the road, soon puts us to sleep, until Vicente wakes us with, "There's Acapulco. You see what I mean?"

APRIL 8

Coyoacán. After a breakfast of "Virgin's milk cheese," which I buy in the market, and the sweet cheese of Oaxaca, which is peeled or unraveled from a white ball, I go to San Diego Churubusco where a wedding is in progress. Following a rendition of "None but the Lonely Heart" by a tenor, violin, and organ, in three different versions of unison, the priest extends the bride's veil over the groom's head and anoints them from an ampulla. As I leave the church a beggar pushes his cup to me; his face and beard are almost exactly the same as those of the Christ image inside the door.

We drive to Tepozotlán in the afternoon, to the Churrigueresque church which I.S. first saw in 1940 and by which he was more impressed, he says, than by any other church in the world. And the rose-colored stone and glittering gold interiors *are* alluring, as one comes to them from the maguey desert, even beyond I.S.'s description of them. The aisle columns are red and the angels are white—like ghosts in the frame of so much color—but the unforgettable part of the church is the chapel of the Virgin of Loreto. It is mirror-lined, "like all places of love—like a brothel," says I.S., "for it is the womb of the Virgin." We look up through a hundred feet of narrowing funnel to the Dove of the Eucharist, which in blinding whiteness reflects an older god, the sun.

SEPTEMBER 9

Helsinki Airport. Midnight. I.S. has had too many schnapps on the plane, but though he says "ish" for "is" in a brief television interview, the Finns can't have noticed, their language being so full of diphthongs anyway. The ride to the city, through moonlit forests, is long, and it is after 1 AM when we reach the hotel, which occupies only one floor, the ninth, of an office building. (The Finnish word for elevator, I note, is *"hissi,"* and the Swedish *"hiss,"* and both words appear on the door but without translation; it is the only Finnish I ever learn.) The view from our rooms of the gull-busy boat basin and the wooded islands in the bay makes the I.S.'s homesick for St. Petersburg.

SEPTEMBER 10

Järvenpää. A white-haired daughter of Sibelius meets us at a pathway near the late composer's house and walks with us to his woodland grave, a large but simple granite nameplate on which I.S. places a bouquet. The house is the cozy residence of a country composer, with a tile stove in each room and wooden floors scrubbed white and smooth; and it is no more than that, meaning that no aura of attempted Beethovenizing hangs over the place. One even has to look for Sibelius's works, in fact, the recordings and bound volumes of scores being tucked away in a cabinet. Back in Helsinki I.S. recalls that he had heard Sibelius's First or Second Symphony with Rimsky, whose only comment was, "I suppose that is also possible." I learn from this anecdote that Rimsky called I.S. "Guimochka, as everyone did who loved me." I.S. says he is fond of the Sibelius *Canzonetta* for strings, "The first half of it, anyway. I like that kind of Italian melody gone north. Tchaikovsky did, too, of course, and through him the taste became an important and attractive part of St. Petersburg culture."

A thick fog has settled over Helsinki Harbor when we return, and all night long we hear the cries of lost boats.

SEPTEMBER 12

The center of the old city is a white square with a statue of Czar Alexander II. (The new city, I hardly need to add, is a mass of gray stone apartment buildings that could have come from and could be shipped to anywhere in the world.) V. goes to the square to look for a hotel she remembers from childhood, but which, she learns, was destroyed during the war. The nearby markets with their heaps of mushrooms, berries, fish, flowers, remind her of St. Petersburg, the more so when she finds that Russian is still spoken by some of the old women who manage the food stalls.

I.S. receives many bouquets at the concert tonight, and after the concert, a dinner by local composers, whose speeches are shy, hospitable, grateful, and very kind.

Stockholm. *En Rucklares Väg—The Rake's Progress*—at the Royal Opera. The stage apron has been extended over the orchestra pit, thus neutralizing the proscenium arch. Moreover, the fullest stage depth is exploited, and very effectively, as at the end of the brothel scene when the actors freeze in the far background in silhouette. A Brechtian poster, *En Rucklares Väg,* is used as a between-scenes drop, replacing the curtain, and this emphasizes the episodes as a progress of pictures in the Hogarth sense. The groupings are Hogarthian, too, and in some of the pictorializations, especially in the earlier episodes, Hogarth is openly imitated; thus the scene of Mother Goose, bottle in hand, falling backward on her couch, is a *tableau vivant* of the painting. The sets, moreover, are changed before the audience's eyes, not furtively, in the dark, but as a co-ordinated element in the movement of the play. "London," for example, is lowered from the sky at the beginning of the street scene, and during the whole of the C-minor Prelude is populated with tradesmen and townspeople. This London scene is visually the most attractive of all, but it is the last that can be described as English in color and style of décor. The costumes become more Swedish after it, and gray and black gradually predominate over pink and orange, but of course this more mute and somber palette also follows the tenor of the play.

1961

I have never seen I.S. more moved by a performance of a work of his—in fact, one seldom sees him not angry—and this in spite of impossible musical cuts, bad *tempi,* and legions of places where the direction is at loggerheads with the book. "Tom's decision to marry Baba has at last been made convincing," he says, "and I want to thank Bergman for that. And to thank him for so much more besides. Ann weeps when Tom leaves for London, and Tom starts to go to her, but Truelove motions him back and goes to her himself. I cannot describe Truelove's gesture, but I believed in it. Also, Tom and Shadow singing from the loges in the auction scene *does* bolster the idea that they are at large. Such small things, and a hundred more, establish the credibility of the play." Best of all, Bergman's groupings manage to be natural without infracting the conventions of opera, for the arias and the actionless ensembles, such as the quartet and trio in the first scene, are sung *to* the audience and stage front. The difference is that Bergman's singers act—move their bodies, use their eyes—as we have never seen singers act before.

One novel aspect of the musical performance is the *sotto voce* execution of the *secco* recitatives, for which the harpsichord is elevated from the orchestra pit to slightly below stage level, where it is, as it should be, closer to the singers than to the orchestra. The card game, incidentally, is played as a *crescendo* on stage, in effective contrast to the dynamically static harpsichord solo.

I.S. is given a standing ovation, not only when he first enters his loge but again at the end of the opera.

SEPTEMBER 14

The Royal Theater at Drottningholm owns more than twenty eighteenth-century sets, and these include not only backboards but perspectival systems of sliding side-scenery as well. The intendant of the theater works the antique machinery for us, displaying movements of clouds and waves, thunder from a drop of rocks in a net, the ascent of a plaster god (or "real" *deus ex machina*). When in official attendance, the King and Queen sat on red thrones in the front center of the audience, but when incognito or with a paramour, the King was sequestered in a latticed loge to the side. The other seats are still designated by plaques for *"cavalieri," "friseurs," "valets."* Forty rooms for actors surround the stage, each one equipped with fireplace, pewter *lavabo,* clothes block, wig dummy, dressing table, mirror. The corridors have been made into galleries of actors' portraits, handbills for such popular plays of the time as Voltaire's *Tancrède,* and theater designs, including many by Bibiena and the originals for Cesti's *Pomo d'Oro.* The wallpaper is a painted, hand-sewn parchment.

SEPTEMBER 16

Uppsala. Ocher-and-red buildings, windmills, farmhouses roofed with sod. The old church on the Royal Ridge occupies the site of a temple to Odin, and, even before that, of a circle of sacred trees. Its holy images, pews, pillars, and pulpit, are as worn as driftwood, but a row of hourglasses still stands on the rostrum, each with a fifteen-minute measure of sand to guarantee against religious filibuster. The church was frequented by professors and prebendaries, many of whom, including Anders Celsius, are buried in the floor. Outside and apart from it is the *klockstapel,* a wooden belfry laced from the waist up with rounded shingles like a coat of mail.

We also visit the home of Linnaeus; the statue of the Arctic explorer Finn Malmgren, who was a distant cousin of V.; the gold casket of St. Erik, and the tomb of Swedenborg, both in the cathedral; and the eighteenth-century Theatrum Anatomicum. Lastly, at the Carolina Rediviva Library, we examine the part-books of Schütz's *Christmas Oratorio;* organ entablatures in Buxtehude's hand dated 1680 and signed *"Membra Jesu Nostri, Organista S. Maria Virgines, Lübeck";* and a collection of drawings by the Swedish kings, of which the best, by Gustavus IV, might have been inspired, at least, by Goya.

Back in Stockholm we go to dinner at the country house of Set Svanholm, director of the Royal Opera, with Ingmar Bergman and his new Estonian wife. Bergman—tall, nose like a clasp, deep-set eyes, a mole on the right cheek—speaks fluent English, abetted by his hands, which become lively and expressive as soon as he begins to talk. Everything he says, moreover, is said very clearly—has been formed by a well-tailored mind—nor is anything about the man in the least tentative. But he is passionate, too, and when he avows that "The artist has only to discover what to do and then with all his strength to purify the doing," I want to discover something right away and rush out and do it myself. When I.S. asks what initially attracted him to *The Rake,* Bergman says "A bad performance." Which opens the door to a discussion of *his* performance.

The Bedlam and brothel scenes were overpopulated, I.S. says. "A few characters can be memorable, never a crowd of them." But Bergman agrees. "In fact, I invented a name for each person, but my work was destroyed when the chorus had to be enlarged for more sound." His first idea, he says, was that the stage should be long and deep enough to permit the actors to appear and disappear in darkness and not through doors. And his second idea was that the opera should be divided into two acts of five and four scenes each, "principally because Act Two, as published, does not have a strong beginning-to-middle-to-end structure. As I see it, the play, up to the unveiling of Baba's beard, is one line, and not only the play but the music; this is the protasis, and the rest is the peripeteia. And I was more concerned with a line for the episodes than with rounded act-structures. I thought, too, that especially in this opera the audience's attention to the stage must not be lost for a single moment, which accounts for—please forgive me—the cuts." Bergman has abbreviated the orchestral march before the brothel scene and excised the whole of Tom's aria at the beginning of the Bedlam scene, two places where other directors have not only complained of I.S.'s misapplied musical thrift but where, customarily, pauses have been introduced because of insufficient musical time. "Another reason for the two-act division," he goes on, "was that I could not have an intermission after the bread machine and allow the audience to go out confused. This scene is the most difficult in the opera both to stage and to believe in." I.S. agrees, and adds: "The waltz music there is deliberately indifferent." (No; it is hurdy-gurdy music, and in that sense mechanical.) Bergman says he dreamed that the machine had a lion's mouth. "I dream about everything I do. Dreams purify my ideas." Which pleases I.S., who says that he dreams about every problem in his composition.

I.S. thinks that Bergman's greatest achievement is in having made Baba believable. "And that is not easy. To reverse a remark of somebody in Henry James, 'She was perhaps a lady but never a woman.' Baba recognizes Shadow for what he is, however, and though she enters the drama as a monstrosity from nowhere, she leaves it as a sympathetic personality." Bergman: "Baba cost me more thought than anyone else. She is the artist in all of us, and not merely the circus artist. This, incidentally, is the reason she represents such a great advance over the original idea of the Ugly Duchess. Her beard must be beautiful, too, not grotesque, and the audience must believe in the reality of what it sees, no matter how fantastic. Besides, the point of the marriage, at least by the time of the breakfast scene, is not its exoticism but its conventionality. Tom is bored with her because she is shallow." Bergman has expressed this, at the beginning of the breakfast scene, by having Baba and Tom lie far apart on a ludicrously large bed.

Bergman believes that the climax of the opera is the confrontation of Tom, Baba, and Ann in the street scene. "That is where Shadow's work is shown in the open, and the reason I bring him on stage: he must look on with satisfaction." I.S. remarks that "The silent movement of people in the streets at the beginning of this scene is the most beautiful tableau in the opera. You have a deep feeling for music." Bergman: "The question for the opera director should always be, 'How much does the music tell us already?' In the street scene it tells us exactly how those people feel. In fact, it tells us that they are not people at all but shadows."

I.S. expands on his impression that the second act was both more Swedish than the first, and more like a Bergman film. "The freaks at the auction, and again in Bedlam—a medieval madhouse, incidentally, more Breughel than Hogarth—were especially Bergmanesque, and so was the solitary dummy at the end of the brothel scene." Bergman's answer is that he had spent so much time on the first part of the opera that too little remained for the rest. "Moreover, I became wary of following Hogarth, who is dangerous because too attractive in himself."

I.S. also remarks that the Epilogue succeeds as it has not succeeded in other productions, "because it did not come as a shock, the audience never having lost track of the 'fable' aspect." This was managed like a Brecht *Verfremdungseffekt,* though Bergman's illusion of reality—cave-of-shadows reality—is exactly what Brecht tried to dispel. Bergman: "The Epilogue is a matter of preparation, which is the reason I also begin each act with it, and thus create a frame for the whole work." (He has staged a dumbshow during and even before the Prelude to Act One, and again before Baba's inventory recitative, which is the overture to "his" Act Two; but these devices are as much to fix audience attention, it seems to me, as they are preparations for the Epilogue.) "What the Epilogue should mean," he concludes, "is that now the play is over and you can go home and talk about the singer's high C."

Bergman's staging of the graveyard scene provokes one criticism from I.S. It is that Shadow enters as well as exits through the ground; I.S. thinks the appearance weakens the effect of the disappearance. But I.S. likes the way Shadow sits on the tombstone at the beginning of the scene. And he likes the silhouette of three Gothic steeples, whose presence is more and more strongly felt as the action develops. Bergman: "The audience is aware of the three spires only as ominous presences at first, but by the end of the scene it knows that they are Golgotha, and the meaning of the play."

In conclusion, I.S. says that Bergman's Bedlamites respond too quickly—stand up too fast—after the first flute duet, and that Tom, after Ann's exit, rises too suddenly for a dying man. Bergman: "Mistakes like these are part of the charm of opera. And they are probably necessary, for they seduce us into trying again."

A few days ago we saw the first act (only) of a really awful performance of *Rigoletto*. This morning, when I unthinkingly whistle one of the *ballo* tunes

I.S. asks whether it is *Rigoletto* or *Traviata*. What he means, of course, is the *Traviata*

which I mention as one of a thousand examples that he hears intervallically first—as he himself claims—rather than rhythmically, so that intervals are connecting roots and rhythms elaboration.

1961

More talk with Bergman about his *Rake*. I.S. asks why the clock in the brothel was not shown. Bergman: "Because it is so obvious in the music. I prefer to see the eyes of the actors watching something that we hear unmistakably as a clock, and to make the real audience believe through the eyes of the stage audience. Shadow," Bergman contends, "should be a kind of lawyer—the *advocatus diaboli*—but critics only understand type-casting. They complained that my Devil was not demonic, just as they complained that Tom pouts and mopes more than he roisters. But the progress of the Rake is accounted for in the sets, don't you think? He really does look a millionaire in the fourth scene." I.S. also asks why the auction crowd is dressed in black, saying that this struck him as Hyperborean and reminded him of the black-robed oarsmen in wood-carvings of toy scullers. Bergman's answer is that black *is* worn in the parish boat races in his native north, but that he had not thought of this while staging the scene. "The reason for the black was to focus attention on Baba and Ann by giving color only to them." As a last suggestion, I.S. thinks that the auctioneer should be removed still farther from the bidders, who sit—and this is effective—with their backs to the audience.

Bergman says he would stage I.S.'s *Oedipus Rex* without masks. "A mask may be beautiful, and it can be a useful façade for all sorts of things, but the price, which is the loss of contact, is too great." As we part, he asks me to keep in touch with him.

Berlin. A tour of *"Die Mauer"* in Mayor Brandt's car, starting at the Brandenburger Tor, where the barricades and land mines are partly concealed by flowers. I.S. points toward what was once the Adlon Hotel, saying that it was where he met Schoenberg in 1912; but between us and it are innumerable death traps, as well as policemen with bloodhounds, binoculars, walkie-talkies, submachine guns at the ready. In the French sector, *"Die Mauer"* is still low enough so that neighbors may converse over it. Old place names survive here, too, some of them now cruelly ironic: "Bellevuestrasse," for instance, a street with the ugliest view of all; and *"Dem deutschen Volk,"* which is above the door of a huge building still hideously gutted and cadaverous from the war. The sidewalk next to the boundary is marked at many places by crosses with wreaths and bouquets commemorating fatal East-to-West leaps. Every house on the line is sealed, the windows and doors bricked up and boarded like a set for *No Exit.* Someone has scrawled *"Wir sind alle Brüder"* on the door of a blockaded church, where even the crucifix is barbwired, a new crown of thorns. One area not yet walled is patrolled by tanks, and in the field beyond them, old men and women can be seen laboring at gunpoint. Several times during this heart-sickening tour we close the windows of our car against the stench of death in buildings still rubbled and derelict from the carnage of 1945.

1961

SEPTEMBER 30–OCTOBER 7

Belgrade. Our passports and currency declarations are collected long before we receive permission to leave the plane. It is a hot, windy night and the streets are crowded with pedestrians. At the Metropole, our rooms face the Sava where it curves to meet the Danube, and the site of Roman Singidunum (which fact reminds us of that great sculptural scroll of the Dacian Wars, Trajan's Column in Rome). They are hardly luxurious rooms to begin with, besides which the telephones have been disconnected, the lights are constantly failing, the handles of doors and bureaus fall off at the slightest tug, and room service takes between two hours and never. But a more serious problem is the water. It works for only a few unpredictable moments each day, and is always scalding. We hoard it, using our bathtubs as rain-catchers, and improvising runnels to flush the toilets, usually burning fingers and drenching clothes in the process.

Apart from ourselves, the hotel's only guests are the personnel of French, Italian, and American film companies whose luminaries—the Americans are Gregory Peck, Mel Ferrer, Jeanne Crain, Akim Tamiroff, John Barrymore, Jr.—almost never leave the bar, presumably because of language difficulties and the lack of any indigenous entertainment worth the while.

Language. The maids, waiters, porters know a few words of German or Italian, but most officials we meet speak only the local language. The I.S.'s are able to follow the drift of this through words with common Slavonic roots, but they complain that these "etymological conversations" are tedious.

People. The women are bulky, but there are more blondes than we expect. The men—caps and dungarees—are large-boned and heavy-set, like Marshal

Tito. Everyone to whom we are introduced—musicians, dancers, theater employees, culture officials—is extremely hospitable.

Politics. No American or western European publication is in evidence at any kiosk, and Italy, a short sea-trip away, seems as remote as Nepal. But we are always aware of Russia. The principal hotel in the commercial district is called the Moscow, and the principal square is the Marx and Engels. As in other "Communist" countries, tips are said to be refused, but they are not refused in the Metropole. The local saying is that "Tips are not given, but they are taken."

Money. The official exchange is 600 dinars to the dollar, but the U.S. Embassy gives us 750. Yugoslav currency is "soft," meaning worthless anywhere else.

Food. The local wines and cheeses are coarse, but some of the German and Italian dishes might be edible if they were not so grossly cooked. We subsist principally on almonds, baklava, Turkish coffee, and a salty Serbian *chèvre.* Slivovitz, the plum liqueur, is imbibed everywhere and at all hours. It is the most enduring and endearing of Yugoslav institutions.

Music. The orchestra is obviously enjoying its discovery of *Oedipus Rex,* and it is a sorry spectacle that such excellent musicians are so completely unaware of this contemporary classic. We attend a seedy performance of *Eugene Onegin* at the small and nonventilated National Theater, and here, as well as later, at our own *soirées,* learn that success is gauged by the quantity of flowers hauled on stage afterward. The applause swells with each bouquet, in fact, as if the flowers themselves were the performers, and naturally the stage looks like a flower show for every artist who can afford it. These nosegays are stored in the artists' large but weakly illuminated dressing rooms during the performance, and when United States Ambassador George Kennan comes to greet us in ours before *Oedipus* and *Perséphone,* I.S. tells him his visit is "like that of a diplomatist at a state funeral."

Marshal Tito's photograph is on walls and desks in every room of the Music Academy, but the only composer's likeness is Liszt's.

Architecture. All government buildings and the newer apartment houses are in a severely unornamented one-party style that is ugly to the point of comicality. But as most churches and mosques are new, large, and ugly too, we perhaps overrate, in contrast, the attractiveness of the old, steep-gabled shops and houses around the market place. Like Athens, Belgrade is electrically bright (when the lights work), and, also as in the Greek city, prettier at night thanks to its Cyrillic signs in neon.

The country. A late afternoon drive to Oplenac, the Escurial of the last Serbian kings. Poplars and plane trees, tobacco fields and vineyards, white-washed farmhouses with thatched roofs. The women wear black shawls, and the men black hussars' hats, leggings, handlebar mustaches. Traffic is limited to bullock carts and canvas-covered gypsy wagons. The Oplenac mosaics, manufactured in Germany about forty years ago, exemplify the bad taste of our parents—which I say knowing that our own good taste will last a far shorter time.

The departure. I.S. at the airport, to a culture official who wants his summation of the visit: "*A la longue* we got rather bored with the hot water."

OCTOBER 12

Zürich. The exhibition of Hittite art in the Kunsthaus includes marvelous orthostat reliefs of jugglers, lutenists, hand-clapping dancers, a fierce griffin with an absurd pussycat mustache, a warrior with an Assyrian beard, a weather god with hammer and tongs. The ceramics include pitchers with pommel handles; rhytons; half-sieve strainers; fertility idols (some as if made with matchsticks, and all as abstract as Arp); curled-toe babouches (as if from the Turkey of the Janissary period); figurines of dancing gods with stilts and horned caps or the tall, conical caps of medieval jesters. Hittite gold, in statuettes of steers, is dandelion yellow, but some bronze and gold objects are striped with silver or electrum. Hittite cuneiform, on clay writing tablets, reminds us of the beach tracks of a flock of birds.

1961

I.S. says that the décors of tonight's *Nightingale* at the Zürich Opera are more African than Chinese. "'Death' is more African liban than Chinese shaman," he says, "and the Bonze looks like a Barbary Captain Kidd." But I am more disturbed by other aspects of the staging. Why, for example, does the palace of the Emperor of China look like a coolie's cottage? And the mechanical nightingale like a pterodactyl? And why, too, should the Japanese emissaries have green faces? A bad crossing? Too much tea?

OCTOBER 16

London. Dinner with the Eliots at the Savoy. The poet is much more hunched than two years ago, and he leans forward when he stands, as if from a yoke. The coloring of his face has changed, also—his lips and large ears are damson now—and its lines are leaner and sharper, reminding us of one of those Hittite ceramic birds.

He complains of the nuisance of having to refuse repeated invitations to the Tagore Centenary. "I took a volume of Tagore from the library the other day, to be certain I had not made a mistake, but could make nothing of it. Difficult to tell that to the Indians, though, or to admit that one does not put their man with Dante and Shakespeare. Bill Yeats claimed to like Tagore, I remember, but he was making a case for the East at the time . . . I receive regular shipments of the works of new Indian poets, incidentally, together with letters inviting my comments. Once I replied, ripping the thing apart, only to find part of my by-no-means-complimentary letter appearing as a preface to the published poems!" (Which is what Gauguin did with a half-critical letter from Strindberg, *i.e.,* printed it as a preface to the catalog of an exhibition.) "In payment I received a Kashmir shawl, which I returned. But soon after that another and much better shawl came with a note agreeing that the first one had not been worthy of me."

Tonight's dinner has been arranged to discuss a proposal that I.S. set "two lyrical stanzas," as Eliot describes them, from *Little Gidding*, though Eliot himself is "doubtful that they can be set." Nothing is said about this, however, and instead the poet and the musician talk about favorite *romans policiers* and about plays of Voltaire neither of them has read. "I knocked down a complete Voltaire at auction when I first came to England," Eliot confesses, "but never came to pick it up; that has been on my conscience ever since." Both men are Simenon addicts, I.S. estimating that he must have read at least sixty of his books, and Eliot avowing that "I can read about Maigret when I can read nothing else." Another mutually admired sleuth is Perry Mason, partly because "the author knows California law"— this from the author of *Prufrock*—and even though "Chandler was a better writer." Concerning the recent *TLS* debate on mistranslations in the *New English Bible*, Eliot owns to enjoying this sort of thing, "when I know, as I do now, that I have the right end of the stick." Suddenly Pound's name comes up, and Eliot confides that "Ezra was always a poor judge of people, and indeed of most things except poetry. He really did believe that his monetary ideas would change the world, however, and we were all tarred a bit by that brush. But he had great gifts, and I owe more to him than to anyone else. Which reminds me that I also owe him a letter; hm, hm, difficult to know what to say."

Eliot is in the habit of exclaiming "Yes?" during each pause in the conversation, but once, after V. recounts some of our Yugoslavian adventures, and at the same time voices some criticisms of Switzerland, he interposes a whole sentence: "Yes, I see what you mean, but I like it because more than any other country it resembles what it used to be."

OCTOBER 20

Oxford. Lunch at Isaiah Berlin's with Robert Graves, who is tall and military in bearing, large-eared, and, today anyway—it is the day of his inaugural lecture as Professor of Poetry—neatly shorn. Like Michelangelo, his nose has been broken, and—doubtless as with the sculptor also—his fingernails are rinded with dirt. When I.S. inquires about his present work, Graves says he is "disguised as a professor, implausibly." Graves then asks I.S. the same question, and I.S. tries to explain that he is engaged in "serial versification"; to which Graves replies that "Poetry is less purely genial than that and more demonstrably linked to moral questions." Graves begins a story: "I started down the street this morning thinking of a woman when suddenly my breast pocket burst into flames . . ." but whether the fire was merely allegorical or actually incendiary we never find out. He reports a conversation with David Ben-Gurion in which the Prime Minister testified that "Israelis are less good taxpayers than the citizens of Protestant countries, but rather better than those of Catholic countries," then moves on to "hallucinatory psilocybin mushrooms," claiming that they "can induce a state of grace." And about Paul of Tarsus: "He was not a Jew, of course, but a Syrian—you remember the Ebionite Epistle?" And Plato, "who did more harm than any one man before Freud." And Aristotle, "a thoroughly unpleasant character." And, finally, Alexander the Great: "Shall I tell you my new idea about him? It will take just three minutes," he says, actually looking at his watch. "Well, that legend of the Priest's serpent at the Oasis of Siwa is nonsense. Alexander decided to conquer the world entirely out of the jealous desire to surpass Dionysus. Like Dionysus, he had himself declared 'Son of Zeus.'"

Composing a "tonal row" and accompanying words of dedication for Isaiah Berlin's guest-book, I.S. asks for an English equivalent to the Russian *"kanitel."* Isaiah says that the word means a silver or gold skein, literally, but, commonly, a long and entangled argument—whereupon someone quotes "or ever the silver cord be loosed." At this, Graves puffs on his cheroot and jumps in with—he is the fastest man with words I have ever seen—"The Yiddish for that is *'magillah'* and the Greek and Latin are . . ." etcetera, etcetera. I.S. to Isaiah, in Russian: "Do you suppose he knows the Etruscan, too?"

Watching Graves listen enviously as I.S. and Isaiah speak Russian, I ask which of his languages he would most readily exchange for it. "German," he says, without hesitation. When he leaves shortly after, to deliver his lecture, Isaiah refers to him as "an Hibernian and an antinomian, as well as a would-be Pharisee, if that would help to depose Jesus and crown the White Goddess. But he is a true poet."

Isaiah reads passages from the Bible for us in Hebrew, not only translating word for word but explaining: "El, Elim, Elohim. Elohim is used to denote the lords of the others, the Hammurabis, the 'after strange gods.'" He promises to prepare a properly accented copy in Russian transliteration of the story of Abraham and Isaac if I.S. decides to use the episode. But he urges him to consider setting "the first and seventh days of the Creation, the two Holiest Days," a suggestion that fails to attract I.S. because of the length. "The music would be longer than a British weekend," he says.

1961

OCTOBER 23

London. At tonight's dinner for I.S., given by the Institute of Contemporary Arts, I sit next to E. H. Gombrich, who talks measurement psychology. At one point someone solicits his opinion of a picture. "I don't know," Gombrich says, his black eyes shining, his long, blunt chin looking more of both: "I am a historian and therefore prefer sitting on fences." At another table, Henry Moore chats with I.S. about the pigeon hazard and outdoor sculpture. I.S. tells him that what he remembers most clearly about Rodin's atelier is "the *démodé* furniture: it had absolutely no connection with what Rodin was doing."

Cambridge. Tea with E. M. Forster in his rooms at King's College. Several times the conversation grinds to a stop, each of them agonizing because Forster's silences are so acutely critical. Each time, moreover, it is Forster who artificially resuscitates the talk, with questions such as: "Did you come on the two-thirty-six train?" When Tolkien's name comes up, he says "I dislike whimsicality and I cannot bear good and evil on such a scale. But surprisingly I liked Thomas Mann's *The Holy Sinner.* Mann always *knew* a great deal, of course, but his other books were so *heavy.*" *Don Quixote* is mentioned, and Forster says, "I never reached the end of it, did you?"— and though obviously I did not, I wonder if I would admit it if I had. He talks about meeting Tagore in 1910, and about a trip to Uganda, this prompted by a question of mine concerning an object on his table, a smooth white box with wires attached to the base, like a jew's-harp. "The natives played these instruments as they worked on the roads," he says. "They cut the telephone wires for 'strings.'"

1961

He refers with evident pleasure to his lecture on music and the arts at Harvard, saying that "Someone had seen from my work how much I cared; I accepted the invitation within an hour of receiving it." And musing on the question of why "humanists" are intimidated by scientists, he says, rather marvelously, "We fear that we cannot tell them anything, and we are self-consciously aware of the nontechnical nature of our language."

A glint lights not only his blue eyes, but everything he says. Except that he does not say it louder than *mezzo piano,* so that I fear his requests for me to repeat several of my own remarks are owing not to deafness but to my savage American accent—that or the incredibility of the content. But one naturally regards the man as a judge. In fact, to him even the weather is matter for judgment. For when I ask if the rain has stopped, he settles silver-rimmed spectacles on his nose, goes to the window, says, "I will try to decide."

London. Cyril Connolly for dinner. He is an amusing *raconteur* but a bored listener, in which role, however, he relaxes his—as he himself describes it—"gimlet glare." He talks about the latest complaint of psychoanalysts, which is that "Women want to go much further back than the womb nowadays, in fact all the way back to papa's penis." And he describes a pre-lunch conversation with the President of Senegal on the merits of certain French wines, only to discover, when the meal was served, that the President was a strict Mohammedan. Connolly has the head of a Bacchus, a flat profile with Pekingese nose, and flat ears growing sprigs of hair—"earbrows," says I.S. later.

OCTOBER 31

Cairo. We are held up, on the way from the city to the Pyramids, by a flock of women in black cerements squatting in the road at the entrance to a hospital and loudly and dismally wailing. This open-air requiem fascinates I.S., the idea of professional mourners as much as the din they produce. But a leper-like pall hangs over them, too, as if they themselves might be from the Kingdom of Death.

At Cheops, now with television aerial, progress is again obstructed by a female mob, except that this time the girls are from Transatlantis and a little inland. They cling for dear life to the red-tasseled saddles of kneeling camels while bravely trying to look happy for a barrage of tripod cameras—their own cameras, inactive for once, dangling against their stomachs as if growing from them like umbilical tumors. Posing tourists this way is an old routine for the camels, of course, in spite of which, and though their thin shanks and shaggy skins show them to be unfit for less humiliating work, they yawp and whine most ungraciously. When the head drover finally shouts the order to rise, they dip backward and kick their forelegs outward like dancers, whereupon the air is rent with a chorus of Ohio-accented screams. Moments later the dismounted ladies, feeling pleased with themselves and exhilarated, as well as immensely relieved, no doubt tip accordingly. Some of them, in turn, prepare to photograph their guides, but are resisted, for the Arabs, like the Chinese, believe—it seems to me, with justification—that the camera steals your soul. I.S. dislikes the Pyramids, in any case. *"Francmaçonnerie,"* he says, and back we go across the Nile.

Each street and alley in the Bazaar is a stage for hundreds of small events, but the stercorous stench prevents us from watching any of them for long. Goldsmiths and silversmiths, brass founders and ironmongers, potters, treadle-loom weavers, dyers and cosmeticists, jewelers with loupes, leather-workers with awls: all work *en plein air.* The shopkeepers greatly outnumber these artisans, but the largest population of all is composed of the ineluctable interlopers, the unshakable cadgers, and the baksheesh-crying beggars.

We stop at the "Nile Vally Perfumes" shop, having been steered there about as casually as a tracer bullet, by a driver whose preliminary parley with the proprietor has clearly concluded in the promise of a mutually satisfying bargain. Although empty on our arrival, the shop is rapidly infiltrated by other people—a team, we eventually deduce, some of whose members simply pose as extremely contented customers while others try to wheedle us into buying or help to display such exotic commodities as sandalwood and musk, attars and sachet powders, mascara, antimony, kohl. The technique of salesmanship is confined to flattering the buyer's taste, and to imply that "Nile Vally Perfumes" runs a secret pipeline to Rochas and Chanel.

In the opening phase the proprietor himself stands benignly apart chewing cachous. But when V. orders a hundred amber cigarettes—at no doubt from four to five times the list price, if one existed—he glides into action. Confident, too, of recovering his investment, he even switches on the lights (we had not realized that there were any), the better to display a dozen rare but resistible products including an "aphrodisiac amberpaste" for I.S., "a blood-warming concoction, sir, very good for elderly gentlemen wishing to re-enter the portals of youth; yes, sir, an Open Sesame." When at last we escape—and it is far from easy—he thrusts a booklet into our pockets. It warns that: "Owing to the great number of designing merchants who vainly try to imitate my wares—an impossibility owing to their excellence—and, furthermore, use a name similar to mine in order to deceive, I have registered in the Courts of Law to obviate entirely. I therefore advise my clients to take great care that my FULL name is printed on each article that comes out of my store NILE VALLY PERFUMES." Some vain imitator probably gave himself away by spelling it "Valley."

Still in the Bazaar, we drink arrack and ‏ﻚﻟ ﻚﻛ‎ (Coca-Cola) at a sidewalk café. Within a radius of a few yards from our table a man is tooling a piece of metal, a boy is honing a knife on a whetstone, a woman is suckling a baby from her mud-caked bosom, a donkey is staling in the dust, and an old man, to whom no one pays the slightest attention, is apparently dying in the gutter. At the next table two turbaned Arabs share a narghile, handing the stem back and forth without wiping the mouthpiece. But we are hardly seated before peddlers besiege us with nougat and sesame-seed cakes, pomegranates and yellow guavas, sandals (a load of at least a hundred draped on cords around the neck), and parrots and lovebirds in cages strapped, à la Papageno, to the seller's back. "O.K.? O.K.?" they say, as who in Cairo does not? And knowing that we cannot refuse them a few piastres, they are not easily eluded. Some are blind, moreover, and some suffer from trachoma and the dread bilharzia. They are a scratching lot, too, with especially itchy pubic regions, unless this gesture is for assurance that the instruments of their gender are still there.

None of the objectives on our after-dinner taxi itinerary is half as engaging as the driver himself. His get-up is part Arab—a gallabiya—and part Chicago-gangster-in-the-twenties—a bevel-brimmed fedora worn at a menacing tilt; but the gangster in him is the most bonhomous imaginable. As with all Cairo cabbies, his goal is to deposit us at one of the nightclubs which pay commissions. And to enlist my compliance in this aim he talks luringly of the pectoral attributes of a certain houri or odalisque at the Arabi Hasha Club. "We go Arabi Hasha, Egyptian place, lovely." But everything Egyptian is "lovely," just as everything American—pronounced as two words, "Emery Cain"—is "verygoodverynice" (one word). Would we perhaps like to visit the Hilton Hotel and hear Emery Cain's music? Is verygoodverynice. Well, actually we wouldn't. What I.S. wants, of all things, is some halvah. And so off we go, only to find that the store recommended by Mr. Verygoodverynice, the Aly Hassan El Hati, in spite of being "Egyptian" and "lovely," as well as very far away and expensive on the meter, stocks nothing even remotely near that line.

Each of Mr. V.'s excursions into "English" is followed by an explosion of self-appreciative laughter and a soliloquy in Arabic. But as a guide and source of information, Mr. Verygoodverynice has shortcomings. One of them

1961

is that he snobbishly reproves our interest in neighborhoods he calls "very cheap parts, strictly for wogs." Another is that he cannot read. "Who is that?" I.S. asks, pointing to a statue of Rameses the Second. "Oh, a statue." "Of whom?" I.S. persists, lowering the aim of his finger to the inscription on the base. "Very famous man." "What man, what is his name?" "Oh, Egyptians never put *names*." But we end up liking this very good, very nice fellah to the extent that we almost swallow his parting bait: "Bye. See you tomorrow. What time?"

At night the streets look as if a Shriners' convention had been roused from sleep and, perhaps because of a fire, only just had time to grab its fezzes and run: a city in pajamas, then, some sleeveless like chasubles, and some striped, as if there had been a jail break. Some of the men also wear colored Kufayah scarves, and some a lace skullcap that seems distinctly an article of bedroom apparel. But the street noise, radios blaring from cafés, automobile horns tooting without let-up, as they do at American weddings, is in no wise nocturnal. Neither is the *tempo* of street life. The waiters hustle their hookahs and coffee trays at a more rapid pace than they do in the daytime, and at one place the pedestrians actually hurry out of the path of the murderous Mr. Verygoodverynice, holding up their nighties as they run like Carpaccio's monks fleeing the lion of St. Jerome.

NOVEMBER 1

At sun-up the river is flagged with sails, the upstream traffic, like in-bound New York commuters, scarcely moving, while the downstream races out of sight as if propelled by nuclear power. A felucca with "FLY TWA" on its sail cruises slowly up and rapidly down the stretch of hotel-fronted river, over and over, like a streetwalker.

We spend three hours in the Museum of Egyptian Art, and another half-hour dodging a dragoman at the entrance. The building itself is hideous, and the crowding of the contents suffocating. A high portion of the latter is macabre, too, inasmuch as the entire first floor is a mummy morgue, and the other floors are abundantly stocked with such items as mummies' rope wigs (which look like clumps of discolored seaweed), and eviscerated organs, which are exhibited together with their resin-soaked wrappings and canopic jars. But because we know Pharaonic culture largely from tombs, after all, the Museum is chiefly and inevitably a repository of funerary artifacts. Moreover, though both the provenance and the eschatology are repugnant to us, it was hardly the same to believers in the Happy Nilotic Hunting Ground of thirty centuries ago.

Even so, the mortuary aspect of the Museum is less stultifying than the sameness. For the same deities, the same postures and patterns, the same sculptural motives, are repeated through dozens of dynasties and thousands of years. In short, the traditions are iron-clad, and anyone feeling the need to "escape from freedom" should spend some time here contemplating the other extreme. Finally, in addition to the gruesomeness and the monotony, many or most of the objects are mutilated or defaced. At least half of the statues are decapitated or dismembered, and many of the torsos are held together by orthopedic appliances and the plaster filler used for surgical models. In sum, every fractured Pharaoh in the building qualifies for the Purple Heart ten times over, and pschent sounds like a dirty word.

We being unable to take Pharaonic art as a whole, what, at the end of the long trek, has given us the most pleasure? Speaking for myself, I would say the representations of birds, fish, and animals—the lions, leopards, monkeys, anubises, horses, rams, and dappled cows. And the Nubian rooms where, uniquely, the statues of the women are the same height as those of the men. And some of the jewelry—among the acres of turquoise and coral-line amulets, scarab seals, sigil and signet rings long since copied and mass-manufactured. Some of the furniture is attractive, too, though not, to my taste, those treasures of *nouveau riche* rococo from the Tutankhamen tomb, that Eighteenth Dynasty Forest Lawn. Ultimately, too, some objects attract simply by virtue of their modernity: a Las Vegas gaming board, for instance, and a carpenter's kit complete with levelers, plumb lines, T-squares, rules.

We hobble out of the Museum at one o'clock on wooden legs, then, stepping through the gates, are nearly run over by a truck of the "Nefertiti Laundry Service."

On the road to Sakkara, in the cooler part of the afternoon, we pass, first, a flock of sheep being driven into a slaughterhouse, each doomed animal daubed on its neck with bloodlike dye; and, second, a wedding procession, which is not a very arresting sight for the reason that the male Arab's dress is so much like a bride's anyway. The bride is enthroned with her maids in a tall donkey cart. No two donkey carts are the same size, incidentally, but the wheels of most are so large that the linchpin is above the height of the animal. They carry fruit, copra, tuns of water, palm baskets, and loads of men looking like prisoners in tumbrils on the way to the guillotine.

To the right of the road is a canal, polluted and uninviting, but a bathtub and laundry, fish pond and sewage system for a million human beings. The Nile, on the other side, is not always in view, but inferable from the masts of dhows and feluccas rising above the levee. The rich land between road and river grows maize and sugar cane, whose tall stalks are made taller by ibises, for the plant bends under the birds only at landings, when they come in like ski-jumpers, then at the last moment tuck in their legs like hydroplanes. But what infinite pleasure to behold this biblical landscape: the fertile fields, the carriage of women with amphorae on their heads, the buffalos slowly turning the water wheels (goaded by officious overseer dogs): the landscape, in short, of Joseph's Egypt, except for our own automobile.

At Memphis we wait while a trainload of apparently disconnected drom-edary heads and humps passes by, these features alone protruding above the frames of the flatcars. "Modern" Memphis is a cluster of duplex mud huts whose upper levels are indented like the adobe huts in Taos pueblo, and whose lower levels are connected to the superstratum by ladders, another reminder of Taos, as well as of Amerindian cliff dwellings. Beggars are even more numerous here than in Cairo. They ambush our automobile while it is still moving, virtually forcing us off the road while demanding to be photographed for money. For money, too, young boys shimmy up the tallest palm trees, barefoot but as fast as monkeys. A short way beyond Memphis, I.S. describes a black goat, tethered by the roadside, as "a color sounding board; just as an orchestra tunes to 'A,' so to a painter the whole landscape would have to tune to this black."

At Sakkara, we traipse by a row of the feet of otherwise demolished statues, like a scene from a surrealist movie; then descend to the tomb of Mera, whose tinted low reliefs of birds and fish, of gazelles, mongooses, ibexes, porcupines, hippos, and crocodiles, are worth all the pyramids of Egypt and other countries in which that dullest of forms has flourished. Mera himself is portrayed in various guises, one of them as a decoy on a hunting expedition, wearing the skin, claws, and tail of a leopard; on another occasion wrapped in a robe and listening to his wife play the harp; and on still another reclining on a high divan while his musical spouse sniffs a lotus. The colors are vivid even through a fine patina of blown sand.

The inland road back to Cairo is congested with men and animals returning from the fields, the men shouldering hoes and flails exactly like those in the Mera friezes. We come to a Bedouin camp, the air above it blue with smoke from cooking fires. The women, carrying jugs single-file to and from a roadside well, are uniformly black-robed and their faces are uniformly covered by sequinned veils, though some wear amber necklaces as well, and the ankles of some are ringed with heavy silver bangles. The evening air is silky, and the only sound in the riverain villages is the murmur of nesting birds.

In the Kumais Restaurant with our new Copt friend, Fares Sarapheem, we squat on low leather cushions around a taller center cushion set with a round brass tray; the walls are covered with damascenes woven with epigraphs from the Koran. As soon as we are seated—in fact, with the speed with which chlorinated icewater is served in American restaurants—a "busboy" deposits a handful of bullet-shaped incense pellets on our tray. He and all other low-level waiters are dusky Nubians, with embossed, tattoo-marked foreheads, whereas the superior waiters are light bronze Arabs, and the head waiter is "white." In short, a hierarchy of pigmentation obtains here, as it seems to everywhere in Egypt, to judge by hotels and private houses, where the masters are identified by lightness of skin, the sutlers and lower servants by progressive shades of darkness. We hear again tonight from brown and khaki-colored people—or at any rate not conspicuously pale ones—the remark that so-and-so "works like a nigger."

The meal begins with prawns and stuffed grape leaves (*warak-enap*), then moves on to *dorad, karouss,* and *fateh,* which is the main dish, a spicy stew of rice and boiled meat. The Western palate—mine, anyway—takes more readily to oriental sweetmeats, and tonight's is the delicious *puri,* a kind

1961

of Shredded Wheat cooked in honey. While we eat, Fares Sarapheem holds forth on the Copts, "the true Egyptians, the Christian inheritors of Pharaonic Egypt. The Coptic language," he goes on, "is a rendering of hieroglyphic Egyptian in the Greek alphabet, with seven additional letters to signify sounds that do not exist in Greek; but it is a dead dialect now, surviving only in the Mass." Then, switching to politics, he says that Nasser's dissolution of the latifundia system has robbed the Copts of their wealth and supremacy. Yet they support his foreign policy because it has kept Egypt free from foreign intervention and foreign commercial domination (the bogey of the British cotton-wallah). "Egypt was a subject country from Cleopatra until 1917," he adds, "and for six hundred years our khedive was the puppet of Istanbul." But I am summarizing and hence deflavoring Fares Sarapheem's very original English, among whose felicities are many honorifics for ourselves, as well as little introductions of the sort: "Perhaps it would be interesting to mention . . ."

Walking from the restaurant to the Kasr el Nil we come upon a blind man singing for alms in the most beautifully floriated style—musical *passementerie*—I have ever heard.

NOVEMBER 2

The Delta road to Alexandria is two-lane most of the way, and it is in good condition all of the way. Police checkpoints, like tollbooths on American turnpikes, are numerous, however, and we are obliged to stop and be counted at each of them; they invariably display photographs of a smiling, toothpaste-ad Colonel Nasser. Of the beasts of burden on the road, the women outnumber both the donkeys and the camels, and *no* woman is empty-handed. They carry head-trays with round loaves of *rayesh,* backloads of panniers and heavy bales, and as often as not, babes-in-arms as well. Woman's uniform is black—otherwise how in this transvestite society would we tell them from the men?—with exceptions in Alexandria, where a few Europeanized rebels (or are they fallen women?) flaunt themselves in washed blues and even pink and orange.

If it were not so cruel, the donkey and camel traffic would be marvelous to watch. Very tiny donkeys carrying huge sacks and a passenger like a garnishing atop are a common sight, albeit a less pretty one than when the animal is otherwise freightless and the rider jogs along, legs out in a wide "V" and sandals dangling from toes. *No* load can make a camel look less supercilious, but the creature's long, knock-kneed, foreleg-amble so reminds us of Aldous Huxley that we are bound if only on that account to regard it with fondness and respect. Never again, though, will I use the expression "camel-colored" (have I ever?). They are a thousand shades of pink, puce, fawn, bistre, black, and even white.

Owing to the lowness of the land, the cemeteries on the south side of each village are elevated, and the chimney-like nodules of the tombs protrude above the walls. We see domed marabouts, too, and from time to time small mosques. Every field has at least one turbaned and gallabiya-ed scarecrow, but not many crows appear to be very scared, and probably as large a share of the crops is consumed by these and other predacious birds as by the farming fellaheen. The latter, naked except for turbans and diaper-like dhotis, seed the fields from shoulder sacks; or work the Archimedean water screws; or, armed with sticks, clout the blindfolded oxen who circle the water wheels.

Mast tips of otherwise unseen feluccas—in altogether unseen canals— move across the flat land like periscopes, but the boats themselves are visible only from bridges. Road-repairing is women's work, of course, and it is evidently the lot of the oldest and weakest to carry the heaviest scuttles of gravel and stone. At one point we see a man in a white jibbah with shiny brass buttons ride by a squad of these laboring women and shade himself from them with a parasol; and whereas he is mounted on an impeccably groomed Arabian horse, a daughter or wife follows him, purple-veiled and presumably the proper number of paces behind, on a mangy mule.

By noon the roadside world is asleep. Even the chickens stop their scratching while men sprawl in mule carts, in rope nets under mule carts, on the ground, in doorways, and perhaps even in the houses, which become prettier and more prosperous-looking the farther we penetrate the Delta. At Tanta, capital of Lower Egypt, the yashmaks are mere bikinis—concealing the face only below the nose and marking, one assumes, a triumph of emancipation—compared with the full masks worn by the women of Cairo. In the next village, Damanhur, a skinned water buffalo is suspended by its tail in the middle of the main street, perhaps to center the flies.

The air is fresher of a sudden, and cooler and more moist, and the vegetation changes abruptly, banyans being common now, and groves of date palms pregnant with udder-shaped yellow and red fruit. The road entering Alexandria is also a quay on its riparian side, and because the longshoremen are bent too low under their loads to see their way, older men lead them by the hand across the teeming highway. There are feazings by each tied-up boat, suggesting that the sailors also perform rope tricks.

The dress of most Alexandrians on the Mediterranean side of the city is European and so are many of their names. Along with the usual "Fawzi" and "Ali Ibrahim" are the "Banco Donizetto," the "Rosenthal Brothers," and "Socrates & Co." But French is the first European language, to judge from the notices on postal boxes as well as from conversation in the Union Restaurant, where we dine on grilled *crevettes, loup de mer,* a compote of dates in warm buffalo milk, and a bottle of white "Clos de Pharaoh." We hire a Hantur, afterward, to go to the Column of Pompey, but stop en route by the gates of a cemetery to listen to the keening of a band of professional *pleureuses* who, squatting on their haunches with black shawls over their heads, look like a flock of ravens.

In the early afternoon the city is emptied as if by a plague, and even on the beaches the only people are two fishermen caulking a caïque. Our new, English-speaking driver is indignant about Lawrence Durrell's "misrepresentations of Alexandria," though it seems to us that the novelist's crime, in this regard, was in having made the city so much more interesting than it is. We follow the beach road to the Royal Palace, now a museum, and to Samalek, the Royal Harem, now a hotel, both prize exhibits in any collection of freak architecture. Except for its "keyhole" Arabic windows, the palace is an example of flamboyant super-crenellated Boca Raton Gothic, and with gargoyles too; and because each new king added a monstrosity, it is possible to regret the fall of the monarchy purely out of architectural curiosity. The lawns are the greenest in Egypt, however, and the gardens, which smell like hair tonic, the best kept.

The sun is low when we re-enter the city, and life has returned to the streets; and not only life, for we are delayed in the Greek quarter by the passage of a cherub-gilded, eight-horse hearse. Elsewhere Muslims are spreading prayer mats on the sidewalks or already praying in fetal position and turned as if magnetically toward Mecca (as white ants are magnetically sensitized to the north). When we start across the salt flats of Maryot, the rim of the sun is still afloat, but it disappears in a sudden dive, like the keel of the *Titanic.* The beginning of the lake shore, where pole-propelled fishing boats (the *tarada*) knife through the dense reeds, is profuse with ducks and other birds, and farther south, in the shallows, a herd of buffalo oozes to the neck in the mud, like overweight bankers in Turkish baths. But how true Yeats's adjective is:

> O what a sweetness strayed
> By the Mareotic sea . . .

Liberation Province begins hopefully, with new houses and newly irrigated patches of land, but the hope quickly fades in a spinifex and scrub desert. We come to a vast nomad encampment, where the men are huddled around fires in front of large flat tents. Camels fodder or squat on the ground looking like a domed oriental city. Otherwise the only habitations all the way to Ghizeh are a gas station at the halfway point and some tattered British barracks from *ca.* 1942. All through the black night our headlights flash on Arabs walking along the road and looking like ghosts as their white robes billow in the rising wind.

NOVEMBER 4

Cairo. We count nine chandelier stores—including the "El Ismail Youssef Mohammed Chandelier Company"—on our way to the Coptic Museum this morning. Chandeliers are a major industry, next in volume to tourism, it would seem, and every sizable home is reputed to possess several of them.

The Museum lies within a Roman redoubt whose walls are three thicknesses of brick and five of stone. The interior is cool and clean, and the contents, in agreeable contrast to the Museum of Egyptian Art, are intelligently displayed. Our difficulty here is in identifying the Coptic in the absence of such obvious iconographic clues as camels, Angk talismans, black-faced saints, the Cross with the three-step standard (representing the three days before the Resurrection). The animal and bird motifs of much early Coptic art—the lions, donkeys, rabbits, eagles, and doves—could be Byzantine as well, for example, and many of its later products are distinguishable from those of Islam only in that they have been stamped somewhere with a Christian symbol, the forms having been taken over intact. Cufic copies of the Gospels are on exhibit, and parchment lectionaries with Coptic and the beautiful right-angular Cufic script on facing sides. Moreover, the Museum itself, with its honeycombed, sunlight-tempering window grilles, and its balcony ventilators, is Muslimite. Finally, then, only the Ethiopian treasures—a barbaric crown of Menelik II and the products of the loom, identified by wonderfully animated figures in many-colored threads—are readily recognizable (to me) as Coptic.

A monk with a sextant-shaped beard, like Tintoretto's Nicolas Priuli, escorts us through the adjoining Church of St. Sergius. This, however, is so Moorish that without our monk we would forget it *is* a church. A spidery old woman in black rags sits on the outside doorstep nibbling nettles.

We eat incomparably better than that ourselves at the home of Victor Simaika, the son of the founder of the Museum, and a cousin of Fares Sarapheem. Mr. Simaika is very *mondain,* or so it would appear from his references to polo games with the Duke of Edinburgh, from the display of photographs with Barbara Hutton and the stengah-drinking set, and from the blizzard of so many other society-column names that there are hardly any gaps between. Mr. Simaika has just returned from the airport, where he has dispatched a favorite Persian cat to Zürich for medical attention (Niehans and Jung, probably). But he is a great charmer, too; indeed somewhat more than that, for without so much as dropping his monocle he confesses to the truth of his reputation as a "big ladies' killer"; which leaves one wondering as much about the large, mysterious females as about Mr. Simaika's methods, whether routine strangulations or what. Otherwise the conversation touches on Evelyn White's *The Curse of the Copts* (apparently many Copts still believe in the ancient malediction); on the Coptic paintings at Faras, on the Nubian Nile, uncovered by the expedition of the Polish Academy of Sciences; on the monachism of Cairo's Bektashi Moslem sect; on the Coptic addition of Love to Paulist Faith, Hope, and Charity.

Mr. Simaika's apartment faces the Nile above a garden of sycamores and jasmine, and as we dine, sails glide by the window like giant moths.

My smallpox certificate having been filched yesterday, along with an otherwise valueless wallet, I go to a hospital to be revaccinated. The operation is performed in a forbiddingly dirty and malodorous room, where I roll up my sleeve with no confidence, and indeed do not receive any cleansing daub of alcohol. Has the needle itself been sterilized? Too late to think about that now, or to pray to American gods of hygiene. In fact, the nurse jabs me as if I were personally responsible for Suez. By dinnertime I have a fever and my arm is a festering mump.

The Mosque of Ibn Tulun is one of the great buildings of the world, yet our driver, a Copt, has no idea how to find it. When, according to the map, we cannot be more than three blocks away, he stops to take soundings from pedestrians, none of whom, of course, has ever heard of it, though everyone knows all about *us:* "American?" "Money, please." "O.K." One urchin climbs aboard, offering to guide us, and he directs us over a wide area before we realize he has merely chosen us to be the sponsors of his first automobile ride. But another waif, this one with a book under arm, volunteers and finally fulfills the service, though when at last we reach the great dun-colored walls, he reviles us because of the size of our—extra large, as it happens— baksheesh. After crossing the ambulatory and swaddling our feet in felt, we enter a courtyard the size of a piazza in a medium-size Italian town. In the right portico, the women pray in purdah behind a wall of rugs suspended from a wire; while in the *liwan,* to the left, the men recite their prayers kneeling in groups of six, of which one member of each group is slightly to the fore. No clergymen or sacramental middlemen are anywhere in sight.

NOVEMBER 5

To untrained and infidel eyes a day in the Museum of Islamic Art is several hours too long or several years too short. And as "taste" becomes an imperative in the absence of religio-historical and religio-cultural blinkers, we force our simple prejudice for things Persian to the point at which we begin actively to dislike things Egyptian, above all the brassware and polychrome lustres. But Islamic art, Persian included, is an art of ambages—of meshing and interlacing, of fretting, filigreeing, foliating, lobing, and lozenging—and its patterns are too complex for our unaccustomed eyes. Even the water jets in the fountains coil like cobras.

From the outside, the Mohammed Ali Mosque suggests a great crustacean, partly because of its mustache of minarets—around one of which, when we arrive, three ravens are wheeling like a propeller. But from the inside, where its many-colored lamps are shaped like alembics and retorts, it might be a laboratory. Saladin's citadel, nearby, is a walled, medieval city, with pennants and oriflammes flying from its towers. But the atmosphere is one of smoke and dust and flies (haloes of circumvolant flies crown us the moment we leave the car), besides which it reeks of filth and urine and of the nauseating stench of abattoirs. Begging is the only occupation of the people, moreover, most of whom swarm about us *like* flies. Many of them are maimed, and many have red, vitreous eyes, or eyes covered with white film; and pitted and scrobiculated faces; and coughs, from the very catacombs of the lungs. For Cairo is appallingly full of sickness, disease, and death. Funerals are held in the streets, in large, carpeted, and well-furnished tents, and it is rare to traverse the city without encountering at least one of them. Vast necropolitan suburbs exist, too, in which hutches are built over the tombs, thus enabling relatives to spend their holy days in proximity to the remains of the departed.

NOVEMBER 6

It is marketing day as well as wash day in the river villages, to judge from the spread of wares on the canal bridges, and the spread of laundry and the copper ewers on the canal banks. South of Aiyat the road signs are in Arabic only, and life is abruptly more primitive; we detour around two men hacking a still-bleeding buffalo in the middle of the road, and going about their grisly work as nonchalantly as if they were chopping a log. But why are we horrified by the *"condition humaine"* in the villages, whereas the pastoral life and the life of toil in the fields, neither of which can be that much better, do not repel us? (Because of the romanticizing notion that these modes of existence are more "natural," meaning that we see no barrier and little difference between a man and his animals? I had better not pursue the thought, in any case, lest my own prejudices be traced back to illustrations on date boxes, so romance-inducing to me as a child.) During *kayf,* the noon siesta, the verges are strewn with exanimate Arabs who look like cadavers, each face covered with a burnous.

When we turn from the river to the desert, forsaking the parasols of eucalyptus and Australian pine for the open sun and sand, the temperature leaps fifteen degrees. The world of Mobil Oil gasoline pumps is left behind, too, and we depend on nomad gas stations—mule carts that roam the desert roads with tanks the size of puncheons or Porto wine barrels, and with siphons hanging from their bungholes like umbilical cords. At a desert guardpost we are greeted with straight-arm Nazi salutes and the password "Nasser"; the police camels here are white, like state troopers' patrol cars in America. A few miles farther, near a walled city with domed dovecotes on every roof, a caravan crosses the road, each camel loaded with hay, through which their humps show like turrets of partly camouflaged tanks.

The desert people are evidently accustomed to great privacy. Men, naked except for their turbans, are cooling themselves in the roadside culvert, and we surprise a Bedouin woman without her veil; she has apparently failed to gauge the approach of our car, perhaps never having seen any vehicle move that fast. Once we nearly collide with a thirty-year-old Packard crammed with at least a dozen Arabs, automobiles being so infrequent that confrontations involve a crisis as to who shall pass on which side.

Then, lo and behold, at El Fayum a new red Cadillac convertible, an oil sheik's bauble, no doubt, shines in the restaurant parking lot as if it had been newly minted this morning and flown in from Michigan minutes ago. A Bedouin woman with a ring through her nose stands staring at it in wonder until, noticing our interest in *her,* she shakes her fists at us and struts off like a peahen. In the restaurant, under a plaque commemorating a banquet that Churchill gave here for King ibn-Saud on February 17, 1945, we eat scaloppini of water buffalo, while outside a snow of ibises settles on the shore of the lake.

We spend part of a forty-hour delay, "for engine repairs," in the airport, part back at the hotel. A Qantas official apologizes for the "inconvenience," but says that it is also "the reason our planes are so safe." I.S.: "Naturally. They never leave the ground." We rise over Cairo and the Pyramids, over the Monastery of St. Catherine in Sinai, over Suez, and Aqaba, over the walled cities and emptiness of Arabia. Somewhere above the Persian Gulf the bar is closed down, just as the bar of the "Super Chief" is closed nearing Kansas. At Karachi a Sikh policeman comes aboard, carrying a lathi, and wearing jodhpurs, a blue turban with a white feather, a neatly twirled black mustache. Four hours later, at Calcutta, the clothing of the boarding officials and of the maintenance squad is reduced to dhotis; both here and in Bangkok these crews are accompanied by mosquitoes and heat. Violent bumping and shaking occur over the Gulf of Siam—"slight turbulence," the pilot says—and the landing at Singapore, where blue-black Malays empty the ashtrays and primp the pillows, is very rough.

1961

Day breaks over the South China Sea and Borneo. The landing strip at Darwin is a platter of red earth on a promontory of rivers and jungle. We enter the terminal for a health inspection and a breakfast of gin and orange juice, then fly for three more hours, over desert, black hills, and, finally, red-roofed cottages on sand dunes, to Sydney, which, says I.S., "looks, from the air, like impetigo."

We cross the Tasman Sea to Auckland this afternoon in a bumpy turbo-prop. To a Sydney Airport official who has been explaining that he must pay overweight, I.S. says, "But I understand the *logic* of it. What I am objecting to is the money." One of our fellow passengers is Field Marshal Lord Alexander, with whom we chat in a V.I.P. waiting room. He reads a Perry Mason during the flight and is greeted in Auckland by hip-hip-hooraying schoolgirls in kilts. Our first view of New Zealand is a rim of very white sand between a light green sea and dark green hills. We stay in the Rodean, a boardinghouse with a view of the bay and not much else.

In the harbor we watch mussel-gatherers follow the ebbing tide, picking the pools in the uncovered land; and watch a trawler, whose Maori boatmen talk like Cockneys, haul in a net spangled with shellfish. England is closer here than it is in Sydney, and not only in cricket fields, bowling lawns, church spires, tall oaks, and Empire names like Khyber Pass Road, but also in the

Constable-like clouds, the shadows, the greens. Each house has its own "tidy plot" and its own flower and vegetable gardens, and—the ultimate English-ness—everyone is a gardener. "That hedge'd take a bit of cutting," our driver remarks indignantly, but though he disclaims a moment later that he is a "horticulturist," the sight of some yellow gorse, "that noxious weed," nearly puts him out of sorts altogether.

He pronounces "Maori" with the German "au" ("Mauree"), and his "Yes" might have a German or Scandinavian umlaut ("Yoess")—when he uses the word at all, that is, for he prefers to say "Righto." His "r" is a combination of Kennedy Bostonian and Dixie. Thus, we are driving an English cah in a land of flowhs, and Wellington is the seat of Pahlamint. The accent of the waitress at the Rodean is more remote; breakfast, for example, consists of braid and eegs, unless one prefers scones (rhyme it with prawns). Small hills are hillies to her, too, and she translates our whiskey orders to "nips"—the furtiveness suggested by her word, however, being appropriate to the restrictive conditions in which the article is both acquired and consumed. And, finally, cockney expressions occur even in the language of the law, for road signs warn the motorist to TIP NO RUBBISH.

1961

Pride in natural New Zealand dominates conversation, and little curiosity is evinced, however strongly it may be felt, about the wonders of other lands. The tone of this talk is that of an appeal to prospective settlers, but the allure—which includes such benefits as free hospitalization—is offset, in my case, by the bachelor tax. Almost as apparent, in the conversations we have had, is the rivalry with Australia: "Our horses are better racers. We have better lobsters . . . ," and so on. (For the Australian attitude, I quote a baggage porter at Sydney Airport: "Going to New Zealand for a few days? That'd be enough, I should think.") This afternoon's tour is accompanied by a steady discourse on New Zealand history and local lore, during which I.S., in the back seat, falls asleep. Then, after about twenty minutes, he wakes with a start, exclaiming "The street!" The driver, at that point talking about the New Zealand Navy, asks "What street?" and I.S., after a strenuous pause, manages to say, "What is the street of our hotel?" confessing later that he had dreamed he was in Paris and was directing a taxi to his old apartment there.

Dinner at the Rodean consists of cockle fritters, steamed *hapuka,* and bread served with about a pound of butter per person.

NOVEMBER 15

We fly to Wellington, with good views, on the way, of Mount Ruapehu, its smooth flanks covered with a snow mantle, and of the Ngauruhoe volcano, which is smoking. The landing, in strong winds, is very bumpy, but Wellington must be one of the world's windiest capitals: we are almost always wet with spindrift blowing from the straits in a semi-permanent gale. Wellington, moreover, strikes us as even more Victorian than Auckland. Its most attractive buildings, those with Gothic windows, iron railings, and iron awnings, are that in any case, but these the Wellingtonians are eagerly demolishing. As we pass a statue of Victoria herself, I.S. remarks that "she looks exactly like a policeman."

Among the two hundred hands I.S. is obliged to shake at a reception given by United States Ambassador Akers this afternoon are those of other ambassadors, the New Zealand Prime Minister, many members of Pahlamint. Large N.Z. lady to I.S.: "Frankly, Mr. Stravinsky, I like the *Firebird* best of all your works." I.S.: "And what a charming hat you have." Small N.Z. gent to I.S.: "People here are very fond of modern music. We had half a program of your own works once" (I.S., later: "My *Scheherazade,* no doubt") "and we've heard pieces by Shostakovich and Ache [Egk]." Wife of high N.Z. dignitary to I.S.: "Do you like architecture, Mr. Stravinsky?" I.S.: "Let me think about it."

NOVEMBER 18

We drive along the straits to the harbor entrance, where a concrete igloo still stands as a reminder of the war. Along the roadside are marigolds, foxgloves, wild sweet peas, wild daisies, golden wattles, pale lupins, roses, and geraniums the size of peonies. Visit from Doris M., a childhood pen pal of one of my sisters, now married to a sheep rancher in Parnassus, a railway junction in Samuel Butler country on the South Island. Doris has never traveled beyond her home island, except once before to Wellington, and that twenty-two years ago. The journey here has been her first in an airplane, moreover, and, of course, she has never seen a symphony orchestra. This is the most exciting weekend of her life, therefore, or so she says. But tomorrow is shearing day in Parnassus, and she must be there by 4:30 AM, when the musterers take to the hills and before the dawn birds can give the alarm to the sheep. She talks to us of sheep-tending: of lambing, docking, and dipping; of the crutching of ewes; of the eyeclipping of heavy fleeces; of the care of the hoggets and the fate of the culls. Her hands are scarred, we notice, not from sheep, of course, but from crayfish, which she hunts in snorkel and fins though without gloves. Another of her seaside pastimes is making earrings from surf-polished marl. And she says that while driving along the beach not long ago, she heard "a fat lady sobbing" but, running to the edge of the water, found a dolphin dying of a propeller wound. "Tears rolled from its eyes, and its cries were terribly human." She talks about blue ducks and the mutton birds (wedge-tailed shearwaters) which migrate from the south of South Island to Siberia, and which only Maoris are licensed to hunt. Cold mutton bird is considered a great delicacy by some, but others consider it indigestibly rich.

No danger, in the St. George Hotel, of our stomachs being put to the test. In fact, the fare must be among the least rich, in all senses, even among the world's worst hotels. Besides which the St. George enforces an intolerably puritanical code. Visitors may call at prescribed times only, as in a reformatory and by suffering some of the same suspicion. Wine, which is available in none of the city restaurants, *can* be obtained in the hotel, but only by registered guests willing to be regarded as depraved. The day, moreover, is as rule-ridden as a boarding school. Coffee is not served at night, but only tea, and it is the other way around at noon. And unless one affixes a special notice to one's door, one is inundated at daybreak with a clattering service of compulsory tea.

We fly to Sydney at sunset, which is in blue, red, and black layers like a flag, above a precipice of cold light. I.S., looped by the time the pilot makes his rounds, tells him that he feels "like a planet."

NOVEMBER 21

I.S. informs a press conference this morning that he is struggling with his "global image," saying, "I feel upside down and way down there. We have a geography of the spirit, after all, and in it, a Great Barrier Reef of the soul." Someone asks whether he has had "any ideas" since his arrival in Australia. "I have 'ideas,' as you say, all my life, and neither more nor less in Australia than anywhere else."

Australian oysters are the best in the world. Or so we conclude after a dinner at Lady Lloyd-Jones's, an 1840's plantation house with attractive gardens and gazebos. Lady L.-J. is very high-spirited herself, and in fact less tame than her lions, who include Patrick White tonight, as well as I.S. A rugged figure with a craggy jaw and a hard stare, White laments "the unofficial censorship in Australia, the provincialism that patronizes second-rate imports above first-rate locals, and the many intellectual deprivations of life in the antipodes." But he prefers to talk about ballet, books, the music of Mahler. When he talks at all, that is, for he is a man of silent temperament—the only nonbuoyant Australian so far—as well as a lonely artist, owing to which he has probably groaned all evening inside. He promises to attend our concert, even though it is to take place, so we have discovered at today's rehearsal, in a vast Victorian cavern with an opulent echo.

1961

NOVEMBER 22

Reminders of Empire: the statue of Captain Cook, the Victorian brownstone houses, the names like Hotel Castlereagh, the zoning by trades—Macquarie Street, for example, being a surgeons' row like Harley Street. But England vanishes with very little below-the-surface scratching. Nor is the physiognomy of Sydney predominantly English, or without good architecture—as well as amusing: the tiny cottages with tall steeples, and the polychrome houses with valentine-lace ironwork. The most attractive buildings, however, those with broad verandahs and white columns, are the work of Francis Greenway, the convict architect whom the free settlers continued to ostracize even after he had built the best of their city.

The Taronga Zoo. Malayan otters have kind faces with Edwardian whiskers, but they squeal like pinched schoolgirls. The kangaroos and wallabies are a distressing sight in the mass, for they seem to limp like cripples then, and their stockades suggest hospital wards whose patients spend their time picking each other's fleas. Koalas are marsupials, too, but nocturnal; thus when a keeper plucks one from the bole of a tree and plumps it in my arms, it turns sleepily from the light. "Cute," V. says, "but add a cigar and it could pass for a banker." When we approach the nearby gorilla cage, its yellow-eyed and inhospitable tenant flings an armful of sawdust in our direction.

The birds are gorgeous and noisy. Except the kiwi, which is not only apteryx but also agoraphobic: it seldom leaves its hut, as if, aware that extinction is near, it wished to co-operate or even to hurry the process. We see red-headed lorikeets, red-eyed manucodes, gaudy macaws, cassowaries, and "satin birds," who fill their nests with bits of anything blue. Some of the birds of paradise have opal eyes and scissor-tails five times the length of their chassis; some are black velvet, with even longer antennae—for jaded lovers, says I.S. Kookaburras, with their recessive lower mandibles and hearty, knowing laughs, look and sound disgustingly complacent.

NOVEMBER 25

Melbourne is a city of stately trees—silver-green eucalyptus, willows, casuarinas—but it is more Victorian than Sydney and less colorful, even when, as now, decked out for Christmas.

We go to Sherbrook Forest in quest of a lyrebird, but hear a tinkly bell-bird instead. The woods smell pleasingly of gum leaf and moss. Then, as we walk through a grove of charred trunks to a fern forest like an illustration in Humboldt, V. remarks that "each tree is an individual." Yet the deeper I wander among the tall eucalyptus, the more I feel the absence of individuality in the loneliness of Australia and in the silence of the wilderness defined by the cry of a bird.

NOVEMBER 29

Melbourne to Tahiti. Nouméa, three hours from Sydney, is a bracelet of white coral, an emerald lagoon, hills striped like tigers, a runway scratched in the livid earth like a vaccination. We walk to the terminal in dry, sun-sapping heat, past some dusky Dominicans in white skirts, rope belts, fedoras; French marines with red pompon berets; "flics" in khaki and képis; women with slit Chinese skirts and faces like statues at Angkor; and some giggling, half-naked native boys, to whom I say *"Bonjour,"* thus provoking an explosion of laughter.

Nandi, a few hours later, is a sauna bath. As soon as we land, over rice terraces and watery valleys, a Sulu in a white apron charges through the plane gaily spraying DDT in our faces. The terminal is new, air-conditioned even on the half-open outside ramps, and equipped with numerous shower rooms, all with electric dryers. The Fijians, sponge-haired and in white skirts with sawlike serrations at the hem, are gentle and well mannered. We buy batik from them, and drink pineapple juice at tables strewn with purple hibiscus. I.S. thinks that Rousseau was right, if by natural people he could have meant the Sulus.

∧ A   ∨ B

A. Venice, at the time of *The Rake's Progress,* September 1951. *(Photo by Douglas Glass)*

B. Munich, October 1951.

C. Hollywood, 1952.

D. With Aldous Huxley in Stravinsky's Hollywood home, 1952. *(Photo by Sanford Roth)*

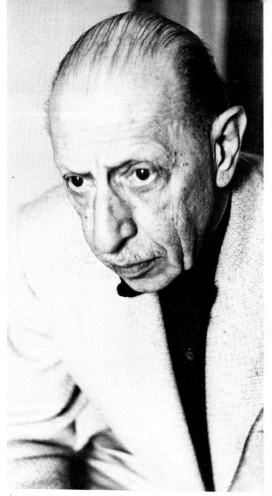

< A   ∧ B   ∧ C   ∨ D

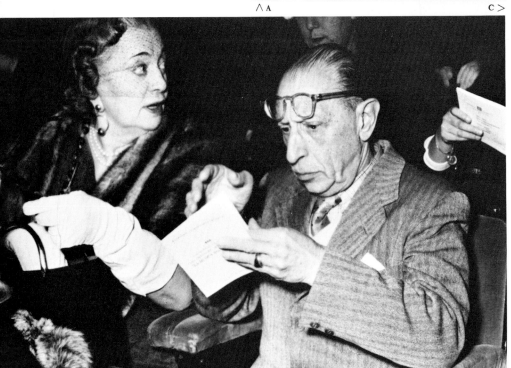

∧ B

A. At a rehearsal of the Philadelphia Orchestra, January 1954. *(Photo by Adrian Siegal)*

B. Teatro Eliseo, Rome. Listening to the author conduct the *Septet,* April 1954.

C. At home, Hollywood, 1954.

∧ Á

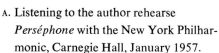

A. Listening to the author rehearse *Perséphone* with the New York Philharmonic, Carnegie Hall, January 1957.

B. Feeding cats in the Campiello "Drio la chiesa San Fantin," September 1957. *(Photo courtesy of* Il Gazzettino)

C. The author with W. H. Auden in the Martini Restaurant, Venice, after the première of *Threni,* September 23, 1958.

D. Rehearsal of *Threni* at the Metropolitan Museum of Art, New York, January 1959.

A. At the ruins of Pachacamac, Peru, August 18, 1960. *(Photo by Vera Stravinsky)*

B. Stravinsky with the author, recording the *Movements* for Piano and Orchestra, 1961.

∧ A

(*Sic:* we have crossed the International Date Line.)

2 AM. Tahiti. The tarmac, on a short, narrow crushed-coral dyke, is lighted not by hurricane lamps but by naked flame torches in iron sconces. Our plane turns gingerly around at the end of it, the wings wobbling over the water like the balancing bar of a man on a tightrope. A reception awaits us by Tahitian belles in blue sarongs and redolent gardenia leis. An elderly U.S. tourist to one of the *Taïtiennes:* "Say, young woman, what's that flower in your hair?" "Tahiti flower." "Oh, I see."

The Hotel Tahiti is a cluster of thatched bamboo cottages on the edge of the lagoon. A perpetual light wind, like the sound of rain, ventilates the inside, but I hear other, less romantic noises as well, including the "chirp, chirp" of lizards and the scuttle of small, unidentified (rodent?) feet.

A rooster debate at 4 AM. Unable to sleep, I go for a walk in the soft silver morning, watching the spray of waves on the outer coral crown. Across the open sea is Moorea, newborn and lovely in the now amethyst dawn.

1961

I say *"Maruru"* ("Thank you"—my entire vocabulary) to the girl who brings breakfast, then show her that the wash-basin faucets produce no water but only a kind of orange pekoe tea, leaves and all. She giggles and explains in verbless but gesture-full *tutoyer* French that this is a result of the rains. Then, looking around the room, she asks if I am alone, and when I admit that this, regrettably, is the case, she disappears for a moment and returns with six other giggling girls who employ the pretext of examining the faucets, but hardly trouble to conceal that I am the real object of curiosity. They wear flower-patterned gingham sarongs and gardenias over their left ears. All have long hair, braided or loose, and all are barefoot. Gauguin was an accurate observer of *taïtienne* toes, as well as of the large flat feet, the thick calves, the shapes of heads and of eyes; but these girls are more beautiful than any *jeune fille* in Gauguin because of the admixture of Chinese.

Papeete harbors a few small steamers, yachts, ketches, but is not a pretty town, apart from a few "picturesque" colonial buildings with colonnades and open balconies peeling white paint. Chinese shops, with advertisements in ideograms and girls leaning over sewing machines, seem, at first impression, to outnumber the French. But the traffic is more interesting than the buildings, especially the motor scooters driven by women in sarongs trailing long hair, and the buses, open to the rear and with benches along the sides to admit large domestic animals. On the sidewalks, French priests and French officials mix with Polynesians of a thousand complexions.

I spend the afternoon on the beach at Fautaua (pronounce five syllables), a cove of sable sand.

At night, orange flares from fishing canoes burn in a score of places at sea. As I watch, from the hotel terrace, two "hostesses" join me, one a pure Tahitian, she says, the other a quarter-cast. Both are pretty, but communication is confined to bar-room French, and to the English names for a few of the less complicated drinks. At midnight some American businessmen arrive and try to dance the twist. (Neither of my companions has the vaguest idea where America is, or, for that matter, Europe.) They wear flower-patterned shirts and crowns of gardenias, awry like Bacchus's girdle of grapes and from the same cause. Within minutes the superannuated American adolescents have paired off with the mature child *Taïtiennes*, for the whole island is a vulva, ready and willing.

I am awakened at 4 AM by a marital squabble in the other half of my hut, the wall between being a thin, resonant tympanum. ("So you think I married you for your money?" the husband yells, but not until next morning do I see that that, indeed, must have been the case; what, however, can have been *her* reason?) Then, switching on the bed lamp, I am vaguely aware of a hairy object on the floor by my slippers, which, putting on my spectacles, I identify as a spider about the size of my hand. (Later I try to recall whether I screamed at this point, but can a totally paralyzed person do even that?) The fright is mutual, evidently, for the monster flies under the bed, on which I now huddle, shivering. Then I remember the bug bomb in the bathroom; and overcome my abhorrence long enough to leap from the bed to fetch it, my flight and arrival causing infinite confusion amongst the cockroaches and lizards night-basking there. I spray the area under the bed, nearly asphyxiating myself, until the spider emerges and climbs to my night table, where I blow the poison at it like an open fire hydrant. Retreating somewhat groggily to the wall, it dodges me there like a PT boat in an air raid, but finally falls to the floor, where it lands on its back with a terrible thud. The legs twitch horribly for a moment, then draw in as, tremblingly, and no doubt cowardly and cruelly, I bear down with the spray can.

1961

The hotel maids, in the morning, laugh at my pallor as they sweep out the corpse and its crabsize legs. The spiders are harmless, they say, but "beware of the centipedes." Henceforth I resolve to spray every surface of the cottage before going to bed, and to sleep sitting up, with my bathrobe over my head and all the lights on.

Still shaky, I go in the afternoon to the Chilean Consul's home at Punavia, in the district of Faaa (pronounce three stutters, like a bleating lamb: the Tahitian alphabet has but thirteen letters), and reputedly the best beach on the island. The women of Punavia, sitting on the steps of their Napier huts and combing their long hair, are so perfectly Gauguinesque that one is hardly surprised by the sign near the little church of St.-Etienne saying "Paul Gauguin lived here 1896–1901." The Consul himself, a white-haired hidalgo with gentle brown eyes, fondles the hackles of a parrot while telling me how he loves Tahiti. He is unshaven, sloppily dressed and greatly embarrassed thereof, but lonely, too, and happy to talk to a foreigner. His *"vahine"* ("wife"—a corruption of "vagina"?) is a teen-age girl with long braids, long fingers, a long—too long—animal laugh. The yard of the consulate is cluttered with idols from Easter Island, assorted refuse, pigs, monkeys, chickens, mynah birds, cats. I swim in the warm lagoon as far out as the coral reef opposite Moorea.

At dinner V. talks about the first Christmas she remembers. "I received a newborn black lamb with a blue bow, and since then lambs and Christmas trees have reminded me of each other." I.S. says he cannot remember his first Christmas, but he does remember a reminder of it: "I was a baby sitting naked on the sands of a Baltic beach—how agreeable to feel the hot sand on one's bare behind!—when my mother gave me a bottle, which I filled with sand and emptied, and refilled and emptied again and again. A pine twig fell beside me and I grasped it and tried to push it into the bottle. But without success, whereupon I began to study the twig, and I thought how like our Christmas tree it was." I.S. also says that he remembers a childhood schoolmate pointing out a cat to him and saying that the cat was skillful in catching fish. "The word 'skill' impressed me, and I have paid attention to it ever since."

DECEMBER 1

Tahiti is tandem-shaped, and we spend the day circling the larger of the two "wheels." The ground almost everywhere is littered with bald, skull-like coconuts, whose husks have been gathered into pyres; the trees wear shiny metal armbands as shields against rats. Other trees include the breadfruit; the mango, which bears purple fruit; the chestnut, whose hard, straight wood is used for making pirogues; and the kapok, whose fibers are used for pillow stuffing. The plants and flowers include elephants' ears, wurra lilies, red ginger bushes, flamboyant pink acacias, yellow hibiscus, and pandanus— these have aerial roots and leaves with "joints" like spiders' legs (which shows what is still on my mind).

Every few kilometers there is a church, usually Catholic and looking as if borrowed *in situ* from a French village, but sometimes Protestant, Mormon, or Seventh-Day Adventist. The most remarkable architectural oddity is none of these, however, but the tomb of King Pomare V. It resembles a bottle of Benedictine, red-capped dome and all—intentionally, it is said, to memorialize the monarch's favorite fluid and the cause of his demise. The only other buildings of any interest are a lazaret, where the lepers sit or stroll on a wide, roofless porch; and the ruins of the Polynesian temple of Arahurahu, where smiling, toothy, pregnant-baby idols stand in a rectangle of volcanic cobblestones on a hillside facing the sea.

We spend the evening with Henri Georges Clouzot, who is fox-eyed, hirsute, and a lively conversationalist about other film directors, actresses (Monroe and Bardot), and painters, for Clouzot's passion, and the reason for his retreat here, is to paint. Nicolas de Staël killed himself, so Clouzot thinks, "because he failed to find the rules and limits of his art."

On the return to Papeete in Clouzot's jeep, in a drenching, straight-down rain, we pass people without coats or umbrellas walking along in the dark, one of them an old man playing a very wet guitar.

DECEMBER 17

Mexico. *"Feliz Navidad,"* the neon signs say all along the Avenida where, also, the lamp posts are thatched with Christmas evergreens. The Alameda, from our hotel rooms, is a child's sugarplum dream of gold, sapphire, and ruby lights, but the wonder of wonders is an electric bird of paradise that changes colors and tail positions three times a minute. A hurdy-gurdy grinds in the street alongside the Alameda, where, too, a balloon vendor apparently either loses the lot or finds a spendthrift customer, for a varicolored cluster floats upward past our window. Somewhere behind the Alameda, in the outskirts, is a ferris wheel of exploding fireworks. "Mexican people have much *revolución,* señor, but they very happy people. You see what I mean?" This, of course, is from Vicente, himself very happy to see us again, as we are to see him. Driving by a cinema with a waiting line five blocks long, he notes that "The people stand many hours, señor. Mexicans have much time, señor."

DECEMBER 18

Today marks the end of the two-week celebrations of the miraculous appearances at Guadalupe, and columns of pilgrims parade to the shrine from starting places miles away in the center of the city. At the head of each of these processions is a band of cornets, violins, guitars, cymbals, and tubas playing very gay tunes. Behind the musicians, boys in black suits, members of some order of hyperdulia, carry banners with the image of the Virgin, while behind them are the ordinary marchers, braided Indian women, for the most part, with babies on their backs and gladioli in their hands.

Going to Guadalupe ourselves, we stand next to a kneeling Indian family, their lips moving in prayer; one of them, a young girl, holds her white Communion dress an inch above the church floor, as if to curtsy, while her brother, a ragged infant of five or six, his feet calloused and caked with dirt, clutches, as if it were his only possession, a green plastic whistle. Suddenly a busload of U.S. tourists empties into the church where, next to the Mexicans, they look as pale as pernicious anemia. "Hold on to your wallets, everybody," their guide says, as they hurry nervously by the ragged boy with the whistle. But they hardly seem to breathe for fear of the germs and the superstition.

One of the chapels displays a glass coffin containing a brown-frocked saint with skin the color of Parian. Coins and paper money are piled on the body, and letters, photographs, wax flowers, babies' shoes are pinned to the surrounding walls. In another chapel, I.S. buys candles to place on the altar table, even though those already there are melting together. The Indians plant their candles, then pray, lying procumbent, or with their heads to the floor like Muslims.

The church of Santiago, built on ruined revetments of Tenochtitlán, is white inside except for black spandrels now looped and twined with ropes of evergreen. In a glass case to the left of the altar is an embalmed saint, like a statue carved in marzipan. But the treasure of the church is a statue of a captive Christ in a pure white robe with a golden hem. We go to the Plaza de Garibaldi to hear *mariachi* music, but Vicente is obliged to corral the players from nearby bars. They wear black velvet jackets and wide-brimmed, forward-tilted sombreros, and their instruments are a clarinet, a cornet, and several sizes of guitar, from the tiny *vihuela* to the big bass. The bass guitarist doubles as the vocalist and, for ten pesos, sings the *"Corrida de Pancho Villa,"* the *"Corrida de Emiliano Zapata,"* and *"Guadalajara."* While we listen to this street concert, a one-legged beggar polishes the car.

Vicente's next stops are the pink palace of Porfirio Díaz and a ramshackle house, nearby, where Zapata lived in 1914: "Zapata no fancy man, señor. You see what I mean?"; and the Zócalo. "Once seventy Aztec temples stood here, señor. I never know how they move so many stones, but I think they must have very strong religion."

1961

To Toluca, on a steep route with many *"curva peligrosa"* warnings. The slopes are thickly wooded, as they were when Doña Fanny Calderón de la Barca made the trip, at which time, however, and one hopes by contrast, the woods were hiding places for bandits. The Nevado de Toluca, with a brow of black clouds, comes into view long before the city.

We go to the Plaza first, a park of ahuehuete trees. Vicente provides an etymology for this name. The Spaniards were unable to pronounce *"ahua,"* he says, meaning, of course, that the Mexicans were unable to pronounce *"agua"*; and we see what *he* means when he describes a group of new buildings as part of a "housing pro*y*ect." The sidewalks around the Plaza are spread with ceramics, blankets, baskets, Christmas *juguetes* (toys).

In the Toluca market, the older the Indian women are, the more they seem to carry; we see one poor crone bent double with a bale of moss that would balk a mule. Most of them are barefoot, too, and purple with cold. The more prosperous female peddlers wear bright blue wool stockings, matching blue ponchos, straw hats, and ladder-like racks strapped to their backs. The men wear cheverel leggings and carry nothing, but knit as they walk. The specialties of the food market are *churros* (a chocolate cake coiled like rope), hot pigs' knuckles, plucked turkeys for Christmas, piles of dried *frijoles,* purple peppers, *pescado frito.*

Toluca is still Aztec, according to Vicente, and the mountain people still believe in Tlaloc, Huitzilopóchtli, Quetzalcoatl. And whatever the truth of this, an indelible and uninterrupted ancient life obviously does survive in this cold, harsh, Andean place. The Spaniards called it the *ciudad de los tigres,* because the Indian braves wore the heads and skins of wildcats.

On the return ride Vicente discourses on bullfighting. "The bull he no cry because he real man, señor. And the bull is only one in *corrida* who doesn't want fight, señor. The crowd want fight. And the *matador.* Then why all the people cry so loud when the *matador* is caught, señor, but they no cry when bull is caught?"

1961

1948
1949
1950
1951
1952
1953
1954
1955
1956
1957
1958
1959
1960
1961
1962
1963
1964
1965
1966
1967
1968
1969
1970
1971

ITINERARY

January 6: I.S. conducts in the Wilshire Ebell Theater in Los Angeles. **7:** We fly to Toronto, where I.S. tapes a television program for the CBC. **14:** We fly via Buffalo to Washington. **20, 21, 22:** I.S. conducts *Oedipus Rex* (and R.C. *L'Heure espagnole*) for the Washington Opera Society. **23:** Train to New York. **February 3:** We fly to Los Angeles. **March 26–28:** *The Flood* is recorded in Hollywood. **April 18:** We fly to Seattle, where I.S. conducts the *Firebird* suite in the inaugural concert (21st) of the Seattle World's Fair. **22:** Train to Vancouver and Toronto (arriving on the 25th), where I.S. conducts, in concert, and records *A Sermon, A Narrative and A Prayer.* **May 1:** Fog having closed the Toronto airport and filled the trains, we go by all-night limousine to New York, arriving only just in time for V.'s vernissage, at the Galerie Internationale. **8:** We embark on the *Flandre,* but go from Le Havre to Paris by car (15th) owing to a French railroad strike. **18:** We fly to Johannesburg. **22, 25:** Concerts in Johannesburg. **June 5:** We fly to Rome, via Salisbury and Brazzaville, then to Hamburg for the celebration of I.S.'s eightieth birthday with performances of *Orpheus, Agon, Apollo,* danced by the New York City Ballet (and conducted, respectively, by Leopold Ludwig, R.C., I.S.). **29:** We fly to New York. **July 12:** Concert in Lewisohn Stadium (New York). **21:** Concert in Ravinia (Chicago). **25:** Concert in Hollywood Bowl. **28:** Train to Santa Fe. **August 21:** We fly to New York, and on the 28th to Israel. **September 16:** We fly from Venice to Paris. **October 15:** We fly from Paris to Rome. **18:** Concert in Rome. **20:** Concert in Perugia. **23:** We fly to New York and Caracas (28th). **November 1, 4:** Concerts in Caracas. **20:** *The Rake's Progress* in Carnegie Hall (conducted by R.C.). **30:** I.S. goes to Toronto by train to record the Symphony in C, etc. **December 4:** We fly via Chicago to Hollywood.

147

Washington, D.C. Visit from St.-John Perse. He says that after his Nobel Prize address, "Some young Swedish physicists told me they were tired of hearing about the opium of the irrational, and they asked if I thought a scientific explanation could be found for the *germination poétique.* I suggested that they substitute 'experimental' for 'opium'—the experimental irrational—to begin with, but I said that poetry can only begin in the inconsequence of the absurd. Of course the application can be scientized, in the logic of the word, though I have not tried to do it myself, or to do anything along those lines, being too busy trying to develop my own intellectual *maîtrise."* And from this he goes on to defend Heidegger's theory of the beginnings of poetry, quoting him on Hölderlin and Trakl, and to attack the "canalization into logic" by English and American "university philosophers." Apropos of this, I.S. remarks that "The university today is only a department store. Worst of all, it no longer allows art itself to be the teacher, but promotes 'the art of teaching' and even 'the teacher as artist.'" Talking next about *"le hazard,"* Perse refers to Einstein's "God does not throw dice," saying that for him, too, the idea of a chance universe is giddying.[1] At this point I.S. interjects that he does not understand chance in art. "One has a nose. The nose scents and it chooses. An artist is simply a kind of pig snouting truffles."

The memory of Joseph Conrad inspires Perse's highest flight of eloquence. "He was the perfect aristocrat and the truest friend I have ever known," says the poet, adding that "Valéry and Claudel were my intellectual friends, of course, but hardly more than that." He then declares himself to be in agreement with I.S.'s remarks on Valéry in the Bollingen volume of the plays, and goes on to tell the story (which I have heard from Aldous) of finding Valéry on a street bench one night, head in hands and the picture of despair. "My wife is going to have a baby," the author of *Monsieur Teste* explained, "hence I shall need money, and have to write again, which of course means the Academy."

"Conrad would never judge a friend either morally or intellectually," Perse continues, "for he regarded friendship as sacred. And he did not love the sea, obviously—after all, his home was forty-two miles inland—but man-against-the-sea, and ships; he could never understand me when I talked about the sea itself. But I think he must have disliked my poems. The only literature that I know he positively hated, however, was Dostoievsky. Telling me about a dinner with Shaw, Wells, and Bennett, somewhere in the country, he remarked that 'These *savants cyniques* of the literary industry talked about writing as action,' which so horrified poor Conrad that he left the table pretending he had to catch an earlier train. Describing the scene—in

---

1. For the philosophy of the nonintentional universe, *cf.* Monod's *Le Hazard et la Nécessité* (Paris, 1970), which concludes that "Man knows at last that he is alone in the indifferent immensity of the universe, whence he has emerged by chance."

épouvantable French, except for one English word I shall never forget—he said that 'Writing, for me, is an act of faith, and they all made me feel so *dowdy.*'"

Switching to his travels in Patagonia and Tierra del Fuego—"The wind, the ocean, the cold, the earth and sky unspoiled by the detritus of man"— Perse sounds like a page from his own *Amers*. And he says that "*La poésie est une façon de vivre, c'est pourquoi je déteste même à parler de 'la littérature.'* The rationalists invented 'literature' and killed poetry—almost."

He says that in 1935 the French government sent him as a special envoy to the Kremlin, "Where Litvinov translated for me but adjusted everything I said. Every evening the dinner table was heaped as if for an orgy, and in fact an orgy of toasting did take place, a glass of vodka being downed in honor of each of the commissars present, with a final toast for Comrade Stalin. I managed to switch carafes and drink only water. Then I noticed that though Stalin drank, it did not affect him. I assumed he had received water, too, and was certain of it when I saw that he ate only goat cheese and fruit. Eventually the commissars found me out. But when they questioned me about it, I replied that, like Comrade Stalin, I did not drink. This was greeted with an explosion of silence, Stalin's water-drinking apparently being an open secret. He looked at me fiercely for a moment, then started to laugh. I had a better opinion of him after that, as I know he had of me, but the next day, in the Kremlin Museum, I was followed by police. When I asked why, Stalin said: 'I wanted to know what interested you most.'" Perse clearly believes that the pendulum of Stalin's reputation has now swung too far toward the Khrushchev view. "Stalin was a man of extraordinary good sense," he says, "and I refuse to believe the stories about him as a table-tapping mystic. He was not vain, moreover, and he was never an actor."

Perse recalls that he met I.S. as far back as the *Firebird,* but that they began to know each other well only in 1921, when I.S. was arranging the piano excerpts from *Petrushka,* and the two of them were often together at the Bassianos' in Versailles. He says that at the première of *Le Sacre* he saw men swinging their canes at each other and opening and shutting umbrellas. "I was with Debussy both shortly before and shortly after, and I remember how excited he was by the music at first and how he changed when he saw that it had taken the attention of the younger generation away from him. He felt abandoned, and be began to criticize it."

Perse also recalls a picture of I.S. in Boston just before his marriage, "Registering in a very proper hotel and asking the clerk in slow, loud, and *épouvantable* English, 'May I have with me a female companion?' Some adoring old-maid disciples of yours overheard and were nearly overcome with embarrassment."

Full-face, Perse bears some resemblance to Poe, albeit a neat and very sane Poe, while in profile he reminds me of E. M. Forster. He is dapperly dressed in a striped suit, vest, and bow tie, and he stands—a head taller than I.S.—like a ramrod. I.S. asks his advice about what to say when he receives a medal from the Secretary of State this afternoon, complaining that "I do not want to be decorated like a general; I want to be *méchant*." To which Perse, the professional diplomat, replies that "Courtesy can be the nastiest thing of all."

Dinner at the White House. The presidential limousine calls for us at the Jefferson Hotel at eight o'clock, but though our arrival is timed via the driver's two-way radio, we are checked in with extreme caution at the gate. A light snow is on the White House lawn, and the ice-covered trees are like crystal chandeliers. TV lights flood the porch, where a mob of cameramen is poised like a football team for the tackle. The Kennedys—both of them taller than we expect, and she more slender and he more Palm Beach color—emerge a moment before we do from our limousine. He greets us in a public-address voice, she in a Marilyn Monroe panting one, and meanwhile the photographers push, shout—"Hey, Jackie, look this way"— and even roll on the ground *à la "Dolce Vita."* Accompanying us through the foyer to an elevator, and from there to an upstairs reception room, the President inquires about Mr. Rusk's medal-pinning ceremony, and the progress of the rehearsals for I.S.'s upcoming performances of *Oedipus Rex*.

1962

The other guests are the Schlesingers and Salingers, Lee Radziwill and Helen Chavchavadze (a beauty in whom J.F.K. is obviously interested), Felicia Bernstein (*ditto,* in whom *I* am interested), her husband, Nicolas Nabokov, Marshall Field, Max Freedman, and the Goddard Liebersons. It is a Kennedy-circle dinner, in other words, with political payoffs, and not an I.S. one (Balanchine, Aldous, Eliot, Auden, St.-John Perse, Isaiah Berlin, Lincoln Kirstein, Berman).

The women sit on sofas by the fireplace and the men stand around the President. For my own part, I drain two large scotches too rapidly and can't get enough caviar, bad as that combination is, to help absorb them. But conversation is self-conscious and makeshift. And I find myself unable not to look two steps away to the young President of the United States; and even less able not to look at "Jackie." Her light gray eyes are prettier than in her photographs, which in any case make them dark brown. Moreover, the thin haggard look, aped by all female America, is nonexistent. Afterward I remember nothing about the room, but on the corridor wall facing the door is a picture of an Indian of the Western Plains, the sight of which unexpectedly gives me a patriotic shiver.

Going to dinner, V. descends the staircase with the President, while I.S. and "Jackie" take the elevator, and I accompany N.N., who is relaxed now and therefore droll and unprintable about the portraits of Taft and Harding on the walls. Ushers lead us to our places as we enter the State Dining Room, the President in the center with V. on his right, and "Jackie" opposite with I.S. on her right; I am the buffer between Mrs. Schlesinger and Mr. Salinger, but the former talks books with me, to my considerable relief, as I am politically up to date only on the Australian election. On the third round of champagne and near the end of the meal—*sole mousse, gigot* (V., later: "A perfect State Dinner for concierges")—the President toasts I.S.; and at two rather shaky moments in her spouse's speech, twinges of anxiety show in "Jackie's" eyes. "We have been honored to have had two great artists here with us in recent months," he begins, and I am wondering if I.S. realizes that Casals is meant by the other. "When my wife was a student in Paris, she wrote an essay on Baudelaire, Oscar Wilde, and Diaghilev." (I.S. later: "I was afraid he was going to say his wife had made a study of homosexuality.") "Now, I understand that you, Mr. Stravinsky, were a friend of Diaghilev. And I have just been told that rocks and tomatoes were thrown at you in your youth." This is based on V.'s briefing during dinner, the story of the *Sacre* première having amazed the President and even made him laugh aloud. Rocks and tomatoes, I explain later, is an American re-rendering—they are thrown at baseball umpires—for I.S. has understood these missiles literally. But the speech is short and, because an American President is honoring a great *creative* artist—an event unprecedented in American history—it is moving. As I.S. thanks him, the anxiety passes from "Jackie's" eyes to V.'s.

Afterward the men gather at one end of the table while the women retire to the Red Room. I.S., forgetting and anyway loathing this barbaric British custom, starts to follow V., both because he is dependent on the translated hints with which she puts him on the track for what he fails to hear, and because he really only wants to be with her. But N.N. shepherds him back and seats him on the President's right. Cognac and cigars are passed around, and with them the character of the President's talk grows more manifestly masculine and even includes a peppering of Anglo-Saxon tetragrams. "How do you feel now, Mr. Stravinsky?" he asks, and Mr. Stravinsky's answer is "Quite drunk, thank you, Mr. President." Marshall Field puts a question to I.S. about Prokofiev and the U.S.S.R., which I.S. does not understand, but, seeing this, Lenny Bernstein comes to his rescue, though instead of stopping there, goes on to describe the reception of I.S.'s own music in the new Russia. "I saw tears in people's eyes and not only for the *Sacre* but for the Piano Concerto, which, after all, is an astringent piece." (I.S. *does* understand this, however, and, talking to me later, is skeptical about the shedding of much lachrymal liquid over the Piano Concerto.)

Duty done, the conversation turns to politics. And here the President shows both his skill as a debater and his ability to bring an argument to a head. He even shows evidence of reading, calling an article on the Berlin crisis in *Encounter* "playing to the gallery." His attention never wanders from anyone else who has the floor, but this may be defensive as he knows that every eye in the room is trained on him. And, finally, he seems to be saying what he thinks. Item: "We are essentially a conservative country, the liberal element always having been a small minority, and by liberal I mean, simply, open to new ideas." When at one point the discussion turns to syndicated columnists, he voices his opinions about them in fair, unguarded, and unminced terms. In fact, he even talks about Cuba without apologetics.

The Kennedys accompany us to the door and wait with us fifteen minutes until the chauffeur, not anticipating our early retreat, is found. And here, alone with us, they are gracious, warm, and totally disarming.

I.S., in the car: "Nice kids."

Back in the lobby of the Jefferson, however, a scrimmage of news hens is waiting for I.S. Surviving that, too, and once we are upstairs, he remarks to V.: *"Le Président me rappelle d'un jeune homme de football qui ne peut pas jouer à cause de son mauvais dos."* But V. is not listening, being only immensely relieved that I.S. did not try to engage the President in a *tête-à-tête* about having his taxes reduced.

JANUARY 19

Lunch at St.-John Perse's with Auden, who is wearing not merely dark, but black, glasses, like a blind beggar. The poets sit side by side, but as neither wishes to speak the other's language, Auden comes through on my side during most of the meal. His opener to Perse seems a bit odd—"By the way, what is the French for *Hühneraugen?*"—but as his most recent poem begins with this word (corns), we wonder if the question is really concerned with French translation or with Auden's own podiatric problems. In any case, V. advises him to try space shoes; the footwear he has on looks as if it had been lent to him by a Breughel peasant.

He is in an epigram-and-aphorism phase, and, for our enlightenment, distinguishes the two in characteristic (a) . . . (b) . . . form: "An aphorism must apply to everyone, past and present, but an epigram need apply only to particular cases and to one person. Thus, Wilde's description of fox hunting, 'The pursuit of the uneatable by the unspeakable,' is an epigram because only certain people at a certain time would understand. On the other hand, his 'A cynic is a person who knows the price of everything and the value of nothing,' is an aphorism because it is universally comprehensible." French examples are cited first, no doubt in deference to Perse, but Auden assures me that La Rochefoucauld's are inferior to the Marquis of Halifax's, and that "Flaubert is only a provincial manufacturer of them." His favorite French example is Proust's "In matters of love it is easier to overcome a deep feeling than to renounce a habit." Then, asking I.S. for Russian examples, and being told that the best are in Turgenev and Herzen, he goes on to say that "I got rather frightened of the Russians after the first sentence of *Anna Karenina,* which, obviously, should be the other way around. Now, if you are going to do aphorisms, surely the first thing is to get them right."

He offers a string of instances from Karl Kraus, whom he calls "one of the great people of the century." And although the crest of his Teutonic period

1962

must soon be due, he quotes his cablegram to Robert Graves on the occasion of the latter's inaugural lecture as Poetry Professor at Oxford last fall, and it is in German. *I* quote the only Kraus I know, about how, in 1919, he proposed to change the national anthem from "God Save the King" to "Thank God for Saving Us from the King," but as this does not contribute to the quotient of aphorisms, Auden only frowns.

Talking about operas, he declares that *Die Frau ohne Schatten* is Hofmannsthal's best, "except the M-G-M ending." Then, perhaps to nettle Perse: "Of course, none of the classical French tragedies can be made into libretti." Commenting on Karajan's *Ring,* he remarks on the conductor's "extraordinary devotion to the dark. Most of it took place in a blackout, for an audience of owls, and Brünnhilde singing about *'Die Sonne'* the whole time. It was not all of the *Ring,* either, the stagehands having struck after *Siegfried.*"

I.S., talking about *The Flood,* says that the visual representation of the Devil puzzles him. "My first idea was to photograph a mobile red spot. But the flood itself is very clear in my mind. I do not want waves, or any movement back and forth. I have an idea instead for a single dancer turning this way and that and bobbing like a piece of wood, always in the same place. I saw an underwater film of the Red Sea not long ago, incidentally, and was impressed by the way the fish came right up to the bathysphere. They were exceedingly confident monsters!"

Auden's best remark of the day is that "Narcissus was a hydrocephalic idiot who thought 'On me it looks good.'" He also pronounces a certain novel "the best queer book of the year," and he maintains that its author, "who is as ambidextrous as a polyp, uses his wife far more as a shield than as a resource." Later, apropos of I no longer remember what, Perse remarks that *"La justice est une invention suisse."* Auden doesn't hear this, but when we laugh, he springs to attention, afraid he may have missed a new aphorism (or is it an epigram?). He departs early, saying he is on his way to attend a Mass for the Africans. "Heaven knows they need it, poor things. The world has had enough of Uncle Tshombe's Cabin."

MAY 16

Paris. Lunch at the Plaza-Athénée with Samuel Beckett, a tall, thin man with a furrowed forehead, a wrinkled and aggrieved face, long fingers, a good deal of potential silver mining in his teeth. His startlingly blue, deep-set eyes, along with the way his hair stands up, suggest a bluejay, except that his modesty and retiring manners are those of an oblate, and that he is soft-spoken in a light, very musical voice. He has motored in from his country house in what he calls his "sardine can," from his description of which we are surprised not to find the tires wrapped in rags.

"I first met Yeats in Dublin, in 1934," he says. "W.B. never gave the impression that he had any sense of humor, but that was far from the case. I knew Jack Yeats better than W.B. Their father, you know, considered Jack the more gifted son. I don't agree, do you?" At one point V. says that in her opinion critics should be ignored—this for I.S.'s benefit, as he is quarreling with one at the moment. "Yes," Beckett replies, "but some of them live such a long time." Beckett is interested in the possibility of notating the *tempo* of performance in a play, and of timing the pauses in *Godot,* and I.S. likes the idea of such controls, of course, but thinks that circumstances are too variable. When we mention the OAS, Beckett remarks that it is beginning "to sound like Péguy."

We go to the "Ancient Art of the Tchad" exhibition at the Grand Palais. Labrets of shell and bone are the commonest artifacts, along with cow masks, and bolas with stone weights shaped and carved (for traction) like hand grenades. The show is also rich in figurines of cows, hippos, crocodiles, and "fretful porpentines," as well as statuettes of dancers with distended lips, and other sanctuary idols from the necropolis of Butte de Médigué.

MAY 17

Brazzaville. 6 AM. A salmon sky streaked with violet and mother-of-pearl. We come in low over the swirling river and its plumes of mist, then tilt toward the runway above tin roofs surrounded by green the color of frozen peas. Even at this hour our spectacles smear with moisture as we step out into the sodden heat, but I.S. pretends to be reluctant to leave the plane for another reason, a concern that the natives may prove to be anthropophagous.

Breakfast is served by French-speaking natives wearing the billowing black trousers of women in Turkish harems. But the walls of the airport restaurant groan with the heads of big game, a fact that inhibits my appetite almost as much as the giant cockroaches everywhere strolling about (and not always strolling, either), and the smell of cooking in palm oil. Some of the souvenir sellers at the entrances to the airfield and restaurant have almost no clothes, some wear standard European dress, some are wrapped in blankets, and some sport skullcaps and ankle-length robes with blue or green stripes. Most are surprisingly short in stature.

Léopoldville, from the air, is a mixture of thatched huts and Le Corbusier. The Congo Basin, thereafter, is covered with a film of blue smoke. We cross the Zambesi, a loop of bronze foil, not far east of Victoria Falls. The red Rhodesian desert is marked by lonely, island-like clumps of trees, jebels— monument-like formations of black boulders—and a dirt track on which a car raises a dust cloud a mile high. The waiters in Salisbury terminal, in their stovepipe tarbooshes, long white robes, shoulder-to-waist sword sashes, and cummerbunds, might be soldiers of Toussaint L'Ouverture.

Near Johannesburg the khaki-colored desert is broken by tracts of trees recently planted against erosion, and the sky is full of slowly dissipating funnels of smoke. The slag heaps of gold mines—gray, white, yellow mounds—are like giant cake molds, or Chichen Itzás.

1962

Johannesburg is a bilingual city, like Brussels and Montreal. And a new city; I.S. is older than it is by a decade. And predominantly "white." Room service in the hotel and all higher types of domestic service are provided by East Indians, whereas lift boys, porters, and menial workers generally, are Bantu. When V. asks our white Afrikaans driver if the churches are segregated, his contented "Yes" is intended to reassure her, which is the reason he does not know what to make of her further question: "And is Heaven segregated too?" The Bantu live in special districts, as do, but apart from them, the "coloreds," meaning Muslims, half-castes, or anyone neither "white"—Chinese and Japanese are legally "white"—nor Bantu. The character of the city, nevertheless, derives from the customs and occupations—pulling rickshaws, carrying head bundles (the women)—of the Bantu. After dark many of them squat on the curb, huddling by gutter fires, for the night is cool at this altitude.

Johannesburg is a refugee city, too, and all European and many other countries are represented in the orchestra. A cellist, Budapest-born, tells us he was a prisoner of the Japanese in Indonesia and that he came to South Africa after the war "because of its opportunities." A Yugoslav woman describes how, four years ago, she and her mother and daughter abandoned their automobile on a highway near the Austrian border and fled through the woods to Austria and eventual asylum here. A young violinist from Amsterdam says she survived the Occupation there by living like Anne Frank. And, from the other side of the political fence, our Italian headwaiter tells us that he was interned in Ethiopia, where he learned to speak Gheez. And our elderly German room maid says she is the widow of a Berlin archeologist who was working in Tanganyika at the outbreak of war, when the British moved him to a camp in Rhodesia, where he died. South Africa welcomes these people because they are "white" and because, wanting to forget the injustices they have suffered abroad, few of them recognize and protest the same things here.

1962

The orchestra and chorus are "white." This leads I.S. to ask whether both mightn't be bettered if the personnel were not drawn exclusively from the ruling minority. "Isn't it conceivable," he asks an Afrikaans musician, "that in so large a country some 'nonwhite' might eventually learn to play the bass drum even better than the 'white' musician now in charge of that instrument? Or, if that seems improbable, certainly you will agree that some 'nonwhites' must be blessed with voices that could improve or at least swell the chorus." The Afrikaans musician's answer, however, is that the nonwhites have their own chorus and it is much better than the white one. But in that case, I.S. says, *he* should have the "nonwhite" chorus, his goal being to give the best possible performance of the music; which is the segregationist argument the other way around, except that "best possible" means "regardless of color," and this is simply not a logical argument in South Africa (though of course no one pretends that logic has anything to do with racism).

The Dutch-descended Afrikaans "whites" are courteous and hospitable in various ways imputed to Southern "colonels" in the United States. Quite naturally they anticipate criticism of apartheid, hence conversation is always straying guiltily toward it. Their argument is that they have developed the country and achieved the highest living standards, for *all* the people, in Africa. Now they are being asked to grant a vote that would reduce them to a powerless minority, forcing them to abandon everything they have labored so hard to build. They claim to be victims of the colonialist inheritance as much as the "nonwhites," furthermore, though world publicity has never dared to state that side of the case. But mainly they contend that the "nonwhite" population is incomparably better off now than a decade ago, which is materially true, no doubt, however incomplete the argument. And, finally, "The 'nonwhites' do not want integration and are not ready for equality"—though no one says whose fault it is that after all this time they still aren't—"whereas apartheid is a tradition as old as European South Africa, in fact the basis of the culture." These arguments are familiar in the Southern United States, of course, for which reason American criticism is regarded as hypocritical: "In the United States, integration exists on statute books," they say, "but from the White House down, American Negroes are a servant class and a zoned people." To which I can only reply, very lamely, that we are at least trying. And, well, a faint cheer for those books.

1962

MAY 20

On our way to the Western Areas Gold Mine to see tribal dances, we pass Diepkloof, of *Cry, the Beloved Country*, and Carletonville, a mining city of fifty thousand inhabitants which a few years ago was an empty plateau. The road follows the great reef of auriferous conglomerates, and the country is humped and pyramided all the way by gray, beige, white, and—owing to the cyanide used in placer processing—green-blue slag heaps. It is also marked by power stations and corset-shaped hoist towers, from which shafts are sunk to below sea level, a depth of 6,000 or 7,000 feet.

Many of the Bantu on the roadside sell oranges and watermelons, but the majority simply loll in the grass or prop themselves against trees. When ambling along the highway they tend to group around someone playing a musical instrument, which encourages a few of them to shuffling dance movements. The most popular of these improvised instruments is a kind of two-string tabor with a flattened-petrol-can sounding box and a piece of railing for the backboard. The men shade themselves with color-striped parasols, the women with heavy head bundles. We reduce our speed near the mines, for it is said that some newly arrived tribesmen are so unaccustomed to automobiles they may actually run out in front of them, like headlight-blinded animals.

The dances are held in the compound of "Blyvooruitzicht"—"*Blyvoraus-sicht,*" or "Happy Prospects," an Orwell-inspired name, I suspect, as the workers live like paid prisoners; that is what they *look* like, at any rate, as they hold out their mess tins to receive a dollop of gruel. The miners work a term of six months, and are then returned "rich" to their villages. They come from tribes as far away as the Rhodesias, Mozambique, and Bechuana-land, as well as from the Union and the Swaziland and Basutoland pro-tectorates.

The dance arena is defined by a circular grandstand filled principally with Basuto and "blanket people"—men in blue-violet karosses and tightly wrapped pink or khaki blankets. The Basuto wear straw hats with pagoda-like knobs, and European trousers artistically patched, *not* necessarily be-cause worn or frayed, but because the wearer likes the pattern. Ears, ankles, and upper arms are adorned with metal rings, but not in any uniform way. In fact, so much individuality is never apparent in any crowd of this size in Europe or America, while more wit is manifest in the costumes of the dancers than in the creations of Europe's most expensive couturiers (if that is a compliment). Here, moreover, everything is improvised from the contents of dustbins. The audience participation is also nonconformist. Thus a man in front of me sways to the sound of his own jew's-harp without a regard for the arena, while others laugh and heckle, and spectators come and go throughout the performance. From time to time, the wind raises scarves of dust and a sickish, ammoniac smell of perspiration.

Each dance moves around the arena, completing a circle, but at about the halfway point the next team, noisily revving up outside like the next bronco in a rodeo, agitates for its turn. And each dance begins with a rally of singing and hand-clapping. When these preliminaries become too protracted, as they invariably do, the leader hectors his company forward with a whistle. He is assisted in this by uniformed policemen who, however, cannot resist dancing along and otherwise getting into the act themselves, to the great delight of the audience. The music is directed to the dan-cers—*i.e.,* is not intended as a concert for the grandstand—and in fact the guitars and concertinas are inaudible to us, though not, of course, the clapping and stamping, which precipitate a dust storm; or the Swazi drum-ming, which inspires feats of rolling, leaping, kicking, high-jumping, and in the spectators as well as the dancers. The musical instruments, like the dancers' costumes, have been put together from crude and improbable materials. The subtlest music is provided by an orchestra of reed flutes, each player contributing a single note, like carillons or Webern. The loudest is a charivari of jingles, rattles, and bells attached to automobile inner tubes wrapped around the dancers' legs. It is used to accompany a Xosa ritual in which the dancers shimmy, shiver, squat, crouch, and fling their arms up like the praying mantis.

One performer wears a miner's aluminum helmet, a belt strung with a dozen neckties, and a flossy mophead tied to each knee. The entire garb of another, a would-be comedian—the catcalls drown the laughter—is a grass hula skirt and a large comb stuck like a cockade in his stubble hair. The onlookers are more amused by the antics of a great muscular creature in a green beret and a woman's fur boa.

The last dance, by a dozen men from the Machupi tribe of the Limpopo River, is the most spectacular, and so is the dress: white skirts and ankle feathers; purple, blue, black, and green tail feathers; deerskin headgear and shield covers. At the climax of this very dangerous-looking ballet, the dancers fling their hatchets to the ground and, in spite of the mine manager's assurances to I.S. that "it is not a war dance," the gesture can only have intended the extinction of the receiving party. And this time, too, the musicians, who wear winglike ostrich feathers, are separated from the dancers, no doubt for safety's sake. They play ratchets and a battery of marimbas made of scrap-metal slats placed on a trestle of empty barrels. The melody is repeated over and over, in *crescendo,* and in several ranges simultaneously, the larger barrels in augmentation against the smaller ones:

It stops suddenly after a tremendous gust of sound, as if truncated by an invisible force, and the dancers plunge their hatchets into the earth in blood-freezing silence, hurling their shields to the ground afterwards and savagely somersaulting over them.

MAY 22

Johannesburg. I.S. receives a letter from a woman in Durban who knew him in the Hôtel des Crêtes, Clarens, in 1913, and who wants to be certain he is "the same Russian composer who used to pound the piano there all day long."

MAY 26

The Ndebeli (Mapok) kraal is in an olive-and-yellow landscape stretching to a pink horizon. Near the gate, a monument to "the pioneers who broke the Zulu nation" reminds us of similar piles of stone in the American West commemorating victories over the Indians. Inside the kraal grounds, Bantu men, accompanied by dogs and long-tailed Persian sheep, raise their hats and wave their knobkerries in friendly greeting. But the land is sadly desiccated and the streams, which have names like "Sand River" or, more hopefully, "Fountain" this or "Fountain" that, are all dry.

The kraal huts stand behind a long white wall on which "windows," "shutters," "doors"—in the form of diamonds and squares, no line of which is exactly straight and whose symmetry is quite drunk—have been painted in bright green, purple, orange. Below and in front of these glittering designs is a kind of sun deck on which the Ndebeli women sit like queens at court, but in heavy raiment. The Ndebelis are a matrilineal society, and a visit to their village makes one wonder about the universality of the Oedipus complex. The power of continuing the culture is believed to reside exclusively with the female. Wives are bought with biblical numbers of cattle, while husbands are sunk in mortgages and denied use of the purchase until paid for in full. The female remains in command after marriage, too—which is less unusual—and she may determine whether her spouse shall share the hut or sleep outside. But one disadvantage outweighs all of a wife's advantages, it seems to me, for these Amazonians are shackled in brass bracelets from wrist to elbow and ankle to knee, and so heavily that they are hardly able to move. Ndebeli women also wear necklaces of woven grass encased in beads, and, like the bracelets, these are welded on, *i.e.,* permanent. And they wear colored blankets and beaded aprons: the sex of even the youngest female baby is concealed by a beaded G-string. Male children, by contrast, are naked except for flies, which nobody heeds, though their mothers whisk them away from their infant sisters. Unmarried adolescent girls are naked from their aprons up, I might add, which enables us to see that from a mammary point of view the female is in decline, in an exact sense, from about the age of thirteen. Not so their meridional proportions. The staple millet gruel is swilled in such bulk that the abdomens of most women are as distended as they would be a week or so before an accouchement. The coiffures of these Ndebeli belles consist of four small hedge tufts, like phylacteries, on skulls otherwise smoothly mown and glistening with pomatum of lamb fat.

The interiors of the huts are painted in the same style as the wall. We buy admittance with gifts of snuff to giggling female elders, and by purchasing beaded figurines. The whole kraal is busily beading to fill a Christmas order from Macy's.

1962

MAY 27

We give a free concert for the Bantu people of Springs, a mining city surrounded by piles of yellow slag. Most houses here are tin-roofed shanties, but new communities are pointed out to us, with expressions of regret that the people are "not yet ready to live in such [palatial] dwellings"—which is the old argument against housing developments in U.S. slums. At sunset, thousands of women appear, balancing tins of water on their heads.

The audience enjoys, above all, the demonstrations of instruments preceding the actual concert, especially the trombone when it "slides," the tuba imitating gastroenteritis, and the percussion. At the conclusion of the program, the Bantu express their appreciation by singing a dolorous Methodist hymn for us, as if on purpose to remind us of the cultural confusion wrought by colonialism. But why should a people with its own rich and varied music greet us with this dismal specimen of its captor's art? (The city Bantu despise their own "Kaffir culture," the Afrikaans people say in reply to that.) Whatever the causes, the effects of the concert are disturbing. But the Afrikaaners are disingenuous in their reasons for allowing it in the first place.

Wasn't the concert primarily a demonstration for our benefit, to make us see that the benighted black is not yet ready for European culture, that the Bantu really are savages? And isn't it just conceivable that the Bantu might resent a concert given uniquely for them, in their own compound, a white orchestra and a black audience? *"Bantu,"* incidentally, means men, and *"Muntu,"* man. But how were the ancestors of these poor creatures to know when they formed the words that other "Bantu" existed in the world and that they were "white"?

We return at night to Pretoria. A vast fire is raging on the veldt, like a prehistoric tableau.

MAY 28

Pretoria is a city of pillared porches and Dutch-colonial gingerbread; and some bronze, too, most notably in the statue of President Kruger, glowering on a pedestal in the Plaza. Our hotel, the Union, is Victorian in physique, style of service, and meals, which include copious breakfasts and teas. The Bantu room waiter has heard that I am American, but he is surprised to find that I speak something more or less resembling English. He asks if I know "the American Negro orchestra conductor, Dean Dixon?" I say I do, and I laud Dixon, adding that I enjoyed playing under him in my student days in New York (which is true), but failing to mention that Dixon was unable (for a racist reason, in my opinion) to find a conducting post in the United States. At the end of the conversation, he says, "Thank you, massa," which depresses me for the rest of the day.

At night, in the street, we listen to a quartet of Bantu minstrels playing guitars and *flûtes à bec.*

MAY 29

On the road to Kruger Park, we pass Bantu boys with calabashes or bags of oranges on their heads; metal-collared Bantu women, as melonous and pro-tuberant as fertility idols, with baskets and rolled-up sleeping mats on their heads; Bantu men comfortably sleeping on two-wheeled bullock carts. *All* Bantu heads are covered, in any case, and all "white" men are bare-headed.

Witbank is a coal and carbide city at the beginning of the carboniferous beds of the eastern Transvaal. But the fields are full of sunflowers—the seed oil is a major export—and gerberas, yellow wattles, arums, aloes. It is the beginning of Swazi country, too, and of domed Zulu-style huts, in front of which tall native women stand erect and motionless, selling watermelons.

Belfast, the highest point of the upper veldt, is in a region of salt lakes, which look even saltier than they are because of white birds on the shores, like the salt crystals on the rim of a "Margarita" cocktail glass. The landscape a little farther along is weird, owing partly to the vegetation—scrubby, black-stemmed proteas, milk-white eucalyptus, blue gum trees—but mainly to the anthills. Small, mumplike papilli, heretofore, they are now eight or nine feet tall, and parched and porous, like the stucco towers of Gaudí.

160

1962

Machadodorp is warmer, a city of willows and lime-colored mimosas. And soon after, the climate is fully tropical: the natives carry umbrellas and live in straw and grass tukals. We stop at a picnic site in which the garbage disposal is left to scavenger baboons.

The road at Kruger Park, inside the Numbi gate, is dusty, tortuous, narrow, but immediately rich with signs of spoor: tracks, ordure, munched and trampled bushes. The shapes of trees are sinister: the flat-crowned thorn trees with the wizened trunks, for one, and the wild figs, the ebonies, the baobabs, the cassias with pendant pods, the white bougainvilleas, the flame of Africa, the red-flowered Kaffir plum trees with hanging finch nests, and the tall fever trees—so-called because they are the complexion of a man with yellow fever. The dry season has begun, and except for the riverbanks the Park is brown.

Suddenly we see a waterbuck in a glade about twenty feet from the road: violently twitching ears, black horns, and on the rump a white circle like a brand. He watches us over his shoulder, poised to run, but does not move until we do. V. says that we should expect to find two cows nearby, but the ladies do not appear and we drive on. This encounter turns the Park into a spell, however, and we go forward—I do, anyway—with clenched nerves.

Two bends in the road later, we come upon an impala herd: brown backs beautifully sheened, beige stomachs, black grill-striped behinds, pinched tails, dainty white feet, black ankles like Russian ladies' fur-lined boots. The antlered leader, in the center of the pack, wriggles his ears and grunts a warning that frightens a young doe and causes it to leap like Pavlova. Impala travel in safari, like a cavalcade of camels, but group when they graze.

A duiker appears next, picking its way in a henlike head-first pecking movement. And then a family of koodoo, whose women and children are feeding; nor do they allow themselves to be interrupted on our account, though the mandarin-bearded buck lifts his streamlined horns and watches us with distrust. Koodoo are identified by large ears, white lipstick, white forelegs tufted at the knees like the Greek evzone uniform, lightly striped coats, long black flyswatter tails, and white tickbirds, which ride perkily on their backs.

We stop at the Pretorius Kop entrepôt to see a pair of West African rhinoceros soon to be released into the Park; full of phencyclidine tranquilizers, they doze like barrels of wet dynamite. At Skurukwan, accompanied by armed rangers, we visit the Hippo Pool; it is the only place in the Park where visitors are permitted to leave their cars, but a man was mauled to death here by a lion not long ago in spite of the guards. The hippos are submerged on a shoal near the other shore, but the surface of the river bristles with their conning-tower nostrils and eyes. Suddenly one of the great graminivorous brutes raises his keel, yawns—a vast, obscene red maw—and snorts—a truck stripping gears—whereupon the whole otiose herd surfaces with an ear-cracking detonation, after which they blow, bellow, gargle, and spout like any gang of beach bullies. Because of this we do not hear, but luckily chance to see, a hippo mother slip out of the foliage on the mudbank near us, where it has been bolting branches and fouling the river. But the sight of a young one sheltering between her rear legs makes me ashamed of my unkind epithets above.

Back on the road, we see purple-gray wildebeeste, timorous creatures with black eyes or mascara; and baboons, sitting like stumps in the center of the road, but not for long. They leap to our hood, fenders, and rear window, which makes I.S. feel "like a politician in a parade." I fetch a candy in the map compartment, open the window a slit, and pass it through; in an instant the receiving baboon is on the windshield pointing to the compartment and demanding more. I.S.: "In another year they'll be saying, 'Go home, Yank!'"

It is now animal rush hour by the river. A sable antelope crosses the road, running with an end-to-end, rockinghorse movement; and a bush-buck lamb; and a hyena, with a sloped, gargoyle-like back; and a steenbok fawn; and a warthog, which, seeing us, charges into the woods with its tail up like a flag. Elephant devastations—defecations and wide swaths of broken branches—have been increasingly evident, but they do not prepare us for the sight of a huge bull of the species bursting into the road about twenty feet ahead. He is taller than the woods and far larger than I remember the proboscideans in circuses and zoos. He thrashes about, moreover, as if greatly agitated, ears flapping like sails. We fear that a herd may follow him or, if he is a rogue elephant and our presence makes him feel trapped, that he may attack. Neither contingency develops, in the event, and he simply turns and re-enters the woods. But an elephant in the wild is an awesome thing, and we hesitate before passing his point of exit.

1962

Skukuza Kamp, the largest in the Park, billets five hundred people in rondavels, and almost as many more in a tented bivouac area. But the Skukuza dining-room décor—animal trophies, witch doctors' mantic objects, Zulu shields and assegais—offers no respite from the Park, and neither does tonight's outdoor film on *African Arachnids*. The flashlight of the ranger who guides me to my rondavel discovers hyena and baboons on our side of the Kamp's low wire fence. They are waiting to burgle citrus fruit and leather shoes, the ranger says, and are adept at opening doors of huts and automobiles. Several times during the night a lion roars, and only a few feet away, so it seems.

MAY 30

We rise at 5 AM and, after a delicious breakfast of Skukuza *pirochki*, drive along the Sabie River in alleged elephant and lion country. Shortly after, the sun rises orange, but turns white in seven minutes. The first animal we see is a baboon sitting at a fork in the road, like a traffic cop. Soon other baboons appear, scratching themselves, nursing pink offspring, clamoring for and receiving tourists' handouts—a defection to the welfare state that is bound to disturb the natural system of dependencies, one would suppose, except that in the abundance of Kruger Park the chain must overlap as well as interlock, impalas, for example, being so plentiful that a lion has only to reach out as they go by, like grabbing a sandwich in a cafeteria.

Then only a few feet away we see two great glistening elephants nonchalantly consuming a tree. They take no notice of us, and go on crunching their morning lumber with as much noise, in scale, as any American at his crackle-and-pop breakfast food. When we start to drive away, a monkey jumps from a tree, grasps our radio aerial, and rides along on the fender like a straphanger in a subway. His face is black, his body gray-white, his testicles billiard-chalk blue; and his tail, in contrast to the baboon's, which loops cheekily upward like a girl's pony tail, drops down straight away.

Rounding a turn, we find eight lions in the road ahead, the elders prowling leisurely in our direction, the youngers playfully pummeling each other. They must have had their *petit déjeuner* by now, for an antelope has crossed the road only a few yards back. (Did the antelope know that the lions were replete, I wonder, or was he simply on the wrong side of the wind?) The lions disregard us, yet at the same time give no ground to our car—as if, like Berkeleians, they could deny its existence simply by refusing to look. But *I* look, and when one of them pads by my window only a foot away, the glare from its cold yellow eyes crosses my heartbeat like a shadow of ice. At first the thought occurs to me that the lion is using the car to cover its scent, but it lopes into a thicket, where it yawns as harmlessly as an actor in a summer theater during an intermission in Shaw's *Androcles.* The young gambol into the bush, too, and have soon melted without trace into the landscape. Who would now suspect this patch of undergrowth to be part lion? And who, seeing what we have seen, would trust the appearance of the jungle?

Birds are everywhere: glossy starlings; blue-casqued guinea fowl; red-beaked honey birds; yellow, waddling hornbills; purple-crested lories; violet troupands; black butcher-bird birdcallers, who impale the victims of their dissembling on thorns; a black bird with a prima donna breast, long flappy wings, and a tail like a ray fish—of such length, in fact, that it seems able to do no more than float from tree to tree like a glider. A single bird in a tree always seems to perch on the topmost limb, like a hatpin, or on the tip of the most extended side limb. Vultures, appropriately enough, seem to prefer dead or totally bare trees, but whirlpools of them going round and round like fathers in a maternity hospital are never out of sight in the sky.

Near lower Sabie, the road runs along an expanse of river, exposing a crocodile on the far bank, its jaws half open in a depraved grin. As we watch, a second crocodile climbs to a rock, midstream, and a kingfisher loops over it like a stunt flyer, alighting on its dripping back to look for encrusted edibles, but, finding none, stands there in daredevil pose, vainly preening.

1962

163

The roadside is dense with impala, their coats, in the early morning cold, a frizzy, goose-flesh fur. We come upon two impala rams fighting inside a widely scattered circle of ewes. They charge like jousting knights, and the ferocity of the combat and the ugly, grunting noises would forever destroy—for movie-bred children—the sentimental Disney image of the doe in a dingle.

About a mile from lower Sabie we espy a leopard couchant in a copse only a few yards from the road. It sniffs the air and twitches its whiskers like any house cat, and it is incomparably more feline than a lioness. Birds scream when it walks—a movement of such litheness that the lion is a hobbler in comparison. And, walking, it displays a sleek white throat, a lustrous rosetted back, and a slowly sloping tail with the upsweep at the end, compared to which the lion's tail is a mere knout. It wants to cross the road to the riverside, apparently, but can find no egress in the rapidly lengthening barricade of tourists' automobiles.

We return to Skukuza on the northern river road, reputedly a good one on which to see zebra and giraffe. And we soon see giraffe, pruning treetops. They are a pure fantasy animal to me, more so here, in their habitat, than in a zoo: in fact, a unicorn would be less surprising. A little later we see several of them at the riverbank. They have white earflaps, are cornuted like Michelangelo's *Moses,* and they cross necks like French generals embracing. They are obliged to spread and sprawl to drink the water, a posture so clumsy that one marvels at the survival of the freak at all. We notice another giraffe peering at us over the top of a tree, like a gardener over a hedge, but finding itself discovered, it ambles away in a long side-to-side movement like roller skating, the hind leg of each side touching the ground first and then the longer front leg.

Zebras are even less trusting. We surprise twenty to thirty of them prancing nervously in a field, and though they are a considerable distance from us, the mares cautiously shield the foals. Every surface is striped, from dewlap to fetlock, whorled nose to Cathedral-of-Siena legs. Some koodoo are grazing nearby, pooling their more powerful auditory radar with the zebra's more acute olfactory sense, "an *entente cordiale,*" as I.S. says.

The chief game warden is our host at the Skukuza campfire dinner—of *polenta* and *sosatie,* which are haslets spitted like shashlik. He is able to keep a close count of the Park's elephants, he tells us, and a reasonable estimate of the lion population, but all other censuses—and especially the impala, which must fluctuate radically at lion lunchtime—are unknown. The warden says that he once saw a crocodile catch and kill an impala at the riverbank and hide the cadaver in a cave. "A 'croc' does not eat any meat fresh, of course, but stores it until it gets 'high.'" And he tells of the discovery of a "cannibals'" ossuary in the Limpopo mountain region of the Park; and imparts fascinating information about a variety of creatures including the edible lizard (the dthub), the fennec, the rhim, the lemur, and the nearly extinct oryx, which is now being brought from Arabia to breed in Africa. But the most appealing of his stories is about a baboon in a tree suddenly seeing a lion directly below, and fainting. We feel more sympathetic to baboons after hearing that.

MAY 31

The sun rises from a lavender sky today, matches every shade on the color chart from blood red to white, and turns the river mist into a cataract of gold dust.

Just outside the Kamp we meet three lions, a "triangle" evidently, with *monsieur* trying to growl away *le gigolo*. And a crapulous trio, to judge by the vultures overhead. Farther on, two more lions, young ones with incipient manes, bound across the road about five yards in front of the car.

A driver coming from the opposite direction tells us of a large herd of elephants around the next bend on the far bank of the Sabie, but almost hidden by reeds and palms and visible only through binoculars. Information of this sort is exchanged everywhere in the Park—"Beyond the bridge about thirty yards to the left we saw an ostrich"—and without it we would have missed a great deal.

The road between Mbyamite and the southern gate is the wildest and loneliest of all, and the animals seem doubly alert, perhaps because of the tall, lion-concealing grass. A saddle-backed jackal, silver and red-clay-colored belly, runs zigzag from us like a professional fugitive; or, as the author of *Venus and Adonis* put it:

> . . . to overshoot his troubles,
> How he outruns the wind, and with what care
> He counts and crosses with a thousand doubles.

1962

The country is wilder and more weird at each turn, and the anthills suggest the chimneys of H. G. Wells's Morlocks or of the subterranean survivors of the next war.

Leaving the Park, I.S. remarks that "Animals do not have to *do*, they just *are*," which sounds like his "A nose is" philosophy.

JUNE 1

On the flight to Capetown, the pilot, for our benefit, circles Table Mountain, the Twelve Apostles, and the Bay area, which obligingly lights up as we land. It is a Riviera climate, with palms and umbrella pines, but the white houses with black shutters and brick houses with iron balconies and tin roofs are remote from the Mediterranean. On the road from the airport political resistance slogans—FREEDOM'S GOING, REMEMBER SHARPVILLE, STOP THE VORSTER NAZI BILL—are as common as roadside advertisements in the United States. We drive past rugby fields and through the market place—

Dutch flower stalls, two-wheeled Bantu handcarts—to the Mount Nelson Hotel, which, for liveliness, would compare unfavorably with a sanatorium for total paralytics.

JUNE 2

The manor house at Groot Constantia—the estate of an early governor, whose vineyards established the wine industry—is a handsome white building with looped Dutch-style gables. It is also a museum of colonial furniture, including teakwood bidets, stinkwood tub seats, armchairs with fan-shaped splats and cabriole legs, Delft celadon wine vessels, and books—a volume of voyages dated Venice 1520 and opened to Vasco da Gama's description of the Cape.

Returning to Capetown, we overtake a column of "nonwhite" boys who, it is later explained to us, are from "a kind of Borstal unit for recidivists." Recidivists at fourteen?

A large reception for I.S. in the City Hall, with lots of speeches and *petits-fours*. The Mayor, with the gold chain of office around his neck, looks like a *sommelier* in a pretentious restaurant. Someone tells us that he is Jewish and that a "Jewish bloc" exists in Parliament, as if this were testament of a liberal régime. V. shocks this person by telling him that her own main interest in South Africa is the Crosopterygian—the armored fish, twice captured in South African waters, from which the amphibian is thought to have emerged.

At dinner we try more ordinary fish: hake, kingklip, snook, steenbras.

JUNE 3

A final excursion today, to Muizenberg, False Bay, Kalk Bay, Chapman's Peak Drive, where a fog rolls in on the surface of the sea like a tidal wave. The sandy lowlands which, from the airplane at night, we mistook for snow, are fringed with yellow heath flowers, blue hydrangeas, pink Watsonia.

JUNE 5

We fly to Rome via Kimberley, Johannesburg, Salisbury, Brazzaville. A sign at Kimberley Airport advertises the diamond mine as "The largest man-made hole in the world," which somehow sounds indecent. The hole is surrounded by scrub desert, mounds of gray slag, strip farms, ponds shaped like boomerangs.

JUNE 11

Rome. Two reminders of Africa, the elephant with the obelisk in front of the Chiesa di Minerva—is this Milton's "elephants endorsed with towers"?—and, in the Campo dei Fiori, the legend "LUMUMBA ASSASSINATO" white-washed on the statue of Giordano Bruno, which marks the site of the great philosopher's burning.

We call on Giacomo Manzù in his Latino Malabranca studio, where he is working on the "Doors of Death" for St. Peter's. Manzù's nose is notched, his forehead is furrowed, and his hair appears to have been transplanted from the crown to the back of the head and neck, where it curls between shirt and ears in classical maestro style. His eyes study I.S.'s head professionally, even greedily, throughout the visit.

The studio is built against an alcove of Roman bricks only slightly higher than the bronze doors themselves—a full-scale skeleton of which stands in front of the alcove, with a Death-on-the-Cross blocked out in gold paper in the upper right panel. The other walls are made of concrete, and Manzù has covered them with tapestries. But these are the only furnishings, the studio being cluttered with easels, cavalettes, and clay casts of the sculptured reliefs for the doors.

Manzù says that the upper left panel will contain a Death of the Virgin, while two smaller spaces, below the Virgin and the Christ, will be filled with *natures mortes.* Next below that are to be depicted the deaths of Abel, Moses, and Saints Joseph and Gregory the Great, and underneath, representations of deaths by earth, air (in space), water, violence (war). Manzù envisions the war tableau as the hanging of a partisan, with the man's mother at his side. These eight central panels will be executed in low relief, the *natures mortes,* along with six squares at the bottom with animals symbolizing death, in full relief—like the efts, insects, and shells on the lid of Jamnitzer's silver box in Vienna. The animals are a porcupine, a serpent, a tortoise turned on its back, an owl, a crow, and a *guira.* When I confess that I do not know this word, the artist quickly draws a squirrel.

The only panel so far completed in bronze is the Death of Gregory, which, for our benefit, Manzù and a helper carry outside into the light. The Angel of Death, helmet visor thrust back, points from the left to the slumped but still-mitred head of the enthroned Gregory, whose long papal cope flows from his head to below the body, which it dwarfs; in fact, the line of this robe is the fixating feature of the composition. Rubbing the patina to show us the true tincture of the bronze, the sculptor says that he prefers to work directly in bronze in spite of the risk because only then does he feel the form is completely his. He says, too, that he makes only a few sketches and a few cloth and paper maquettes, whereas he may try as many as ten castings; and he displays a laundry list of trial moldings for the animals of death, on which seven or eight scratches follow the name of each animal. He also professes to make no more than a single copy, saying that "Two is already mass production," and he tells us that he refused the Vatican's request to include the Resurrection. "Resurrections are baroque—too baroque for me, in any case—and their drama is diluted, whereas death is purely dramatic."

The only other opus in the studio is the head of a cabaret girl, a striptease *artiste* with an unforgettable twist of *je m'en fiche*-ism on her lips.

We drive with the sculptor to his regular studio, which is in an industrial outskirt, guarded by high walls and hounds. The yard is full of sculpture, as is the three-room atelier, which, owing to the many busts and figures wrapped in canvas cloaks and hoods, might be a morgue. The shelves of the main room are stacked with unfinished figurines, puddings of gesso, and a hardware store of hammers, hatchets, picks, pestles, spatulas, chisels, drills, and saws. A plaster bust of Kokoschka lies in a corner next to a terra-cotta head of a boxer, and in the center of the room, two otherwise nude bronze ballerinas stand tautly on their slippered toes tying ribbons in their hair. As we admire them, Manzù pats their behinds, with pride but also with concupiscence.

His still-life chairs piled with vegetables and fruits are so real that we want to touch them—and do: a cold, slightly macabre sensation. These technical exercises, as Manzù calls them—and he shrugs his shoulders showing them—disturb us in the same way as the sculpture in the Campo Santo at Genoa. Is it because a *nature morte* in three dimensions and actual proportions is as morbid as Madame Tussaud's? Or because a *real* chair in bronze seems a waste of that substance as well as of sculptural energy?

At one point he remarks that "Unlike the poet and the painter when they complete their work, I, when I finish mine, must still endure the suspense of the *fusione*." I.S. answers this by quoting Strindberg: "'The art of the future will, like nature, leave a lot more to chance.'"

Manzù's palms are itching to do I.S.'s head, but he says, "I cannot just begin to sculpt. I have to study photographs, think for a long time and be inspired." I.S.: "In my case the 'necessary angel' appears only when I am already working, and then sometimes the lady takes a lot of nudging before her wings begin to flap."

[**Postscript, June 26, 1971.** I go with V. to see Manzù in his new home at Campo Fico, a hillside near an old Roman town, Ardea, which may seem prettier than it is simply because the drive through the suburbs of the new Rome is so awful. *"Attenti al cane,"* a notice warns at the gate, but I suspect that "attention" to a high wire fence should have priority, a chewing by canines being a less terrible prospect than electrocution. We ring up, drive up, park behind the maestro's new Cadillac—not the only sign of the increasing marketability of his art—and are warmly received by him, and only once growled at by the *cane*.

The maestro is so portly now that one wonders how he can work at all from certain angles. Otherwise he seems the same, which is to say that his hair is still migrating from his head neckwards, and that his quick brown eyes are both as soft and as strong as ever. The route to the sitting room passes a shelf of the maestro's Al Capone hats, two pieces of his sculpture, and a long gallery of Japanese prints. The walls of the room itself display some of his own drawings, but its furniture—a low glass table and bucket chairs capacious enough to contain the maestro—is *very* modern.

I explain that V. wants a simple stone with the name (no dates) and a cross. The stone should be white, Manzù suggests, and probably in two layers, the upper slightly indented. "I can procure the marble from the Vatican, but the cross must be gold as befits a great king." The name could be done in tesserae, he adds, but he says he would want time to consider the idea—and so would we. I promise to send the measurements of the plot from Venice next week, and he promises to join us there at the end of August and bring a model of the tomb. Then, telling V. that I.S. was the greatest inspiration to him all his life, his eyes suddenly fill with tears, whereupon V. embraces him, and says—revealing more of her own loneliness than she ever allows any of us to see—"I can't get over the feeling of expecting him to come back."]

JUNE 14

Piero's *"Misericordia"* polyptych, now in the Istituto Restauro, is surrounded by detailed photographs of every stage of its cleaning. According to one of the restorers, the cape that the Queen of Heaven spreads above an apse of kneeling worshipers is an oil emulsion, whereas her other garments are pure tempera, which may indicate that they were painted at different periods. One of the kneeling figures wears a black hood, as members of Tuscan *Misericordia* societies still do. According to popular tradition, the man on his left, whose face is the most arresting in the group, is a portrait of the artist. But to my amateur's eyes, the Sebastian in the left panel is more of a Masaccio than a Piero. It is, in any case, the face of a dumb and brutalized peasant rather than, as usual, that of the mere disappointed lover. The marginal surfaces of the wood beneath the painting are daubed with Piero's trial color mixes.

1962

Also in the Istituto is an icon from Santa Maria in Trastevere, a *toile* already restored—transferred to cedar boards—a millennium ago; and it is the discovery of this early effort at preservation which has excited the workmen, who think it may be one of the oldest icons extant. The face is in the Fayum tradition, but the rest of the picture is full of movement, the Madonna dandling the Infant as if she were giving Him a first walking lesson. The pedestal for her left foot is, or appears to be—this part of the picture gapes with lacunae—the prostrate person of a pope.

But to me the most affecting of the to-be-restored treasures is a chipped and candle-blackened *"Ecce Homo"* signed, in a painted banner on the frame, *"Antonellus Messinius pixit."* The eyes of Antonello's young redheaded model are bloodshot, as if from conjunctivitis, and a noose and its shadow hang around his neck. The flesh is flecked with tears of blood and transparent perspiration, and if the painting has a fault it is that the painter prided himself too much on this pearly perspiration.

AUGUST 29

Lod Airport, Tel Aviv. As we leave the plane, a chorus of schoolgirls welcomes I.S. with songs; or at least that is what, by their open mouths and thrusting bosoms, I suppose them to be doing, but a jet is threatening to take off in the vicinity and we hear nothing. The girls pelt us with carnations when we move within range, and I.S. gathers some of them from the ground into a bouquet, with which he waves a return salute. This is the warmest reception ever, from people, photographers' bulbs, the setting but still sweltering sun. "*Shalom! Shalom!*" everyone is saying, and cordiality flows around us like a warm bath.

At the Dan Hotel the room clerk speaks Russian, the receptionist Spanish, Italian, and Greek, the *maître d'hôtel* German, the telephone operator English, the chambermaid French, the elevator boy—a *sabra*—Hebrew only. We exchange vigorous handshakes with all of them, and are greeted by all like long-lost relatives. "Welcome home," the room waiter says, with an enthusiasm befitting the return of the *juif errant,* except that his confidence in me seems to wane rather quickly, for by the end of the meal he is procuring illicit cream (forbidden after meat) for my coffee. The delicacy of the dinner is a kosher red caviar on unleavened bread.

Tel Aviv, on one side of our rooms, is a cliff of balconied apartment houses, like commodes with the drawers open. On the opposite side, under a sky like a planetarium, the sea is sprinkled with lights from fishing boats. Besides the surf, the only sound is a wail from a café somewhere down the beach.

AUGUST 31

Awakened by shouting, I hurry to the window in time to see a dozen women, sufferers from nothing more serious (I hope) than over-adequate adiposity, drilling on the beach like a squad of recruits in the Marines. The instructor shouts and the ladies salaam; or, arms akimbo, and then folded behind their fleshy backs, twist and bend their obese trunks; or roll on the ground, apparently trying to bounce; or lie as nice ladies should not, kicking their legs like overturned beetles. They droop a bit after the workout, but no one is noticeably more svelte. Perhaps the simpler solution would be to cut down on the curds and whey.

On another part of the beach, two girls are displaying about all that legally *can* be displayed of precisely the flesh that these elders of the sex would like to be left with, but displaying it for the benefit of two bald but otherwise hairy men who are too absorbed in conversation to look. At this point I.S. enters my room, takes in the scene, observes that "Businessmen should not talk business undressed, especially when they look like orang-utangs." And, looking at the girls: "What counts is not so much the unclothed body, but movement, and not matter-of-fact movement, but gracefulness."

I begin this morning's rehearsal in Mann Auditorium with misgivings, having been told that nearly everyone in the orchestra once was, and in most cases still considers himself to be, a conductor. But the players are as co-operative and as adult—musicians in groups often being quite child-ish—as any with whom I have worked. They are quick, too, which is not surprising, except that we had anticipated a show of polite resistance to our all-modern program, the stalwarts reputedly being not only conservative but Viennese-conservative; and, in truth, the very first beat shows that the mold of their style *is* the sentimental tradition, and that Old, but not old-enough, Vienna is their first love. Yet their musical performance, good as it is, is less remarkable than their linguistic one. I.S. addresses them largely in Russian, but from time to time in French, Italian, German, and English as well, yet in no instance is translation required; after hearing their own exchanges in a dozen other tongues, I deduce that *any* language would be understood, if not by the triangle player, then by the trumpeter or the harpist. In fact, the only missing linguistic ingredient is Brooklynese, that loveliest of brogues. Nobody says: "Khau do you do?" and "Don't be noivez."

During intermission a joke goes the rounds, one of many sparked by the recent visit of Willy Brandt. It seems that Herr Brandt had expressed his pleasure to Mr. Ben-Gurion that the Mann Auditorium had been named for a "great German writer" (author of *Buddenbrooks*). "But it is named for an American writer," the Prime Minister reportedly answered. Herr Brandt: "Really? I do not think I have heard of him. What did he write?" "A check," said Mr. Ben-Gurion, and one imagines this example of the patriarchal powers of repartee touring the country, and the family pride it leaves in its wake.

After the rehearsal we go to Jaffa, "for purposes of sightseeing" as the driver explains. But the truly impressive "sights" are people, most memorably an ancient rabbi wearing corkscrew side curls, gabardine coat, and a black hat over his yarmulke; a small boy leads him by the left hand, for his other hand taps the pavement with the white cane of the blind. In the same neighborhood, the narrow streets near the harbor, another religious venerable wears the Daniel Boone cap of the twelve peltries representing the twelve tribes. But to us it seems impracticable and extremely uncomfortable that these people have transplanted themselves from Chagall's Vitebsk to the heat and humidity of a Miami climate with no modification in clothing. Our friend, the Haganah veteran Ahron Propes, agrees. "The wardrobe is a survival from a mystic way of life," he says, "and it should be adjusted." But no one will say how or venture to introduce a rabbinical summer style. And this ambivalence toward religious orthodoxy, and indeed every kind of hereditary religious dispensation, is one of Israel's profoundest problems, both individually and at the government level. "I am not a believer," an American acquaintance tells me, "but when I am here I put on my hat and talith and go to the synagogue; and though I have long since drifted away from any semblance of the dietary observances, in Israel I follow them strictly." And the statement is typical. But when rigid traditions are no longer needed to preserve identity, how long will they last?

Our driver is a refugee from Germany, except that "refugee" is never used here; Israel is "home," and today's refugees are "newcomers." A hitch with the British Army during the war left him with an odd brand of English.

Thus, he refers to "Christ's crucification." And as a cicerone, though he can supply biblical references for everything we see, they are scarcely recognizable to anyone brought up on King James. Fortunately he has another lore, a bag of stories about the 1956 campaign. "Arabs run better without their shoes," he says, "and as they were always running, the Sinai Desert, when we got there, was a harvest of old shoes."

It is the eve of the Sabbath, hence the two candles and two loaves of bread in a napkin on a table at the entrance to the dining room. The headwaiter asks us not to smoke, as we enter, then, taking us for "newcomers," he bids us "welcome home." And rightly, I am beginning to think, for we do feel at home here. And as if to convert feeling to fact, a letter awaits me in my room from a woman in a kibbutz who, seeing my name in a newspaper, claims kinship, and substantiates the connection with a long list of wrong relatives. So much for "Jewish names."

SEPTEMBER 1

1962

"Shabbat Shalom," the room waiter says this morning, and the greeting explains the frugality of the breakfast, the creation of fire being forbidden on the Sabbath. Another, more welcome, consequence of holy writ is the suspension of rehearsals, for our bodies are still functioning on Pacific Standard Time, a discrepancy of eleven hours which leaves us with a diagonal feeling and the need of a time pill. One unforeseen complication caused by the Sabbath is that no laboratory technician will take I.S.'s blood, and his weekly examination is due today. A doctor comes instead, but after punctiliously fulfilling the Greek—Hippocratic—part of his duties, he no less strictly obeys the Hebrew part by refusing to sign I.S.'s medical logbook and thus defile himself with a pen.

Public transportation services, including some international airplane flights, are halted until sundown, and automobile traffic is thin—in some areas virtually at a standstill—so that "Sunday driver" would have a different meaning here; driving to the Weizmann Institute ourselves, we wonder whether bystanders are thinking us flagrantly sacrilegious. Recalling that the interdiction against travel on the Sabbath does not apply to journeys by water, I.S. describes how the younger Jews of Ustilug used to sit on water bottles in railway coaches. I should add that, since his arrival in Israel, I.S. has been repeatedly reminded of Ustilug, at first simply by scraps of conversation with elderly settlers from Russia, then by a quality of "coziness" which he holds to be peculiar to Russian Jews. Yesterday he was presented with a history of the Jewish community of Ustilug compiled by descendants of families who had lived there, and I have rarely seen him so moved.

Meyer Weisgal, director of the Weizmann Institute, is refreshingly unorthodox as an academic dignitary. "Jesus Christ" is his favorite expletive and his imagery tends to the earthy, "bald as a camel's ass," for example, being his description of a colleague's tonsorial problem. During lunch at his home with the Minister of Education, Abba Eban, a discussion develops about anti-Semitism in the Soviet Union and recent Soviet newspaper attacks on "the philosophy of the Bible," though on evidence few of the attackers have read "The Book," which has been on the Soviet *index librorum prohibitorum* these forty years. Mr. Eban attributes the Soviet refusal to allow its "Jewish" musicians to perform in Israel to "fear of defection." But here the I.S.'s, meaning only to keep the discussion afloat, nearly sink it with some testimony of exactly the wrong kind. They say that a waiter at the Dan, a newcomer from the Soviet Union, has told them that in his experience "Racism did not exist in the Red Army, whereas in Israel, peoples from different countries and with different shades of skin are constantly waging disputes."

In the afternoon we visit a kibbutz of exotically dressed newcomers from Algeria; and Ashkelon, birthplace of Herod the paranoid. Sections of pipeline for the rerouting of the River Jordan, nearly large enough for an automobile tunnel, have been rolled to the side of one stretch of the road.

SEPTEMBER 2   **1962**

Caesarea. Our French-speaking guide is a fluent quoter of Josephus and a learned commentator on such subjects as Roman castrametation and the origins of the cunei, the diazoma, and the skene. A stone has been uncovered in the amphitheater, incised with the name of the procurator Pontius Pilate. On him, incidentally, as on all Roman officials, Christians eventually took iconoclastic revenge, decapitating every Roman image in the country except a statue of a woman in Ashkelon, which may prove the rule, its resemblance to an early representation of the Madonna very likely being responsible for its escape.

Reaching Haifa at dusk, we drive directly to a lookout near the gold dome of the Bahaists, for the view of Acre lighting up across the harbor. Many Druses are in the streets, mysterious people with long veils trailing from white turbans.

Our Haifa concert takes place in a cinema between screenings of *A Streetcar Named Desire*, in what may well be the hottest room in the world. The slightest movement provokes a flood of perspiration; my spectacles steam over like frosted glass when I conduct, and I am soon swaddled by my clothes as if I had fallen into a swimming pool. After the first movement of the Symphony, I remove my tie and unbutton the upper part of my shirt, and at the end of the third movement, peel my jacket as well. This greatly amuses the audience, it seems, and the prolonged applause at the end of the piece may be less an expression of enthusiasm for the music—which they may suspect of having been the *Istar* Variations—than of curiosity to see what will come off next. No wonder then, that when I pull a bath towel from under my score, after the Violin Concerto, and pass it to the soloist, Zvi Zeitlin, whose own handkerchiefs and hand towels are waterlogged, and when he mops and then I mop, this humid scene wins a thundering ovation.

Life along the road to Nazareth and Tiberias is mainly pastoral, with but little husbandry, and Arabs, wearing aquals and kaffiyehs, are more numerous than on any of the other routes we have traveled. The economy of Nazareth itself, a hideous city, seems to depend entirely on souvenir-selling; and as the water of "Mary's Well"—"Where Jesus drank"—is bottled and sold, so, no doubt, are the local earth and local air. A church "as large as St. Peter's" is promised for the city a few years hence, and, indeed, size is the only attribute in which it would be possible to have any confidence. An hour beyond Nazareth, the Sea of Galilee comes into view, and the purple-and-beige mountains of Syria. Our ears crackle as we descend.

Tiberias, a stone village with iron balconies, is forlorn and oppressive: the only life is in the Sea, where the fish leap, and on the beach, where the bathers are both human and goat. At Capernaum, we are admitted by a Franciscan friar who is lonelier than a lighthouse keeper and so pleased to have visitors to whom he can speak Italian that he may never be able to stop. He wants to talk about the arts, of course, and give a rest to his tourist routines about Christ's life here as a nemoricole, and about the quarry of old stones—Roman olive-oil presses, largely—of which he is custodian. But for I.S., the dereliction of Capernaum, coming after the tawdriness of Nazareth, is a shock. Only a very dingy chapel, which the city fathers of Nazareth might have dumped as surplus goods, marks this supposed site of Christ's first miracles. And instead of an élite honor guard of one of the holy brotherhoods, the place is inhabited only by this garrulous and destitute monk, who falls on us like the last defender of the fort in *Under Two Flags*, the sole survivor, now half crazed from the solitude and the heat; or, rather, Capernaum being some 600 feet below sea level, the solitude, the heat, and the bends. But how much of the shock is also due to conditioning by Art, the Holy Land of our imaginations having been formed in large measure by, for example, Tuscan and Umbrian landscapes in *quattrocento* paintings?

Prejudices of art raise no obstacles to biblical visions on the road to Jerusalem, in any case, and this in spite of the wrecks of trucks and tanks left by the roadside as memorials to the blockade-runners of 1948. Biblical mirages are conjured up at every turn, in the Judean hills, a man on a ladder picking a fruit tree, for instance, becoming a picture of Absalom suspended by his hair. At times the territory of Israel narrows to a defile not much wider than the road, which means that we ourselves are only a bull's-eye from barbed-wired Jordan. The higher we climb, the more barren the brown, terraced hills, until suddenly looming before us like a white crown is the city of the mellifluous name.

Jerusalem, from our rooms, is a white wall turreted in front and machicolated to the west, and for these and other features it bears a remarkable resemblance to the city of Carpaccio's imagination in the *"Prédication de Saint-Etienne,"* in the Louvre. Below the wall is the gulch of Gehenna, a dry moat, and beyond it are round Turkish towers, square Gothic towers, the Tower of David, cross-topped cupolas of Eastern churches, Muslim orbs. The Jordanian frontier is marked by a row of carrot-shaped cypresses and shrubberies hollowed like bagels, beyond which is a no-man's-land of rubble and desert. From the angle of another hill, a short walk east of the hotel, we can see the Mount of Olives, Gethsemane, the Valley of Moloch, and Golgotha. For still more views we drive along the border as far as Manhat, which, lying directly on the line, has been evacuated, a dead city under the eye of a ghostly Ottoman tower. At sunset the desert turns violet, and its cities—Moab, Gilead, Bethlehem—salt white. Back in Jerusalem in the blue light of evening, we leave for our concert under a barrage of church bells from the Old City, as discordant as the different versions of the Only Veracity they advertise.

The presence of President Ben-Zvi at the concert obliges I.S. to lead the *"Hatikva,"* a dreadful dirge in D minor ("the Sanhedrin Blues," I.S. calls it) reminding us of *"Má Vlàst."* He is nervous about this, and after an uncertain first beat, when he finds the orchestra quite capable of sustaining the mournful melody on its own the relief is so great that he swerves into the remainder with blood, schmaltz, tears, and even a final Bernstein lunge.[1]

SEPTEMBER 5

We tour the city in the morning, going first to the Mandelbaum Gate, where buildings are sandbagged and a *détente* seems to be as far away as ever. But another borderline, less violent if at times hardly less troublesome, exists in this neighborhood within Israeli territory: the ghetto of the extremist Neturi Karta sect, the Me'a She'Arim. These zealots live only for the Sabbath, measuring the hour and the day in terms of time from it. They are, of course, rabidly opposed to the Erastian state of the Zionists, on the un-arguable grounds that it was created not by the Messiah but by men. They are a considerable nuisance to the state, refusing to pay its taxes and to serve in its defense, though more than that, too, for they are the atavistic conscience of the whole country. What most impresses us about them is that they have so successfully marooned themselves and their gnostic way of life, or way of waiting for God, in the heart of a modern city. The fathers and husbands go about in sackcloth and cover their wives and daughters in long dresses, coarse black stockings, and woolen wigs—lest they tempt other men—while half a block away *Lolita* is playing at the cinema.

The Dead Sea scrolls, at Hebrew University, look suspiciously new, and in fact the black script on the clean white parchment sheets, sewn together like frames in spools of film, is easily legible and can be read without

---

1. Next day's newspaper notices cited the discernment of the interpretation, but what they said about the remainder of the program provoked I.S. to remark that "The Talmudic tradition is still active in music criticism."

difficulty by schoolchildren. And this state of preservation of the language is far more remarkable to me than the state of preservation of the scrolls. A commentary on Habakkuk is on exhibit, as well as a copy of the Book of Isaiah, and the Essene text "The Sons of Darkness and the Sons of Light." Each scroll is displayed with the jar in which it was found, together with photographs of the jars in the caves at the time of their discovery.

We go from the University to the presidential "Log Cabin," which, along with its incumbents, is a national symbol of pioneer Israel. There an adjutant reads citations for I.S. and myself, after which Mr. Ben-Zvi presents I.S. with an antique vase, and myself with a medal and standard. The ceremony over, the President switches from Hebrew to Russian, which appears to be the domestic language of elderly officials—white-haired cabinet ministers, octogenarian social planners, and such. It develops that Mr. Ben-Zvi and I.S. had known the city of Poltava at approximately the same date, and as they exchange recollections of it, other guests join in. At one point a parlor game of renaming Russian writers as Jews—Pushkinson, Gogolman, Lermontovich, etcetera—gets under way. When we leave, Mrs. Ben-Zvi beseeches I.S. to "say a good word for Israel when you are in the Soviet Union."

Back in Tel-Aviv we dine with Theodore Kollek, who is said to typify the new Israel and who undeniably does present a striking contrast to the Russian refugees of the morning meeting. Kollek is a husky, hard-drinking, cigar-smoking man of action, as well as an intellectual whose off-duty passion is archeology. He has a small Luristan chariot ornament with him, in fact, which he found on a dig not long ago, but I admire it too much and he gives it to me.

SEPTEMBER 7

We spend the morning packing and receiving visitors. One of them, the proud parent, as she says, of a new Mozart, is proof that the great traditions of *chutzpah* are alive and well, for she plainly implies that it is high time I.S. renounced his own footless activities in favor of a full-scale dedication to her whiz-kid son and his certain-to-be-world-changing genius. Another caller, this one evidently a *meshuganah,* wants to commission a concerto for shofar and orchestra.

We leave early for the airport, allowing time for the Haaretz Glass Museum in Ramat-Aviv. The director of this attractive new circular building leads us through, discoursing the while on glassmaking techniques: the discovery of the sand-core method and the method of coloring by cobalt and manganese oxides; and the marvering and crizzling of the parison, which is the glass in its bubble-gum state. Like many other chronologically arranged museums, the Haaretz constitutes a strong argument for the decline of culture. In glass manufacture, moreover, the downgrade is noticeable as early as the Late Bronze Age. The gradient is not always even, to be sure, and beautiful individual objects were produced in all periods, but the direction of the slope, as it courses through the Persian, Phoenician, Sidonian, Hellenistic, Roman, Byzantine, and Islamic periods, is unmistakable. The decline, furthermore, is characterized by the same process in every culture. For it is always a matter of more bulk and volume, more gilding and incrustation, in short, MORE. And it is almost always marked by a turning away from the functional in favor of the purely decorative, and by a final stage that descends from the highly baroque to the merely bizarre. The Haaretz, in sum, is an argument for "old bottles" (leaving aside the question of wines), of which the very oldest—cosmetic phials, finger bowls, an aryballus—are all small and, in form and color, very simple. In the Roman period, which is already a long way downhill, the stock of utilities has expanded to include such instruments as the strigil, but meanwhile the old forms have been vulgarized, and pure colors have given way to color effects, including iridescenses and rainbow patinas. Ancient Hebrew glasswares are identified by ashtaroths, menorahs, corn sheaves, clusters of grapes.

Leave-taking at the airport is misty-eyed and smothering. Another departing passenger, watching the fuss around I.S., asks me if I know "who the old guy is," but without waiting for my reply goes on to remark that "On second thought, whoever it is must be an old *goy* or they wouldn't pay that much attention."

SEPTEMBER 10

Venice. I.S. is already working on *Abraham and Isaac*. After dinner we watch a battalion of German tourists grouping for a crepuscular gondola ride. "They do it with more discipline than other people," I.S. notes, "which may be part of the reason that Stockhausen's title seems so apt." As one group glides by, under the Ponte San Moisè, he bids them *"Lustige Fahrt,"* but the language even in his mouth is an abrasive contrast to the chatter of passing Venetians.

Full of calorific Italian cuisine, we take a gondola ourselves to the Campo San Zanipolo, going by way of the Rio di Palazzo—many more of whose *diamanti* have been dislodged since we last saw it—and returning by the Greek church, whose minacious bell tower may topple at any minute into the canal. Our conversation at the Zanipolo is about Tiepolo's "Abraham and Isaac" in the nearby Santa Maria dei Derelitto.[1] And about the coming evacuation of Venice—eviction, in the case of the last *homo sap.* on the last garbage scow—and the final gurgle of the scuttled city as San Marco sinks under the waves, a *"Cathédrale engloutie."* We talk, too, about the gaps to

---

1. One of the orphanages which supplied players for the famed nun-orchestras of the Vivaldi era. Its façade is grizzly, yet the grizzly barbarian faces are not an uncommon Venetian motif (*cf.* the belfry door of San Bartolomeo, as well as the Ponte de le Guglie—where, however, they are less human than leonine). Each face is mustachioed and each gnashes sabre-like fangs, while one of them, convulsive or drunk, curls its tongue to the side. Directly above are four *Telamoni,* and above them, on the cornices, statues of the Virtues, one of them black, like the Virgin in the Scalzi, another ringing a schoolbell, and a third holding foundling babies in her arms. But the street is narrow and the upper part of the church scarcely visible.

be filled in the libraries, before the Flood (now that a competent history of the gondola has appeared, that Guariento has come into his own, etc.). Books are needed on the decorated ceilings in the great *palazzi,* for instance, and on the *cortili,* the loggias, the bridges and their iron railings (all different), the iron window grilles, the (now muzzled) well-heads, the chimneys, the street lamps and votive lamps, the calvaries and shrines. Several volumes should be devoted to the aspect of the city strictly as viewed from canals (*i.e.,* excluding views from *campi, calli, salizzade*); and to particulars of Venetian iconography, such as the fascination with animals and birds, for it is no accident that the best-known rhinoceros in paint is Venetian (although Dürer's engraving does the animal much more justice); and some of the best-known dogs (I am thinking of the courtesans' poodle looking straight at the photographer), to say nothing of the lions, the bronze horses, the dromedaries (in Gentile Bellini and on the wall of the Palazzo del Cammello), the crocodiles (on the pedestal in the Piazzetta), and—in spite of Michaels and Georges aplenty to kill them off—the dragons. Venetians, moreover, still predict the weather from the altitude of swallows (low-flying ones spell rain), and birds still chirp in window cages all over the city, drone louder than an electric generator on San Francesco del Deserto, and "coo" in the Piazza, these last despised, partly, I think, because they do not hop but walk one foot after the other, like businessmen.

Another book, V. says, should be devoted to the eighteenth-century paintings of acrobats in four, five, and six pyramidal tiers (her own first commission as a painter having been to copy a picture of one of these human lattices). But before any of these tomes is added to the shelf, I say that a book of angels is needed, Venice being, above all, a city of angels, whether dancing (on the Salute), trumpeting (on the corner of the Giglio and under the cupola of the "Ascension" in San Marco), floating (on the Riva del Vin side of the Rialto Bridge), or simply exposing their celestial forms (the Scuola di San Teodoro, where one of them, however, looks slightly bat-like—a bat out of Heaven, then?).

But I.S. says that the musical Venice is the most important, "the Venice of Schütz and the Gabrielis, of choirs and organs, of brass instruments in stone streets and churches; and the Venice of opera, of Monteverdi and Cavalli, whose theaters have been destroyed. And this Venice cannot be preserved. Witness the sewing-machine performances of Vivaldi, whose music is comparatively recent and simple."

But one form of music survives: the bells. For life in Venice is still regulated by bells; people still set their watches by the *nona,* still start and stop work by the *marangona.* And the bells tell not only the hours but also the character and remembrances of the hours, including our own mortality.

The music of the three-tone bells (San Marco's five and the Frari's four are too many), thanks to the illusions of changing speeds resulting from the constantly changing positions between the three isorhythmic parts, can be mesmeric. The bells of Santa Maria del Giglio, for example, begin with the *"mi,"* followed by the *"re,"* which limps after the higher part in ever shorter steps, then passes it, whereupon the *"mi"* sounds like the gimpy one. Finally, the *"do"* enters and seems to take sides with the *"re"* against the *"mi."* The *"do"* is the last bell to sound, trailing off, like an *ejaculatio,* with ever longer pauses after each fainter peal. The whole performance, moreover, lasts less than two minutes. (An *ejaculatio praecox,* then.)

SEPTEMBER 21

Paris. Fifteen months of uncertainty coming to an end, we fly to Moscow in a Soviet TU-104, downing vodka and *zakousky*—sprats, herring, caviar—served by hostesses who have not been to charm school and have no camera smiles. Nearing Moscow, the plane dips low over forests turning yellow, meadows still green, boat-busy rivers, lakes, canals. The landscape is rich and tidy, unexpectedly so, for I have pictured a muddy, sprawling country on the lines of the Russia I.S. likes to characterize as a combination of "caviar and *merde.*" I.S., straining to see, is excited and open-mouthed, and V. is choked with emotion. Aground, we taxi past airplanes, unseen in our world, from Poland, Bulgaria, China, and halt by the terminal. A reception committee pushes to the door, and at the same time I.S. emerges, bowing deeply—a gesture out of another era as his dark glasses are glaringly symbolic of another kind of life (Hollywood, I regret to say). We move toward television lights, blinded like moths.

Among those helping us to the waiting room are the familiar faces of Tikhon Khrennikov and Kara Karayev; and the familiar-by-resemblance face of a woman with the slant Tartar eyes Picasso saw in I.S., who sings to me in a high voice, *"Je suis la nièce de Monsieur Stravinsky."* A short, stout woman, who could pass for Jacob Epstein, says *"Ich bin Yudina"* and plants a wet kiss. Another woman, telling me in English that she is the daughter of the poet Konstantin Balmont, hands me a birch-bark basket (whose contents, however, a twig, a leaf, a blade of wheat, an acorn, some moss, I am not particularly needing at the moment).

Inside the terminal, hand-shaking is almost continual, and so are the repetitions of *"Dobro pozhalovat"* from large, round, smiling faces. Most of those present have waited a seesawing year for this moment, and some have hoped or feared a far longer time; to Yudina, for one, it fulfills a lifelong dream. Which is the reason why the atmosphere is like a child's birthday party, and the reason why everyone, and not least among them I.S. himself, is bursting with relief. Finally, a neat, bright-eyed young woman called Alexandra Alexandrovna introduces herself as my interpreter, and we pack into a limousine.

The divided highway—through birch and pine woods, in a cold pink sunset with an Edvard Munch feeling—has less traffic than any major road in the United States, but more than anticipated, a thought that suddenly makes me aware of my cold-war conditioning. Moscow is lighting up as we enter, and V. vainly studies the miles of new apartment buildings on Leningrad

1962

179

Prospekt for landmarks. At the National Hotel, the airport committee, only slightly diminished, awaits us all over again, but this time they seal their welcoming with vodka and sweet champagne. It is the event of Russian musical history, some say, and others tell me they are still rubbing their eyes, never having believed it would happen. When I.S. reads a telegram from Shostakovich, national sentiment flows with the national champagne and gets even thicker.

We escape to the restaurant with Xenia Yurievna, the new-found niece, who says that thirty thousand people have queued up for I.S.'s Leningrad concerts, and says it so earnestly that I fear she may have arrived at the tally by her own footwork. The restaurant seems to have ambitions as a nightclub—moldy jazz-type noises are coming from a band in a far corner—and that may explain why single men are relegated to a smaller, adjoining room. The waitresses are blond, uncorseted, and unhurrying, and the customers—among them Indians in saris, a party of Italians very happy to find *espresso* on the menu, and Chinese who are the "best-dressed" people in the room—appear to have all the time in the world. Except for the portrait of Lenin on the wall and the absence of neckties, the restaurant is not unlike many in the East Fourteenth Street neighborhood of Manhattan. The Chinese are "conditioned," too, as much as we are, V. says, a conclusion she reaches after watching them cut their food into tiny, chopstick-size pieces.

The hotel lobby serves mainly as the place of embarkation for a pair of dilapidated elevators and a staircase with Atlases who appear to be holding up the second floor. (Nothing is holding up the drapery over the Atlases' private parts, however, and for this reason they look as if they were about to drop the second floor.) At the front desk we receive tourist folders of the "Lenin-Stalin Mausoleum," which betray an unsuccessful attempt—it has been blacked out but is still distinctly legible—to cancel the "Stalin." At the second-floor desk we receive our room keys from a concierge in a white *kokoshnik* such as the nurses wear in *Petrushka*. Following her down the corridor, I note that cuspidors have been placed at several convenient points, perhaps with a view to serious service owing to the nauseating smell of fish glue.

The I.S.'s suite, vacated by the Prime Minister of Singapore minutes before, might be called the Napoleon Room. The ceiling fresco is a "Lancret" peacock and nude *femme fatale,* the draperies are in Empire-style crushed velvet, the furniture includes chairs with fasces arm rests, and the "Sèvres" vase, on a pedestal in the corner, is adorned with Imperial gold eagles and a likeness of the Corsican himself. Somewhat out of style with this are the modern five-pronged lamps and a sub-Landseer portrait of a heroic dog. Starting tomorrow, all of our meals will be served in this medium-sized ballroom, Alexandra Alexandrovna says, and waiters and maids soon come to take our orders for breakfast (caviar and coffee). These people are as curious to talk to the I.S.'s—returning White Russian celebrities being rare—as the I.S.'s are to talk to them. We learn that they work and rest in twenty-four-hour shifts, which can hardly make for the greatest efficiency, but which they claim to prefer. One girl, telling V. that her vacation begins in a few days, begs for a bit of rouge.

I walk, before bed, in Red Square, which is empty except for a few trucks and a few other pedestrians. The night is crisp and crystal clear, and the red stars on the Kremlin towers burn like beacons.

SEPTEMBER 22

I rehearse the Moscow National Orchestra in Tchaikovsky Hall, a glossily resonant room also serving as a portrait gallery of composers. The conductor, Ivanov—yellow hair and the face of a good woodsman in a Russian fairy tale—introduces I.S. to the orchestra, which receives him with applause and bow-tapping. But the greeting seems a little quiet and cool to me, and I confide this impression to Alexandra. Her answer is that "We do not glamorize artists here as you do in America, where, for example, Ulanova's *claques* are an embarrassment to the Bolshoi Ballet. We have no cult of personality here." Not since Stalin, anyway, I want to say, and also to protest that I.S. and Ulanova are hardly analogous cases. But, in truth, I like this refreshing democratism, and the absence of that detestable *"Sehr-geehrter-Herr-Professor-Doktor"* protocol; and I like seeing my name in the *affiches*, when I recognize it, in the same type as everyone else's, instead of, as it is for my concerts with I.S. in Europe and America, in the pica otherwise reserved for piano tuners.

The orchestra is a good ensemble, quick to adopt our alien demands of phrasing and articulation, and harder working than European orchestras generally are. And *Le Sacre,* played with an emotion I can describe only as non-Gallic and un-Teutonic, is a different piece. The sound does not glitter as it does with American orchestras, and is less loud, though still deafening in this small, live room. Obviously the musicians prefer the lyric dances to the rhythmic ones, but even in the broadest *cantabile* they do not chew into the visceral fat or weave with passion as Russian violinists are wont to do abroad. And this sobriety is very much to I.S.'s taste. His only criticisms, in fact, are that no one is attentive to tuning—I think they consider our own concern with it exaggerated—and that the harp, in *Orpheus,* is thick, honeyed, and weak in volume: two players share the part, but it is less penetrating than ever before. Another, but satisfying, oddity is the bass drum. The instrument is open on one side, or sawed in two, and the clear, *secco* articulation from the single head makes the beginning of the *Danse de la terre* sound like the stampede I.S. had in mind. He also likes the *rape güero,* which, he says, should be heard above the din of the whole orchestra like a giant locust rubbing its appendages together. And, finally, I.S. thinks that the timbre of the bassoon is different, and that "The *fagotti* at the end of the *Evocation des ancêtres* sound like the *cinq vieillards* I had imagined."

But in every respect the music is radically unlike the conductors' showpiece it has become in the West.

Following a reception at the Composers' Union, with Khrennikov, Shaporin, Dankovich, and Kabalevsky, we make a tour, starting at turbaned St. Basil's and the Kremlin. Alexandra and Karen Khachaturian, the nephew of the composer and our escort from the Composers' Union, use pre-1917 names that the I.S.'s are likely to recognize. Thus we go about anachronistically being told that the green building on our left is "the Hall of the Nobles," and the rose-colored building on our right is "the English Club, which you know from *War and Peace.*" The colors of the old city, of the low, flat nineteenth-century houses with double windows and circular archways, are pastels of peach and pink contrasted with strong blues, ochers, greens. But these attractive houses survive only helter-skelter among mammoth gray apartment and office buildings. At Sparrow Hills on the south bank of the Moscow River—the site of Napoleon's first view of the city— we leave the car for a walk. It is a russet-and-gold afternoon, and a gauze of blue smoke hangs over Moscow. The I.S.'s are silent and more moved than I have ever seen them.

Nor does the mood change back across the river at the Novodevichy Monastery (which means "New Maidens," a redundant name unless the place was intended for repentant fallen women—*i.e.,* "new maidens in heart"). This excursion is at V.'s insistence and, I think, against the wishes, unexpressed, of Alexandra and Karen. The Novodevichy, decaying behind ancient walls, is an island of the Old Russia. In the gardens, old women in black kerchiefs, tattered coats, and lifetime shoes are kneeling and praying before graves with crosses and statues of angels. Entering the church, we find a priest in a white cassock officiating before an elderly congregation, some of the more fervent members of which lie kow-tow and entirely prostrate, the position I.S. used to assume at his own devotions in the Russian Church in Hollywood.

This unexpected look behind the door has driven a wedge, however slight and transparent, between the I.S.'s and their escorts, though the visit was not in any outward sense opposed by them, and perhaps I am mistaken in feeling that silent resistance. (I have felt it more strongly than the I.S.'s, in any case, but then, twenty-four hours in the Soviet Union have helped me to realize how much farther advanced is my, and my generation's, disease of self-consciousness than theirs.) Inside the church, nevertheless, we are all three aware of a certain anxiety in our chaperones, attributable less to the large numbers of people there, I think, than to the glaring fact of their poverty. And the conversation in the car, later, is inhibited. Karen talks about "the *new* Soviet life," the free education, the free medical care and free medicine, the free utilities, the small—nine-rubles-a-month—rent, the wonders of the Metro, and of the street automats, where a kopeck in a slot procures not only a sandwich but also a spray of perfume. Alexandra, taking another tack, uses the Novodevichy as an example of religious toleration. And she talks about the church as a relic of an older generation—"Why, even my own mother knows a priest"—soon to die a natural death, and therefore of no consequence. But the I.S.'s are disturbed not for any religious or political reason but simply because the Novodevichy is the Russia they knew, the Russia that is a part of them.

Tonight, exchanging impressions with the I.S.'s—this is the first time we have been alone long enough to do so—I am conscious of a desire to push into black or white, even at the cost of exaggeration; and aware of a need, for the first time in fifteen years with the I.S.'s, to feel some co-ordination between my impressions and theirs, a confirmation that our experience has been in some measure the same. The I.S.'s complain that the foreign picture of the Soviet Union is absurdly misleading, even concerning such uncomplicated questions as the condition of consumer goods. For V. has come with trinkets, as Peter Stuyvesant came to the Indians, except that she is now ashamed to give, and is even embarrassed to dispose of, them. The I.S.'s are indignant, moreover, at having suffered so many months of worry; and they are ashamed of their suspicions, as recently as yesterday, about "being taken in by flowers and flattery." Moscow is not "grim," they say, and the people do not appear more "oppressed" or "happier" or "unhappier" than people do elsewhere. And though suffering and pride go well together, the pride we see here is of an altogether different order. Furthermore, the I.S.'s say that the disappearance of servility and *nichivo*-ism is "hardly believable." As V. puts it, after a trip to the post office: "Servility has been replaced by civility." The man who drives our limousine is not a "chauffeur," the girl who cleans the room is not a "maid," the woman who checks our coats is not an "attendant," the boy who operates the elevator is not the "lift boy." (What they *are* I do not know, but the most common greeting is still *"Tovarich."*) All of which is only to indicate how overwhelmingly "pro" the judgment is at the end of one day.

But do the I.S.'s share my feeling that in spite of all the similarities slightly transposed, and in spite of admirations and sympathies aroused by everything we see, the feeling remains that intellectually speaking we are on a different planet from the Paris which is only a long lunchtime away? And the answer, alas, is "No," they do not. For they are home. The schizophrenic split between the U.S. and the U.S.S.R. has suddenly ceased to bother them, nor have they been brainwashed even by forty-eight years abroad. Their abiding emotion is an intense pride in everything Russian. (How wise, if unjust, of immigration departments to put the birthplace question first and the citizenship question second.) Only two days ago, in Paris, I would have denied that I.S., and to a slightly lesser extent V., could ever be at home here again, meaning by "here" not the political Soviet Union, of course (though even that could be arranged), but "Russia." Yet half a century of expatriation can be, whether or not it has been, forgotten in a night.

1962

The passers-by in front of the Conservatory at 9 AM include women in boots and kerchiefs and men in leather jackets, some with berets and some with Lenin beards. Nobody looks like Marx or Castro.

We note many solid improvements in the orchestra this morning, above all toward steadiness of rhythm in the strings. And I note further transformations in I.S. V., at breakfast, attributes at least part of the change to the removal of "money and taxes" as subjects of conversation, "thereby freeing about 60 per cent of his talk for other topics." But another reason is that I.S., speaking his own language, was always a different person; and now, exchanging talk with the musicians, he is more buoyant than I have ever seen him. But, then, this is also the first time in his life that he has conducted a Russian-speaking orchestra. Incidentally, the fact that no one speaks a word of any other language makes us feel the decades of isolation more strongly than anything else, orchestras usually being so polyglot. The players call him "Igor Feodorovich," and the family feeling in any group of Russians is quickly established. To the eye, I.S. remains outside the family only by virtue of his elegant manners, typified in that courtly bow from the door of the airplane.

1962

Returning to the hotel, we find V. tearful. Her cousin Valodya has brought a packet of family photographs and an account of her mother's death during the war, the first news that V. has had of her mother in thirty years. This is the moment she has dreaded ever since the trip became a possibility, though she has sought it, the certainty of it, too. She spent the earlier morning, moreover, searching for the home of her first marriage, but though she found the street, and no building on it had been destroyed or changed, she failed to recognize the house. And this has been almost as disturbing.

In the evening we go to *Boris* at the Bolshoi, whose plush, gilt, and glittering chandelier are monuments to the *ancien régime*. Our loge, directly over the orchestra pit, is half shrouded by a red canopy, but I.S.'s presence is known and creates a stir. The conductor, on the other hand, is hardly acknowledged on his entrance, which, Alexandra explains, is because "He hasn't done anything yet," though even when he has, and the other performers too, the appreciation of the audience strikes us as remarkably restrained. But the visual aspect of the performance *is* superior to the musical. The sets could be *tableaux vivants* in the Kremlin Museum, and actors more richly robed would be difficult to imagine. I.S., who has not heard the music in thirty years, is both moved and—by Rimsky-Korsakov—annoyed. "Mussorgsky accompanied Pimen, writing, by a single bassoon; but Rimsky, to be certain everyone got the point, added other instruments—and reduced an original idea to a commonplace. In a word, Rimsky not only deformed Mussorgsky but tried to export him." I.S. remarks that the music of the Coronation Scene "must have" inspired the death march in his own *Nightingale*. He says, too, that Mussorgsky's Fool undoubtedly provided Berg with a model for the same role in *Wozzeck,* and he says that it is obvious how the Czarina's unaccompanied song at the beginning of Act Two became Mélisande's *"Mes longs cheveux."* But I.S. likes the Polish scene above all, "that marvelous revelry which, alas, musically speaking turns to marmalade at the end." During the intermission following this scene, he is actually feeling almost compassionate about the Poles. "What a history! But, then, if you pitch your tent in the middle of Fifth Avenue, it is more than likely that you will be run over by a bus."

Another late-night séance, the I.S.'s again complaining of the misinformation of other visitors and conveniently forgetting that few others have had a red (no pun) carpet tour comparable to theirs. But I.S.'s *volte-face* has now reached the point at which I would hardly be surprised to find him appearing in the role of defender of the faith (Lenin's). His "defense of Russia," in any case, is virtually complete. "What a beautiful factory. *Chudno* apartment house." Heads roll in Hollywood when dinner is five minutes late, but a two-hour wait here is commended as "excellent service"—which it is, compared with some even longer delays. But perhaps this change is also caused by his resumption of that Russian time scale according to which a visitor arrives for tea and stays to talk until midnight. When the dinner finally does appear, moreover, he will comment on "the marvelous salt!" while failing to mention that the *pièce de résistance* would effectively resist an electric saw. In point of fact, if tonight's meal had been served to him in France, De Gaulle himself would have received a telegram about the decline of civilization, whereas here it was *"vkussno"* ("very tasty")—a judgment, I should add, not based on any sustained attempt to eat it.

Ralph Parker, Hurok's representative, to whom I confide some of this transformation, asks whether I think I am now seeing "the true Stravinsky." Well, all I.S.'s are true enough, I answer, but the picture I had drawn of him is now being given its background, certainly, and that background does wash out a great deal of what I had heretofore supposed to be "traits of character" or personal idiosyncrasy. And certainly I can now understand the Soviet view of I.S.'s expatriate years as a pillar-to-post course from circus ballet to Roman Catholic Mass to Hebrew canticle, a view blind to the value question of how perfectly fluted I.S.'s pillars are and with what exquisite capitals he has adorned those posts. For a time, too, I will try to listen to his music from their perspective, *sub specie patris.*[1]

V. says that I.S. is slipping into diminutives—which he affects to scorn in Russians abroad—and she adds that, contrary to foreign information, diminutive forms are not more endemic than they were fifty years ago. Tonight, for example, he has apparently asked the waiter for a spoon-*chik,* which, V. says, is a *"petit-bourgeois* solecism of a very revealing kind," though

---

1. I have, and have discovered Russianisms even in *Pulcinella;* the D-minor tenor aria, for example, is a Russian dance, and the horn counter-melody at No. 65 is far closer to Tchaikovsky than to Pergolesi. The Symphony in C now seems to me as "Russian" in its way, too, as *Les Noces,* and Russia haunts *Oedipus Rex.*

185

she has always held that I.S. is a hundred per cent Russian, whose international sophistication was invented by and is to some extent an imitation of Diaghilev. I.S. has also begun to address his niece Xenia as "Xeniochka," which seems remarkably inapposite. For though Xenia is a courageous and good-hearted woman, she appears to regard her uncle as something a new Soviet invention has retrieved from the moon.

SEPTEMBER 24

An interview with I.S. in this morning's *Pravda* concludes with a spurious quotation: "I salute the noble Soviet Union." Ralph Parker calls, says it is a stock phrase tacked on to every interview, advises us to ignore it. But the difficulty in I.S.'s case is that he has annoyed the Western press by receiving *Pravda* and refusing them. When they call to ask for his denial of the statement, therefore, they are well aware that he cannot give it without insulting his hosts. But Parker succeeds in pacifying the principal foreign reporters with the argument that I.S. is not a United States cultural exchange artist, but a guest of the Soviet government. (The "U.S.A." appears only after my name on placards and programs, but *could* it have been put after I.S.'s name?) I.S.'s confidence is a little undermined by this breach of faith, as he calls it, and though he does not mention the matter to Alexandra and Karen, when they appear, both of them behave rather sheepishly.

Among the surprise visitors at the rehearsal today are our Mexican banker-friend, Carlos Prieto, and Lily Brik, Mayakovsky's *amour,* whom V. last saw in Petrograd just before the Revolution. Lina Prokofiev, last seen in Paris in 1938, is also there, though Parisian Russians have advised I.S. that even to inquire about her could do her harm: she was sent to Siberia for eight years during the Stalin era, supposedly for consorting too much with British and Americans—she speaks perfect English—in the embassies. Madame Prokofiev is accompanied by her son Sviatoslav, a gangling, slightly grosser image of the composer.

At this same rehearsal, the conductor Rozhdestvensky makes a present to I.S. of a cover of the second volume of Debussy's *Préludes,* on which, after the printed words *"pour piano,"* the composer has written, *"et surtout pour amuser mon ami Igor Strawinsky, ton ami Claude Debussy, juin 1913."* Rozhdestvensky says he purchased the page for a few kopecks at a Moscow bookstall. It provides me with an opportunity to make inquiries concerning I.S.'s house in Ustilug, whence it must have come, but no one except Xenia Yurievna has even heard of Ustilug, and she knows little except that in 1914 I.S.'s Beliankin cousins moved his possessions from there to a warehouse in Poltava. Xenia does have a photograph of the Ustilug house with her, though, and of the *shtetl,* the Jewish village, but as I.S. feels more strongly about this happy home than about his largely unhappy childhood one in St. Petersburg, he looks at it only very reluctantly; Ustilug is a subject he will not discuss. The Debussy autograph most likely indicates that his possessions there, manuscripts, paintings, books, were looted during the Revolution and eventually sold.

In the Oruzheinaya Palata (Kremlin Armory Museum) this afternoon, we find ourselves looking less intently at the exhibits than at the other visitors: Tartars, Mongolians, Chinese, Red Army soldiers, kerchiefed Russian women, Uzbeks in black-and-white hexagonal caps. Wearing felt overshoes and in tow of female lecturers, they glide clumsily over the polished wood floors like tyros on a skating rink. An ecclesiastical museum, first of all, it is rich in crosses, Bibles, and clerical garments, all lustrously jeweled: a gold surplice brocaded with 150,000 pearls (*Henry V:* "The inter-tissued robe of gold and pearl"); a Bible encrusted with a tutti-frutti of rubies, diamonds, emeralds; another Bible set with tear-shaped amethysts. The Imperial jewels—in orb and scepter, in throne seats, in baldrics, in fur-trimmed crowns and ermine-lined robes—are no less rich, of course, and the Czars' horse equipages (saddles, bridles, stirrups, whip handles, harnesses, pommels, cantles, a horse's bit with a topaz stud the size of a bird's egg) are the most extravagantly jeweled objects of all. One of the horse blankets, the tribute of a shah, is made of the feathers of five hundred yellow parrots. But the Oruzheinaya is a museum of fabrics and needlework, too, of winding sheets and palls in gold and silver thread, of silks and satins, taffetas and velvets, of sleigh rugs with cloisonné spangles. And it is a museum of the Imperial utensils, the silver plate with niello tracery or appliqué gold.

Lermontov's *Masquerade* at the Maly Theater tonight is well acted and so lavishly decorated that the stage picture could be a collective dream-wish of upper-class elegance. (Incidentally, the I.S.'s been told abroad of a shortage of actors with convincing "aristocratic" accents and "refined" intonation, but they find no evidence of that lack tonight.) The *mise-en-scène,* whose rapid pace depends upon ingenious uses of the revolving stage, seems to follow the old Meyerhold production. And the long evening is cleverly relieved, if not shortened, by some incidental dancing to a well-chosen potpourri of Prokofiev. But what an odd play! While the first two acts are in some ways hardly less powerful than *Othello,* to which the plot contains a not overstrained parallel, the third act is unmitigated bathos. Instead of a dramatic solution, the author simply pops an "evil genius" out of the bag and lays the tragedy to a forgotten vengeance-seeker of long ago.

The most amazing performance of the evening is not on stage, however, but in the seat next to me, where Alexandra, line for line and for four and a half hours, pipes a nicely resourceful translation of this difficult verse play into my ear. (She apologizes in advance to our neighbors, but no one glances at us with annoyance, or even pays us the slightest attention.) In the intermissions we drink tea with the stage director and scene painter and talk theater with Alexandra. Her passion, and largest source of income, is translating plays, and she asks me to recommend new American ones that she might translate, stipulating, however, that they be "something like Wesker."

1962

We pay an official call on Ekaterina Furtseva, the Minister of Culture, an attractive blonde—she is referred to privately as Catherine the Third—with abundant *charme slave.* Madame Furtseva talks to us about the future, giving poetical recitations of art production statistics and enticing descriptions of new orchestras, new ballets, new schools in Tashkent and Siberia, which she graciously invites us to visit.

At the Lenin Mausoleum we jump the queue, a caterpillar of booted and bundled, capped and kerchiefed people winding a half mile around the north corner of the Kremlin. (We have guilt feelings about doing this, to be sure, but we *couldn't* have waited six hours, and those who have waited seem so long-suffering.) We join a double file inside and descend a staircase in strict silence. In front of us are turbaned heads from the southeast, fur-covered heads from the far north, and dark faces, light faces, yellow faces, square faces, slant-eyed faces. Soldiers keep the traffic moving in the marble corridor below, and soldiers face the glass catafalque from each side, themselves standing at near *rigor mortis.* The hair and brows of the small recumbent figure in the black suit are red, not black as in photographs, but surely the figure is not an embalmed body at all but a wax doll. And, just as surely, it makes no difference. Seeing is believing, whether it be Muhammad's toenail, a splinter of the True Cross, or the "real" remains of Lenin. I.S., later (is he changing back?): "The religion of Lenin is the opiate of the masses."

The Leningrad Ballet performs *Orpheus, Petrushka,* and the *Firebird* tonight in the Kremlin Theater, a new auditorium with seats for six thousand and devices for radioed translations at every one. The theater is also equipped with escalators, lounges, bars, through which we are guided by Khrennikov's daughter Natasha. The English-speaking composer Kabalevsky sits behind us during the performance, and though reputedly opposed to I.S.'s visit, weeps at the end of the *Firebird*—which, come to think of it, is not incompatible with anti-Stravinskyism. Both the music and the staging are hardly recognizable at times, especially in *Petrushka,* which seems so much less "Russian" to us than the Fokine-Benois staging. The *Firebird* is the best performed and the best received of the three, but, then, it is the prototype of the Soviet ballet in many respects, including length and sentiment. Shortly before the lights are lowered for it, the audience discovers and applauds I.S. A moment later, Khrushchev, accompanied by several members of his cabinet, enters the loge directly across the hall from ours, whereupon the whole audience stands and applauds. But soon after the *Firebird* begins—or seems to: the *tempo* is strange and the sound unbalanced—someone directly below shouts "*Viva* Khrushchev!" The cry is taken up by other voices, and an attempt made to turn it into a rhythmic chant, but shushing noises are heard, too, and they are soon in the majority. Still, the demonstration is quelled only when the lights are turned up for a moment. "Cubans," Alex-

1962

andra says, without much sympathy for them. "It happens all the time." Khrushchev stands and applauds I.S. at the end, but vanishes before the first curtain call.

Kolya K., a poet (self-declared) aged twenty-six, has haunted the hotel lobby for three days in hopes of viewing I.S., but this afternoon he is partly placated by being allowed to talk unofficially with V.—though deeply offended by her when she refers to his hero, Yevtushenko, as "a tribune who might have been a poet in another time and place"; but, then, V. says the same of Mayakovsky, and that is an even more unpopular verdict. Brecht is a Kolya idol, of course, whereas Rilke is unknown to him even by name, and Edna St. Vincent Millay is his favorite twentieth-century English-language poet. His pantheon of painters is even more curious in that it contains no Renaissance masters at all, but only such "moderns" as Cézanne and Renoir, whom K. defends as *avant-garde* causes. Confessing his inability to appreciate more recent art, he tells us that on a trip to Paris he saw "a clump of barbed wire, at an exhibition, that was called 'Dream.' Now what has barbed wire to do with dreaming?"

1962

On the topic of the arts under Stalin, he says that the dictator is supposed to have remarked, apropos some poems by Simenov to his mistress, that "just two copies should be printed, one for him and one for her." On the new climate of "liberalism" toward the arts, K. feels that "The most dangerous enemy is the foreign press. Many government officials want to support the so-called rebel poets, musicians, painters, but as soon as they are published, performed, exhibited, the foreign press pretends that they are defying the régime, which Yevtushenko, for example, most patently is not." The essence of K.'s political argument is that "The Russian people have risen from a terrible history to the highest place. They have never known what you call prosperity, but soon *will* know it, and inevitably, as they go ahead, the United States will become more and more bitter. We do not want war, if only for the reason—to obviate other arguments—that we have so much to develop here. And we believe that as long as Khrushchev is in power, war is not a probability. We think, too, that the Americans should realize this and help him against the militarists and the Stalinists. But is it true that the Americans have bomb shelters? Surely they can't be *that* silly?" This is the first time that the cold-war scare has been mentioned.

Later, V. repeats the gist of this conversation to I.S., who says that Stalin is "important" because "He attempted to, and, I am afraid, for a time did, prove that people do not matter."

Tonight's concert in Tchaikovsky Hall is one of the most moving in my experience, and it is for I.S. as well, though the applause may be more for the returning prodigal son than for the music. *Orpheus,* in any case, is attended with much reading of program notes, coughing, and other signs of restlessness, and in every section of an audience that is at least as stratified as ours, with eager youth in the balcony and apathetic age *parterre*. I.S. conducts his wind-band arrangement of the "Volga Boat Song" as an encore, but the severity of the instrumentation—the audience has waited in vain for the strings to play on the second time around—diminishes the ovation somewhat and slightly depresses the mood; besides which, the music itself, apart from I.S.'s version of it, refers to the wrong Russia and the wrong past. Yet the applause, in rhythmic unison, goes on and on until I.S. appears in his overcoat, holds up his hand for silence, and tells the audience, "You see a very happy man." Afterward, in the dressing room, the orchestra players bring gifts, for me a lacquered box with a "Firebird" on the cover.

SEPTEMBER 27

The former Yusupov estate at Archangelskoye, one of the great *podmoskovnaya* (suburban villas), is now a showcase of nineteenth-century country life. Geese waddle on the lawns, and drays, whose horses have the large surcingles and horseshoe-shaped shaft-bows (*doogah*) of nineteenth-century illustrations, are on the roads. The villa is a heavy, ocher building with a tall, untapered dome like the smokestack on an ocean liner. The dome, on the inside, is an oval crown of eight Corinthian columns supporting a white cornice. But the room is barren, whereas the side rooms are galleries of pictures and furniture, including cabinets and chairs of Karelian birch, and rugs woven in the Yusupov mills at Poltava. In the actual living rooms the ceilings are low, to concentrate the warmth.

1962

A party of Cameroons is also visiting the grounds, accompanied by an Intourist lecturer in Arabic. Suddenly one of them recognizes I.S. from a photograph in today's *Pravda,* and one and all gather around for autographs, to the obvious annoyance of the abandoned lecturer, who is obliged to stand dumbly by while the I.S.'s talk to her charges in French and English, and to each other in Russian. Would the Cameroons, who seem to be regarding their visit as a lesson in medieval history, believe that I.S. had been to school with, and that V. was a friend of, the man whose home this once was?

In the car, later, V. says that "Yusupov was so perfect a gentleman that when he came to call on us in the Crimea during the Revolution—we were living in a single room at the time, without any furniture—he did not look about for a chair, but sat on the floor without hesitation, as if it were the most natural thing in the world for him to do."

Returning to Moscow on a different, less rural road, we pass log-cabin *izbas* with fancy wooden-lace window frames; every habitation, even the tiniest *izbushka,* is equipped with at least one television pole. We also pass the enshrined hut that was the scene of Kutuzov's council before Moscow. Kutuzov is no longer merely the hero of strategic retreats, Ralph Parker says, but a newly rehabilitated aggression symbol, and Parker adds that the grounds of Borodino have apparently been adjusted to this interpretation.

Prokofiev's *War and Peace* tonight helps to confirm the interpretation, too, for while Napoleon appears in it as a small-time Fascist neurotic, Kutuzov, the solitary, is a genius as big as Russia and rather larger than history. The opera is a succession of historical friezes. Visually it might be compared to a series of museum panoramas, which, as pictures, are good to look at. But the book cannot be parceled out or reduced to operatic mold. And even if Prokofiev had limited himself to two or three tableaux, Tolstoy's characters would still be too roomy for him. The music is more pleasing, nevertheless, especially in the long first-act cotillion, than I.S. makes out, and the performances, most memorably of a soldier in black boots dancing a mazurka, are excellent. We sit in the Imperial Loge (or whatever it is now called) just above some Kazakhis wearing skullcaps, beards, and caftans cut like Victorian frock coats, and, in the intervals, meet the cast and feed on *pirochki* and sugary champagne. I.S., later, feeling tipsy, complains that the champagne "had the wrong nuance."

From the opera we go directly to Moscow Television Studios for a late-night interview. Answering a question about his next composition, I.S. lays an egg as large as Kastchei's, but less magical. When he says, "I am writing a biblical cantata, in Hebrew, for the people of Israel," faces fall and the program limps to an end. After it, Ralph Parker says that the stony reaction was owing partly to the Soviet attitude to the Bible, partly to the feeling that Israel is no more than a ward of the United States, and partly to a wish that I.S. would use a text in his mother tongue. A newscast immediately before our appearance shows Khrushchev being cheered along the route of his Turkestan tour, and after this the arrival at the Moscow airport of the new United States Ambassador, Foy Kohler, who looks as grim and unfriendly as Gromyko is made to look in the United States.

SEPTEMBER 28

The Scriabin Museum, which is in the composer's former apartment in the Arbat district, cannot differ much since Scriabin's time, Madame Blavatsky still being a "presence," along with the *clavier à lumières,* which looks like a harmonium and seems an unlikely contribution to the great composer's vision of a synesthesia and the *"déroulement de tous les sens."* The caretakers, two old ladies madly in love with "Vanya Cleebourne," introduce us to a young "electronic composer" who plays his "tape filter" for a film, *Cosmic Space,* the techniques for which are mysteriously purported to have been developed from Scriabin's ideas concerning the *clavier à lumières.* We hear a recording of Scriabin's "Black Mass" Sonata, too, played by the late white (red?) hope of Soviet pianists, Safronitski. The museum possesses a letter from I.S. to Scriabin expressing great enthusiasm for one of his later sonatas.[1]

Among sundry other visits, we go to the Kamerny Theater, where, early in 1917, V. played in Beaumarchais's *Svadba;* the Kamerny is on the Nikitski

---

1. 1971.   My ignorance of Scriabin's music at this time, along with a tendency to take I.S. too much at his own word, are the reasons for my failure to recognize the considerable influence of Scriabin on the early Stravinsky.

191

Boulevard, the "bark" of the old city, on the analogy that Moscow grew in concentric rings, like a tree. And the Chekhov House, a red brick *fin-de-siècle* eyesore. And the Tolstoy House, which is in a neighborhood of attractive lime-colored buildings with white, arched window frames. A tall dovecote stands at a nearby street corner.

During the intermission of our concert tonight, a repeat of the first one, I.S., pale and perspiring, complains of nausea but refuses to see a doctor. I send Alexandra for one anyway, and she returns with an elderly woman who tells me that I.S. was a legend to her even in her childhood. She finds his pulse weak and refuses to sanction any more conducting, at which I.S., furious, drinks brandy and coffee, stalks on stage, and does rather better than two days ago. But the forty-minute intermission has put the foreign press on the trail, and newsmen, when we return to the hotel, are perching like carrion crows outside our rooms. The medicos who come to examine I.S. there are dumbfounded at the extent of his private pharmacy and incredulous at the—true—story that just before the concert he swallowed ten drops of an opium paregoric and washed it down with two tumblers of whiskey.

SEPTEMBER 29

Most of the day is spent answering cables about I.S.'s "stroke" and denying press reports that he had one. At night we go to the Obratszov Puppet Theater, which is featuring a parody program of music and musicians. It is very funny, too, and even at worst, without *longueurs.* Child prodigies are mocked by an infant in a perambulator howling for its bottle and babbling baby talk, but then smashing into the Rachmaninoff Second Concerto. Gypsy-style "dark" singing is lampooned by a teen-age girl with a bass-baritone bray, and American-style tap dancing, Hope-Crosby-style comedian singing, and "sexy"—"sex appeala," the Russians call it— adolescent blues singing are all neatly spoofed. What interests me in these burlesques, however, is the typifying of American physical characteristics, "how the Russians see us." But the drollest of the American parodies is a take-off on television commercials, an elaborately developed choral fugue about vitamin pills "that keep you alive until you die." Well done as they are, these gently anti-American satires are not the highlight of the show— although they receive the most vigorous applause, nevertheless, from an audience that, to judge by the U.N. switchboard of languages in the lobby, is at least half foreign. I should add that the performance can be followed without knowledge of Russian, though at certain points the spectator must at least be able to recognize it, as in the skit with a French poodle which growls angrily when its pretentious owner bids it *"Bonjour,"* but barks with pleasure when she says *"Zdrastvooite."* The highlight, for me, is a parody of younger-generation poetry readings. The readers invariably have huge mouths, terrible grammar, and atrocious manners, rudely clearing their throats and expectorating on the floor. One of them, after affectedly announcing "The first chapter of my new novel," utters a few obscure and disconnected words, then says, "I will skip the next sixteen chapters as they are concerned entirely with the psychological development of Chapter One." The word "psychology" takes a severe beating, and not only here, as we have learned in conversations.

SEPTEMBER 30

Today, V.'s name day (St. Vera's), occasions festivities on the part of our nonbelieving hosts that would shame the church-going White Russian regulars in Hollywood. They bring gifts of broadloom linens, an electric samovar, lacquered trays (recalling the old arts of Palekh and Mstera), wood and terra-cotta miniature animals. And they bring a new conviviality, too, in which all trace of the official manner of a week ago has disappeared.

OCTOBER 1

Today's *Pravda* carries a large photographic spread of hate-ugly faces with captions about "the racial war in Mississippi." And the Russians ask us, with genuine incredulity, how such things are possible "in a country as advanced as *Ameriki.*"

Along with several Russians, we attend a lunch given by Ambassador Kohler at the United States Embassy. The Ambassador proposes a toast in Russian, but switches to English midstream, asking an aide to translate the latter part. What he says, in substance, is that I.S., as a Russian American, is a unique link in cultural relations. But the Russians—among them Madame Furtseva, Krilov of the Soviet Embassy in Washington, and Khrennikov—listen with blank faces, do not reply, and do not applaud. Their attitude is that I.S. is not a United States cultural exchange artist but a guest of the Soviet Union. Yet I.S.'s position *is* extraordinary. One of the few Russian creative artists since the nineteenth-century literary giants to have attained a high order of world prestige, he has been *persona super non grata,* until now, only in Russia. After lunch, privately, he makes the point that the cultural exports of the United States and the Soviet Union are essentially the same: pianists, orchestras, ballets, "not creative talent, in other words, but performing talent, which, I suppose, is all that can be exported, though the prospect of more and more *Wunderkinder* playing Tchaikovsky concertos is hardly my idea of a musical Eden." He observes, too, that whereas the artist in the United States complains of the government's rejection of responsibility to support the arts, in the Soviet Union he might decide that the highest duty of government is to leave them alone.

In the evening we attend a reception given by Madame Furtseva, the Minister of Culture, and selected Soviet composers, in a private room at the Metropole. This turns into the most extraordinary event of the trip, a kind of Last Supper for nondisciples, during which I.S. reveals his Russian-ness more completely than at any time in the fifteen years I have known him. Nor is it any wee supper, either, but an excellent dinner of white veal and *Kievski kotleti,* proving that good food exists if ordered by the right people. Madame Furtseva presides, at the center of the table, with I.S. to her right and Shostakovich to her left; to see the two St. Petersburg-born composers together is to be struck, above all, by the similarity of their complexions and sandy hair. V. sits across from Furtseva, between Aram Khachaturian and Kara Karayev, and I sit between Karayev and my earphones, Alexandra, who translates word for often unbelievable word.

Shostakovich's face is the most "sensitive" and "intellectual" we have seen in the U.S.S.R. Otherwise, he is thinner, taller, younger—more boyish-looking—than expected, but he is also the shyest, most nervous human being I have ever met. He chain-smokes, chews not merely his nails but his fingers, twitches his pouty mouth and chin, wiggles his nose in constant adjustment of his spectacles, looks querulous one moment and ready to cry the next. He stutters, too, and his hands tremble, and when he shakes hands, his whole frame wobbles (which reminds us of Auden), besides which his knees knock quite audibly when he speaks, at which time the others look anxiously toward him, as indeed they might. He has a habit of staring, then of guiltily turning away when caught, and all evening long he peeks illicitly at I.S. around the nicely rounded corners of Madame Furtseva. But the thoughts behind those frightened, very intelligent eyes are never betrayed—or at least *I* cannot read them. A new wife sits beside him, an adoring pupil, one would guess, but by age, looks, and an equally shy, serious, and distant manner, a daughter.

Then it starts. *Confiteor me.* Each musician proposes a toast, which is in effect an invitation to return to the fold; and each begins by baring his soul, confessing to some guilt, some shortcoming of his own, some misunderstanding of I.S., some prejudice or lack of sympathy. (And *I* confess, too, but only to this parenthesis, that whether or not the nature of these revelations is biologically "Russian"—and the answer may be simply that what is "candor" to some is "lack of reticence" to others—a propensity to them is also part of the make-up of I.S. Oblomov may have disappeared in the Revolution, let me add, but Stavrogin is still very much around.) Naturally, very little of this is needed to turn the room into a Finnish bath, in whose vapors everyone, proclaiming and acclaiming each other's Russianness, says almost the same thing. I.S.'s human qualities are lauded—they are Russian qualities, after all—and the man, well, all who have met the man have seen how truly genuine he is. (No one says a word about the composer, and only Shostakovich toasts future works by him, though, to be fair, none of them has or could have any notion of the real stature of the composer.) Again and again they abase themselves before the mystery of their Russianness. And so, I realize with a small shock, does I.S. His replies, in fact, are soon overtaking the toasts. In a perfectly sober speech—he is the least alcoholically elevated of anyone in the room—I hear that "The smell of Russian earth is different"—it is—"and such things are impossible to forget"—they are; and so far so good. But he goes on to tell Khachaturian and Khrennikov of his desire to know more of their music, which is less good, not only because it is a polite untruth, but also because they have avoided any mention of his music. All that Khachaturian has said was that I.S. had been a "legend" to him all his life, "but now that I have seen the man I am greatly moved by his sincerity" (cheers), which *non sequitur* leaves little doubt about the nature of the "legend." But I.S.'s serious confessing gets under way in his reply to Madame Furtseva—who, after a patriotic preamble, has advanced the somewhat dubious proposition that "All really great men are optimists," this by way of comment on an "optimistic" remark by I.S. Not "in effect," then, but in actual quotes, here is I.S.: "A man has one birthplace, one fatherland, one country—he *can* have only one country—and the place of his birth is the most important factor in his life. I regret that circumstances separated me from my fatherland, that I did not give birth to my works there and, above all, that I was not there to help the new Soviet Union create its new music. I did not leave Russia of my own will, however, even though I disliked much in my Russia and in Russia generally. Yet the right to criticize Russia is mine, because Russia is mine and because I love it, and I do not give any foreigner that right." (*Bolshoi* applause.) It is an astonishing speech to at least *this* criticizing foreigner who, accordingly, is beginning to feel more foreign every moment: so astonishing that, as I see when we are back in the hotel, the I.S.'s are embarrassed to have had it overheard, even by me. But it *is* believable, and so is every word he says tonight except the professed interest in Khrennikov's and Khachaturian's music. I.S. *does* regret his uprooting and exile more than anything else in his life, which I say not because of a few emotional speeches, though they have come from the depths, but because of the change in his whole nature here. Now, looking back at Hollywood, the perspective from Russia outside, I can see that his domesticity is purely Russian; in fact, he will eat his soup only from the same spoon with which he was fed by his *babushka* seventy-five years ago. And in Hollywood, or anywhere, he will go through the day, if possible, speaking only his mother tongue. Just five years ago in Baden-Baden he flew into a rage on hearing the news of Sputnik, forbidding us even to mention the achievement. Was the power of this jealous hate (the result of the mother's deprived love) responsible for his at times too conspicuous "Western sophistication," in the sense that the latter became a weapon to prove his superiority, and that of other cultures, to the Russia that failed to recognize his genius? I offer no answer, but am certain that to be recognized and acclaimed as a Russian in Russia, and to be performed there, has meant more to him than anything else in the years I have known him. And when Mother Russia restores her love, forty-eight years are forgiven with one suck of the breast—several sucks of vodka, in fact, at this amazingly Dostoevskyan dinner.

1962

195

A reception at the Canadian Embassy. Stalin, paying a visit here once, saw a photograph of King George V, mistook it for one of the Czar, thought he was being insulted, and fled. So the Ambassador says, anyway, and he tells another, now popular, story about the child who asks its *babushka* if Lenin was a great man. The answer, of course, is "Yes." The child then asks the same question about Stalin. A very bad man, says the *babushka*. "And, *babushka,* Khrushchev?" "Hush, my child, he is still alive." The Ambassador has a collection of abstract paintings by Karitnikov and other artists who are not exhibited publicly. Seeing I.S.'s interest in them, he takes us to the Kostaki "gallery"—in fact, Kostaki's own three-room flat in a huge apartment house several versts from the center of the city. And it is well worth the trip, for Kostaki has beautiful icons as well as important works by the pre-Revolution *avant-garde,* including early Kandinskys—an especially fine one on glass—Gabos, Larionovs.

Tonight is our first concert with Kiril Kondrashin's orchestra. The musicians are younger than those of the Moscow State, which means, as it would anywhere in the world, that the ensemble is more exact and the varnish on the sound less thick. After the performance of the *Capriccio* I receive a presentation copy, inscribed by about fifty of the players, of their new recording of Shostakovich's Fourth Symphony, this together with flowers from *The New Statesman* and from the soloist, Tatiana Nicolayevna, who plays as though she could have won several events in the Olympic Games. Rehearsing the *Capriccio,* incidentally, has been the oddest musical experience of the trip. The orchestra parts have been copied from a pirated score and are full of mistakes: missing accidentals, wrong clefs, etcetera—some of them grotesque solecisms, as in the case of several wrongly and lugubriously flatted sevenths in the finale of this jolly piece.

1962

Ralph Parker gives a farewell buffet for I.S. and some of the performing plutocrats, including Rostropovich, Gilels, Kogan, Oistrakh. Parker now functions as unofficial liaison man between our hosts and ourselves. He is, moreover, our chief outside source of information, which is to say that he relays the tenor of the Soviet reaction. Parker has a gently mordant manner, but is passionate about painting. Over the years, now twenty-one in the Soviet Union, he has developed the discretionary habit of whispering. He will sweep into a room as if to shout "Eureka," but then, seeing Alexandra there or another possible informer, will sidle up and softly buzz his tidings in your ear instead. I.S. has named him *"Signor Sotto Voce."*

Fog obscures the towers of the Kremlin but does not delay our flight to Leningrad—after a lunch at the airport, ordering from a menu in Russian and Chinese. In the plane (one class), Alexandra engages me on the subject of psychoanalysis. "Self-indulgence," she says. "People should be taught to master themselves with willpower and to solve their own problems." I try to argue from utility, pointing out that capitalist psychotherapy with its bourgeois-objectivist rationalizations has helped many people to lead useful lives. And I suggest that it will appear in the Soviet Union *pari passu* with the rise of a cultural élite, but when I talk about the Freud-Marx synthesis of such Western Marxists as Marcuse, I am made to feel blaspheming. And whereas Alexandra has read more widely in several pre-twentieth-century literatures than I have (which is not saying much), she has never heard of any of the writers I take to be twentieth-century greats. "Freud" leads to "Society," which, she says, is simply a question of "What is good for the people." I agree, but then imprudently ask who decides what that good is, whereupon she accuses me of "Philosophy, which is only putting the world in parentheses. The good is better living conditions and the freedom to pursue one's inner life." And with this she moves on to "the parasitism of the bourgeoisie," and to the question of whether the United States is "a common denominator society, using 'individualism' as a slogan." But Soviet planes are fast, and no conclusions are reached.

The Leningrad welcoming committee is smaller, older, poorer than the Muscovite. One pale elderly gentleman greets I.S. and starts to weep. It is Vladimir Rimsky-Korsakov, and I.S. has failed to recognize him, apparently because he has a mustache instead of, as when last seen (*ca.* 1910), a beard; but the real reason, I.S. tells me later, was that "He said 'Igor Feodorovich' instead of 'Guima.' He always called us, me and my brother, Gury and Guima." Vladimir lives in the English Prospekt apartment house in which I.S. wrote the *Firebird.* Relatives of I.S.'s friend and co-librettist Stepan Mitussov are present, too; and a nephew of Diaghilev, a man with old-fashioned and most unproletarian manners, who speaks English and French; and a daughter of M. K. Ciurlionis, the Latvian Odilon Redon; and again the daughter of Balmont, with another basket of posies and moss, as well as a photograph of her father with goatee and shoulder-length hair, like Buffalo Bill. The Leningradski, *these* Leningradski at any rate, are more cosmopolitan and European than the Muscovichi. They bow, kiss hands, and do not shy from foreign, especially German, expressions.

After a long drive through postwar suburbs, I.S. recognizes the Imperial Riding School, and from there on it is home. To right and left, everything is *"chudno"* and *"krassiva,"* and he has a story to tell about each building. We drive along the Neva to the green-and-white Winter Palace—rose-and-white when the I.S.'s last saw it—and down the Nevsky Prospekt to the Yevropaisky Hotel. V., who lived here on visits to St. Petersburg in her student years, says that the furnishings, the German piano, Louis Seize clocks, Empire ormolu in beds, desks, chairs, are unchanged (in spite of reports that the furniture had been used as firewood during the war when the Yevropaisky was a hospital—or has it all been restored?). In the evening we go to the spectacularly beautiful Alexandrinka Theater to see Tolstoy's *The Living Dead*. But the title is also a description of the performance, and as our seats, in the first row, tip uncomfortably forward toward the orchestra pit, and as the gypsy singing, in Romany, is a Himalayan bore, we leave after the first act.

When I enter the hotel roof restaurant a late-night floorshow is in progress, in which a magician is sawing a woman in half to the accompaniment of "VI-VA KHRUSH-CHEV" and applauding-in-rhythm by a party of Cubans at the center table. (Are they vivisectionists?)

OCTOBER 5

After an early morning rehearsal we drive to Peterhof, now Petrodvorets, and Oranienbaum, the city of I.S.'s birth, now Lomonosov. The road is virtually deserted except for women shouldering large nets of cabbages which, Alexandra says, they are taking home to salt. At times the Gulf of Finland is in view, as are the derricks of the Kronstadt shipyards. War scars are everywhere—charred buildings, woods half cropped by artillery fire—and Petrodvorets itself was severely shot up, being the object of a systematic German attempt at demolition. But it has been admirably restored. A Russian tank stands as a monument at the point of the farthest German advance.

1962

The principal Petrodvorets palace is rated as Rastrelli's magnum opus, but the romantic rusticating of nature, as arranged by Rastrelli and others, is at least as great an attraction. We roam in bosquets, in Peter the Third's Dutch tulip garden (this is where Lermontov conceived *The White Sail*), and on avenues of poplars and fir trees where the leaves of the former have fallen or blown over the latter like yellow snow. And we walk by fountains, cascades, statuary—the gold Samson of Russian might destroying a Swedish lion—and a pool in which, two centuries before Pavlov, fish swam to be fed at the sound of a bell.

Except for the forest of TV poles, the long rows of unpainted wooden *dachkis* in nearby Lomonosov—which was not captured by the invader—can have changed but little since the time of I.S.'s birth. But I.S. has not seen the city since he was a few days old (if he saw it then), and he has no clue as to the address of his first home. Lomonosov is an *embarras de richesses* for fanciers of rococo, what with Catherine's pale-rose Chinese palace and her delectable "*palais des montagnes russes,*" Menshikov's palace, domed like a grand duke's crown, and the low, long, flat, and colonnaded Peter-period palaces. Near the last is an artificial lake on which the Czar fought mock naval battles.

Dinner is in Monferrand House, now the Leningrad Composers' Union. We sit with about thirty guests at a "T" table, I.S. presiding at the intersection, directly under a portrait of Glazunov. From this ironic position issues what is surely the Union's first two-hour monologue on serial technique. But it is received by people incomparably better informed than any gathering has been so far, and in comparison with their Moscow colleagues the younger people here are *frondeurs*. The atmosphere is that of a provincial club welcoming a hometown hero, yet the evening is lively and without any of the stuffiness of a "historic occasion." Clearly the hometown boy has never enjoyed himself more, and only Glazunov seems not to be having a good time.

One of the "12-tone" *apaches* is Dmitri Tolstoy, son of the writer, Alexei. A stately, Pierre Bezuhov, pyknic-cyclothymic young man, he gives short piano pieces to I.S. and myself, written for and dedicated to us. But after proclaiming himself an admirer of I.S.'s music, he begs him, ludicrously but touchingly, to "send a score of the *Firebird,* and anything else you have written."

At midnight, when we return to the hotel, about a hundred people are waiting on the pavement in front of Philharmonic Hall. Each of them represents a block of a hundred seats, and according to Ralph Parker, this or another hundred—for each watch may be divided into several reliefs—will remain there all night. Parker says that the queue is a year old, that each place in it has had to be checked every month and, as the date drew near, every week, and finally, twice a day (before and after working hours). An eighty-four-year-old cousin of I.S. has told Parker that her number in it is 5001, hence she will not be able to attend the concert but will have to watch it on television.

OCTOBER 6

The "Scythian" gold in the Hermitage basement includes art and artifacts from the whole Russian geography, and from history as well as prehistory. Early Sarmatian culture is represented, treasures from the Chaltamlik burial sites, works of Greek-period craftsmanship from Theodosia and the Bosphorus, and objects from Peter the Great's Siberian collection. All the gold is light in color; and the forms, whether of ornaments or utilities, rarely tend to the geometric and abstract. The principal objects are harness buckles, scabbards, goblets (one with a relief showing a tooth extraction, not unlike backwoods dentistry today), laurel leaves—a surprising number of them— carcanets, crowns. The vast display of bibelots includes tiny gold flowers, acorns, sheaves of wheat (for prehistoric Miss Balmonts), and sea urchins, dancing humans, birds in flight. But perhaps these are totems, like the bulls, eagles, serpents, and winged humans that our young girl guide reproves me for comparing to angels. (They are "geniuses," she says.) Czarist-era gold, in clocks, snuffboxes, toys, has this in common: it is all useless, all too richly jeweled—a gold-lion paperweight with diamonds for teeth—and it all looks as though made by Fabergé. The visit to this Scythian Fort Knox entails a mile hike through corridors stuffed with grotesquely large bowls—the largest, a jasper punch-bowl, would do in Beverly Hills as a swimming pool—most of them made of purple agate, lapis lazuli, malachite. A collection of what appear to be enormous bathtubs is stored here, too, but in fact they are tureens for cooling champagne (jeroboams only, one assumes). We leave the Hermitage feeling Lilliputian.

The Composers' Union invites us for a concert of I.S.'s Septet and Octet and an exhibition of Stravinskyana. When we arrive, about five hundred people are gathered in the paneled oak library under likenesses of Tchaikovsky, Mussorgsky, Lenin, Glinka, Glazunov. The instrumentalists, all young students, are excellent, but their *tempi* are erratic and the finale of the Octet is played faster than I had ever supposed possible. The music stops, too, even if a phrase is in mid-career, exactly where the sides come to an end in somebody's old recording. For the Septet, Professor Maria Yudina steps to the piano, an instrument she plays with skill and control, though the music, the Gigue anyway, makes little sense and cannot have pleased the audience, no matter how earnest the applause.

It is Madame Yudina's night of glory. She escorts I.S. through the exhibition, listens to the Octet sitting at his side, receives him on stage after the Septet. Some of her stage behavior might have been learned from Klemperer, which is to say that she does not bow or smile, or acknowledge even our most energetic applause with more than a trifling nod. She has been known, reputedly, to cross herself with passionate ostentation before playing, which can scarcely ingratiate her with Soviet audiences. And she has also read impromptu lectures to them and poems by Pasternak. Once, too, she supposedly stopped in a Prokofiev sonata, saying, "After Beethoven I simply cannot continue with *this*!" Yudina has carried I.S.'s banner in the Soviet Union longer than anyone else, and in recent years, through I.S.'s Paris friend Pierre Suvchinsky, she has been in communication with Stockhausen and other composers of his generation. Not surprisingly, she does not sit very smoothly with the powers of the Composers' Union, and when, at their luncheon party today, she pops a book from under the table and attempts to make them listen to her read religious philosophy, the expressions of dislike exchanged on both sides nearly degenerate into an open squabble. Yudina's Stravinsky collection fills walls and glass cases in several rooms, and includes photographs of Schoenberg, Berg, Webern, many of them probably being seen for the first time publicly in the U.S.S.R. Indefatigable in I.S.'s cause, she flies to Moscow late tonight to play his Piano Concerto, and will return here for a second performance Monday. In profile, playing, she looks like my idea of Bach without his wig. Full face, in the street, with her cane and handbag—from which she is forever pulling books, jars of honey, sweets, poems by Pasternak—she looks like (and is) a Doctor of Philosophy.

OCTOBER 7

I.S. listens to tapes of four new Soviet compositions, at the Composers' Union. The first is a cantata, a triptych on texts by Essenin, Blok, Mayakovsky; and the music, by Sviridov, a pupil of Shostakovich, is steady, solid, unhurried (all euphemisms for "boring," of course, but I am at least trying).

It does not venture beyond a primitive triadic scheme, and the most pleasing instrumental idea, the octaves between the piccolo and contrabassoon, was more effective in *Alexander Nevsky*. In the context of the Sviridov, the second piece, a quartet by Salmanov, qualifies as experimental music. It does little more, however, than naïvely repeat a Bartók *pizzicato-glissando*, unless the device comes from Gnessin, who was Sviridov's teacher. The third piece is a sonata for violin and piano by Ustvolskaya, another student of Shostakovich (also with exposure to Bartók: those sad, falling minor-thirds). Mirzoyan is the composer of the final piece, a symphony for strings and timpani that starts with a steppe-like *Largo*, goes on to some *Schelomo* (and is equally profound, I regret to say), and concludes in a fast movement, half rhapsody, half Moscow two-step, and all *kitsch*. After these samplers, no doubt chosen to please good old radical us, how can I.S. continue to proselytize for a school whose musical logic is at least a light-year away, and whose emotional world is on the other side of the galactic field? But he has had the same reactions. He tells me afterward that he had been writhing inside, adding that "That was the real *rideau de fer.*"

In his reminiscences, both spoken and written, I.S. has hardly mentioned the green, white, and gold Nikolsky Sobor, which is an architectural marvel even in this city. This is all the more surprising in that the Nikolsky is only a long block from his childhood home, and the belfry, a separate building, is in view from the street in front of his house; not to mention that belfry—he never has—is like living a block from, but not mentioning, the Taj Mahal. But I.S.'s descriptions of his neighborhood in his books are also greatly misleading as to scale and space. The Nikolsky is a double-decker church, of which the upper part is a sun-filled but now otherwise empty room, the lower part a sanctuary for old women. The low-arched lower floor is dimly lighted by oil-wick lamps suspended from the ceiling and by the tallow candles of the old-women votaries. V. buys a candle herself, but is made to pay four times more than anyone else, which may be social justice of a sort (Robin Hood), but which leaves her with the inference that in the New Russia this kind of experience occurs only in churches. I.S.'s niece's husband, and *his* son-in-law, accompany us on this expedition, albeit with an air of derring-do. Both have lived a block away most of their lives, and both are architectural engineers, but they have never been inside the church before. They look on with amazement as I.S. dips his fingers in the stoup, crosses himself, genuflects. Leaving the Nikolsky, we pass a synagogue, bulb-domed like a church. A sizable group of the bearded and black-hatted is gathered in the street before it.

The Krukov Canal, in front of I.S.'s old apartment, is about twenty-five feet wide. All of the buildings on the other side are new to him, he says, but the iron railings are the same, and so are the wooden footbridge at the corner and the cobblestone street; tramcars, moreover, still skid loudly by on their rails. A plaque commemorates the residence of "the composer and conductor" Napravnik in the house next door to the blank wall commemorating the twenty-four-year residence there of the composer of *The Rite of Spring.* I.S. says nothing as he looks at the door I have so often heard him describe—it opens directly on the street—and shows no trace of emotion.[1] Contrast this with his reaction, around the corner, to the Conservatory and the Maryinsky Theater. An involuntary "Glazunov" escapes him (after fifty years!) in the instant in which he recognizes the former, whereas, looking the other way, at the green-and-white Maryinsky, his face ripples with pleasure. Anyone who had seen this could not doubt that he had learned to hate music at the one address and to love it at the other.

We go to a family dinner at Xenia Yurievna's, number 72 Ulitsa Glinka. I.S.'s old apartment, next door, at number 66, is identical to this one, Xenia says, a statement that drastically reduces the scale of I.S.'s published recollections of it. Xenia's husband fought at Stalingrad, and from there to the end of the war, which came for him at Magdeburg. Xenia herself was in Leningrad throughout the siege, serving in an *opolchenie* at first and then with a burial battalion, for at least a third of the city's civilian population died from starvation.[2] Xenia's children and in-laws, all in their twenties, are attractive, shy, cheerful, scientific-minded, and they all have a smattering of English. Her Stravinsky collection includes many ancestral portraits, medallions, and photographs—most remarkably, a daguerreotype of Ignatievich, I.S.'s great-grandfather, a mutton-whiskered gentleman here aged 110. (Ignatievich died aged 111 as the result of a fall suffered while climbing over the fence on his way to a forbidden outing, a doctor having ordered the old tomcat to stay home, and the family having locked the gate.) Many of the photographs of I.S.'s father show him in the costumes of such of his basso roles as Holofernes and Sparafucile. Of the several hundred family group photographs, I. S. is present in perhaps a third, and of that third, about half were posed in Ustilug and Pechisky. In one photograph of I.S. in his room here, dated 1899, the walls are as crowded with pictures and mementos as they are now in Hollywood, but Berlioz was prominent among the pin-ups then. The most striking photograph of all, however, shows I.S. writing down the music of an ancient, and itinerant and blind, concertina player.

Xenia also has a painting by I.S., a small landscape, in oils, dated 1900; and packets of letters from I.S. to her father, Yuri, which break off *ca.* 1929 and, after a decade of silence, conclude with a note from Editions Russes de Musique in Paris announcing the deaths of I.S.'s mother, wife, and daughter; and several letters from Rimsky-Korsakov, though whether or not with references to I.S. I have no time to discover; and programs and press books covering virtually every performance of I.S.'s music in his native city both before and after 1917: of, for example, Petrenko singing the *Pastorale,* Gorodetzky's *Spring,* and, with Warlich and the Court Orchestra, *Le Faune*

---

1. "But I couldn't let myself," he said, when he read this.
2. See Leon Goure, *The Siege of Leningrad* (Palo Alto, Cal., 1962).

et la bergère, January 22 (O.S.), 1908; of Ansermet conducting *Mavra* and the Symphonies of Wind Instruments in the season of 1927–8; of Klimov conducting *Les Noces* in 1926 and *Oedipus Rex* in 1928; and of Stiedry conducting the Little Suites and *Le Sacre du printemps* in the same year.

One would have thought such an evening must be a deeply disturbing occasion for I.S., but I see no sign of it. V. says, however, that he reverted to childhood expressions several times during dinner.

Still later in the evening we go to the Maryinsky Theater—to see *it,* of course, and not *Lohengrin,* which is in the way. (I.S. has asked to see *Kitezh,* in fact, but the Composers' Union resisted the idea with mysterious excuses; finally, a susurration from Parker explains that the performance is famously bad.) Once again, I.S. is wildly wrong on scale: at seventeen hundred seats, the Maryinsky—light blue and gold, with a blue ceiling and a chandelier—is less than half the size of his description. He says that when he was a child the hem of the curtain was embroidered with medallion portraits of singers, one of them his father. According to the intendant, the *Lohengrin* was originally mounted in honor of Ribbentrop's visit in August 1939 and was scheduled for performance again on the day of the German invasion. (I am misquoting him, though, for he will not say "German," but only "Fascist.") Tonight's performance is the first since then, he says, but we would have been happier with the ban.

Upstairs in the foyer, a bust of Lenin now stands where I.S., as a boy, saw Tchaikovsky.

OCTOBER 8

Following the morning rehearsal, I.S. talks informally to a group of young musicians. But some of today's questions are of a different stamp: "Doesn't serialism constrain inspiration?" "Isn't it a new dogmatism?" I.S.: "Certainly it is a dogmatism, but don't dismiss it because of that. So was 'the old system' constricting and dogmatic—to bad composers." Then, turning to Khrennikov, he says, "You, too, Tikhon Nikolayich, will be trying it soon." Everyone laughs at this, including, most magnanimously, Tikhon Nikolayich himself, who recently informed a composers' conference that "the 12-tone system has no place in Soviet music," and to whom, therefore, the laugh must have had a cutting edge. All the same, I.S.'s colonizing has gone about as far as it can go on a verbal level, except that he could recommend pieces to be performed, but has not yet done so. My own feeling is that to the custodians of this outward-growing, big-statistic society, Webern's music can only seem like the nervous tics of a moribund culture. *I* feel no need for it here, in any case, and no correspondence between it and what I have seen of Soviet life, while on the other hand a Stravinsky-shaped vacuum did at least exist.

The turquoise palace of Czarskoe-Seloe, now Pushkin, was savagely gutted by the retreating "Fascists," but the cupolas again gleam as though newly splashed with gold, and the wing containing Cameron's Chinese Room,

Peacock Room, Blue Drawing Room (with intarsia woods from North Vietnam), as well as the bedroom and green dining room of Catherine II, is a masterpiece of restoration. The satellite buildings in the surrounding parks are inspired by French *dix-huitième* examples—a Trianon, an *orangerie,* a monopteral pavilion—and so, perhaps, are the groves of sycamores and the gardens trimmed like canapés. In the tall birch forests children are making sport of gathering leaves.

A stone marks each verst on the royal road from Czarskoe-Seloe back to Leningrad—where, at Nevsky Prospekt, we are held up as a ski team on two-wheel roller skates poles along in snow-country costume. "They are practicing for the Olympic Games," Alexandra explains. And no wonder if they win.

Shortly before our concert tonight, I.S. receives a last-minute request for tickets from some teen-age members of the "Stravinsky Club of Kharkov"— and he arranges to get them in.

Then, reaching the podium, he turns around and tells the audience that he attended his first concert in this hall. "Sixty-nine years ago I sat with my mother in that corner"—he points to it—"and heard the *Symphonie Pathétique,* conducted by Napravnik to mourn the death of Tchaikovsky. Now I am conducting in the same hall. I am very happy." This moving little speech is even more of a success than the music, which, after all, as I.S. quips, "was half-Tchaikovsky" (*Le Baiser de la fée*) "and half Rimsky-Korsakov" (*Fireworks* and *Firebird*). We had asked the Composers' Union to invite Nadiejda Rimsky-Korsakov, the composer's daughter, to the concert—the *Fireworks* having been composed to celebrate her marriage—but learn (a whisper from Parker) that the old lady declined because she had always known that I.S. was not fond of her husband—the composer Maximilian Steinberg—or, for that matter, herself.

1962

OCTOBER 9

It is a wet day, but we walk from the Hermitage Bridge to the Pushkin Museum, where punts and kayaks are in the Moyka River. The Museum's relics include the vest the poet was wearing at the fatal duel; his death mask, which emphasizes the large brow, the dilated nostrils, the small mouth; and his library, perhaps as many as half of whose books are in foreign languages.

From Pushkin we go to V.'s former residence at the Moyka corner of the Champs de Mars, a sand-graded parade ground when the I.S.'s knew it, but now a garden with a mammoth war memorial; and to Aptekarsky Ostrov, the island where she was born[1] (but which would have been a more appropriate birthplace for I.S.: "*Aptekarsky*" means apothecary); Kammenoi Ostrov, where we see a tree planted by Peter the Great and now in the middle of a street; the Peter and Paul fortress; a corvette, the first to mutiny

---

1. At Pesochnaya Ulitsa, 4.

in 1917 and now a naval museum; and the house of Kschessinska, where a plaque on the balcony commemorates Lenin's first address to the people. V. also shows me where she crossed the ice in 1917 to hear Gorky speak.

According to Alexandra, we cover fourteen kilometers of the Hermitage this afternoon, and I do so being constantly surprised by the dimensions of familiar pictures—the *"Madonna Conestabile,"* for instance, which is so small it can almost be circumscribed by the hands of a pianist. But nothing I can say about the Hermitage will satisfy me.

Leningrad is tall, regular, Western, straight—in contrast to circular, haphazard, oriental Moscow. And in Leningrad, the royal city, the people look more drab than they do in Moscow, the proletarian one, if only because the buildings are so sumptuous. I.S.: "The best thing in Leningrad is St. Petersburg." And St. Petersburg is a city of romantic bridges and islands, and of small cobblestone streets and byways not yet macadamized like the large thoroughfares. It must be one of the few great cities of the world in which the ugliest buildings are churches. Thus the Issaksky, which is a heavy, black roost for Imperial eagles, and which deserves to be in Berlin; and the Kazansky, which imitates St. Peter's and deserves to be in Rome, Georgia; and the Spassa Nakrovee, which consecrates, or desecrates, the site of Alexander II's assassination; and the Gastinny Dvor, the "upside-down trousers," as I.S. calls it. And St. Petersburg is a polychrome city. Thus the Dance Academy, a building the size of an American aircraft factory, is ocher; the Gorky Theater is green; the Anichkov Palace is red; the stables by the Champ de Mars are peach-colored; and the Yusupov Palace, in which Rasputin's murder took place (the first few stages of it), is yellow. And St. Petersburg is a city of classical angles and perspectives, and of planned space—I am thinking of the semicircular space cut back from the corners of streets contiguous to the Fantanky River. But at night, St. Petersburg is a lonely, melancholy city, like Venice in winter. I.S.'s old neighborhood is all but deserted after six o'clock, and very dark, street lamps being far apart. At midnight, romantic mists hang low over the canals and the city has a ghostly gloom. One imagines the Yusupov Palace full of light and gaiety, as it once was, but the beautiful old building is empty, dark, and dead.

Tempting generalizations I will never pronounce in public: Russians are: hospitable; sentimental; "optimistic"; patient (an amazing capacity to stand in queues, especially in Leningrad, though Parker says that some of this is laziness: "They would rather stand on line than work"); garrulous (heavy artillery wouldn't interrupt most of them, but the voices and the language are less grating, at length, than French and German); direct—the compliments, not to say encomia, they address to us and each other in their toasts—but not frank (they will hide the real reason for anything they do not wish to reveal, like dogs burying bones); fundamentally friendly (they are more friendly to us than we are to them, certainly); generous ("You like it? Here, take it," and never the spirit of *"Klein aber Mein"*). Their manners are not "good," but they more than make up for that by their very ready affection; I, at any rate, have never known a more affectionate friendship in so short a time than I have had with Karen Khatchaturian, though we are able to talk to each other only very haltingly. Russians have no commercial spirit—none of our venal pursuit of money—and even in the arts, no wasteful competition. Thus, while Russian composers may dislike each other just as intensely as European and American composers hate *their* colleagues—some of them ought to, for sure—they nevertheless co-operate and function as a political entity in a way that Western composers might envy. Lastly, "sophisticated" conversation—meaning, I suppose, a certain range of reference to modish mental *bric-à-brac*—is in short supply. It is replaced by "enthusiasm."

After our concert tonight, we rush to the midnight train for Moscow, carrying bouquets along with our bags. Then, as we pull out of the station, a Diaghilev, a Tolstoy, a Rimsky-Korsakov, and a Balmont run alongside for a moment, like another era trying to catch up.

1962

OCTOBER 10

The sun rises through green forests touched with gold, and from Klin to Moscow we press our noses to the corridor windows, watching people in shawls, caps, and boots going about their work in a land of brightly colored barns and *izbas*. It is the world of I.S.'s *Pribaoutki*, and of Kandinskys and Jawlenskys and Chagalls of half a century ago.

At the National Hotel, a letter awaits I.S. from a Polish branch of Stravinskys living in Danzig, complete with genealogical tree. At noon, Khrennikov and Khachaturian arrive laden with farewell gifts of samovars, gold spoons, gold tea-glass holders, inscribed scores.

Tonight's farewell banquet at the Metropole is a happy occasion, free of speeches and of formality; in fact, it becomes somewhat too relaxed as pellets of bread and even apples are flipped about the room. Husbands and wives sit next to each other at these affairs, and the wives we meet are all professional women, chemists, archeologists, physicians, scientists. Shostakovich, this time at I.S.'s side, seems even more frightened and tortured than at the first conclave, perhaps fearing that a speech is expected of him. He converses neutrally, at first, then like a bashful schoolboy blurts out that the *Symphony of Psalms* had overwhelmed him when he first heard it, and that he had made his own piano score of it, which he would like to present to I.S. Seeking to return the compliment, I.S. says that he shares some of Shostakovich's high regard for Mahler, at which point Shostakovich starts to melt, but quickly freezes up again as I.S. continues with: "But you should go beyond Mahler. The Viennese troika also adored him, you know, and both Schoenberg and Webern conducted his music." Toward the end of the evening, and after several *zubrovkas,* Shostakovich touchingly confesses that he would like to follow I.S.'s example and conduct his own music, "Except that I don't know how not to be afraid."

I.S., going to bed, says he has been imagining a conversation on the other side:

> "The Russians have skyscrapers."
> "Yes, but they are built on mud and will soon collapse."
> "Well, they do have very good roads."
> "Of course, but they are the work of slaves."

OCTOBER 11

A telephone call at noon from the Kremlin fixes an appointment with Khrushchev, who returned late last night from a twelve-day tour and has just arrived at his office. We enter by the Bashnya Borovitskaya at one-thirty, our driver simply saying "Nikita Sergeich" to a guard who asks for no identification. We go beyond St. Ivan's, gleaming white and gold, to the Council of Ministers Building, from which Suslov, leaving, waves a greeting but walks by, which surprises Khrennikov who has expected him to be present at the meeting. A solitary soldier stands at the door, and a civilian secretary who leads the I.S.'s to a tiny elevator and climbs the two flights with me. We pass a large cloakroom and walk through a long corridor to a waiting room resembling a doctor's office, with a table of foreign-language magazines and a portrait of Marx on the wall, like the doctor's old professor. After five minutes here, the same secretary ushers us to a long room with a long conference table covered in green billiard cloth. Khrushchev, behind a desk at the far end, sees I.S.'s limp and hurries to his side, where, I.S., addressing him as "Nikita Sergeich," apologizes "for taking time that must be doubly crowded after your absence." Khrushchev—hardly taller than I.S., with small, brown, swivel eyes (you would not be able to look if they were larger)—gives us short, energetic handshakes with a pudgy, short-fingered paw, and says, "But I wanted very much to meet you." We sit at the far end of the billiard table, I.S. and V. facing Khrushchev, myself and Khrennikov next to him. Lenin is present, too, in a photograph on the wall behind Khrushchev's desk, as well as in a frame on his blotter next to a file marked "*Tass,*" and Marx, over the door, beyond several racks of pull-out maps.

Khrushchev rests his rimless spectacles on the green felt, asserts his elbows there, and begins to talk about his trip. "I had been promising to visit Turkestan and the Aral Sea region for a long time, and though I was too busy to do it now, I felt it could not be postponed. What I saw impressed me so much that I returned by train, to give myself time to think about it." He describes the irrigation of the "Hungry Desert," in which "skeletons of camels have been found, though human beings have never been able to exist there. We have built a thirteen-hundred-kilometer canal and redirected the once-dried-up Amu-Darya. Rice and cotton are already growing, and in a few years the whole region will flourish." Anticipating the future, and not only of those regions, Khrushchev beams with pleasure and becomes even more energetic. He smiles, too, exposing a gallery of dental gold, but does not smile *all* the time, which is one's impression of him from newspapers. "The world's largest and fastest supersonic jets are being built in Tashkent," he goes on, glowing at the prospect of the Soviet lead in "inertial navigation." And he describes a territory, near Samarkand, in which "the English found gold—mere gold—but where we have discovered fountains of naphtha and inexhaustible deposits of copper. The gold is still mined, of course, but as a quaint sideline industry. The women in these regions like to show off their wealth by wearing heavy red velvet, even in that oppressive heat, but they live in squalid houses that they will not improve because of an old fear of being taxed. When refrigerators, television sets, and laundry machines reached the stores there, not long ago, everything was sold in an instant and paid for literally from barrels of money." Elaborating on the good living conditions on the Soviet side of the border, *versus* the misery on the Indian side, his tone becomes aggressive and boastful. (I.S., later: "I think he wants India.") I.S. asks if the people in these regions speak Russian or if he uses a translator. Khrushchev: "All *my* republics speak Russian; I have never used a translator in our country."

I.S. translates for me, however, this being the only occasion at which Alexandra has not been present, although a speech studded with statistics and geographical names is easy to follow, besides which the speaker could hardly be more concrete. (Afterward, the I.S.'s remark his "very correct Russian.") Khrushchev is acutely sensitive to whatever we say, and even more sensitive, I think, to whatever we might say; clearly, he does not want I.S. to talk about music. (But what *are* his thoughts about this emissary from the czarist past?) He does almost all of the talking, in any case, and as he can scarcely contain himself on the subject of his trip, nearly all of the forty minutes are devoted to that. We exchange observations about Moscow, however, and when the I.S.'s tell him how beautiful they find the city, Khrushchev says: "Yes, I drove around really looking at it myself, not long ago, and I was impressed; but for eight hundred years it was a pigsty." As we leave, he repeats Khrennikov's invitation to stay in a *dacha* in the Crimea, carefully including myself. I say *"Bolshoi spassiba,"* and he, graciously, *"Prieyzhiety opiat"* ("Come back"). I.S., in the car: "He is like a composer showing you the composition on which he is at work, and of which he is very full and very proud."

Sheremetievo Airport is an obstacle course of reporters, tape recorders, television cameras. An American reporter to V.: "I understand you had an interview with Khrushchev." V.: "Oh no. It was simply a visit, not an interview. *This* is an interview." Reporter: "Well, did you talk about music?" V.: "Mr. Khrushchev is not a musician. We did not exchange banalities about music, therefore, but listened to him recount fascinating things about his trip."[1] Reporter to I.S.: "Will you say something about the beauties of Russia, Mr. Stravinsky?" I.S.: "Beauties are to be loved, not talked about." And, "Mr. Stravinsky, what was your impression of Khrushchev?" I.S.: "That no palace eunuchs are running his affairs."

A hundred new friends and now familiar faces crowd around, stuffing our arms and pockets with presents (bottles of vodka, tarlike lumps of pressed caviar, photographs, flowers) and our hearts with kisses, embraces, tears.

OCTOBER 14

Paris. Lunch with Jean Genet, a small man—for some reason I had expected a large one—and in spite of the leather jacket, open shirt, necktie slack like a noose, unexpectedly soft-boiled. His gray-brown eyes are frightened but at the same time as impertinent as a stethoscope. He likes or doesn't like, and he lays it down short and sharp, frequently with *"Ça m'emmerde,"* or *"Ça m'embête,"* but after a round or two this is predictably perverse. Thus, when the name Dostoievsky comes up, he says *"Tout ça m'emmerde beaucoup,"* while his reaction to Tolstoy is *"Connais pas."* He was unable to finish Kafka's *The Trial,* he says, *"parce qu'on a trop parlé de ça."* He laughs with us from time to time, but then looks dangerous again and ready to bite. And when the punch line of someone else's joke has already been delivered, he has a prickly way of following it with *"Eh, alors?"* He contradicts, when someone describes an actor as handsome—*"Même à dix-sept ans il était très moche"*—and he finds a film *"Abominable"* when everyone else speaks well of it. He flatters I.S., or tries to, telling him that his voice is "like the sound of the percussion instruments in *Histoire du Soldat.*" However, when I.S. asks him, innocently, "Do you like to read at night?" he pretends to think deeply for about thirty seconds before coming back wickedly with *"Oui, peut-être."*

1962

OCTOBER 21

Assisi. I.S. is much upset today by the news of the death of Goncharova. We lunch with the painter Bill Congdon, reminiscing about our meeting in the middle of the night in the Azores and about our exploration of San Zan Degolà in Venice together, shortly after the frescoes were cleaned.

OCTOBER 28–NOVEMBER 3

Caracas. The principal hotel having been bombed by saboteurs, we stay in the Circo Militar, an officers' club—actually a private village—"erected in the great days of the dictatorship" and a shining example of the corruption of the "in" party. The officers' entertainments include a cinema, a stadium, swimming pools, and a perpetual concert piped into every room and hall and even into outdoor space. The gates are watched by guards with sub-

1. Next day in the Western press: "As Khrushchev is ignorant of music, he talked banalities about his trip."

machine guns, however, and though the marble bars, ballrooms, restaurants are empty except for us, every table is fully, mysteriously, set at every meal.

Caracas resembles Los Angeles—in the freeways on which traffic regulates itself entirely by threat, and in the glass elevators, like thermometers, on the outsides of buildings. But it is defaced by more outspoken political graffiti: *"Vivan las guerrillas," "Muera Fidel," "Romulistos asesinos,"* and so on, back and forth. *Un*like Los Angeles is the mountain wall between the city and the sea, the peaks of which, like elderly courtesans, lift their veils only at night.

The United States Embassy, where we attend a reception, looks over the city from a hill. "It is like San Francisco without the bay," the Ambassador observes to me of the view, but what with the ring of armed guards it *feels* more like Alcatraz without any San Francisco. A time bomb was exploded in the Embassy laundry chute a few weeks ago, and the Ambassador himself is unable to attend our concert because the police cannot guarantee to protect him in the University auditorium.

The lisp and elimination of the "s" are more marked here than I have ever heard; the musicians address I.S. as "Maetro Travithky," and when I announce Debussy's *Gigues* for rehearsal, it is repronounced *"Heeg."* At the rehearsals I.S. tells the *Petrushka* pianist to open the lid all the way, to use the left pedal only, to play *forte* and *secco;* and as I have heard these directions a hundred times, I should record them as definitive. He also instructs the strings to play the triplet in the *Cantique* (*Four Etudes*), including the augmentation of it in the first and last measures, with three up-bows on one bow.

The hills across the highway from the Circo swarm with shacks, some of them made out of billboards, with the advertised products—a woman drinking Pepsi-Cola, for instance—still showing. Rich people tell us that the indigent people who have drifted here from the jungle consider themselves better off than ever before, no matter what; and the "what" means no plumbing, no water, no latrine but the street, no electricity except by filching from other people's outlets during the night. We have been warned against walking here—the dirt labyrinths are impassable to automobiles—but walk, nevertheless, for as long as we can stand the stench, which is long enough to discover, of all things, a Russian church. Nor are we attacked or threatened except by girls of nursery-school age who turn toy submachine guns in our direction.

Commenting on the extremes of poverty and wealth, Federico Schlesinger, late of Vienna and now proprietor of a local hotel, says that "Venezuela does not spend its money but throws it away." One of Federico's own treasures is a tooled morocco guestbook inscribed by every celebrity who has dared to come within the three-mile limit. Irritated perhaps by the fulsome testimonial of a previous signer, Ernest Hemingway has written, I suspect with malice, "To Federico, may his luck continue."

I visit the Institute of Scientific Research, several thousand feet above the city, and its director, Marcel Roche, who describes the work being done to combat the *schizotrypanum cruzi.* This is transmitted by cockroach vermin and, he says, has already caused cardiac damage to at least a tenth of the population.

At a late-night farewell party, in the garden of Ríos Reyna, president of the orchestra, girls with tall, spun-sugar coiffures sing attractive Creole songs, but my own attention is held by giant moths alighting on the walls, and grasshoppers with chassis the size of large peapods.

NOVEMBER 17

New York. Auden for dinner, in the restaurant of the Pierre Hotel. His face hangs in loose folds, somewhat like an elephant's behind, and in great contrast to his extremely tight trousers, the cuffs of which are as much as ten inches above his flat, platypus-type feet. He says that in the club car of the train on his way to lecture at Yale, two Yale boys sent him a note: "We can't stand it a minute longer: are you Carl Sandburg?" He wrote back: "You have spoiled mother's day."

After asking the waiter to bring him a "veg," he tells us that "Cardinal Newman could have become a saint but thought it too fruity to do a miracle." Then, for no apparent reason, he tells us that when he was examined for United States citizenship, "It didn't look too good because I admitted I was a writer, though when I said that, the interviewer told his secretary to put down 'Can read.' One question, incidentally, was 'Do you intend to kill the President?' but I am certain if I had answered 'Yes,' no one would have noticed."

He talks about his ideas for a libretto on the *Bacchae,* confessing that "The *Elegy* was our version of *Arabella.*" Switching to other operas, he describes the beginning of the second act of *Die Walküre* as "a Victorian breakfast scene, Wotan meekly cracking his morning egg behind *The Times* while Fricka furiously rattles the teacups. *Pelléas,*" he says, "is an underwater opera. Nobody can be that refined; the piece succeeds because it flatters the audience. But imagine devoting an opera to people with manias for losing things!" Apropos a line in *Vanessa,* he wonders "where the author had seen 'weeping deer,'" and, in defending opera against other types of music, he remarks that "People who attend chamber music concerts are like Englishmen who go to church when abroad."

His literary references nowadays are exclusively German. Thus, "Lichtenberg's notes on Hogarth contain a better translation for '*The Rake*' than '*Der Wüstling,*' but I can't remember what it is." He complains that "The Germans tend to regard one of their classic authors as Jesus Kleist," and he proposes as a new classification for a whole category of females: "the Rilke-girlfriend type." He gets lost on a trip to the "loo," however, and this must have given him an unpleasant turn—"*schwarze Gedanken,*" he would probably prefer to say—for shortly afterward he announces: "When my time is up I'll want Siegfried's Funeral Music and not a dry eye in the house."

1962

1948
1949
1950
1951
1952
1953
1954
1955
1956
1957
1958
1959
1960
1961
1962
1963
1964
1965
1966
1967
1968
1969
1970
1971

ITINERARY

January–February: Hollywood. I.S. composes *Abraham and Isaac.* **March 18:** We fly to Oberlin. **21:** I.S. conducts the *Symphony of Psalms* at Oberlin. **22:** We fly to New York, and Toronto (27th). **31:** We fly to New York. **April 9:** We sail on the *Bremen* for Hamburg, for the first staging of *The Flood.* **May:** Budapest, Zagreb, Paris, London. **June 10:** Fly from Dublin to Hamburg. **12:** I.S. conducts *Oedipus Rex* at the Hamburg Opera. **13:** We fly to Stockholm, Milan (20th), and New York (29th). **July 1:** We fly to Hollywood, and Chicago (11th). **13:** Concert at Ravinia. **14:** Fly to Santa Fe. **August 7:** R.C. conducts the U.S. première of *Lulu.* **18–19:** Drive to Hollywood. **25:** Fly to New York. **29:** Fly to Rio de Janeiro. **September 9:** Fly to New York. **17:** Fly to Hollywood. **November 5:** Fly to New York, Rome (11th), Palermo (16th). **25:** I.S.'s last concert in Italy, on the night of President Kennedy's funeral, in Santa Maria Sopra Minerva (Rome). **26:** Fly to New York. **December 5:** Vernissage of V.'s second exhibition at the Galerie Internationale.

APRIL 20

Hamburg. *Mahagonny* at the Staatsoper, our first evening in a two-week "theater cure." The staging, by a Brecht pupil, is admirably severe, especially in the groupings of the chorus. But after applauding the director, one hastens to credit the composer. I.S. will say no more than that "There are good things everywhere in the score, only it is not everywhere good." Nevertheless, the wonder of *Mahagonny* is that so prodigal a musical substance was lavished on so flimsy a play. (Berg must have known *Mahagonny,* incidentally, and it seems to me that Lulu has a touch of Jenny, and Berg's Athlete more than a touch of Weill's. Perhaps even the choice of instruments in Berg's *"Garderobe"* scene was influenced by the sax and banjo in Weill's jazz band and the zither in his glutton scene.) But whatever the quality of

212

the music, how dispiriting a work it is: a lively beginning, then a three-hour downward plunge with nary an upward swerve; one leaves the theater at the end quite literally in the dumps. No doubt this long decline is responsible for a deleterious effect on one's judgment, too, so that most of what one remembers as "good" seems to have occurred comparatively near the beginning; the boxer's death, for example, and the brothel scene (*"Erst wasch die Hände"* and *"Jungens macht rascher"*), and the scene with the glutton (an *"Er ist tot,"* a "hats off," and a "that's that").

But Hamburg is no Berlin-in-the-twenties. Risqué lines and situations are greeted with uncertain titters, and all over the theater Herren and Frauen Schmidt exchange whispers and knowing nudges. Furthermore, the reception as a whole is exactly the opposite of the authors' intentions. The audience sits back and enjoys it as it would a musical or operetta, albeit a strangely depressing example of either.

After the performance, the scene in the restaurant of the Vier Jahreszeiten might be a continuation of the last scene of the opera. There the final abasement of society is represented by pickets with placards saying FÜR GELD! while in the restaurant bellhops in floor-length aprons march about carrying the same kind of signs but summoning people to telephones: BITTE HERR STOLZ!

1963

APRIL 25

The Gründgens staging of Schlegel's *Hamlet* at the Deutsches Schauspielhaus is a language lesson, whatever else, for the English lines leap into the mind like subtitles in a foreign film—if one catches the German trigger words that release the springs. In my case this involuntary translation mechanism seems to give many of the German phrases an unbecomingly comic sound: *"Ein Meisterwerk ist der Mensch,"* for example, and *"Hat der Kerl kein Gefühl für seine Arbeit?"* And even the forms of address, *"Gnädiger Herr"* this and *"Gnädige Frau"* that, strikes me as ludicrous, partly because they are used here in Hamburg for the I.S.'s, who always laugh at it. The German vocabulary seems much smaller, too—more like a translation of Lamb than of the original—so that we are aware of repetitions of phrasing. (But what can any translator do with a succession of words like the Ghost's "unhousel'd, disappointed, unanel'd"?) Another, but unexpected, impression is that the language, though Germanic only, is softer than the combination of Latin and Germanic in the English.

Exactly how close the translation is as meaning I am unable to say, but the action often seems to indicate that any connection is tenuous. "Who is there?" Marcellus asks, and the guard counter-challenges, "Nay, stand and unfold thyself." But this Marcellus is long since unfolded and, even allowing for poor visibility, stands less than a foot away. Nor does Hamlet himself take any pains to act in reasonable conformity with what he is saying, or what one remembers him saying in English. To begin with, he is wholly devoid of a poetic or intellectual temperament, but is a great one for leaping

213

and somersaulting, playfully wrestling with and knocking Rosencrantz about, half throttling his mother, prematurely practicing balestras on Laertes—the loudest Laertes, incidentally, in the history of the theater. In fact, Hamlet is faster moving than anyone else on the stage, which contradicts not only the usual picture of the character but also the specific suggestion in his mother's speech during the duel that (like Aeneas, incidentally) he is heavy-set. In one scene he rolls and squats as if he might be preparing for a performance somewhere else as Puck, and in the *prie-dieu* scene he comes tearing in like a professional sprinter, or as if following a canine interpretation of "a Great Dane." In short, no indecision, no pale cast of thought, but a great deal of roistering and rapidly translated action. Which is part of the reason that the play feels so prosaic.

The decorative and atmospheric aspects of the production are no less odd. Several series of "abstract expressionist" panels are imposed as backdrops or subliminal advertisements. Unobtrusive at first, they become less abstract with each scene and more expressionistically involved, eventually forming an intolerable symbolic accompaniment to the play. Thus a great deal of gray is exhibited when the outlook for Hamlet may seem to be taking that complexion, and of red when we should sense that blood is about to be shed. In the graveyard scene the panels are smeared in a way that seems to pose a riddle, which focuses attention on the solution of the symbolic conundrum rather than on what is otherwise the most successful scene of the evening, a masterpiece of *Schadenfreude,* in fact, which the gravediggers play like contemporary Berlin wits. But whatever *do* those panels mean? Dirty laundry? That the cemetery is not in a posh neighborhood?

As for the costumes, Horatio looks like an orchestra conductor or *maître d'hôtel,* Polonius like an idiot Wilhelm II, Fortinbras like a space-traffic policeman, the Norwegian army—green leather uniforms and crash helmets—like shock troops of the near future. Still other periods are suggested by the music and the choreography. The former consists of spurts of pseudo-Handel on the organ (which, however, may be preferred to the usual rancid sackbut sennets), the latter of "modern-dance" ballet—in the dumb show, during which Hamlet never so much as slyly glances at the King. It remains to be said that this action thriller takes place in two dramatically shapeless divisions, separated by an intermission just long enough for philosophers to read Karl Jaspers's program notes, *"Hamlets Wissen."*

After the performance, I.S. observes that "The play is like a turkey which nobody knows how to cut because Hamlet himself is developed so far out of proportion to the other characters." But is it partly because of the German language, I wonder, that "philosophical" passages seem to stand out?— Ophelia's "We know what we are but not what we may be," for instance, which makes off with the cake of Existentialism—and the belief beyond appearances and sciences ("There is a special providence," etc.). Nor had I ever noticed before to what extent Polonius's boringness is a family disease, both children being afflicted with it as well. And I had quite forgotten Hamlet's generosity to artists, *i.e.,* when Polonius orders the actors to be treated "according to their desert," and the Prince counters with the order, "Use them after your own honour and dignity: the less they deserve, the more merit is in your bounty."

Tonight's opera is *Don Carlo.* But the staging lacks action, and some of the little there is goes wrong, such as the sword-drawing in the street scene, which also marks the breakdown of credibility in the work as a whole and is a weak curtain-closer. Nor do the sets offer much compensation, their main feature being a row of overgrown asparagus meant to represent trees. The drama falls off so sharply after the Grand Inquisitor scene, in any case, that the rest is hardly more than a costume concert. And to make matters worse, the Inquisitor is miscast, a feeble elder rather than a holy terror; the orchestra does the casting here, incidentally, implacably setting the scene for a person and a voice more powerful than Philip's. But despite the shortcomings, I.S. is rapturous. "What scope and vitality Verdi had, and with what scale he could endow his people! How I would like to have known him! His was the true spirit of *libertà,* too, and he, not Wagner, was the true progressive, not merely the Verdi of the Risorgimento and Cavour's parliament, but the composer of the *Don Carlo* duet:

1963

which, to me anyway, is so much more likable than that other *Blutsbruderschaft* music which fat people in horns and hides howl at by the hour."

When I.S. takes his seat in the middle of the third row of the Staatsoper, a moment before the lights dim for *Der Rosenkavalier,* the audience applauds him, and very warmly. He acknowledges the ovation with a deep bow, but whispers to me that "It is because everybody is very happy to see me sit through four hours without syncopation." But he *doesn't* sit; or at any rate, he doesn't sit still. "How long can this false counterpoint go on?" he mutters in a *voce* not *sotto* enough, and, "How can anybody swallow all of that *Schlagsahne?*" At intermission he remarks that "Prurience is intolerable even in Mozart." During the later acts some of his comments are: "Strauss holds his breath too long"; and, "Bad taste and vigor go well together"; and, "If Richard, then Wagner, if Strauss, then Johann." After the performance he notes that "Strauss may charm and delight but he cannot move. That is partly because he was never committed. He didn't give a damn."

KERJÜK AZ ÖVEKET BECSATOLNI! DOHÁNYOZNI TILOS! (FASTEN SEAT BELTS, NO SMOKING) flashes a sign in the Ilyushin turbo-prop carrying us from Amsterdam to Prague to Budapest. And as if simply out of spite against so many letters, two of the shortest words in English instruct prospective occupants of the WC to "PU SH" the door. Prague Airport is not only empty and ominous, but just before take-off, two policemen enter the cabin and check every face against a photograph. Budapest Airport, a half-hour later, is totally dark and, except for our welcoming party—a press photographer and three Italian-speaking women from a concert agency—likewise deserted. As we step down, the photographer seems to be asking V. if she would care for some chocolates—"*Csókolom, csókolom*"—until we learn from the Italians that "*Kezét csókolom*" means "Kiss the hand."

The city might still be under a wartime curfew; the streets are very dimly lighted and virtually without traffic, vehicular or pedestrian. But shell-holes and other damage from the fighting of seven years ago are visible even in the gloom.

The Grand Hotel, on Margit Sziget—Margaret Island, in the Danube— stands behind a levee in a park of chestnut trees, now in blossom. No renovation appears to have disturbed the Grand since the good old days of Hapsburg decay. The bedroom furniture is turn-of-the-century imitation rosewood; the paintings, landscapes and portraits, are framed in gold guilloche; the beds are covered by eiderdown dumplings; the windows are draped with velvet curtains, each large enough to conceal the modesty of a small operatic stage. Less charming, for nonantiquarians—or should I say *even* less charming?—is the plumbing. The water, both "cold" and "hot," dribbles out lukewarm and sulphurous, and the toilet gurgles vindictively for an hour or so after each use. (So does the neighbor's, a high transom permanently open to the adjoining apartment forcibly informing us of all activities there.) But the first clue that some ill may have befallen the old Empire is in the WC. Each morning a dirty paper band is laid across the toilet seat. It says "Sterile," *in Russian!*

The contrast between the faded Franz Josef appointments and the clientele is bizarre. Most of the guests are political missionaries, a description that includes several different delegations of Africans; a party of Frenchmen who, whenever we pass them, always seem to be muttering something against General de Gaulle; and a sizable contingent of Chinese. The latter, wearing stiff-collared Mao tunics, share endless speech-making dinners with Hungarian officials—in, I.S. says, very correct Russian. Nor are the entertainments of this extraordinary aggregation less odd than its appearance. At about five o'clock each afternoon, in a dance pavilion adjoining the restaurant, an eight-man jazz combo starts through a repertory of American hit tunes of the thirties, of which the favorites are "Stars Fell on Alabama" and "Smoke Gets in Your Eyes." The floor then rapidly fills and color-integrates, except for the Chinese, who not only do not participate but also at this time clearly regard their western and southern allies as puerile offenders against intellectual dignity. It is a vivacious crowd, nevertheless, and the Hungarian girls wear their hair like nests, in the American way. (Or is it the Thracian way? *Cf.* Archilochus: ". . . the ungodly Thracians with their hair done up in a fright on top of their heads . . .")

The food, except for *caffè espresso*—coffee bars are two and three to the block in the city—is ostentatiously bad. But a few imports are available, including Scotch whiskey, English gin, French sardines, French champagne ($40 a bottle), French wines (according to I.S. all Hungarian wines taste "like shellac"), Icelandic caviar (*sic,* not "outlandish," though it is that, too). The U.S.S.R. being at the same time the largest exporter of caviar in the world and Hungary's biggest brother, the presence of an Icelandic brand strikes us as spectacularly eccentric. Is it protest, or penance, or both? Surely no one could *prefer* it to the Russian, as the I.S.'s too openly demonstrate by clamping their noses against its repellent ichthyoid odor. I.S. notes, incidentally, that "despite all the rumors of famine, everyone looks remarkably fat," but V., after observing the bolting and guzzling at neighboring tables, says that the fat is emotional and the crapulousness a sign of deprivation.

The Hungarian National Radio Orchestra is rich in tone and precise and fluent in rhythm, and the concert is the most satisfying on our tour as well as the most warmly and, I think, discriminatingly received. But the rehearsals are more gratifying than the concert because they take place in the small, acoustically perfect Franz Liszt Hall. The players' first foreign language is a grudging German, with English a close second, French a poor third. Hardly anyone speaks Russian, and in spite of the parity with Hungarian on toilet seats, the language of the occupier is certainly not popular. The few Hungarians who talk to us about the U.S.S.R. are far from enthusiastic, in any case, and those who have traveled there are openly disparaging.

We attend a reception by the Union of Composers, a well-informed multilingual group that includes a very pretty girl who, it is said (though that is beside the point), has written a highly successful opera. Delegates from the Union of Soviet Composers are present, too, and they give us recordings of our Moscow concerts last year. Zoltán Kodály has promised to come, but as he is I.S.'s age and has only recently taken a bride of twenty—following the death of a first wife some thirty years *his* senior—his absence is accountable.

Although the director of the Hungarian National Ballet apologizes for "the very tired orchestra," *Le Sacre du printemps* is musically accurate and the group-calisthenic choreography is at least well done. Moreover, I.S. says that the *temenos*—the magic circle—is right, as well as the descent of the *Elue* into the cave. This season's repertory, the director goes on, totals sixty operas. "In a city as small as Budapest, an opera can be given only a few times, whereas in a city the size of New York, a very few operas can be played again and again. Still, our ballet has performed *Le Sacre* forty times

1963

this year, which I think is as good a record as New York." He is incredulous, of course, when I.S. tells him that the complete work has never been staged by an American company.

After the theater we go to a restaurant in Buda to hear an orchestra of cimbalom, clarinet, and strings. All of the pieces begin with moody cadenzas and eventually turn into rhapsodies. The players wear muzhiks' blouses. During their vodka breaks, they stand, click their heels, and raise their glasses to I.S.

MAY 9

As we leave the hotel for the drive to Zagreb, a girl hands I.S. a note

> Dear Mr. Stravinszki! I please one autogram
> because I very like *Petruska* and you,
>
> > Podmaniczky, Judith

which he signs in the Hungarian manner: "Stravinszki, Igor." Travel fever shows in the eyes of the people who come to see us off, and we feel like departing prison visitors.

A long avenue with ocher churches and ocher trams leads to fields of black loam in which stooks of straw are stacked like tepees. Here, and all the way, most agricultural workers are women. From time to time a Red Star on the gate of a collective farm reminds the motorist who is in authority, but these stars are greatly outnumbered by crucifixes and shrines. A plaque on one of the low, thatched-roof houses of Martonvásár commemorates Beethoven's stay there in 1808; at least that is what it seems to say, but when I try to read it, or pronounce any Hungarian aloud, our driver is seized with such fits of laughter that I fear we may land in a ditch. A catastrophe of the sort is only narrowly averted, in fact, when we come to Székesfehérvár (say-cash-fé-hair-var), a city with Roman and Byzantine ruins and a turquoise-and-marigold rococo square. By the time we reach Nagykanizsa (nadg-caneezha) and Siófok, where we eat in a "bisztró" on Főút Street—a name, we now know from experience, that will not sound as Chinese as it looks—I have learned to hold my tongue.

Lake Balaton is half hidden by a blizzard of dandelion fluff. The fields and forests to the south are richer and larger, but the farmers work with primitive hand implements, including hand barrows, and they seed the earth from aprons—as, doubtless, their ancestors did a thousand years ago. At the frontier, gun-toting guards, barbed wire, and a double barricade on the bridge explain the claustral look in the eyes of those who came to see us off this morning.

On the Yugoslav side the road is unpaved as far as Čakovec, and thereafter, in the mountains of Illyria, worse than anything the word "unpaved" can suggest. The land is poor, too, and the few strips that have been plowed on the steep hills are hardly wider than toboggan slides. Almost without exception the people wear gray or black clothes, as if in mourning for some

1963

national disaster—which indeed seems to be the case. The houses in Čakovec itself bristle with TV antennae, but this does not inspire confidence in the local prosperity, and, in fact, a work crew, idling in the yard of a derelict factory, looks to me as if it had given up hope and was simply waiting about in the chance of being rescued by helicopters.

Our Hungarian driver pronounces "Čakovec" Aristophanically, "Ka-ko-kek," but the Yugoslavs to whom he appeals for directions fail to associate any part of their geography with this word. Nor are the "aids to pronunciation" in our guidebook any help in this case, or, for that matter, in any case but the most desperate. Thus *"Gdje je najbliži restoran?"* is the Croatian for "Where is the nearest restaurant?" (Nearest? A question of starvation?). And "Could you recommend me [*sic*] to a good hotel?" is *Možete li mi preporučiti jedan dobar hotel?"* We will remember the Croatian for "restaurant" and "hotel," at least, however we manage the anterior matter.

At Zagreb we drive around the Strossmajer Gardens and the vined and turreted old city, entering the megalithic new city via the "Square of the Victims of Fascism." Hundreds of vanguard musicians, here for the Biennale of Contemporary Music, are billeted in our hotel, and electronic composers, microtonalists, etcetera, are milling about the lobby and bar.

1963

MAY 9–14

Zagreb. I like the "Jugs" but could not live in their East-West, North-South, Latin-Slav, Catholic-Orthodox cruciform culture. And I admire their bravery. They were criminally underrated and criminally neglected by the Allied governments in the war, at one time holding down more German divisions than we were in Italy. And we still patronize and neglect them, in spite of which they are full of good will. But I note one national idiosyncrasy. It is that whereas they can be relied on to follow instructions to the letter, they will not extend the principle of them a step beyond, to unspecifiable eventualities. Thus the ushers at the late-night far-out concerts are very strict in keeping people from entering the hall during the performances, but when a young man jumps to the stage from a nearby loge, like John Wilkes Booth, and begins to strangle an *avant-gardiste* making jejune noises on a clarinet mouthpiece, they do nothing to restrain *him.* (Or are they way ahead of me?)

The Zagreb musicians learn I.S.'s *Movements* in less time than any orchestra has learned it heretofore, and their reading of it, with the excellent local pianist Jurica Murai, is music-making of a high order. After the concert, I.S. remarks, apropos the *Monumentum,* that the harmonic tension is short-changed in transferring the music from voices to instruments. "What is radical to sing sounds merely tame and archaic when played."

MAY 16

Paris. A journalist calls asking I.S. to tape record a get-well message to Cocteau, as Braque and Picasso have already done. But he refuses, and so

219

firmly that parts of the telephone fly off as he recradles the receiver. Then at lunch, with all ears to him, he says that *"Cocteau ne peut pas mourir sans faire réclame."* The remark is partly a reversion to type, for just as I.S. became more Russian in Russia, so in Paris he quickly returns to and fulfills the expectations of a society whose smartest applause is reserved for the most barbed *bons mots.* Yet his feelings about Cocteau *have* changed. Only two weeks ago the news of the heart attack (and the thought of the subtraction and the narrowing circle) deeply upset him. But when he learned that his old friend had begun to recover, certain signs of annoyance began to appear, as though, having already written off an account, it was a nuisance to reopen the books. I.S.'s feelings about Cocteau always have puzzled me, however, and though V. attributes them to the pernicious influence of Diaghilev, surely I.S. must have known Cocteau on independent terms at least at the time of the *Oedipus* collaboration. I have heard only sharp remarks about him, nevertheless, in all my fifteen years with I.S., and the last time the two of them were together, in Paris a year ago, I.S. jibbed at keeping the appointment.[1] At about that time, too, and after repeatedly prompting himself to "put something about Cocteau in one of our books," I.S. produced for that purpose a thousand or so partly libelous words, later blue-penciled and edulcorated under pressure from V. to the two paragraphs in *Dialogues and a Diary*, which he considers high praise.

One of the luncheon guests is a biologist who talks about the possibility of life on other planets, based on noncarbon elements. How I wish I could follow even the half of what he says concerning the chemistry of carbon compounds and the red shift, but I am a scientific illiterate, understanding less of the world around me than a three-year-old Eskimo.

Dinner with Ionesco, Giacometti, Nathalie Sarraute, *et al.* One's first impression of Ionesco as he enters the room is of a Chinese actor—the slightly slant-eyed mask with remnants of hair tucked about the ears and lower cranium by a skillful make-up artist. Behind the mask is a permanently worried face, with a deep frown and sulky eyes. No smile escapes it all evening, but after watching it pan through a few jokes, one wonders whether in fact the zygomatic muscles are still capable of pulling out of the pout in such unfamiliar directions. Would he be less cross if his striped serge suit and checkered shirt were less stridently in conflict? I think not, for on second glance one sees that this is the actor's costume, exactly what the well-dressed Béranger would wear, besides which sharp or too noticeable clothes help to mortify shyness and punish self-consciousness, as well as to shield us by advertising how well guarded we are; and that, M. Ionesco certainly does want. *"Ça dépend,"* he says, again and again, fiddling with his fork, molding

---

1. On May 16, 1962, I accompanied him to Cocteau's apartment, to which we were admitted by the housekeeper, Cocteau being in a café. A young man, emerging from a shower and dressing rapidly, went to fetch him, and a few minutes later Cocteau came running up the stairs, gasping and panting in consequence throughout the meeting.

and unmolding bread crumbs and restricting the conversation to inhibited artificialities.

When someone refers to the New York production of *Rhinoceros,* Ionesco condemns it, "except for the freak virtuoso performance of Zero Mostel." He greatly dislikes Broadway, of course, and New York even more. "It is a *chien ville.* Most cities can be classified as either dogs or cats. Naples and Venice are cat cities, London and New York are dogs, and Paris is both." (I think of how Auden, to whom classification games of this kind are old sport, would relish this feline-canine form, and with what *a priori* certainty he would set about assigning the cities of Central Asia; nor would Auden miss the point of Ionesco's preference for a Paris he considers ambiguous.) From New York we switch to the Soviet Union. But it, too, is unloved; or, rather, so virulently hated that he strikes at it blindly, like a boxer stung to the quick. The Russians buy and read more books than any other people, V. says. "You see them reading in buses, on benches, in queues, during intermission at concerts." "Yes," Ionesco agrees, "but such bad literature." V. mews back at this with, "True, it *is* likely to be only Pushkin or Gogol, and no one would claim sophistication such as ours for the Russians. Still, masses of people read poetry there as masses of people in Paris do not." Ionesco: "But such bad poetry. Yevtushenko." This time, remonstrance comes from Mme Sarraute, who has just returned from Moscow and has been talking about her experiences there with I.S. (she speaks perfect Russian); but rather than let the argument get farther out of hand, Ionesco simply shelves the U.S.S.R. as a *"révolution technocratique."*

He is guiltily talkative, though, about his recent house-call on General de Gaulle, which he describes as an act of courage on his part, "for the reason that French intellectuals are one hundred per cent against De Gaulle, and I am what people call a Saint-Germain-des-Prés intellectual." Whether or not he feels that his motives may appear shaky, or that "courage" does not have quite the right ring, he tries to cover his tracks to the General's door by calling it an anti-conformist gesture, which is on the order of Cocteau's attempt to justify his standing for the Academy on the grounds that as the honor is no longer honorable, to receive it constitutes an act of rebellion.

We come away yearning for the raw technocratic materialism of the *chiens villes,* of course, and complaining about Parisian insularity and, at the same time, pretense to the planet's acutest criticism. Michel Butor, who walks back to the Berkeley with us, explains that Ionesco must have felt intimidated because "He is not really like that." (I.S.: "Fewer and fewer people are what they seem.") "He can be five different characters in an afternoon," Butor continues, "and the whole gamut from morbid to gay. His politics are mixed up simply because he has suffered both from failure and success, and is afraid in equal measure of both the *avant-garde* and the reaction." I.S.: "How interesting to be five different people! And, after all, if you have the talent to create a variety of *personnages* for the stage, why not also create them for yourself?"

Bergen. A lunch by H.M. King Olav V in the Royal Lodge at Gamlehaugen. The hotel maids have been squealing *"Kongen, Kongen"* all week long at the sight of the invitation on my dressing table, and since yesterday, when H.M. appeared at my concert—thus obliging me to conduct the Norwegian anthem and "God Save the Kong"—their attention to me has improved to a point where they re-mop my floor every ten minutes. Gamlehaugen village is a thirty-minute drive from Bergen, by forest and fjord, and the Lodge itself, which is Rube Goldberg Toonerville Gothic, complete with widow's walk, is a short distance beyond. The royal colors flying from the roof, the sentinels' boxes at the main gate, and all the rest of the *mise-en-scène*, are out of an operetta.

I am ushered from the door to the main room by a protocol officer who also presents me to the monarch, a pleasant and ruddy (in fact, alcoholically florid) gentleman whose graciousness conceals every hint of the intense boredom he is reputed to suffer at all concerts, hence no less last night at mine. (When, after the Beethoven Violin Concerto, the audience began to applaud in rhythmic unison, His Majesty rose to leave, which meant that the audience had to rise, too, and the applause to freeze in mid-reverberation.) From H.M., I am handed along to admirals and generals with ever-diminishing clusters of medals and braid; and to high clergymen, M.P.'s, millionaire shipbuilders, Miss Sonja Henie.

My place at table is between a bishop and a knight, where I feel like a pawn. Nor is solitary drinking permitted. One must fix one's eyes in those of a partner during the whole draught, as if in a state of hypnotic fascination. The vintages are excellent, and as a guest is naturally inclined to fortify himself on such occasions, and as he may never again succeed in drawing the attention of another free pair of eyes, small wonder that one drains one's glass at each opportunity. The Kong himself drinks the health of each of us individually, starting on his left around the three-pronged table from his position at meridian. One watches for the royal nod as one's turn approaches, then one hoists oneself with one's glass and locks H.M. in the eye-to-eye embrace, this time, however, omitting the *"Sköl."* But none of this is as stiff as I am making it sound, and the excellent *"Lunsj"* (lunch) of *"Sprösteke Kylling"* (spring chicken) is expeditiously served and happily unaccompanied by any testimonials. Still teetering from the toasts, we move to a verandah afterward for cognac and liqueurs. Here are tasseled cushions, frilled armchairs, chintzes, *Jugendstil* tapestries of Norse mythology: blond goddesses, lilies and swans, krakens, *Yggdrasil*.

The conversation of the shipbuilders centers on the Munch Museum to be inaugurated in Oslo next week. "It has now been determined," one of them says, "that sixty-six-and-a-half degrees Fahrenheit—not sixty-six—is

1963

the optimum room temperature for the oil paintings. But I remember Munch's studio when the paintings were strewn all over the floor, and if they were in his way he would walk on them or stack them outside in the snow. Now, too, we pay fifty thousand dollars for the kind of picture he would give to the grocer in settlement of a bill. In fact, those grocers are sitting on their Munchs, so to speak, waiting for us to buy them, as American farmers wait to sell their land to builders of turnpikes."

Back in Bergen with nothing to do (having missed today's installment of the perpetual Grieg concert), I walk by the quay and the gabled houses. A more vigorous promenader than myself is Björnsen—the statue of him, that is, at the head of Ole Bull Street. Its stride is the most powerful, living or graven, I have ever seen.

MAY 29

Oxford. The I.S.'s lunch at Isaiah Berlin's with Professor Gilbert Ryle, a big-boned, major-in-mufti type, with bald, brindled cranium, thrusting jaw, and "intellectual" brow; one feels that without further make-up—he arrives in a parka, tweeds, specs, pipe ("Damn the dottle, let's get our teeth into the problem")—he could take to the stage playing the part of a private eye (Bulldog Drummond). About two minutes of conversation make clear that the Professor is a purely British phenomenon, deeply suspicious of "continental intellectuals" or, indeed, of anyone from "abroad." If he were to make an exception, moreover, it would undoubtedly favor a lean, outdoor-type Australian pragmatist, say, over some pasty-faced Middle European logical positivist, even if the ideas of the latter on how to "do" philosophy were closer to those of the Professor.

"Why are your chaps always bringing up Dewey and James?" he asks. "The world would have been so much better off without those Great American Bores." No answer is expected, of course, the impossibility of expostulation having already been conceded. Besides, more seriously offending countries have yet to be dealt with. (When they have been, one sees to what extent philosophy is a national and school bias. "Steeped in port and prejudice among the monks of Oxford," Gibbon wrote, escaping the fate.) Noncompetitive philosophers such as those of the U.S.S.R. rate only indulgent amusement, and, for laughs, a Soviet philosophical journal is quoted on the Professor himself; it has called him both a "bashful materialist" and a "creeping empiricist." The stronger medicine is reserved for closer trans-Channel targets. "One of my greatest satisfactions as an editor was in publishing a review of the works of one Teilhard de Chardin, rumored at that time to be a biologist. What a lot of lemon juice we poured on *that* old teleological pancake." Nor does Merleau-Ponty fare any better: "French *clarté,* indeed! And, by the way, have you noticed how many French intellectuals have become retroactive heroes of the *maquis?*" Mention of a contemporary Viennese philosopher provokes the remark that "The first person pronoun, found twice in Aristotle, occurs seventeen times in one of

Herr P.'s shorter footnotes; he can hardly bear to use any other word." Two Israeli philosophers are dismissed with the comment that "Neither is actually very good at listening," and an overenterprising British colleague is swept aside as a "literary civil servant. One wonders about these people who try to take the pulse of every new movement. I mean, where do they get all the fingers?"

But the acid tickles more than it burns. On the subject of "philosophers' jamborees," he notes that "The *real* philosophers are the translators. Picture two thousand of us in an auditorium in Brussels with Professor Gorgonzola on the rostrum being translated line for line: 'The ontological postulate of the, and . . . oh, pardon me, Professor, but I didn't get the last phrase.' Well, *I* got it. Rubbish, of course." And he goes on to tell us of an invitation to a similar picnic "somewhere in the Great American West. They wanted me to 'express my views on philosophy,' as they put it, in a five-minute television interview, to which I replied that I doubted if I could make anything clear to anyone out there in less than five years."

Talking about the problem of trying to keep up with new publications, I.S. cites the case of a friend who has learned to read while he walks. "But he looks like the absent-minded professor or the last eccentric." The notion of crossing the quad with a book to one's nose greatly delights Professor Ryle—"Oh, jolly good, very impressive indeed, splendid, splendid"—but he does not agree that eccentrics are disappearing, "at least not when I look around at my colleagues in the common room." An aroma, unmistakably of that location, is twice uncorked, first when he replies to one of our queries with "That's a further question which I will answer when you've answered mine," and again when he illustrates a limitation of the word "correct," in the sense of behavior, with the example of Lord So-and-So, "who when told that his wife had been killed, responded with 'What a pity.' This, you see, is perfectly 'correct,' but you would agree that something is missing." Once or twice I wonder whether the best of his *aperçus* ("Every generation or so philosophical progress is set back by the appearance of a 'genius'") do not roll off somewhat too readily, so that confidence in their hundred per cent spontaneity is undermined, and one could begin to suspect that a repertory is being worked off, in the manner of Tchichikov or Mr. Jingle.

A bowl of cherries is handed around after lunch. (The Professor's appetite is commensurate with his frame, and when the main course is finally cleared, he resists three attempts by the waiter to remove his bread plate.) "I have a cherry tree of my own," he says—to my surprise, as I had pictured him in landless bachelor's digs—"but have not yet tasted its fruit because the birds get there first." V. recommends a certain kind of protective net now available, but the Professor's answer is that "The tree is thirty feet tall and I'm not," which is empirically verifiable, to be sure, as well as, one fears, an example of more than a little philosophical activity.

The meeting's only real mishap, however, occurs when somehow the word "music" slips out. The Professor glums thereat, and is soon beating a retreat back to, as he says on the way out, "academe." (But when did he leave it? Can he possibly have regarded the visit as an excursion into "real life" as he defines that concept in his new lecture, *A Rational Animal*?) When he has gone, I.S. compares him to "a very brilliant schoolboy who, without meaning to, has made us feel like very dull schoolboys." But the truth is that whereas the Professor has enlightened and exhilarated us, we have failed, for our part, even to provide him with good cutting matter for his wit.

Back in London we divide the evening between a new *Figaro* at Covent Garden and a fiftieth-anniversary *Sacre du printemps* at the Albert Hall. The *Figaro* is a gala performance in the presence of the Queen Mother, whose loge we face during the national anthem. But the glittering and bedizened audience is in striking contrast to the set for Act I, which might be a suite in the Dorchester Hotel and doubtless is applauded for that reason. As for the performance, it is souped up, over-molded, too pushed and high-powered, with a scale of dynamics more appropriate to Varèse. "Mozart is poorer than that," I.S. says.

We arrive at the Albert Hall during the *Danse de la terre* and find half of the orchestra following Maître Monteux's actual beat, and the other half following what they, and no doubt *le maître,* too, know the beat should be. He comes to I.S.'s loge after the *Danse sacrale,* and the two tiny gentlemen pose together as if for an advertisement on the longevity value of modern music: "Why we didn't retire at sixty." "Monteux is shrinking," I.S. observes to me afterward. "He seems only half as heavy as when I saw him last," which was at another *Sacre* blowout in Paris eleven years ago. And the question of the old maestro's physical reduction seems to disturb I.S. all evening, in spite of V.'s reassuring *"multum in parvo."* I.S. seems not to have been in the least touched by the occasion, however, and he is loudly critical of the performance. Only late at night, re-entering the Savoy, does he simmer down about the wrong *tempi* long enough to call *le maître "un très brave homme."*

1963

MAY 31

We drive to Canterbury, then to Saltwood Castle for lunch with Sir Kenneth and Lady Clark. The Kentish woods are carpeted with bluebells, and pink hydrangeas are blooming in country gardens. The fields of hops near Canterbury are honey-colored like the newly scrubbed sandstone of the cathedral itself.

To go from the cathedral to Saltwood is to go from the scene of Becket's murder to the scene of the hatching of the plot, or at any rate the pledging to it, for it was at Saltwood that the villainous conspiring knights met, afterwards extinguishing their candles to avoid each other's eyes—according to Tennyson, who was imbuing the murderers with a degree of conscience they hardly seem likely to have had. As for more recent Saltwoodiana, it is said that one prospective caller rapped at the portcullis but was turned away with the explanation that "Lady Clark is busy weeding the battlements." According to another anecdote, the chatelaine once reproved a serving wench for "fingering the tulips before the Kents come to dinner." But the best of this Firbank anthology is a story about some distinguished ladies at a court ball who complain to each other of the nuisance of having to send to the bank once or twice a year to fetch their tiaras, at which point Lady C. enters remarking that *her* tiara has become terribly worn. But to visit Saltwood is to see that the battlements *would* need weeding.

Except for a television aerial on a parapet and a flivver parked by the moat, doubtless belonging to scullions or varlets, the picture of the castle could be titled "Saltwood as Becket knew it." When we arrive, Sir K. himself is seated under a chestnut tree, but with pencil and pad in hand rather than halberd and shield. He shows us through the castle, which, beginning in the entranceway with a collection of narwhals' horns rivaling that of the Musée Cluny, is one of the great private museums of the world. Every room and corridor displays masterpieces in impeccable taste and of perfect pedigree, and even in the "loo," the wallpaper pattern is by William Morris (who may also have been responsible for the plumbing: "Only the Queen Mother knows how to use our WC," Lady C. says, innocently adding a new anecdote to Saltwood lore).

From those weedy battlements, Sir K. can survey his demesne over the milky haze of the downs to the sea. It is the sea of Turner's "Storm at Folkestone," which hangs in Sir K.'s library, and about which he talks with great eloquence, though I can render no more than the gist of it: "Turner was always living in houses along the River Thames, you see, and getting up at dawn to study morning light on water. Now look at that light. And at this circular movement. He thought in circles, you see; I doubt that his hand could have moved at all if it had had to do classical symmetries. In fact, I would call him the arch anti-classicist."

At table, Sir K. talks about twentieth-century Russian painting, putting forward the notion that "instead of trying to suppress modern painting, the Russians might reasonably have claimed to be its discoverers, what with Malevitch, Gabo, Archipenko, Soutine, Chagall, El Lissitsky, Tatlin, Kandinsky, De Staël, Poliakov, Berman, Tchelichev, Goncharova, and Larionov. The difficulty is simply that all of these artists soon became refugees. But Kandinsky's case is the most curious because he was potentially if not in fact a *great* painter up to the time when he went back home and became a commissar. (I'm sure he liked that, for a time anyway.) After his political experience, reality went underground, and he painted only squares, circles, abstractions, all very dead. There, perhaps, is a clue to 'modern art.'"

The lunch being rather heady, I recall only one other remark: "Real gourmets always take red wine with salmon." And in rapid succession I feel that I am, (a) an unreal gourmet, (b) no gourmet at all, (c) anti-gourmet.

Back in London we dine at the Garrick Club with Henry Moore, an open and immediately likable man with clarion opinions and an appealing debonair giggle. At one point the talk drifts toward the quagmires of "taste." "Taste is for pederasts," I.S. says, "and for most other people it is simply a matter of familiarity. Other people's toes are ugly, but not our own because we grew up with them and got to know them well in the piggly-wiggly stage." Here Moore supervenes with, "But there is something much bigger than taste, and that is the sense of a terrible importance." "Which sculptors have this sense?" I ask him, and he replies with certainty and no hesitation to each of the names I propose: "Rodin was a great sculptor, Brancusi was only and totally a sculptor, Matisse was a sculptor, Picasso is a sculptor, Wortruba is a sculptor, Giacometti is a great *artist,* Marini is a bit of a sculptor, Manzù is a real sculptor, but a bad one." A few minutes later, as he is telling us about a Cycladic vase he has just purchased, words suddenly fail him, and he takes a pen and draws the object for us with a few swift strokes. "Well, as you can see," he says, "that's not a ceramic at all but a sculpture."

JUNE 1

1963

We call on David Jones in his bed/sitting-room on the second floor of a lodging house in Harrow-on-the-Hill. But it is more cocoon than room, and even as silkworms go, the tenant is delicate and withdrawn. His face is boyish, owing in part to bangs and a glabrous skin, but he has a boyish grin, too, which vanishes suddenly, leaving one aware of how deeply troubled his expression was before. His extreme shyness and lack of animal confidence retreat somewhat with each link in a chain of cigarettes, yet never to the extent that our presence is less than a terrible burden on him (the cocoon is so close), and of course our feelings of intrusion are all the stronger in that his solitary confinement is obviously self-willed.

Paintings, drawings, manuscripts, books are scattered everywhere, and he complains of having to unpile his bed every night and to pile it up again in the morning. It is strewn with sheets of foolscap now, the calligraphic hand on each page of which trails off to the lower right as if the writer were unable to follow the shape of the paper or confine his thoughts to it.

As the first picture he shows is of a lion he drew at the age of six, one wonders if he has ever willingly parted with any of his work. Whatever the answer, the most potent pictorial image in the room is a colored drawing of a woman's head, faintly reminiscent of a Henry Moore. The more recent "Tristram and Yseult Aboard Ship" is Pre-Raphaelite, and more than faintly. ("I know only a little about ships," he says, "enough for a little ship, perhaps, but you must know a lot to do a big ship.") The latest picture, a labyrinthine but still unfinished "Annunciation," recalls Blake. I.S. likes this "Annunciation," and he very gently remarks that it seems complete to him now, but might, with more elaboration, become too complex. Mr. Jones acknowledges the danger, but says he wants to add a bit more color, "If, at the same time, I can keep it a drawing. Of course," he subjoins in a much more cheerful voice, "I don't much like anything I do."

At one point he seems deeply distressed trying to remember the word "wire," the which broke on one of his pictures. At another, when he counts on his fingers, eyes closed, in an effort to recall whether he is a Capricorn or a Scorpio, it is as if he had long been removed from any quotidian count of time. The mood changes again when he exhibits one of his plaques of Latin lettering *à la* Eric Gill, telling us that he "posted it to a convent in Wales, from which, after a great delay, it was returned with the explanation 'No one has any use for Welsh in Wales any more.' Evidently even fewer people have any use for Latin," he adds, and a seraphic smile forms, but this time fades very slowly.

We turn about the room, examining long undusted books, a majolica angel, a cross of palm. Why? And why have we come? Out of admiration for a writer of genius, perhaps the greatest living in English prose, as I think, and if it *is* prose. But I have a reason of my own, quite apart from the I.S.'s, and which might be called a quest for inspiration: for David Jones has attained a life of purity, while my life is one of pastiche.

Mr. Jones has made a beachhead on one of his thickly littered tables and landed a spirit ring there, a small mound of sugar, a punctured can of milk, and a meager assortment of other comestibles. It is teatime, and a kettle hangs from an andiron, but we trump up a pressing reason to depart. As we go, Mr. Jones tells us that he has been ordered to pay back-taxes on some long-since-spent award money from an American foundation, and that he does not know what to do. And he is obviously penniless, and terrified of the consequences.

On the return to London, we find ourselves haunted but also lifted by his aloneness. At what point does the self-consciousness of the solitary man—"Sisyphus was a bachelor," Kafka says—and the pedantry, the paranoia, and the overdeveloped sensibilities that are his commonest forms of hypochondria—at what point do they begin to shut him off from the outside? When did David Jones begin to believe in his illness, in other words, and is it agoraphobia, that typological disease of the inward-turning, or is he a *malade imaginaire?* Real or imaginary, is the malady traceable to the war, to experience shared with men that could never afterward be recalled with women, let alone shared with them, therefore resulting in a withdrawal from their society? That great dramatic monologue, *In Parenthesis,* is no withdrawal, in any case, but an affirmation of the world. The *Anathemata,* on the other hand, *is* a retreat, behind language, symbols, obscure reference, and the windowpanes of his room; and it is, to me, a breakdown in communication just as *Finnegans Wake* was after *Ulysses.* To me, I repeat; for the breakdown in communication may well be on one end only and the *Anathemata*'s only fault, and the onus of this Philistine judgment, my own ignorance.

JUNE 2-9

Ath Cleath. The "center of paralysis," Joyce called it, and more indulgently— for it is dirtier than Chicago—"dear dirty Dublin." Many sunburned and freckled priests are in the crowd at the airport, as is a flock of Sisters of St. Vincent de Paul in swanlike *chapeaux à corne.* How musical their voices are, in contrast to the flat, pinched, and but slightly varied vowel sounds of the London bloke! Nor is there any reluctance to speak. "Now would that be Mr. Eyegore Strawinsky?" a bystander asks me, half singing the question. The Hibernian lilt is less noticeable in our driver, but he quotes Yeats in describing parts of the Ould Sod which he thinks we should visit, an itinerary that does not include North Ireland for the reason that "it is still occupied."

The Joyceana in the Sandycove martello, now "James Joyce Tower," is a thousand times more modest than that of many an American university, but at least *Ulysses* is on sale here, as it is nowhere else in Dublin. We climb to the small bleak room on a spiral fire escape in an appropriately spinning wind—shivering in our topcoats, too, though the beaches beneath the tower are dotted with purple-blue bathers.

Residential Dublin, rich and poor neighborhoods alike, consists of rows of identical brick houses, each with clusters of chimneys like sows' teats. The rich homes of Merrion Square—Yeats's, Sheridan Le Fanu's, Wilde's among them—have rounded-arch portals, white pilasters, brass knobs and knockers. A plaque on the poor, Synge Street birthplace of G. B. Shaw describes him as an "author of many plays," but the slightly richer brick childhood home of James Joyce, in the still poorer purlieu of Rathmines, is unmarked. On our way there, V. wonders aloud whether any other modern city of the size can have spawned so many major writers, and at once the driver advises her that "To be a writer here, lady, all you have to do is to keep your ears open." And as if to prove his point he is soon giving us a vivid story, in steep b'jayses brogue, of how Brendan Behan, having tucked away too many noggins, started a brawl with some famous bowsies and ended up in the pokey. But I.S. wonders why, of all the writers Dublin born and bred, so few have been buttered here. (Paronomasia is a contagious disease in Dublin, thanks to the emphasis on the music of the language; puns are homonyms and musical accidents first, after all, the words bumping together by the attraction of their musical similarities, the connecting co-incidence of sense being discovered only after the musical event.) But the driver is unbudgeably convinced that Shaw, Wilde, Beckett, and the others evacuated the homeland for no other reason than to escape the climate.

The illuminated books in Trinity College Library are a fantasy world of birds and beasts both fabulous and real. Yet the Mandala-like mazes of ornament and the script itself are no less marvelous, above all the minuscules in the Book of Armagh, whose syllabic flags (accents? ligature signs?) remind me of Cufic. The books' first attraction, nevertheless, is color, including that of the bindings, many of them madder-stained pigskin with linen cord and iron hasps. Compared with these Celtic manuscripts, the oldest paleographic treasure in the Library, a Ptolemaic stone with texts in hieroglyphs, en-chorials, and Greek, is drab and disappointing.

1963

The National Museum is hardly less rich in spoliation of the monasteries. Here the treasures are jeweled crucifixes, croziers, missal cases, pricket candlesticks, and hundreds of other ecclesiastical utilities and adornments. Still, the collection of Bronze Age gold interests us more. The most common objects are torques, gorgets (for wimples), and posy rings with bezels carved in the shape of clasped hands, or *ouroboros*. Otherwise, lunular and penannular forms predominate, as they do in—hence reminding us of—Nigerian art.

In the late afternoon we drive to "Howth [Hoath] Castle and Environs," where the seaward slopes are golden with gorse, returning through Phoenix Park, Chapelizoid (Chapel-is-id), and Summer Hill, Sean O'Casey's slum, where we attract some Unsmiling Irish Eyes. The tide is out and the swans are stranded in the sulphurous Liffey mud.

A trip to Clonmacnoise via Athlone and, on the return, ivy-covered Clonony Castle and Kildare. The road leaving Dublin is shaded by beeches and elms, and on either side are stone-walled lanes, stone bridges, hems of stone fence enclosing fields and dells. Most roadside cottages are stuck together and repeated, as if by multiple mirrors, yet individuated by their flowers, especially lilacs and whitethorn. In the main street of Mullingar, four men are dancing a reel to the accompaniment of a fiddle and hand-clapping onlookers. South of Athlone we enter peat bogs, shaved of their scutch grass and ready for cutting, which is generally done by machines now, though at one point we overtake a mob who, shouldering the old double-edged sleans, might be a contingent of the rabble on the way to the Revolution of 1789.

At Clonmacnoise, seven ruined churches and a cemetery of old Celtic crosses sleep on a hill by a bend in the Shannon. The smallest churches are simple biliths, or walls slanted together corbelwise, but the one called Ui Ceallaigh (O'Kelly's) has a vaulted roof. Hand querns and other stone implements of the destroyed monastery are scattered on the grass, but the best-preserved of the ruins is a crannog tower with a cap shaped like the nose cone of an ICBM. We wander in the sweet air, thinking Clonmacnoise one of the sacred places of the earth.

JUNE 23

Milan. The custodian of the crypt of St. Ambrose jangles his keys like the sacristan in *Tosca* to remind us of the need for fresh boosts in his economy. Ambrose's skeleton lies in a glass catafalque, flanked, at a slightly lower elevation (as befits subordinates), by the skeletons of Saints Protasius and Gervase. The Ambrosian skull is mitered; those of his two escorts carry gold crowns; but the tightly clamped teeth of all three are stained as if they had been lifelong chewers of betel. The royal purpure, the scapulars, the jeweled slippers, the branches of silver palm are a dramatic contrast to the skeletons they accouter, and the picture seems more an allegory of medieval kings illustrating the temporality of earthly treasures than a triptych of Christian martyrs. A gold phoenix perches like a vane on the top of the catafalque, ready to crow the Resurrection.

In the *mostra* of Iranian art at the Palazzo Reale, Islamic Luristan is richly represented, but the Hittite section is disappointing except for two gold tablets covered with thornlike script, and a pair of gold *mitènes*—fingerless gloves, with a gauze of gold mail on the back of the hand fastened to gold rings at the hilt of each finger; they could be worn, without encumbrance, for piano practice.

We spend the drowsy afternoon at the Certosa di Pavia. Soft, foamy summer clouds. Bronzed fields of wheat. Wild poppies and wild sweet peas. Ilex. The scent of lime trees by Leonardo's canal, of mintlike privet in the Certosa grounds, and of new-mown grass everywhere.

The open door of the church exhales drafts of chilled air like cold breath, but apart from this natural air conditioning, I do not like the interior: an angel has been packed into every archivolt, an ornament squeezed into every squinch. A party of tourists is marauding the quiet, among them a woman whose automatic "What?" after every remark of the guide so resembles the bark of a dog that one would like to offer her a biscuit.

But the only sounds in the cloister are the buzzing of flies and the turning of gravel by a hand shovel, an old-fashioned noise agreeably defining the surrounding peace. The cloister comprises twenty-four duplex cells topped by a fence of twenty-four Gothic chimneys. Each cell is equipped with a revolving dumbwaiter for meal trays (like the MacDowell Colony), a strapontine table and bed, a garden, a well, and a leafy pergola in the community vineyards. In sum, the Certosa was a meditators' co-op ruled by ascetic disciplines that kept its exclusively noblemen inmates in trim condition for *this* life—establishing records for longevity, in fact—whatever it did for them in the next. Why, then, do *I* shudder at it? Symmetrically balanced space such as this, after all, is supposed to generate a sense of euphoria in the laterally symmetrical bodies of chimpanzees and men. Is it because I doubt my power to summon the positive, favorable images necessary for prolonged solitude? Or that even though my life is a chaos of distractions, I do not believe that I can resist them by the method of prayer reading, of the Hindu endlessly reciting his *japa*?

The late-night rehearsal at La Scala of the Hamburg productions of *Oedipus Rex* and *The Flood* is a demonstration of how, in my imagination, the Axis must have worked. The German stagehands take to their tasks like an army on the Blitzkrieg, and a Panzer army to boot, for they are equipped with two-way radios and closed-circuit television. In fact, the smoothest, most impressive performance of the evening occurs when the stage director, Dr. Rennert, exasperated to breaking point by the misfocused lighting, orders the entire *Oedipus* set dismantled and rebuilt to the reach of the beams, a job that the German crew completes in a mere eighteen minutes, but that would have defeated the Italians for a season or two. The Italians, of course, are in charge of the lighting, and, as noted, they do about as well with it as, two decades ago, they did with other matters in North Africa. Throughout the rehearsal a *"maestro direttore"* shouts and begs through his telephone: *"Luigi . . . la luce . . . per piacere, Luigi, pronto, la luce . . . si, la luce, ma adesso, adesso . . . la luce . . . L-U-I-G-I,"* while the impatience of the Germans shows more openly by the minute, until we expect them to seize the apparatus, as once they took over the Italian army and eventually even confiscated Italy itself. And whereas the Italians only pretend, and unconvincingly, to crumble and fawn before their superiors, the Germans reply smartly with *"Jawohl, Herr Doktor"* and actually click their heels. (I.S.: "People must be born *'Herr Doktor'* in Germany; it's practically a hereditary title, like *'Prinz.'*") The standby Italian stagehands squat on the floor, too, huddling together like prisoners of war and wearing the bewildered expressions they were often seen with in wartime newsreels. In fact, the one apparent difference from 1945 is that they are able to desert their German masters and disappear for long *espresso* breaks.

Oedipus Rex is creditably staged, though the goriness of the eye-gouging would be more appropriate to *The Cabinet of Dr. Caligari,* and the cardboard effigies—exposing heads only, like old-fashioned photographers' dummies— give the impression that the chorus is in mud baths. The one musical failure is that the Shepherd is miscast. The singer is both too heavy vocally (a mere Bo-Peep is required) and addicted to bleating, as though, being too long removed from his fellow Thebans (?), he had taken to the language of his flock.

Even greater credit is owing the Hamburg Opera for the first staging of I.S.'s latest problem opus. *The Flood,* in Herr Rennert's view, is a résumé of I.S.'s theatrical forms. Thus the arias of Lucifer-Satan represent the element of pure opera, *The Building of the Ark* the element of pure ballet. The narrator, moreover, is a Stravinskyan device as old as the *Soldat, Oedipus, Perséphone, Babel,* and as new as *A Sermon, A Narrative and A Prayer;* the precedent for pantomime goes as far back as *Renard.*

And Herr Rennert has some capital ideas. One of them is broadcasting the voice of God from various parts of the hall like an electronic concert, and at the same time lowering His words from Heaven on plaques like the Tables of the Law. The difficulty with this is that in so large a theater as La Scala the electronic God is too portentous for the modest frame of the music. Tonight, furthermore, the plaques either do not appear in time or else disappear too quickly, before any of us has read them through, for no other apparent reason than to prove that the hand is quicker than the eye. Add to this the lateness of the lighting ("Luigi . . . *L-U-I-G-I* . . . ") during the bass drum[1] introductions to God's speeches, and the spectator's frustration is understandable.

It is a good idea, dramatically, too, to keep Lucifer-Satan on hand

1963

---

1. The drummer should use a wooden stick, depress the center of the head with the flat of his left hand, and strike close to the taut edge of the vellum.

throughout, as Rennert does even during the flood itself. But the Lucifer must move, dance as he sings, as the music tells him to, and not simply plant himself to the side of the stage. Still, the failure of the scene is owing only partly to this diabolical paralysis. Another factor is the lack of any transformation in Satan after the Fall. (He switches masks, it is true, but the new one bears an unfortunate resemblance to Papa Katzenjammer, and the comic touch at this point is disastrous.) Furthermore, the *Melodrama* is an inset; it must be separated from the action before and after, at least by lighting, and Satan must do something to indicate the change of scene, even if only to step into a telephone booth to say "Eve."

The parting curtains reveal a solitary bench, stage right, and behind it a cloakroom rack on which are hung the masks of Satan and the Noah family. The actors, shawls partly covering their street clothes, enter stage left, followed by the chorus, uncostumed but carrying football-type helmets at their sides; they do not look in the least athletic, however, but like factory hands when work lets out after an exceptionally fatiguing day. They halt unmilitarily at stage center and don the helmets, at which point the music begins. Then, the *Te Deum* over, they fan out to stage aprons on either side of the orchestra pit, watching from there as part of the audience. The final *Te Deum* is sung there, too, after which they "exeunt severally" in the worst sense. But while these arrangements do at least solve the problem of disposing of the chorus, the interruption of the music for time to ferry the singers across the proscenium and into the bleachers is fatal.

Another, no less mortal, disadvantage in this tonight-we-improvise beginning is that it contradicts the music. The *Prelude* must be free of visual associations, hence played before a closed curtain and in darkness. It is essential, too, that the curtain open in synchronicity with the twelve-note harp ladder—which, incidentally, requires an expressive *ritenuto*. In fact, all four twelve-note ladders were intended to accompany curtains, either of material or of light. The bassoon version of the ladder, the dissolve from Eden, should be synchronized with a *crescendo* of light from deep darkness to the equivalent, in wattage, of a *mezzo-piano;* for the stage remains murky and shadowed afterward in correspondence with the new, minatory note in God's music, that masterstroke which adds a dark cloud of *ponticello* violins and violas to God's voice and doubles the two lines of the voice itself (the Eastern and Western Churches?) equiponderously with piano and harp.[1] The third musical ladder should follow a small ray or spot of red light from a total blackout to the Devil,[2] while the fourth is coordinated

1. The change of color and the restoration of the octave in God's music *after* the flood are no less simple and subtle inspirations, and the accretion of a few flute, harp, and celesta notes during Noah's speech "The earth is overflowed with Flood" instantly and magically transform the atmosphere.
2. One reviewer shrewdly described the work as anti-clerical, the music associated with the idea of sin, the sin business, being decidedly nasty in contrast to the innocent *paterfamilias* music of Noah.

with the slow final curtain, whose cue is the chord of cellos and basses. But in the Hamburg production no visual connection is established with any of these musical staircases, nor is it in any way apparent that they are the frame of the work.

If the *Te Deum* is to be sung as a concert piece, ignoring the enlarging movement (composed with television in mind) *in* the music, then it would be better to hear and not see the angels—Local 27 angels, at any rate. But I should also note that the Hamburg staging stops the music a few measures before the return of the *Te Deum* to allow more time for the narration, and that this pause is another fatal one. The fault here is partly I.S.'s, however. The music *is* perilously short—and as a bridge it seems to me too pat, in the same way that the reprise of the opening of *Agon* is too pat. I remember I.S. with stopwatch in hand, one morning, asking me to read the narration "in a brisk *tempo*," after which he said he was pleased since he would have "only ten more seconds of music to compose." But is the whole of *The Flood* too short? Not for the cinematography I.S. had in mind, though he cut both the text and the ballets to less than half of what the original television producer had calculated as acceptable minimum timings. A short piece is not made longer by adding pauses, in any case, and some of the impression of scrappiness in the Hamburg interpretation could be overcome simply by not stopping so long between each bit and piece and the next.

The Hamburg Narrator is wrong, too, as narrators generally are. (It seems to me that dramatic authors must regard their narrators as "natural" children, *i.e.,* reminders of weakness.) He is, after all, and in principle, *only* a voice, yet for want of cinematography, this all-too-embodied voice all too often receives the full burden of visual attention, as in the case of the entire *Genesis* speech. More imaginative use is made of him in the *Catalogue of the Animals,* where he becomes an on-the-spot television news reporter swiveling, microphone in hand, from Ark to audience and reeling off the names of the arriving couples as if they were movie stars at a Broadway opening.

Still, the *Comedy* is the Hamburg production's most serious failure—or uncomic failure. The music is disastrously cut, in the first place, and in the second, though it demands action—running, slapstick—no one moves. Lastly, a half-minute of silence has been inserted to get the Noahs aboard, though, once there, they stand frozen, looking as tragic in their deadpan masks as anybody in *Oedipus Rex.*

The ballets are more successful in conception than in execution. Both are costume pieces, the carpenters who build the Ark (hammer-and-nail sex symbolism) wearing space-cadet jumpsuits, and the girls who dance the flood (reversing Balanchine's identification of the beleaguered and beleaguering sexes) dressing like waterdrops (female sex symbolism). The ship itself, I should add, comes out as an all-purpose galleon suspiciously resembling the titular vessel in last week's *Flying Dutchman.* At the first bolt of lightning, a solo waterdrop splashes in from the wings, followed in a trice by a cloudburst of her colleagues who then enchafe the Ark. The picture here, of the eighty or so animals—supernumeraries in street clothes but with *papier-mâché* animal heads, horns, tusks, trunks, bills, manes—crowded together like refugees and riding out the storm, is so moving that it nearly rescues the whole performance.

AUGUST 30

Rio de Janeiro. The afternoon sun turns the fog to mica but does not lift it until twilight. Then, in an eerily apocalyptic moment, the Corcovado Christ looms through the dispelling vapors like the airborne Christ statue in *La Dolce Vita.*

I have increased my Portuguese by ten words today, thus jumping the total to eleven. But progress, even on this scale, is a questionable asset. For one thing, our driver takes too much heart from it. Supposing us to have been shamming until now, he fires away with such speed that I am at a loss to interject even a punctuational *"Sim?"* (Yes) or *"Espere um instante"* (Wait a minute); and as nothing else in my vocabulary will turn him off, I switch in desperation to an equally unresourceful Spanish (*"Caramba"*). Then, searching for a store in which to buy whiskey for I.S., I discover that sign language can reduce even the most garrulous of direction-givers to the same means. When at length the whiskey store is found—after several tryingly Trappist scenes—I rehearse my pronunciation of *"Não"*—a less nasally feline noise than the one Brazilians make—until the clerk holds up a bottle of one of I.S.'s brands (*"Sim"*).

In the evening all Rio seems to be holding hands, and more than hands when the darkness deepens and the beach is strewn with twining couples. V., surveying this sabulous Agapemone, cites the influences of topography—the sugar-loaf phalloi—and the sensual sound and scent, the loneliness and timelessness, the continual caressing of the sea. But I.S. thinks that the human topography, the ballooning bosoms and thrusting *labia majora* of the Copacabana professionals is the more actively conducive landscape.

At night, too, the city's huge mendicant population takes to outdoor cubbyholes and crevasses while the most destitute simply coil up on the open ground, protected only by newspapers or rags. When we park for a moment on a hill above the bay, a bundle shifts position in the gutter—an old woman, as we discover when the poor crone raises her blanket of sacking as if to ask us why we have disturbed her sleep. But she disturbs mine, too, returning again and again in a procession of people remembered: the Negro laborers with bare backs, bare feet, and fanciful folded-newspaper hats; the Negro belles in percale and dimity dresses and with orange-rust hair; the girls in a street-side lace factory manipulating their bobbins with, for Rio, unwonted dexterity and speed; the cariocas in stand-up street bars drinking round after round of coffee (do they ever work?); the near-naked waifs stealing precarious rides on the wide runningboards of the *bondes* (open trolleys).

All Rio is rebuilding, which means that the regional and characteristic are being replaced by the international and indifferent. It seems, too, that the few doomed remnants of colonial styles still extant are always found side by threatening side with the newest opus Niemeyer. This is the case with little laundry-blueing Santa Luzia, now hedged around by skyscrapers; and the case, too, with a score of old frame houses nearby, all with tall shutters, wrought-iron railings, walls of pellagrous paint. It is a popular local irony that the most graceful of the surviving old structures, the Casa de Saudi, was until recently an asylum for lunatics.

But colonial church architecture is disappointing. The façades are elegantly simple, but most of the interiors are tropical tangles. São Bento is a case in point. Its walls crawl with *rocaille* and creep with vegetal ornaments, so that only after long peering do we discover human figures in the lush carvings, like hidden faces in Henri Rousseau jungles. The exceptional church, with an interior no more complex than the exterior promises, is the white, octagonal Outeiro da Gloria, which sits like a coronet on one of the older city's highest hills.

1963

The Zoological Gardens are a *jardin des plantes*, as well, if only incidentally, the walks being shaded by banyans and colored by hibiscus and bougainvillea. The sight of animals from northern habitats suffering from the heat disturbs V., however, and she tries to comfort one old bruin with compatriotic feeling—"*Ve govorite po Russki?*"—though at the same time, and perhaps for the same reason, she refuses to speak German to a seal that looks like Bismarck and wears an even unhappier expression than the bear. I.S., observing the anthropoids, wonders what it would be like "to go about on all fours with one's behind in the air, and a plaque on one's cage containing a Latin binomial and a paragraph of false and irrelevant information, like program notes at a concert. Except that nowadays the animals are no doubt sexually attached to the keepers." Near the exit some flamingoes stand immobile in a pool covered with pea-green scum, like fixtures on a Miami lawn.

We have been told to come at two o'clock for today's rehearsal of our concert of sacred music in the Igreja de Candelaria. But the doors are still locked at two-thirty, and the musicians do not begin to appear until three, at which hour it is discovered that the orchestra librarian has neglected to bring the parts. Half of the players never turn up at all, moreover, while those who *do* eventually present themselves allow us a mere thirty minutes' working time, the union foreman having decreed that no matter how late in starting, the rehearsal must end punctually. Our complaints are heard out with amiable shrugs, but thrown out of court (the foreman's) with the argument "This is not a factory"—as if anyone who had spent as much as a day in Rio could believe in the rule of stop watches, even in factories. The rehearsal pleases, nevertheless, such as it is, if only with respect to the Latin diction of the chorus. The Brazilian pronunciation, a squall of sibilants, softens every edge (*"genite,"* for example, becomes *"zhenite"*), and smooths all "k" and "ch" sounds with gently hissing cedillas (as in *pacem*).

On the return to the hotel we stop at a *favela,* a hillside Casbah smelling of carrion, cooking-in-oil, *merde.* It is a political entity, said to be virtually outside the jurisdiction of the Rio police, the physical density of the place, no less than its secret customs and codes—which reputedly include kangaroo courts—being well-nigh impenetrable. Not far along, our path is barricaded by a sow and her farrow, but we have no wish to continue. Later, discussing the experience with Brazilian acquaintances, I am surprised not so much by the absence in them of a moralizing tone—such as affluent North Americans use in berating *their* slum dwellers for laziness and lack of aspiration—as by their poorly disguised disapproval of V.'s readiness with a *cruzeiro* for every beggar and by their lack of sympathy with her remark, "The only moral question we can ask is why we should deserve to have anything to give." At the same time, neither V. nor I.S. would ever think of questioning the political and social conditions responsible for the *favela.* And they are able to regard its Cubistic superimpositions of basketwork huts as "beautiful," whereas I am incapable of beholding such sights scenically, or in fact of seeing the "view" in any picture that also exposes misery, though this is to admit that my idea of social structure and social morality is materialist first of all and doubtless much less profound than theirs.

We dine with Jocy de Oliveira at the C. restaurant, which affects the Regency style of Dom João: tall mirrors and high ceilings, gaitered and liveried waiters. The first and last courses—the *cachaça* (cane-sugar alcohol) cocktails and the coconut entremets—are the best of the dinner, and the best of the conversation is about Euclides da Cunha, though I.S.'s talk on another subject is so typical that it is what I will record. He explains to the *maître d'hôtel* taking our salad orders that a "paregoric dressing" would be the only safe kind for him, then goes on to give the full intestinal news of the day. But when I first knew him his matutinal salutations used almost invariably to include an inquiry about my "regularity," as well as a description of his morning fears, even if allayed hours before. And it is characteristic of I.S. that where bowels are concerned, total strangers are chosen for the frankest confidences, and if attentive enough on such favorite topics as diverticulitis, pyloric spasms, enema dreams, and log-jam nightmares—as tonight's *maître d'hôtel* pretends to be, though his understanding of French is obviously limited to the menu—they are generally found to be, like this waiter, *"muito simpatico."* Dining rooms are I.S.'s preferred setting, too, and

237

the mere mention of prunes, *crudité,* or "roughage" during a meal can lead to some extremely unappetizing digressions. I have often wondered whether this *Tisch-Gespräche* owes anything to I.S.'s German nurse, Bertha, but in any case it shows the identification of "pre-napkin" and "pre-lapsarian" in his mind, and indicates a traumatic toilet training.

SEPTEMBER 2

Not surprisingly, our concert at the Teatro Municipal begins an hour late, a time spent in a sweltering greenroom under a portrait of Gomes, the composer of *Il Guarany.* The audience is loudly, even vocally, appreciative, and the performances are good, my own failure of nerve when sharing concerts with I.S. not having "frozen me up." I.S. is besieged by admirers backstage afterward, Governor Carlos Lacerda among them, Sir John Barbirolli, and Heitor Villa-Lobos's widow, who bestows an *abraço* and reminds I.S. of her husband's visit to him in Hollywood many years ago.

At a reception following the concert, an American doctor, here for an International Congress on Tropical Medicine, fills me with sleep-destroying information about the local forms of filariasis, the "snail vectors" of which are a principal topic on the Congress's agenda. He believes that Darwin suffered from a form of this disease.

1963

SEPTEMBER 3

A drive to Tijuca to visit the niece of Machado de Assis. Her home is near the base of a steep mountain, climbed almost continually by a file of black women with head loads, and called "the *favela* of the ants," though we never learn whether the name is metaphorical (for the labors of these female safaris) or a description of actual entomological activity. No sooner have we made the acquaintance of Machado's niece than her husband hustles us off to see an Order of Merit awarded him by President Roosevelt in 1944 and a photograph of himself in San Francisco among the Brazilian signatories to the Charter of the United Nations.

The descendants of, as they pronounce it, "Machadasi" are not conspicuously conversant with the writings of the founder of their fame, and they seem a little nervous that his spreading reputation may oblige them to read him. One of Machado's books has lately been published in Moscow, they tell us, in a tone that seems a blend of pride and alarm.

Machado's injunction to burn his manuscripts having been less ambiguous than Kafka's, the store of his literary leftovers is small. But a batch of family letters survives. Showing us one of these, in a neat, clerk's hand, from the novelist to his fiancée, the niece blurts out that her uncle was "not white" (a concern for our reaction?) and that his fiancée's family opposed the marriage *"parce qu'il avait de couleur."* A few photographs have been preserved, too, but only one is worth the mention, a too-sweet portrait of a young but motherly woman. This picture had held Machado in a state of trance, his niece says—onanistic trance, *I* would say, to judge by the poem he addressed to it, with its fixation on the woman's gloves, and by comparing the sentiments of these verses with the sentiments in his classic of disguised onanism, *A Woman's Arms.*

When these relics are removed, whiskey, tobacco, and salvers of sandwiches are passed around. The niece's daughter takes a cigarette, which I light for her, only to find her staring at my matchbook, from a Hollywood restaurant, as covetously as a Conquistador eyeing a gold ornament on a savage. She is a phillumenist, it develops, and her collection of these folders exceeds three thousand. We promise to send additions.

SEPTEMBER 6

Shortly before midnight we drive to a secret rendezvous in the hills where a *macumba* ceremony is to take place. The trail to this eyrie is marked at each turn in the road by candles, and at major intersections by piles of poultry eviscerations as well. The actual entrance, at the foot of a hill mounted by some sixty steep stairs, is designated by a whole galaxy of candles and a portable shrine. At the top, two women, white-robed like Sisters of Father Divine, lead us to a grotto of holy images, black-faced Josephs and Marys, St. Sebastians and St. Georges. Leaving the grotto and taking us to the *heiru* (hairoo), a rolled-dirt compound slightly larger than a tennis court, our guides stop every few steps to chalk crosses on the ground in front of us. In the *heiru,* we are installed on a bench near the center sidelines where, however, the extremely rich insect life—its stridulations are like a Cuban percussion orchestra—loses no time in finding our bearings. V. is afraid of caterpillars, she says, but I.S., hearing a snort from something unseen in the woods, only hopes that "nothing bigger than bugs decides to fraternize."

One end of the *heiru* is formed by a candle-decked altar with a painted backcloth of moon and stars. At the other end is the circle of the dead, a cairnlike pile of stones enclosing a wooden cross marcelled with white ribbons; everyone gives this the widest berth. About three or four hundred people stand beyond the fenced sides of the *heiru,* men and women segregated like the score or so of white-robed celebrants gathered within; presently V., too, is led to the women's side. Meanwhile, a man in a white suit stenciled with insignia on the sleeves comes to warn us not to cross our arms or legs lest the spell (*candomblé?*) be broken (and ourselves disclosed as enemy warlocks?). This is said in utmost earnest. But when I.S. asks whether the women in white organdy dresses and silver neck crosses, in center court, are "the vestal virgins," he breaks into profligate laughter, assuring us, when his breath is caught, that *"Ça n'existe pas ici."* And, in truth, these necklaced women *are* matronly in their proportions, or at any rate far from wraithlike, which for some reason reduces my (never bounte-

1963

ous) faith in them as spiritual agents. (Are they in fact the exact opposite of I.S.'s suspicions, namely, instruments of what anthropologists call sexual hospitality?) Among the spectators almost all of the men and most of the women are smoking cigars, and everyone except ourselves is "black."

Tonight's ritual is that of *ubanda,* or white magic. How this has been determined—phases of the moon? haruspication of those roadside entrails?—we never learn, but it is for this reason that the celebrants are continually touching the ground: the gesture signifies the burial of black magic. Tonight's principal celebrant, greeted by a stingy drum roll as he proceeds to the center of the *heiru,* is a bearded, turbaned, darker-in-hue Billy Graham; which is to say that the manner of his delivery is partly evangelical, partly heart-to-heart sex talk; and though I cannot follow the matter of it, the gist, judging by the repeated words, seems to favor the "spiritual" over the "material." It fills an hour, in any case, and survives as many false endings as Beethoven's Fifth, yet because of the audience, especially the animal audience, we are never bored. Flocks of doves that had been fluttering about the *heiru* before the sermon now settle in the surrounding sapodillas—like baseball fans in the bleachers, except that they listen with Sunday attention and quiet. When, at about the halfway point, one of them flies to and perches on the Billy Graham's head as if bringing him a message, we are prepared to believe in metempsychosis. And we are also inclined to suspect preternatural influence or ESP in the perfect timing of a chanticleer's bugle notes at two major pauses in the prolix speech; in the transfixed expressions and maudlin nuzzling of a pair of heretofore ferocious mastiffs; and, above all, in the behavior of two geese—"One spiritual and one material," as I.S. says. Whereas these geese have claxoned obstreperously before the sermon, during it they lie silent and rapt at the Billy Graham's feet. The moment he finishes, however, making the sign of the cross, they waddle a yard or two from him and consecrate the matrimonial rite, the gander rowing his wings over the goose like a *premier danseur* in a ballet about a boat. The act inevitably appears to have been sponsored by the Billy Graham, who watches conspiratorially, in any case, as a *cri de coeur* heralds the climax and as excited flapping and postcoital cooing confirm it. A D. H. Lawrence parody scene? Yes, but an affecting one, owing to all those mesmerized doves in the trees.

One of the Father Divine girls now replaces the Billy Graham, whose retiring tattoo is as niggling as the fanfare that hailed his entrance. Three men join her, then dress each other in scarlet mantles and nightcaps that resemble the tasseled nuptial hats of Mohammedan brides in the *nichau* ceremony. They plant candles in the ground at the center of the *heiru,* then light cigars, the incense and lustral smoke from which, on every side of the *heiru,* nearly asphyxiates us but is a great tonic to the mosquitoes. At this point everyone kneels to sing a litany, which clots with passion as it grows louder. A chant, "Jesus, Mary," follows

accompanied by clapping, drumming, stepped-up earth-touching, and it lasts until the Father Divine girl rings a plantation-type dinner bell. This is the cue for a hag, heavily strung about with beads, to become possessed, but it also sets the now becalmed geese honking plangently enough to save Rome. The beaded hag emits an eldritch scream, with a wind-up like whooping cough, then throws herself to the ground panting "Ya, ya, ya, ya, ya," and puffing her cigar to a blaze. But it is an unconvincing performance, and when the others in her coven fling themselves to the ground and follow suit in all the rest of the mummery, we depart. These seizures take place against a chant that repeats the word "Negro"—"*Nay-gro*"—monotonously, again and again, but as we stumble back down the mountain on the candle path another litany has begun, and I go to bed (5 AM) humming the response:

and , *et cetera.*

SEPTEMBER 7

It is Brazilian Independence Day, and we take another midnight drive, this time to a *samba* ceremony. Like the *macumba,* it is alleged to be clandestine, though one wonders how a corroboree of three thousand people can be much of a secret. Again we are the only "whites," but tonight's tumult, unlike last night's, portends the Black Revolution. In order to penetrate the crowd, we are obliged to link hands like mountain climbers, therefore being unable to clamp our noses against the acridity; every sebaceous gland in the steaming room must be hyperactive. And what a room! The far wall is covered with a backdrop representing the black-and-white mosaic waves of the Copacabana sidewalk. In front of it is a platform on which about twenty musicians are playing both standard and native instruments, most of them percussive; the percussion section, in any case, throbs like a migraine at the core of every piece and even causes the brick walls to vibrate. Nor does the dancing afford any relief. One expects so much sizzling flesh to ignite into something saturnalian, but nothing happens except the weaving and swaying of the *samba* line—the memory of portages and the coffle—always the same, endlessly repeated. Pulling each other outside again, to the ozone of the street, we stop to ask a direction to Rio. An old man is sitting on the curb and alternately piping on a penny fife and singing a melancholy *saudade,* the music of which is almost worth the ordeal of the *samba.*

NOVEMBER 16

Palermo. So many bombed buildings are still unrestored and even uncleared in some areas of the city that the war might have ended yesterday. On either side of one narrow street near the market, struts and wooden soffits have been inserted between the buildings to keep them from caving in. But the market itself, though heavily damaged, is thriving, and is in fact the liveliest center on the island. And most deafening, beginning at the entrance, where fiacre drivers solicit their fares with whipcracks as loud as the revolvers of on-the-town cowboys. The market itself is powerfully vocal, the contents of every booth, table, trundle, costermonger's barrow being advertised by stentorian voices sustained by bellows-like lungs; we hold our ears while a rapscallion a few steps away cries his produce in a great high-to-low arc of impressive resonance and duration. The fruit and vegetable stalls are first: strings of red peppers, pyramids of tomatoes and artichokes, clusters of grapes, mounds of melons, prickly pears, purple eggplants, persimmons, lemons, figs, and pairs of pendant, testicular squash. The displays of spongelike *funghi* are striking, too, and of mortadella loaves, and spherical cheeses, and heaps of polenta, and many kinds of grains in turned-down burlap bags, and towers of tangerines: tangerine perfume saturates even this stew of odors.

The butchers' shops are in the center of the market. Here are hares and lambs still in their skins; ropes of black sausages, flitches of bacon; slimy messes of gizzards, tripe, entrails; and trussed and gibbeted poultry, plucked and red as if flayed. At the fish stalls surrounding the Church of Santa Eulalia of the Catalans are sardines, wet and glistening like tinfoil; tubs of turtle claws, black mussels, pink langoustines, squid, calamari; and countless shades of blue, gold, and bronze glazed-eye fish. We watch a fishwife flip a mullet on the scales, then let go with a great Santuzza cry of passion, which, however, does not succeed in distracting the customer, who follows the dip of the beam with distrust and begins to haggle with her as a matter of course.

Each booth has a Madonna with tiara of candles, a wedding or family photograph, and an oilcloth backdrop depicting a harvesting scene or one of fruit-picking and of loading the mule carts, labors invariably supervised by low-flying angelic hosts.

We go from the markets to the baroque, buttock-style Oratorio of the Knights of Malta; and from there to the Oratorio of San Lorenzo, Serpotta's masterpiece, a wedding-white confection that boasts Caravaggio's "Nativity." There, however, the sight of a donkey with mountainous bales strapped

1963

to its sides, shackled to a curbstone—all Sicily depends on a cruel system of donkey slavery—causes the I.S.'s to forget about Caravaggio and instead buy lumps of sugar and fetch a pan of water for the overburdened beast.

No performance is scheduled today at Maestro Giacomo Cuticchio's marionette theater, but we rap on the door anyway—it is in a bomb-made alley doubling as a chicken coop—hoping to induce the celebrated puppeteer to favor us with a private one. For answer, he invites us to see the *fantoccini* in their back-stage cupboards, where they hang from racks like the poultry in the market. Then, showing us how they work, he is soon treating us to a full performance. A small doe-eyed girl with large earrings appears and begins to crank a mechanical piano, and we move to a backless bench in the audience.

The frame of the tiny stage is covered with a curtain advertising Maestro Giacomo's motto and formula:

ARTE — MORALE — DILETTO

But as soon as the curtain is rolled—like a windowshade—we are deceived by scale. The marionettes seem to be from one to two feet tall, rather than, as D. H. Lawrence described them, two-thirds of human height. They are manipulated by wires instead of directly, digitally, which accounts for their jaunty, hip-swinging, bowling walk. All of them wear shining armature, silver in the case of the hero knights, Rinaldo, Tancred, Orlando, but burnished bronze for "Papa Leone," as well as for the ladies, whose cuirasses, incidentally, are accommodatingly bosomy. The armor and plume of the traitor knight are black, and, reversing David and Goliath, he and his fellow villains are small and thin (Ibsen's Lean Person), the most generous hearts being found in the burliest brutes. The coats of mail and turbans of the Saracens are black, too, as are, of course, their Stalin mustaches. The Spanish knights are hardly less swarthy or more sympathetic, though they are allowed to wear red kirtles and boleros. But then, painted donkey carts on every road in Sicily today depict the same warriors in the same scenes from the same *Orlando furioso*.

Maestro Giacomo begs off the strenuous work of a battle scene, but gives in when some children join us, and puts on a really ferocious fracas. The story seems to compound an episode from the Crusades with one from Charlemagne, but which ones I cannot say, nor is Giacomo's thundering dialect narration any help. A dragon identifies St. George, of course, as the crown, scepter, and red Frankish beard identify Carlo Magno, and the horns and cleft feet the Devil—a very human creature, incidentally, who, at the end, is brought to book fettered like a felon, then hauled away by angels armed like the hero knights, but less heavily, as befits an aerial unit.

Each of the four changes of scene exposes a deeper interior stage. The final one, which represents a plain before Jerusalem, is reserved for the most spectacular carnage. This ultimate battle begins with solo combats and ends in a general clash, after which the lopped limbs and other severed parts—the marionettes are built in sections like cuts of meat on butchers' charts—darken the stage horizon. The most impressive aspect of this Armageddon, however, is the noise, the clatter of swords, shields, visors; the neighing of steeds; the stomping, shouting, grunting, and groaning, like a Japanese movie. The slaughter over, the death rattle of the tinny piano stops, the lights go on, and Maestro Giacomo emerges like a conductor from a hidden orchestra pit, mopping perspiration, bowing to our applause, and then piecing the sautéed Paladins together again and racking them up in their closet.

Tonight's dinner at the Circolo Unione concludes, but might better have begun, with a gigantic green *cassata siciliana.* Our host, Barone Agnello, the principal patron of the local orchestra, is famous locally for having been kidnaped a few years ago and held by brigands in a mountain fortress. Our hostess is his sister, a beauty who might have modeled for a Francesco Laurana queen. As represented by the Circolo, Palermitan society is insular and separatist; Rome is regarded as remote, and a trip there as something of an undertaking. But it is literary-minded like that of Bogotá, Humboldt's "Athens of South America"; they read much and go *north* in the winter. Table talk is in heavily accented French, which is a lifesaver for me, their Italian being more rapid than that on the peninsula, except in the case of the Barone himself, whose diction is as deliberate—the word *"contento"* rolls out *"cone-taint-toe"*—as if he were giving a speech lesson. They speak a parody dialect among themselves, which, they say, is not to be confused with the parody dialect of the *"borghese,"* but resembles it in that neither has the future tense. Their speaking voices are musical but weary, as if oppressed by the long catalog of their cultural surfeits and depredations, Greek, Roman, Carthaginian, Byzantine, Saracen, Norman, Catalonian, Hohenstauffen, Hapsburg, Bourbon, U.S. Army. The Barone positively drones through a word like *quattrocentesco.*

1963

NOVEMBER 17

The long corridors of the Villa Igiea, our hotel on the bay below Mount Pellegrino, were exploited photographically in *L'Avventura,* but the hotel's most promising future as a film prop is as a background for ghost and murder stories. The corridors are not merely penumbral but as dark as the Tunnel of Love. And it is possible to get permanently lost between the lobby and the bar, and momentarily lost in one's own room; small wonder that a number of distinguished suicides, Raymond Roussel's among them, occurred here. But all is forgiven for the morning view, that first slot of sun on the smooth, metallic sea, and the soft, still morning air broken only by the vascular put-put of a fishing boat.

The Villas Valguarnera and Palagonia, both in Bagheria, are dying of the endemic Sicilian diseases of deturpation and indifference. But while Valguarnera is a still-sumptuous ruin, Palagonia, unless a rescue squad acts immediately, will soon disintegrate altogether. It may be described, without helping much, as a later cousin to Bomarzo; but it is even odder because surrounded by ordinary buildings, which reason also accounts for some of the oddity of the Rodia Towers in Los Angeles. Goethe, whose augustness left no room for unwholesomeness, was shocked and exasperated by it.[1] And he had actually seen, but avoided meeting, the Prince who created it! If only the great man had been able to put aside his passion for progress and good works and turn his powers of observation to abnormal psychology! The Prince was a bimetallist, of course, with interesting complications: those hundreds of mirrors inside the Villa and all that perverse statuary on the garden walls: goblins, dwarfs, hunchbacks, Moors, animals with human heads, winged fauns, griffins, misshapen and disfigured classical divinities, obscene goats—in short, an All Hallows' Eve. But a musical one. For the strange assembly is playing cymbals, zithers, flutes, guitars, long-necked cellos and basses, all modeled from engravings in Bonanni's *Gabinetto armonico* and carved in black tufa.

1963

From Bagheria we drive to Cefalù, stopping in a spooky *trattoria* on the way. And on the return we encounter a funeral procession. An immense hearse leads it, drawn by a team of glistening black horses with black pompons and black panaches, but carrying only flowers. The coffin follows on the shoulders of four elderly pallbearers, and behind it, walking alone, the widow, thickly veiled. A group of girls in convent uniform follows her, praying aloud, after which come the solitary mourners, curiously gotten up because it is *cacciatore* season: many of the men wear leather buskins and have guns slung on their backs and dogs chasing at their heels. The next village has turned out to await the procession, its automobile headlamps lighted as a sign of respect. The windows of almost every house, too, are draped with quilts and bunting as brightly colored as Joseph's coat.

NOVEMBER 18

Eight thousand skeletons are displayed in the Capuchin catacombs, which we visit this morning; or, rather, if skeletons were what they were, we would not be quite so horrified. But in fact many of them are still remarkably fleshy and only slightly decomposed. (Are the walls made of limestone?) Some have very long hair, too, some are of a rather off-putting pistachio color, while some, at least for my sensibilities, are simply too recently deceased (1929). These corpses hang along the corridors in a most macabre way, moreover, seeming at times to move, so that the visitor imagines the sound

---

1. "The cornices slant this way and that so that our sense of hydrostatic balance and the perpendicular, which is primarily what makes us human beings . . . is upset." Elsewhere, writing of a monastery, he remarks that "a celibate group can create the greatest of works . . . but one old bachelor—witness the case of Palagonia—has rarely produced anything sensible."

of scraping bones and the rustle of dried intestines. At one point the lights falter, as no doubt they are made to do for every tourist. But after that we make our exit, not escaping, on the way, a "Children's Corner" in which scores of infants are dolled up in their burial best, a sight so strongly lacking in appeal that I emerge into the daylight probably looking pistachio-colored myself.

The *"Trionfo della Morte"* fresco in the Palazzo Abatellis is as powerful as the great Angers tapestry of Death on his green horse. But here Death, screaming mouth in an oval rictus, rides an elongated, half-skeletal animal, forehooves in the air, like the horse in Leonardo's "Study for the Battle of Anghiara." This Death, moreover, is an archer shooting his arrows through lords of wealth and power, his victims, for a change, being not peasants but princes and popes; the picture is a kind of "Death strikes high society."

Minutes after leaving the Abatellis, we encounter a brutal reality. An old woman, only a few steps ahead of us, starts across the street without looking and is crushed beneath a bus. It is a shocking, sickening, horrifying sight, but a crowd is soon pushing for a better view, and the police almost have to hack their way through it to cover the body with newspapers and, until an ambulance comes, stand guard by this gutterside *cappella ardente*.

Why does this incident apparently upset me so much more than it does any of the others with me? I cannot say (for them), but I do know that there is too much careless, callous, and unnecessary death in Sicily. And that death here always seems to be very close, an impression caused in part by the sight of so much misery and poverty, a sight that beautiful buildings and noble landscapes only mock. For in view of the ragged *ragazzi* of Palermo, the cultivation of aesthetic emotions, or any kind of emotion except pity and indignation, is indecent. And to answer the suffering of these people with such complacencies as "Not by bread alone" (as if anyone has a right to say *that* before everyone has bread) is criminal negligence—and American no less than Italian, too, for our own government has not yet understood that there are no longer any "standards of living" to be protected for the simple reason that there is no longer any place to hide.

NOVEMBER 19

To Segesta and Selinunte, with a driver more interested in showing some of the sacred sites associated with Salvatore Giuliano. One of these is the scene of the bandit hero's murder, which took place "not in Castelvetrano, whatever history and the police may have established, but right here in Monreale." The driver says that when the film about Giuliano was shown in its hero's native village, Montelepre, the *contadini*, finding it insufficiently epic, pelted the screen with eggs. Going from Montelepre to Partenico, however—from the violent to the nonviolent reformer—the driver's arguments are all loaded the other way. Danilo Dolce's balloon must be pricked.

1963

I mention an evening with Dolce and Margaret Mead at Auden's in New York and he says, "You foreigners have all been duped. Dolce is great only as a *filibustero*. He has a dozen illegitimate children and lives with a married woman who has a dozen more of her own; he is apparently trying to populate Partenico all by himself." But Dolce's real sin, as the next remark partly proves, has been in offending Sicilian pride. "He has exposed our poverty abroad successfully enough but has failed to make our rich Sicilians aware of it, and we have more millionaire *principi* now than ever."

From fifty yards away, the temple at Segesta looks as if it were made of cork. Closer still, the surfaces prove to be pitted and eroded like the barks of old olive or camphor trees. A flock of swallows scuds away as we approach the ruin, but the only other sound during our visit is the distant glitter of a goat's bell. Inside the temple, in the full sun, some of the columns are iridescent, with lustrous veins of red, orange, and gold. (Goethe, incidentally, found more profitable matter for contemplation in the structure of the wild fennel growing near the temple than in the dead building itself, concerning which he drew a moral similar to the one about the friability of the tufa at Palagonia. But he did not like the countryside, either, which he described as brooding in a "melancholy fertility." I am not elated by ruins myself, however, and should not ridicule my own weakness in the other.) We climb from the temple to the amphitheater, which overlooks the sea, and where lintlike pieces of clouds tuft the surrounding peaks.

The foliage south of Segesta is turning autumn colors, muted as yet or fuscous and tawny, except for a few flame-red pear trees and bright yellow aspens. Every arable ell has been plowed, but the soil is poor and pockmarked with cacti. "Life," in the town of Vita, can only refer to chickens and mules, the latter, drawing carts, plumed like Theda Bara. Santa Ninfa, on a knoll, is livelier, and its agglomeration of angles makes an attractive Cubist picture.

Whereas the skeleton of the temple at Segesta is gnawed but still standing, every bone of Selinunte has been violently and as if systematically broken. In fact, the place is still haunted by the noise that must have followed the exertions of the sundering Samson, as discobolus-shaped capitals and giant salami-slices of columns crashed into the earth like flying saucers.

"Psst. Psst." *That,* at any rate, is not an imagined sound. It comes from a man of unprepossessing appearance—what appears of him, for he is largely concealed behind a cracked stylobate. He extends a cupped hand containing, we suppose from his manner, a lubricious photograph, but it proves to be a figurine, which he claims to have excavated today and wishes to sell. And his story is probably true, tomb robbers being employed nowadays for their expertise despite the risk to the petty archeological cash. These scavengers are obliged to accept such employment, moreover, for it is unlikely that they can make off with anything as major as a metope and difficult any more to find receivers. The scamp will not give up, however, and he pops out at us all along the path (*"Psst, psst, professore"*), even following our car on a bicycle for a time when we leave.

At Gibellina, on our return to Palermo, the land, in color and texture, looks like elephant hide. Alcamo, just beyond, is said to be the "heart" of the Mafia country, but perhaps a better word would be "arsenal."

We call on the Principessa Lampedusa in the evening, but narrowly escape dismemberment by a giant Cerberus at her *porte-cochère* and, inside, are nearly turned back by a concierge with a built-in look of disapproval. The Principessa, a large, vehement, coronary type, receives us on the *piano nobile* attired like a doge: coif, mink shoulder rug, black robe, velvet slippers, jeweled hoops on both forefingers. The daughter of a singer, and herself gifted with a round, uvular, bass-clarinet voice, the Principessa vocalizes her vowels so that the word *"vuole,"* for instance, comes out *"voo-oh-lay,"* in three warbled syllables. An impressive linguist, she converses with V. in Russian and moves through all the major European languages with the greatest of ease (while rather loftily implying that she can as easily manage the minor ones too).

She is even more dogelike in her salon, plumping herself into a curule and assigning us to smaller chairs on either side of this throne, as if she were holding court. Save for one dim lamp, the room, book-lined from floor to ceiling, concedes nothing to the last hundred years, nor does it appear to have been disturbed in at least as long a time by the vulgar enterprise of dustcloth or mop. A console on the Principessa's right holds a framed photograph of her late spouse, as well as a pile of foreign-language editions of his book. The conversation is almost exclusively related to these objects, and on the subject of her husband's novel the Principessa is a formidable monologist indeed. *"Ah, Lampedusa, quel homme!"* she croons. *"Il avait des sentiments si fins. Comme je suis triste et seule sans lui. Imaginez-vous qu'est-ce que c'était la vie avec lui."* But we cannot oblige, and need not try very hard as she is soon giving us her own very substantial account. The story of the publication of the *Gattopardo* is as good as the novel itself, however, and if made into a movie, with the Principessa playing herself, it would be destined for an even more spectacular film career.

But the Principessa is autocratic. And worse than that, in fact despotic, with her servants. She interrupts herself to deliver some sharp commands to a rheumy-eyed old codger standing slump-shouldered in the doorway, and a no less browbeaten footman in a long-unlaundered white jacket is ruthlessly told to fetch another cognac, then harshly admonished for failing to pass the *hors-d'oeuvre*. Otherwise she keeps to the main path of her narrative, stepping out of it only now and then when an imperceptive critic has to be disposed of, or anyone who has stood in the way of her husband's book. And here one cannot but admire the swift, clean strokes of her axe as "whish" goes the head of Donnafugato, whose criticism is *"Tutto falso,"* and "wham" goes Orlando, who was incompetent "because he did not even know Lampedusa."

Smoking being permitted in Palermitan audiences, by intermission of our concert tonight the air is as dense and blue as a *fumerie,* or the club car on the "Super Chief." *"Agnus Dei"* sings the chorus, and "Scratch" goes the response of someone lighting up in the first row.

After the *"Vom Himmel hoch"* variations, I.S. remarks that the chorale melody was too obtrusive. "Instead of a *point d'appui,* it lumbered along in clumsy contrast to the lightfooted artifices of the variations." But a no less serious fault in the performance is the lack of articulation, the unwillingness or inability to play "off the string." Left to themselves, the violists would execute every line for "tone," which is to say not merely *legato* but *portamento,* and the harpist, instead of attacking every note *smorzato,* would glue them all together.

1963

The Gancia is virtually the only large Palermitan palazzo to have escaped the bombs of 1943, for which reason, and because of the railway-station proportions of its main *salone,* it was used for the ballroom scene in the film of *The Leopard.* We are shown through by the present owner, Prince Wolff-Stomersee, who hangs on I.S.'s words as if he intended to have them carved in marble. (Which is the reason I.S. sidesteps every trap laid for his opinion: he will seldom pop when put on a griddle and expected to do so.)

In the wall by the main entrance—where one might have found the umbrella stand in a Victorian mansion—is a rounded indentation like a piece of well-worn billiard chalk. It was used for snuffing torches.

To Agrigento by way of Mussomeli, where loaves of hay, hollowed like tents, are pitched between black wheat-soil hills; and Castello Diana, which the *Guide Bleu* describes as "an impregnable fortress" but which seems reasonably pregnable to me. The muleteers in this region wear long capes of archiepiscopal purple, which cover their heads, cowl-like, and flow over the flanks of their animals. These people seem more Arabian or African than Italian, but are in any case a reminder that whereas the coastal cities of Sicily may belong to Italy, the harsh, half-savage interior is an altogether different land.

The interior of Agrigento Cathedral might be Mexican, except that the columns have been quarried from the temples of older religions. Workmen are repairing the coffered ceiling, held up to it on a tall wheeled tower like a mangonel or other Leonardo da Vinci poliorcetic engine, but, as we watch, a cataract of wood and plaster crashes around our feet.

The Museum of Archeology is safer. To judge by the profusion of Demeters with breasts like brioches, *in*fertility must have been a problem; but the fault may have been a corrupt bachelordom, penises commonly being represented as curled, like anchovies on *hors-d'oeuvre*. The Silenuses bear a striking facial resemblance to Cyril Connolly.

The temples of Agrigento have not suffered destruction on anything like the scale of Selinunte. Juno's roof appears to have been swept off in a tornado, nevertheless; and Concordia has been made to swallow, though it has not digested, the church of "St. Gregory of the Turnips." (Such names—"Our Lady of the Asparagus" is another—imperil the tourist's sense of romance, nor is the discovery that "Selinunte" means celery rather than the moon goddess compensated for by gastronomic anticipation.) Violence of a personal kind seems to have befallen the Telamon statue, which lies on the ground fractured into armillary layers like the *pneu* figure of the *Guide Michelin*.

The land near the Lampedusa town of Palma di Montechiaro is parched and white. Thereafter it flattens toward the beaches and dunes west of Gela, which are still marked by German "pillboxes" and *chevaux de frise*. Seeing these fortifications, our driver recalls the news of the American landing here as it affected him as a child in Palermo. "The Germans acted as if we had betrayed them, and they would kick anyone who came near them. The G.I.'s, for their part, were friendly and generous, but the first one I saw gave me chewing gum when I had asked for *caramella,* and not knowing what it was, I swallowed it." (I, too, remember the news of the landing at Gela. Or, rather, the eye of my memory funnels back to that day, long dead and buried, and I see myself, dog-tag 32748830, standing in an endless line outside the mess hall in the New Orleans Staging Area, while newsboys on bicycles ride by shouting *"Times-Picayune, Times-Picayune:* Landing in Sicily"; except that *"Je est un autre,"* and I can no longer enter that other mind.)

Etna comes into view a half-hour north of Gela, with a plume of smoke like a *bersagliere*'s feather. Then more smoke appears, but nearer home, in fact from the hood of our car. We stop halfway up the hill, and the driver steps out, but only to look, listen, and wait. Nothing happens, of course, nor, after a dozen more tries, does the motor show any signs of "turning over." Instead, *we* turn the car around, aim it downhill, push it, jump aboard, but soon reach the bottom without having coaxed even a faint tracheal cough from the engine. And here, for the first time, we notice the loneliness of the surroundings and the rapidly descending dark. So, apparently, does the driver; the looking and listening are agitated now. Then very luckily, even providentially, two motorcycle policemen, the first I have seen in Sicily, come cruising by. What is the trouble with the car, they ask, and aren't we aware of the danger of stopping in these bandit-infested hills? But, *mirabile dictu,* they have just heard an announcement on their radios of our concert in Catania tomorrow night, thanks to which they requisition the next passing automobile to take our driver to the nearest town likely to have a mechanic.

About forty minutes later, during which interval a number of other drivers stop to survey our situation—no doubt attracted by the possibility of seeing some spilled *sangue*—a mechanic actually does materialize, a short, dark, highly excitable man in a beret and very roomy overalls. He sets about his business by looking, listening, waiting, and some not very energetic pushing. Then in desperation he inclines his ear to the hood, as a doctor would to a man whose heart has stopped beating. The result is a decision to operate, a very grave step evidently, calling for no end of shrugging and arm-waving. And at long last the car *is* actually opened up, and a large and frightening array of tools flourished, among them a giant monkey wrench, which, if accidentally precipitated in the now-exposed viscera, would undoubtedly justify several months in a garage. At length the beret and upper half of the overalls disappear into the nether regions of the unhooded area, accompanied by, to some extent, *la polizia*. And a long time later the beret and overalls emerge, rather blacker than before, and make for the front seat of the car, where knobs, gears, clutches are then poked, pressed, pulled, pushed, pedaled—though to no effect, and without a churr of response. At last the partly submerged *polizia* surface as well, and also try the driver's seat, performing there in the same way and with the same result.

Finally it is decided to commandeer one of the kibitzing bystanders to tow us to the next town, for which eventuality, miracle of miracles, beret-and-overalls has brought a rope. When at long last a towline is secured, the "*ciao*," the "*grazie*s," and the hand-wavings at the breakup of the party would befit a departure for the moon; and, indeed, the last-minute debate that develops about the signaling system to be adopted during the voyage would seem to imply that some monumental feat of engineering really was about to be asseyed. Then at long last, off we go. Or, rather, off *they* go, for the rope slips loose at the first tug by the other car, thereby provoking a tremendous expenditure of oaths and accusations between beret-and-overalls and the indentured other driver. A fifteen-minute *pausa* ensues while new knots are tied, this time of Gordian complexity and security. And, strange to tell, this time we actually move.

Our new driver is delighted to have us aboard, he says, and in truth he appears to be *molto contento* with the whole adventure. He speaks a few words of "Inglis," he says (not speaking them), for he was captured on the second day of the war, then taken to Cairo and later Palestine, where he married. *Certo,* those were the times. And what do we think of it all now, of "*la* Roosia" and the "*Cinesi*"?

At Caltagirone we hire a taxi. And this driver, too, as it happens, speaks *un poco inglese,* having spent the war—ah, those were the days!—in Glasgow after managing to be captured in Algeria. "*E molto bello, Glazgo, ma freddo, freddo.*" And what do we think of Mussolini? He wasn't all bad, you know. And the Americans, who have all the money? Well, America is better than *la* Roosia, anyway, because of *la democrazia.*

We reach the hotel in Catania at ten o'clock and hear the thunderclap that "*Il presidente Kennedy è morto, assassinato!*" Stunned and unbelieving, we sit by the radio most of the night.

Black-bordered photographs of the late President are on walls all over the city, the flags on every public building are at half-mast, and the line of black, empty *carrozze* at the hack stand in front of the hotel looks more than ever like a train of hearses. We go to Siracusa and wander without point in museums and churches, climbing a wobbly ladder for a closeup of Caravaggio's "Death of Santa Lucia," burrowing in "The Ear of Dionysus," a cave with freakish acoustics: in one place a tearing Kleenex sounds like an express train. Back in Catania, after our concert, I.S. composes a cablegram for Mrs. Kennedy, but V., seeing him mark it "night letter," argues that "at a time of personal and national tragedy you cannot show that you have thought of saving money." I.S. insists it is not parsimony, however, but good sense. "Furthermore, I do not see why I shouldn't always use good sense, and especially during national disasters."

Rome. While our train stops at Naples this morning we see a newspaper headline, *"E morto il piccolo maestro, Aldous Huxley."* So it has happened, and exactly at the time the doctors predicted. I mourn him; and mourn myself, for his death is the death of a part of me. At one time, and during a period of about five years, we met never less than once, and more commonly several times, a week. Then, after Maria's death, his remarriage and his and our travels separated us until lately he seemed to have become part of an already completed past, whose feelings, moreover, were complete in themselves. Can those feelings be articulated and interpreted today, but avoiding today's new pictorial edition of them? And is it possible to revive a memory without memorializing it? Or possible to deny that essential part of the origin of valedictions, the *need* to mourn?

All recent memories of Aldous are vividly clear, in any case, and the picture they form is heartbreaking. The last decade of his life, from the discovery of Maria's cancer, was never free from the mental cruelty of incurable illness, for hardly had he watched her struggle end when he entered the same lists himself. Call it "his way" that one never heard him complain; or ascribe to the desire to "guard his grief" that he kept others from touching his wounds. But he was a very brave man. Alone and nearly blind, he went on working, supporting a host of dependents. For he *had* to produce a book a year, and *had* to and did lecture until three months before his death, which was that of Pirandello's *"l'uomo dal fiore in bocca."* Nor was mortal illness the only specter. The failure of a play on Broadway, the waste of time and mind on film projects, the generally belittling reception of books: these were hard knocks, the more so for a man once so popular. At the time of McCarthyism he was even subjected to an official indignity. "Would you refuse to take arms against an enemy of the United States?" he was asked. And Aldous Huxley, a man far more deeply responsible to

1963

Society,[1] human as well as American, than most of the citizenry he honored by living in its midst, was actually denied American citizenship because of the pacifist clause. May a Dantean bootlicking punishment—Aldous's feet were not small—await his inquisitor and judge.

As Maria's health declined, Aldous, struggling to save her, tried everything from hypnotism and acupuncture to the newest "expander-of-consciousness" drugs.[2] He even flew with her to Lebanon to see the magician Tara Bey, whose American tour, a few years before, the Huxleys had underwritten by their intellectual support. But because Aldous did not tell us when the cancer had entered the cobalt stage, her death came as a shock. What an agonizing sight he was then, so miserable and so alone. I see him at the funeral, groping his way down the aisle, his bowed head still a head taller than anyone else in the church. And I see him at the graveside, giving his arm to Maria's sturdy, dry-eyed mother, who did not appear to need it. Maria, who shared so little of the world of his imagination, who was bored by his beloved music, who could read to him hours at a time without listening: this same Maria was his seeing eye and the eye of all his affection, and he was as helpless as an unfledged bird without her.

In the lonely weeks after her death, we kept him company as often as he would allow. But painful slips would occur, including that sign of delayed shock, the solecism of the present tense: "As Maria tells... I mean, used to tell me." And because we tried to avoid her memory in our own remarks, conversation was both ghost-ridden and leadenly self-conscious. We and all of his other friends worried about him alone in that empty house, where, as I took him home at night, he would let me walk with him to the door and fit the key in the lock but would otherwise resist boy-scouting. His refusal to accept help crossing streets was a great anxiety to *us,* and we would watch, or not watch, these passages, fearing the worst. He entrusted himself to his hearing and memory on his afternoon walks, but even those acute faculties were hardly adequate in Los Angeles traffic. In the last years he suffered one serious fall.

Now, as I write, memories of the early 1950's return, but helter-skelter. I see Aldous at the cinema, but why there I am unable to say. Except for documentaries—I remember taking him to an Italian film on Bosch, to an anthropologist's film on a tribe of Central American Indians, etcetera—he loathed "the movies." Is it because he cut such a bizarre figure, sitting by himself in the front row and moaning comments like "Inconceivable

1. At least twice, to my knowledge, he took the trouble to testify in Sacramento against power-lobby legislation. On one expedition there, he defended a would-be manufacturer of battery-powered automobiles against the vested oil interests, and on another, took up the cause of the importer of his perforated-celluloid eye-focusers, when manufacturers of optical instruments had successfully banned them.
2. He had urged I.S. to take mescaline and LSD in the interests of science, to see what effect they might have on a creative musical mind, but to I.S., music, as he heard it in his chemically normal mind, was enough; to have taken mescaline would have been, to him, like Keats putting cayenne pepper on his tongue to "hop up" the taste of claret.

tripe," "Monstrous oafs," "Semi-minus epsilons"? Ordinarily his Chinese perforations served him at the cinema, but he would switch to a magnifying glass for a better view of . . . well, Fräulein Dietrich's charms as exposed in *The Blue Angel,* for I remember seeing that with him in a seedy theater on Wilshire Boulevard. But Aldous also braved the cinema for the sake of I.S., who, like Wittgenstein, would go for relaxation to almost any movie, no matter how bad, and as many nights of the week as I would take him.

A sheaf of pictures comes back, too, of Aldous listening to music, which was one of the delights of his life. But on this subject I can tell the story of the "he" only by intruding the story of the "I." From 1952 he regularly attended rehearsals and concerts of "pre-classical" music—Monteverdi, Schütz, Couperin, Bach—that I was performing; I should add that he was interested in, but did not love, new music, or indeed much music of any kind after Beethoven, with the exception of Verdi, and especially *Falstaff.* In 1954 he fell under the spell of Gesualdo di Venosa, whose last four madrigal scorebooks I had transcribed, and whose texts he translated for me; in fact, he introduced my concerts of this music in Santa Barbara and Los Angeles with racy public lectures on the North Italian courts of the time. The quality of his musical ear was such, I can attest, that he was able to perform the Speaker's part in the *Ode to Napoleon.* We worked on it together for a time with the idea of recording it, but his voice was too subtle even for the microphone, and the repetitious poem exasperated him.

Another typical picture now reappearing is of Aldous the museum addict, his lanky elastic-vertebrae back bent toward an object which he studies through a pocket glass like a bacteriologist. The museum might be Pasadena's Huntington Library, where I remember turning the pages of a Shakespeare folio with him, and a copy of Haydn's Symphony No. 101 in the hand of Richard Wagner; or the Museum of Modern Art in New York, where he hated most of the pictures[1] but would return again and again to Monet's "Water Lilies." Monet's sight, when he painted the picture, was almost as poor as Aldous's, hence it seemed to have been composed to Aldous's scale, and in any case he did not use his glass when looking at it.[2] (The amount of reading, writing, manuscript-correcting, proofreading he could get through with that glass was astonishing, incidentally, and I do not think that he used dictaphones or tape recorders until the very last years.)

In still another glimpse, I see him threading his way through the thick

---

1. "Why should we take Mondrian seriously?" he said to me there one day. "After all, he was a bad academic painter before he did abstractions, and he could not draw." Well, neither could Cézanne draw, I should have argued, and *was* Mondrian such a bad academic painter? But Aldous was anti "modern art."

2. Monet's spectacles were exhibited in the Musée Marmottan, 1971, and like Aldous's they were very thick, while the lens on one side was almost opaque with what looked like brown paint (which may have been an effect of time, except that both lenses were tinted a light green). But what pleasure Aldous would have derived from these pictures of *nymphéas* and *nénuphars,* which compose differently at different distances but would have composed close up for him!

of a Hollywood party at Glenn Ford's. He winces at the party voices, but fastens like an anthropologist to the film moguls and to the actors with pink shirts and bare feet; and I knew that the next time we saw him we could expect to be treated to comparisons with wilder New Guinea. (My own conversation with him that night was about insomnia, and I remember being advised to "eat a stalk of nerve-relaxing celery just before going to bed.") Aldous was surrounded at these affairs by flocks of adoring females, ranging from elderly women in saris to culture-struck nymphets for whom the initial attraction may have been the unfamiliar charm of the English language (*versus* the "beat" talk of their boyfriends). But everyone felt the magnetism of this shy, soft-spoken man with the noble head and cameo features.

I should note, too, that Aldous was anthropologically interested in juvenile delinquents of another order than the luminaries of filmdom. In fact, he was rescued by a gang of boys from the fire that destroyed his home. As he described it later, "The gang came to warn me a good fifteen minutes before the arrival of the television trucks, which, in turn, were half an hour ahead of the fire engines that could have saved the house. After the boys had led me to safety, through the one passable street, I noticed that some familiar faces among them were missing, and I expressed my concern about them. But the leader told me not to worry because they were merely out starting more fires."

"*È morto il piccolo maestro*" says the newspaper. And even before his long, drawling body is cold, the reputation industry will have decided just how "*piccolo*" he was, and done its work of summing up, which is obituarese for hatcheting down, the failures being so much easier to see than the enduring value. But how predictable the whole process is, being so exactly in accord with the birth dates of the clerks who practice it. Aldous Huxley, a good and gentle man, and a better writer than those who will now bury him in their weekly columns, dear Aldous will be patted on the head and put away as an "era."

And myself? For I, too, am a clerk with a birthday, and as an obituarist am even unholier than thou. I can only say that for me the man and his work can never come unjoined, and that the joining place is not on the bookshelf but in the heart. Which is the reason I will not be able to read him again for a long time. For I would hear his voice and that would measure the void.

1963

1948
1949
1950
1951
1952
1953
1954
1955
1956
1957
1958
1959
1960
1961
1962
1963
1964
1965
1966
1967
1968
1969
1970
1971

ITINERARY

January 5: I.S. to Philadelphia by car. **10, 11, 13, 14, 20:** Concerts with the Phila-delphia Orchestra in Philadelphia, New York, Washington. **31:** R.C. to Toronto. **February 5:** I.S.'s leave New York for Los Angeles by train (joined by R.C. at Buffalo during the night). **March 3:** I.S. buys a house at 1218 North Wetherly Drive. **8:** We fly to Cleveland. **12, 14:** Concerts and recordings (*Jeu de cartes, Ode*) with the Cleveland Orchestra. **15:** By car to Cincinnati for V.'s vernissage (16th). **18:** We fly to Hollywood. **April 29:** We fly to Detroit. **May 3:** I.S. conducts the Philadelphia Orchestra in Ann Arbor, after which we drive to Toronto. **8:** We fly to New York and Hollywood (18th). **June 11:** We fly to Denver for a concert on the 13th. **14:** We fly to New York and London (15th). **16, 17, 18, 23:** I.S. records *The Rake's Progress.* **29:** I.S. conducts the *Symphony of Psalms* at Oxford. **30:** We fly to New York and, July 5, Hollywood. **July 16:** We fly to Chicago. **18:** I.S. conducts at Ravinia. **20:** I.S. flies to Hollywood (R.C. to Santa Fe). **August 14:** The I.S.'s fly to New York. **17:** We fly to Paris and, the 20th, to Jerusalem. **23:** Première of *Abraham and Isaac* in Jerusalem. **24:** *Abraham and Isaac* in Caesarea. **25:** We fly to New York and (31st) Hollywood. **September 8:** The I.S.'s first night in their new home. **13:** We fly to New York, Paris (16th), Berlin (17th), Paris (24th), New York (27th: Drake Hotel). **October 5:** We fly to Hollywood. **November 22:** We fly to New York. **December 6, 7, 9:** Concerts in New York (Lincoln Center), Washington, and Boston. **11:** I.S. records his instrumental songs.

JANUARY 21

New York. Auden for dinner. He drinks a jug of Gibsons before, a bottle of champagne during, a bottle (*sic*) of Cherry Heering (did he think it was Chianti?) after dinner. But the different qualities for delectation in these

256

fluids hardly seem to count compared to their effect as a means of conveyance—supersonic jet, one would suppose—to the alcoholic Eden. Despite this liquid menu, he not only is unblurred, but also performs mental pirouettes for us, as if the alcohol were transformed into an intellectual ichor. V. believes in a physiological explanation of the phenomenon. "He must have multiple stomachs, like a cow, the gin going to the omasum, while the wine stops in the reticulum and the kerosene stays in the rumen." I.S., for his part, is impressed above all by the display of liver power, "though livers learn, of course, and Wystan's would naturally be the most intelligent in town." My own fascination with *homo bibulus*—to round out the appreciation—is with the capaciousness of the plumbing: not a trip to the "loo" all evening. Labial difficulties occur, to be sure, but they are overcome by a sort of isometric exercise, a screwing up of the rugosities of that nobly corrugated face, and by bursts of music, including some very melodious singing of bits of Rossini's *Petite Messe solennelle*. Otherwise the only sign of tipsiness is an initial lurch at departure, after which a gyroscope seems to take over.

I.S. wants to compose an elegy to the memory of President Kennedy, "either six or nine stanzas of two long lines and one short. I have a choral piece in mind, and low in *tessitura*. Probably I will use a male choir, though whether or not with instruments, I cannot say." [1] These carpenter-like measurements delight Auden—"I'm an old hand at this sort of thing"—and he decides then and there to do a double octet and a quartet. "I'll throw in a bit of 'Grant Us Thy Peace,' of course, and I won't forget that 'his name was John.'" (I.S., later: "Wystan is wholly indifferent to J.F.K.; what he cares about is the form. And it is the same with his religion. What his intellect and gifts require of Christianity is its form—even, to go further, its uniform.")

1964

Because he has just written a lecture on Shakespeare's Sonnets for the BBC, we hear some opinions about scholars. Hotson, for one, "is frightfully learned but all wrong," while Rowse is "good on the background but quite dotty on Shakespeare." The work of another distinguished authority is dismissed as *belles-lettres*. But the main difficulty appears to be that "it won't do just yet to admit that the top Bard was in the homintern, or, for that matter, that Beethoven was queer." He then mentions a public reading on his agenda, but forbids us to attend. "I never allow anyone I know to come to those things. First of all, I want to keep my tricks to myself, and second, I'm always afraid someone in the back of the hall is going to shout something like 'We've heard all that before,' or 'Get her!'"

He says that Hammerskjöld's Diaries, to which he is writing a foreword, reveal an early belief in a mission and a tragic end. The reference to

---

1. This suggests the combination of the *Introitus*, composed over a year later. As soon as the *Elegy for J.F.K.* arrived, March 3, 1964, I.S. decided that the words were better suited to a solo voice. But the association of solemnity with a low-*tessitura* male-voice choir is at least as old as Compère's *Quis numerare queat*.

Hammerskjöld's death leads him to the story of the suicide of the Austrian poet whose house he now owns and inhabits, and who "was a bit late in seeing that Hitler wouldn't do." ("Won't do" is one of Wystan's hardest-worked expressions.) Then, switching to the English scene, he remarks of certain elderly writers that "The Lord should hurry and take them now that their time is up." Compton Mackenzie is an exception, reprieved because "he still has to do his book on the great liars, T. E. Lawrence and so on." Wystan contends that a doctor who conceals the gravity of a patient's condition from him is guilty of great wickedness. "As the Psalm says, 'Lord, make me to know the measure of my days.' And, anyway, we need time to make peace with our competitive friends." Called to his father's deathbed not long ago, he greeted his expiring parent with—so he says—"Well, Dad, you're dying, you know." And he adds that, "Ideally one should die upstairs, like Falstaff, while a party is in full swing below, and people are saying things like, 'Now why doesn't the old boy get on with it?'"

The talk turning to music, he offers an estimate of the influence of Max Bruch on Elgar. Then, speaking of Britten's *A Midsummer Night's Dream,* he suggests that "it is a mistake to conclude each act with people going to sleep." And speaking of *Rasputin* by Nicolas Nabokov—"A composer who will never realize his talent because he cannot bear to be long enough alone"—he declares that "The idea should have been rejected out of hand. It won't do, for the simple reason that the *true* subject is hidden, as the audience is aware and *quid pro quo.* What *Rasputin* is *really* about, of course, is a prodigious penis."

Getting on to historians, he says that if a certain professor "has missed the whole point of a small event like the General Strike—which, as a witness, I know he did—how are we to trust him with the Middle Ages or the Russian Revolution? Obviously the underlying reason for the strike was the middle-class English boy's desire to drive a bus or a train." He describes another historian's "attack" on Hannah Arendt's *Eichmann* as "the point of view of the disguised *goy,* of the Jew who has it made," adding that he would have defended the book himself "but for the automatic answer that *goys* like it."

He bemoans an upcoming dinner party by "a social register bluestocking who addresses me either in words of six syllables or Greek, and, worse, quotes bits of my poetry at me." He then claims to be able to recognize every line of verse he has ever written, but says he often fails to identify excerpts from his prose. His German quotations tonight—the Teutonic period is still at high tide—are all from Qualtinger, but at one point he says that Rilke is "the greatest Lesbian poet since Sappho." Yevtushenko he dismisses as "the poor man's *Howl.*"

SEPTEMBER 23

Berlin. Auden for dinner, in great form despite some ventral expansion, giving us of his best "unacknowledged legislator" manner, and successfully (in fact easily) defending his title as the world's most delightful wit. Although here at Ford Foundation expense, for a Congress of African and European writers, he confesses himself "unable to follow nigritude." Nor does he share our enthusiasm for the tribal dances of Dahomey, which we have just seen at the Berlin Opera House. (Did none of that beautiful bird-mummery—for the dancers are like grounded birds—impress him? Nor the way the dancers run about like birds plucked of their feathers? Or climb to the tops of poles and flap like birds who have lost the secret of flight? Nor even the scene in which the male dancer's ruffs vibrate like a cock's wattles, while the female, with hair like a willow tree, waits for him to regain his vigor and the young males hover ever nearer, threatening to understudy him?)

On the subject of this afternoon's session, the poet's loneliness, he holds that "In spite of all that *einsam* rubbish, poets are no lonelier than anyone else. Poetry itself is lonely, of course, in the sense that few people read it. But why bother about that when we know that the few really care? And anyway, who would want to be read by the cinema-novel public?" Or as he has put it elsewhere: "After all, it's rather a privilege amid the affluent traffic to serve this unpopular art."

Some of his pique against the Congress is evidently caused by the language in which the meetings are conducted. "Why," he asks, "should I be compelled to listen for hours at a time to Pierre Emmanuel's rhetorical frog effusions?" But anti-batrachian remarks of the sort flow on unabated all evening, and at one point he even says that "Rimbaud, Baudelaire, and Proust would be much better if they had written in English. As for Mallarmé, well, *chic* nonsense is the most appalling kind."

1964

It seems that when he entered the hall for our concert last night with a raincoat over his arm, an usherette stopped him and said that the coat had to be checked. "I protested, of course—*Krieg* is a language the *Krauts* understand—and told the Waltraute that the right to hold one's coat in one's lap is surely not legally *verboten* even in Deutschland. At this point an *ober*-Waltraute intervened and, fearing a scuffle, said I could take it with me but would have to wear it, which I did. It was a very hot concert."

He talks about the film that the Austrian government has been making of his life in Kirchstetten. "One scene is in church—not terrible appropriate, perhaps (a naughty bar might have been more suitable), but you can hear me singing. Besides, the priest loved being photographed and got all dolled up for it. You can also hear me speaking *Kraut,* ungrammatical, no doubt, but chatty, and I get in some *echt* expressions."

Switching to poets, he expresses admiration for Robert Frost, "in spite of his mean character, for he was jealous of every other, and especially every younger, poet. So was Yeats a jealous old man, who behaved abominably to younger poets. But Yeats was untruthful, too, which is the reason I dislike his poetry more and more. Why can't people grow dotty gracefully? Robert Graves is aging well, by the way, except that he has become boastful, implying he's the oldest poet still fucking. Now obviously it is normal to think of oneself as younger than one is, but fatal to want to *be* younger."

He condemns Shelley ("a thoroughly uninviting character") for share-holding in cotton mills, but may be seeing the poet in the light of Dickens's "Merdle" as he condones Wordsworth's similar investments in railroad stocks, adding, however, that "I'm fond of trains." As for Byron, he was "a master, not of language but of speed. If Goethe had been able to understand him in English, he wouldn't have liked him at all." Goethe's love-life, he goes on, shocks and bores him. "He moves along so smoothly, then every once in a while along comes one of those awful outbursts of '*Mein Liebchen.*'" He mentions a desire to translate the *Römische Elegien,* but says that so far the task has seemed impossible. "I also want to do a poem explaining why photography isn't an art," he says, "and of course any claim for the cinema as an art is rubbish. For the moment I have a medieval anthem in the works, one of those the-latter-half-is-the-mirror-of-the-first-half things. I promised it to Willie Walton at a party when I was in my cups."

Is he in his cups now? He chews out a waiter for bringing him a glass of water: "I haven't had any of that for thirty years and don't propose to start now." (When Stephen Spender joins us later and I.S. asks him what *he* would like to drink, Auden whispers to me, "Cocoa, I should think.") There is no mental fuzziness, in any case, though diction is less distinct, and though, with the ebb and flow of *alcools,* as "frogs" say, conversation becomes more and more of a one-way street. His memory is unfailing when it comes to quoting poetry, which he spouts as if he had been struck by the hoof of Pegasus. But when he is obliged—as who isn't?—to rummage for a name or date, his twill-weave facial integument (with a wiggly wen) contracts while his right hand stirs what might be an unseen pancake batter. These, however, are the only outward signs of the throes of thought.

1964

Moving on to Wagner, he remarks that "Mrs. Hunding didn't keep a very proper hearth for the old dear. Incidentally, quite the worst example of stage-timing I have ever seen occurred the other day in a performance of *Siegfried,* the anvil breaking in half just as the hero was raising his sword to strike it."

On the subject of the forthcoming American election, he thinks we should bear in mind that "It might be better to be governed by a crook than a fool." He plans to visit East Berlin tomorrow, in spite of the ordeal of the border police, who now wheel reflectors under every car, like the mirrors dentists use for upper teeth; and in spite of Stephen Spender's remark that it is like a "genteel prison." "Well," Auden replies, "all that can be said about a genteel prison is that it would appear to be better than a nongenteel one."

His departure is heralded by some fresh abuse of "the frogs," whose "famous *clarté* is thicker than the thickest *Wiener* treacle. The French, my dear, are hardly white." Tomorrow's conference is foreseen as "a day among the Laestrygones. But if anybody brings up the subject of literary criticism, I will bolt. After all, we were put on this earth to *make* things."

1948
1949
1950
1951
1952
1953
1954
1955
1956
1957
1958
1959
1960
1961
1962
1963
1964
1965
1966
1967
1968
1969
1970
1971

ITINERARY

January 11: We fly to Los Angeles. **24:** I.S. greets an Israeli fund-raising dinner at the Waldorf in New York via CBS television from his home in Hollywood. **March 16:** Filming begins for the Liebermann-Leacock "Portrait of Stravinsky." **31:** We fly to Austin to begin filming the CBS television "Portrait of Stravinsky." **April 4:** We fly from San Antonio to Hollywood and, on the 15th, to Chicago. **17:** Première of *Variations* and *Introitus* with the Chicago Symphony. **20:** We fly to New York. **May 1:** We sail on the *Gripsholm* for Göteborg, where we fly to Paris via Copenhagen (10th). **15:** We drive to Vevey, Basle (17th), and Paris (19th). **June 1:** We fly from Warsaw to Paris. **6:** Train to Rome. **12:** I.S. attends a concert in the Vatican and receives a decoration from the Pope. **13:** We fly to New York, Hollywood (18th), Indianapolis (28th), going from the latter by car to Muncie where, on July 1st, I.S. attends staged performances of *Histoire du Soldat* and *Oedipus Rex*. **July 2:** We fly to Chicago. **8:** Concert in Ravinia. **9:** We fly to Vancouver for concerts on the 12th and 13th. **14:** We fly to Hollywood. **August 19–26:** I.S. records *Pulcinella, Le Baiser de la fée, Variations*, etc. **September 2:** Concert in Hollywood Bowl. **3:** We fly to New York, Hamburg (6th), and London, where, on the 14th, I.S. conducts the *Firebird Suite* (televised) in Festival Hall, his last appearance in England. **15:** We fly to New York and, on October 10th, to Cincinnati. **October 15, 16:** Concerts in Cincinnati. **17:** Fly to Hollywood. **November 10:** I.S. completes the *Exaudi*. **27, 29:** I.S. records his *Cantata, Concertino*, etc. **December 10:** We fly to New York. **15:** R.C. conducts in Toronto, Ithaca (17th), and records *Svadebka* in New York (18th).

Paris. A visit to Giacometti. He is thinner than last year, but otherwise looks the same, *i.e.,* like an unmade bed. Apart from the rumpled clothes and dishevelment, his skin is as coriaceous as old luggage, his hair has apparently never been violated by a comb, his fingernail dirt is paleozoic, and his tartared teeth alternate yellow, black, and absentees like the keyboard of a broken harpsichord. But in the street, where he comes to greet us and to see us off, he blends into the *quartier,* and the *blousiers* who pass by talking about food, with *baguettes* under arm, do not even notice him.

His studio is no tidier, but the clutter gives an impression of spareness, like the art it contains. We enter through an alley, whose walls Giacometti has fitted with Renaissance (Della Robbia?) and other low reliefs. The room is small, with a high skylight. We notice the graffiti first, for all of the walls are scratched, scribbled on, painted, like those of a catacomb or cave. Next we are aware of the sculptured figures, a hundred or more of them, it seems, some as small as lead soldiers, others larger than life. A few of them appear to walk about the room, but most are gathered in a corner where their thin gray trunks look like trees after a forest fire. Two others are wrapped in canvas tied with rope, and from time to time Giacometti sprinkles these newest creations from a watering can, as if he were tending flowers.

1965

We sit on a cot after clearing it of paints, bottles, papers, books, sketches, canvases, palettes. (I note that whereas the palettes are blobbed with bright colors, the paintings themselves are all dark gray.) The other furniture consists of a battered table, a potbellied stove, and a small tree which comes up green through the dirty floor like a medieval miracle. His paintings, all in great need of dusting, are turned to the wall; nor will he show them to us except very reluctantly and while supplying a running commentary on the degree of failure in each: *"Je n'ai pas réussi . . . je dois travailler . . . c'est mauvais, ça . . . toujours la même chose, chaque fois la même."* And he almost succeeds in convincing us, for the uniformity in the portraits of seated people and in the sculptures of walking men *is* a bit stultifying. He withholds the shrug of failure, in fact, only for a sheaf of pencil portraits of Matisse done in 1954, even owning, or almost, that one or two of them might actually be acceptable. "Matisse was a difficult subject," he says. "He hated to pose and would give me only two minutes at a go. And to make it even more difficult, he kept telling me as I worked that nobody knows how to draw any more: 'I can't draw, Giacometti, and certainly *you* can't,' he would say, and of course he was right. He knew he was dying, and said he regretted it because he needed twenty more years to accomplish his work." A dozen times during the visit Giacometti interrupts himself or ourselves to remark *"C'est curieux, ça,"* about something which does not seem at all curious to me. Shortly before we leave he pours scotch for us from a bottle with a whiskey label, but the drinks taste like turpentine.

Henri Michaux for lunch. His eyes are so striking—a little exophthalmic, a little too high up and close together, a little oriental ("like two jewels in a Chinese idol," I.S. says, and *"Il n'y a que des yeux dans ce visage"*)—that I hardly remember his other features. I do recall light red, dandelion-fluffy brows, however, but only because the cranium is otherwise so entirely molted; and something rodent-like about the forehead and mouth only because benevolent rodents are so rare. For Michaux is a polymath mouse; a mouse that sits on its hind legs and clasps the table with long, white, very clean paws; a mouse out of *Alice,* intellectually superior to ourselves both naturally and by experience. And, as one would expect, such an extraordinary creature emits an extraordinary laugh, the most serious, most thoughtful laugh I have ever heard. It also offers an incidental dental survey that proves him to be a chrysostomos in the literal as well as the poetic sense.

Do his gray flannels and blue sports jacket express a desire for a way of life that his shyness and claustrophobia—"In airplanes I look at my watch all the time and wonder when my head is going to explode"—will not allow him to lead? When he is unfolding an idea, in any case, a different character emerges, as if the machinery were being removed from automatic controls, and when mescaline is mentioned, his phrasemaking is both more rapid and more novel. One of the joys of this drug is that "While the thing outside you, the thing you have made, becomes greater, you yourself become more and more detached from it. As the lines in your drawing begin to seem more important to you, so you forget about your own importance, and the result is that you feel *royalement bien.*" But I.S. takes issue with this, saying that he has no wish to leave himself outside or behind, and that detachment does not attract him. Whereupon Michaux graciously provides him with the counter-argument. "It is true that life has difficulties enough without adding new ones. That, after all, was Balzac's stand against drugs, and it may be preferred to Baudelaire's drug-taking for literary exploitation." But Michaux's use of the word "understanding" during mescaline intoxication raises another demurral from I.S. "I prefer thinking to understanding, for thinking is active and continuous, like composing, while to understand is to bring to an end."

Proposing a new category of "superbly boring literature," Michaux says he would award the palm to Proust's letters. "The ennui is really masterfully composed." From Proust he turns to Lou Andreas-Salomé, who "could wiggle her shoulder in a way to imply that Nietzsche"—he pronounces it to rhyme with pizza—"was somewhere within. She used geniuses like make-up, wearing Freud like a face powder, showing off Rilke as if he were a new kind of lipstick. She was a flaming redhead, and when I first met her was stoking a blaze in her fireplace which exactly matched the color of her hair. She talked about Rilke then, until after a while it occurred to her to inquire about my own profession. I will never forget that look of disbelief when I said that *I* was a poet. But what a temperament she had! *Une femme ravagée, mais ardente, ardente!"* And as he goes on to imitate her Russian accent, I wonder if his obvious sensitivity to accents is owing to his own Belgian one, for he does not gargle his "r's" in the way that Parisians do.

Talk about Tibet and a recent trip to Katmandu lifts him to the day's highest pitch of excitement. "How primitive and empty we are—Americans, Russians, Europeans—in comparison with these people, though next to a Montagnard, even the Hindus are hysterics. And what a *maîtrise* of philosophy and psychology they have attained, and not only in their tantras but also in their lives. You feel, with them, that they are simply waiting for us to grow up to their height." Which is pretty much what *I* feel with Michaux.

Giacometti, come to draw I.S., arrives just as Michaux is leaving, and as they pass each other, the artist compliments the writer on his new paintings. They are amateur work, Michaux says, and Giacometti does not dispute the word, but he confesses that he sees no difference between the paintings done under the influence of mescaline and the others, an observation that earns him the silent study of those two piercing oriental jewels.

After the physical neatness and mental positiveness of Michaux, Giacometti is almost too extreme a contrast. For the artist is obsessed, if not with his failure, at least with the idea of his failure. And the conviction that he will fail yet again is apparently a necessary goad for each new attempt. His talk, in the main, is a nervous patter of questions, *"Eh?" "N'est-ce pas?" "Non?" "Vous croyez?" "Ce n'est pas vrai?",* which he accompanies by tapping his nicotine-stained fingers on the tablecloth and turning his very kind light brown eyes in a restless search from face to face. *"J'ai beaucoup travaillé mais la sculpture est là, et je reste toujours là,"* he says, tracing two areas on a napkin to show how he cannot bring them together.

Preparing to draw, he sheds his jacket, thereby exposing several inches of underpants overlapping the soiled blue shirt above the belt line, the belt itself having missed at least half of the loops. He then rolls up his sleeves and with the blade of a small pocket knife whittles several hard-lead pencils to fine points. Proposing to practice on me before trying I.S., he explains that, just as a pianist must wind or unwind a piano stool to exactly the right height, so for him the main problem is in finding the exact distance. In fact, he works very close to me, but shifts positions twice. When I ask whether he would like more light, the answer is that the light is immaterial to him. "If we change it, it would only be different, but not easier or better." He takes a sheet of slightly rough paper, adjusts his spectacles, folds his right leg over the left, peers into my face. *"Je ne vois rien,"* he says, not very flatteringly, then: *"Je suis complètement incapable . . . je suis à zéro . . . je dois recommencer . . . je me trouve toujours devant la même difficulté et je ne peux rien faire."*

Finally deciding to take the plunge, he begins to draw, looking rapidly back and forth from my face to his paper, about three dozen times in all. He talks incessantly; and we are a little like the loquacious dentist and the gagged patient, for if *I* talk or budge, he will destroy the drawing. He works at great speed and makes almost no erasures, but the moment he finishes, exclamations of failure pour out in a torrent: *"Mais, c'est mauvais, ça . . . c'est mal fait . . ."* When *not* drawing, he chain-smokes (Camels)—ashes falling where they may—and his cigarette cough could be studied for extra realistic effect by even the most accomplished of Mimis and Violettas. After completing two drawings of me, he starts on I.S., who steers him to the subject of Picasso. *"Il m'étonne,"* says Giacometti, *"il m'étonne comme un monstre, et je crois qu'il connaît aussi bien que nous qu'il est monstre."* Two very fine portraits are achieved during this one-way conversation.

MAY 17

Vevey. I.S. conducts a search "on camera" (CBS-TV) for the *pension* in Clarens where he composed most of *Le Sacre du printemps,* though Les Tilleuls, as the residence is called, was already tracked down during a rehearsal excursion yesterday, and is well known locally in any case. But whereas yesterday's experience very obviously affected him—to judge by his blindman's buff directions to the driver and the general fuddle in his usually infallible memory for this sort of thing (he has no recollection of having shown the house to me in October 1951)—he seems calm today returning to his old home, and unafraid of whatever peeps into the past the visit might hold in store.

In spite of the plural name, the entrance, 51 rue Gambetta, at the intersection with the avenue des Châtelards, is shaded by a single linden. Entering the *pension,* I.S. is allowed to climb one floor too high before the CBS men direct him back to the *première étage* where, thanks to their fieldwork, one buzz of the doorbell admits him to his old lodgings. He goes at once from room to room impatiently looking for his quondam studio, but soon announces it is not here and that therefore this is the wrong apartment. At which point CBS springs its coup, a red-nosed and frumpish old lady, Madame Louise Rambert, who actually lived in the building at the same time as I.S. and has never changed her address since. Madame Rambert fusses her way in, alarmed and confounded by the TV cameras, the powerful lights, the sound equipment, and the crew who, in full gear, standing by for a Stanley and Livingstone scene, *do* look as if they might be part of a Martian invasion. When the old lady sees I.S., her voice chokes and she is on the verge of bursting into tears, except that the explosion takes the form of volubility instead, a cascade of memories from which there seems to be no prospect of shelter. And I.S., though usually contemptuous of anyone who allows the past to obtrude in the present, is obviously deeply interested in, and moved by, the old lady's recollections.

The two of them sit in an alcove with a view, down the hill, of La

1965

Pervenche, another of I.S.'s homes; and beyond that, and below some railroad tracks, to the site of yet another residence, the former Hôtel du Châtelard; I.S. recalls that work on *Le Sacre* was interrupted each morning by a train and that he used to wait for it with hatred and baited nerves. Still farther below is Lac Léman.

The old lady says that Madame Stravinsky did her hair in a bun, and that she and her children were always very wan and sickly. I.S., she continues, spent all day in his studio, which was on the *rez-de-chaussée,* though he denies this, maintaining that it was on the same floor as the apartment. When Madame Rambert reminds him of some fellow tenants of the time, among them a German ex-admiral and an Austrian countess, he himself supplies additional details about these people. Madame Rambert, of course, would like the CBS crew to know that the address had aristocratic as well as artistic tenants once, partly by way of apology for the present occupants of I.S.'s old apartment, a family of migratory workers from Spain. She recalls, too, that the other residents used to complain that "Monsieur Stravinsky plays only wrong notes," which, however, does not amuse I.S., who returns in a heat to the charge of 1911: "The wrong notes for them, but the right ones for me."

1965

Eventually Madame Rambert leads a disbelieving and protesting I.S. downstairs to the room she assures him was his studio. And this time recognition is immediate. His face floods with pleasure, entering this amazingly tiny and constricting room, reminders of long-dead friends and loved ones being pushed aside by reminders of the creation of a masterpiece. He walks to a sofa, exactly as he says he used to do fifty-four years ago, and, sitting there, tells us and the U.S. television audience that he was fully aware at the time that he was "writing something important." In fact, he inscribed some words to the effect that *Le Sacre* was composed here, on the inside door of the closet—nicked them out with a knife, like a schoolboy's declaration of love on a tree, as I have heard him say on other occasions, when, too, he has said that the verb was active ("I am composing"). We look for this carved autograph, but the incumbent of the apartment, Madame Carrel, says that the door was relined a decade ago and that she knows of no one who would be able to say whether the signature had been found on the former surface.

It is wondrous that *Le Sacre* was born here, that such power—I picture I.S. at the piano with handfuls of volts—was unleashed in this dingy cubbyhole. (Does the room resemble his childhood bedchamber in St. Petersburg? It is exactly the sort of room, in any case, claustrophobic to me, that he loves, and not only loves but compulsively needs, to crowd still more with the objects and artifacts that to him signify order.) But the wonder is also in the neighborhood, in the townsmen with whom I.S. was rubbing elbows, and in those fellow boarders, the admiral, the countess, Madame Rambert herself, and, at one time, just down the street, Maurice Ravel and his Basque-speaking mother. How, in this torpid village, which was also the scene of *La Nouvelle Héloïse,* did I.S., or the powers that mediate, manage to keep the fuse to his taproots so directly, fully, and perfectly open? But then, the same question might be asked in connection with Schoenberg's *Moses,* part of which was composed at Territet, only a little farther down the lake; and of *Tristan und Isolde,* that most un-Swiss flood of passion, which was brought forth not so many kilometers from here.

When I.S. departs, the old lady, now in a high state of emotion, gives him an ink-press *cliché* of Les Tilleuls and begins to weep; her moment has come and gone, the witness has been called, the content of waiting emptied. But the encounters of the morning must have run an even more difficult course for I.S. What the "universal eye" of television has tried to do is to rub his nose in former emotion in the hope that he would be able to say what it is "like," though of course he cannot say, but can only repeat conditioned answers a little differently, changing a bead here and there in the mosaic of semi-fictions out of which "true" history is composed. Ultimately, too, ghosts, souvenirs, and even the opening of tombs may be less hard than the realization that the fifty-four intervening years have produced no composition to equal the one composed here, this at any rate being the weight of opinion behind the promiscuous lens that has been prying down on him all morning, focusing on *Le Sacre* of all his life work.

1965

MAY 23

Paris to Warsaw in a Caravelle, which I board through the rear door like stuffing going into a turkey. My first glimpse of Poland is of lettuce-colored fields, thin strips of newly plowed land, and a highway without traffic which must have looked the same forty years ago. The closer the view the more skeptical I am of the stewardess's promise that Warsaw is "a gay city," though it could be that with her along. Did she notice an effect on me of the other passengers, all of them returning Poles and every face an advertisement of how grim life in Poland must be?

The airport porters find me worthy of sustained curiosity, but this is regrettably not the case with the girl from the PAGART agency sent to nursemaid me through customs and currency control. A veritable Berlin Wall of indifference and *sang-froid,* she selects certain of my questions to answer, but shoves the others aside as if I had simply not asked them. Except for a few brick and tile-roof prewar buildings, and some barrack-style postwar ones, the road to the city is lined mainly with empty or rubble-filled lots. The Warsaw skyline itself is dominated by the tower of the Palace of Science and Culture, which so resembles one of the towers of Moscow University that I am misled to expect a city with Russian-style architectural features.

The Europejsky Hotel—the name seems to suggest that Europe is somewhere else—is modern with respect to date and the intention of its conveniences, but it is so bleak and institutional that I expect to hear the clank of a lock and chain after crossing the threshold. While Miss Permafrost enrolls me at Reception (and probably with SMERSH as well), I wait in

267

the restaurant, which is as large as a city block in Peoria, and as square. Nor do the potted palmettos standing at lonely intervals around the room conjure any atmospheric benefits of southern seas, or serve any other decorative purpose that I can discover. Are they bugged?

The menu, on the other hand, *is* exotic, but linguistically rather than in the actual promise of culinary delights, one of which is "gravy soup." The foreigner orders by reading translations in any of four languages and pointing to the Polish equivalents, for none of the waiters is able to speak more than a word or two of any other tongue. This is surprising, at first, in view of the wartime diaspora, but as the room staff proves to be just as crampingly monolingual, the reason must be attributed to "security." One built-in defect of this pointing system is the lack of allowance for variable detail ("Can you bring mine without the sauce?"), but a more serious difficulty is that most of the dishes listed do not exist. No fruit of any kind is available, not only no Viet Cong pineapple and Cuban cantaloupe (lots of Cuban crystal sugar, though, or is it ground glass?), but even no Polish cherries or grapes. Each dish is priced by weight, as caviar used to be priced in Western restaurants. Thus, so and so many *zlotis* will buy 38.08 *og*s (grams) of beans or 15.29 *og*s of jello. Miss P. recommends ham, and advisedly; in fact, after only a few experiments I resolve to stick to a Gadarene diet for the duration. The wine, a Bulgarian off-white with the consistency of mineral oil, is served with a towel tied around the neck of the bottle like a flapper's scarf in the twenties. The dessert is a plate of almonds in a dune of hot salt.

I accompany Miss P. on a tour of inspection of the I.S.'s suite, now being readied for their arrival Tuesday. Its vast and cavernous living room could well be, at other times, the main meeting place of the Central Committee of the Party Presidium. The only furnishings are a round table with six straight-backed chairs and a huge painting of a naval disaster. When I reckon aloud that the ceiling must be forty feet high, Miss P. provides the exact information. "The entire apartment is above a hundred square meters," she says, in a special tone of achievement and as if we intended to spend our spare time flying toy airplanes. But rentals *are* determined by spatial volume, just as foods are priced by weight. "This is because of the inspectors," Miss P. adds, but without explaining who these mysterious people are, or otherwise developing this promisingly Gogolian, or Scotland Yard, theme.

But I must stop saying "Miss P." She has a beautiful name, Jolanta (the "J" pronounced as a "Y," as in Spenser's "His sports were faire, his ioyance innocent"), and is herself, by very evident attractions, deserving of more personal, in fact full-scale, attention. She is tall, strawberry blonde—when at last she removes an absurd Andean-Indian woman's bowler—and very fair of complexion. But her light brown eyes are afflicted with a slight strabismus—of which she is overconscious, trying to find an angle to conceal it when she talks—and her fingers are nibbled at the tips like a pianist's, which they probably are, as they seem to be performing piano exercises wherever they alight. Finally, her manners are ladylike and pre-proletarian, which sets her apart. I suspect a deep romantic temperament beneath the capping of *froideur* she is showing me, but a de-brainwashing would be necessary to prove it—though that, come to think of it, could be an agreeable assignment. Yet one thing puzzles me: her quick and open expression of dislike for everything Russian. Is it to draw me out, a part of the East-West game? I think not, but if she is a stooge, congratulations to the Party on such a beautiful one. If only she would lose that New-Year's-party hat!

My room is a different matter. It is mascot-sized—its measurements could best be expressed in *ogs*—and might have been chosen by a status-conscious capitalist. After squeezing through the door, I see that to "stay flat in bed" would be an impossibility, though a heavy comforter has been folded over the middle of the mattress to disguise the fact. Of the lights, the one on the ceiling hums E above middle C loud enough to cushion the explosions produced by passing tramcars; and the reading lamp, which has the strength of one aged lightning bug, is remote from the bed, even when its strangling length of wire—if it should come to that—is stretched to the full.

Strolling alone on the Nowy Swiat, later in the afternoon, I enter the Church of the Order of the Visitation, attracted by its Venetian façade; Warsaw is an Italianate city even now, at least at first glance in the direction of its church architecture. The church is surprisingly crowded; and I find full congregations in three other churches, too, all with fairly large sprinklings of young men in cassocks and calottes. Does the West underestimate the Church, I wonder? One forgets that even the radical agrarian reform program of the National Liberation Committee of 1944 did not apply to Church-owned estates. Clerical habit is more common in the streets here, in any case, than in any other European city except Rome or Dublin.

And sidewalk traffic, in other ways as well, is much less drab than it is in the political parent, Russia. A type of trench-coated, beretted, and brief-case-carrying pedestrian is endemic here, as he is in Moscow, but the quality of these accouterments is at least marginally better here; and Warsaw—though I should have begun with it—is bountiful in good-looking women.

The window of a bookstore on the Nowy Swiat contains a large display of photographs of death and devastation resulting from U.S. air raids in North Vietnam. But compared with some of the protestations to the same purpose currently decorating the walls of Paris, it is mild and inconspicuous, and less damaging to the U.S. "image" hereabouts, I would think, than some of its own propaganda pictures of the apple-pie-eating spouses and base-ball-playing progeny of the latest astronauts.

Two American exchange students, here to study cinematography, take me to dinner in the Club for Film Artists and Writers, a prewar building, I assume, though it is difficult to distinguish the restored from the genuinely old. The women here, the waitresses no less than the actresses, are strikingly handsome, with auburn hair, milky skins, high bosoms, the dark eyes of

269

Maria Walewska. Best of all, the American students confirm the French air hostess: Warsaw *is* a "fun" city, they say, and the "loosest" in Europe.

MAY 24

Jolanta, this morning, is unable to conceal her annoyance because of my unchaperoned sortie to the Film Club, and she goes so far as to request particulars of other places visited and of people met. Is she required to fill out a report, I ask, but with that her tone changes, and back we go to the superior nursemaid of yesterday. It is now becoming clear that if we are to act out a charade, she as Ninotchka, myself as "the American," then the rule of the game will be that the more serious she is, the more I will be obliged to laugh. But is the plot also beginning to resemble *Ninotchka* the play? Flirting with her, in any case, could easily become involuntary.

Arriving for rehearsal in the concert hall on Henryka Sienkiewicza Street, I am shown to a dressing room whose furnishings include a portrait of Artur Rubinstein's father-in-law (Emil Mlynarski, founder of the Warsaw Philharmonic) and a clock with a heavily premonitory tick and a minute hand that jerks like a taxi meter. The conductor, Witold Rowicki, introduces me to the orchestra, then delivers me to one of those mysterious "inspectors," a panjandrum who announces the order of the pieces to be rehearsed and calls the intermissions, during which everyone drinks tea, Russian style, from a glass. I address the musicians in English which the concert master translates, prefacing each remark, before relaying it, with the Polish for "colleagues." At one point a player voices a question in German and I answer it in that language. This causes a commotion: will I please continue in German, as more than half of the orchestra understands it, whereas no one knows more than a word or two of English or French; and from then on we communicate in the language of the wartime invader, a fact no one seems to feel as an irony.

The players are willing, patient, good-humored, slow; but I, too, am slow—to adjust to their radically different scale of time, which is that they are not going anywhere and have lots of it, and that I have a date in Paris next week and am in a hurry. They play with energy and passion, but their instruments are poor in quality, their mode of attack is not well or uniformly defined, and their ears are innocent of any training in intonation. (I.S. has often remarked that in the first decades of the century little attention was paid to intonation even in the best orchestras of western Europe, let alone eastern.) In view of the holocaust that took place here, however, it is a wonder that an orchestra exists at all, and a miracle that it is such a good one.

Lazienki Park, where I walk with Jolanta in a light rain, is surrounded by the kind of wrought-iron fences that were melted into the war effort elsewhere; were the Nazis never short of scrap metal? The semi-wild beauty of the park is contradicted only by the professional nut-begging of a large population of red squirrels. But the romantic trappings, the ghostly palace

1965

swaddled in mist, the swan lake, the forest of tall larches, poplars, beeches, firs, have no outward effect on Ninotchka. Her only emotion, so far as I can see, is patriotism, the colors of which, in the little lecture she delivers in front of a monument to Chopin, are as bright as the Polish flag. This is an official stroll, she seems to say, and I must not expect her to exceed her office by a whit or a word.

Taxis are not plentiful in Warsaw, and most of the few that exist would have been declared unfit, even in 1914, for General Gallieni's trip to the Marne. As all drivers are empowered to sell taxi service, we hire a ride back to the hotel with one of the beret-and-briefcase types.

I go with Jolanta to an evening rehearsal by the National Ballet of *Le Sacre du printemps,* in the not-yet-finished—there are no seats!—Teatr Wielki. This is said to be the largest opera house in the world, but the less said about its other qualities, especially of architectural imagination, which gave out near the level of the basement, the better. The *Sacre* choreography is of the so-called kinesthetic variety, but with odd alien touches. Thus the "adolescents" imitate ponies, and their dance alternately suggests a school of equitation and a Western, except that the Indians do not actually whoop. Thus, too, hands tremble over heads in *Spring Rounds,* I think to suggest sprouts on the way up. And this sort of thing, *i.e.,* tying the music to something not essentially musical instead of leaving it to its own description, can soon reduce even *Le Sacre du printemps* to gag music. The triviality of these exterior associations is obvious, but isn't *any* visual complement, accompaniment, commentary to a piece as powerful as the *Danse de la terre* bound to be absurd? The ballet ends with the *Elue,* one of those tender shoots, falling on her back where she writhes, curls, and grinds as the male audience would want her to do in bed.

MAY 25

I have been trying to picture the ruins of Warsaw at the end of the war, but Cibrowski's *Warsaw, Its Destruction and Reconstruction,* which I receive today, does the job for me horribly well. Photographs of the rubble heaps of 1945 are on facing pages with photographs of the same sites from exactly the same angles today; and it is apparent from these comparisons that the feat of reconstruction here far surpasses that of any other city, German, Dutch, and Russian included. But to look at this book is to lose the power of criticism and to come away feeling guilty for ridiculing not only the new architecture, as I have done, but anything whatever.

The book does not include a photograph of the prewar Ghetto (or is this a tautology, in that a postwar Ghetto does not exist?). But if the enormity of the crime against the Ghetto is unimaginable, one nevertheless has some sense of it simply because nothing stands in its place, the site now being an empty square formed by slab-style apartment houses. Of the largest home of the Jews in Europe, however, no trace is to be found. A monument has been erected, a prismoid pile of black granite flanked by black marble

Menorahs which, to remind the world that the Jews of Warsaw chose to die fighting, are sustained by pairs of rampant Maccabean lions. The monument itself contains an unfortunate attempt to depict the murder of the Ghetto, a sculptured relief of resisting people, all impossibly heroic—as if anything so monstrous could be represented in a vignette tableau, even a good one. (What should be erected here is a candelabrum of seven eternal flames.) Someone has chalked the figure 6,000,000 on the base of the stone, and as I stand looking at it an old woman in black, leaning on a small boy, slowly makes her way up to it, kneels, and spreads a handful of posies under the six circles.

Later, I question Jolanta about the Jewish population of Poland today; announcements in Hebrew can be seen on the kiosks in the Nowy Swiat, a play by Isaac Babel is on the local boards, and a few dishes on the hotel menu are described as Jewish, though one wonders whether there are Jews to eat them. But all she will say is that "We make no distinctions," and her pretty face turns poker. Then suddenly, unasked, she tells me that "Polish youth have no sense of belief that such things as Oświȩçim really happened"—and this, no doubt, is true, for what else is the failure of history? (V. says that the Poles she knew in her childhood never used the word "Hebrew," but only the contemptuous "Zhid"; she also recalls a childhood visit to the Warsaw Ghetto with her father, saying that it was famous for its beautiful women.)

Jolanta is changing, nevertheless, and I suspect that in no great time and with no undue pressure the Ninotchka carapace can be penetrated and even crumbled entirely. The first crack in it, still hardly visible on the outer edifice, is that she has begun to show strong feelings, if only feelings of national pride. She is no mercenary, then, and if a bureaucrat, at least one with a soul for the job. What she wishes to bring about, the cause she is working for even through me, is the cultural autonomy of Poland and a new *Regnum Poloniae* of the arts. And I offend her most, I have been slow to realize, when I fail to distinguish the Polish from the Russian in that, to me, gray area where the two seem to shade into each other. In remark after remark I have implicitly blanketed the Slav under the Russian, and consistently failed to identify that which for her is so vividly individual; and I am aware of this even now only because she is so quick to correct me. It embarrasses me now that I ever could have questioned the ingenuousness of her Polish sentiments and suspected her animadversion to the U.S.S.R. of being simulated. Big Brother *is* listening, of course—we may already have swallowed detector capsules, and the chauffeur and the waiter could very well be governmental gumshoes—but not through Jolanta's attractive antennae, not at any rate in the way I at first assumed.

Patriotism and the suppression of feelings to duties exact their price in a woman, however, a price of femininity, usually, though that, too, may be a planned part of the job—to keep a quarry at bay. Jolanta, in any case, needs an eye-do and a hair-do for a start. But what rules has she been given concerning me, I wonder? Surely it is unintentional that her lips open farther outward and more flower-like pronouncing English (she now addresses me as "yourthelf") than Polish, and as surely she cannot be completely unaware that the result is a tempting, if somewhat graceless, pucker.

For I.S.'s arrival this afternoon, CBS has asked the Ministry of Culture to "lay on a gay crowd, if possible in regional costume." But the request is turned down with the explanation that "Poles are not a gay people." "What about the Polonaise and the Mazurka?" CBS comes back, but the Ministry will not be drawn into a more specific definition of the national temperament, which, after all, is nowadays a question of ideology. (Whether "gay" is the word, and the larger question of "Poles" apart, the people of Warsaw seem to me remarkably cheerful and light-humored.)

Cameras crackle like a pine-woods fire when I.S. leaves the plane. But as he steps to the ground there are signs of a bibulous lunch. Soggy with Polish vodka as he proves in fact to be, however—does he mistake the TV men poking their light meters in his face for breathalyzing traffic cops?—his happy-to-be-here speech manages to say all of the right things.

The I.S.'s are hardly out of the airport before they begin to react to the Poles as Russians of fifty years ago might have done, and a few minutes of conversation are enough to revive the national prejudices of their youth. These amount to something like the so-called natural Russian anti-Semitism, of which the richest examples are in Dostoievsky and Rozanov, though if I remember correctly Dostoievsky's anti-Polish sentiments are hardly less strong. (Doesn't Dmitri Karamazov denounce someone as a "typical cheating Pole"?) I.S., in any case, recalls Russian expressions mocking "Polish" pomposity, and "Polish" servility and obsequiousness—which V. describes as especially dripping: "I am already on my knees" or "Already prostrate before you" ("*Padom do nog ooshe lezhoo*")—while the hypocrisy of the Poles, both I.S. and V. aver, exceeds even that of the Viennese, whose alleged failings, or successes, in this field are so famous. And no doubt these attributions are true to a degree, for how could the character of a people with a thousand years of that geopolitical background, or non-ground, *not* develop in these directions?

V. asks Jolanta about changes in the language, which before the war still employed the polite form of the second person and was therefore well suited to the fawning and the niceties the I.S.'s have been ridiculing. Her answer, which is that the spoken language has been greatly vulgarized since 1945, puts her firmly on the side of the *ancien régime*. And at this I.S. confesses that "To Russian ears, Polish sounds like a comical *argot*, full of mal-apropisms or, if not that, of closely related but strangely off-target words, like saying of a good perfume that it stinks." The transliterations on the dinner menu amuse the I.S.'s, too, but when they speak Russian to the room waiter, who looks like Nijinsky, except for Boris Karloff bangs, *he* laughs,

1965

273

too, so the exchange evidently works both ways. And some laughter, at this point, is welcome for whatever reason, V., after a stroll through the lobby, having announced her intention of "staying in bed until the plane to Paris."

MAY 26

The orchestra does not know how to greet I.S. when he appears in the auditorium at my rehearsal today. Some of the players applaud, some stand, some remain seated, but all hesitate until Maestro Rowicki gives them a signal, at which they leap to their feet and give forth with a genuine, if too-late-to-be-spontaneous, ovation. This uncertainty followed by late but fervid action is interpreted by V. as an example of the effect on the Polish character of historical habits of palliation. She claims, moreover, that I.S. shares this character, that it is a mark of—as she says with no great fondness for it—his Polish side. "Thus when I ask whether he would prefer this or that and he says, 'I don't know, what would *you* prefer?' I recognize the voice of his Polish ancestors." And not only do I see what she means, but I also think I am now able to see wherein some of his manners are more Polish than Russian, and whereby the almost over-politeness marking him out in Moscow three years ago was more than a question of czarist *versus* commissariat styles.

1965

In fact, we soon *do* hear some of those voices, in the persons of relatives, cousins-german every one, so they pretend, for people named Strawinsky are swarming to him like a gathering of the clans. But the name *is* said to be common here, and the letters and calling cards piling up with the concierge—telephone directories do not exist—are proof of it. A distant female cousin, heavily armed with family photograph albums, calls on him during lunch today, but though he claims to recognize some of the faces in her files, we correctly deduce, when she pulls him out of earshot, that genealogical research is a lesser object of her visit than *zlotis*. One *bona fide* relative is Dr. Konstanty Strawinski, the director of the Zoological Institute of the University Marie-Curie Sklodowska in Lublin; but he has contented himself with a letter.

Another correspondent, but no kin, is the poet Anatol Stern, who encloses a reprint of an interview that he conducted with I.S. in the Warsaw Bristol Hotel in 1925. In it the ill-humor of both I.S. and V.—indiscreetly identified as a "Russian lady-friend"—with Warsaw, the hotel, and the interviewer himself comes through saliently and characteristically, though not, apparently, to Mr. Stern. Still another letter, from the daughter of I.S.'s family doctor in Ustilug, reminisces about I.S. at Ustilug in her youth. This Dr. Backnitsky was a friend and correspondent of the Marxist philosopher Plekhanov, whose letters I.S. also read, "as they were written in an unusually intelligible German." Regularly, since the war, I.S. has sent money to the doctor's daughter.

I drive with Jolanta to Chopin's birthplace at Zelazowa Wola. The road is brick-paved for about half the way, and better suited to the wagon traffic of the time of its construction than to automobiles. We pass trough-shaped carts, horsedrawn but with rubber tires of heavy trucks, as if the mechanization process had broken down after this first step. No farm machinery is in evidence, but only hand implements, yet most of the low-lying thatched-roof houses along the road have TV aerials. Jolanta says that much of the land in the region is privately owned. And, she adds, a few privately owned restaurants survive, too, "the only good ones in Poland," though everyone expects these mavericks to be taxed out of existence.

The Zelazowa Wola relics are unremarkable—a plaster cast of the composer's left hand, some nursery chairs and other petite furniture, manuscripts of juvenilia—but the STEINWAY stenciled in large white letters on the grand piano ("Chopin's choice"?) *is* surprising in a country so wholly without advertising. The attractions of the place are the sylvan walks and a willow-washed stream. But these fail to work any spell on Jolanta, who is doubly careful today to treat me as an assignment. And in any case, Poland having a pluvial climate, we are soon running from torrential, after four days of merely heavy, rains. I note that the Poles do not like to hear the name of their national musical idol pronounced as if he were a Frenchman.

Back in Warsaw we attend a reception by the Union of Composers at their home in the Rynek Starego Miasta, which is in the heart of the old city—or, more precisely, of the rebuilt old city, for it was pulverized during the insurrection of 1944. Since then, every edifice has been reproduced in replica, the Rynek (market) again being recognizable from Canaletto. Much as one is compelled to admire the spirit behind the rebuilding, however, these five-year-old medieval houses, in which even the creak of the ancient floorboards has been restored, are as eery as a movie set. I prefer the new city, no matter how ugly.

The composers are shy, hospitable, well informed—as people who stay home and read *are* well informed. And their pride and patriotism are on a par with Jolanta's; one of them tells me that though Moszkowski may not have been any great shakes as a composer (no argument), "he *was* Polish." Again and again I.S. is asked for details about Szymanowski, whose *Stabat Mater,* written in the shadow of the *Symphony of Psalms,* is thought hereabouts to compare not unfavorably with it; but Szymanowski was more V.'s friend than I.S.'s, and she has not come to the party. Before deciding on the Polish trip, I.S. feared he would be "kidnaped by the official musicians and the academics of the older generation." And to some extent this might have happened; none of the younger progressives, not Penderecki, Serocki, Baird, Gorecki, or even Lutoslawski (whose *Three Poems by Henri Michaux* is Polish music's current pop-modern display piece) is present.[1] But official-dom *is* conservative, and a guest of I.S.'s stature could hardly expect to escape it. I nonetheless regret the absence in this group of any of those representatives of the musical renaissance—composers, conductors, instru-

---

1. We learned later that they were attending a modern music festival in Germany.

275

mentalists—who have not only enriched Poland but brought it world prestige. And if I emphasize the latter it is for the reason that while the Polish arts movement may have come into being in protest against the Stalinist East, yet it is the Western export business that they—Grotowski, Penderecki, the writers and film directors—have most eagerly sought.

Speaking for myself, too, I would like to hear something from any of the group about the music of the Jagiellonian Dynasty, about the influence of Marenzio in Cracow, etcetera; and I would like to hear from unabashed living lips (except that they could only be abashed ones) more of the Marxist interpretation of Renaissance culture as propounded in the State Publisher's luxuriously embellished editions of early Polish music. In *Music of the Polish Renaissance,* for instance, "ideological progress" is equated with "the democratic current of homophonic structure," and "the abandonment of forms for the select few in favor of simpler but more expressive types." And in *A Thousand Years of Polish History,* published in 1964, "the flourishing of Romanesque art" is attributed to, of all things, "social and ideological fermentation." Now it seems to me that if the phenomenon of art can be accounted for by any circumstances other than the appearance of talent, then Poland today is an argument for the theory that great suffering provokes strong feelings and that these feelings *might* at least be artistically fertile. But no one, abashed or otherwise, will tangle with that very unprogressive idea.

Toasts are proposed—in French, the language of most of the conversation—each one ending *"Vive Stra-win-ski!"* I.S., toasting the Union in turn, strays into politics, and even begins to castigate Russia, blaming her for the largest share of Poland's miseries. He has taken for granted that his audience is anti-Russian, as Poles generally were in his youth. Twice, too, he refers to the Iron Curtain, and both times one can fairly hear the creak of those new-old floorboards.

1965

MAY 27

The Cleveland Orchestra, on its way home from the U.S.S.R., rehearses this morning just before we do. And what a contrast to the Warsaw Phil.! The American ensemble seems nearly perfect, the playing so polished and refined, and above all so beautifully in tune—the notes sitting squarely in the center of the pitch, whereas with the Warsaw Phil. they tend to circle around it, trapeze-like. Yet we have become accustomed to the Poles, even to the extent that the efficiency and finesse of the Clevelanders are working inverse returns, actually making us feel somewhat fond of those very crudities in the Warsaw Orchestra which the Cleveland machine has been at such pains to steamroller out.

Appeals to the Soviet embassies in Washington and Warsaw, as well as directly to Madame Furtseva in Moscow, have failed, and we learn today that permission for I.S. to visit his old home in Ustilug will not be forthcoming. Ustilug is in a pink zone, automatically off bounds to foreigners.

We had hoped for permission, nevertheless, as the reasons for the zoning, according to the Poles, are not military but economic. The neighborhood is reputed to be poor and squalid, with many people poorly clothed and shod; understandably the Russians prefer to keep such places swept under the carpet, or at any rate not advertise them on American television.

From 1919 to 1939 Ustilug was a hundred miles or so within Polish territory. At some time during the latter part of that period, I.S. managed to sell a part of his land there to the Polish government through his relative, Grigory Beliankin, who visited I.S.'s former estate. But when the Soviet Union annexed eastern Poland up to, approximately, the Curzon Line—in effect moving the whole country a hundred miles to the west—Ustilug came out on the Soviet side of the new frontier by the margin of the Bug River. I.S. has received letters from actual and would-be[1] visitors to the village since the war, and photographs of his home there have appeared in both Russian and German publications. But Warsaw is as close as he will come to it again himself.

1965

In the course of a conversation with a young Polish writer about the comedies of Alexander Fredro, I learn that Joseph Conrad is widely read here and that Polish translations of him are "well redacted." Interest has revived in the work of Conrad's father, Apollo Korzeniowski, too, and only last year his play *For the Love of Money* was produced in Warsaw with considerable success. Korzeniowski was as enamored of the English and French languages as his son, and he became an expert translator from both; in fact, two of Shakespeare's plays are performed here exclusively in the versions by Conrad *père*. Then, quite by accident, the talk turns to politics, and my young acquaintance reveals himself as a neo-orthodox Marxist. To him, history is a kind of Gulf Stream, a steady current flowing in a fixed direction. Moreover, the travel time to any point in this current, meaning to any point in the past or from the past to the present, is equal, and involves no awkward apparatus of cultural contexts and comparisons. The only factor, and it applies everywhere and unmodified, is the evolution of the Marxist concept. Westerners, he contends, are overconcerned with pattern in history, including, as it may be, the pattern of change. This leads them to discover parallels that are not really parallel, rhymes that do not rhyme. "The

1. "Lublin, December 8, 1968. Dear Mr. Stravinsky, Among your mail will be this modest letter. I decided write you because of my holiday event. On summer this 1968 year I traced your home and your youth on the River Boog and I have heard many good things about your family. It were so: holiday 68 I went to a Polish village on the edge of the River Boog. I lived there and I talked with the old peoples living there. Among others, I have heard about the village on the Russian edge today. The old peoples told me that in this village lived in former times good lords named Stravinskys. They were very kind lords and their fame is living the peoples on both edges of the river. The peoples says that in Stravinskys palace visible on the Russian edge there were great dances and musics of several tens years ago. I heard and I asked many questions so I suppose this is your familiar possession. I am very curious if I am right. I would be very happy to hear your answer. Excuse me for my mistakes with English language. I hope I traced your home place and I would like to know it for myself. Respectfully, Tadeusz Wojnicki."

capitalists still look for a cyclical repetition of the stock market crash," he says, "and they still look for the overthrow of the socialist revolution, after which they expect to return to their old innings." But it is on the subject of corrupt individualism in the West that the young man is most convincing; and it must be admitted that the picture he draws of us, each in his "existential void," is, from here anyway, extremely attractive.

Jolanta's conception of history, on the other hand—as I discover in a late-night conversation, our most intimate so far—is expressed entirely in cultural terms. To begin with, she draws a firm distinction between Slavic and Germanic cultural watersheds. Then, too, she subscribes to the idea that the Soviet Union is simply the contemporary manifestation of Russian history, as Nazism was of German history. Furthermore, she believes that "while nationalism may have declined at the end of the war, owing to the large, Late Roman Empire-type East-West division, it is again more important than ever in the socialist countries." But *is* the East-West fracture so very sharp in Poland, I ask, and she persuades me to "look at the country from the point of view of a middle ground, an Eastern language with a Western alphabet, an Eastern people with a Western church." And what does "the West" mean to her? "Ideas of liberty and democracy, never much cultivated here," she answers, very readily. "Nevertheless, we believe that our socialism is more profoundly democratic in its aims than your democracy."

If Jolanta is changing, so am I. And if we are correctives to each other, the corrective action is also bringing us together. The worm has turned so far, in any case, that I have become almost overly respectful of her Ninotchka seriousness, and correspondingly ashamed of my native inclination to laughter, with its detestable implication of superiority. How embarrassing now to recall my bumptious behavior on arrival, the tactless references to the West, the specious analyses and superficial comments on everything I have seen! Jolanta, at the same time, has somehow become infected with my former laughter; which would be less regrettable if she knew how to laugh, and did not respond so excessively in terms of volume, and were not seduced by only the lowest and most depraved examples of my own "wit." Thus when I inquire about what one does for nighttime amusement in this gay city, the Ninotchka guise instructs me to go to that Stalinoid monster-building, the Palace of Science and Culture, "and look at the Book Fair." But then when I underline the problem—"I mean, what does one do between one and four AM?"—the point is at length seen, the funnybone greatly tickled, and the night air shattered with the reaction. How far, how far will this dangerous transformation go, I wonder, for she is also becoming a little impish and coy, as when, at parting, she bestows a cold peck of *amitié* on each cheek, Slav style, but lets me see that she is well aware of how much more I would prefer the in-between. If she continues to concede at this rate, it will be difficult before long to distinguish the truly adamant from the false.

A shopping expedition, to buy a rug for V. and wine for I.S. Clerking, it seems, is for women only. Another apparent qualification is the ability to maintain a total indifference to customers, for wares are displayed only on request, and then reluctantly, with no effort to engage any interest. This absence of the commercial spirit has a surprisingly depressing effect, too, except that, considering the merchandise, neither party in a buying-selling transaction could be expected to show much exhilaration. In one food store, about fifty people are standing before a clump of what will surely prove too few sausages (*kilbassa*) to go around. And in another an even longer line has formed to buy tins of peanuts "From Hanoi," as the label too pointedly advertises in English. For this second store (in which we find one bottle of Beaujolais) is open to tourists, as well as to Poles, and it is also licensed to accept their *zlotis*, most stores not off-limits to foreigners altogether being designated "for foreign currency only." Hard money is of course avidly coveted by a government desperately trying to keep prices pegged to the international index at the official rate while its own currency is worth six times less unofficially than officially. In fact, the government is said to be so dollar-hungry that the black-market speculators parading like prostitutes between the two "American" hotels are widely suspected of being Treasury Department employees.

1965

The audience at I.S.'s concert tonight has come as much to see a famous live animal as to listen to music. But it is a very gala event, and along with several standing ovations, I.S. receives countless bouquets of carnations in the national colors of red and white. We then go to a post-concert concert, a jazz *jeunesse musicale,* as the American film students call it, neglecting to say that the jazz is not of the grooviest. The audience is good-looking, well dressed (spitcurls and Beatle-type forelocks but no beards), well behaved. During an intermission I am introduced to an older woman who tells me that she "grew up under Stalin and therefore never dreamed of seeing Igor Stravinsky." At this point, a younger girl contributes the only political utterance of the sort I have heard in Poland: "Things were going so well under Khrushchev, but now we are very frightened again."

Oh, you poor stomped-upon Janus-headed Poles—though not even Januses, for as real estate you belong to the East (that watchtower of the Palace of Science and Culture standing over your town) no matter how ardently you pursue the *ignis fatuus* of a middle ground.

A new attitude is immediately noticeable in Jolanta this morning, and from her first words I am aware that she is not being frank. We have hired a car to go to Malbork on Monday, and from the very variety of her arguments against the trip, it is obvious that her superiors have countermanded it. The simple truth, as it later appears, is that they themselves wish to entertain

I.S. on that date at a formal luncheon and have charged Jolanta to maneuver us out of the other arrangements. Yet I foolishly act as if she herself were guilty of a misprision; and this exaggeration makes me aware of how much I have put my trust in her, which in turn leads me to reflect on her responsibilities as an employee. After all, her orders, from the beginning, must have contained lists of things we were not to know and things we were to be prevented from doing or made to do. Hasn't she, in effect, been steering me from the moment of arrival? As I am by no means the first of her charges, hasn't each stage of my adjustment been coolly observed by a professional eye? And isn't she also aware, as the psychoanalyst is aware when a similar crisis overtakes *his* patient, of the true nature of my feelings for her? And to how many of her charges has that happened before? This sobering thought leaves me feeling not only naïve but also nakedly transparent. It also hurts.

MAY 30

Today being the first without threat of rain, we drive through the Praga to Wilanow. It is National Election Day, too, and though we see no signs of hustings or election fever (how *could* there be any with a choice between Gomulka and Gomulka?), every factory on the way is flying the Red Flag of the Revolution side by side with the red-and-white Polish flag.

1965

The view of *Urbs Warsowia* from the Praga is a popular angle in old prints, the viewer looking over plumed riders on prancing horses in the Praga foreground, and noble ladies in fur-lined pelisses (I am thinking of Watteau's "*La Femme polonaise*"). It was also the Red Army's view in 1944, when they failed to cross the river and raise the siege from the insurgents, standing by for political reasons (as is now generally believed) while a quarter of a million people died. But the Vistula, from here anyway, does not play as vital a part in the life of Warsaw as the Danube does in Vienna and Budapest.

MAY 31

We pack, pay bills, spend leftover *zloti*s, and go to the composers' luncheon in the rebuilt Poniatowski Château at Jablonna. The trans-Vistula landscape—brown wooden houses, pigeons perching in mud pools, fields of broken corn stooks, farm lands covered with mulch—reminds the I.S.'s of Russia, as does Jablonna itself, with its circular saloon and veneered-birch furniture.

Amazingly, the cuisine is of a quality to match the surroundings. The chef, now eighty-six and former chief cook to the Czar, is sent for at one point (he looks like Bruckner) and presented to I.S., whose hands he kisses as a peasant would have done a century ago; everyone applauds him and says that his *service royal* is the only good cooking in Poland, but no implications are drawn from the fact, at least not out loud. At table I try to make Ger-French conversation with, on one side, Stefan Sledzinski, the president of the society, who chairs the proceedings, and, on the other, the writer Tomaszewski (a face like that of the Polish hero Lelewel, but with blunter features, like a Wit Stwosz peasant). Toasting comes to the rescue, at long last, except that I fail to recognize myself in the one to "Robertowi Craftowi," owing to the tail ornaments, and have to be nudged. At the heady high point of the *fête*, the composers stand, face I.S., and sing an old Polish song in unison (not very good unison, for composers): "May he live to be a hundred." Then a remarkable event occurs. I.S. suddenly, and, I am convinced, unconsciously, switches from French to Russian. And in a trice the entire company follows him, as though they had only been waiting out of politeness for him to give the signal. And whereas most of them had been dropping mildly denigrating digs about the Russians only moments before ("They have not played as much modern music as we have"—which is true—"and therefore their orchestras are not as quick as ours"—which is false), all seem perfectly at home now speaking the Russian language.

Post-prandial drinks are passed around. But I escape with Jolanta to the Château park, where we follow a meandering path to the roiling river. Here are the tall, soughing trees, the lush meadows with buttercup and dandelion, of my adolescent daydreams of Tolstoy and Russian novels. And here, finally, on the riverbank, against a bilious soundtrack of frogs and a dovelike wind, it is the turn of the middle, which is yielded silently, seriously, persistently, and with no outwardly escaping sign of pleasure.

Back in Warsaw I try to collect the impressions of a week, wondering if even one or two have survived the mass reversals. But none has; and the subject of my Polish peroration must be my reason for the impossibility of composing it. Part of it—the brevity of the experience, the lack of language, and the lack of both general and specialized knowledge—is obvious. And at least one other difficulty is the same for every foreigner: Warsaw is not only not Poland, but is hardly even a continuation of the city it once was, having been clinically murdered and, as doctors say, left alive only biologically. Yet the greatest obstacle to the visitor is the ambivalence of the Poles themselves—as shown in that nonplussing switch to Russian at Jablonna today. In Russia, by contrast, the attitude to the Westerner is always clear, because substantiated by power. But what are the psychological strategies of a people whose map has changed with every major European power shift and who, during the whole of the nineteenth century, were deprived of both political and territorial existence? (It seems to me that the ethnological problems of the territory are soluble only by transplanting minority populations to new demographic gravity centers, by moving the people of Lwow westward for instance, as Muhammadans were migrated to Pakistan from other parts of India.) And what of a people who, when reconstituted at Versailles, found themselves a century behind the West—whereas before the Partitions, in the age of Stanislaus Leczinski, they had been in the very vanguard of the Enlightenment? Were they not an easy prey, first to corruption and later to fascism? And, finally, what are the feelings of a people who, at the end of a terrible war of liberation, find themselves more hopelessly the instrument of another power than ever before?

To read even as little as I have in Polish affairs is to be astonished by the survival of Polish culture at all. The explanation can only lie in the integrity of the people. They were a heroic people during the Occupation, when in spite of the suffering, no Quisling appeared and collaboration was almost unknown. And that heroism continues now, for life is in many ways even harder today. Under the Nazis there was at least the mitigating hope of the overthrow and final defeat. But what are the chances of change now? In fact, every reference to "the West" or "the Line" (the Iron Curtain) seems to contain a choke of emotion. Living conditions are grim, too, and not only materially. The censorship is among the cruelest in the world, and while money and other contents of legal mail from relatives in the West are confiscated, or at any rate fail to arrive, to carry a letter in or out is a prison offense. Naturally the Poles are suspicious of us. It is a condition of survival in the underground where, swallowed but not eaten, they still live.

JUNE 5

Paris. We go to the *"Spectacle Igor Strawinsky"* at the Opéra, *Le Sacre du printemps, Les Noces,* and *Renard,* staged by Béjart and conducted by Boulez. The *Noces* musicians are in the pit, the chorus in the center wearing brown robes with cowls. The half-lowered backdrop seems to represent an *Arabian Nights* city, hence is too oriental by several thousand versts; it is also greatly indebted to Goncharova's curtain for the 1929 revival of the *Firebird.* No less remote are the village weddings, not only of the subtitle but of the whole character of the work, the bridesmaids in their taffeta dresses and ermine muffs resembling ladies-in-waiting to a czarina. V., who was to have played the bride in the original performance and who rehearsed the role in Monaco, recalls that she stood stage center during the combing and plaiting of the tresses, which were several yards long.

The second scene is no closer to the geographical target, the costumes of the "best men" being a cross between gaucho and Music Hall Cossack, while their dance is half Siberian, half Argentine folk ballet. Beginning with this scene, the spectator's attention is divided by a choreographic device. The bride and groom, got up like fairy-tale royalty, are split in two; or, rather, doubled, like the Sorcerer's Apprentice, except that the doubles are naked, presumably embodying the betrothed pair's visions. (Or dirty thoughts? Like "blues" songs, the text is coded with sexual meanings.) But though this could be diverting in a satire on a Victorian costume piece, for example, it is wholly out of place in *Les Noces.* The visions, dancing like shadows by the sides of their projectors, imply a psychological interior which, no matter how shallow, is contradicted by the hard musical surface. And this gratuitous psychological dimension dilutes or sells short the severity of the musical emotion, which, at the end anyway, is tragic emotion of a rare kind. The sentiment of tonight's staging, by contrast, is that of an exotic

1965

"musical." Besides which the visions are optically confusing, the eye naturally preferring to travel with the naked *Doppelgänger* rather than with the overclothed original, and the naked thoughts obtruding too much, getting in the way of their thinkers at first and then taking over from them completely. *Les Noces* is musically mechanized ritual. Failing to match the demands of the score as such, the choreographer's next best course is to stage the piece straightforwardly as an album of village wedding scenes.

To judge by the costumes, the geography of the third tableau is even farther afield. The headgear might have been confected by a Cambodian pastry cook, the bride's mother's minks by a Parisian furrier interested in the program credits. But the great scene of the two weeping mothers is ruined less by couturiers than by an excessively slow *tempo,* when in fact no change is warranted at all.

The final scene is the worst. The backdrop is covered with icons befitting a church of the Hagia Sophia class; the bride is veiled like a Muslim; and the groom is hatted like a Tibetan yak, perhaps to keep company with the five no less oddly clad clowns—marriage brokers?—who pop on stage to "play" Pelegai. But the supreme vulgarity is saved for the very end. As I.S. conceived it, when the wedded couple enter the nuptial chamber, the relatives and guests seat themselves on a bench against the wall outside the door. The immobility of the scene, frozen in the music, frozen on the stage, and everlasting in its minute and a half of time, is unique in the theater. But instead of this realization of one of the simplest and most beautiful pages in modern music (drop the "modern," too), the "visions" are joined upstage, where they copulate in synchronicity with the piano chords. Commenting on this afterward, I.S. remarks that "The most dangerous compromisers of art are the second-rate geniuses: stage directors, film directors, TV directors, orchestra directors."

The staging of *Renard* is less offensive both because the scope for harm is so much smaller and because in this case a degree of experiment is justified. In this version, Stravinsky's *dramatis personae* are given spectators' vantages to the rear and sides of the stage, thus forming a stage arena, while the action, a total enigma to me, is entrusted to the animals' human representatives—more visions, perhaps—in Flapper Period bathing garb. This aquatic troupe is taxied onstage by a Hispano-Suiza during the introductory march and taxied off by it during the final one. The ballet world being what it is, the villain Renard—who has a marvelous slink and great guile—is a woman.

The backdrop, half lowered from the boom, exposes a collage of photographs, most prominently of Diaghilev, Astruc, Groucho Marx, Picasso's I.S. And this time the orchestra and singers are perched on a pile of automobile tires, about twenty *pneus* high, at the back of the stage. The screaming singers—all senses—are almost miraculously bad (though only minutes ago the feat of finding a worse vocal quartet than that in *Les Noces* seemed impossible), and the voice of the tenor crying the cock's part is in more terrible tatters than the fowl itself, after mauling by the fox.

When the *"Spectacle"* is over, Boulez, who has conducted the triple bill without visible exuviations—a literal example of "It wasn't any sweat"—tells us that part of his success formula is: "Be a Robespierre in rehearsals, a Danton in concerts." But *he* is Napoleonic.

JUNE 6

Lunch with I.S., the Suvchinskys, Boulez in a restaurant near Versailles.

1965

1948
1949
1950
1951
1952
1953
1954
1955
1956
1957
1958
1959
1960
1961
1962
1963
1964
1965
1966
1967
1968
1969
1970
1971

ITINERARY

January 18: We fly to Minneapolis. **21:** Concert in Minneapolis. **22:** Fly to Los Angeles. **27, 28:** Concerts with the Los Angeles Philharmonic. **February 1:** I.S. and R.C. fly to St. Louis for concerts on the 5th and 6th, returning on the 6th. **18:** We fly to San Francisco for concerts on the 23rd, 24th, 25th. **26:** Fly to Los Angeles. **March 6:** Fly to Rochester. **11:** Concert at the Eastman School. **12:** We fly to New York, and Hollywood (19th). **April 6:** I.S. completes the *Rex Tremendae*. **27:** I.S. completes the *Lacrimosa.* **May 5:** I.S. conducts *Perséphone* at the Los Angeles Music Festival. **8:** We fly to New York, Paris (12th), Athens (23rd), Lisbon (27th). **June 1:** Concert in Lisbon, I.S. conducting *Oedipus Rex*. **2:** We fly to Paris and New York (21st). **July 1:** We fly to Los Angeles. **5:** Concert in Hollywood Bowl. **14:** I.S.'s fly to New York. **24:** I.S. conducts the *Symphony of Psalms* in Lincoln Center. **25:** I.S.'s fly to Los Angeles. **August 13:** I.S. completes the *Postlude*. **25:** R.C. returns to Los Angeles, after conducting second *Wozzeck* in Santa Fe. **September 12:** We fly to Louisville. **17:** Concert in Louisville. **18:** Fly to New York. **October 8:** Première of *Requiem Canticles* at Princeton. **12:** We fly to Hollywood. **November 7:** Concert at California Institute of Technology, Pasadena. **12:** We fly to Honolulu. **20, 22:** Concerts in Honolulu. **23:** We fly to Hollywood, and Columbus (25th). **29:** Concert in Columbus. **30:** We fly to Portland. **December 5, 6:** Concerts in Portland. **7:** We fly to Los Angeles. **15:** R.C. records Stravinsky excerpts for United Airlines film. **19:** I.S. attends performance of the Schütz *Christmas Oratorio,* Los Angeles County Museum of Art. **23:** We fly to Chicago. **28:** Concert in Chicago.

New York. The Pierre Hotel. Wystan Auden for dinner in the I.S.'s suite (1716). Besides the glittering jewels of his intellect, he wears a dark brown flannel shirt, black necktie, wicker beach shoes, and—on departure, shortly before midnight—very dark glasses, like a jazz musician. After confounding the waiters by ordering mushrooms as a "savory" and using "Quite" for "Yes"—"More wine, sir?" "Quite"—he expatiates on "anti-opera." The high-cult examples, he says, are *Fidelio, Boris, Pelléas,* but he chooses to dwell on two out-of-the-way specimens, "Janáček's *House of the Dead,* which has no characters and no tunes, and Godard's *Dante,* pronounced 'Dant.' Whereas the whole Act One of *Dante* simply sets the Florentine scene, the subject of Act Two is the entire *Divine Comedy.* Act Three unites Dant and Beatrice in, of all places, 'a nunnery, near Ravenna.'"

But Wystan is more in his element with German operas. "Elektra is so definitely non-U," he says, "that a singer who fits the part shouldn't attempt Isolde." This leads to the observation that "The dramatic movement in the first act of *Tristan* is limited entirely to exits and entrances." Telling us about the numerous excisions in the new Viennese production of *The Rake's Progress,* he proposes that in future the publishers should proscribe all cuts by contract with the opera house. "And, after all, *The Rake* isn't exactly *Götterdämmerung,* where the stage director can claim he has to give people a chance to pee."

Talking about more recent operas, he expresses concern "lest the Britten pendulum swing so far the other way that people begin to say they are *all* bad. . . . By the way, I understand that *Cleopatra* is to be tried out here, even though Verdi saw that it wouldn't do—although it might have done in Boito's Italian. Now obviously the only Shakespeare that could be turned into English-language opera is *Love's Labour's Lost,* and that would take a great deal of turning." Gently teasing I.S. about money ("Has he scads now?" he asks me), Wystan suggests that *millionen* would be a good word for him to set to music. "Think how you could aspirate the final syllable, Igor, and keep it going, page after page, like the compounding of interest."

Confessing homesickness for his house in Austria, he says that he buys a Viennese newspaper from time to time, "to see what the weather is doing there—I don't need to be told what it is doing here—though having bought it, I sometimes peek at the obits, too." Recalling his Ford Foundation year in Berlin, he describes a brush with the law one night on suspicion of inebriety. "The Berlin police pay people to inform on pedestrians who appear to be tight. *I* was informed on once, and the police refused to believe I was a Herr Professor. I had no trouble passing their mental tests and co-ordination tests, of course" (who *would* have, under any conditions, with *that* intellect?) "but evidently the alcohol in my blood was too high" (as well it might be after a demijohn of Chianti). Back home in Kirchstetten, however, he is always immaculately abstinent driving his Volkswagen; and was ever so "in motor cars," he adds virtuously, since first piloting one in 1925. The date reminds I.S. that *he* began to drive in the same year[1] but gave it up because the *gendarmes* stopped him so often, and because he habitually burned up the brakes; which, Wystan observes to me, "is another figure in the pattern of the pills and the salting away of securities in Helvetia."

Turning to literature, he complains about "scholars who refuse to consider the possibility that Shakespeare could have made a mistake." He also cites several mistranslations in the new Bible, but otherwise avoids ecclesiastical and theological talk, apart from one reference to the Pope as "publicity mad," and the remark that "When God said 'Let there be light,' He must have realized He was saying something extraordinarily pretentious" (which, I think, is a variant of Phocion). He says that T. S. Eliot wrote "very good ribald verse that will probably *not* be collected. I once submitted a poem to him, for *The Criterion,* that included a then unprintable word, and he suggested the more decorous: '. . . like a June bride . . . sore but satisfied.'"

Books mentioned include Auerbach's *Literary Language;* Tolkien's *Silmarillion* ("J.B.B. is 'in' with the teen-age set, you know, and no longer a property of dotty schoolteachers and elderly cranks"); *In Cold Blood* (can he really have read *that,* or did he simply sink a trial shaft?); *The Ambidextrous Universe* ("One knew all along that it wasn't symmetrical, of course—after all, even nucleic acid is left-handed—but my generation was brought up to think of God as Someone like Zäzilie, Christian Morgenstern's symmetry-loving housemaid"); the new David Jones ("I'm sorry my name preceded yours on the subscribers' list, Igor, but it was only because of 'A,' which I can't help; still, the way it was printed did make it seem as if I were somehow next in rank to the Queen Mum"). Apropos the Capote book, he says, "I understand that the author is remarkably changed now, and looks like a banker—which I suppose he is." And, the question of capital punishment arising in connection with it, he says that "At least in England they don't keep them waiting about for five or ten years." I reply that in the Christie case they should have, and I ask whether he thinks a death sentence is ever justifiable. "Well, there *have* been people on whom I can picture it being carried out. Brecht, for one. In fact, I can imagine doing it to him myself. It might even have been rather enjoyable, when the time came, to have been able to say to him, 'Now, let's step outside.' But of course I'd have given him a good 'last meal.'[2] Still, you must admire the logic of a man who lives in a Communist country, takes out Austrian citizenship, does his banking in Switzerland, and, like a gambler hedging his bets, sends for the pastor at the end in the event there could be something in that, too."

Once when I.S. and V. converse in Russian, he remarks on the beauty of the language. As he has never hinted at a remotely favorable opinion

1966

1. His driver's license is stamped "Paris, December 2, 1925."
2. According to Glob's *Bog People* (London, 1969), the condemned man (or *élu*) in Iron Age Denmark was fed a gruel containing some sixty different varieties of grain, evidently to induce the return, or propitiate the gods, of spring.

of it before, this raises the alarming thought that his German period may be running out. Or, rather, it would have raised it except that he is unusually mellow tonight in other ways as well. Randall Jarrell's death has shocked him, though he observes that "It's not very nice for the driver of the truck you decide to jump in front of." Then, as if reflecting on his own mortality, he says that "A schoolgirl, quoting from one of my poems in a class recently, astonished her teacher by insisting that I was among the living. In fact, not long ago a newspaper did refer to me as deceased. I saw the correction myself in a later edition: 'Auden not, repeat, *not* dead.' Naturally I tried to inquire what it was thought I had died of."

MAY 12

New York to Paris. Airplane conversations between strangers seem to follow a pattern. Stage one begins with a rummage for mutual acquaintances, shared opinions, shared impressions of places. The common knowledge even of a restaurant or hotel will help people to feel weighted together, proving to them that "the world is very small," when in fact it proves only that people of pro-rata incomes tend to be found in the same places, and hence on the same highways leading to those places. Stage two, marked by the settling-in-of-cocktails, moves on to exchanges of scraps of personal confidences. And often to more than scraps. My remarkably unreticent neighbor, a New Man type—Foundation representative, or Rand mathematician, the sort of person who would chat with you about Quine's set theory or Bohr's complementarity principle, if you knew anything about them—manages to deliver himself of a very substantial installment of autobiography between some twenty or so foot-trampling trips to the lavatory. (When it turns out that he is on his way to an important lunch tomorrow in the Congo, I confess that I have had some "contact" with the Congo myself, but not that this was limited to flushing the toilet over it on a flight to Rhodesia.)

1966

Stage two depends on the quantity and effectiveness of the libations. Owing partly to the tensions of flight, partly to the limbo psychology that abrogates not only responsibilities but also the sense of time, the Establishment narcotic is an especially potent confessing drug in airplanes (to say nothing of its biochemical effects—on blood sugar, on the salt content in the hypothalamus, etc.). Alcohol at high altitude pushes forward suddenly-remembered connections, stories, comments, which are of supreme importance for a moment and insist on being voiced, but which turn away as peremptorily as a cat and a moment later defy recalling. If we are but loosely in control of our thoughts ordinarily, how much less so are we under alcohol and over 40,000 feet?

Stage three, flirtation, depends on individuals, but a great deal of it transpires in airplanes. The reasons re-include those for stages one and two, with the added factor that flying itself is sexually stimulating, both mentally—all flying dreams are sexual, after all—and physically, in the tingling sensation aroused by the wheels touching the ground, in the pressure of braking, and in the desire to re-embrace life, each landing being a birth. Yet the central sexual ingredient in air travel is none of these but the stewardess, toward whom the male passenger harbors, and often openly attempts to navigate, the most ardent wishes.

She, moreover, is not merely a new amalgam of receptionist, party hostess, geisha, waitress, mother, mistress, nurse (bringing clean napkins every few minutes as if symbolically changing our diapers), but an entirely new aspect, or hitherto unexploited aspect, of Woman. Just as landscape painting did not exist before Giotto, though landscapes evidently did, or the cult of literary tears before *Manon Lescaut,* though the flow of actual ones must have been fairly constant, so the combination of beauty and bravery as a commercial asset was unknown before the age of air travel. A handsome girl, ever the most desirable traveling companion in any case, is now the most exemplary as well, for her valor or indifference shames the passenger and helps him to collar his cowardice.

Our stewardess's lecture on flotation seats and life-raft inflating, on the donning of life jackets and the manipulation of lanyards, sounds like so much fun-filled fashion modeling. But her perpetual cheeriness gives way for a moment when, nearing the French coast, the plane begins to bump coltishly and to yaw and shake. In fact, the sternness of her command to buckle seat belts and gutter cigarettes is then in such contrast to her usual manner that I suddenly become aware of the Holy Bible on the magazine rack, along with *Playboy* and *Time.*

1966

I.S. objects to the stewardess tone of voice, nonstop smile, incessant salesmanship ("Your personal airline," she says, parroting the slogan of this giant, totally impersonal airline), and interminable translations of such useless information as "The outside temperature is minus forty-two degrees Centigrade," and whether or not "Captain Smith hopes you have enjoyed your flight. 'Bye now." "*Le capitaine* Smeet . . ." etcetera, etcetera. I might add that the stewardesses' very busy path to the cockpit with trays of vodka, wine, cognac, champagne, and even Pernod has not greatly increased *my* store of confidence in *Hauptmann* Schmidt.

I.S., far from sozzled, though he has been slaking his thirst with several kinds of antifreeze, talks to me about Chekhov, whom he is systematically rereading, and with whom he identifies to the extent of defending *Ivanov* against last night's Broadway cast: the wife who might have been reading from a teleprompter; the uncle who, judging by the way he has picked each overly decrepit step, might have been on an obstacle course; and the Ivanov himself (Gielgud), whose main method of expressing bitterness and suffering was to curl his mustached lip, which merely conveyed the impression that someone in the vicinity had made a rude smell. "The plight of provincial Russians wanting to go to Moscow is no longer very spellbinding," I.S. admits, provoking no dissent from me. "Yet Chekhov manages to make us care whether they go or not, and he manages it, as he manages everything else, with the greatest tact."

Apart from Chekhov, I.S.'s in-flight reading is confined to Michel Phillipot's monograph on himself, which he is obelizing—correcting, annotating, rephrasing, deleting words and substituting better ones of his own, even rewriting in whole chunks, polemicizing with the author and posterity.

Approaching Paris, we drop from photophobic sunshine through the iridescence of an afterstorm and toward a cloud bank on which the shadow of the airplane flashes like a wheeling bird. At a still lower layer of weather, we dive through the storm itself—which is like traveling backward in time. The encasing element establishes relativity and creates an impression of the velocity of the plane, which is sobering, not least in the specific sense of the dispersion of alcoholic vapors. In consequence, already pouchy faces seem to become pouchier and roomier for returning anxieties.

At Orly I watch an old woman standing as if hypnotized by the beam-controlled, electric-eye glass doors, but I notice that older people, *i.e.,* with acquired rather than innate confidence in mechanics, lead with their arms extended as they approach the miracle.

Malraux's newly cleaned Paris is the color of white skin from which black greasepaint has just been removed.

MAY 22

I.S. is complaining of a *crise de foie* today, as might be expected after so many bibulous meals; nor are we allowed to remain in ignorance of his fecal fears, besides which his luncheon conversation includes an absorbing scatological disquisition, with digressions on purgatives and piles. But how much more at home he is in Paris than in California! He prefers the gender language, for one thing, and for another, though he scoffs at French society, he is also entertained by it, especially by that climate of intrigue compared with which the smog-darkened atmosphere of Los Angeles seems pure and clean. In Paris, above all, conversation has not yet been superseded by television, though the cutting off of all that oral libido, the national satisfaction of the mouth, would be impossible to imagine, in any case. At the same time I wonder whether his Russianness is not at least as apparent here as his Europeanness is in America, French social structures being so much more closed than American.

We drive to Chartres in the afternoon, but every approach to the cathedral is blocked by the booths of an agricultural fair. Returning through Maintenon, we eat Camembert sandwiches Chez Loulou, then go on to Paris 2, which is the French idea of American *luxe intégral:* termitary architecture, swimming pools, shopping *géants,* and other tokens of *le bonheur*—as distinguished from *la culture,* which Americans cannot hope to understand, of course, let alone possess. In Paris 2, unlike Paris *tout simple,* the bidets do not outnumber the bathrooms, the elevators do not hobble, and the telephone earpieces do not reverberate like seashells—*"Ne quittez pas, monsieur."* This horrendous Utopia adjoins the toy village of Marie-Antoinette.

Athens. Lunch in the stuffy hotel dining room, where I.S.'s two small cut-lets are wheeled in in an egg-shaped silver container the size of an iron lung. During the meal an elderly woman approaches our table flourishing a photograph of herself with I.S.'s brother Gury and reminding I.S. that they knew each other in St. Petersburg in 1900. Whatever his curiosity, if any, I.S. is in a foul humor today and in no wise disposed to grapple with unforeseen reminders of the tenderest years of his past. He scolds the woman for disturbing him and sends her away. The upshot of this is that V., although wholly uninterested in the woman's story, feels sorry for her and follows her to the lobby to hear it through to the bittersweet end. I.S.'s reactions in such cases seem capricious and are in fact unpredictable. Yesterday he might have invited the intruder to a banquet.

We drive to Corinth in the afternoon, a five-hour jolt on a nonroad in 1956, now a ninety-minute spin on a divided superhighway. Automobiles are a hundred times more numerous than a decade ago, too, and the jogging donkey carts of that remote date are rarer in the same ratio. In fact, all of Greece is so transformed, touristically speaking, that the view of the Hilton from the Acropolis is as frequently spoken of now as the other way around. It is even said that in the most popular vacationing waters, warning signs have had to be floated against dropping anchor on the scuba divers.

1966

Shrines survive along the road and, near Athens, a few touchingly ugly churches with cypress-shaded cemeteries; the roadside exposures of all other buildings are covered with hoardings. Only the sweeping hillsides seem the same as ten years ago, which is to say stony and lacking in tilth. At Megara, the scent of pines, anticipated from memories of 1956, is swamped, if it exists, in the fetors of refining petroleum and, more agreeably, in clouds of spume blowing over small islands that seem to have fallen like crumbs from the cake of the mainland. The tourists at Nero's canal lean over the sides of the bridge like seasick steamship passengers at the taffrails, and at Corinth the proportion of tourists to natives must be roughly equivalent to that of Persians to Greeks at Thermopylae. Where a decade ago I posed against the deserted ruins—for an excitable photographer, wearing an artist's smock, Lavallière cravat, Taras Bulba mustaches, and ducking his head under a black tent to take the picture—tourists now pose and snapshoot each other by the hundreds. On the return to Athens we are detained at a railroad crossing by the almost toy-sized but clangorous and fuliginous—like black wool—Sparta Express (?).

Our concert, in the Amphitheater of Herodes Atticus, goes very smoothly, blessed by an ambrosial night and the circumstance that I am not, as so often, distracted by awareness of myself, as if from another plane or body, or from the helicopter of my superego, which can make a deafening noise.

A singer's mistake puts I.S. into a lather, however, and when the impresario appeals to him to take extra applause-milking bows, he refuses, brandishing his cane. After the concert we go to Piraeus and listen to bouzouki music.

Lisbon to Paris. Suvchinsky meets us at Orly, and we drive directly to the Boule d'Or, where the conversation quickly gravitates to Boulez. "He talks only about *'les problèmes de la direction'* nowadays," Suvchinsky regrets, "and although he has unquestionably mastered many of them, how can a man with both creative talent and brains want to be an orchestra conductor?" B. is in the throes of a *"crise de colère,* or *crise de César-Napoléon,"* according to Suvchinsky, who thinks it may be the reason for the herpes zoster with which B. is now afflicted.[1] Suvchinsky has been telephoning B. in his Baden-Baden bastion, attempting to stay him from publishing an open letter blasting Malraux and, of all unblastable people, Milhaud. But Suvchinsky is less concerned with the vicissitudes of career-maneuvering than with the younger generation's dismissal of B.'s music. "*'Bien décoratif,'* they say, and they compare the end of *Pli* to Ravel, and the *Improvisations* to Reynaldo Hahn."

This talk says more about a contemporary success story, however, a Julien Sorel updated, than about B., who naturally attracts some of the brambles formerly reserved for X., Y., and Z. Toward the end of the dinner, and no doubt feeling guilty, following the pattern of gossip of this kind, Suvchinsky suddenly remembers how much we all love B., recalling the morning he fetched I.S. with a car at the Gare de Lyon during the taxi strike of November 1956, and the day in August 1957 when he played Stockhausen's fascicular piano piece for I.S. in the rue Beautreillis cubbyhole.

1966

Walking in the rue St.-Honoré this morning, I am accosted by a display of Schoenberg recordings in a shop window. Then in the next instant I recognize them as *my* recordings, and in the same instant feel ill. Why does the sight of my name in print, or of a photograph of myself, or any kind of publicity concerning myself, or even the sound of my voice on a playback or in an echo chamber during a long-distance telephone call, upset me so much? I put the question to I.S. later, but instead of explaining the neurosis, he adds to its documentation, saying that I neglected to sign the first letter he received from me, because of which he had to track me down through Nicolas Nabokov. At night I.S. attends a concert in the Hôtel de Sully.

I go with I.S., Xenakis, and Béjart to a screening for French critics of CBS's I.S. documentary. They unanimously condemn it, of course, as an

---

1. It is a viral disease, in fact, as we learned when I.S. caught it, in December 1968.

American-style cover story with interpolated gratifications for minority groups, music critics excepted. And above all, they object to the popularizing diversionary gimmicks: the reception by the Texas cowboys, the hansom ride in Central Park,[1] the ballet of little girls—to whom, nevertheless, I.S.'s parting words, "Grow up well, little *demoiselles*," provide one of the film's most endearing moments. Nor do they approve the relentless hyperbole of the narration, the oh-so-famous Mister Balanchine, the great, great Mr. Benny Goodman, and now just look who this is, and in fact it is, the Pope himself. (And very pleased His Holiness was to be on American television, though the Vatican concert honored not only I.S. but also Malipiero and Milhaud, both unceremoniously shunted to a back row by an obliging Papal Public Relations Department at the request of the CBS cameramen.) But what the French critics see as most American of all is the McLuhanite message of the TV screen itself, which says, in effect, that great artists are rewarded with riches, the company of the famous, TV biographies.

The Giacometti episode alone wins praise, but as much for the reason that it is conducted in French, I suspect, as for the relief it brings from the tone of an overly excited TV commercial surrounding it. Giacometti never notices the camera, never emerges from his absorption in his work, and talks only of his failure. ("*Je n'arrive pas. C'est abominable.*") But none of today's viewers notices that in I.S.'s drawing of Giacometti, the artist's eyes are closed as if he were a dead man, which in fact was I.S.'s presentiment that May day of 1965, six months before the sad event.

"Is the film a true portrait of I.S.?" one of the disgruntled critics asks me afterward, meaning, I take it, that while I.S. has said and done everything he is seen to say and do, have the editing, cutting, transposition of contexts unduly distorted the resulting picture? I answer that the contexts of the critic-fustigating are immaterial and that the drawing of a few more beads, or potshots, in the direction of Richard Strauss requires no contextual preparation. (I.S. had answered a student's question as to "what specifically" he dislikes in the music of Strauss with "I do not like the major works, and I do not like the minor works," adding, off camera: "Strauss's music is over-homogenized.")

Moreover, the film inevitably offers many valuable reflections of I.S.'s mind. One such is a statement about preferring "the worst communism" to anarchy. Another is his misquotation of Tertullian's "*Credo quia absurdum*" ("I will give it to you in the original Latin [!] of St. Paul: '*Credo in absurdum*'"), which can be interpreted as an indication of his dogmatic side and of his supposed respect for rubber-stamp forms (formulae, formats), time-hallowed ideas, apparent traditions. For the received idea of I.S. as a composer for whom rules precede emotions and frames come before pictures is still widespread in Paris, but it is also, or was also, a self-promoted view, and a hedge against other people's rampant feelings.

1. This, incidentally, was staged only a block from the house where, six years later, I.S. died.

293

If the film misleads, however, it is not in any out-of-context or too locally circumstantial remark, but in the inference that Poland was important in I.S.'s life and his concert there something of a pilgrimage (it was neither), and in the implications of the Vatican episode. The Throne of St. Peter, in a sudden, ill-advised gesture of recognition toward the arts, decided to honor four composers of four faiths, choosing Sibelius to represent the Protestant (did they know he was dead?), Milhaud the Hebrew, I.S. the Orthodox Church, and Malipiero the Roman. But I.S. has not been *pratiquant* in *any* faith for more than a dozen years, and if religious affiliations could be classified by feelings rather than by declarations and acts of worship, he might be described as a lapsed Jansenist; in fact, his beliefs are secret and defy labeling.

One frame in the Vatican sequence deserves but does not receive comment or caption. It occurs after the *Symphony of Psalms,* when I.S. kneels to kiss the Fisherman's Ring but slips and momentarily loses balance. Seeing him totter, an old gentleman with pince-nez steps forward from an aisle seat, on the viewer's left, to lend a hand. It is Giovacchino Forzano, librettist of *Gianni Schicchi.*[1]

In view of the expenditure of so much footage elsewhere, it is a pity that the post-concert dinner at the Hilton, given by Puccini's nephew Giulio Razzi, was not filmed. I.S., flanked by two exclusively and effusively Italian-speaking ladies, both unknown to him, soon got very drunk, and by the time testimonials drew round, his head was on his arm and his arm was on the table. Seeing this state of affairs, V. walked around the table behind him and whispered in his ear that he absolutely *had* to acknowledge the host's gratulations. This piece of intelligence took some time to sink in, but when it had, I.S. bravely raised his head, slowly but clearly formed the syllables "*Gra-zi-e,*" then sank back into his lees.

JUNE 30

New York. The steam rising from open manholes and grates of subway catacombs is like Doré's *"Inferno";* and the whistles of doormen for taxicabs, like shrieks of Beelzebub, make the picture lifelike, or afterlife-like. But unlike Dante's Florence and Ravenna, which have remained much the same for some time, New York is a never-completed city. "What will it be like in five years?" I think aloud to my driver, on the way to the Port Authority Bus Terminal. "Mister, I'm wondering what it's going to be like in five minutes," he says, and, when we reach our destination: "Have a nice trip. Please write."

I spend the afternoon with Marianne Moore eliminating archaicisms from the Narrator's part in *The Flood.* The poet is Twiggy-thin, wispy, and as bent as a woman carrying a shoulder load in a Hiroshige print, but she

1. Forzano died in Rome on October 28, 1970.

bustles about her apartment at high speed and works with enviable energy and concentration. The book-lined walls are further embellished with pictures of birds and animals, and with photographs, one of them of a young, unfamiliarly fleshy and smiling T. S. Eliot.

Miss Moore has marked scansions and circled words that, she contends, "can be read but not narrated—if the audience is to understand." But her own reading is difficult to follow: her alveolars do not come through, her volume is small, her delivery is uninflected—if refreshingly nonemphatic— and she fails, orally, to cross her "t's" ("cree-a-[t]ure"), so that the unfocused vowels surging around the unpronounced consonants are as broad and undefined as the river—at springtime—whose name classifies her accent.

But the blur in enunciation is in striking contrast to the matter enunciated, for her thought is marvelously distinct, her intellectual vigilance unflagging. Of the libretto generally, she commends the idea of assigning the lines from the Bible to a narrator and the guild-play lines to actors, adding that "The stylistic fusion of Genesis, Anonymous, and *Paradise Lost* is natural." She is also the first critic of the opus to remark that the sea itself is the symbol of chaos, and to catch the connection with *Timon* in the "salt flood." As for the replacements of the words she rejects as too obscure for a textless audience, I concur in every instance, if only, in one or two of them, in gratitude for the privilege of watching her work.

1966

She fetches several "bulwarks" (dictionaries)—one at a time, to my relief: those precarious, stilt-thin arms and legs!—including German, for she has revised bits of the German translation as well. But a sere and yellowed rhyming dictionary is the only one of these tomes that we use. In fact, she systematically ransacks it, pointing a long fescule-like forefinger to keep her place in it as we discuss the candidacy of each word. Her method is to preserve the rhyme words wherever possible, and exchange the bodies of the lines, which is like *bouts-rimés;* only failing in that will she re-order the rhymes themselves. Quantities are of negligible importance in these transpositions, and templates and purely musical ornaments are ruthlessly expunged. Her goal is the elimination of ambiguity and obscurity, and in achieving it, anachronisms may be allowed and stylistic questions may fall by the board. Her rules, in short, are rules of thumb and ear: *her* thumb, *her* ear.

"I cannot use a word I feel contempt for," she stipulates, changing "Hares hopping gaily can go" to "And hopping briskly hares can go," and explaining that "'briskly' has more dignity." She amends "Here cats can make it full carouse" to "Here cats make full carouse," and repairs

> And here are bears, wolves set
>   Apes, owls, marmoset

to:

> And here are bears, wolves, leveret,
>   Ape, owl, and marmoset

which is superior but may raise the question whether the singular might have been too sophisticated for the fifteenth-century guild plays, coupling being the *raison d'être* of the Ark. She also changes "Here are lions, leopards in" to "Here come lions . . . " and finally alters the "briskly" *versus* "gaily" stanza to:

> Both cats and dogs also
> Otter, fox, fulmart, too,
> And, hopping briskly, hares can go.

Her most drastic revisions are in Noah's last speech, where she re-renders "And multiply your seed shall ye" as "And so shall your lives be saved" (which lacks a syllable for the music), and "Sons, with your wives shall ye be stead" as "Sons, with your wives gain new estate." Objecting to "bairns" (which Basil Bunting is trying to keep in circulation), she adjusts "Your bairns shall then each other wed" to "The youths and maids shall then be wed." Finally, she changes "And worship God in good degree" to "And thus your God be served"; and "Shall forth be bred" to "Shall thus be bred."

Accompanying me to the street, Miss Moore provides a rare spectacle for the devotees of extraordinary millinery among her neighbors. *La dame au tricorne* is bareheaded!

JULY 21

1966

Santa Fe. I leave for El Paso in a chartered Cessna at 7 PM and from there at midnight for New York, joining an American Airlines flight from Mexico City. The worst of the Cessna is the noise: raspings and explosions as we roll down the sizzling concrete-and-melting-tar runway and slowly lift into the sky, and thereafter a deafening drone. The flimsiness of the plane—the pilot flings my bags aboard like a balloonsman loading ballast—and the thinness of its insulation are the more evident the greater the altitude. I feel pangs of acrophobia which, however, disappear in an unnamed worse sensation when paroxysms of shuddering seize the plane. What is the meaning of those drops of oil shivering on the window, I ask, by pointing to them, but the pilot assures me that "It was like this three days ago." (A tertian ague, then?) He shouts this information above the roar of the motors. Otherwise communication is by sign language, which includes a great deal of gesturing toward the instrument panel on his part, and a corresponding amount of ambiguous shrugging and head-shaking on mine, my mechanical aptitude being such that I can hardly tell the difference between a flooded carburetor and a flat tire.

Numbed by the noise, I begin to fly backward in time (as positrons, or electrons, are said to travel temporally backward) until transported to a similar evening hour when, standing in a field loud with katydids and tightly holding my father's hand, I watch the take-off of the first airplane I have ever seen. The aviator spins the two-bladed propeller himself, and runs back from it several times before the motor, which makes stuttering, dynamite-like detonations, finally turns over.

I see myself as well, a short time later, greatly disturbed by the story of an ace stunt flyer and daredevil parachutist whose chute had failed to open and who volleyed to his death at the Kingston Airport a hundred yards from a horror-stricken crowd; this plummeting-man image, along with dreams of burning dirigibles, has remained in my mind's eye until now. In the same year, and in spite of this incident, I flew with my father in a Ford trimotor, rising over the city higher, it seems, than I have ever flown since—though it must have been lower, in fact, as I could see both the Ashokan Reservoir and our house, which looked like a toy. I remember that we were unable to talk against the blast of the motors at that time too, and that the noise bothered me more than the bumping or the paper bags marked "For Sickness"; I used to hide in the cellar or attic on the Fourth of July, and at the circus, waiting for the man to be catapulted from the cannon to a net, suffered agonies of suspense—as much because of the explosion, I am ashamed to say, as for the safety of the man. Then thirty-five years hurtle by, and I am I, here and now, attributing the unlocking of memory to similarities of sensation between the two airplanes, and thinking that the most evident difference now is that I am probably greener in the gills.

Like a scenic-route bus driver, the pilot—who, I now notice, grips his steering wheel much less tightly than I grip mine—points out the site of the first atomic explosion and calls out the names of mountains, rivers, towns, sometimes shouting anecdotes connected with them, of which I usually fail to get the drift. Again as it was thirty-five years ago, we fly low enough to follow an automobile map and to construe details of the landscape down to a haystack and even a cow. Vast sheets of water, gleaming from the desert like metal reflectors, are evidence of recent storms, as the choppiness, scudding clouds, and aerial bombardment-like flashes are promises of about-to-be ones. Suddenly the pilot begins to twiddle the dials and hammer the instrument panel with his fists as if it were a rigged pinball machine. Removing and shaking his earphones—his only "gear," for he is dressed like a rancher—he tells me that the radio is out of order and that a landing at El Paso Airport is unthinkable without it. Accordingly, we head west of the city for "a small strip along the river where if the weather is clear we should be able to touch down without difficulty." And it *is* clear, clear*er* at any rate, a sliver of sunset still showing on one side of the plane while nets of stars ignite on the other, and the lights on the converging highways below turn on at a switch.

The Rio Grande coils blackly between the electrically gaudy American and the electrically faint Mexican cities. We come in, swaying like a swing, at hardly more than rooftop height, then bump down cushionlessly on a short, narrow, ancient concrete strip, rebounding as if we were on a roller coaster. "Fillerup?" a cowpoke with paprika freckles asks, as I emerge, weak-kneed, onto the wing and into a light warm rain. I count out $220 for the pilot and take a taxi to the main airport.

New York. Visits from H. before and after my morning rehearsal at Phil-harmonic Hall. During it she goes to one of her tri-weekly talking sessions, now in their twelfth year—H.'s illness is that she is very seriously rich—so that by my arithmetic her analyst has heard more stories from her than the Sultan from Scheherazade. I tease her about this, reminding her of Karl Kraus's "Psychoanalysis is the disease of which it pretends to be the cure"; likening analysts, as outlets for talk, to manicurists and coiffeurs; and warning her that today's aggressiveness, like tomorrow's meekness, is all a matter of how her shrink pulls the strings.

For the first visit, H. is caparisoned in ultra-super sheath pants, solid gold waist chain, ear ornaments resembling the appliance that used to be worn before the advent of The Pill. For the second one, this outfit is exchanged for a paneled bakelite micro-mini with fluorescent buttons, fishnet stockings, hoop earrings the size of canaries' trapezes. H. herself sometimes seems as easily changeable as her wardrobe, but that is untrue, and she is charming, genuinely unaffected (no air about her of "I don't mind if you don't matter"), as well as shy (less genuinely, more like a Mark-4 tank), and personally winning in every way. Still, the talking cure is not yet a complete success, and more sofa work is undoubtedly in store—to judge by her habit of packing her bags at four in the morning and tiptoeing out, like Santa Claus, or a thief, for the declared reason, if caught and pressed to reveal it, that "I feel rejected."

1966

Louisville. The Liebermann-Leacock film of I.S., which he sees for the first time after our rehearsal this evening, is the most natural view of him, above all of his genial side, ever likely to be made. It is also the least scripted, least manipulated by technicians, advertisers, ax-grinders, of all the filmed portraits of I.S. In fact, its only misrepresentation is that the time sequence has been jumbled for effect. And its only drawback is that, like all one-man documentaries, it is essentially an obituary. But it would be worth seeing for five remarks alone. The first is I.S.'s disarming explanation, in reply to a question about his anti-Wagnerism, that "Everybody who makes something new does harm to something old." The second is prompted by a question, raised during a tea party with Christopher Isherwood and Gerald Heard, about the creative process. "There is no creative process for me, only the pleasure," he says, adding, off-sound: "Imaginative processes have their laws, but if I could formulate them, they might stop being useful to me." Then in response to a question as to whether he cares if his music is performed, he says: "Of course I am interested to hear if I was right or not." But the most valuable two remarks in the film occur (transposed) at the end. "I am always happy when I am awakened," he says, "and it is the same with composing." And finally, the eighty-four-year-old composer remarks that

"In the morning we think differently than in the evening. When I come to a difficulty, I wait until tomorrow. I can wait as an insect can wait."

NOVEMBER 14

Honolulu. I.S. describes the tuning up before the orchestra plays as "The ritual of 'A,' which, as soon as it has been observed, permits every chord thereafter to be out of tune." But Itzhak Perlman's playing of I.S.'s Violin Concerto at today's rehearsal pleases the composer as much as any performance of his music for a long time. When Perlman mentions Isaac Stern in connection with his study of the Concerto, I.S. tells me that he thinks of Stern's appearance as "still embryonic, a kind of unborn Beethoven."

A letter from L. rawly exposes what I have known for some time, but out of vanity not been willing to admit. And I mind especially, and no less vainly, because other people must have seen it so transparently.

> When amorists grow bald and amours shrink
> Into the compass and curriculum
> Of introspective exiles, lecturing ...

Stevens's lines come to mind as, swimming across the warm lagoon and the warmer reef to the surf (the loneliness of the long-distance swimmer), I find myself to be the only over-twenties, to say nothing of thirties and forties, in a group of still bald-chested surfboarding boys. This suddenly makes me aware that age differences had been suspended, and that the mask I must have been wearing against myself has now been lifted. But I must oust the feeling, or cauterize it.

Will writing about it help? One of the oldest forms of surgery, after all, is the Anatomy of Love, and an exploratory operation can at least discover whether the ego is tumorous. Thus:

1. All love is self-love, all talk of sacrifice for the other is rhetoric. ("Talk," yes. But the formulation is eighteenth-century, and the ground on which such remarks were once made has been superseded by psychology.)

2. Love is like talent in that he who knows it truly—*i.e.*, has not mistaken an identity or used it as a form of conquest—can never lose it entirely. (Pointless, and the area of confusion is too great.)

3. We are more agreeable when in love than at less enchanted times, partly because the best of reality is intensified for us and the worst hidden. (Still *dix-huitième* and valueless in the absence of statistics.)

4. The opposite of love is the fear of possessing or, which is the same thing, of being possessed. (Undevelopable in these terms.)

5. Love is uncharitable; we cannot beg it. (A cliché.)

6. The paradox of love is that we are more aware of its limitations during it than at any other time. (A Stendhal novel in this.)

7. Infidelity is natural to all "true" lovers, for "true" love is dependent

1966

299

and the deprivation of the other "unbearable," whence the recourse to substitutes, as exemplified in the supposed high incidence of posthumous cuckolding, and the need of all about-to-be-unfaithful wives or husbands to assure themselves and their adulterers that they really love the wives or husbands they are about to betray; these assurances are, of course, perfectly "sincere." (Too many hidden assumptions.)

8. Even a single experience of the depths of love's labour's lost should have taught us that our "inconsolable" feelings will change. Yet we continue to pretend that it is within our power to mortgage future ones, as if we could promise a love that "death cannot abate" or pledge our love "forever," by which, even in love's exaggeration, we do not mean some extension beyond time, but an experience endlessly in it, and therefore above all, now. (Obvious.)

9. After the first fall, experience in love does not count, in the sense that we do not learn any more from more of it. How otherwise explain Lothario's successiveness and the length of Leporello's seed catalog? And how explain the experience of encountering a former till-death-do-us-part lover a cold interval later and wondering how we "ever could have"? (Obvious but worth repeating.)

10. While our "rational" parts are fully aware of the circumstantiality of life, our far more powerful "irrational" ones prefer to cling to false absolutes, including the idea of an absolute love. (A parochial observation.)

1966

11. Memory is no less circumstantial, and in the radically different circumstances of Hawaii it is already dimmer and less poignant; even that last encapsulated moment together, our last full exchange of love, is beginning to dissolve, as capsules will; and involuntary, purely glandular proclivities, the recognition of which made me feel disloyal only a week ago—acknowledgment even of the existence of anyone else representing a move away from L. and confirming the possibility of a post-L. world, which in my "heart" I did not want—are now invested with a decidedly voluntary element, if not yet a full return to normal nympholepsis. (Personal.)

12. We talk about swallowing our vanity and our pride, but love is the bitterest and least digestible—it is more often and more convincingly described as sickness than as health—of these in any case unnourishing metaphorical meals. (Literary.)

13. The unresponsive mistress may prove to have been a more fertile theme for poetry (Campion, Donne) than the fully cooperating, and aggressively abetting, one in the line of Marvell's *To his Coy Mistress.* (*Ditto,* and remains to be seen.)

14. All lovers are ridiculous. (See 1–13 above.)

I empty out today's bag of platitudes—the circumstantial brain—on the beach, to escape not only the throb of Hawaiian music in the bar, but the people, for if the air is "like silk," as everyone says, and the sea "like satin," then the texture of the tourists is gunnysack. But will I, after this little

A. At Lewisohn Stadium,
New York, July 11, 1962.

B. With Mme Furtseva, the
Minister of Culture, and
Mr. and Mrs. Dmitri Shos-
takovich; Moscow, 1962.

∧ A   ∨ B

A. At a rehearsal conducted by the author, Moscow, 1962.

B. Applauding the author's performance of *The Rite of Spring,* Moscow, 1962.

C. The *dramatis personae* on the S.S. *Bremen,* April 1963.

∧ B

∨ C

< A

∧ A   ∨ B   ∧ C

A. At home, with dictionary, 1967. *(Photo by Roddy McDowell)*

B. On his eighty-fifth birthday, Coronado Beach. *(Photo by Vera Stravinsky)*

C. At home, a year later. *(Photo by Bobby Klein)*

∧ A   B >

c >

A. The *dramatis personae,* two decades down, New York,
   September 24, 1968. *(Photo by Arnold Weissberger)*

B. Hôtel Royale, Evian, August 1970. *(Photo by
   Rita Christiansen)*

C. The Essex House, New York, March 1971, with Mme
   Natasha Nabokov. *(Photo by Ed Allen)*

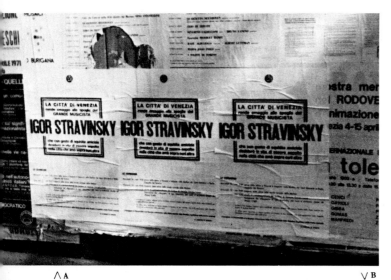

∧ A

∧ B

A. A wall in Venice,
   April 13, 1971.
   (Photo by Ed Allen)

B. Approaching San
   Michele, April 15,
   1971. *(Photo by
   Ed Allen)*

exercise of penmanship, be able to work at last? "Weeping Eros is the builder of cities," Auden says.

Hollywood. A visit from Yevgeny Yevtushenko, which the I.S.'s much enjoy, the family affection Russians are able to turn on at first acquaintance, even Russians holding such different views as the I.S.'s and Y.Y., amazing me once again. Yevgeny Alexandrovich—the conversation is immediately on first-name terms—arrives with translator and publicity team in tow, but as soon as he has been pictured peeling his jacket under the tropical glare of his photographers' lamps, this entourage retires to another room. V. chats with him about Gorodetsky, Kuzmin, Vladimir Nabokov,[1] and other writers she had known in the Crimea during the Revolution, and of whom, she says later, Yev. Alex. reminded her. He listens carefully to her description of Osip Mandelstam in the Crimea in 1917: "Mandelstam was always ardent and always hungry, except that, as everyone was hungry at the time, perhaps I should say even hungrier than other people. Having very few clothes, he parsimoniously hoarded the best of them, including an emergency shirt, as he called it, and a pair of almost-fully-soled shoes. He called on us once wearing a raincoat and nothing else, and paced up and down by our cupboard the whole time like a peripatetic philosopher, not to keep warm but to find out—sniffing like a Platonic philosopher—whether our larder had any food. I remember a train trip with him to Simferopol. The cars were so crowded with soldiers and refugees that babies sleeping on the floor were helmeted with pails to keep them from being crushed by people struggling to push through. Dressed like a Muslim woman for protection from the soldiers, I sat between Mandelstam and Sudeikine." Yevtushenko tops this tale with an account of Mandelstam's death, "drowned by bread, literally choking on it. His dying request was for *Russian* bread." (Y.Y.'s words, my italics.)

Of all the cultural ambassadors from the U.S.S.R. to have visited the I.S.'s, Yevtushenko is the first to notice the contents of the house. He looks at everything, in fact, inspecting objects as one would do in a flea market, and admiring the paintings, especially one by V., thereby being presented with it on the spot, which is called Russian hospitality. Near the end of the visit he suffers one minor setback, trying to turn the talk to Shostakovich and provoking I.S.'s point-blank dismissal; but he recovers in time to mention several favorite compositions by I.S. himself.

Why am I recording this not very momentous encounter? I had not intended to, in any case, nor was I attentive during it until I saw how animated the I.S.'s became speaking the *lingua materna* not, for a change, with other *émigrés*, but with a representative of the younger generation of the actual Russian-speaking state. It seemed to me, too, that they were more natural with Yev. Alex. than they are with their closest American friends.

1. V.'s English tutor in Paris was the novelist's brother, Serge.

1966

1948
1949
1950
1951
1952
1953
1954
1955
1956
1957
1958
1959
1960
1961
1962
1963
1964
1965
1966
1967
1968
1969
1970
1971

ITINERARY

January 1: I.S. conducts in Chicago, then flies to New York. **12:** I.S.'s fly to Hollywood. **15:** I.S. attends concert in Inglewood (Wagner, Mozart, Tchaikovsky, Beethoven, conducted by R.C.). **16:** I.S. attends concert in Los Angeles County Museum of Art, Monteverdi *Vespers*. **18:** I.S. conducts his last recording, the 1945 *Firebird* Suite. **February 14:** We fly to Miami. **24:** Concert in Miami. **25:** We fly to Los Angeles. **27:** Concert in Beverly Hilton Hotel. **28:** We fly to Seattle. **March 1:** I.S. conducts *Histoire du Soldat*. **2:** We fly to Hollywood. **April 7:** R.C. flies from New York to Lexington for a concert and lecture. **May 12:** We fly to Toronto. **17:** I.S. conducts the *Pulcinella* Suite, his last concert (televised, CBC). **18:** We fly to New York and Los Angeles (31st). **August 21:** I.S. enters the Cedars of Lebanon Hospital. **24:** I.S. is transferred to Mt. Sinai Hospital. **September 4:** I.S. returns from the hospital.

JANUARY 9

New York. A breath-fogging night. Dinner with Marcel Duchamp, who is tight-lipped and *sec*, but in aspect only. And what an aspect! The profile might have served for a Renaissance numismatic or medallion portrait, whereas the posture and the backward tilt of the head are characteristic of equestrian heroes—Pisanello's "Leonello d'Este," for example, a far-fetched comparison that I attribute partly to something equine about Duchamp himself, partly to his talk about the armor of scorpions. He is neat, well barbered, tightly tailored. He sports a daunting pink shirt and blue necktie, but when complimented on this natty combination dismisses it as a

Christmas present. Conversation gets under way with the mention of Giacometti, but when someone remarks that this mutually lamented friend must have been "a *triste* person," Duchamp objects to the word: "Not *triste*, tormented." Certainly neither description could ever have applied to anyone with the raptorial acuity of Duchamp himself.

But what *are* the feelings of a man who, when the subject gravitates to airplane crashes—I am flying tomorrow—contributes the thought that "Death in the air is a good way to go because you explode"? (*Vs.* death in bed from a heart attack because you implode?) They are not morbid feelings, certainly, the thought being purely logical to him, with no more emotional coloring than one of his chess moves. But what may seem untrue to type in a crystallizing mind such as his is the keen susceptibility to outside amusements. He tells a story about the Queen of England at an exhibition of his work at the Tate Gallery questioning an embarrassed curator about an object Her Majesty did not seem to see was ithyphallic. But he quickly follows this drollery with the observation that "A freedom we are all much in need of at present is freedom from bad wit."

Tunneling a chimney through an after-dinner cigar with an ice pick, he handles the awkward awl so adeptly that we watch as if he were sculpting a new anti-masterpiece, which of course he is. But just as he once vandalized the "Mona Lisa" with a mustache, so the cigar ruins the Pisanello profile.

1967

FEBRUARY 14

I spend the day writing captions and an "Afterword" for Arnold Newman's photograph album, *Bravo Stravinsky:*

I

During the morning of December 13, 1966, Stravinsky, who always knows exactly when his imagination is at the starting line, expressed "the need to put an idea in order." About thirty-five minutes later he had completed a sketch, which, however, did not extend from that "idea." Soon after, Mrs. Stravinsky clapped her hands together in the hall below her husband's studio, her signal that lunch is ready, and Stravinsky applauded back, his signal that he is, too. At table, to show what he meant by "putting in order," the composer placed three wine glasses in parade formation, then interchanged the first and third, saying, "It is all a question of knowing that the notes must be this way and no other."

Stravinsky has identified the sketch as "part of a string passage in the middle section of a symphonic piece," and the presence of instrumental indications (violas and cellos) in this initial stage argues that the springs of his invention are concrete. Nor does the scissoring out of a twelve-note series—which is the beginning of a formulating, not of an abstracting, process—contradict the claim. The composer's next step was to chart his fields of choice by drawing derivative serial forms. These he attached to the side of his piano writing-board, like dressmakers' patterns, pinning the sketch itself to the center, whence it became the incremental center of the composition. From this point, too, he worked exclusively at the piano, not having touched the instrument that morning but composing, as he said, in his inner ear.

303

Clamping the left hand over the mouth is Stravinsky's equivalent gesture for head scratching.

I I

Stravinsky is adopted by a stray kitten. The composer says he feels closer to some animals than to a great many humans, and he will interrupt work to watch animal programs on television, and to visit the zoo before the art gallery in a new city. During the nineteen-fifties, when he spent part of each summer in Venice, musicians and others who wanted a glimpse of him knew that he could be found at a certain time and place each day feeding cats. The Stravinskys kept a clutch of chickens when they first lived in California, and they would have added cows, goats, and a whole *Renard* barnyard as well, but for zoning laws and neighbors who, in the composer's words, "wanted every lawn to look as tidy as a cemetery or golf course." The Stravinsky house was a rookery, a bird cage, a wildlife refuge. Canaries had the run of the living room, munching the leather book bindings and target-practicing on the lampshades, while as many as forty lovebirds (some making love, some just necking) could be counted in the kitchen. At table, obstreperous parakeets, gifts of Emil Ludwig, took turns pecking food directly from the composer's mouth—and depositing nibs, feathers, and unmentionable other matter uncomfortably near one's own *déjeuner*. For a time, too, an extraordinarily un-shy hummingbird used the composer's hand as a helipad.

I I I

Vera (*née* de Bosset) Stravinsky did not become a full-time painter until 1950, but within a decade she had mounted very successful exhibitions in Rome, Tokyo, Tel Aviv, Milan, Mexico City, New York, Santa Barbara, Los Angeles. In Paris in the twenties and thirties, she directed an atelier that supplied costumes for ballet and opera, designing some of the products herself and some in collaboration with, among others, Matisse and Rouault. In Hollywood during the war she founded the gallery "La Boutique," which became a center of local artistic life, especially for artists in exile. Madame Stravinsky's favorite painters are Turner, Redon, Klimt, Klee, Nicolas de Staël, but she cites floral and marine forms as among the primary influences on her painting. Her first pictures were impressions of redwood forests in rain and fog, and of California oil refineries at night. She works every day, household schedules and her husband's concert nomadism permitting, in a studio behind and separate from the Stravinsky house. And her husband visits her there every day, invariably responding to her work as he is doing in the photograph: with resounding osculations.

I V

Patience royale, the painter steering, the composer ruddering. When Stravinsky plays solitaire, it is not a quiet game, and an eavesdropping collector of late-Czarist-period Russian *gros mots* would surely be able to increase his store. Solitaire is the perfect pastime for Stravinsky between spells of composing: it occupies only a small and automatic part of his mind, leaving the musical digestion parts uncompetitively to their own processes.

A regular occurrence at noontime meals, but an alarming one to guests, is the composer's bout of sneezing. ("There are conditions under which the most majestic person is obliged to," as George Eliot wrote.) "Here comes my allergy," Stravinsky will announce (allergy to *what,* Scotland grains?), and then, always either nine or eleven times, sneeze. The third party in the photograph is the "onlie begetter" of these rambling interlineations. He is known to the other two as—imagine a deep-sloping Slavic intonation—*"Bobe."* In Russian it means "bean."

V

Word investigations and lexical comparisons are a regular part of Stravinsky's day. He will not allow an uncertain term to pass until he has satisfied himself with a full etymological as well as, if any, a current-usage understanding of it, after which he will further pursue it for equivalents in other languages. At present he reads and writes in English more regularly than in Russian or French, but in conversation favors these other languages, and in that order. He was in his fifties when he began to study English methodically, at a Paris Berlitz, in preparation for an American tour.

The score of the *Requiem Canticles* stands on the piano music rack, the upper right corner of which is fastened with paper clamps arranged to look like the prow of a gondola. The bronze stylus on the ledge above the keyboard is Stravinsky's patented invention. It has drawn the staves for most of his music since *Petrushka.* The pictures on the wall are of Claudio Monteverdi playing a lute; four photographic negatives of drawings by Cocteau; and Michel Larionov's drawing of a cat, intended as a cover design for Stravinsky's *Cat Lullabies.*

V I

The locket over Stravinsky's bed contains a miniature icon that his son Theodore copied from an old master. Diaghilev admired it, and since the impresario's death it has accompanied the composer as an amulet on all of his travels;[1] the chain of Mexican gold, an heirloom and the gift of the composer Carlos Chavez, was added in 1940. The shelf beyond the bed displays several eighteenth- and early-nineteenth-century icons. The photographs below are of the Turin shroud and the "Zurbarán" Lamb in the San Diego Museum. Further along the wall are daguerreotypes of Stravinsky's maternal grandparents and, directly below, an English watercolor.

V I I

Vera Stravinsky's life has been hardly less eventful than her husband's. Born in St. Petersburg of French and Swedish ancestry—but no Russian, in spite of Thomas Mann's description of her "specifically Russian beauty . . ."—she was a well-known actress in her youth, both on the stage (the Kammerny Theater, Moscow) and in films (Elena in *War and Peace*). She learned to play the piano at an early age; an aunt was a "professor" of the instrument in the St. Petersburg Conservatory. At that same time one of her uncles, the cellist Malmgreen, was employing the teen-age Stravinsky to play piano accompaniments; but the young composer and his future wife did not meet then, or ever in Russia, and in fact discovered this connection only recently. Mlle de Bosset's acting career ended with the Revolution, whose first throes, in St. Petersburg in March 1917, she witnessed crossing the frozen Neva to hear Gorky speak, and several times being exposed to the cross-fire of street-fighting. In May 1917 she fled to Yalta, with her husband, the painter Serge Sudeikine, and from there, two years later, to Tiflis. By May 1920, the couple had saved enough money to buy passage on the *Souhira,* a French steamer bound for

1967

---

1. And now to his grave.

Marseilles. But about three hours out of Batum they were pirated—by "Georgians who spoke Russian like Stalin," Mme Stravinsky recalls. Except that she was Mme Sudeikine then. Apart from herself, everyone aboard was relieved of his portable valuables. Not only was Mme Sudeikine *not* plundered, however, but the gallant corsair chieftain left a purse of Turkish lire at her feet, when he parted—a tribute to her beauty, of course (see the portraits of her at the time by Jacovlev, Sorin, Bakst), for the discriminating swashbuckler could not have been aware of her warmth and generosity, her talent and intelligence, her goodness and grace. But gratifying as this adventure must have been to the recipient, it could hardly have increased her popularity with the other passengers, most of whom, fortunately, left the marauded boat at Constantinople. She still wears one of these coins as an amulet, incidentally, and regards its protective powers as second only to Stravinsky's gift to her, a gold bracelet that says "I love you."

VIII

Yevgeny Yevtushenko is fast-moving (and rapidly appraising), but he arrived at the Stravinskys, with a cameraman and news bureau in tow, an hour late. The Stravs briefed themselves during the delay, however, and thus were able to greet him as "Yevgeny Alexandrovitch." Conversation began with a discussion of Anna Akhmatova, Mme Stravinsky recently having received an ink silhouette of herself from Akhmatova, dated St. Petersburg during the Revolution. Yevgeny Alexandrovitch offered to recite a poem of his about Akhmatova's funeral, if the Stravinskys would care—well, yes, they would—to hear it. The rendition was stirring, and the most accomplished of maudlin actors might have envied the voice and delivery, even if these attributes do not show to best advantage in stageless, pulpitless, and merely medium-sized parlors. When the recitation had finally ebbed, the poet candidly confessed his inability to warm up (that was cold?) before audiences of "less than two thousand people." But the Stravs liked the poem and said so, thereupon being rewarded with two encores, about which the only area of judgment open to me was one of admiration for the poet's memory.

1967

"Are you coming back [to America]?" the Stravinskys asked, as Yevgeny Alexandrovitch bade them "*Dezvidanyiya.*" And the poet's anachronistic answer, "God knows," reminded us that he is a compatriot of Daniel and Sinyavsky and, by that fact alone, a man of courage. His visit made the Stravinskys homesick.

IX

Picasso's portrait of the resident, and a partial view of the Stravinsky living room, here with Christmas tree. The composer, in his library, examines old programs with Sol Hurok, who once danced (!) in *Petrushka*. At one point Stravinsky observed to the impresario that "All of these people are now dead," a wrenching remark because he seems so little attached to the past and so rarely expresses feelings about it. (The contents of a man's rooms speak back and forth to him, nevertheless, and Stravinsky's are heaped with mementos.) The magazine in the foreground is opened to a photograph of Vera de Bosset as the Queen in Diaghilev's 1921 revival of *The Sleeping Beauty*.

X

The manuscript on the left is an excerpt, words ("I'd give a rouble for her") and rhythms only, from *The Wedding*. It is from Mme Sudeikine's autograph album for March 1921. "I forget the rest," Stravinsky has added. The adjacent costume sketches by Eugene Berman are for a staging of Stravinsky's *Renard* in Rome, October 1966. The small encroaching photograph dates from Stravinsky's thirty-first birthday; it was taken in a sanatorium in Neuilly, where he was recovering from typhus. The picture of Rimsky-Korsakov, next right, was made by Stravinsky himself in the older composer's St. Petersburg apartment. Next to it the Stravinskys flank their hosts at the White House, January 18, 1962. Again to the right is Stravinsky's portrait of Diaghilev, drawn in a Paris restaurant on a scrap of paper whose folds and blemishes, according to the composer, corresponded so strikingly to the subject's features that the portraitist had to do no more than "fill in." The photograph in the upper right corner poses Stravinsky and Otto Klemperer in Leipzig, 1929. In the one next to it the Stravinskys are in New York, in 1965. To the left again is a group of Diaghilev dancers. Giacometti's portrait of Stravinsky, top center, separates two of the composer's favorite photographs of his wife, one from Rome at the time of her first exhibition there, in 1955, the other, with her Angora, "Mashka," on the garden steps of the De Bosset country home at Kudinovo, near Moscow. (Another pet at Kudinovo was a cow, "*La Générale,*" and just as royal families traveled with their own bottled water, so the De Bossets journeyed with fresh milk, taking "*La Générale*" with them, in a box car, on their trips from Moscow to St. Petersburg.)

The framed triptych mounts Stravinsky's own photographs of Nijinsky (Monaco, 1911) and Diaghilev (Nice, 1910), along with an unremembered someone else's photograph of Stravinsky, Diaghilev, Lifar. Stravinsky's caricature, "*Tête de Picasso,*" is as powerful a study of the artist as the artist's of the composer. The oval snapshot, inscribed "Paris, May 1920," poses Stravinsky together with Mme André Derain (seated), Edward Clark, Ansermet, Derain. The adjoining photograph of Stravinsky with Debussy was taken by Erik Satie in Debussy's home, 80, avenue du Bois. The book about the California corpse business by the man in the bowler amused and horrified Stravinsky to the extent that he actually undertook his own investigations at Forest Lawn and the Hollywood Pet Cemetery. In the photographs to the right, Stravinsky is shown first with C. F. Ramuz, and second with Diaghilev, here looking like a "mod" Home Secretary, as he welcomes the composer at Croydon airport a few days before the English première of *The Wedding.*

XI

Beckman Auditorium, the California Institute of Technology, Pasadena, November 3. Stravinsky the conductor is often regarded as a lifesize (still small, though) metronome. And so far as it goes, he does not object to the description. "If the conductor beats time precisely and at the indicated speed, the music will take care of itself," he says. Which isn't true, of course, but it shows to what extent Stravinsky would like to harness the profession. In fact he will grant little difference between the orchestral and streetcar branches of conducting; the practitioners of both types, he says, need do little more than start and stop their vehicles and keep them on the rails. (It follows that he dislikes the performances of all freeway-type conductors, and that sports-car conductors are anathema.) But all of this is only in principle, and principally for other conductors. He goes about the matter differently himself, for the inexorableness of the composer and the inexorableness of the conductor involve substantial changes of view. In brief, the performer edits the creator in numerous small but, concerning diction, radical ways. Which is the principal reason that Stravinsky's own performances of his music always reveal something new about it.

XII

Stravinsky listens to a Beethoven symphony as apparently he alone is able to do: with innocent ears and as if for the first time. Beethoven has occupied his mind more than any other composer in recent years—the Beethoven, above all, of the late sonatas and quartets.

The drapery in the unwigged, dome view of the composer is not a "Mother Hubbard" but the upholstering of his chair. After the rehearsal, some Cal Tech students invited him to a "wine" party (Glenlivet for the composer, Gallo and Manischewitz for the young boffins). He accepted and enjoyed himself answering their questions, "Because of the chance that one of these young people may keep going."

XIII

December 15. The composer listens from the control room while excerpts from his music are recorded for a travelogue, and during the playbacks he discusses the performances with the players. The choice of these excerpts, the mating of photo-geography with episodes from, largely, ballet scores, was a welcome diversion for the Stravinskys. The winning combination was undoubtedly that of the "Apotheosis" from *Apollo* to underscore (undermine?) a tour of the District of Columbia's most hallowed monuments. The other most ingenious matches were the use of the last section of the "Interlude" from *Agon* as a requiem for Arlington's Unknown Soldier, and of the beginning of the "Nurses' Dance" in *Petrushka* to accompany a narrow-gauge Rocky Mountain train ("huffa-chuffa"). Yet even the most promising of these marriages proved to be less than ideal, for the reason that the forms of strong music assert themselves too strongly, which is to say independently, and ultimately, therefore, subversively. Nearly all of Stravinsky's lighter music had to be rejected, too, because of its fundamental irony, until eventually, and no less predictably, *The Firebird* became the filmmakers' chief resource. It is, after all, the richest in mood clichés of all of Stravinsky's scores. In fact, each of the passages chosen had long since borne the moviemakers' own stamp of a description or character, the "*Berceuse,*" for example, answering to the "eeriness" of Monument Valley to their complete satisfaction. Stravinsky: "Eerie it may be, but I scar-cely thought, in 1910, that I was composing music for Utah landscapes."

1967

After the recording session, someone asked the composer a general question about the use of music in films. "But it shouldn't be used," he said, "except where logically required by contexts, such as in scenes of concerts and in furnishing the imagination of a musically minded character. There can be no real relationship between what one sees and what one hears, but only habit relationships, all bad. Most filmmakers continue to treat music as sound effects and wall-to-wall emotional carpeting, nevertheless; or, in other words, on more or less the same level as cat food. And as if trying to tie it to concrete sentiments and things were not bad enough, they also attempt to synchronize its own events to movements of the camera, making the horn 'sting' coincide with the 'zoom-in,' the 'expansive theme' with the 'pan-across,' the orchestral *crescendo* with the visual 'tilt-up.'"

XIV

The Stravinskys live a mere few hundred yards north of the Sunset Strip, and hence a still smaller distance above the present hairline of the hourly more harrowing smog. The neighborhood itself might be a large-scale Happening. Only a short walk from the composer's home are such famous "topless" and "bottomless" restaurants as "The Naked Lunch" ("Serving Double-Breasted Milkshakes") and "The Body Shop" ("Kama Sutra Is Here"). Tribes of Neanderthal Men (so different are the new coiffures from the Castrovian modes of a year ago) now prowl streets lined with billboards advertising aerosol snow ("Have A Kool Yule") and "Christmas Trees Painted Any Color You Want," decrying "Blue Fascism" (the police) and paging "Lee Harvey Oswald, We Need You Now." Whatever notice the composer takes of these surroundings, he is fully aware of the social erosion in them. Stravinsky *is* political-minded, but he has not been politically involved to any great extent since the outbreak of the First World War, when he predicted and welcomed a Russian revolution (see Romain Rolland's *Journal des Années de Guerre*).

Nor does he have any connection with movieland Hollywood, his friends among the stars (and nebulae) of filmdom dating back to the Dietrich era, and including the wrinkle-proof Blue Angel herself, a "fan" of the composer's and now a neighbor. In the photograph, Stravinsky is greeted by "Mrs. Miniver," an acquaintance from his summers in Santa Fe.

X V

The sketchbook of the *Requiem Canticles* is also a necrology of friends who died during its composition. The composer once referred to these pasted-in obituaries as a "practical commentary." Each movement seems to relate to an individual death, and though Stravinsky denies that it really does, the framing of his musical thoughts by the graves of friends (that touching cross for Giacometti) exposes an almost unbearably personal glimpse of his mind.

In some of the photographs the composer is comparing corrections between his manuscript and that of a copyist, and, in the last one, between his manuscript score and a page of the original sketch. The latter is virtually a complete text of the music—the next, full-score stage, being little more than a copying job, at least for Stravinsky. Early notations are generally preserved in duodecimo sketchbooks (such as the one with the necrology), which are diaries not only of his musical thoughts but of some of his thoughts *about* music and other matters as well. He will refer to all three sources until a work is in print, and until that time none of the three is ever far from his person. The sketch of the *"Rex Tremendae"* shows that the pitches of the notes have occurred a stage ahead of their metrical groupings, while that of the *"Exaudi"* offers specimens of the composer's instrumental shorthand, and of his method of marking serial groupings. The *"Tuba Mirum"* sketch invites the reader to hypothesize the composer's thinking from a larval stage to the final score.

X V I

Stravinsky's redrawing of Edward Lear's cover for *The Owl and the Pussy-Cat* adds waves because, as the composer explained, "My music is rocking the boat." *The Owl and the Pussy-Cat* was the first English verse that Vera Stravinsky committed to memory. Later she became almost as fond of Francis Steegmuller's French version of it, and it was the latter that originally attracted Stravinsky to the poem. "To Vera," the dedication reads, and the owl may well have had the pussy-cat's gentle voice and modest pianism in mind while writing the song. The elegant fowl kept the composition a secret, in any case, until he had sung and played it to his feline love—not, of course, in a pea-green boat, but in his soundproof roost.

1967

309

The first rehearsal of the song put the composer into a pet, and he is jumping down everyone's neck: *Sauve qui peut.* Having completed the music only a few days before, he is naturally very full of it and of exactly how it should be performed. "Straighter, quieter, without *vibrato,* more spoken and more simple," he says, and some sharp "no's" punctuate the proceedings when these strictures are less than perfectly heeded.

X V I I I

Halloween. The composer of *The Owl and the Pussy-Cat,* arriving for its first performance, at a Monday Evening Concert (Hollywood), is greeted by Arthur Morton, the composer of *Peyton Place.* Stravinsky listened backstage. But whatever his thoughts about his own creation, he left the concert overwhelmed by Beethoven's Sonata, Opus III, played by Michael Tilson Thomas, which concluded the program.

X I X

Maria Milena, named by her father after the Princess of Montenegro, was born in Lausanne while Stravinsky was composing the last act of the fairy-tale opera *The Nightingale.* Stravinsky is a family man. He would like to be surrounded by his children and grandchildren—and now great-grand-, too: Svetlana Stravinsky, born February 1967—but since the War only Milena sees him regularly. With her husband, André Marion, she moved from France to Los Angeles in 1947, and has lived only a few blocks from her father ever since.

1967

X X

The composer packs his concert uniform first, as he prepares to depart for Columbus, Ohio; and he is the first passenger aboard the DC-7. The flight was not smooth, the plane bumping in an atmosphere like "snow" on a TV screen, and later in a Walpurgis Night. "If we didn't have seat belts, we would be clinging to the ceiling like bats," Stravinsky remarked, and when he was again on terra firma, confessed he had been afraid we were going to be "front-page news." He enjoys flying, nevertheless, and positively basks in the attentions of the stewardesses, except when they call him "folks" and wake him up with mid-flight bulletins on the outside temperature, "as if we were planning to eject ourselves." The landing at Columbus was not only abrupt but of the kind referred to in space-speak as "eyeballs-out." When the composer left the plane, however, all of the stewardesses, and an old lady who looked like George Washington, asked for and received his autograph.

X X I

The auditorium at Columbus adjoins a casket factory—advertising itself in realistic mauve neon—on the wrong side, from the center of the city, of the Scioto River which is pronounced like the Bridge of Sighs and provokes similar deflations. The program was difficult—a "fix-bayonets-men" expression from the band as it came on stage—but well played. The most responsive instrument in the orchestra, how-ever, was Mr. Newman's camera. Whether Stravinsky was cueing the bassoons, the trumpets, or any other section, Mr. Newman was always in its midst and always on the beat. Finally, but sad to relate, Mr. Newman unwisely concealed himself beneath the bass drum during the *Firebird,* from which vantage he was carried out after the concert suffering from shell shock.

XXII

The Stravinskys watched a film during the flight from Chicago to Seattle, but the composer's apparent absorption in such entertainments does not invariably guarantee that he is successfully following them. Near the end, in fact, he inquired about the identity of a character who had already appeared several hundred times: *"Ktoh eta?"* (Who is that?) V.S.: *"Ubitsa, koneechna."* (The murderer, of course.) I.S.: *"Kak ti eta znyesh?"* (How can you tell?) But the befuddlement may have been a result of cocktail hour, which is what Stravinsky likes best about flying, except when the sudden tide of alcohol washes away the good fences between good neighbors. It began, for him, with a course of medical *hors-d'oeuvre:* Glutovite, for the memory; and "leapies" (pep pills). "There is no way of knowing whether they help," he says, "but if you are willing, maybe they do." And down they went, followed by a variety of libations including some under-the-counter refills from his own stores.

XXIII

Stravinsky's piano is sent to his room in the Hotel Pierre during each of his longer New York visits. It is muted with felt, like the one in his studio at home, and he quickly furnishes it with his writing tools, and decorates the tables and walls around with pictures of his own, rather than of the hotel's, choice. He has not yet done so in the photograph because he is impatient to play notations made in the last few days, when he was without an instrument. He pretends to believe, incidentally, that coincidence is the only force at work, or play, when a line he composes contains twelve different pitches in succession, though if this phenomenon were reported of some other composer he would be the first to see that hearing and thinking in units of twelve is to some extent a matter of habit. Perhaps I should add that Stravinsky seldom volunteers much information about work-in-progress, the crisis in the soul, in his case, being reflected by moody silences. Another reliable sign that creative problems are under attack is a return to the Eighteenth Amendment—repealed, of course, the moment they have been solved.

XXIV

The conductor at this first full rehearsal of the *Requiem Canticles* is neither auditioning for ogre parts in Grade B thrillers, nor suffering withdrawal pains—nor even, so far as he knows, reverting to a less underwrought previous existence: he (the "onlie begetter") simply comes on that way. Nor is the chessboard floor a Newman "property," but genuine décor of New York's Henry Hudson Hotel.

The interaction of conductor and composer is a vital condition of Stravinsky's art, and his need for performing experience has been lifelong. He always conducts along with the actual conductor at rehearsals of his (and other people's) music, and he will beat meter patterns and give cues even while listening to a piano sonata. Incidentally, his baton during *this* rehearsal was somewhat unusual: a tissue of Kleenex. Listening to a new work for the first time, his attention seems to be channeled exclusively to questions of performance, above all to balance, meaning that which is not heard distinctly enough; and to tempo, of which there are usually only two kinds for him: too fast and too slow. As the rehearsal proceeded, he adjusted notations of dynamics and articulation and was always ready with bits of advice to the players, but of his thoughts about the music itself, he vouchsafed almost nothing.

XXV

Princeton, October 8. The composer presides at the dress rehearsal, which was open to musicians and students, most of whom were hearing the *Variations* (1964) as well as the *Requiem Canticles* for the first time. The fact that music of such newness could be composed by a man in his mid-eighties amazed everyone, but especially the young people who were just learning to become the old man's contemporaries.

In the "greenroom" before the concert, the composer studied the score of his *Symphonies of Wind Instruments,* then planned his post-concert "getaway"—with the thoroughness of a bank robber. During intermission he received Dr. Robert Oppenheimer, who had led the standing ovation at the beginning of the concert as well as defied an injunction in the program not to applaud at the end of the *Requiem;* only four months later a recording of the *Canticles* was played at another gathering in Princeton in Dr. Oppenheimer's memory, and at his request.

The audience included a top dressing of composers, all of them in larger and smaller, direct and indirect ways, indebted to Stravinsky. He talked to each of these colleagues after the concert, and to many other people, listening sharply to every comment on the new work and no less sharply to every absence of comment, sixty years in the arena not having insulated him from opinion.

XXVI

Stravinsky and Marcel Duchamp are seeing each other for the first time since about 1920. A meeting of two veterans, then, two who challenged and changed the values to which they were born and now almost sole survivors of a revolution in art and anti-art. It is difficult to realize now that they both occupied lonely outposts once, and that some of the currency of our whole world was at one time theirs alone. "Well, maestro," Duchamp said when they parted, "see you in another fifty years."

1967

XXVII

Stravinsky listens for the first time to a test pressing of the *Requiem Canticles,* deploring the errors, now irremediable (the fault of a corrupt text), that deform the performance. George Balanchine, on the other hand, whether or not he notices these shortcomings, is deeply moved, and moved in his own terms, imagining a choreographic presentation, sacred texts notwithstanding. "Every measure that Stravinsky ever wrote is good for dancing," he says, and proceeds to prove the claim choreographically—arm and hand movements only and no embellishments of costume apart from his rumpled shirt and bolo tie, souvenirs of his frontier days (*Western Symphony* and Maria Tallchief). Stravinsky has a choreographic imagination, too, one hardly needs to add, but when he is with Balanchine, defers to the professional.

AFTERWORD

Mr. Newman's photographs have been grouped in a narrative order and in accordance with their own attributes. But as this is generally the reverse of the actual order, a chronology and slightly more fleshed-out background of the composer's activities during the period covered by the book may be useful.

The period extended from the beginning of October 1966 through the first week of January 1967, the place at both terminal dates being the composer's rooms in the Hotel Pierre, New York. Mr. Newman accompanied the Stravinskys to Princeton University on October 8 for the dress rehearsal and first performance of the *Requiem Canticles,* the occasion that inspired him with the idea of the book. In addition, he spent part of a week with them at the end of October and beginning of November, and another week in mid-December, in Hollywood, and he joined them for a concert in Columbus, Ohio, November 29. In all, photographing took place during some three weeks within a span of three months.

It was not an exceptionally eventful period. In relation to the composer's principal, if, at times, seemingly-lost-sight-of, business on earth, it began with the completion, in mid-October, of *The Owl and the Pussy-Cat,* which had been partly composed in mid-August. A new piece was begun in December—as traced in the book's first photographs, a note-by-note record of the composer actually composing, that was realized only because he had forgotten Mr. Newman was already in the room taking stills of the objects. Stravinsky's secondary work, performing his music, was also light during the three months. Concerts were few and the repertory not taxing, and he did not record at all. Nor was his social calendar heavily inscribed, though, as always, the uninvited visitors outnumbered the invited, Stravinsky being a tourist attraction even in the city of Disneyland and movie stars. Books claimed the largest part of his leisure. He reads continually, with the range of a polymath and the speed of a reviewer, claiming that old age is the best time of life to be a student.

Happily, but rarely true for a period as long as three months, the composer succumbed to no illnesses (apart from hangovers). On the contrary, in fact, his health improved auspiciously. He has a blood disease (polycythemia), and he suffered major cerebral thromboses in 1956 and 1959, the first causing a temporary loss of speech (a short circuit in the Convolution of Broca), the second partially paralyzing, and leaving permanent claudication in, the right leg. At the end of August (1966), the disease apparently switched course, or at any rate failed to respond to its containing treatment. When the composer arrived in New York, following a concert in Louisville, September 17, Roentgen rays were prescribed, and he was exposed to them several times during the week of rehearsals for the Princeton concert as well as in the week following. In fact, a threat of leukemia hangs over his head, a threat of which he was fully aware, during the entire series of New York and Princeton photographs. But the beneficial effects of the radiation exceeded every expectation, as the composer learned after returning home, where, within two weeks, analysis showed a perfect restoration of all chemical percentages and balances.

The chronicle of outer events during the three months included brief treks for pairs of concerts to Honolulu (mid-November), Portland (the beginning of December), and Chicago (the end of December). Portland was less exotic than Honolulu, in spite of perpetual rain and, at the Hilton, mentholated toothpicks and Japanese waitresses—very pretty as they lined up to sing "Happy Bird-Day to OO," and intelligent as well, having quickly learned to ask the composer: "You wish care more Scots whiskey pease?" But the Oregon concerts were satisfying—what a wealth of good underpaid musicians there are in America!—and Governor Hatfield not only came backstage but later sent a medal, which I remark because politicians are usually more careful to keep their distance from the arts, at least in public.

1967

The Stravinskys arrived in Chicago at the winter solstice and under a gooseflesh sky, a harsh contrast to the pavonian colors and rich sea changes of the Hawaii they had so recently departed. The waves of Lake Michigan appeared to have turned to ice at their crests and the surf to have frozen in mid-spray, but the Stravinskys, answering the call of their septentrional childhoods, went out into the snow to "play." The composer received ovations from the Chicago audiences, the "tusch" from the orchestra, and the usual reviews from, so he remarked, "deathwatch-beetle reviewers." ("Stravinsky is the greatest living composer, and I say that sincerely," wrote one of them, to whom sincerity appears to be an exception.) Between times he saw a Neil Simon play and read two volumes of French history, as well as the hourly newspaper reports on Casals's ninetieth birthday. (One of them, beginning "The master inhaled the morning air, exhaled it, again inhaled, then gazed into the face of Vice-President Humphrey, now tear-stained and smearing its make-up," stayed Stravinsky from sending congratulations himself, but he expressed his sympathy several times as well as his fervent hope that Casals's age had not made him sound like the Jack Benny of the cello.) Still another kind of recognition came in the airport on the way to New York, when a teen-age boy, passing him, turned to shout to a companion: "Hey, man, the cat in the wheelchair is IGOR STRAVINSKY!"

". . . when we read the poetry of *King Lear* what is it to us how the poet lived? . . . Peeping and prying into greenroom gossip of the day, the poet's drinking, the poet's debts. We have *King Lear:* and it is immortal." Thus George Russell in *Ulysses.* But Stephen Dedalus's answer, that Shakespeare *is* Hamlet, constitutes the more modern argument. "As we . . . weave and unweave our bodies . . . from day to day, their molecules shuttled to and fro, so does the artist weave and unweave his image . . . so through the ghost of the unquiet father the image of the unliving son looks forth."

Whatever our own views, privacy—which is more and more difficult to define in the Modern State as there is less and less of it—is already, and no doubt permanently, invaded. We are all "on camera." Nor are closed-circuit television, radio-wave detection systems, infra-red photography, wiretapping, and the other ever-improving "bugging" devices likely to restore the castle to the home.

Mr. Newman's "*Histoires Naturelles*" take the viewer into the home, yet do not invade it. But are his pictures true? Is the cameraman more closely bound by fact than the writer, or are the illusionist tricks of both simply too different to be compared? Whatever the answer—and I think it is that verbal accounts can say both more and less than photographs and are therefore not in the same senses either true or untrue—at least none of Mr. Newman's photographs was posed. There are no pin-ups in the book and, to my nose, no whiff of the incense that naturally clouds around the composer nowadays. Neither was any situation staged or conjunction of people arranged: Mr. Newman's camera was never coercive. Once, at the beginning of term, he exhorted the "maestro" to repeat a gesture, but the maestro did not comply and was never again prompted. He went about his routine (some routine!) apparently oblivious of the lenses, though whether he really was oblivious, except in the composing sequence, is difficult to say. One night in a restaurant he called for pen and paper and drew the muzzle-end view of a camera. It looked ominous. (See the Newman Collection, No. 7693.)

As with descriptions in a diary, each of these photographs not only frames but inevitably dramatizes a moment—to the exclusion of other moments, the reader may object, adding that selection distorts by grouping fragments of a large picture to form a different, smaller picture, satisfying another purpose, and providing, at best, a misleading view of the whole that is life itself. Yet memory acts in the same way, and so does art. Mr. Newman has memorized a Stravinsky for all of us, and all who have known the man must agree that each of these recollections is characteristic of one of his many characters.

APRIL 3

After conducting the Boston Opera's third and last performance of *The Rake* last night, I drive to Kingston, and from there to my sister's home at New Paltz. "Samantha has recovered," she says, surprised herself to be pleased at the news, Samantha being a white rat rescued from a laboratory at Cornell by my niece, and since then living encaged, but far from all of the time, in New Paltz. Three mornings ago she was discovered on her back, breathing heavily, legs outstretched and deathly stiff. Until then, the rodent had inspired only the strongest revulsion in my sister, but the sight of the stricken creature emboldened her to reach into the cage, wrap the invalid in a blanket, and rush it to a veterinarian, even though worrying the while about bubonic plague. The diagnosis, as it happened, was merely acute constipation, the treatment an injection of antibiotics and a spoon-feeding of prune juice, after which the patient, tightly cuddled in a blanket, was discharged. This morning Samantha's legs began to flex, and tonight she is her old self again, playing in the living room with the cat and dog, her best friends except when she receives more than her share of attention—which tends to bear out Lorenz's theory that real aggression takes place only within the species. My niece believes that because Samantha has not seen another rat for two years, she may be assuming herself to be one of us. But, speaking for myself, I hope she takes me to be a sinking ship.

1967

APRIL 4

Kingston. Reading Wallace Stevens's letters this morning, I come across a paragraph dated August 1942 that bumps head-on into my own life. Describing "a visit to the Dutch Church at Kingston . . . one of the most beautiful churches that I know of," Stevens says, "the janitor told me that at one time there were nine judges in the congregation . . . and he gave me a pamphlet by one of them . . . Judge Hasbrouck, containing an article on this particular church. The Judge starts out with this: 'When Spinoza's logic went searching for God, it found him in a predicate of substance. The material thing.'" Now, "'the predicate of substance' in this case, was this church: the very building," Stevens says, adding that, "if a lawyer as eminent as Judge Hasbrouck went to church because it made it possible for him to touch, to see the very predicate of substance, do you think he was anything except a poet? Another thing that this episode makes clear is that Spinoza's great logic was appreciated only the other day in Kingston."

It was also being read at the same time and place, though I doubt with very much appreciation, by me. A passionate interest in Spinoza came over me in my eighteenth year, but I have no idea why, except perhaps a quest of reasoning power for its own sake. Determined to master his "great logic," I mounted assault after assault on the *Ethics,* only to recoil again and again from some step in the narrowly consecutive argument over which I had stumbled and could not get past. Then in due course I developed a strongly secular bias that relegated Spinoza's monism to my Index, along with all related claims that the mind of God is reflected in His works, and that human notions of evil are only further proofs of God's perfection.

With Stevens's letter in mind, I walk to the Dutch Church, which is the center of the city even now, as it was of the stockade of 1658. The outlines of the latter are still marked by ridges and glacis, and the eighteenth-century houses within are surprisingly rich both in numbers and quality; nor are the few modern buildings with Dutch gables a serious eyesore.

The fastigiate steeple is the visual radial point of the entire valley. Halfway up is a small window in which, after dark, a ghost was known to appear to children, and for this reason I would avoid short-cutting through the churchyard cemetery at night. George Clinton, the first Governor of New York and later Vice-President of the United States, is buried in this picturesque boneyard, along with many veterans of the War of the Revolution whose graves are marked by iron wreaths stuck in the ground in front of their headstones, like tie-pins. Civil War graves, most of them grouped around a statue commemorating the 120th Union Regiment, are even more numerous. But the most interesting stones of all are the ones scratched with crossbones and skulls and morals in terse verse. According to legend, a system of underground tunnels used to connect the church with burial vaults, and the thought of this, together with a reading of *Edwin Drood,* fired my Gothic-novel imagination—to the extent that my claustrophobia may be more literary than real even now—with ghoulish thoughts of incarceration in subterranean charnel.

The interior of the church could be a syndics' meeting room in a late-seventeenth-century Dutch town. No cross or other Christian image is exposed in it, and it is Dutch-clean: the walls and ceiling are immaculately white, the floors are newly red-carpeted, the pews and their knee-high gates are spotlessly upholstered. When no pamphlet-distributing janitor appears, I sit in one of the pews for a moment and involuntarily see myself, aged six, deposited by my mother at my first choir rehearsal, where the older boys sniff me over as if I were a new dog. Then in the very effort to banish this memory, I begin to explore it, wondering, first, what I owe to my years as a pre-cracked (vocally speaking) chorister. An ear well trained in four-part harmony and voice-leading, for one thing, and hence a love of J. S. Bach. But also a somewhat morbid concern with death. For the choir was employed at funerals, and imbursed for them at grand enough sums (albeit scaled

316

down from the oldest alto bullies to such lowly sopranos as myself) that my fellow *decani* regarded the passing of any well-heeled churchman as greatest good fortune. Yet for me these were dreaded occasions, and I would cry at night long after each of these gruesome ceremonies, foreseeing my own mother's death. And although I was supervised when reciting my bedtime prayers, I am certain no one ever suspected the reason for my only half-suppressed sobs. The cure for them, in any case, was the reading of an extra chapter of *Uncle Wiggly,* a fact recently restored to my memory by seeing the word "pipsissewa" in a newspaper and realizing that it is a real flower, which I did not suppose—such being the parlous state of my nursery culture—when hearing the name read to me in *Uncle Wiggly.*

The Holy Communion disturbed me, too, but much later, in my twelfth or thirteenth year, and as a result of conflicts prompted by arguments divulged to me by my older and more enlightened sister, then immersed in "atheist" literature. These tracts—Bertrand Russell's *Why I Am Not a Christian* was one—seemed to dwell on the barbarity of the theophagous impanation ritual ("This is the body . . . Take ye and eat"), so that when finally receiving the Eucharist myself, I felt profoundly deceived. The perfumed sweet wine ("The blood . . . Drink ye") and the pasty paten, shaped like money and served on a ciborium that looked like a collection plate, cheapened and degraded the symbolism, in my eyes, while the prayer, "Jesus Christ our only mediator and advocate," made Him sound like a union boss.

1967

But I have not come to the Dutch Church looking for memories. I do not repine for, indeed would not willingly relive, a single moment of that past—though I do not deny a moment of it either, having more or less (and at last) come to accept who I am. What *would* interest me is an encounter with myself as an object, a meeting that could be brought about only by the discovery of my childhood poems and letters and musical compositions. Yet I am certain that with that material in hand I would avoid the error of most autobiographers, which is in forgiving themselves.

Dutch names—Neukirk, Swarthout, Van Deusen, Tenbrouck, Hasbrouck—are inscribed on rosters in the entranceway. Encased there, too, are the colors of the 120th Union Regiment, and a letter from General Washington thanking the city for its hospitality to him in November 1772.

MAY 17

Toronto. A CBC concert in Massey Hall, I.S. conducting the *Pulcinella* Suite, after which I conduct *Oedipus Rex.* As we leave the hotel for the Hall, I.S. happens to pass before a crowd come to stare at Princess Alexandra. What compounds the irony is that no one in the gathering can be aware that the unscheduled parade of the little old man is a far rarer sight than the one they are waiting for, creative geniuses being so much harder to come by than merely well-born ladies.

317

Backstage, someone puts a question to I.S. about his "wooden Indian" staging concept of *Oedipus*. But I.S. denies that it is so very different from his earlier theater works with voice. "The singers are in the pit and the dancers on the stage in *Renard, Les Noces, Pulcinella* as well, and the title part in *The Nightingale* should be performed in the same way. The music is more important than the action, as the words were more important than the action in Shakespeare." For tonight's performance of *Oedipus,* he has asked us to repeat the *Gloria* before the Speaker, as in the original score, and to begin the first note of Oedipus' *"Invidia fortunam odit"* with Tiresias' last note, an overlapping *not* in the original score. Tonight's performance convinces me that the repeats in Jocasta's aria and in her duet with Oedipus, both added in 1949, are miscalculations. But why were so many useful directions in the original score not retained in the 1949 edition? The indication to take the $\frac{4}{4}$ episode in that same duet in cut-time is one of them, and another is to conduct the measure of Oedipus' 2 against the orchestra's 6 in 6 (1 before $\boxed{58}$), it being rhythmically slack in either 3 or 2. But tonight's performance is the most satisfying vocally I have ever heard, from the chorus to Ernst Haefliger's Oedipus (*langsam* and *sehr ausdrucksvoll* as it is), Jean-Louis Barrault's Speaker, and Marilyn Horne's Jocasta, which not only is rich in tone but also is sustained at the stately metronomic *tempo*.

For the first time in his life I.S. conducts sitting down, which probably gives him more trouble than he avoids by not standing except that he *is* unsteady on his feet and, in spite of the chair, grips the podium railing with his left hand during much of the performance. Remembering how vigorously he conducted in Chicago a mere five months ago, V. is alarmed watching him. Worse still, as she can plainly see, the orchestra is not really following him but the *tempi* of my morning run-through of the piece. At the start of the *Tarantella,* moreover, about half of the players interpret his first gesture as a 1 beat, while the other half read it as a 2 beat. This results in about ten measures of excruciating "augmentation," after which the playing thins out almost to the point of stopping completely.

The performance over, I.S. moves to a chair at the front of the stage, averts his eyes from triple-pronged TV exposure, hears out accolades in both French and English by dignitaries who then bemedal him. This ceremony very evidently affects him, too, as it would not have done a year ago; in fact, he probably would have been contemptuous of it then; and not merely the ceremony, but the special warmth of the audience, whose applause has distinctly said: "This is the last time we see Igor Stravinsky." As I know him, no one is more aware of this than I.S.

In the greenroom afterward he tells one of the medal-conferers that he suffered an "occlusion" two months ago, adding that "my blood is like purée." The remark startles us because until this instant he has betrayed absolutely no sign of suspicion that a stroke is what might have happened.

I am unable to sleep after the concert, seeing the I.S. of the past, as if on one side of a divided movie screen, skipping across the stage to the podium, his movements twice as fast as anyone else's, and in this, as in everything he did, leaving everyone around him far behind; and on the other side, I.S. tonight, old, frail, halting, and, I fear, conducting in public for the last time. What makes it all the more disturbing is his super self-awareness. A long decline and withering away would be a great cruelty to him.

New York. The findings of an electroencephalogram and of other tests performed on I.S. yesterday amaze his physician, Dr. Lewithin. The receptivity tests show that the responses are as rapid as in a man of thirty. Nor is there any sign of senility, of the brain-softening normal in a man of I.S.'s age, or any onset of brain sclerosis, the doctor assures us. But then, I.S. lives entirely in his brain. And he is greatly interested in the encephalogram himself, comparing it with "an electronic score with six-line staves and unreadable *avant-garde* notation," and adding that the eighteen electrodes attached to his head made him look like "a bald woman trying to scare up a mane of hair."

At the same time, Lewithin warns, the composer's body is a ruin. Two blood-lettings and three Roentgen-ray treatments are scheduled for the week, and these are a matter of life and death, as I.S. not only knows but is already processing and overcoming in his powerful psychological machinery. Armed with an understanding of the apprehensible biochemical facts, he will begin to "think positively," harnessing his formidable "esemplastic will" to the favorable factors and ignoring the unfavorable. But a more difficult enemy to subdue is another part of the same mind, that intelligence which has not aged with the body and remains so ruthlessly aware of it.

1967

Attending to a medical problem of my own, I go this morning for X-rays of the kidneys, the first stage of which is a two-hour wait in a room permanently piped with very loud pop. Finally, served up to the photographing eye semi-naked on a freezing platter, I am interrogated about my susceptibilities to sodium injections; and am advised, now that it is too late to retreat, that "some people become violently ill." In the event, the injection, in the median cephalin vein, *is* followed by cramps, tumescence, hot flushes, vesical burning, and a tidal wave of nausea. (Psychologists would classify me as an "augmenter" rather than a "reducer," but I do not see how that helps.) At this point the radiologist warns "me"—actually carcass number so-and-so—that the slightest movement on my part during the next thirty minutes, let alone retching, will spoil the test and oblige me to start over on another day, with three ounces of castor oil. I "endure," of course, and an hour later learn that I have prostatic calculi and must go on a régime of Eau de Vittel.

To the Met in the evening, still feeling radioactive, to see the Royal Ballet's *Romeo and Juliet*. But the Met itself is the more arresting spectacle. The whole ensemble—lowest-bidder architecture, sculptured plaza, Chagalled foyer, retractable chandeliers—might have been intended for an Eastern European People's Republic, then sold to the capitalists by some sharp Ministry of Culture *apparatchik* who saw that it had gone wrong. Eastern Europe, however, is where two of the principal ingredients of the evening, Prokofiev's music and Nureyev's Slavic charm, do come from. In fact, Nureyev's broad Slavic face is as radically in contrast to the pinched Anglo-Saxon features of his fellow dancers as the exhibition of his other attractions (*Chacun à son goût*), the muscle-bound buttocks and steel-thewed thighs, is in contrast to the concealing of the charms of Juliet and her attendant goslings by floor-length skirts.

Act One offers two opportunities for musical depth, Juliet's return to the deserted ballroom and the balcony scene. But Prokofiev makes nothing of either, merely substituting loudness for intensity of feeling, as if "passion" and "full orchestra" were synonymous. The music accompanying Romeo's approach to the balcony is so over-agitated, moreover, that it momentarily casts the hero as the villain. And, finally, Prokofiev cannot perorate, but only repeat, and in the empty lengths of repetitions even balletomanes must soon be lost. I should have noted in the first place, though, that the play is poor material for a ballet, pantomime being a poor exchange for poetry. And the choreographer seems to agree, at least in those far from rare instances when the dancers stand about gesturing like singers whose sound systems have gone dead.

1967

JUNE 18

Hotel del Coronado, Coronado Beach. "Are you Mr. Stokowski, the conductor?" the receptionist asks, and I.S. nods affirmatively but is less amused later seeing his own name in a letter from Public Relations asking whether he would mind being photographed.

The hotel is old, but less so than local veneration—which seems to put it on a par with Cheops—implies, being in fact ten years younger than I.S. It might have come from another country, as well, but the question of which one would be hard to decide. It sets out to be tropical, and overdoes it. And colonial-oriental, though I may be over-ascribing this side of it, owing to prior knowledge that the original construction force was comprised largely of Chinese coolies. Still, the window ventilators, transoms, verandahs, balconies, wicker furniture, valentine-lace panels, and tinderbox whole would not be out of place in Hong Kong, and the only feature of the Repulse Bay Hotel missing here is the ceiling fan like an airplane propeller in each room. The pavilion tower reminds I.S. of a Russian church, in the cupola, but of a stave church in general shape as well as in its dark red shingles. Yet the religion urged on the congregation inside is from Utah, each dressing table being furnished with a copy of *The Book of Mormon*.

Some congregation! "Ex-passengers from the *Queen Mary*," I.S. says. And the Coronado *is* spinsterish, prudish, dead-as-Lugano, and as sad as all old-fashioned resorts. We follow a creaky mahogany and dark-oak corridor to an elevator cage, then to a kind of Crystal Palace dining room in which a dozen or so occupied tables are huddled to one end against the gloom of two hundred or so unoccupied ones. Mammoth coronado-shaped chandeliers are suspended from the high, woven-basket ceiling, but they shed precious little light. Whether because of the inhibiting emptiness of the room or the annoying sobriety of the other diners, we drink too much and become too loudly effervescent.

Henry James, writing from the Coronado, in April 1905, complains of having been kept awake by the "languid list of the Pacific." But it is a very noisy rumble, at least from the waves curveting on the rocks opposite my window. The beach is wide and the sand very fine and soft, though only apparently white, one's footsoles being tarred after even a few steps. During low or eddying tides the shore is a congeries of vegetation from "the ooze and bottom of the sea": clumps of kelp and amber algae; chains of seaweed with spiculed, fin-shaped leaves; a plant, from some fantastic underwater garden, with a long mosquito or snout-of-an-oiling-can proboscis.

Jellyfish quiver in the sand—shaped like the human pancreas, or like *tête de veau,* or glycerine-like and purple-veined—and amputated jellyfish tentacles, like soft icicles, are common. We uncover a dead gull, claws up as if to fight off an enemy, and a dead skate, cuneal wings partly buried in the sand; V. extends her camera over these birds as if it were a Geiger counter and as if she feared their spirits. Live, all too live, are the beetle-size beach crabs, which Japanese fishermen gather for bait, meanwhile leaving tall fishing poles and pails of gasping perch untended in the dunes. (I remember Auden comparing himself to the beach crab—Talitrus—saying that, like it, he knew when it was mealtime not by hunger but by knowing the time of day.)

In mid-afternoon, scores of tentlike sails appear, tipping and careening in the wind. An airplane begins to skywrite, too, scraping a white path on the blue surface like a figure skater; but the wind strengthens, the aerial chalk blurs, and the drifting bits of alphabet are soon indistinguishable from natural clouds.

I.S.'s birthday party is launched with a bottle of Stolychnaya and docked with a cake baked by his daughter and brought into the room by her parading with V., who carries a tray with eighty-five lighted candles. We sing "Happy Birthday," which, I.S. remarks, makes it *"son et lumière."* But he says little else, and it is hard to know his feelings.

After he cuts the cake, we open some of the four hundred cables and telegrams that have been piling up all week from all over the world. But whereas the President of Germany, for example, has wired a two-page homage, no word has come from any public official in America, where "The poor procession without music goes." Nor has any message come from the

Mayor of that despoliation of the desert in which I.S. has lived for twenty-seven years. In fact, the only acknowledgment of the anniversary in his home community was a concert by the "Beverly Hills Symphony," conducted by himself four months ago at a greatly reduced fee not yet received. So, let the record stand. While the greatest living composer's eighty-fifth birthday is being celebrated all over the world by entire festivals and countless individual concerts, performances, and publications, no organization in the vale of smog-induced tears that *he* has so long honored by his residence so much as thought of dedicating a program to the event. Not the local—exceedingly local—Philharmonic, it goes without saying, but also not the Ojai Festivals, which were pleased to have him at a third of his normal fee at a time when they could use his name, but which had been distracted this year by the glare of momentarily more expensive, if in the long run much cheaper, attractions. In fact, the *art* critic of the Los Angeles *Times,* two months before the date, alone recognized the necessity, for Los Angeles's sake, of a concert, and attempted to organize one, but the Musicians' Union refused the request of the musicians who wished to contribute their services on grounds that it would "set a precedent." A precedent for whom? Is a deluge of Stravinskys imminent? In Los Angeles?

As V. unwraps gifts that have accumulated during the past weeks, identifying the senders for I.S., I cannot help thinking of how utterly lost he would be without her, and hope for his sake that it is destined to be the other way around. She translates bits of talk for him that he fails to catch and supplies quick Russian synopses of American jokes. And he, to be with her for even a few minutes, will take the long walk to, and even brave the terebinthine fumes inside, her studio. She, of course, is kinder and more patient with him each ever-more-difficult day, and she has lately begun to take him with her to the supermarket because he can hold on to the cart instead of his cane, and even push it, thus feeling useful to her.

1967

The emotional strain of the birthday must be very great, and some of the messages, especially from old friends who broke down and said the things old friends always want to but seldom do say, must have moved him; a letter from Nadia Boulanger, for example, was transparently about death. I.S. was never one to brood over the certitudes of insurance companies, of course, nor has he betrayed any sign of dotardly sentiment concerning his age today. Still, I will be happy to see him more combative again. Which is why his answer to a well-wisher's question whether he would like to live to the same age (111) as his great-grandfather—"No, taxes are too high now"—is reassuring; and why we are greatly relieved when, after the party, he says he is in a hurry to be rid of the birthday and resume composing.

JULY 15

Hollywood. Nureyev and Fonteyn for aperitifs—directly from a rehearsal, which partly explains his get-up: white tennis shorts, white sweater, white sandals. He may be "faunlike" from the front, as is said, but seeing the back of his head first, with the long, shaggy, Beardsley-period hair, one could easily take him for a tousled woman. He is quite unlike the thrasonical exhibitionist of newspaper copywriters, nevertheless, and no one has ever been more gracious and gentle with I.S., to whom his first words are: "This is a very great honor for me and I only hope I am not taking your time."

He talks about Bronislava Nijinska's revival of *Les Noces,* saying that he himself has learned a great deal from it. The I.S.'s, in turn, talk about their reception in the U.S.S.R. But this makes him uneasy, and when V. quotes Nancy Mitford on the "clean feeling in the Soviet Union that money doesn't matter," he cannot help breaking in. "Of course it doesn't. There is nothing to buy: no automobiles, no houses, no edible food." But he speaks gratefully of Madame Furtseva, who "discovered" him during a Kirov Ballet season in Paris. "She pointed to me at a reception for the dancers one afternoon, and told one of her minions, 'Next time this one will dance the solo.' That did it."

Explaining his defection shortly after, he says that "We were quartered in a very poor hotel near the place de la Bastille and never saw anything of Paris. Then one day I learned how to use the Métro and took it to the Champs-Elysées. Suddenly Paris seemed to me the most wonderful place on earth, and it was while walking from there to the Seine that I resolved never to leave. But tell me, why are Russian *émigrés,* in Paris, California, and everywhere else, so nostalgic for a Russia most of them have never seen?" V. suggests that part of the answer is in Russian literature; and it is true that many of the refugees she knows are walled up in a world of Russian books and have never even learned the local language. Nureyev's rejoinder is that "A refugee should live according to the way of life in the country of his adoption." Just as *he* lives?

Next to I.S., thin and shrunken like Mahatma Gandhi, Nureyev is almost impertinently healthy-looking. Entering the room he identifies a postcard-size Klimt, and he continues to study the art objects on tables and walls, glancing back and forth from them to I.S., as if trying to crack the "object language" of the house (people being implied by their possessions, after all), which, as he must see, is simply I.S.'s obsession with the minuscule.

Dame Margot, lissome and lovely, describing her arrest in San Francisco a few days ago on suspicion of possessing marijuana, says that she was searched skin-deep by a jailoress who had been to all of her performances and claimed to "idolize" her.

I.S., who had tried to avoid the visit at first, was especially lively during it, partly because of a hint from V. that his state of health is reported nowadays, a consideration that had never seemed to occur to him before.

In the evening we listen to Fischer-Dieskau recordings of parts of *Winterreise, Dichterliebe,* and the Opus 39 *Liederkreis,* as well as a batch of Brahms *Lieder,* and the *Spanisches Liederbuch.* I.S.'s fingers play along with the piano in the Schumann songs, one of which, *"Am leuchtenden Sommermorgen,"* he asks to hear three times. He also cues vocal entrances, flips pages back in search of a detail or comparison, and two or three times turns ahead impatiently to the next song. His highest expression of approval is a staccato grunt, but the same kind of noise turns into a groan when something displeases him, or is *too* beautiful ("Beautiful, but not for me"). Brahms, on the whole, wearies him: "There are too many *Regenlieder,* and compared with Schumann it is formalism; what I admire in Brahms is his knowledge, which isn't quite the right thing." But he likes *"Herbstgefühl,"* and *"Du sprichst,"* and the third of the *Ernste Gesange,* while of the Wolf songs he falls heavily for *"Herr, was trägt der Boden hier."*[1]

JULY 26

Santa Fe. Tonight, in prickly heat and dry lightning, and after four weeks of rehearsing, I conduct the American première of the original version of *Cardillac.* And tonight, anyway, my feelings are that Hindemith's goldsmith is at least not an unalloyed disaster—and this in spite of the composer's lack of aptitude for the theater, and in spite of several patches of really wretched music (villainous muted brass, etc.) and umpteen patches of indifferent music (fugal exercises not only conveying no message bearing on the dramatic action, but sometimes seeming to belong to another opus entirely, as if some packer at the Hindemith factory had mixed up the parts). The work is surprisingly stageworthy, too, even though the cast, except Cardillac, is made up of mannequins unbreathed on by any form of life, and though Cardillac himself, after his metallurgical recitative with the Gold Merchant, declines into the mad-genius inventor of the comic strips. The saving grace is that the subject has inspired Hindemith—no mean feat—so that he surpasses himself at times, his routine self running after, even if rarely catching up to, his inspired self, and in one scene even trying to scale a peak (blowing very hard into his hands to stave off frostbite, actually). The performance goes smoothly, too, except that the offstage conductor apparently has an attack of offstage fright.

1967

JULY 27

I leave a party for the *Cardillac* cast at I AM. Then during breakfast comes the appalling news of an unscheduled Wagnerian finale: a fire, starting at about 3 AM, has burned the stage and auditorium to the ground, incinerating as well not only the *Cardillac* sets, costumes, and orchestra parts but also cellos, basses, harps, and in fact everything combustible in the theater area,

---

I. In a single afternoon, May 15, 1968, in San Francisco, he arranged the piano part of this song, along with that of *"Wunden trägst du mein Geliebter,"* for three clarinets, two horns, and solo string quintet. One of his reasons, so he said at the time, was that "Wolf used octaves only for more sound. He had a marvelous ear and a marvelous sense of invention, but very little technique." Another reason, however, was that he wanted to say something about death, and felt that he could not compose anything of his own.

which is now a sickening prospect of ashes and charred remains. The second performance being canceled, I drive to Albuquerque and fly to Los Angeles.

Seeing the I.S.'s again after even a short separation moves me nowadays almost more than I can bear. They are the two most marvelous people in the world, the last survivors of a bigger and better humanity, a whole continent in themselves. But they are so old and creaky and fragile now, and so terribly alone. They know the hour of my flight, and when to expect me; if I am late they will go to the window again and again and play their rounds of solitaire more anxiously. When I do arrive, the sight of them in the doorway, to which they come at the sound of my taxi, is upsetting. They seem, especially after the ride through the junkyard and *dreçk* of Los Angeles, desperately out of place as well as out of time; for I tend to think about them, when I am away, as they were in the past. To see them after an interval, therefore, is a sudden acute reminder of age, a reminder full of the pain of impending loss. I simply cannot accept their passing as natural, as I have had no insurmountable trouble doing in other cases, but then, to me I.S. is a part of the order of nature. Dinner with them tonight is sad, all the sadder because they are so happy to see me.

AUGUST 21

New York. An alarming call from V. during my recording session tonight saying that I.S. has a bleeding ulcer—that he has in fact lost more than half of his blood—and that he has been taken to the Cedars of Lebanon Hospital. I arrange to fly back immediately.

1967

SEPTEMBER 13

Hollywood. The fourteen days in the hospital and nine subsequent days in bed at home have been extremely weakening. I.S. has lost 18 pounds—one wonders from where, as he was so tiny anyway—little of which can be regained on his present frugal diet. His rib cage reminds us of photographs of Buchenwald, and he complains that every nerve ending in his skin-and-bones body is raw and painful. The hematocrit still stands at only 35, too, whereas the platelets have risen to 1,200,000. While the one component of the blood is anemic, in other words, the other is too rich; and further to complicate the matter, the indicated medication for each is "counter-indicated" by the other. The level of his uremic acid is high, as well, and each finger of his left hand throbs like toothache from what has now been diagnosed as gout. Worst of all, and unspeakably depressing to observe, is the defeat—I pray only temporary—of that powerful will. He does not even read today, and when I switch on the television for him to watch his favorite African animal program, he refuses to turn toward the screen, saying, "I only like to look at it in Vera's room." He tells V. that he saw his birth certificate in a dream last night, and "it was very yellow."

V. has draped a towel, with a print of a cat on it, over the couch in his room, as if to represent her *in absentia,* though she seldom is absent any more; and this *does* seem to raise his spirits when she is out of the room. How fitting, if it is so destined, that his last creations should be a statement of religious belief, and that a Requiem, and then a personal piece for the human being who has meant most in his life.

SEPTEMBER 25

A marked upturn today, symptomized by an old-time tantrum over some of the contents of the mail: a fulsome fan letter; an application form for a self-paying *Who's Who;* a request to fill in a sexual questionnaire (I.S. is regularly circularized for this); a tape of a "ballad composed on a harmonica by an airline pilot during flight," herewith submitted for I.S.'s opinion, which is: "I will be afraid to fly again." Reaching for a Kleenex and finding it to be the last in the container, he flings the empty box to the floor. V. gently admonishes him, as one would a small child, telling him that the box will probably have to remain where it is until a pile accumulates, "Then perhaps the thrower will realize that we have no one to pick up such things."

The night table at the side of the bed holds an array of pens, music pads, pliers, secateurs, along with the Fabergé gold clock that Alexander II gave to and inscribed for I.S.'s father, and the small gold cross and silver roundel of the Virgin which I.S. has worn around his neck since his baptism.[1] Books, dictionaries, boxes of Man-Size Kleenex are stacked on the floor around the bed. To remind him to drink water, V. has written "Water" and "H$_2$O" on a dozen sheets of paper and taped them to the walls and furniture and the wastebasket with a photograph of Tchaikovsky on it, and has strewn and propped them everywhere else. V.'s Russian translations of medicine schedules are attached both to the head of the bedstead and to a dressing table otherwise crowded with trays, thermos bottles, glasses and cartons of milk with Mickey Mouse straws in them, packages of crackers, paper cups for quarter-hourly doses of Gelusil, plastic and glass medicine vials. I.S. keeps his own pharmaceutical inventory, however, and his own records of medicines consumed, entering this information in a red diary, an extraordinary chronicle that sometimes takes note even of a cough or a sneeze. On better days, prescriptions are spelled out in full, and reactions elaborated in detail, but on worse ones the identifications are brief: "Took one *foncée* capsule at 2:30, two white ones at 3:45."

He sits up during most of the afternoon today, telling me with some of his old zest that the Japanese ideogram for noise is the ideogram for woman repeated three times. (He has learned this from Hideki, our cook and, until recently, driver: he is so small that, at first glance, other drivers do not see anyone behind the wheel at all.) He also talks about Gorky's *The Mother,* which he is rereading. "I read it when it was first published, and am trying it again now, probably because I want to go back into myself. But it is not

---

1. And which were buried with him.

326

good. Gorky is not the 'big' writer I had hoped he might be, the writer that Tolstoy is even at his worst. Gorky's indifference to 'style' would be legitimate only if he had invented something to replace it. And surely it is more important to show what one likes than what one dislikes." The comparison with Tolstoy brings to mind Gorky's famous remark about his great predecessor, which, I suddenly realize, exactly describes my own feelings about I.S.: "I am not an orphan on the earth as long as this man lives on it."

George Balanchine comes for dinner, snorting and sniffing as if from hay fever, twitching as if he might have caught the *tic douloureux*. His clothes—check pants, silver-buckle shoes, double-breasted blue blazer with gold buttons, sideburns to the ear lobes—are moderately "mod," but on arrival he goes to the basement music room and puts in a half-hour of very conservative piano practice. At table, describing the *Salome* ballet now planned for Suzanne Farrell, he uses mudra-like movements, and asks me to choose music for it by Berg; but *Reigen*, the only possibility I can think of, is too large orchestrally, and like the Variations and Adagio from *Lulu*, which he has also been considering, is too brooding in character and too explicit dramatically. I wonder if Balanchine's inspiration has been kindled in any degree by the circumstance that the seven-veils striptease, like that of Astarte-Istar, would inevitably conclude in a complete disrobing nowadays, while the dance would be able to show Salome, like the Queen in *Alice*—"Off with his head!"—wanting a different part of the victim's anatomy than the one she gets. Herod, too, would be revealed today as the archetypal Humbert Humbert, marrying the mother for the daughter (or the Baron de Charlus buttering up Mme de Surgis because of her sons).

Mr. B. wants I.S.'s new piece, whatever it is, and in reply to the composer's damper that very little of it is finished, says he would settle for even two minutes of music because "They are bound to be an atomic pill." Showing the score of *The Owl and the Pussy-Cat* to Mr. B., I.S. says that the song "should be impersonated: a little hooted, a little meeowed, a little grunted for the pig." Just before leaving, Mr. B. asks a number of questions about *Russlan,* which he will direct in Hamburg. He still looks to I.S. for ideas—as well he might, considering that some of his most successful ballets (*e.g.,* the Bizet Symphony in C) began in suggestions by I.S.

When Mr. B. first enters the room, I.S., very self-conscious about his weight, says: "Like all Americans I am reducing."

OCTOBER 8

At about 4 PM I.S. complains of a chill, and his teeth, as he says, begin to *"klapper."* By 5 PM he has a 101° temperature, which, in his weakened state—he can hardly navigate across the room now, and his shoulders and torso are as fleshless as a coat hanger—is alarming: pneumonia or even influenza could kill him. But his lungs are clear, and the fulminant pains he complains of are abdominal. When I ask him to describe them, however, he sits bolt upright and says "FEAR." Soon after this he begins to urinate

327

every few minutes, which could indicate an infection from bladder crystals formed by the high uric acid.

Re-entering the room at 7 PM I find him praying, *"Gospodi, Gospodi,"* over and over, with his head turned to the wall. At long length (it is Sunday) a doctor arrives and prescribes Gantrisin. At the beginning of the doctor's examination, I.S.'s pulse is very fast. Then as soon as he is convinced that a bladder infection is the true complaint, his pulse rate drops to normal and his temperature to a bit below that; he has had a death scare, and was as frightened of pneumonia or 'flu as we were. All night long, says V., who spends it on a couch at the foot of his bed, he twists, turns, fumbles with the sheets trying to make a nest, but is unable to forget the specter.

The fact that a man's life has been rich, long, and perfectly fulfilled does not make him any readier to leave it; the contrary, rather, and the more so in I.S.'s case because of his knowledge, and ours, that there is more of it in him. Nor do "naturalness" and "justice" enter into consideration, except from afar, where the termination of a life of sixty-five years of continual creation must seem more just than the savage extinction of wholly unfulfilled young lives in a senseless war. But what may seem the most natural of events at a distance can be the most unnatural at close range. Death, at any age and in any circumstances, is immeasurable loss; but if I even *try* to measure the loss of I.S., it comes to something very like life itself. And though it may be special pleading, while joy to future millions will be the consequence of his existence, many if not most other existences only compound the general misery. But, strangely, that thought affords me neither compensation nor consolation.

1967

> . . . blown husk that is finished
> But the light sings eternal . . .

So Mr. Pound sings. But the light eternal hardly matters to me now, only the life which I pray will go on in that—well, I.S. is still far from a husk.

I realize now that in recent years I have hidden my true feelings for him precisely because of this dread. Yesterday evening those feelings came irrepressibly flooding out as the result of an extraordinarily clear hour with him, during which he talked and discussed his ideas with me in the way it used to be between us years ago. And I understood then that he has no thoughts of *not* going on. But he *can* go on, of course, only in that undamaged and undaunted mind of his, which is the tragedy.

Ever since I have known them, I.S. and V. have kissed each other at first sight of the new moon, a promise of renewal. The moon is new tonight, but they do not see it. And there does not seem to be any future.

OCTOBER 28

I.S., at dinner with Suvchinsky, is keen and alert, as he has been since the arrival of his old friend yesterday. We listen to *Les Noces* together, and, after I.S. goes to bed, to the *Requiem Canticles.* The latter, Suvchinsky suggests, "are ritualistic but in an ancient, atavistic way, being neither Pagan nor Christian, though without intentionally avoiding both [as *King Lear* seems to do]. The Postlude," he continues, "is one of those endings, like that of *Les Noces,* which do not end, or end in infinity. And this is where Stravinsky adds a dimension to Western music, beyond the classical composers. Think, for comparison, of the ending of a Beethoven or Brahms symphony, which simply thumps more loudly with each repeat."

Suvchinsky contends that a neurosis is at the root of I.S.'s passion for order, with which I agree, citing a relevant new study on "Religious Order and Mental Disorder in a South Wales Rural Community" (in *Social Anthropology of Complex Societies*); and that I.S.'s Russian background constituted a greater handicap to his development as a composer than the misunderstanding and opposition that were Schoenberg's lot. "If you had seen what he came from in Russia, in both the family and musical senses, you would believe in genius." (I already do.) "Stravinsky's creative psychology, that of a 'walled-in' artist, was fully formed by the time of the *Firebird,* and it never veered in any essential thereafter. Obviously he neither invented nor followed any doctrine of 'neo-classicism,' but simply made music out of whatever came to hand. Which was all he *could* do, given the limitations of the tradition from which he sprang. But it is high time the Diaghilev myth was exploded. So far from discovering Stravinsky, Diaghilev never really understood how big Stravinsky's genius was." And with this, Suvchinsky repeats I.S.'s story about Diaghilev's reaction to the ending of *Petrushka:* " 'But you finish with a question?' " "Well," I.S. used to add, "at least he understood that much."

NOVEMBER 2

I.S.'s "gouty" left hand has suddenly turned black. A new team of doctors, in consultation early this morning, attributes the discoloration to circulatory blockage from a sludge of platelets, a rate of some 2,000,000 at last count (*vs.* a 200,000 normal). The finger pains of the past eight weeks were caused not by gout, in other words, but by circulatory failure, and all the anti-gout medicines he had been taking were not merely powerless to relieve the hand but were dangerous for the ulcer. The discovery is not only frustrating but also infuriating. Why were a competent vascular cardiologist and a gout specialist not called in two months ago, or as soon as the colchicine and the wonder-drug anti-gout medications failed to alleviate the pain? And is sudden gout even a remotely reasonable prognosis for a man of I.S.'s build, temperament, and lifelong habits? How, furthermore, could four doctors, whom I would not now trust with a hangnail, accept the gout theory of the fifth while overlooking the possibility of circulatory blockage, and this in a man who has had polycythemia for twelve years and whose platelet count stands at two million? That is a miracle of modern science.

To try to dilate the coagulated capillaries, it is decided to block the nerve with Novocain injections; and as this entails a risk in a man of I.S.'s age, the operation must be performed in the hospital. Choking with tears and fears, I pack his bag and take him to Mount Sinai in the early afternoon, practically carrying him from his room to the car, for he is heavily drugged and scarcely able to walk.

The injection is not administered until seven o'clock, however, after a second consilium with a second vascular cardiologist. But when we return to the hospital at eleven, the fingers are even more horribly black. Gangrene is now mentioned, and the gruesome possibility of amputation, and we are further warned of a high danger of pneumonia, I.S. having been so long in bed. I drive V. home, then go home myself, but I cannot pass I.S.'s studio and bedroom or look at his dark window from my room, or, of course, sleep; and when going to bed I remember and use all of my childhood prayers.

NOVEMBER 3

The finger color has improved slightly since the third Novocain injection, but the hand is still gangrenous. Sick as he is, however, and despite the haze of pain-killing sedations, I.S. shines like a beacon, replying precisely, ironically, originally, I.S.-ishly, to a forensic inquisition by his doctors, and replying to them in English and German, moreover, and to myself and V. in French and Russian, without once mixing or confusing the languages or fumbling for a word. To one of the new neurosurgeons, who asks if he dreams under the drugs, his answer, to our great relief—he was always a hyperactive, total-recall dreamer—is that he does and that the dreams are "good." When the doctors leave the room for a consultation, he drops his voice to a whisper to ask V. if she has been painting, apparently having no sense of his own volume, except that at the same time he overhears *our* whispers even through the pall of the drugs.

His extreme fastidiousness is giving him no end of trouble. He insists on staying in the *gabinetto* unaided and on brushing his teeth unseen, and he charges me to explain to a voluble nurse that he does not mean to be rude but is unable to converse with her. To me he says: "I can offer you nothing here but *ennuis.*" As I leave, the nurse, no doubt annoyed by my anxieties and imperfectly stifled feelings, follows me into the corridor with the advice that "It is a mistake to get so involved." Is "involving" oneself a matter of choice, then, and would a noninvolved life, if it were possible, be worth anything?

NOVEMBER 4

The nerve will not be blocked today, the index finger being slightly less black this morning, and the palm of the hand a little rosier. Because the amelioration is ascribed in some degree to a trickle of alcohol in the intravenous fluid, it is further decided that I.S. should be allowed to *taste* the stuff, if it *can* be tasted through all the lactation he would have to swallow before

1967

330

and after. He is to receive three half-jiggers of scotch, at wide intervals, each of them blended to obliteration with milk. The prescription provokes a flap among the floor nurses, who say it is the first time that "drink" has been administered in the hospital in the social sense.

But I.S. is untrusting. Nor will he take my word for the contents of the bottle, until I uncork and hold it to his nose, after which we can almost see his olfactory bulb turning on. What follows is a Finnegans wake. He sits up—as if from smelling salts after a dead faint—eyes widening with each inward waft. Then to prove that we are not misleading him with a stratagem of flavoring or perfume, I play Petronius and sample the liquid in front of his eyes. After that the head nurse fills a paper cup to the halfway mark, inserts a straw, holds it to his mouth. And I.S., drugged to the bones with codeine, Darvon, Demerol as he is, nevertheless protests the miserable dram—"Half?"—but resigning himself to it, throws out the straw, and with inimitable I.S.-ian panache touches his paper cup to mine. And whereas he has slowly and torturously sipped his milk and medicines these three months, he downs the whiskey in one gulp. A smile spreads over his face, it seems for the first time in an age. And we tell him that a new era has begun, quoting Goethe on the beginning of the French Revolution: "From today forward, a new chapter in the history of mankind," etcetera. But in fact the whiskey, strongly opposed by the gastroenterologist, is a desperate expedient, almost the last trick up those white surgical sleeves.

1967

NOVEMBER 5

The left index finger is still blue-black today, but the others are normal, and the nacreous, color-of-death streaks in the palm of the hand have disappeared. I.S. insists that all of the fingers hurt, adding characteristically that "Each pain has its own manner." No less characteristic is his response to a doctor who asks if he can endure the pains from three to five minutes longer without more codeine. Out of a profound stupor—his eyes roll like ball bearings when he first tries to open them—but also out of a fathomless vitality comes the accepted challenge: "Five minutes."

Returning to the hospital in the afternoon, I spoon-feed him and hold his bad hand: he says the warmth diminishes the pain. A naturally affectionate, but also a deeply lonely man, feeling now pours out of him. And not a little of it pours into me. For we are very close now, as we were in our first years together. He asks me to sit by him all the time, and will allow me to leave only if I promise to return immediately. This directness of feeling, which in other circumstances each of us would be the first to flee, makes it difficult to control my not heretofore suffusion-prone eyes, an absurd propensity that I try to excuse by arguing that death is different in I.S.'s case because he can still create: witness the sketches on his piano, and his talk even now about his musical ideas. And in truth it is this power of creation in him that has always fascinated me, and which is more than the ordinary fascination of the creative for the uncreative. Yet this is not the principal reason why I cannot bear that the light of this most intensely alive human being I have ever known be extinguished, this man to whom I have been closer than to anyone else since childhood, and around whom my own life has revolved for twenty years. My uppermost feelings are simply those of love for a best friend and admiration for the fantastic fight and will and courage of an old man.

To what extent death is in *his* thoughts I have no idea; that will appear later, if he lives. But it is clear that much of his mental suffering in late years has been caused by the lack of a proper sense of himself as aged. In his own mind he is not eighty-five.

A resurrection has occurred between my second and third visits tonight, and of all providential ironies the whiskey may have turned the tide. His face has more color, the grasp of his hand is firmer, his voice is stronger, his conversation is quicker, and his criticisms of the nurses are as caustic as they would have been if he had not been ill. He wants to know today's date, and, on hearing it, seems as surprised as Rip Van Winkle was on being told how long *he* had slept; but then, only yesterday he was uncertain whether he was even in the hospital, at one point asking the name of the hotel and the city. The finger is clearer tonight, and as the doctors concur in ascribing at least some of the improvement to the whiskey, we tipple once more.

NOVEMBER 6 **1967**

An electric vibrating mattress has been brought in, to stimulate circulation, and the left arm is thickly swaddled in cotton to increase the flow of blood. A fluid of glucose, vitamins, alcohol, and vasodilators is fed to him intravenously through his right arm, which is bandaged in several places, besides, and as needle-marked as the "golden" arm of a "mainliner." His watch is now on his right wrist, having been transferred from the left—but only after a struggle that did not succeed in removing his two wedding rings and family signet ring from the painful fingers except during an X-ray, and then virtually by force.

We spend the entire day in the hot, stale, ill-lighted, and medicine-flavored room, and return again in the evening, after attending a Monday Evening Concert to hear the four-hand version of *Le Sacre du printemps.* The concert includes a group of Schubert songs as well, sung with no *Schwärmerei* and little enough voice; Webern's piano minuet, which is just long enough for the question to cross one's mind whether any composer has ever been so quickly and so cruelly picked so clean; Stockhausen's *Adieu,* which contains some novel wind-instrument sounds suggesting weeping; and I.S.'s *Pastorale,* which, with quarters rather than eighths as the unit of beat, is nearly twice too fast for its character. The *Sacre* performance is rousing, though the timbre is monotonous, the main lines are frequently overbalanced, and the *tempi,* pianos being unable to sustain, are generally too fast. But the effect on me, and of the concert as a whole, is extremely depressing. It has made

I.S. himself seem remote and expendable; and made me realize that his music can never have an independent existence for me, as it has for the audience. The evening is a foretaste of a time in which his absence will be felt and regretted by no one but me; which means simply that I have never been able to separate the man and his music.

At the hospital afterward we find him drugged but lucid: Suvchinsky describes him as a *"flambeau."* We do not stay long, the room being as stifling as a greenhouse, but because I.S. begs us to, with imploring looks as well as words, the departure is very painful.

NOVEMBER 11

The patients' list today includes Jennifer Jones, brought in during the night, like Botticelli's "Venus" still dripping from the sea. The nurses are goggle-eyed not with scientific amazement at her apparent amphibiousness, however, and the phenomenon of Anadyomene, but for the banal reason that Miss Jones is a "movie star."

I.S. has a new nurse today, a tough old trout with a scabrous tongue and the personality of a warden. She treats him as if he were an ancient, puling baby, and deeply offends his decorum with questions such as "Do you use Poly-Grip on your dentures?" and remarks like "I've wiped more bottoms in my time . . . " The patient serves as a lever of compensation in her own life, as I have come to think most patients do for most nurses; which is the reason she so clearly resents V.'s place next to the bed and I.S.'s rapt gaze toward her, as if she were a peri from another world. "Can you see this?" V. asks, holding up a book of photographs for him to peruse, and he says, "I think so, but I would rather look at you." What I am beginning to fear now is that unless I can find a way of spreading her burden, V., too, will collapse.

1967

NOVEMBER 13

A *Dies Irae,* the worst crisis since August. A new abscission must have occurred in the index finger, which is blacker than ever. Even worse, or at least equally upsetting, is I.S.'s semi-delirium. His senses of time and distance are virtually inoperant, and his memory is a jumble. He repeatedly asks where he is and confounds names and places (though verbal resemblances are evident in this, the name "Dr. Marcus," for example, starting him off on Markevitch). He talks to the nurses in Russian, too, mistaking them for V. But worst of all, he says he cannot see and is clearly unable at times to identify objects in the room, or even ourselves. At one point he tells me that "I have left my passport behind and cannot return."

Fearing that he has had a major stroke, I ask for a consultation, convene the two neurosurgeons, and return to the hospital in the evening to witness their examination. The result is an amazing display of I.S.'s always amazing and still very much intact mind. It is true that he is fond of medical interrogations, but he rises to the occasion tonight with some impish *mots d'esprit*

333

as well. Dr. Rothenberg: "Will you answer a few silly questions, Mr. Stravinsky?" I.S.: "No." But the questions come. "Do you ever see double, Mr. Stravinsky?" "Yes." "How long has this been going on?" "All my life, when I am *soûl.*" "What month and year is it?" Here the best I.S. can say for the former is "autumn," but he gets the year right. "Did you see people or animals in the room at any time today and later realize that they weren't there?" "Yes. Two boys were sitting in that chair this afternoon." "Did you see a black cat?" "No." But he claims to see vivid color mixtures in the curtain even now, at the same time telling us that he knows it is a drab brown because it was that color yesterday. A reading test then reveals that he sees the letters a half-inch to the left of the print at the same time as the print itself. But what distresses him even more than this, he confesses, is his inability to relate events. "Something is wrong both in my sense of time and in the reasoning faculty," he says, and goes on to describe the symptoms of this mental state with a power of reason and an awareness that a philosopher in perfect health and a fourth of his age might envy. In fact, one of the doctors, in the interests of an analogy I fail to follow, puts a question to him about time in music but bungles his concepts, whereupon I.S. sets him straight by distinguishing "time as a matter of speed, and rhythm as a matter of design."

The doctors seek to assure him that his new complaints are owing entirely to the effects of his new drugs. "I am *consolé,*" he concedes at last, adding that "I looked hard in myself for the cause of the failure and was distressed because I was unable to reason about it exactly enough.[1] I want to be more exact in my thoughts." But *is* he *"consolé"*? He pleads for "a more powerful pill, so that I will not have to think any more tonight." A stronger sedative is forbidden, however, because of the danger of pneumonia if he does not move enough.

1967

The examination has allayed V.'s worst fears for a bit. His imagination is unimpaired, certainly, and his repartee says the same for his spirit. But it is obvious that he has had a new thrombosis. And what of that black finger? And of the effects of more pain and more drugs when he has already endured so much of both for so long? As Exeter says of the King:

> Now he weighs time
> Even to the utmost grain.

NOVEMBER 14

Finally, a criminal eight weeks late, I.S. is given an arterial injection of radioactive phosphorus, by a doctor in a rubber suit and what might be

---

1. His habit of intellectual self-accusation, a lifetime trait, was a great trial to him during his convalescence, simple failures of memory being enough to precipitate fits of anger. In Zürich, almost a year later, his inability to recall some incident during a discussion at table one evening seemed to have been responsible for a nightmare. Hearing him get up at about midnight, I went to his room and found him sitting on the edge of his bed with his truss in his hand to use against "the guards" who, in his dream, were coming to take him "to the madhouse."

a welder's helmet. Three nurses, like the three queens accompanying Arthur to Avalon, wheel the patient to a lead-lined room in the basement, and immediately afterwards a thrice-daily series of abdominal and subcutaneous heparin injections is begun.

The mental wanderings are even worse than yesterday. Before the trip to the X-ray room, he asks us to look after his wallet, which he has not had on his person since long before the hospital. (This may be no more than a habit of concern about his pocket valuables when disrobing for X-rays in the past.) But on the return to the room, he asks if we have "enough *Frantzuski Geld* to tip the porters." When dinner comes, moreover, he insists on eating from his own tray, thinking himself in his room at home, and when V. says that it isn't there, he points to where she can find it. Then as we leave for dinner ourselves, he asks to come to the restaurant with us. He will be able to do that very soon, I tell him. But after considering this for a moment he replies, heartbreakingly, "Oh, I realize I am not able to eat with you, but I could watch." He also begs to be taken for a "promenade" in the car. And no doubt troubled by his mistake in thinking he was home, he asks how it is there now. Very bad, I say, for we miss him all the time. "You remember how you used to describe us as a *'trio con brio'?* Well, please hurry and get well so we can be one again."

He has a period of hallucinations—a heparin side effect, the doctors say—apprehending people who are not present but failing to see us and his nurses when we are only inches away. Once he asks why there are two watches on his right wrist from which even the one has now been removed. His comments, in Russian, V. says, are "nonsensical" and "delirious," which greatly upsets her; nor is she impressed by my argument that this unreality is better for him now than the truth. Then suddenly, in the midst of the rambling, he drops a remark showing such a perfect sense of reality that we know that underneath it all his mind is holding on tight. Overhearing us mention a music critic whose name has not come up in years, he wants to know whether the said critic is dead or alive. "Dead," V. says, but I.S. is suspicious. "No, he is probably alive and in Argentina."

His mind seems to be divided into two parts, of which only the part dealing with the outer world and the present is confused. But this, too, is natural, given the disruption of his time sense by medicine schedules and drugs, and the dislocation as a consequence of staring at hospital walls, not, after all, so unlike the walls of his bedroom at home.

The other, the creative part of the mind, appears to be unaffected. In the evening, during one of his lucid spells, I tell him that the BBC would like him to compose from six to ten seconds of music which, together with a multicolored eye by Picasso, would form the signature of a new color-television channel. The creative mind instantly seizes the idea and moves ahead with it like a prow. "The limitation to six seconds rules out chords, as well as rhythms in any conventional sense, though many notes can be used at once. But an eye means transparency, which means in turn that the sound should be produced by very high instruments, possibly flutes, compared with which oboes are greasy and clarinets oily."

I leaf through a book of Watteau drawings with him, but he complains that the reproductions do not show scale. And he is annoyed by a phrase in the commentary about the new sophistication in the appreciation of Watteau at present. "Whatever comes later is more sophisticated," he says "which later-comers should remember as they look forward, as well as back."

NOVEMBER 18

The depredations are showing. I.S. is so thin now that his nose seems to have grown, and his long-untrimmed mustache overhangs his lip, suggesting a walrus or fox terrier. But the finger remains blue-black and painful—less so in the mornings, when he is still comatose from the sedatives of the night. As for the intensity of the pain, the doctors assure us that he performs for our sympathy, which is normal patient behavior, and that he has often dispatched his nurse for codeine or Darvon but fallen asleep before she has had time to give it to him. Some pain he has, nevertheless, and he moans from it throughout the afternoon. Once the nurse gives him a pill, warns him it is a big one, goes to fetch water to help him swallow it, but when she returns, he says: "Already done."

As a result of yesterday's midnight consultation, which introduced a new vascular surgeon into the medical-opinion pool, new ingredients are compounded in the I.V., arm and hand exercises are begun, and mild heating therapy is applied to the forearm and hand. Thanks to computerized filing systems, too, a former victim of the same ailment has been traced, and his case history, treatment, progress, studied and compared. The man was I.S.'s junior by twenty years, however, and his hand became gangrenous after a coronary. We learn from his deposition that recovery was extremely slow and that in the matter of pain he would "prefer ten coronaries to that ache in the fingers."

1967

The main effect of the change in the I.V. fluid since the midnight medical pow-wow is soporific, the new strategy apparently being to keep the patient "under" until the radioactive phosphorus begins to work, which is like waiting in a heavily besieged fort for the relief column of cavalry. But why am *I* suffering so much, asks a new and analysis-jargonized ("accident-prone," "fantasize," "intropunitive") nurse? Father figure? Identification? I do not give my answer, which is that I love him, for of course she would translate the primitive word into a neurotic symptom.

But what *are* the answers to her questions? To borrow Rank's terminology, wasn't there a narcissistic basis for the object-choice of I.S. in the first place (*i.e.,* twenty years ago)? And, to borrow Freud's terminology, haven't I identified my ego with the disappearing object? Perhaps, in both instances; and certainly I can be fooled by my ego as well as the next person. But the main hinge of Freud's explanation, the transformation of the object-loss into the mourner's ego-loss, certainly does not apply.

The new I.V. formula, with the new anticoagulant, Priscoline, has not changed the finger color, but it makes I.S. so drowsy that I get only a few words out of him the whole day. When I enter the room, he says, "They are giving me phenobarbital now, probably to keep me polite." A great while later he adds, as if he were reading our own minds: "My impression is that the doctors haven't the faintest notion what to do." Once, too, he describes the finger pain as "crackling," and at another time as "needling." Yet I suspect that a resourceful nurse could keep him off painkillers entirely. He displays the finger ceremoniously to the new, analysis-wise but otherwise resourceless one, saying, "*We* can't touch it." His failing sight is far more alarming than the finger, however, and while he identifies us by our voices, hardly turning his head to left or right, what he *does* see—the anti-corona of someone walking past the bed—is not there.

NOVEMBER 20

"Where are you?" he asks, hearing me enter the room this morning, and as I approach the bed, he puts his good hand to my face as if he were totally blind. He is so heavily drugged, too, that he speaks only at great intervals. "How long will it last?" he says at one point, and again, "How much longer?" Then for the first time in all these months: "I don't want to live this way." I try to make him believe that he will soon be home and composing, but he nods his head weakly toward his left hand, saying: "I need my hand; I am maimed in my hand." I am more worried about his eyes, however, and most worried of all about the amount of fight left in him. Already, as the Duke of Albany says in *Lear*, "The oldest hath borne most."

1967

NOVEMBER 23

It is Thanksgiving Day in the most wonderful way possible, for the long-prayed-for miracle has happened. The finger color has returned to normal, and I.S. has not complained of pain or taken painkiller in seventy-two hours. His sight is not restored, and he is unable to distinguish faces in what, as he describes it, seems to be a dioramic blur; but his eyes turn rapidly toward and focus quickly on us. He sits in a chair for a while, too, which makes him look much thinner than in the bed. And while he is up, his daughter reads to him, and is quickly pounced on for mistakes in Russian pronunciation. Incredible man! Only three days ago he was in a semi-coma, his left hand a half-silted estuary of gangrene, his body worn out by months of sickness and pain, through which, however, and as Suvchinsky said, he himself was a torch. And now he has come out of it, actually recrossing the Styx. "How much is it costing?" he asks me suddenly, and in all these weeks no words have sounded so good. I.S. is back in decimal-system reality. Thank God.

He is pepped up—from glucose—jumpy, brittle, anxious, ready to fly off the handle at any and everything. "I have had enough medical philosophy," he informs his most discursive physician, and to a nurse who advises him to "Relax," his retort is: "What? And leave the driving to *you?*" He is suffering drug withdrawal, of course, and a mountain of after-effects. But I like the friction.

V. is ill and in bed today. Her own diagnosis is 'flu, but I think "battle fatigue" would be more accurate. The crisis last weekend was too much for her, and she has kept her fear too long inside.

NOVEMBER 28

I bring I.S. home at noon, his departure having been delayed by requests for autographs from every nurse on the floor, which he gives, of course, embellishing some of them with musical notations. Outdoors, out at last from that stultifying hospital, he looks as pale as junket and, dressed in a suit, terribly thin, shrunken, and frail.

As I help him from the car into the house, he says that it must seem to me as if I am "towing a wreck." But weak as he is, he props himself on the couch and will not go to bed. Contemptuous of medicines now, he balks at his quarter-hourly doses of milk. "Milk is the Jesus Christ of the affair," he says, to which profanity V. responds with: "Now at least we see how much better you are." But he is not having any of that. "Not better, bitter," he corrects. Then, to divert him, V. plays patience and asks him to keep the tally for her in his head. His scores, she says—not meaning any pun—are perfect.

1967

He asks for today's newspaper (which says that Zadkine, another coeval, has died) and the post. The latter contains Malraux's *Anti-Mémoires,* with the author's dedication: *"Pour Igor Stravinsky, avec mon admiration fidèle."* But I.S. jumps on this. "When was he ever *'fidèle'?* He said once that music is a minor art." And so I.S. is still I.S.

Later in the day, when the doctors call to congratulate themselves, he flummoxes them, too, as he has done at every stage, telling them that "The finger and the eyes are from the same cause." The chief neurosurgeon corroborates this to me privately, in fact, saying that not one but three thromboses occurred just before that tardy radioactive phosphorus, and that some peripheral vision in the left eye is permanently lost. At the moment, however, I.S. is distressed less by the damage to his eye than by a gas pain; and when the doctors seek to remind him that he has not suffered alone, he snaps at them with "Maybe, but you don't have this gas pain." (Apostrophizing them later, he remarks that "It was very well-paid suffering for them.") But he is beginning to talk like a doctor himself. "Is the pain merely spasmodic," he asks, "or could it be organic?" One of the medics, in parting, tells him that "Healing takes longer at eighty-five, Mr. Stravinsky," but I.S. turns on this with "Damn eighty-five."

He watches *Daktari* in V.'s room tonight, but tosses and turns in his bed afterward, tormented, he says, about the state of his mind. At eleven o'clock

I go to V. to see if she is all right, and find her in her dark room, quietly crying, tears streaming down her face. Not once during the whole ordeal did she ever lose control, and only now is it clear that she had begun to lose belief and was only continuing to pray that he would ever be home again. After an hour of trying to talk her into some "peace of mind," I am summoned by the night nurse to help with I.S., who is not asleep in spite of his pills. I try to fake some more good cheer with him, but he says he is "in a bad way psychologically." When I leave him he answers my last inane "Please stop worrying" with "I am not worrying any more, only waiting," which wrenching remark kills the possibility of any sleep of my own. "Old people are attached to life," Sophocles says, condemning it as a fault.

DECEMBER 1

Hallelujah! The platelets have fallen to 900,000, and the white count—"my blood policemen," as I.S. tells it, though he is also using such nonmetaphorical terms as oenosyllophyl—is down to 17,000, from 37,000 only a few days ago. His diet is less strict now, too, and henceforth the taste of milk can be cut with larger swigs of scotch. This news raises I.S. out of the apathy—black melancholy, rather—into which he had fallen the day after his homecoming, when he had apparently expected to be able to skip rope. After dinner we listen to Opus 131 and the *Dichterliebe,* the first music heard in the house since he entered the hospital. And with the music he comes to life, grunting agreement with Beethoven at numerous moments in the quartet and beating time with his left hand, which is protected by an outsized mitten, like the claw of a fiddler crab. Whereas he has been unable to read words, his eyes travel easily with the score (being guided by a quite exceptional "ear").

DECEMBER 6

It is a marvelous day, brilliantly sunny and warm although the San Bernardino Mountains glitter like Kilimanjaro with new snow. But my leave-taking is the hardest I have ever had to go through. It will only be a few days, I tell I.S., and I blame his music as the reason for the trip in the first place. To which he says, *"Je crache sur ma musique."*

DECEMBER 15

New York. To the Met's new *Carmen,* as the opera is billed, though both musically and visually it is unrelated to the traditional character of the piece. The set for the entire opera is a bull ring of Colosseum proportions. In the first act it is an esplanade for strolling couples, fashion models apparently dressed in lavish Goya and Manet costumes. In apposition to this preposterously rich apparel, the children are gotten up like Cruikshank chimneysweeps or the waifs in photographs advertising the plight of starving earthquake survivors.

The principal shortcomings of the musical reading are simply that the *tempi* are too fast, the orchestra is too loud, and the performance is innocent of all nuances, shadings, inflections. Singers and orchestra are seldom synchronized, moreover, despite Maestro Mehta's heroic strivings—between prize-fighterly cues to cymbals and brass—to bring them together. Nor is Grace Bumblebee's beautiful voice enough equipment for the title role; she does not move like the sultry heroine, and is no temptress.

But no matter, either. The Met audience, corporation presidents and their blue-rinse spouses, applauds each ill-conceived and worse-executed stage trick as if the music did not exist.

DECEMBER 16

Hollywood. Meeting me at the door, V. says that I.S. had been waiting for me since early morning but became tired and fell asleep. He is awake when I enter his room, nevertheless, and when he sees me, actually sheds tears. He is utterly changed, better than I had ever hoped to see him again. But, V. says, a delayed shock has occurred. A veil has dropped over the worst of the illness, mercifully eradicating all memory of the hospital. In fact, he has refused to believe he had been ill at all, on the grounds that he had had no temperature, and while remembering that we were all much concerned about his hand, did not recollect that it had ever pained him. He flexes the hand as we converse, tightening and loosening its grip on a toy-sized football.

But the greatest difference is in communication. Whereas two weeks ago he would follow our conversations abjectly, contributing little himself, talk flows from him now. Telling me about a Christmas letter from the conductor James Sample, he recalls several incidents touching the lessons in composition which he gave to Sample's father-in-law more than twenty-five years ago,[1] and describes how he wrote much of his pupil's symphony for him. After dinner we listen to the quartet movement which I.S. calls the *Sehr grosse Fuge,* and to the Debussy *Etudes,* which, not for the first time, he names as his favorite piano opus in the music of this century. He says he dreamed about Debussy a few nights ago and "clearly recalled the strong scent of his eau de Cologne when we last embraced each other."

Both I.S. and V. seem happier and are looking better than at any time since August, for which I thank God *and* I.S.'s invincible spirit.

DECEMBER 25

It now seems likely that the viral infection to which I.S. is supposed to have succumbed on the nineteenth, and against which he was murderously dosed with antibiotics, was a new thrombosis. But it is difficult to be certain, precisely because of the debilitating effect of the anti-viral drugs. He is extremely low, in any case, seems to have aphasia at worst, and at best,

1967

1. I.S. noted each one of these in a diary.

forms words with great difficulty. He cannot walk at all without the aid of his nurse, but resolves to come to the dinner table because it is V.'s birthday and Christmas—in *that* order: "Christianity is a system," he says, "but Christ is not a system." His only other words during this extremely depressing meal are a *cri de coeur:* "Something new has happened to me. What is it? I was walking so well last week."

At the end of the dinner he says *"Ne bougez pas!"* then climbs slowly up the stairs with the help of the nurse, and again all the way down, bringing me a Christmas present, a gold clasp. "It belonged to my father and to his father," he says, and he apologizes because it isn't wrapped.

It seems so brutal that, having endured so much, and at last reaching the threshold of recovery—walking unaided and even mentally digesting his ordeal—this brave and miraculous man should again be struck back. What can we do now except pray that the thread by which his life seems again to be suspended will prove, as it did before, to be as strong as someone else's rope? But when I greet V. with a "Merry Christmas and Happy Birthday" this morning, all she says is: "I went to his room a few minutes ago and thanked God that he was still breathing."

1967

1948
1949
1950
1951
1952
1953
1954
1955
1956
1957
1958
1959
1960
1961
1962
1963
1964
1965
1966
1967
1968
1969
1970
1971

ITINERARY

February 10: We fly to San Francisco (St. Francis Hotel). **13–15:** Concerts in Oakland (conducted by R.C., I.S. in attendance), flying to Los Angeles after the concert of the 15th. **March 19:** The I.S.'s fly to Phoenix. **21:** *The Rake's Progress* in Phoenix (I.S. in attendance). **22:** We fly to Los Angeles. **27:** *The Rake* in Los Angeles (I.S. in attendance). **April 2:** *The Rake* in Los Angeles (I.S. in attendance). **May 3, 4:** Balanchine visits I.S. **14:** We fly to San Francisco (Clift Hotel). **21, 22:** I.S. attends performances of his *Psalms* and *Oedipus Rex* at the University of California, Berkeley. **25, 26:** I.S. attends performances of the *Octuor, Les Noces, Histoire du Soldat* at Berkeley, flying to Los Angeles on the 26th. **September 6:** Televised (NET) concert of *Svadebka,* preliminary versions, Los Angeles County Museum of Art, an ovation for I.S. **8:** We fly to New York and, on the 24th, to Zürich. **October 23:** Fly to Paris. **November 8:** I.S. attends a performance of *Le Sacre du printemps* at the Paris Opéra. **14:** We fly to New York. **18:** I.S.'s fly to Los Angeles. **December 9:** I.S. has herpes zoster.

JANUARY 1

I.S. is none the worse today for some sips of champagne at 12:01 AM, but he releases a thunderclap by remarking that certain legal actions, of which he has just learned, were necessary, "in case I had died in the hospital." During the struggle no acknowledgment even of the possibility had ever crossed his lips. Then at lunch, we prod him to exercise the bad finger, but

342

he says: "I will be able to use the finger only when I can get it out of my mind."

One of his Christmas presents is a canary. When I remark somewhat acidly on the impressive volume of its "song," I.S. challenges my word: "Musical elements—pitch, color, intensities, rhythmic patterns—yes. And the bird even gives notice before signing off. But the result isn't 'song.'"

We listen to *Messiah* in the evening, and although I.S. tends to resist Handelian grandeur—"Handel was the commercial composer of his time, Bach the inward one"—he cannot resist this excellent performance (by Colin Davis, whose *tempi* and articulation are superior, but who does nothing about *notes inégales*). We listen to bits of *Hercules,* too—Dejanira's mad scene, Iole's recitative "Forgive me, gen'rous victor"—but give up because the performance is excruciating.

JANUARY 16

Stephen Spender telephones from London, asking I.S. to answer the Litvinov appeal. I.S. consents, tells me what he wishes to say, and we draft the following statement together, a revised Russian version of which he will record next week for the BBC:

I remember the sufferings of my teacher Rimsky-Korsakov from the threat as well as the actual exercise of czarist censorship. Now, sixty years later, while the world stands in admiration of so many achievements of the Revolution, Russian writers and readers still live under the censor's Reign of Terror.

But the spirit of the Revolution is with the condemned writers, who must be counted among their country's most valued patriots if only for the reason that they love her language; except that writers cannot live, and neither a poetry nor a people can grow, under censorship.

The Soviet Union can prove its greatness more profoundly by pardoning the condemned writers than by the conquest of all outer space.

1968

Privately, however, I.S. denies that czarist and Soviet censorship are even comparable. "There was hope under the old régime, now there is none. But what an idiotic idea is this 'patriotism.' The world being what it is, how can a writer or anyone else be patriotic?"

JANUARY 25

We play Schubert's E-minor four-hand Fugue and some of his F-minor Fantasy together this afternoon, after which I.S. reveals that he does not want to go on with his own piano opus because he has "a bigger piece in mind." But no further information about this newer composition is forthcoming beyond the assurance that it is not to be a string quartet. As for the abandoned piano opus, he says that "I had no sooner forbidden myself to use octaves in one piece than I saw what richness I could extract from them, and I used them in the next piece all the time."

V. is disturbed because I.S. cannot remember where they were married. But why should he remember New Bedford, Mass., from a visit which lasted only an hour or two, twenty-eight years ago? Furthermore, after nineteen years of what already amounted to matrimony, the ceremony itself could hardly be expected to become the most indelible of events. Still, the lapse *is* curious in that the day before the thromboses, last November, I.S. began to talk about his life in Massachusetts in 1939–40, a subject rarely mentioned previously, and to talk about it with exceptional distinctness. Is this merely the long arm of coincidence, or were the cells encoded with those particular memories in that particular file of the information bank undergoing exposure as a result of strain just before the eclipse?

Listening to *Pelléas* after dinner, I.S. says that he likes it much more now than the last time he heard it. When was that? I ask. "With Debussy."

FEBRUARY 10

San Francisco. The view from our hotel rooms features an electric letter-board flashing time and temperatures in the name of Equitable Life Insurance; a second electric sign that intersperses news of local and world disasters with appeals to drink, smoke, deodorize, and wipe with products that are bigger, better, newer, cheaper, sexier; tomorrow's skyscrapers—slanted jibs of cranes, girders, showers of sparks from welders—dwarfing today's skyscrapers and giving promise of more and larger executive suites; a column, possibly a reject for a Central American version of the place Vendôme, topped by a globe and a coyly draped but disproportionately diminutive dancing nymph carrying a thyrsus and trident.

A hurdy-gurdy, performing for the empty benches of Union Square below, reminds I.S. that this low-fi but loud music machine—it is audible even above the demolition squads—"was so popular in St. Petersburg that to find more than one competitor grinding at the same time, as in *Petrushka,* was not an uncommon sound or sight. Sometimes they were accompanied by dancers, too, and I watched more than one hurdy-gurdy ballerina from my window, as a child, and, with my brother Gury, threw coins tied in a rag to the *artiste.*" Another, much louder, concert is pealed up to us in late afternoon by off-key carillons somewhere in the all-too-near environs. This angelus consists of the principal theme of Tchaikovsky in B flat minor, and because of it even the pigeons flee their eyases on the ledge below us, whether or not it be anthropomorphism to say so.

"Loud" is again the word for tonight's Chinese New Year parade, the firecrackers suggesting not merely an old-fashioned Fourth of July but the blunderbusses and cannonades of the Revolution itself. The din and wail of Chinese music combine ominously with the subterranean rumble of the cable-car chains; but the procession, too, is sinister, with its real (caged) gorilla—this is "the year of the monkey"—and sinuous, scaly, block-long cardboard dragon, to propitiate Confucius knows what malevolent powers. Some of the marchers carry paper hares and paper tigers, and some of the

1968

344

onlookers hold clumps of balloons which resemble models of molecular structures. But San Francisco itself has a Chinese aspect tonight in the shapes of hills under the nesting fog, in the stylized Chinese clouds, and in the Chinese moon over the Bay.

We visit the Haight-Ashbury and the Barbary Coast North Shore tourist districts. The former might be a movie set for an earlier America. The nomadic, semi-pastoral people carry duffel bags and guitars, and they wear long hair and Smith Brothers beards, frontiersmen's leggings, Civil War capes, dungarees, Indian ruanas and headbands (there is berdache—Indian transvestitism—too). A sign in a store window here reads: MIRRORS FOR SALE, NEW AND USED. The North Shore is different, catering to that privilege of businessmen, the tax-deductible night out. It is a flesh market, sold on the hoof. There are advertisements for "Bottomless Shoe Shines" and "Topless Weddings," for "Thoroughly Naked Millie," "Miss Freudian Slip," "Naked Orphan Fanny," "The Nude Bat Girl" (what can be the added attraction of an aliped?). One establishment lures its customers with a busty, sparsely clad girl standing in a glass telephone booth elevated to about twenty-five feet above the sidewalk. We are lured here ourselves for a moment, in fact, though more, so we say, to observe the scopophiliac audience than the entertainment, which is very dull. Owing to the mental level and the potential lactation, the place would be much more useful as a nursery.

FEBRUARY 11

1968

A Navy training jet has grazed the Bay Bridge in thick early-morning fog and drowned. Hardly any traces of debris are found, and though frogmen discover an oil slick—a clue to them, as spilled blood is to the police in a murder case—the plane is not recovered by nightfall.

We drive to Muir Woods, over the red bridge from which known *salto* number 340-odd has been tabulated this week—the number of unknown opters of this way out (down) being estimated at between three and ten times as many. San Francisco, from the bridge, is a white, Arabian city, and Muir Woods is a small pocket of Natural resistance.

At the evening rehearsal of his "requicles" in Oakland, I.S. asks the chorus to speak in triplets, in the *Libera me,* and to speak, not mumble; but then the words come out as if from the cheering section at a football game.

The violist, Germain Prévost, a friend of I.S.'s for fifty years, tells me he finds the composer spectral and weak-voiced, but less peaked than might have been expected after such an illness. It is true that I.S. has never regained his full voice (there were spells of total aphonia in the hospital), but we are accustomed to the new timbre and do not notice the difference. Undoubtedly he strikes other people as very thin, too, though to us, comparing the present with a few weeks ago, the face seems almost bloated, as in the portrait by Auberjonois, who made him look fishlike, slanting the eyes and distorting the head like the sculptures of Lepenski Vir. "Eat more," the portly Prévost advises, and I.S. says that he swallows two raw eggs "like oysters" each morning. Prévost's autograph album, submitted for fresh inscriptions, contains a manuscript poem by Schoenberg and the chronicle of a concert tour in the twenties featuring I.S.'s *Concertino*. Evidently what most impressed Prévost about the *Concertino* was I.S.'s demand and receipt of 500 francs per performance.

After the rehearsal, talking about love in the Pill paradise to K., a member of the Sexual Freedom League, I put forward the *a priori* (*a* priapic?) opinion that groups such as hers are expressions of reaction to Salic laws, and more important to women than to men because they give women the freedom to choose. "Obviously," says K., an informed student of mating behavior and an advocate of sexual freedom *à la* Fourier, "the point for men is that the prospect of new females increases the possible number of copulations— *brevis voluptas*—as is the case with other male mammals, bulls, for example, being able to mount new cows and Pasiphaës shortly after dismounting old ones." Whatever the truth of these contentions—and *a priori*-ism is proved or disproved not by more philosophy but by experiment—K. believes that all participants in group sex suffer from third-sex repressions. She also says that group sex is engaged in in total silence, and that names are never used. Pot is seldom taken at Bay Area League meetings (orgies?), she says, but she justifies her own occasional use of it by citing the laudanum-taking of De Quincey, Coleridge, Elizabeth Barrett. K.'s talk has made me feel very ancient.

FEBRUARY 13 | **1968**

After the concert, I.S. stands to acknowledge the ovation and, Russian style, applaud his applauders; but the audience rises, too, and blocks the composer, who is probably the smallest man in the hall, from the view of all except his immediate neighbors. Emotional dangers beset him from several sides tonight, the concert marking at the same time his first appearance in public since May, first exposure to live music-making, first audition of the *Requiem Canticles* since Princeton. No wonder he trembles slightly in the car afterward. But back in the hotel it is clear that he has had a boost from the experience, and a much-needed restoration of confidence. V. says she is now convinced that he can and will compose again.[1]

His comments on the concert show that, as always, it is impossible to know what is going on in the engine room when one's view is limited to the top deck. "The Symphony in Three Movements is naïve in construction," he says, which emboldens V. to ask if he entertains a similar opinion concerning the *Scherzo à la Russe*. The answer is no. "The *Scherzo* is exactly what it

---

1. On April 17 he began to compose an extra instrumental prelude to the *Requiem Canticles*, for a performance of the work in memory of Dr. Martin Luther King. He started with the first two notes of the violin solo in the *Canticles*, the interval that appears in so much of his mourning music and the same notes that he played on the piano when he touched the instrument for the first time after his illness. The prelude was abandoned when he saw that it could not be completed in time for the May 2 performance date.

346

should be." He is well aware, too, that only a small part of the ovation can have been generated by the *Canticles*. "People come first to see if *you* are still there, and second to see if you are still there in the music, hoping, of course, that you aren't." With this he begins to autograph a pile of scores—pirated editions of his early ballets, in the main. As if the buccaneering were not injury enough, one of the stolen publications of *Le Sacre* adds the insult of subtitling it a "Ballet Suite." I await an outburst, but, untrue to form, the composer calmly and neatly blacks out the offending description, saying, "Why not call it Gavotte?" Signing a score of *Petrushka,* he tells me that one of his aunts, "married to a man with whiskers like a Schnauzer," refused to see the ballet because she was "not going to the theater to look at a lot of peasants."

FEBRUARY 21

New York. To *Die Walküre* at the Met, two acts of it, that is, for it affects me like chloroform. Visual interest is sustained in the first act, for a time, by the arboreal confusion in Hunding's tree house. The two limbs that sprout like phalloi from either side of this mammoth log—the only one, incidentally, in the whole forest primeval—appear to have been grafted from a cactus (*Girl of the Golden West*?); and although a Plantagenet profusion of branches was probably not to be expected, the poverty of connection implied by only two—and those from a cactus!—is really too poor and too bastard. Besides, there *must* be another part of the forest. The tree is hewn through at the base, not merely like the redwood that straddles a highway somewhere in northern California, but as openly as the Eiffel Tower. Siegmund's sword, uneasily sheathed in the shin bark, is hardly as big as a thorn, in proportion, but it is a most sensitive thorn, blushing at every mention of its name, flickering and gleaming at every hint of the "sword motif." No one is surprised, therefore, that when finally extracted, after much strenuous but unconvincing tugging, it comes out as highly charged electrically as a bolt from Thor.

1968

The "action" in the Fricka scene, what I see of it in my sleepless moments, takes place on what might be the rim of a recumbent flying saucer, or other UFO; but whatever it is dwarfs the gods who, by my prejudices, should look like Giulio Romano giants in a clouded skyscape. The duel takes place in a kind of mobile Monument Valley, where two great monoliths come together most effectively.

MARCH 3

Hollywood. "I have been thinking about the Picasso eye," I.S. says, out of the azure, and as the subject has not been mentioned since the hospital, the remark falls across the conversation like a news caption on a television screen during a "detergent opera." "A thousand notes could be spent in those few seconds, but what matters is that the form—the music must begin and end, after all—reminds the listener of an eye. I have considered many ways of composing it and many kinds of measurement. But my brain is not clear enough yet, and my body has to be re-educated. I was thinking as I left my bed this morning that I walk like a turtle."

It is impossible to restrain I.S. from commenting aloud at *The Graduate* tonight, as always at the cinema, and from loudly and frequently applying to V. for Russian translations. At one point he provokes a chorus of shushes and a scramble for new seats. In fairness to our fleeing neighbors, too, it must be admitted that his observations are annoyingly detached (if also marvelously acute, especially on errors of length), or would be to anyone engrossed in the film.

I leave the theater ahead of the I.S.'s to bail out the car from the parking lot and meet them at the curb, but return to find them drawing blank stares from the long line of young people filtering inside, people as faceless and undifferentiated, even by the effects of Crest on their grins, as eggs on a conveyor belt; which makes the two old people seem more radically differentiated than ever and turns the flow of my own abundant philoprogenitiveness away from the egg faces and toward them; and which further makes the old man's desire even to *go* to the movies (and it is his second time for *The Graduate*) seem like a manifestation of the same tremendous life force that impelled him, at the age of most of these eggs, to stay home and compose *Le Sacre du printemps*.

MARCH 21

Phoenix. We are suffering from euphoria, for a change, owing, I think, to differences of climatology (if the word can be borrowed back from political jargon) and the sudden excess, after Los Angeles, of chemical-free and even orange-blossom-scented air. Another explanation for the feeling of looseness is inadvertently proposed by the pretty, snub-nosed photographer who meets the I.S.'s at the airport. She says that certain supersensitive small parts of her cameras come unfastened during flights. What then, *I* say, of the effects of flight on such a comparatively sensitive appurtenance as the human nervous system?

We stay in the Casa Blanca Inn, in the desert near, and with a view in zoom-lens distinctiveness of, two humps of rock inevitably called Camelback Mountain. The mosque-shaped central building, as well as each outlying motel unit, is protected by spiny saguaro, prickly pear, bristling ocotillo, tall cucumber-shaped and small porcupine-shaped cactus—a statement that probably reflects my low tolerance of the golfers who are our only Inn mates. Beyond the swimming pools, the fairway, and the putting greens, the desert is tinged with lupines and golden poppies. In Arizona, the color of spring is gold.

Just how mortal the desert can be is made clear by a traffic warning: DON'T END UP A LITTLE WHITE CROSS—unless, of course, the sign was erected by a society of agnostics or by B'nai B'rith. We refrain from questioning our driver on this point, in any case, because to do so would be to interrupt

348

an exceedingly slow-moving disquisition on the, as it turns out, not inconsiderable differences between a butte and a mesa; and we are already late for the dress rehearsal of *The Rake.*

This takes place in an auditorium designed by Frank Lloyd Wright for, it is said, an emergent African republic that in the event failed to emerge. It was completed by one of Wright's pupils three years ago and is something of a freak, possibly because the change of destination did not effect any impious modifications of the master's plans. In any case, the building would certainly look better in Cairo or adjoining the Casa Blanca Inn. Then, on second glance, whatever it is seems to be more sea- than earth-going; a stranded ark, perhaps? The side entrances are in the form of gangplanks and the wall lights are shaped like portholes. But for a building so recently finished, it is astonishingly tacky and out of date (Wright the irrepressible stuccodore), and the atmosphere it provides is more appropriate to a Ziegfeld folly than to a "mod" opera.

Before beginning the rehearsal, I introduce I.S. to the assembled cast, chorus, orchestra, bystanders; except that the only person actually to stand, out of respect for the composer and older man, is our friend Robert Tobin; which means that some of those present have undoubtedly taken Mr. Tobin (who is distinguished-looking) to *be* the composer.

Following the rehearsal, we go to a diner, but the food—plastic shrimps, chopped-rubber-tire hamburgers, a "shortcake" made of old pancakes—is a front for jukeboxes with video screens showing "conservative striptease." Finding no restaurant open after the performance, we go to bed hungry. At 3 AM, V. is awakened by a noise she thinks was made by a rat, but it is I.S., half-starved, nibbling a *gaufrette.*

1968

The musical reading of the opera is excellent, and would have been even better with some fifty more rehearsals and several other changes of circumstance. The Rake's English, for one of them, is unintelligible, owing in part to tracheal congestion—to judge by the struggles with mucosities and the emanations of Vicks reaching to about the thirtieth row. Perhaps from the same cause his pitch is only intermittently *not* a quarter-tone flat, but the fitfully in-tune notes, obtained at the cost of an excruciating *fortissimo,* are worse. The harpsichord is distinguished by a no-less-painful pitch discrepancy, but in the other direction, and the instrument is amplified to something near the level of the Mormon Tabernacle organ at triple *f.* In the first scene a singer anticipates an entrance by several beats, and the others follow him, sheeplike, instead of taking their cues from the orchestra, with the result that the dénouement occurs somewhat sooner on stage than in the pit. In spite of this, I.S. tells me at intermission that he feels as if he were "in a *fauteuil*" when I am conducting the opera. But at times tonight I feel as if *I* am on the edge of a very wobbly seat.

I.S. likes the male Baba vocally ("voyce of unpaved Eunuch," as Cloten says in *Cymbeline*), and the sound *is* good, except for an alarmingly clamant bark on the A in *alt.* "After all," I.S. remarks, "the opera takes place in

349

the age of Farinelli, when operatic sex-swapping was conventional." True, but in the period of tonight's staging, universal transvestism constitutes a stronger justification for the switch. Perhaps unnerved by considerations involving his, or her, muliebrity—or bilateralism—tonight's Baba is forgetful. "Speak to me," she croons, and the Rake, dependably flat, wonders "Why?" but gets only a freezingly long pause, then a backing up, by Baba, for yet another try at "Speak to me," as if she had suddenly found herself to be extremely fond of that particular line. At this point, and because her next lines are *a cappella,* I clear my throat and prepare to give way to a swell of lyricism myself.

But the breakfast scene (in which the running commentary of photographic slides includes a view of Baba doing a sit-in at the "Last Supper") is too campy with a male Baba, and anyway—a more fundamental objection—the opera needs a second woman, even a bearded one. Then, too, hermaphroditism seems to be less happily represented by a division down the middle, as the case is here, than by the over-endowing of the female, as in that Hellenistic reclining nude in the Villa Borghese. In last year's Boston performances, the resurrected Baba—after the hibernation under the wig—was projected on the curtain through closed-circuit television. This suggested psychic manifestations and ectoplasmic transubstantiation, and was superior as an idea to the new one, in which the garrulous androgyne reappears on a standard-size television set exactly like the evening news.

The psychedelic lighting has greatly improved since Boston and so, on the whole, has the stage management, despite minor logistic failures in chasing people on and off the sets in time, no doubt blamable on green thumbs in the local stage crew. Half of the scenery is rather surprisingly carted off *during* the Cabaletta, for instance, word probably having got back that intermission had already begun—which indeed it would have if Anne had been two inches farther upstage and hence carried along. Nor are mishaps of the sort confined to people. In the best tradition of Environmental Theater ("All the world's a stage"), objects are continually dropping in, falling down, bursting, all apparently of their own accord. Even the Rolls-Royce hearse enters too fast, recoiling from its stage blocks like the El Capitan overshooting a station and jerking to a stop. But at least the Rolls does not catch fire, as it did in Boston, where some Fundamentalist was apparently trying to smoke out Shadow—forgetting that the brumous pit is his natural element—and obliging the stagehands to jimmy the windows in a very real rescue operation.

As each performance occasions further thoughts about the opera itself, this one leaves me with the conviction that the lack of dimension in the characters is a graver weakness than any fault of dramatic structure. In any case, the rustiness, or even the absence, of a few dramatic hinges is not necessarily calamitous in a form so dependent on suspensions of disbelief as opera, to say nothing of the unrealities and fairy-tale premises of this

1968

particular opera. The Rake's three wishes have not become more subtle over the years, to be sure. Nor has the nursery-rhyme plot—"a year and a day hence"—grown more compatible with Hogarth and Everyman, however well it may suit the Faustian element in the mixture. What does stand out more than it used to is the Rake's unbusinesslike agreement to the leap-year pact. In fact, it now seems inconceivable, and is certainly not putting too naturalistic an interpretation on the opera, that the Rake can accept Shadow with no notion of who he is, and with no further questions about that long-forgotten uncle, the mysterious benefactor, who does not re-enter his nephew's thoughts until the graveyard scene: not inconceivable in a fairy tale, but certainly in a dramatic spectacle inviting a degree of audience concern over the fate of the characters. It hardly matters that Shadow's "We will settle our account" follows too quickly Truelove's "The sooner that you settle your estate," but it is important that when the Rake's hash finally has been "settled," Shadow's gift of an escape clause—"only what you yourself acknowledge to be just"—is forgotten. Still, these are technical mistakes, not violations of the genre, and the opera survives them.

Thanks to the music, it also survives the one-dimensionalism of the characters. But the strain is greater. While no one in the opera is a believable person, Shadow, Baba, and Sellem, who least need and least pretend to be, are more so than the hero and heroine, and by the time of their final exits, this exotic trio has won a substantial measure of our sympathy and aroused our desire to know more about them. All three are intelligent and engaging, and Sellem, who could have been tiresome in another composer, is so much the opposite that we regret his failure to appear in the Epilogue—insofar as it is worth regretting anything about the Epilogue besides its existence. (In this staging he reappears as the turnkey in Bedlam.) Still, all three are strictly one-dimensional, for Shadow's confidences to the audience hardly invest him with an extra layer of depth, though they do form a stylistic link with the Epilogue, hence are a clue to staging it (if it must be staged). In spite of his parsonical black, and that other well-known clerical disguise, a bad case of Pulpit's Disease, the "king of tears" cuts a more dashing figure than the Rake, and the role is the stageworthiest in the opera by a long shot.

Audience involvement reaches its highest intensity at the Rake's demise, nevertheless, because at this juncture the drama is real and the poetry and music are both perfect in themselves and perfectly fused. But until the graveyard scene, sympathy for the Rake is minimal, and our interest in him mainly confined to his music. His very first aria exposes him as a cad ("Why should I labor for what in the end/She will give me for nothing, if she be my friend"), and is a marplot dramatically in that it precludes true "love interest." Nor is he very clever; in the bread-machine episode, the parable of the Multiplication of Loaves, his intelligence appears to be so perilously low, in fact, that when Shadow compares notes with the audience—"My master is a fool as you can see"—the latter, accustomed to suffer operatic fools gladly for their music, is convinced that this one will end up in Bedlam from natural causes.

Anne is no less vacuous. But she is strangely blinkered, too, and she and the Rake go through the middle part of the opera passing each other like ships in the night. Clearly the Rake is happier with Shadow, as the Don is with Leporello; at any rate, the callousness of his description of his former betrothed as "only a milkmaid" is scarcely thinkable under any other interpretation of his sexual temperament. Partly for the same reason one cannot feel bitterly sorry for her, and for this and other reasons as well—for example, when she can say nothing more about the Rake's betrayal than "It is I who was unworthy"—we wish her Godspeed back to the dairy.

Whether or not the words are, or can be, superior to the meanings, verbal infelicities are by no means rare.[1] Some of the difficulty appears to be with the period of the language, the pastiche of it being at times stilted ("Nick . . . you have some scheme afoot"), and at other times too broad, as in the inclusion of quotations from *Henry IV, Part 2* ("I am exceeding weary"), Dryden's version of Book VI of the *Aeneid* ("Restore the age of gold"), the same poet's "The green sickness" (Epilogue to Mrs. Behn's "The History of Bacon in Virginia"), and even a well-known line from Wordsworth's *Poems of 1807*. Period aside, some lines are ambiguous to the ear. Thus, "Let all who will, make their joy here of your glad tidings" ("Let all who will make their joy hear of," etcetera). Another example is "Bowers of paper only seals repair," which conjures a vision of sea lions at first, until we begin to wonder what a bower of paper might be (the top floor of a Wall Street office building stocked with lavatory tissue for a "ticker-tape" parade?). Ambiguous, too, in the reference of the plural pronoun, is Truelove's "While they're in mind I'll tell you of his needs," which sounds as if it had been written in German first. And Shadow's "Lawyers crouched like gardeners to pay" is remarkably cryptic, considering the dramatic business in hand. In this scene, incidentally, Shadow reacts to the word "God" in Truelove's "May God bless you" by interrupting the conversation, but at the beginning of the very next scene refers to himself as the Rake's "godfather," which is not a likely irony for him at this point. Nor, two scenes later, is Shadow's "the giddy multitude driven by the unpredictable Must of their pleasures" altogether waterproof. I do not doubt that the gray majority may at some time have experienced the sensation of giddiness as a whole (though I do not entirely believe it, either), but certainly the predictability of its pleasures is absolute and foregone.

1968

1. On the other hand, most of the once awkward-seeming musical accentuations no longer ruffle. I should add that at the time of *The Rake* Stravinsky was steeped in Elizabethan music, which offered him precedents aplenty in the matter of accented weak syllables: Morley's "and sweet wild ros*es*," for example, and Wilbye's "with smiling glanc*es*." His preference for the French scansion of franglais words, as in the allocation of but one note to "uncle," was a problem, moreover, only when he first started to compose. It is at the opposite extreme from Handel's German habit of pronouncing *everything*, even making a dissyllable of "whole."

Whether the double meanings are intentional I cannot say. Certainly the Ophelian repressions betrayed in Anne's dreams of wedded bliss—"The joyous fount I see that brings increase," and "the touch of his" (his what?)—seem to be; and so does Shadow's question to the Rake, "Does your machine look anything like this?" But long before the Rake can confirm that of course it does, the audience knows the answer, at least in this staging, and in this prepuce-less age (unaware that foreskins were Pharaonic trophies, as scalps were to the Sioux); for the machine is a modern phallic fantasy, not only in design but also in operation, lighting up with each discharge of bread-loaf like a one-armed bandit registering a jackpot, and thus, incidentally, identifying sex and money. The machine naturally wins the loudest and most spontaneous applause of any of the performers.

But the words, words, words themselves are a verbal fault compared to which these are peccadilloes. The audience is regularly told more (as well as less) than it needs to know. (So is the score reader. "The crowd murmuring," says a marginal direction before the line "We've never been through such a hectic day," but try murmuring "hectic" for a start.) The Rake's soliloquy at the beginning of Act Two, for example, is full of good lines, but for a poetry reading at the "Y": not enough of them count dramatically, and the shape of the scene is imposed by the music. The next scene, too, Shadow's tripartite aria, depends very heavily on the music, the verbal argument being almost purely rhetorical and the dramatic action nonexistent. Yet when the words *are* dramatic and active, which is the case in the Bedlam scene, the effect is powerful enough to carry the weight of all the failures.

As for the staging, not all of the "mod" correspondences are successful, but many fit surprisingly well, and even those that do not are redeemed to some extent by the evidence of a lively imagination. This much must be said because the reviewer's ploy is to make heavy weather of the unorthodoxy and to pose as a defender of the sacred original, which he has heretofore loathed. And it must be said, as well, simply because *any* proof of imagination in opera is rare and in need of support, American patronage tending to help the workshop and the study group rather than the real thing. Miss Caldwell's imagination is evident all the way from her programming—in following the Boston première of *Lulu* with *I Puritani,* for example, and, this year, in saluting the Mexican Olympics with *Montezuma's Revenge*—to her last desperate improvisations on opening night. She has authority, too, and superb musicianship, as proved by the *Tosca* she conducted a few days ago on no notice when the scheduled maestro turned up so much the worse for drink—the offstage life of her company is more theatrical than the on—that he had to be ejected from the theater, a building so poorly insulated that his vociferations from a new location outside were distinctly audible in the quieter moments of Act One.

The first act, "mod," goes down remarkably well. At least *something* happens in that starchy opening scene, and if the Hell's Angels motorbike

1968

353

and the Harold Lloyd–era Rolls are gimmicks, then gimmicks are useful in teasing some life into a formality ("O clement love") bordering on parody. But while Pop Truelove as a lunchpail-carrying, aitch-dropping railroad worker is a solid improvement on the absurdly portentous father-in-law figure "Dear Father Truelove," this change in social position raises a difficulty at the end of the opera, for he appears there, and must appear, in Sunday clothes, after not having been seen since Act One, Scene I, some two and a half hours earlier, and at that time wearing overalls. Programs rustle all over the theater when the stranger himself fails to give any clue, his daughter's misbetrothal evidently having turned him tight-lipped. (He contributes but four words to the Epilogue.)

The beginning of the second scene is even more convincing "mod," partly because the discothèque dances (boogaloo, swim, funky Broadway) fit, as well as spoof, the corny march music. But one episode fails. When Shadow, acting as MC, has adjusted a reverb mike to the Rake for his *ad lib* song, and "Love, too quickly betrayed" gets under way (more than a hint flat), the "mod" apparatus suddenly seems tawdry and irrelevant. But, then, the stage looks a little forlorn whenever the music engages any depth of feeling. Nor is Shadow baleful enough in these surroundings, and it is precisely at the end of this scene that he should first gloat a bit and bare his fangs.

The third tableau is cumbersome. We do not need the Big Dipper and an ocean of pallid lighting to know that it is night. Good diction would be lodestar enough—would in fact obviate the scene shift in the first place, for it is six minutes in coming and then lasts only nine. The one rule here, to which all other considerations may be sacrificed, is not to interrupt the transition from strings to wind trio. Anne's two plummy arias could be delivered in front of the curtain. Come to think of it, that is the best place for them.

The next scene, the Rake wringing his withers in his London pad, is very busy with lighting and other distractions, not all of them intentional. They detract from the mood of the music, too, without making a wordy and undramatic scene less so. Nor is the street scene short on visual targets, though the stage picture was more effective in Boston, where filmed rain made it still more complex. The crowd could be more nondescript than it is, more like a troupe from 8½, though the neighborhood is not a very likely one to be invaded by protest marchers. Finally, it seems to me that Ingmar Bergman's two-act division, concluding the first act with this scene, is still the best way to shape the opera.

The auction scene is Miss Caldwell's most complete success. Sellem—Hawaiian shirt, hippy beads, gardenia over the ear—is a combination Guru, con man, TV automobile salesman. He sits crosslegged on a Simeon-like stylite hoisted from stage level, and as he reels off the objects under the gavel, photographs of them are flashed on the curtain in the manner of a fast-moving slide lecture. The bidders, who have infiltrated the audience in Café La Mama style, move closer to the orchestra as each lot is sold, until they stand by the pit itself for the balance of promises and a better view of Baba resuscitated on TV.

The graveyard, on the grounds of an abandoned, weed-fronded church, is for automobiles, and the lighting is provided by the headlamps of Shadow's Rolls-Royce hearse. The idea is brilliant, but the execution is marred by trapdoor crudity and the position of Shadow's descent, which denies even a glimpse of Satanic transformation; in a staging so tricked out as this one is, surely some earth-rattling or a sulphurous whiff could have been introduced at this point, where something really *is* needed. Furthermore, the switch from cemeteries for people to cemeteries for automobiles renders Shadow's rope useless—unless he intends to perform an Indian rope trick—for the set has no tree, yardarm, or other hangman's drop.

I regret to report that the Bedlam scene is weak and scrimpy, and that the "mod" approach founders in it, the only time in the opera. Nothing after the curtain is as good as the montage of projections before it, of green embryonic faces like those in Tchelichev's *Hide and Seek,* of Hogarth's madmen.[1] Nor is the stage picture convincing. It is dominated by the Harley-Davidson, now thickly bandaged, hence Surrealist as an art object and awkward as a utility, for the gauzed pillion offers "Venus" a clumsy "throne."

Throughout the scene, the madmen shield themselves from the audience and each other (even group therapy has broken down), lying behind the ends of hospital beds. These bedstead grilles are handy, if transparent, symbols for tombstones, prison bars, sickness and isolation, but are ineffective for the reason that the patients never appear. Visual scale is lacking, too; somehow the picture suggests a group of bassinets in a maternity ward. But isolation to this extent may be the wrong idea. The lunatics are a chorus, after all, and Miss Caldwell's Odyssean first notion, which was that all of them together should weave a shroud or other fabric—crazy quilt?—would at least have refined the choral performance. But the scene does, and still would, lack movement. The choruses, even "Madmen's words are all untrue," are dance pieces. Whether Balanchine ballet—the Minuet is a fast, quirky dance as I.S. conceived it—or Peter Brook hoppings-about and holy-rollings, like chickens turning on a spit: some kind of movement is indispensable. That goes for the Mourning Chorus as well. (How beautiful the suspensions are in the bassoons and English horn at the end of this piece!) "Tread softly round his bier," the madmen chant, but no one in this mysterious asylum even shows himself.

The Epilogue is a disaster. But a photograph, flashed across the curtain at the end, of I.S. playing cards—of I.S. the artist, finessing his work, of I.S., indomitable—trumps it and is at the same time a "real" *coup de théâtre.*

1968

---

1. Not the least recommendation of the décors is that the black-and-white sets imitate eighteenth-century engravings, burin lines and all.

Hollywood. Twenty years ago today I first met the "Stravs," that same day on which Auden delivered the book of *The Rake;* and to mark this vicennalian anniversary, I.S. gives the sketches of *The Owl and the Pussicat* [*sic*] to me. But the greatest gift is that we are celebrating together as, so short a time ago, with I.S. straddling two worlds in Death Row at the hospital, I hardly dared hope we would.

At dinner, Christopher Isherwood—still boyish, eyebrows now like tussocks—wonders how such an anniversary can be designated, whereupon we decide to call it a marriage of Craft and Art. Then, as the I.S.'s have a corner and more in Isherwood's autobiography as well, he asks them for *their* impressions of *me* at that first meeting. But the I.S.'s are able to recall only that I was "very nervous, hardly said a word, and had apparently never before touched alcohol!" Well, I am still nervous at times, but do talk a bit now and then, and do not invariably refuse a glass or two of certain anodynes. Finally, Isherwood wants to know "whether it was love at first sight," and I am happy to say that all three of us at the same time answer YES.

Zürich. Our hotel, the Dolder Grand, belongs to the Engelbert Humperdinck period (the *original* Engelbert Humperdinck), to judge by the gingerbread towers, but the period of the weather is the Wet Age. Mists and fog alternate with drizzle and pelting rains, and vapors deliquesce like steam from doused fires above the golf-green lawns and pollarded chestnut trees below the hotel. At noon today, as if in response to the morning-long barrage of church bells, a sudden wind sweeps the snow peaks and sends sailboats skeetering over the lake. It sends me outdoors, too, and into the woods—more Humperdinck—where the shuffling leaves take me back thirty years.

1968

The hotel seems to have been prophylactically insulated against any form of mirth, and whether for the sins they may have beheld, or as insurance against leaks of laughter, the rooms are diurnally punished with furibund rug-scourgings and vacuumings. Nor can the tidyings-up, at various unpredictably inconvenient times during the day—the bedspreads resmoothed, the pillows newly primped, the Kleenex freshly pressed—be intended for any other purpose than to make us feel otiose and immoral. But the Dolder would be a perfect retreat in which to knit a novel, as V. says, and it *is* a good place to put on weight, which is what I.S. needs. In fact, the restaurant is a holdout on a grand scale against quick-fix, precooked, and semi-reconstituted airplane meals. Kangaroo-tail soup, roast thrush, smoked swallows' nests (an acquired taste), and saddle of chamois *poivrade* (served with *pommes* Goethe, *points d'asperges* Eisenhower, or other cultural side dishes) are regularly available, along with the perennial *Birchermuesli*. Considered simply as a room, too, the restaurant compares favorably with the rest of the hotel, the lounge being a gallery for *September Morn*-type pictures, the bar a mausoleum with pianist.

Our fellow boarders include a Libyan prince who looks like Sam Jaffe as Gunga Din, and a sister of the late King Farouk, who looks like nobody knows what, for the reason that she has not left her room in eight years or exposed more of herself than a phantasmal arm extended from behind a door to receive a letter or telegram and give a tip. According to our Austrian *Stubenmädchen,* the Princess bolts herself in the lavatory during meal deliveries and room cleaning. The *Stubenmädchen* reports great quantities of books, too, and racks of never-worn Parisian dresses, and she romantically attributes the Princess's purdah, or super-Garbo seclusion, to blighted love.

Shah Pahlevi is another of the hotel's regulars, partly, it is said, because of vast personal fortunes in local banks, access to which is no doubt assured by a permanently revved-up 727 on the palace runway back home. Our room waiter's description of the Shah's entourage reminds me of a Saudi prince and fellow hotel guest in Geneva in 1951, whose caravan included a portable harem complete with eunuchs who camped in the hallway outside the royal concubines' doors—where monogamous guests leave their shoes. I remember seeing four of the royal Fatimas one day in the back seat of a six-door Cadillac parked in front of the Hôtel des Bergues. They were wearing black robes, black triangular veils, gold bracelets, and one of them was pouring water from a gold jug—which, I suppose, is the Royal Arabian equivalent of a thermos bottle.

1968

OCTOBER 7

We overhear an American in the bar telling a companion about one of Zürich's temples of the gnomes. "You enter by a special door," he says, "where a guard impounds your passport and obliges you to write the number of your account on a paper, with which he disappears into the interior, where your handwriting is verified and your face identified by him against a photograph. Another guard then escorts you to a conference room—incarcerates you there, in fact, to the extent that he continues to stand watch outside the door; the bank wishes to protect the privacy of its celebrated depositors and spare them embarrassing encounters with each other, the Shah bumping into General Franco, for instance, or Truman Capote colliding with Gore Vidal. You imagine that the room is rented out in the evenings to abortionists or psychoanalysts—when not occupied by the usury squads of the Swiss Monetary Police. Then, discovering it to be sound-proof—a clank of chains next door, or even a murder, would not be heard—you realize that, off hours, it must serve some still more sinister purpose, such as a confessional cell for high-ranking criminals.

"The furniture is sparse: a leather couch, a leather-backed chair, a table stacked with picture magazines of Swiss scenery and skiing resorts, mimeographed sheets of stock-market quotations, and a telephone—severed, no doubt, or tuned to a record saying 'Normal service will never be resumed.' At some point you are aware of a peculiar aroma—money, obviously, except that apart from those market averages, nothing in the bank even hints at anything so crass. One of the very last features you are likely to notice is the barred window, if you *do* notice it, for it is the most discreet barred window imaginable. They alone remind you of the bullion somewhere below, and of all those nests, glittering with golden eggs, of the rich and super-rich.

"Your banker, when he arrives—eyes sterling cold, clothes as crisp as newly minted money—puts you on sufferance by requiring you to recite your account number, as if it were the password in a speakeasy or the combination to a safe. He is courteous but uninterceptible, male-voiced but sexless, and the mini-skirted courier who joins him after the inspection of credentials is cold enough to copulate adiabatically. She brings a folder containing the numbered but nameless records of your investments, which you are allowed to study but not to remove. In fact, no documents of any kind are exchanged. Instead, you receive an accounting in the mail, unsigned but with a printed card: 'Compliments of the Schweizerische Bank Verein.' Then, as soon as your business has been transacted, you are bundled out of a back door, after an all-clear from the guard lest in that instant Harold Wilson be entering or leaving as well."

OCTOBER 10

On the way to Lucerne today, I.S. expresses the need of a "Watyer Closyet"—Russia evidently had so few of these facilities that it did not bother to make up its own name—but he rejects an Esso station after discovering that a previous user "had very poor aim." A similar complaint could be made about the swan-fouled lakeside walk in Lucerne, except that this seems to be deliberate, an act of mass excremental retaliation for the polluting of the boat basin, from which apparently even the youngest cygnets have soiled their down.

The caretaker of Wagner's villa at Triebschen is unbelieving after reading I.S.'s signature in the visitor's book, but she recovers her composure (and composer) in time, and guides us through. The collection of musical instruments on the second floor contains many beautiful examples by Renaissance and Baroque craftsmen, along with such Wagnerian instruments as the tenor *Tuben,* not only of the *Ring* but also of *Le Sacre du printemps.*

OCTOBER 11

I.S. receives the manuscript full score of *Le Sacre du printemps* from his son in Geneva today, but the sight of penciled changes made during the first rehearsals reminds him of the première, which thought so irritates him that he adds a P.S. on the last page, berating the first audience for "the derision with which it greeted this music in the Théâtre des Champs-Elysées, Paris, Spring 1913." The score is bound in red morocco and linen, and many pages are reinforced with transparent tape. The Russische Musikverlag stamp is on several pages, too, the manuscript actually having been lent out to conductors and used in performances. Among those penciled pre-première amendments are the following additions: the trombone parts two measures before 22 ; the bass drum part one measure before 22 , and, *ibidem,* the *fermata* on the F (not sustained by the tubas in this score); the piccolo trumpet part at the beginning of the *Jeu de rapt;* the horn and trumpet parts in the first two measures of 62 .

The Russian title, *Gra Umikanüa* (*The Mock Abduction of the Bride*), has been deleted here, and replaced by *Jeu de rapt,* but at what date I.S. no longer remembers. *Spring Rounds* is called simply *"Khorovod"* here, and the music at 64 still bears the separate heading *"Idut-Vedut,"* and the *Dance of the Earth* is still *"Vyplyasyvaniye Zemlee,"* with no French translation supplied. Finally, the manuscript title of the *Action rituelle* is "Consecration of the Place," and the title of the *Evocation* is "The Evocation of the Human Ancestors."

The only major revision shown in the autograph is at 28 , where the quarter-note theme was first composed for horns, and where, in rewriting it for trumpets, Stravinsky cancels the entire page (18 measures) and rescores it on an inserted one—which, however, is bound in the wrong order. But I should also mention that the eighth-notes in the *Kiss of the Earth* are in the solo cello part, rather than in the solo bass; that the bassoon lead-in to the *Action rituelle* is marked *forte;* that the bass drummer in the *Evocation* is directed to use a wooden stick and to touch the head of the instrument with his hand to try to produce a high B flat; that the score specifies four timpanists, the timpani parts in the main part of the *Danse sacrale* being doubled.

On the title page of Part Two, the composer advises the publisher, in Russian, that "Pages 69-87, containing the *Danse sacrale,* will be sent shortly," and that the music between rehearsal numbers 86 and 88 is out of sequence. The score is signed and dated "8 III/23 II 1913" (*sic:* New Style first, then Old Style) at the end of the *Danse sacrale,* and signed, dated, and located, "Clarens, 16/29 III 1913," at the end of the third measure of 85 .

1968

OCTOBER 19

To Einsiedeln, crossing the lake on the causeway at Rapperswil, where V. photographs the cloister and Schloss. The valleys are still green, but the vineyards are yellowing and the ivy is already mulberry red. South of the lake the road is clogged with wains.

The exterior of the Benedictine monastery at Einsiedeln—*"Coenobiu Eremitaru"* on old maps—reminds us of the Escorial except for the church in the center with volutes like treble clefs, which is typical South German Baroque. The interior is disappointing, partly because we have anticipated the gleaming white and gold of Wies and the other Bavarian masterpieces, but a choir of shavelings kneeling before the Madonna and Child in the nave chapel is singing a Vesper service with the greatest refinement of intonation I have ever heard. Outside again, in the arcades which form a semicircular approach to the church, we buy photographs from a man who manages to inject so much kindness into the transaction that he sticks in my mind, together with the idolatrous choristers, for the rest of the day.

OCTOBER 23

Paris. Our rooms at the Ritz are not merely holding-actions against the "de-erotization of the environment" (Marcuse), but veritable love nests, as strategically mirrored as brothels, though in style kin to Gavarni's foyer at the Opéra. The beds—pink-silk spreads, goddess figureheads on the foot-boards—are double, and so, in a squeeze, are the *chaises longues.* Moreover, the allotment of space for the boudoirs would be unthinkable in any city except Paris, and unthinkable there since about 1900. Erotically conducive, as well, are the log-grate fireplaces, the coved doors, the carnival-mask (*cache-sexe*) lampshades, the key-and-keyhole light switches, the cushioned footrests for the *maquillage* and dressing tables, the chain in the bathtub to summon the *femme de chambre,* the bedside push button for *service privé,* and—not least—the view from the window of one of the largest phallic monuments in Europe, in the place Vendôme. Less erotic, even allowing for kinks, are the umbrella stand, the chandelier, the five-minute choke of the wall clock, the tarnished gilt moldings, the striped upholstery, and the escritoire; but the only serious *an*aphrodisiac is the price.

According to the doorman, the hotel had only nineteen guests during last May's revolution-that-got-away, but the staff of four hundred was always on the job. Sugar had to be rationed from the second day, he says, but while he elaborates on this and other hardships, I wonder about the continuing provocation, to Cohn-Bendit and company, in the steady flow of Mercedes, Rolls, and Alfa Romeos stopping at the entranceway.

1968

OCTOBER 26

Tonight's concert in the Théâtre de la Musique is the culminating event of a *"journée Xenakis."* The other principal event is billed as a discussion-debate which, however, does not entail any lobbing back and forth but only some very heavy "questions" that are really self-answering statements much longer than the "replies." Pop-cult hero Lévi-Strauss himself attends the debate, and young people, dandy rather than hippie, overflow both affairs. They lather into a Beatles-type hysteria several times at the concert, but were perhaps already in it beforehand as any causal connection between the character of their responses and the contents of the program is slight. I sit not far from Messiaen, in a loge apparently designed for people with no knees.

Few contemporary composers can survive the exposure of a one-man concert, let alone a one-man day, and Xenakis is not among them. But this difficulty is nowhere dealt with or acknowledged in the purple program folders, whose Xeroxed sheafs of press clippings, biographia, film-strip photos of the master at work, and a booklet of Pataphysical bull entitled *La pensée de Xenakis* spill across the stage most effectively later in the evening when jettisoned in that direction by the protesting minority.

One of the publicity releases assures the reader that Xenakis's "time" is "in some cybernetic future." But tonight's reception shows all too patently that his time is right now, and that the future, cybernetic or otherwise, is precisely what he will soon have to worry about—as soon, in fact, as the next performance. Again, despite all the advance warnings about the abstruseness of the composer's cogitations and the inaccessibility of his mathematical methods, the music itself is both devastatingly predictable (or, in fashionable cant: "The mind makes probabilistic assessments") and astonishingly naïve, the latter being the case with several timpani rolls of the type that one had thought to have gone out with the *Symphonie fantastique*.

The program's centerpiece is an avalanche of electronic noise called *Bohor,* which, if pronounced as one syllable, is also a partial description of the effect. It is an experiment in sonic torture, inflicted by "quadruple stereophony"—bruited, in other words, by eight loudspeakers shaped like dryers in a beauty salon and aimed at the audience like death-ray machines. A jet motor seems to switch on *in* one's penetralia, whereupon one stops one's ears but only with the effect of tiring one's arms. When the theater itself begins to tremble like a tuning fork, the reactionaries head for the exits—as I would myself, except that I go on thinking from second to second that it cannot last a second longer. It seems obvious after a while that the machine must be stuck or the tape derailed, inasmuch as the noise is so little varied. But whatever the explanation, *Bohor* should be played, or detonated, if at all, in a football stadium for an audience in air-raid shelters several miles away.

The one point of interest would be in comparing impressions of duration (ten minutes? an hour?), but even that is frustrated, for when the aural holocaust has finally subsided, the outburst of booing, jeering, catcalling—accompanied by a hail of program folders like the refuse thrown into a bull ring after a bad *corrida*—nearly equals *Bohor* in volume. The counter-assault (*"Bis!"* from the Beatle-maniac majority) has hardly got under way when the string orchestra returns to the stage, and the demonstration turns to whistles imitating the slow glissades, which in the main are what the strings play. As the conductor signals the start of the next piece, a shout, *"Du Mozart!"*—a "plant," I suspect—goes up and is answered by a rich assortment of uncomplimentary epithets, the most popular of which is *"Con!"* But surprisingly, the opus passes without further outward incident. And without much inward incident either. In fact, the layout of contrasting blocks of sound effects is much the same in every piece, except that "contrasting" misleadingly implies movement. If this is "sound architecture," as advertised, then it should go back to the drawing board.

But the real trouble with the concert after *Bohor* is that live players, a

1968

361

conductor, "trad" instruments, and the concert routine itself seem so glaringly obsolete. The conductor's straight beat patterns are without evident bearing on the rhythms. Nor are the instruments functionally adapted to their work, the design of a violin, after all, and its tuning in fifths, corresponding to an evolution in music itself. In sum, Xenakis's *"pensée"* seems more fittingly served by filters, sonotrons, oscillators, potentiometers, sinewave generators, ring modulators, and the other hardware.

The composer receives his ovations in the blue-denim uniform of a factory worker and footwear showing him to be ready for tennis. Well apprised that the turnover in the reputation stock market is more rapid on the Paris Bourse than anywhere in the world, however, he emerges afterward inveighing against the Parisian process of becoming *à la mode.* BECOMING?

I emerge thinking about Verdi's "Progress could be in the reverse direction." I think about it, with rapidly diminishing interest, until 2 AM, at which hour girls for hire—"shop workers who want to buy more clothes," R. says—are trying to give a basic idea of their wares in nearly every doorway of the rue de la Paix all the way back to the Ritz.

NOVEMBER 18

Pompano Beach. The state of culture as advertised along the mental five-and-ten of Route U.S. 1A: invitations to bowl, rollerskate, have your fortune told; play shuffleboard, miniature golf, jai alai; buy plastic driftwood, electronic fish-finders (isn't that "unsporting"?), "Spanish Colonial Furniture. Custom Made"; patronize "U-Save Shopping Centers," "Drive-In Funeral Homes," "Happy Hour Cocktail Lounges," a "Jungle Garden Safari" ("See 100 Lions in the Wild"), the "Wigwam Village of Tuckabuckaway and Tribe" (those thrifty Seminoles?); try a garage selling "Personalized Waxing" (how personal can *waxing* get?), and a First Church of Christ Scientist selling a sermon: WHERE WILL YOU SPEND ETERNITY?

1968

I go to the beach despite wilting heat, a louring sky, too many people, and paralyzing blue-bladder hydrozoans (Portuguese men-of-war, which, when punctured by sharp sticks or stones, as small boys delight in doing, explode like party balloons). The people are a breed (retired necktie salesmen? ex-shillelagh manufacturers?) peculiar to, though not bred on, the peninsula. Their interests, to judge from my involuntary eavesdropping, are confined to logging the weather (the satellite views of the weather on the telly here look like X-rays of tubercular lungs), Dow Jones Averages, and "back-home." Their daughters—some of them desirable, in décolleté-of-the-derrière bathing suits, but all of them intolerably young—are throwing frisbies, which are plastic discs the size of phonograph records, launched backhand, like quoits. Those Route 1A–type advertisements pursue the customer even here, however, trailed from small airplanes at strafing height. MINNIE PEARL'S CHICKEN: ALL U CARE TO EAT, one of them reads, somewhat ambiguously, it seems to me, in the verb.

1948
1949
1950
1951
1952
1953
1954
1955
1956
1957
1958
1959
1960
1961
1962
1963
1964
1965
1966
1967
1968
1969
1970
1971

ITINERARY

April 20: The I.S.'s fly to New York. **27:** I.S. attends a concert of his music at Stony Brook, Long Island. **May 1:** Nicolas Nabokov for dinner with I.S. at the Pierre. **July 1:** I.S. goes out for his first promenade since leaving the hospital. **9:** We fly to Hollywood. **September 3:** I.S. goes out to dinner (at Lawrence Morton's) for the last time in Hollywood. **October 21:** I.S. receives Svetlana Stalin. **December 16:** I.S. receives Harold Spivacke from Library of Congress, apropos gift of manuscripts.

MAY 2

New York. Following a consultation with his doctors, we take I.S. to the New York Hospital at noon; he has complained since yesterday of sharp pains above the left knee, which may indicate that the clot, discovered January 18, has grown. In fact, the femoral artery is found to be entirely blocked, and circulation in the by-pass veins so dangerously reduced that surgery is necessary as soon as the patient can be prepared. The preparations, incidentally, require that I.S. autograph a release, which, he says, "is like signing your own death warrant." The operation begins under halothane

363

and sodium pentothal,[1] with simultaneous oxygen feeding to ventilate the heart, lungs, and blood; and it lasts from 7 to 10 PM. A catheter, inserted into the artery, removes an eleven-inch embolus by air pressure from below.

MAY 3

We learn this morning that another clot was found in the other arterial branch, and that a second embolectomy will have to be performed today, as well as a left lumbar sympathectomy, to open all of the pipelines as widely as possible. The alternative is amputation, which he cannot survive. But can a man of eighty-seven, already weakened by long illness, survive major surgery for the second time in twenty-four hours?

We wait outside the operating theater all evening. At about 11:20 I am taken to an Intensive Care Unit occupied by a patient whose bandages are like the padding of an ice-hockey goalie; another patient, muzzled with breathing machinery, whose heartbeats bounce across the screen of a cardiac monitor in the form of green blips; and I.S., who is clear-headed, sprightly (from digitalis?), and wholly in character. When I tell him that V. is anxious to see him, he says, "Why? What's the matter with *her?*"

MAY 12

I.S. has been moved from his small, bleak, Spanish-Harlem-view cubbyhole to the spacious room 1719, which is reserved for sick bigwigs; it looks over the barred sun terrace of the psychiatric clinic, a few floors below, to Welfare Island, where rookie firemen extinguish practice blazes in dummy buildings. As he is able and eager to listen to music now, I play a recording of Handel's *Theodora,* assuming it to be emotionally unharmful to him. "It is beautiful and boring," he says, not far along, "Too many pieces finish too long after the end." He sleeps afterward, then on waking becomes intransigent, refusing to talk and excluding us all from the privacy of his mind. He is literally skin and bones now, but will eat no more than a smidgen of caviar, and that only for the ration of whiskey allowed with it, for he knocks back the liquid in an amount disproportionate to the small substance of the solid. The skin of his buttocks hangs like laundry when we lift him, and his fingers are so thin that his sapphire signet ring, an apotropaic power to him, will not stay on; his slippers, too, have to be cross-gartered to his ankles like ballet shoes, but with bandages. On the other side of the ledger, the danger of infarction has passed, the carbuncular swelling has diminished, the toe is no longer pustular, and sensation is restored to the foot. The surgical scars, too, from which long threads protruded a few days ago like hairs of a large insect (or Gregor Samsa metamorphosed), are healing, and the skin around them, covered with black-and-blue maculae, is squamous and starting to peel.

1969

---

1. Which he described later as "Felicity: it seems as if you have just extended your arm for the shot when you are told the operation is over."
 (Sylvia Plath: "Fuzzy with sedatives and unusually humorous
     . . . At the count of two
     Darkness wipes me out like chalk on a blackboard . . . ")

When I enter the room at noon, I.S. proudly tells me that he has scored four more measures of the B-minor Fugue. But in mid-afternoon his temperature flares up to 39° (the New York Hospital uses the apothecary system), from the 38.2° that has been "normal" since the operation, and that has aroused suspicion he may have the so-called hospital infection ("staph disease"?). His cough is more congested, too, like croup, and the respiration rate has accelerated to 44. X-rays are taken and bacterial cultures dispatched for analysis, but whatever the diagnosis, it is not the pneumonia all of us fear[1]—the "all" including doctors and nurses whose anxiety is unprofessionally apparent but humanly welcome. I stay at the hospital until midnight. After that a nurse calls me hourly to report small fluctuations of temperature.

An offended letter from X., whom I.S. failed to recognize in the intermission crowd at Stony Brook last month—reasonably, it seems to me, I.S. having seen X. only twice in two years, once before the long illness in 1967 and once sixteen months later. Like other acquaintances of I.S. of other eras, X. is very free in advising me about what is best for him, exactly what he needs, where he should go, what he should do, what my own attitude should be. The last should not, above all, include any unrealistic optimism, for if I.S. has failed to recognize X., things must be bad indeed. Return to Hollywood, says X., leaving I.S.'s own feelings out of consideration—whether he himself might wish to escape the depressing reminders of his illness there— and unable to imagine the sheer physical impossibility of life there now for both I.S. and V., neither of whom can manage the stairs any more, let alone look after the house.

1969

But I myself am unable now, or unwilling, to sympathize with the point of view of people like X. I do not doubt that I have been guilty of mistakes and misjudgments in trying to take care of I.S. But I have given all of myself to him and to the job, at least, and if I hadn't a great deal more might have gone wrong and his musical life would have come to an end. As I see it, I.S.'s true friends are indebted to me for that.

The responsibility for every decision has been mine, furthermore, with no help from the X.'s, or, for that matter, from anyone in I.S.'s own family except V. And the responsibility is becoming intolerable, and my own equilibrium ever more difficult to maintain, as I am increasingly aware thanks to my habit of assessing every liability of a course of action for V., then giving my own opinion, and finally backing down from that and opting for another course simply to shirk the blame for any unfavorable consequences.

1. It was, but we were not told until later.

But it could be that I am becoming ill myself. Abulia, perhaps. (Or is it bulimia?—nervous overeating.) And self-justification, certainly.

MAY 25

I.S. has taken an upturn and emerged from the limbo in which he has been suspended for three weeks. Best of all, that incredibly tenacious demon of his is still there. "I want to work," he says, "and if I can't work, I want to die." Accordingly, we hoist him out of bed to a gantry-type table with windlass-like level-adjusting device, where, cocooned in blankets and with his feet resting on a pillow labeled "Feet," he transcribes Bach. Glancing back and forth from his score to the printed copy, which is propped on a reading stand, he might be a monk copying a manuscript, or Jerome translating the Bible. (I am thinking of Carpaccio's "Jerome" in San Giorgio di Schiavone.) Some twenty minutes later we lift him back to bed, with the difference that a small gleam of confidence is showing in his eyes; but he is soon up again, and up and down a total of four times during the afternoon. He wants to listen to music, too, but "my own only if you have nothing else." In fact, I play his tiny two-trumpet *Fanfare,* which draws the comment, "Well, I have nothing against *that.*" We also play the Mendelssohn Octet, Schumann's first string quartet, Beethoven's C-minor Variations and the Serenade (Opus 8), and Messiaen's *Cinq Rechants.* He follows all of the scores but betrays no sign of pleasure or pain except during the Mendelssohn (pleasure).

His bed oscillates like a bunk on a slowly rolling ship. It is covered with a sheepskin paillasse, but he is so thin now that his back is soon sore at every point of pressure and his position must be shifted every few minutes. About once an hour, moreover, he is obliged to lie totally flat while his left leg, which he crooks like a pelican most of the time, is forcefully—painfully—straightened. "I hurt everywhere," he grumbles. But the *longueurs* of medicine schedules, of permuted tests for prothrombin time, of bombardments from a humidifier (like the steam from a manhole cover in a New York street), to say nothing of the indignities of bedpans and the occupational disingenuousness of nurses, with their alternating Grosspapa-talk and baby-talk ("upsy-daisy")—these must hurt and gall him most of all.

Still, he *is* better, and a thousand hosannas for that, his amazing recuperative powers having again proved themselves, astonishing those who see only the outward and belying decrepitude. His temperature is normal, too, for the first time since May 20, though whether as a result of the river of intravenous effluents poured into him these five days, I cannot say. Once, in a pique, he moves his arms as rapidly as he ever did conducting an orchestra—which provokes a sibylline nurse to remark that "Obviously God doesn't want you yet, Maestro." But he will not eat. Nor heed our arguments that only by eating can he return to his piano, which he says is his one

1969

366

wish. And the hunger strike is more difficult to break than the silence strike. In fact, he can seldom forbear to provide the word one of us may be groping for in some backchat he is not supposed to be tuned in to; or resist the temptation to correct my French (no end of opportunities; I am unable to pronounce the French *"muscle"* to his satisfaction, for example, and the word regularly recurs in reference to the dystrophy in his abdomen and left leg). Once when he seems to be on the verge of talking on his own volition he stops short, dramatically (aposiopesis), and expresses the futility of it all with a wave of the hand. Yet when a head floor nurse—a "yenta" whose own vocal equipment could drown out the brass section of the Hamburg Philharmonic—asks him if he will please say something, anything at all, just to oblige us, he fairly yells at her: "MERDE!"

From the hospital, where the parking attendants now call me "Doc," I go to the ballet, where the main attraction, more stared at during intermission than the stage during the performance, is Mrs. Onassis. The seats are knee-jamming and ill-raked, and the applause is misplaced except for a brief volley mocking the retractable rock-candy (?) chandeliers, as well as, I like to think, the abstract antlers (?) above the proscenium arch. The *tempi* are stretched to groaning point for Fonteyn, while Nureyev, now Tarzan-maned and with hocks like a Percheron, seems to spend less time dancing than bowing, which he does with his right arm straight up like a chief of MGM Sioux. But, then, I am hardly present, being unable to take my thoughts from room 1719 and the man lying there, who has enlarged the imagination of the world as much as anyone still alive in it, but who had to be helped this afternoon in transposing a clarinet part.

1969

JUNE 18

I.S. returns from the hospital—having been on the rota for discharge since Sunday—and not only from the hospital but from a place so close to The Other Side that few who have been as far ever return. Before he leaves, the floor nurses bring him a birthday cake with musical notes on the icing. He smiles, seeing it—a genuine smile, not the new ritalin-induced one—and when the women in white break into "Happy Birthday," he conducts them. The party continues in the hotel, where thirty baskets of flowers await him, and where, as V. opens gifts and telegrams, he sips champagne. One of the gifts is a full score and recording of *Le Coq d'or,* to which he listens for about three minutes before it puts him out of sorts.

Going to his room at night, I find him wide awake (and his nurse unarousable). "I'm accustomed to the undulating bed," he explains. "Besides, I am afraid of dreaming music, and I realize now that I will never again be able to compose." I protest, of course, and try every tack I can think of to persuade him he is wrong. But he doesn't believe any more, and is impervious to cheer. In fact, it is becoming difficult now even to record the depression.

Hollywood. At 12:20 AM I.S.'s nurse calls to say that his temperature has mounted to 104° and that his respiratory rate is alarmingly fast. I telephone a doctor, who instructs me to bring him to the Emergency Entrance at U.C.L.A. Medical Center, which I do in an ambulance because I am not certain of being able to carry him safely inside once we arrive. The doctor in attendance is busy antidoting mushroom-poisoned (botulism toxin?) hippies. When finally he examines I.S.—under my proctoring, as we have returned from New York only two days ago and the nurse is only sketchily aware of his medical misadventures there—the verdict is pneumonia. X-rays reveal no more than the thirty-year-old tuberculosis scars, however, and two other doctors, arriving for consultation, are as baffled as their New York colleagues were by the similar incident on May 20. An oxygen cylinder is wheeled into the room, nevertheless, and I.S. spends the night unhappily with a plastic mask clapped over his nose and mouth. It is 4 AM when I take V. home.

I.S. himself, temperature and respiration normal, returns in the afternoon, undiagnosed. V. fears that his tuberculosis may have become active again. (An enclosed, dormant TB bacillus is virulent if released, and could be even after two thousand years.) She believes, moreover, that people are born to their diseases—that Bartók was born to his leukemia—and that I.S.'s born-to disease is tuberculosis. Poor V. She can only wonder from which direction the next blow impends.

1969

I.S. enters the Cedars of Lebanon this afternoon for further tests, on the hunch of one of his doctors that the coughing spells, the halituous constriction, and the râle may be due to clotting in the lungs, a not-uncommon development in polycythemiacs. But the diagnosis on his admission card is tracheal bronchitis. As he coughs only when swallowing liquids and *not* when he eats, is it possible that the spasms are caused simply by pressure on the esophagus?

"The tests will prove nothing," the patient protests. "*Le mal est dans mon âme.*" Overhearing our discussion as to whether a practical nurse will be needed for the night, he cuts in, snappishly, with, "All of my nurses are *im*practical, anyway, and since I already have pains everywhere else, why must you give me a pain in the neck, too?" But when V. asks if he wants anything, the answer is, "I want to compose." Later, leaving the hospital, she reasons that "He would suffer less if he had a smaller share of intuition, but then he wouldn't be *him*."

Yesterday's lung-scanning has unfounded our fears of clotting but has not dispelled the specter of tuberculosis or ended the suspicion that the alveolae may be dilating or that the small lung sacs may be fibrillating, as they do with emphysema. Are the doctors, obviously unable to account for the coughing fits and violent rises in temperature, simply grabbing at straws?[1]

He is discharged from the hospital at noon, the worst of the experience for him having been that he received someone else's lab report yesterday, and it was less good than his own. But he needs analeptic medicine now, or, like an athlete, anabolic steroids. He weighs only 87 pounds!

Three of Haydn's Opus 76 quartets, in the evening, elicit his long-unheard grunt of pleasure (once at m. 45–50 of the Largo, and again at m. 169–172 of the Presto, of no. 5, and then in the last ms. of the Adagio of no. 6). And his attention strays only during the thicker layers of unctuousness in the performance. "That the music may seem to be 'like Beethoven' is hindsight," he says. "Certainly it should not be played as if it were *by* Beethoven." But he does not cough at all during the hour and a half of music, and he has not had any linctus. We carry him upstairs afterwards on a seat of crossed hands.

AUGUST 26

The turnover in nurses has been so rapid of late that I.S. pretends he cannot remember their names. He has taken to summoning them with "Hello," therefore, spoken weakly at first, then repeated three or four times, parrot-like and *con crescendo*. If a response is still not forthcoming, he will shout it in a *Boris Godunov* voice one is surprised to find he still has. But he is always aware of his nurse's language, and always chooses the right one (whether Russian, German, English, or French) in which to be understood by her when criticizing her to V. This afternoon, for example, he greatly offends his doting Russian *nanya* by asking us, deliberately within her earshot: "Why must I spend the whole afternoon in the company of an idiot?"

At table now, too, he prefers to officiate and to direct traffic, if he can get away with it, rather than exert himself. Thus he will nod his head or crook his index finger toward an item of food on his plate that he wishes to be fed, but if no nurse is around, will eat perfectly normally by himself.

A birthday dinner for Christopher Isherwood, after which I listen with I.S. to *The Stone Guest,* following a score he acquired in Kiev in his youth. "If you were to ask me about the music today," he says when it is over, "I would be less generous than I once was. I prefer the libretto to the music, now, and so far as the performance is concerned, I prefer the diction of the singers to their singing. Still, it is an original score, whose best and worst qualities are the same: the evenness." Isherwood, meanwhile, has fallen asleep in front of the television, waking at 1 AM.

SEPTEMBER 14

We fly to New York, via Newark, and go to the Plaza Hotel.

1. One more crisis of the same kind occurred at the beginning of August, at which time, too, the tests for tuberculosis were positive; but this was reversed before the move to New York.

1969

Berlin. At my dress rehearsal this morning, I decide, together with Nicolas Nabokov, not to play I.S.'s new Bach transcriptions, too little if anything of I.S. being discernible in them as they stand now, virtually unedited.

I fly to Munich with R.—at 7 AM and in heavy rain—change there for Zürich, and in Zürich for Basle, where a brass band parading on the Rhine Bridge and a band concert on a river barge rock me in my room at The Three Kings, but not to sleep. In the afternoon I go to the bank to arrange for the transferral of I.S.'s former attorney's power of attorney and thus make possible the repatriation, as quickly as possible, of I.S.'s and V.'s money.

I drive with R. to Zürich for the four o'clock flight on Swissair to New York. Mont Blanc is unclouded and so is France, from Burgundy all the way to the Channel. New York is a multi-layered traffic tangle: in the air (a two-hour "holding pattern"), at the airport, waiting for baggage, in Customs, queueing for taxis, on the expressways, crossing Sixty-first Street to the hotel. But I.S. looks almost hale—except that his calves are as thin as those of Donatello's "St. John" in the Frari—and his weight is up to 106, which is the same as it was before the operations.

1969

We move to the Essex House, V., already acclimatized to New York, bravely signing a two-year lease.

Inscribing a copy of *Retrospectives and Conclusions* for Lucia Davidova tonight, I.S. writes his name in Russian on the flyleaf, then turns to the biographical blurb on the inside of the dust-wrapper, and below the phrase "lives in California," adds the heart-breaking words "No More."

I.S. files suit to recover his manuscripts from his son-in-law, Andre Marion, and former lawyer, William Montapert, to whose joint stewardship they were entrusted in February 1967. The story is carried nationally, by newspapers and television. But not, of course, the *full* story. When I.S. requested the return of his manuscripts after becoming a New York resident two months ago, he was answered with the demand, by Marion, to sign a "release." This claimed as its basis a "dispute over the ownership of certain manuscripts." But I.S.'s manuscripts were incontestably his property, nor had he ever indicated his intention with regard to them, except to give them for tax deductions to institutions. It also described some seven or eight categories of employment ("business and investment manager, holder of various powers of attorney, bookkeeper, recipient and disburser of funds, corporate officer and director of Verigor International, manager of Stravinsky's farm," etc.) for which the I.S.'s had apparently been paying Marion, but of whose functions Marion denied any knowledge when V. sought his help during the hospital crisis last May.

The "release" further demanded I.S.'s protection from prosecution by the government (as if he could contravene an official investigation): ". . . Stravinskys agree to hold Marion harmless from claims of any governmental agencies, whether State, Federal or foreign . . . and hereby expressly waive the benefits of the Civil Code of the State of California which reads: '1542. A general release does not extend to claims which the creditor does not know or expect to exist in his favor at the time of executing the release.' This is intended as a general release," the document concluded, "and not a mere covenant not to sue." But why in Heaven's name should Marion have reason to fear that his father-in-law might wish to sue him? And what could he possibly have to hide from government agencies, local, federal, and even foreign?

I.S. cannot be party to such an agreement, of course, and especially not to recover what, after all, is his own property. Suit is his only recourse now.[1]

DECEMBER 11

I draft a letter to L., in answer to one from him concerning my strictures of Los Angeles for its disregard of I.S. on his eighty-fifth birthday.

1969

Dear L.:

I am glad to have your views on my "general condemnation" of Los Angeles in its treatment of Stravinsky. But my remarks were provoked only by comparing what Los Angeles did in observance of Stravinsky's eighty-fifth birthday (*i.e.,* nothing) with what was done in other cities of the world, many of them with far fewer resources. And I continue to see the matter differently.

Obviously I should have been more explicit. I should have mentioned the failure of the Los Angeles universities to mount a Stravinsky festival, as Berkeley did. And no less obviously I should have excepted you, Ingolf Dahl, Sol Babitz, and a few other individuals.

But why do you mention John Vincent and the *Cantata* "commission"? For although it is true that Stravinsky did eventually receive a minute sum for the piece above his conducting fee, this was used to cover costs of part-copying and of importing a tenor. And weren't you present at the rehearsal when Stravinsky volunteered to pay for an extra oboist out of his own pocket *and was accepted*?

And Werner Janssen, yet, among the wronged! Stravinsky used to tell it the other way around, and the evidence of his archives supports him. But, then, the archives tell much the same story from Janssen all the way down. It is a story of skimping on rehearsal time, of the composer being asked to waive music rentals and performance fees, of programming based on first-performance publicity.

1. The case was settled out of court, and the manuscripts returned at the end of December.

But what has happened to *you*? Not long ago you would have been the first to agree with my "condemnation." When Stravinsky was only eighty and not yet safe to praise, you helped him to write letters protesting the Los Angeles *Times*'s defamation of *The Rake's Progress*.

You say that the Museum concerts were "costly" as well as "sincere appreciations of Stravinsky's presence in the community." *I* say that they were not costly enough. Nor do I consider the three Stravinsky concerts an extravagant number, even if personal homage had been left out of it. Besides, "the Museum," in the sense of initiator, does not exist. The concerts took place for one reason only: because *you* were there. Nor was the third and final one, the belated so-called birthday concert, anything more than a face-saving afterthought. If Basle, Berlin, Edinburgh, etc., earn an "A" for good intentions simply by announcing their programs a decent interval in advance, then Los Angeles deserves a "Z." And even at that final event Stravinsky *was* exploited. Television had him for nothing.

So, not pretending to any detachment and claiming a perspective no larger than what I have learned by reading Stravinsky's mail, I feel that Los Angeles's treatment of him on the occasion of his eighty-fifth anniversary was shabby. And what matters far more, the Stravinskys felt it, too. Yet I concede, and Stravinsky concedes, that it was probably no worse than it would have been if he *didn't* live there.

Yours, etc.

DECEMBER 17-18

I bundle I.S. into the car for an evening ride through Central Park and down Fifth Avenue to see the Christmas lights. Then, back in the hotel, we listen to the Adagio and Fugue from Opus 106. ("What do you think of that?" I ask at one point in the Fugue, but he shuts me up with *"Je ne pense pas, j'écoute."*) V. advises him to go to bed early. "Auden is coming for dinner tomorrow and you will have to be sharp. Please try to be a little less gloomy, too," she adds, to which his answer is: "Then give me a larger scotch." She also reminds him that "Nicolas Nabokov is coming in the morning to say *au revoir*" (I.S.: "Without saying *bonjour* first?"). And she suggests that he be a little more *méchant* with his nurses, "just to get back in form." (I.S.: "I already started today.") When Nabokov does come, and talks at length about his recent trip to the U.S.S.R., V. asks I.S. if he remembers who attended the banquet in *his* honor in Moscow in 1962. I.S.: "Well, *I* was there, in any case, which means that *you* were probably there, too." And, it is clear, the presence of nobody else in the world would matter in the slightest. Nabokov asks him to autograph *R. & C.,* and V. encourages him to "add a few notes of music as well." "Which notes?" he asks, whereupon she hums something that he writes down in a novel way. (But he *never* autographs the same way twice, and he *always* has ideas. Thus, meeting our friend Hans Popper in Tokyo, after having seen him in Vienna and New York shortly before, I.S. decorated Popper's keepsake album with a map ingeniously relating the three cities, and in no time at all, with no apparent forethought.)

1969

1948
1949
1950
1951
1952
1953
1954
1955
1956
1957
1958
1959
1960
1961
1962
1963
1964
1965
1966
1967
1968
1969
1970
1971

JANUARY 4

Auden for dinner. I fetch him in a limousine, taxis being scarce both because it is Sunday and because the unremoved snow in streets like his keeps them away. But the chauffeur's raised brow when we enter the neighborhood is not a reaction to driving conditions, and twice he inquires whether I am certain of the address.

Auden is gentleness itself with the I.S.'s, and the evening is smooth, quiet, affectionate. How different he is from his new public persona. Not long ago, he wrote that "A writer's private life is, or should be, of no concern to anybody except himself, his family and friends." Why, then, does he invite so many journalists to his Austrian hideaway? And why is he apparently gratified with their descriptions of his very private life?—as in the recent *Esquire* piece, and the one in the current *Life,* which he actually commends to us. At the same time he has become almost impossibly touchy (from loneliness and frustration, no doubt, Chester hardly being a family), as well as tyrannical and quixotic in his opinions, tending to speak almost exclusively in absolutes: "This is right, that is wrong; one must, one mustn't." Approbation, condemnation: each is total and final. Consider his rave review in *The New Yorker* of Eiseley's *Unexpected Universe,* a likable book, certainly, but by no means free from "romance of Nature" gush. (Describing

373

Captain Fitzroy of *The Beagle* in the act of slitting his throat, Eiseley writes: "In the dim light the razor glinted." How does *he* know? Did Fitzroy leave a last-minute note? And does it matter?)

But the marvel of the poems continues and pardons all; and not only of the poems, but of the man who wrote not long ago, that ". . . every time we make a nuclear bomb we are corrupting the morals of a host of innocent neutrons below the age of consent." At sixty-three, however, is he not a little too aware of his POSITION? And is he not becoming the Good Gray Poet long (one hopes) before it is necessary (if it ever should be)?

JANUARY 6

Yesterday afternoon R., I.S.'s nurse, comes to tell me that I.S.'s left foot is cooler than the right. V. calls his regular doctor, who, after examining it, declares it is only a spasm. But the symptoms are the same as a year ago, January 18, when a clot was found; and because to hesitate could be fatal, I call N.N. and ask him to send *his* doctor—who duly arrives, says it *is* a clot, and prescribes anti-coagulants. The foot is warmer today, and my own *apologia pro vita sua* is defined: I am an Early Warning Station.

But *not* a Boswell. Which I say because no reference to me neglects to call me that. This may be owing in part to the Great Cham's own observation that "Nobody can write the life of a man, but those who have eat [*sic*] and drunk and lived in social intercourse with him." Except that the second half of the statement— ". . . but few who have lived with a man know what to remark about him" —takes away what the first gives. The difference is that Dr. Johnson needed a Boswell and I.S. doesn't, even though he himself clearly thought of me as one, even going out of his way to tell me secrets—about his brother Gury's homosexuality, about his nurse Bertha—that he seemed to want recorded. But if I reject the Boswell role, it is to claim one more like that of a Goncourt (in category, of course, not quality). In fact, the beginnings of a Goncourt partnership go back to our first week together, for I.S. inducted me into his letter-writing from the start. And the method was exactly that of the Goncourts' "dual dictation." I would lean over his shoulder as he wrote, each of us acting as the other's intercessory, contributing words or phrases, suggesting changes, beginning sentences which the other would finish, as we still do in conversations. For this reason I can go through my journals and point to words and expressions that were his; and go through his writings, stumbling on phrases (flippancies and pomposities, all too frequently) that were actually mine. In short, and presumptuous as it is for me to say so—as well as difficult to substantiate because our only taped conversations, at a public forum in Cincinnati a few years ago, reveal me only in my feed-in function and him only in his "public personality" one—a merger (exchange, symbiosis) *has* taken place between the senior and the junior, the creative and imitative components of our firm. And, ill-assorted a pair as we are in many ways, our musical responses (which is what brought us together, after all) are kindred, though of course they

1970

374

are *his* responses, to which I am merely conditioned. Finally, other resemblances to the Goncourts obtain in our menage: but that is another story.

MARCH 3

In reply to the inquiry of a friend concerning his children, I.S. says that "Except for Theodore, they have been more concerned about my wealth than my health." Yet in fairness to the children, their father's double life has left them in an anomalous position throughout the longer part of their own. In fact, their strongest emotion toward their parent must be, and very likely always has been, fear. Nor can it ever have been very easy to have such a man for a father. Even biologically their first legacy was the threat of the recessive gene, for they were born of first cousins.

But apart from that, all great artists are selfish: they *must* be, to get their work done. And they sacrifice the people around them. I.S. sacrificed his children to his art (and sacrificed them to V. as well). I can imagine, from my own early years with him, exactly what life must have been for them. When he was composing, he would sometimes come to the table several days in succession without saying a word and forbid everybody else to speak as well. He was also capable of throwing things, of locking himself in his room, and of shouting orders at anyone in his vicinity, which meant, first of all, his family. Even at eighty-six, ill, and in bed, he could and did so terrorize his daughter on at least one occasion that she came from his room in tears, saying: "It was always like that with Papa! He always got his own way."

Nor is the wealth *versus* health remark fair in another sense. The truth is that the children have been remote from their father not merely during his illness but for the past thirty years. They did not see him at all in his first decade in America, and in the twenty years since then, the two sons have spent little time with their father, being busy with their own work. The older son, who lives much farther away and can much less afford a trip, *did* visit his parent just before his eighty-fifth birthday, however, and came again to see him in New York last November. Of the reasons for the remoteness—understandable envy of the superior qualities of the step-mother, envy even of the very minor talents of the scribe—not the least is that the children are older and mentally less elastic in their sixties (as I am in my forties) than I.S. is in his eighties.

The real puzzle, however, is in connection with the I.S.'s gift of their Arizona citrus groves last year to the three children in equal shares. The gift never got beyond the daughter and her husband,[1] who simply did not inform the brothers of the parental intentions, and V. found this out purely by a fluke, in conversation with the older son. But, as V. says, describing the imbroglio to a friend today, "The strain of premature interest in matters of inheritance began to show in the daughter and son-in-law two years ago. In fact, their

1970

---

1. Except under legal pressure many months later.

375

remark that 'The paintings are disappearing from the walls of father's house'" (Picasso's portrait of I.S., actually lent for an exhibit in The Hague) "repeated to us by their and our lawyer, first alerted us to the true attitude. I then discovered that my husband's will" (which, incredibly, she had not read!) "denied me the right to a will of my own; that my husband's son-in-law and lawyer had blanket powers of attorney as well as exclusive access to his European bank account, of which they would have become the sole parceners."

What makes this sordid turn of events all the more puzzling is that so far from following traditional novercal behavior, V. has always acted with the greatest munificence. It was she who convinced I.S. to buy new houses for the children, etcetera, etcetera, which he never would have done on his own. And, of all ironies, it was *her* idea to bring the children from Europe after the war, to take care of I.S. in his old age if anything should happen to her. And even now, her only feeling in the matter is one of concern for the damage to I.S., both physically and morally, and which the doctors have assured her has already set back his recuperation.

And the feelings of the paterfamilias himself? Does he feel like King Lear? He had ranting, Lear-like moments at the time of the manuscript suit, but this soon turned to irony, and once he compared the whole affair to *Gianni Schicchi.* Still, one day not long ago he said: *"Il arrive un moment où on ne veut plus savoir."* And this very afternoon he inquires as to the whereabouts of the manuscript of *Jeu de cartes.* "It is in the other room," I say. "Do you want to see it?" "No, but I would like to know what the price tag on it says."

1970

MARCH 5

During the night, after months of painful deliberation about the matter, V. composes a letter concerning I.S.'s funeral and burial in the Russian corner of the cemetery island of San Michele (Venice). She does not represent this as I.S.'s own wish, which none of us has ever been able to determine because of the unmentionableness of the subject; in fact, all we know for certain is that he does not want to be cremated and scattered to the winds. And all V. says is that she believes he would have concurred with the decision. (Well, you couldn't say that it would have *pleased* him.) Then this morning his nurse fetches me, saying, "The maestro wants to talk to you about Venice"—which shows me how little I know about this deeply psychic man.[1]

Later in the day we play the recording of the *Requiem Canticles,* which V.'s letter has specified as the work *she* wishes to be performed in his memory, when that terrible time comes, "since *he* and *we* knew he was

---

1. Shortly after Stravinsky's death, V. lifted his Russian Bible and a picture of St. Michael fell out, a copy of an icon in St. Petersburg that I.S. had had since childhood.

376

writing it for himself." But at the *Libera me,* where, it seems to me, the music leaves the concert hall and actually becomes part of a Requiem service, she rushes from the room in tears.

I.S. awakes with a fever. Examining him two hours later, Dr. Lax diagnoses pneumonia in the lower left lobe. Tetracycline, digoxin, and other medications are sent for, and happily the temperature does not rise.

The fever has disappeared, and I.S. greets us in the "good-morning-everybody" mood of the Emperor of China in *The Nightingale,* after *his* nightlong struggle with "Death."[1] To the doctor, however, I.S. describes his condition as *"Comme ci, comme ça."* Which, says Lax, "is not only proof that his spirit is intact, but a precise scientific answer . . . I have never seen such inner vitality and life force," he goes on, "to say nothing of the alertness, the powers of observation, the acuteness of the critical faculties—for he can formulate the subtlest distinctions. And the inner physical elasticity is no less amazing, considering the restricted outer mobility. Few people of his age are able to respond to medication not only the way he does but at all."

And speaking of China, the eclipse of the sun today, which I.S. watches, is accompanied by an eery quiet, the opposite of the great din that the Chinese keep up during eclipses to frighten off the evil spirits. Is it because the whole city has stopped to sky-gaze? And does the greenish, deathly penumbra remind I.S. of the shadow that has passed over him during the night?

1970

On the "Seaboard Express," nearing Palm Beach, memories of an automobile trip through Florida with the I.S.'s twenty years ago come crowding in on me. We entered the state from the west then, partly because I was gathering local color for an article on such improbable one-time residents as the author of the "Ossian" forgeries, McPherson (in Pensacola); Prince Achille Murat (in Tallahassee); Maeterlinck (in St. Augustine); and Delius (Solano Grove, the would-have-been Laurentian pantisocracy or Rananim). In February 1950, we drove from the Prince Murat Motel, Tallahassee, to

1. In December 1971, V. thought of having the following fragment of dialogue from *The Nightingale* engraved on the side of I.S.'s tombstone:

> Nightingale: . . . and over there beyond the white wall
>   there is another garden.
>   Death: I like to hear you singing. Why have you fallen
>   silent? Sing on!

Opening his score at that place to check the Russian, she discovered a mark in his hand, the only one in the book.

Tampa and St. Petersburg; and from there went by ferry across the Bay, in spite of I.S.'s fears that the boat would capsize and he would "drone"—in which prospect V. attempted to console him by the thought that at least the water would be "lucky [*i.e.*, luke] warm."

In Sarasota, finding ourselves short of money and unable to pay our hotel bill, I.S. asked Mr. and Mrs. John Alden Carpenter, who had a winter home there, for a loan, and thanks to their generosity we were seen through to New York.[1] We visited the Museum,[2] then drove to Key West, and finding no rooms there, back to Miami. The next day we went to an alligator farm, the only incident of the trip that I.S. still remembers because the keeper told him that a giant gavial, between whose jaws he had inserted a strut in order to show the teeth, was born during the lifetime of Dante. (I.S. still pronounces the last syllable of "crocodile" as if it were a pickle.) We spent that night in Daytona, and the one after that in Charleston, where V. had lived for a month shortly after coming to America in January 1940.

But these daydreams are interrupted by the arrival of the train at Palm Beach. Or, rather, at the black-belt backyard of Palm Beach. Social stratigraphers must have an easy time of it in Florida, status being almost entirely a matter of distance from the beach. The farther inland, the lower the social order, and for black people the railroad tracks provide an additional demarcation to stay on the wrong side of.

APRIL 6

Pompano Beach. I have hardly begun to bask in the sand and eye the Nereids when V. calls from New York to tell me that I.S. has pneumonia and is to be taken to the hospital. She is naturally distraught, but has tears in her voice, too, because of anxiety about his heart, this for the first time. It seems that weakness has been detected in the left ventricle, and from her description it sounds as if there may have been symptoms of the Stokes-Adams Syndrome. Not yet having unpacked, I go directly to the airport and add my name to several waiting lists for cancellations, flight reservations being unobtainable because of the air-controllers' strike. Then, luckily finding a seat out at seven-thirty, I arrive at the Essex House in time to hear the eleven o'clock newscaster announce that "The condition of composer Igor Stravinsky, now in the Lenox Hill Hospital Cardiac[!] Unit, is described as critical."

One prays, of course, in spite of Galton's *Statistical Inquiries into the Efficacy of Prayer* (*i.e.*, *in*efficacy), which I have just been reading. And the thought of Galton makes me wonder about a statistical inquiry into the

1. I.S. had known the Carpenters since his first American tour in 1925, and he had stayed with them in Chicago in 1940. She was Adlai Stevenson's mother-in-law.
2. One of the curators, the late Everett Austin, another friend of I.S. in his first years in America, was among the first sponsors of "Monsù Desiderio," whose work he acquired for both Sarasota and the Wadsworth Atheneum in Hartford. A dozen years later, Eugene Berman gave a "Monsù" to I.S. on his eightieth birthday.

1970

378

efficacy of "symbiotic relationships," if the phenomenon can be extrapolated and distinguished from "coincidence," whose numerical expression is comparatively simple. For this is the third time I.S. has been taken to the hospital when I have gone away, in as many years.

Not *that* thought keeps me awake, however, but the emptiness of his room, which is across the hall from mine; and the silence, for I have listened to his cough, his calls for the nurse, his movements in and out of bed every night for the last six months. And not only listened, but gone to his room several times each night, quite regularly at his worst hour, 4 AM, talking to him, giving him water, primping his pillow, helping him to turn or sit up, or simply holding his hand when he seemed confused or surprised, perhaps waking from a dream, his eyes questioning for a moment, and the next moment knowing the answers all too well.

V. asks me to leave all the lights on in his room tonight. But I hate to enter it, hate to see the icons and the photograph of the Turin shroud in the empty corner; and the Bach fugue he had been playing, still open on the piano; and, worst of all, that terribly sad wheelchair *by* the piano. Only three nights ago we listened to the *Canticles* together, after which I tried to encourage him to compose "even two notes." "But they must be the right two," he came back, and the whole meaning of the man was in the answer. (Last week, a nurse who urged him to "try" to compose was rebuffed with "I never *try*. I compose or I don't compose.")

APRIL 7

The first volunteer pallbearer is the BBC. Its New York office calls early this morning to ask "whether Mr. Craft will be available for an interview if Mr. Stravinsky dies."

I go with V. to the hospital, but we are obliged to wait more than an hour before seeing I.S. Meanwhile we watch his heartbeat on a master console of monitors, one for each patient in the Cardiac Unit, which reminds us of Space Flight Control, Houston. The range of I.S.'s graph seems small (indicating weakness?) and the beat itself syncopates about once every two trips across the screen. But the others are more erratic. One of them seesaws bumpily, one is as jagged as lightning, one is like last week's stock market, one is alarmingly flat, and one hovers very high above the equatorial line, like a profile map of the Himalayas.

I.S. is in a pressure breathing unit, with clumps of wires like the viscera of an old radio set attached to his chest. He has a nasal cannula, too, like a diver's noseguard; and a catheter, which drains into a plastic canteen and which is the worst of these trammels, he says, provoking an unassuageable urge to urinate. He begs to get out of bed, turns from side to side, and finally kicks his blankets away, revealing strap-on sheepskin heel-pads (as they are called, though the heels are uncovered) with which he looks incongruously Mercurial. But he betrays not the slightest opacity of mind, and knows exactly what he wants, whether word, object, or action.

1970

He is a minefield of medical problems, to be sure, what with polycythemia, chronic bronchitis, and numerous other complications to be contended with. Yet we are not disheartened by the visit. His strength, both inner and outer, is far from depleted, and his lifeline is more steel cable than silk thread. He may once again play havoc with medical laws of averages.

An avalanche of well-wishing cables, telegrams, letters from all over the world (and unlike last year, almost no quack-religious Get-ready-to-meet-your-Maker mail). Xenia cables from Leningrad, Aaron Propes from Jerusalem. Proud parents in Holland say they have named their new-born baby after I.S. ("Igor," presumably). A lawyer in Portugal, using no other address than "Neuva Iorque," seeks to convey his gratitude for the music. A school in Delaware petitions I.S. to get well with pages of its pupils' signatures. Scores of letters from every European country express appreciation for the music and hopes for its creator's quick recovery. A cardiologist in Ventura, California, telegraphs that of all the hearts in the world, I.S.'s "is the most worth keeping going." But whereas the Composers' Union in Moscow has been quick to send its sympathies, few composers in America—for all the dozens I.S. has lettered to Guggenheim juries, seconded for nomination to Academies, recommended to publishers—have thought about him, or at any rate acted on the thought. Among the exceptions, however, is Leonard Bernstein, who has shown the greatest feeling for I.S. since the beginning of his illness.

As for the messages from anonymous lovers of his music everywhere, the people I.S. *doesn't* know, these attempt, simply, forthrightly (no panegyrics, no dithyrambs) and often very movingly to tell him how much his music has meant to them. And I should add that "everywhere" includes New York. Scores of people here have stopped at the hospital to inquire and leave messages, some signed with peace decals and the word "Woodstockers." Two young Juilliard students have even made their way to and stood vigil at his door.

1970

Entering the room toward evening, we find I.S. alone in a chair, trembling—from cold, he says, and his saffron, Buddhist-monklike robe *is* three times too big for him. He has been given a bell to ring, but owing to its strange shape didn't understand what it was; and the nurses twittering in the corridor just outside his room have, unrung, not looked in at him for some time. We cover him with blankets and hold his hands until the chill is over and the pulse meter, which had been running riot, subsides. But he has had a fright, and in consequence presses V.'s hand to his cheek and never turns his eyes from her. Is he in pain? we ask, and he ventures a cautious nay-shake. Does he feel exhausted, then? No, again. In that case, is it boredom? A large "Yes." But the only alleviation we can promise is that tomorrow he will have his own nurses and at least be able to amuse himself outwitting them, as he does at home. Is tomorrow's moonshot of any interest to him? It is, on the contrary, the essence of *acedia* (though I should add that the astronauts' dream-world weightlessness and slow-motion dancing used to fascinate him). Is he pleased by our report of the many performances of his music in New York this week? He could hardly care less. What does matter, and uniquely, is our insistence that he can, and will again, compose. At this, anyway, he smiles. But can it be possible that he is still undiscouraged, that he still wants to go on? I myself had feared this time, not that he would capitulate, but that he might at least allow the dangerous debate to get on the floor.

APRIL 13

The retention of urine since the decatheterizing—which on other occasions was followed by enuresis—has not been noticed until too late. (One wonders what happens to quite ordinary, as distinguished from VIP, patients, who are *not* in Intensive Care and cannot afford the supplementary ministrations of private teams of round-the-clock nurses.) By evening the Blood Urea Nitrogen count has shot so high it flies off the chart. The symptoms, which V. and I recognize long before the lab tests have been completed, are, of course, the same as they were in October 1967: trembling hands and chattering teeth.

One of our own standby nurses—herself with an intensive-care cough, aggravated, perhaps, by her odd perfume (glue?)—tells us that the nurse who performed the suctioning operation on I.S.'s bronchial tubes during the night asked for and received an autograph immediately after.

1970

APRIL 14

I.S., now in another Intensive Care Unit, is especially miserable today ("So far, so bad"), owing to a splint bound to his left elbow to keep the I.V. in place. He changes position quite suddenly once, causing the complex in his cardiac monitor to invert and bringing a nurse on the double. She adjusts the focus of the machine, spreading out the rills (like an affine-geometry transformation) to read the graph from a different and enlarging perspective, but nothing is wrong.

A woman burned nearly to death is installed in the next cubicle. And obviously it would have been better if she *had* died, for it is certain she will never regain consciousness, or be able to maintain even the most tenuous connection with life, except by machines. It seems, too, that her family is fully aware of this. Yet while the whole horrifying spectacle directs my thoughts to the problem of death control (hardly less important in the future, perhaps, than birth control), I overhear the family talking in the corridor, and they, at least, no matter what, do not want the woman to die.

In another cubicle a man lies near death from knife wounds inflicted in the unsafety of a local jail. He must be in a bad way, in any case, being in an oxygen tent most of the time, and all of the time chained to plasma pumps and I.V. Yet three formidably armed cops, bandoliered as if for a siege, stand in shifts at the foot of his bed, presumably to stop him from going on the lam even by dying. Meanwhile, the patient, who might have a case against the city for its *lack* of protection in durance, is visited by several pretty girls. The last of them, a freckled redhead wearing a wedding ring, is accompanied by a "spiv" lawyer who cross-questions the nurse-in-charge as to whether "experimental" drugs have been used.

APRIL 15

The apical averages and B.U.N. are normal today. And, just as I.S. is aware of most things about himself in advance, so he knows now, by some sixth sense, that he has surmounted another crisis. (But how *can* he still respond to antibiotics, after the saturation bombing of the last ten days?) His eyes— which changed color in November 1967, the left turning darker, and the right, both iris and pupil, becoming more blue—are alive with the knowl-edge. A tough old nurse tells us we should be relieved: "Most of them go from Intensive Care to Perpetual Care." Then, leaving the room for a moment, she warns I.S. not to "run away." Which, I suppose, is an example of nurse-ry wit.

APRIL 17

I.S.'s elder son arrives from Geneva, but too late to go to the hospital. He spends the evening telling stories about his father, of which the best is one about I.S. trying on Wagner's beret, in the Werner Reinhart collection, and finding that it almost covered his shoulders as well as his head; and another about his father interviewing wet-nurses at a breast-feeding agency in Lausanne and insisting on sampling the milk of each candidate himself. Theodore says that his father had a marvelous collection of antique wood-sculpture puppets that he painted himself, in many colors, and that both Jawlensky and Malevich, who were I.S.'s neighbors in Switzerland during the first war, greatly admired the composer's talent as a painter.

1970

APRIL 29

After returning to the hotel this afternoon, I.S. sits at the dinner table with us and even listens to music afterward: the Schubert B-flat Sonata, first, but not much of it, both because it ill suits his mordant mood and because, as he says, "The theme itself is everything; it doesn't need development"; then the Fourth Symphony of Beethoven ("*Ça nourrit l'âme*") and my own new recording of Gesualdo's Book Six, which at last avenges Maria D'Avalos by plunging the knife into the Prince of Venosa himself: the performances are murderously bad; then Boulez's Flute Sonatina (I.S.: "Let's hope he doesn't write a sonata"); and, finally, I.S.'s own String Concerto, which he obliges me to switch off before the end because of the messy, out-of-tune string-playing. "The record will be advertised as a 'document of the com-poser's wishes,'" he says. "Still, the *tempi* are right, and because of that I suppose I must accept it."

Dr. Lax, on a routine visit, tells I.S. he is in good health. I.S.: "I wish you would come when I am sick." But he is crusty and capricious with everyone today, and so spiteful to his nurse that even after defeating her at "three-dimensional checkers" he knocks the "tryptic" over and sends the lucite marbles rolling about the room. The asperity undiminished at table, he demands a proper whiskey-glass for his scotch and a proper spoon for his demi-tasse (he flings the teaspoon to the floor), and he describes the omelette as *"une sottise réchauffée."* It is really wonderful to see him like this again. The temper changes only when we play the *Canticles.* After it he leans over and tells me that "The last movement was composed for Venice."

We land at Geneva (from New York) at 7 AM. *"Prudence,"* a large sign advises on the south-shore exit from the city, while other signs, in the city, say *"Silence"* and *"Ne crachez pas sur le trottoir"*—the latter in mosaics *in* the *trottoir.* Immediately on the French side of the border, the emphasis switches to food, from *"casse-croûtes"* (snacks) all the way up to *"alimentation générale."* In one small village alone we count three shops selling *"charcuterie."*

The Hôtel Royale in Evian is a glorified sanatorium for the very *vieux* and the very *riche,* the latter including both *nouveaux* and second-generation types (themselves "elders of scions," you might say). On one side are Alpine vistas and Grand Roc and, directly in front, the lake—arctic-white when we arrive but when the mountains on the Swiss side emerge, like a heat-vapored valley in the California desert. Then in late afternoon the surface becomes glassy, and the boats—spinnakers, racing sculls, a speedboat buzzing like a Brobdingnagian wasp—seem to be sailing in the sky. Immediately below our rooms are shrub terraces and beds of roses, coleuses, begonias, hortensias; and below that, poplars, pines, and tall red oaks. At night the Swiss shore is defined by the lights of the towns in which I.S. wrote so much music, and its distance is measured by the beetle-like Evian-Lausanne ferry plying between.

1970

I.S., in the church at Neuvecelle, which is just beyond the hotel and a field of clover and buttercup (we have literally "gone to grass" here), dips his fingers in the stoup, touches his forehead, then uses the water to smooth down his hair. He is in marvelous form (though the latest analysis shows mild anemia) and more active both physically and mentally than at any time since he was in Europe two years ago; it is as if the ordeals visited on him in his New York dog days had never occurred. But after lunch a visit from his granddaughter and great-granddaughter, who are leaving for a holiday in Corsica, upsets him briefly, as no doubt it did them. "What is the little girl's last name?" he asks, and the granddaughter answers "Stravinsky." "Has she no father, then?" "No."

At St. Gingolph, a village half in Switzerland, the streets are so narrow we are obliged to enter the Swiss half in order to turn our (large) car around, which means that re-entering France we are obliged to clear the border controls. Storms are breaking in a dozen directions at this end of the lake, but many sails are out, and, in view of the reputation of the water for iciness, a surprising number of swimmers. At several points along the shore, plaques remind compatriots—SOUVENEZ-VOUS, FRANÇAIS—of victims of the Nazis shot while attempting to escape to Switzerland. We pass a hayrick loaded with greens and as fragrant as a salad.

Dinner with Arnold Weissberger and Milton Goldman on the hotel terrace, which has five waiters per table, *versus* the five tables per waiter average in New York. Another advantage here is that a few francs and a bottle of white wine are enough to bribe the "Tea for Two" orchestra into a permanent intermission. Milton G. poses a riddle, dog-eared perhaps, but I am not up to date: What is the question for which "9W" (the highway on the west bank of the Hudson) is the answer? And the answer, of course, or, rather, the question, is: "Do you spell your name with a 'V,' Herr Wagner?" ("*Nein,* 'W.'")

JUNE 15

Evian is a health resort, and bingeing is less conspicuous than rechabitism, dieting more in evidence than gulosity. Yet the Royale does not lack for gourmets, the most deeply devoted of whom is in residence at the table on our right. This gentleman—who also appears at times to be rather deeply ingrained in alcohol—directs all operations concerning his own fare, at one point summoning the whole staff for a conference, at another obliging the *maître d'hôtel* to swallow a scoop of a Cavaillon melon himself for confirmation as to some insufficiency of flavor or freshness. The second, but by no means the main, course in his "lunch" today is a trout drowned in Armagnac and grilled before our eyes on a crackling pine-branch fire. The gourmet bones the fish himself, of course, starting from the tail and folding the skin back like a coiffeur center-parting a head of hair. Yet this elegant performance, followed by no less elegant ones at subsequent stages, concludes with an indecently loud and vigorous quarter of an hour's probing with a toothpick.

1970

Later, by the swimming pool, the same ever-famished one kisses the hands of the female bathers of his acquaintance, absurd as that seems in view of the brevity of their garments—so loose and low in the bottom in the case of some of the younger naiads loping about that my own impulse is to go about pulling them up. (Some are transparent, too, there and elsewhere, and in at least one instance the upper containers seem to exist only that the contents may be kept outside. False nipples are "in," too—though also outside, of course—but the French bosom, on the sampling of the Hôtel Royale, is seldom outstanding, and in the over-thirties more often than not

384

resembles fried eggs. Bottoms, too, seem to have a national character here, Boucher-*cum*-Bouguereau in the case of the French female, jodhpur hips in the case of the British.)

Although the sky is always dramatic and expectant, storms are nonetheless sudden. They usually come from the south, over the mountains, which are snow-topped (when you can see them). And it raineth every day.

Marcel, our *niçois* room-waiter, not only leaves no "e" mute and inglorious, but singsongs the language like a stage Italian immigrant speaking English. *"Une tête comme ça,"* for example, comes out *"Un-e-têt-e-com-me-ça."* Even so, the words are less important than the operatic gestures that accompany them and outline the actual proportions of this big—*i.e.,* smart—head. Marcel is a philosopher, storyteller, almanack, quack physician, and, it follows, a man of enormous if winsome conceit. Like Figaro, he can turn the tables on those he serves, as I discover when he deliberately confuses my name, calling me Mr. Stark (Kraft). He has recipes, remedies, prescriptions, explanations for everything from the weather—"If you can't see Switzerland, it is bound to be good"—to a long catalogue of maladies both physical and mental. "Carrots clear the complexion," he says, and "Asparagus are healthy for the kidneys, but not if eaten too often." He advises me to singe my hair to delay the retreat—or, as it has seemed to me lately, rout.

As a waiter, Marcel supplies mind-reading service, appearing at the propitious moment with the martinis we didn't ask for but are delighted to have, sending an *omble chevalier* when in his opinion we have chosen something less likely to please. *"Il est dynamique, comme un Américain,"* he says about someone else (with more richness of vowels than this spelling indicates), but the description would apply to himself if only American "dynamism" were more likable.

Not surprisingly, Marcel's storytelling is theatrical, but it contains insights and illustrates moral virtues besides—counting sympathetic observation itself as a high moral virtue. (He has—no virtue—shrewdly observed our preferences from the first and thus made himself the master of our tastes.) To illustrate his point that children lead their parents about nowadays, he says he wanted to spend last Christmas in Rome, but his son, now twenty-five and a Mercedes salesman in Berlin, wished to go to Brussels. And Brussels prevailed, except that at Cambrai father and son were detained by the police for crossing a double line on the left. As the policeman approached their car, which had a "D" license plate (for "Deutschland"), Marcel Junior instructed Marcel-the-one-and-only to "Pretend you don't speak French." Hence the policeman's *"Qui parle français?"* was answered only by Marcel's uncomprehending smile. *"Trop 'links,'"* said the *flic*, showing off his German before letting the frightened foreigners go. But Marcel's point is that his son had thoughtlessly exposed him to risk, and he dubs the story the *"Bêtise de Cambrai."* His younger son would not have done that, he goes on, proudly

1970

informing us that this further offspring is "the first in our family to wear spectacles, our first intellectual." But V. questions him about the older brother. "How could you have a son of twenty-five?" she asks, and his long-drawled answer is: *"Par-ce que j'ai fait un-e bêtis-e."*

Marcel is assisted by a dark, handsome, fifteen-year-old and still gauche Sardinian, Raffaello, who stands to attention while Marcel bids him take copious mental notes on a wide variety of matters. During the more pro-tracted of his partner's yarns and vaudeville acts, Raffaello's faraway eyes betray no flicker of concern for the outcome. But when Marcel says some-thing particularly outrageous—*"Je suis une vedette du cinéma,"* for instance (he once *was* a stand-in for John Gavin on long shots, apparently, and he claims to have received 2,000 francs for saying *"Scusi"* in a Sophia Loren film); or, *"Ce soir j'avais un peu plus de fantaisie"* (this refers to a new arrangement of his thickly brilliantined hair)—Raffaello flashes his stagey superior a withering look of disbelief.

Once, describing a scene in a cowboy film, Marcel not only blazes away from the hip but also blows the smoke from the barrel before holstering the imaginary weapon. It is a convincing bit of buffoonery, but as Raffaello does not watch, cannot be brand new. Later Marcel confides in us about his minion, saying, *"Il est très sensible, Raffaello, mais un peu sauvage. Il faut faire attention avec lui."*

JUNE 18

Waking from deep dreams this morning, I.S. says: *"Je veux que Bertha vienne me féliciter."* Is he thinking himself back eighty years, or simply telling us that he would like to see his old nurse again? In either case the remark tends to confirm, as he has always claimed, that Bertha was closer to him than his mother in his infancy and impressionable years. The burden of the anniversary *has* been weighing on him, however, and he has been talking about the remote past as, unprompted, he seldom does. Shortly before lunch he complains of nausea, and of "another pain, just behind the nausea," which I mention only because the identification of a pain "behind" a pain is so typical of him. But at lunch he has no trouble in the deglutition of two prodigious helpings of caviar, nor do we see any ill effects from the vodka and champagne on top of a stiff medical aperitif. He replies to our toasts to eighty-eight, moreover, with allusions to ninety.

As Auden wrote of Mozart's two-hundredth:

> How seemly then, to celebrate the birth
> Of one who did no harm to this poor earth,
> Created masterpieces by the dozen . . .
> Nor while we praise the dead, should we forget
> We have *Stravinsky*—bless him!—with us yet.

A cable, at night, informs us of the death, in New York, of I.S.'s physician and friend of many years, Leon Lewithin. A year ago today, Dr. Lewithin

1970

supervised I.S.'s discharge from the New York Hospital. He would hardly have believed then that a year hence his patient would be flying to Europe, though that was what he planned to do himself.

The only sounds reaching our rooms at night are the chugging and the two-note hoot of a rickety train, the Poe-like plaints of crows, and the bells of Neuvecelle celebrating the hours.

JUNE 21

Marcel loses his bet in the races at Deauville today; he had gambled on the numbers of his sons' birth dates. But his spirits are undampened; and, having worked in Deauville at one time, he treats us to a description of the arrival there of the Friday afternoon *"train des cocus"*—husbands down from Paris for the weekend.

He acts out the Evian cure for us, too, playing the concierge who delivers the bottle of spring-fresh water outside the door at 6 AM like a milkman; and the sleepy guest who fetches it, cuts his thumb removing the sharp tin cap (half of the people in Evian go about with Band-Aids on their fingers), drinks two glasses, then returns to bed and snores for another hour or so before eating too much breakfast.

JULY 4

Several times during a walk with V. in the dewy fields this morning, she stops to pick mushrooms that I do not even see and almost trample. Naturally, I prefer to blame this blindness on differences of culture rather than on personality.

Suvchinsky having arrived from Paris last night, we drive around the lake to Clarens and "Les Tilleuls," the birthplace of *Le Sacre du printemps.* The sight brings tears to Suvchinsky's eyes, but leaves I.S., to all appearances, unmoved; in fact, he seems more interested, back on the French side, in La Tourronde, a one-time home of St. François de Sales. Suvchinsky being my only *tutoyer* friend, I am rusty about verb endings and obliged to think twice before every remark addressed to him. But it seems odd to say *"tu"* to him and, after twenty-three years, *"vous"*—as well as "Monsieur" and "Madame"—to I.S. and V., though it would be still odder to use the intimate with them.

1970

JULY 12

Marcel has again gone unwisely to the guichet, this time staking his all on a horse called "Igor." But others must have wagered, too, for the *"comptes rendus de la course"* blare from transistors on the terrace all afternoon. At dinner, the now two-time loser talks scoffingly about *niçois* superstitions: about never opening an umbrella indoors; never passing a saltcellar directly from hand to hand, and never thanking for salt (because you thank for what it may bring); never stopping to converse in the doorway or on the threshold of a house; never putting the picture of a loved one on a sideboard shelf or other eminence whence it could fall; never measuring a child's height (it might be for a coffin); never putting flowers on a bed (it could be for a grave).

Bastille Day. A listless morning—the mood of the *cor anglais* in *Tristan,* I reflect, until the hotel comes to life (breakfast trays appearing on balconies, waiters going through their paces on the terrace, bathers by the poolside smearing themselves with suntan oil) and I realize how inapposite the musical reference is: our own condition, socially speaking at least, is exactly the opposite: we are not lonely enough. By noontime Switzerland is pre-monitorially clear, and the surface of the lake is so unrippled, despite the internal hemorrhage of the Rhône, that the rhumb line of the ferry vacillating between the two countries survives for a quarter of an hour after each passage.

Nor does Wagner's pipeherd express the mood at dinner, which is simply the *flânerie* of the overfed. The actual dinner music, on the other hand, is a collage of *La Traviata* by the "Tea for Two" band and snatches of martial airs floating up from the festivities in the town below. V. recalls that she first saw the opera with Lina Cavalieri, "the mistress of a grand duke who rewarded her, a little too specifically, perforce, with a gold bidet whose fountain was diamond-studded."

After dinner we watch the fireworks display from our balcony. They begin with magnesium flares and detonations, introduced by long, swooping whistles, like an old-fashioned bombardment. But the girandoles and the spangles that hang in the sky like parachutes, then fizzle and dissolve in an instant, are worth the noise. One great burst of white chips falls all the way to the ground, like manna. V. is nostalgic. Her liaison with I.S. began in Paris on *le quatorze,* 1921.

1970

I.S.'s niece, Xenia, arrives from Leningrad (via Paris, by train) for a three-day visit, the purpose of which is immediately clear. The U.S.S.R. wants I.S. to "come home," and—as they say in the Wild West—dead or alive. If it is the latter, he will receive "the world's best medical care, as well as a house, car, chauffeur, and every comfort and even luxury." If it is the former, he may be assured of the highest state honors as well as a niche next to Pushkin or Tolstoy.

But he is already enjoying at least some of the luxuries for the living right here (though here, incidentally, we are struck by the contrast between the old-fashioned gentility of this comrade of a Communist state, and the boorish behavior of the hotel's *haute bourgeoisie*). Xenia is a little slow in grasping the point of some of our conversations, but understandably, never having been outside the Soviet Union and only infrequently outside Leningrad. Yet she is really only interested in what we have to say about the U.S.S.R., being importunate, for example, to hear our opinion of the Daniel and Sinyavski affair. And when the S.'s describe their meeting last year with

Svetlana, née Stalin, Xenia actually takes notes. A tea drinker in the Russian tradition, she remarks on the comparatively rare addiction to this brew in France. But when V. mentions her own preference for Peking tea, Xenia's hands go up in protest (a tempest in a teacup): "Oh, no, please. *Nothing from China.*"

Or Israel. Xenia says that both wars passed near I.S.'s old home in Ustilug, devastating the neighborhood, but not his house, which sustained only a scratch—a chimney, shot off but now restored. The house is still known locally as I.S.'s, she adds, and a few elderly people claim to remember him there. Then, for my part, I tell her that during our first tour of Israel eight years ago, a kibbutz of émigrés from Ustilug presented I.S. with a history of their former Russian community. And at this, hardly less agitated than by the thought of Chinese *chi,* Xenia says that "Probably they lie"—though one wonders what there could possibly be to lie about in that.

As for her Leningrad news, we learn that Nadiejda and Vladimir Rimsky-Korsakov are still alive, and that not long ago, she, Xenia, shared the exercise yard of a Leningrad hospital with Shostakovich.

Like all Soviet citizens abroad, Xenia seems to wear blinders, seeing neither to right nor left, which, no doubt, is the inculcation of the idea that all this will pass away—as, no doubt, it will.

JULY 22

We drive via Geneva to Annecy, Talloires, Bonneville, Taninges, and, via Thonon, back to Evian, commending, as we leave each town, the French practice of canceling the sign of its name, as, for example,

1970

Campers' bivouacs are everywhere, and *pique-nique*-ers who literally squat on the roadside as if some indispensable condiment were provided by car and truck exhausts. The mountain-and-gorge scenery is enhanced by one spectacular château, that of Menthon, but the towns are farragoes of modern maisonnettes, chalets, barrack-style apartment buildings, and, as I.S. says, "The villas of retired dentists, each with a copy of Rodin's 'Thinker' in the garden."

Back in the hotel we learn that a third transfusion of *globules rouges lavés* will be necessary next week, the worst of which is that an amount of painful harpooning is entailed nowadays to find an infrangible vein.

AUGUST 5

I.S. calls me in the afternoon, saying, "I have two things to tell you. First, I, personally, do not feel very well. Second, I am *très inquiet* about Vera"—V.

389

having gone to Geneva for the day. But the order of the anxieties is typical; he would have said exactly the same twenty years ago.

A touching reply from him tonight, when I promise to play music with him tomorrow afternoon: "Good. I am free."

AUGUST 24

We return from Geneva in late afternoon, and at six Lord Snowdon calls. Joining him in the bar, I find him taller than photographs have led me to expect, and more freckled, more wrinkled, more blond—as well as less, in fact not at all, o'erweening. His young assistant—Beatles hairdo, black velvet suit, pink shirt unbuttoned to a gold cross, high and super-shiny shoes—opens with: "I'd like to drive a very fast car through this hotel." And His Lordship—himself rather trendily gotten up as to hair length, shirt, cravat, gold-chain bracelet, gadgety Omega wrist-clock—orders a vodka and tomato juice (*not* described as a "Bloody Mary") and opens with a reference to something of mine he has read. I retaliate with a compliment on his film about old age, which inspires him to put on a droll imitation of the jactations, German accent and all, of the great rejuvenator, Dr. Niehans.

AUGUST 26

Geneva to New York. The send-off party at the airport does not include I.S.'s younger son; but this is hardly surprising as he has spent the summer only 150 miles away without so much as telephoning about his father's health. The reason, as repeated to us, is that "I can't bear to see Father so old and frail." Which raises the question of what condition a man in his eighty-ninth year should be in in order not to upset his son.

OCTOBER 23

New York. But who *can* say what condition "Father" is in? (I have just come from a doctor to find out what condition *I* am in, and, whatever the verdict, so much of the medical machinery resembles instruments of torture that I feel fortunate in having survived the checkup. I am wired for a cardiogram like a man condemned to the electric chair; my head is fitted to the chin rest of an X-ray machine as if for guillotining; I am obliged to run up and down stairs like a hazed recruit in the Marines; and—the ultimate indignity—I am placed on an operating table and made to go on all fours for a rude and painful probing of the prostate.)

To return to I.S., he is, of course, very frail, a bright light in a thin shell; and partly because of this, has acute ochlophobia: he dreads his afternoon sorties on Fifty-ninth Street, and is no sooner out than he insists on returning. But he is not declining into "anility"—softening and slowing down, yes, but not crossing over—as someone who doesn't know him assumed in a recent article. And the vital signs are all very good; his blood pressure is perfect, his heart is "that of a man of thirty" (Dr. Lax), and the neurological evidence has not shown any cardio-vascular "spasm" for at least eight months.

1970

Although we were assured, too, a year and a half ago that the sympathectomy would deprive him of the use of his left leg, he is able to walk with the support of a walking machine, and his muscle tone improves with each visit of the therapist. Owing to poor circulation, he has some necrosis in his left toe, but that condition is responding to dermatological treatment. He uses four languages, both in reading and in conversation; plays the piano daily; sometimes wears a hearing aid, but removes it when listening to music and nearly always complains that the volume is too high.

The state of his mind is far more difficult to describe, but always was; one *never* knew exactly what was transpiring there. Certainly *I* would not attempt to diagnose it even now, though I am closer to him in some ways than V. I *do* know that at times he behaves like a character in Beckett, turning off simply because he feels that nothing *can* be said or is worth saying. Yet he takes in everything. N.N., on a recent visit, reading aloud and translating the paragraph which I.S. appended in 1968 to the last page of the *Sacre* manuscript score, found himself stuck for a word which I.S., who did not even seem to be following, instantly supplied ("guarantee").

Thus, too, at dinner tonight, when V. cannot remember the Russian and German words for certain precious and semi-precious stones ("jasper," "chrysoberyl," "garnet," "amethyst," etc.), I.S. provides them with the speed of an infant prodigy on a rigged quiz show. Nor has his lifelong quest for precision lost any of its force. The well-worn dictionaries and encyclopedias are still stacked on his reading tables and still resorted to. "Which is more correct, 'every day' or 'each day'?" he asks me this afternoon, and a friend who asks whether he is "drinking," is rather curtly told that "I *drank*, of course, a while ago, but obviously am not drinking now."

Nor has his fussiness at table diminished an iota. He still gathers crumbs, sweeps and tidies the tablecloth, shunts aside and calls for the instant removal of each (or is it every?) plate and glass the moment it is emptied. And certainly his acquisitive powers are intact, as we see tonight when he switches from his customary "Hello" to "Hi," to acknowledge in kind the greeting of a substitute nurse.

But if his critical faculties are unimpaired, he remains loyal to most of his old prejudices. He has been execrating Berlioz as harshly as ever, for example, dismissing most of *Les Troyens* (to which we have been listening recently) as *"N'importe quoi,"* and replying to my question about what he would like to hear after tonight's dose of it, with "Something better." When at length I am able to prise a more specific critique out of him, it is that the music does not evidence any real harmonic and melodic gifts; and he cites the "flatness" of Chorèbe's *Cavatina*, speculating about what Verdi might have done with it. (Nor is the comparison unfair, for the big choral scene, *"Châtiment effroyable,"* is handled in a Verdian manner, and—so *I* think—almost as ably as Verdi.)

What he likes in *La Prise de Troie* are some of the orchestral novelties: the high strings and woods at the very end of Act Two; the two-note

391

orchestral figure at *"J'ai vu l'ombre d'Hector,"* and the six measures in eighteenth-century-suite style which follow. What he dislikes are the long March and Hymn, with its dull *"Dieu des mers"* choral echoes. And the waltz finale, which he describes as "bad French ballet music," thereby committing, if possible, a double pleonasm.

NOVEMBER 2

I.S. receives an offer of a huge sum to appear on a television talk program. When V. tells him the kind of questions he would be expected to answer, however, he interrupts her, protesting: "Is this already a rehearsal?"

Buñuel's *Tristana,* tonight, is disappointing, except for the restfully vitamin-deficient color. But the predominance of eerily filtered yellows and the viridescence may be symbolic of the heroine's gangrenous and later-to-be-amputated leg. What we actually see of her complexion, however, is so pale that one suspects Buñuel of whatever is the next stage beyond necrophilia (laying a ghost?), for at times he seems to suggest that she is not merely cold but also not really there. She—Mlle Deneuve—is icily beautiful, but her beauty is compromised less by its temperature than by the over-dubbing, her lips being contorted by the discrepancies between the sounds they form and the ones we actually hear. (The same may be said for the facial expressions with which she accompanies her rendition of Chopin's "Revolutionary" Etude; and as I seem to be dwelling on the subject of synchronization, I should add that the titles, apart from many wrong nuances, are left too long on the screen, the eye having assimilated the sense in most cases long before the words appear; which is one up for McLuhan.)

The grimness and social cruelty of Spain are not overdone, I think, but some of the other messages—the anti-clericalism, the sexual hypocrisy—are embarrassingly tendentious and simplistic. Nor is the erotic element effective; a glimpse of Mlle D.'s left leg, early on, is too pointedly aimed for the dramatic irony of the many later gruesome views of its wooden replacement lying about on chairs and sofas. But I should have begun by saying that the picture is ruined even earlier for me by a fatal, un-blot-outable resemblance between Mlle D.'s wheedling guardian-lover and Vincent Price.

1970

NOVEMBER 12

I.S. is in high spirits today, though the lab reports that his hemoglobin is as low as 6 and his hematocrit is down to 20; a transfusion is scheduled for tomorrow. He pens a message for a Festschrift to be presented to Aaron Copland the day after tomorrow (ironically in our own hotel): "Dear Aron, 70 is pretty good. Congratulations, Stravinsky." V., however, happening to read this testimonial, remarks that Mr. C. spells it "Aaron." Whereupon R. suggests that I.S. write a small "o" over the "A," like a string harmonic, this being the Scandinavian vowel-repeating sign. But I.S. vetoes that idea on the reasonable grounds that "Mr. Copland isn't Scandinavian." And he rewrites the whole, grumbling that "If he doesn't like this, *je m'en fous."*

R. reads to him then, but he is impatient and keeps asking, "How long does this description go on?" "Well, you can't get into the book without an introduction," R. argues, not mollifying him in the slightest. *"Well,"* he says, imitating her, "it's very boring. Let me read it myself, if I must." But when R. gives it to him, he slams it shut. "You're not being very nice today," she says, going out. And this time he withholds his retort. Then five minutes later, not at all contrite, but having found the compromise that suits him, he calls to her, saying, "After all, I've decided I'd like to read a bit *this afternoon.*"

NOVEMBER 17

Not the least blessing of David Storey's *Home* tonight is in compensating for last night's *Sleuth,* the latter a short story with *grand guignol* ending, never as good as the Agatha Christie it seeks to parody, and made into a long evening of forced jokes redeemed only by the three minutes during which the future murderer plays a recording of the end of the first movement and the beginning of the second movement of Beethoven's Seventh.

Home is a good enough play superbly performed. An inassessably large part of its appeal, however, is in the contrast with the various kinds of theater which it is *not,* these ranging from several species of New Theme Drama to the equating of the physical closeness of the actor with closeness in communication. Among other welcome absences are those of shouting, both in what is said and in how; of all Bedlamite, mad-as-a-hatter, *Marat–Sade* funny business; and of the philosophy of "the kids," Mr. Storey's people being naturally ravaged elders. As for positive virtues, the language of clichés is well observed. And there is one very shrewd structural invention, the introduction of a fifth character, the lobotomized boy wrestler, at the beginning of the second half of the play. Until then the straying thoughts and the forgetfulness of the two leading men could be attributed to daydreaming, as their somewhat excessive reactions to trivia might be indicative of "nervous disorders" well within the bounds of "normalcy." And until this point, too, even the women, who are more obviously "off" than the men, and whose imaginations are more lurid, might pass simply as eccentric boarders in a seedy "rest home" instead of inmates in a lunatic asylum. It is by drawing his women from a lower social order than the men, incidentally, that Mr. Storey finds his dimension of comic relief, for the shabby-genteel Jack and Harry are quite incapable of the coarse jokes of their female counterparts. But the boy wrestler puts the play where it is.

The beginning may be, and the end definitely is, too long, with moments that threaten to become over-poignant, not to say sugary, as in the case of the slow, final blackout, which has been prepared for, however, by an amount of mood-filled cloud studying of the *Dances at a Gathering* type. Moreover, the two-couples idea threatens to become as symmetrical as a tennis match—mixed doubles inevitably following the men's and women's singles—though better that than the formlessness which would have been

1970

393

inevitable otherwise. As for the cast, the women are natural comediennes, but whereas Richardson *is* the character Jack, Gielgud—who, like a wooden image of some Neapolitan saint, can cry real tears on cue—remains too much Gielgud. But Mr. Storey is the star. He can show not merely the despair and emptiness behind the mental door, but also the small-scale bravery that can keep them there and enable people incompletely in charge of the knob to go on. And in doing so he has both entertained and moved—me, at least.

NOVEMBER 22

Before we go in to dinner, I tell I.S. that V. has trudged about to buy the ingredients of his favorite soup, *"Shchi,"* and that he must remember to say he likes it. Then at table, when I ask his opinion of the wine, he says, "I can't tell you; I'm still thinking about the soup."

We listen to Prokofiev's First Violin Concerto, which I.S. likes; to two late Haydn piano trios, of which he is particularly fond of the first movement of No. XXX in D; and to Liszt's *Transcendental Etudes,* one of which, *Feux follets,* might make a good solo number in a ballet, he suggests, though another, *Mazeppa,* makes him laugh out loud. Moving on to Beethoven's Eighth, he notes his oversight—in a recent interview citing a type of "Pastoral Symphony" melodic design recurring in other symphonies—in neglecting to mention the variation in the violins beginning at m. 44, as well as the music at m. 70, both in the Allegretto. After that, hoping he will have had enough music for the night, I say, "What could we possibly listen to after the Beethoven?" "That's easy," he says, *"lui-même."*

It is a year today since I.S. filed suit to recover his manuscripts, after a personal letter to his son-in-law failed to retrieve them. But it is much longer than that since either his daughter in Los Angeles or his son in Urbana has come to see him or even telephoned about his health.

1970

DECEMBER 1

V. purchases an apartment at Seventy-third Street and Fifth Avenue. The Essex House, long since become intolerable, is now being "remodeled," a process that adds hammering and sawing to all the other noises—a soggy rendition of the Triumphal March from *Aida* in the corridor at 4 AM today by a chorus of carousing conventioneers—and the reek of dust, plaster, and paint. But apart from that, the new apartment has four Park-side rooms, as well as easy and private access for I.S., which will encourage him to go out with greater regularity. The yearly costs should drop to a fraction of what they were, too. And, finally, the I.S.'s can at last remove their furniture, pictures, books, and bibelots from storage, where they have been for more than a year.

But today's *New York Times* carries an article to the effect that the manuscripts and archives are for sale at $3,500,000, and it names the U.S.S.R. as a bidder. Taking a clue from the Morgan Library, to whom the collection had been offered, a *Times* reporter interviewed I.S.'s agent, who divulged both the top asking price and the information about the inquiry from the Soviet Union, which was no more than a lure to induce some buyer to come forward here; the U.S.S.R. does not part with hard currency in such amounts, and, anyway, in a lump-sum sale, as one to the U.S.S.R. would have to be, little would remain for the S.'s, after taxes, commissions, lawyers' percentages. In spite of which, the telephone is busy all afternoon conveying congratulations to the new "millionaires."

DECEMBER 2

A summer's day—so warm, in fact, that some of the trees in the Park seem confused in the absence of a proper cue whether or not to go ahead and shed their leaves.

Auden for dinner, in top, even euphoric form, dispensing greatly needed shots of mental B_{12}. "I've just done Igor's obituary for *The Observer*," he tells me in an elated—or at any rate not conspicuously bereaved—voice. "I talk about him as the great exemplary artist of the twentieth century, and not just in music."

But he eulogizes I.S. more than I have ever heard him do before, asking him to distinguish between the love which he feels for him and the mere admiration which he feels for Wagner ("who was indisputably a genius, but apart from that an absolute shit"), and attributing his own discovery of the sense of the Modern to I.S.'s music. I.S. dislikes being told such things to his face, of course, and a few weeks ago was very rude to N.N. for telling him much the same. But he is on his best behavior tonight—he *can* be *très enfant de la nature*!—listening and watching very intently, and observing to V., in Russian, that "Auden has marvelous ideas." He obdurately refuses to talk, otherwise, except once when V. asks why he did not respond to a joke: "I smiled inside," he says.

1970

Auden is preparing a lecture on Freud for a public reading in Philadelphia next month, and his homework is taking him back through the *New Introductory Lectures* and *The Interpretation of Dreams* ("Now the trouble with dreams, of course, is that other people's are so boring"). All that we hear about its content, however, is that "It makes a case against analyzing works of art as if they were people. I was delighted, by the way, to find that Freud has so much common sense. I mean, for example, he *does* see that a cigar could be simply a cigar. . . . Incidentally, I have been doing a bit of amateur psychiatry myself. Young people. You know the type: every experience of life by age twenty—except work. Most are on drugs, and all have sex problems, Gay Liberation Front, and so on. But I'm no advocate of the purely Uranian society myself. I mean, *I* certainly don't want to live *only* with queers."

He reels off a list of books we should have read—Blythe's *Akenfield*, Leontiev on Tolstoy (well, I *have* read that), the new biography of Scott, etcetera. "By the way, how much Scott have you actually *read*?" he asks, but, luckily, doesn't wait for an answer. "Rereading him now I see that he was more of an eighteenth-century rationalist than I'd thought.

"I have given up sleeping pills," he confesses. "Too difficult to procure in Austria. Instead, I keep a glass of vodka by my bed, which tastes better." Is his greater sociability attributable in any measure to this chemical change, I wonder? *Some* of it, in any case, is owing to expanding royalty statements. "I can't complain any more," he says, "and my credit in the neighborhood has increased remarkably ever since some TV cameras began following me about." I ask about the fortunes (Tyche sense) of his operas, and am told that "Henze wears a Mao tunic now, but with lots of money in the pockets."

The great poet has not given up gaspers, though, and in fact forges a chain of them, from a pack of Lucky Strike, at regular intervals. "We all know that smoking is bad," he says, "but I can't see why anybody should ever want to stop drinking." In that case would he care for another martini, I ask, and the answer is "Jolly." He has a remarkably spruced, almost-washed appearance tonight, and his slippers are in better repair than the floppy tartans he was wearing last time. His mind, of course, is *always* tidy, and even after the martinis, the claret, the champagne, he can remark that "Every artist must see for himself the relationship and balance between tradition and change. But does anyone see it any more? Now surely you, Igor, composed what you *had* to compose without asking yourself first: 'Well, let's see, what sort of thing should I be doing now?'"

Switching to his social life in Kirchstetten, he says that "The Burgermeister cannot be invited to dinner because he hasn't got a degree, and for this reason it would embarrass him to be asked; but the chemist can be asked simply because he has one—at least I *hope* he has. Incidentally, the village priest's name is Schicklgruber, and he is actually a relative." Wystan's own religious affiliations have lately turned to the Greek Orthodox Church, because "I can't put up with all the Reformist nonsense in my own."

When I congratulate him on *The Aliens,* he owns to being "pretty well pleased with it, too," and as for *A Certain World,* that, he admits, is "at least fun." Then promptly at nine o'clock he looks at his watch, mutters something about bedtime, and bolts from the table and the apartment.

1970

1948
1949
1950
1951
1952
1953
1954
1955
1956
1957
1958
1959
1960
1961
1962
1963
1964
1965
1966
1967
1968
1969
1970
1971

JANUARY 1

Pompano Beach. I play tennis this morning for the first time in years, paunching about, panting and perspiring, sometimes missing the ball entirely, three times sending it on a straight-up aerial course, twice lobbing it over the fence, and once adding it to the game in the neighbor court, where it must have made the players feel like jugglers.

Orthography along Federal Highway One tends to purely alphabetic forms. Thus "ex" is "x," as in "xpert," a motel calls itself the "C-Breeze," a new household appliance is advertised as "E-Z-ER," and the established way of writing a certain synonym for rapid is "kwik." But some of the other innovatory English is difficult to accustom to. Item: "Orange Juice Freshly Squozen."

At the beach I lie under a sea-grape tree with a trunk resembling above-ground roots. The dunes are littered with palm fronds, coconut husks, shells (I find an exquisitely gadrooned one). Swift-legged sandpipers, like tightly wound-up toys, flee and follow the surf an inch apart. A dead fish is washed ashore, a gull instantly swoops on it, plucking out its eyes. The majority of bathers today are elderly women who regale each other as "gals" and regularly anoint themselves with protective lotions. Another of their ghastly

397

euphemisms is "shedding a tear" (for micturition). Some of their male coevals are as much in need of "bras" as they are themselves, if not more so (two sets of boobs).

The expression "rubber goods" does not mean here what it does on Eighth Avenue, nor are there any uterine *double-entendres* in "inner tubes," "skin-diving sheaths," etcetera. The reference is simply to bathing caps, snorkels and fins, inflatable beach furniture, surfing mats, rubber surfboards with sharklike rubber fins, and tublike rafts that are large enough to hold three paddlers as in the nursery rhyme. I ride the waves myself, trying to catch them between the curl and the break, my only thought being how quickly "Thought" disappears under the pressures of the apolaustic life.

The sky, lightly flaked at first, turns stormy, like a Winslow Homer, in late afternoon, at which point a blimp appears above the beach trailing an advertisement from the nacelle: TRY THE LIBRARY AT THE HILTON.

JANUARY 16

New York. A cold spell, everyone breathing steam, and buildings, too, smoke plumes hovering over parts of Harlem like anti-aircraft balloons. Earflaps and woolen headgear, unexpectedly rural touches, are seen in the Park and on Fifty-ninth Street, but a pity on all those unskirted knees.

After two hours at Bonnier's, V. buys a Calder-type toy, a bouquet of hollow, billiard-size balls attached to flexible wires and anchored in a wooden plaquette; when knocked together, these globes emit a limited variety of soft, more-or-less-agreeable clucking noises. But how are such objects packaged and transported? This one, at any rate, is fitted into a cylindrical plastic tube, large enough for a missile or nerve-gas shell, perhaps, and with a violin-case handle at the center. Boarding the Fifty-seventh Street bus, however, V. cuts a wide swathe, as if the other passengers suspected the contents of being exactly that; until, that is, she is overheard asking the driver if he stops at Carnegie Hall. And at this, speculation turns on the nature of the instrument in the parcel, V.'s Russian accent obviously marking her as a musician.

At teatime the I.S.'s receive a visit from the violinist Leonid Kogan, whose accent is even more Russian, but who does not mention fiddling. In fact, the *Mavra*-like conversation is about the servant problem in the U.S.S.R. As bad as here, he says.

JANUARY 20

Playing patience with I.S., R. tells him not to forget to make a wish if he wins. He does win, naturally, whereupon R. asks him to reveal his wish. I.S.: "To win."

To Peter Brook's circus-like *Midsummer Night's Dream,* the bad taste of which, as I.S. would say, is often quite profound (though I.S. would have been struck by the line, "I never heard so musical a discord," and cite it as the sort of observation of which his own teachers, including Rimsky, were

1971

incapable). The play itself may be boring, but that can justify only the intention, not the quality, of Brook's distractions, which include the fat man's pants falling down, and not once but twice. Nor does Brook's busyness dispel the tediousness of the lovers' symmetries, so that one wonders if the thing will in all senses ever come out of the woods.

With the Liebersons, Bernsteins, and Avedons to a screening of Ken Russell's *Delius,* which we hate at first, but are moved by, at the end, and so deeply that when the lights go on, I find V. in tears. The film contains striking resemblances to I.S. in his present condition, the locking-in musical imagination, the portative papal chair, and—perhaps in a similar way, as V. no doubt thinks—the death.

New York. Asked by a friend what he would have chosen to be if he weren't a composer, I.S. frowns suspiciously and says, "Why, who wants to know?" (He might have chosen to be a linguist, among many possible alternative careers, as I realize at table when he conjugates a Russian verb for my edification—a hopeless goal.) Pursuing the matter from another angle, the friend then asks him to "suppose that when you were a young man a beautiful goddess had offered you any career *other* than that of composer, what would you have chosen then?" "Well, if she were *really* beautiful," he says, "I would probably have chosen *her.*"

By all reports his mother's style of repartee was much the same. Thus, at a performance of *Les Noces,* Madame Stravinsky *mère* is said to have reassured someone who had expressed concern lest she *"siffler la musique,"* that she would most certainly refrain, *"parce que je ne sais pas comment siffler."*

1971

Pompano Beach. Calling New York this noon, I talk to I.S., my first long-distance telephone conversation with him since August 1966. And it is startlingly like old times, his voice sounding much deeper than it does in person nowadays. His breathing is clear, too, which I say because it *can* sound like a soda fountain. After a moment of indecision as to which ear to apply to the receiver, he comes on gruff and laconic, as he always was on the telephone. "It arrived to me" (*i.e.,* happened), he says, explaining an indisposition, but "I gathered all my forces"—which sounds like a general recalling a campaign but simply means "force" in the sense of physical and moral strength. I suggest some music to listen to on the day of my return, and his reply is "I have nothing against it," but though the negative seems to imply a residue of skepticism, the expression is actually a sign of something akin to enthusiasm.

A dependable guide to the true situation of motels and hotels vis-à-vis the beach is the degree with which they overdo their claims to be directly on it. Thus, while the "Briny Breeze" and "Vista del Mar," modest enough in name, are only a few blocks from the shore, the "Sea Spray," "Surf-Side," "Sea Wash," and "Sandy Toes" are miles inland. On the whole, too, their true proportions can be deduced simply by inverting the measure of exaggeration in their self-descriptions. Thus, the "Ocean Manor" and "Castle-by-the-Sea" turn out to be glorified bungalows.

Whatever the Miami hotels intend with *their* names, the partiality to the Scottish and the French is hardly borne out by architectural resemblances, at any rate in "The Kenilworth," "The Ivanhoe," "The Balmoral" (there is also a "Prince of Whales"), "The Versailles," the "Eden Roc," "The Fontainebleau," and "The Fleur de Lit" (*sic:* this may be a way of indicating room service beyond the routine).

But whereas hotels frequently advertise their accommodations in acronyms—"SGL," "DBL"—most flying ads are spelled out to a tee. One small airplane buzzes our beach at crop-dusting level, trailing what looks like a tennis net lettered: "KEEP FLORIDA GREEN: BRING MONEY." And another low-flying machine drapes the warning: "LIFE BEGINS AT 40 BUT EVERYTHING ELSE BEGINS TO GIVE OUT, WEAR OUT, SPREAD OUT: WATCH YOUR WATE." This is a pitch for the macrobiotic, unbleached bread and health food markets, and for still more of the unhealthy-looking types who seem to be their principal patrons, and in whom last year's saccharine panic evidently failed to arouse any suspicion. Related appliances such as "wiglets" are widely available hereabouts, too, and related stimulants such as "Stagarama" cinemas. But to most outward appearances, the "life" that "begins at 40" centers on lawn-trimming, bridge, and the phosphor dots.

I am alone on the beach this afternoon except for a man feeding dog biscuits to gulls unable to fend for themselves. "After all," he tells me, not quite analogously, "the mother wolf nourishes her youngest and weakest cubs first." One-legged birds, losers of contests with rival predators of the deeps and shallows, are surprisingly common. These unipeds reduce their landing speed with a flurry of flapping, but alight off-kilter, nevertheless, and attain balance only by hopping about. The older birds are yellow and scruffy, the younger ones sleek and white-and-gray, like West Point cadets, which I say for the further reason that they look so much like sentinels. Nor is there any amorous billing and cooing among them, but only the squawk of the pecking-order top sergeant.

MARCH 1

New York. An article on euthanasia in this morning's *Times* provokes some pertinent remarks from I.S., which I note down for an interview with him on the subject.

Talking about the Mayakovsky vogue, I.S., who knew the poet in Paris, remembers him as *"très arrogant,"* while V. recalls that when she first saw him, in Petrograd in 1917, the point was that he should not see her. "I was in a cabaret in the Champ-de-Mars one night when Mayakovsky came in, but Sudeikine quickly put a napkin over my head and pushed me under the table. Mayakovsky was supposedly irresistible to women."

We listen to *Pli selon pli* after dinner, I.S. pillow-enthroned, like a pasha. But he is in a mischievous mood, counting the remaining pages of each section of the score as I hold it for him, and muttering, *"Tout ça, c'est bien égal."*

At midnight the sky is topaz where the glow of the city strikes the fog bank. But in spite of the cold and damp, or because of it, the male professionals are out hustling on Central Park West, as are their brawnier female rivals on Central Park South, some of whom are basking under the infra-red, meat-grill marquees of the Fifty-ninth Street hotels. A young man, long hair greatly in need of a shampoo, is picketing the Plaza, but for a remote cause, it seems to me, in view of the overloaded nags on this very block who haul the tourist hansoms. STOP THE BRUTAL CANADIAN SPORT OF CLUBBING BABY SEALS TO DEATH, his placard reads on one side, and on the other, instead of letting it go at that, KILL SEALS HUMANELY. Why not simply leave them alone?

MARCH 3

I.S., at a two-year peak, composes this morning for the first time in months, as we are suddenly aware because of the greater intensity of his playing, and the complexity of the harmony—though talking about it later he says that he "had an idea beginning with a combination of *tierces*." His memory is wide open, too, and his verbal powers are quick and fluent. I ask about his working method in translating *Les Noces* with Ramuz and he describes how, after he had prepared several crude French versions for his collaborator, they would refine one of them together, always settling for the best musical solution. "Would you like to hear a recording of *Noces*?" I ask, but he refuses, saying, "I like to compose music, not to listen to it. All my life I have been pursued by 'my works,' but I don't care about 'my works.' I care only about composing. And that is finished."

1971

MARCH 4

Still in marvelous form, he composes again today, this time for about an hour. Besides which, he is clairvoyant, above all about himself, though he also describes everybody's mood in the morning before seeing anybody (which, around here, may be simple prediction). "Sometimes I am frightened because I can't remember," he says. "Tell me, when did Bertha die?"

MARCH 12

I.S. makes the *Congressional Record,* his tax predicament with regard to his manuscripts and personal papers being cited by Senator Church in connection with a proposed revision of the law. "One extremely important collection denied to the Music Division [Library of Congress] has received recent public attention," the senator remarked. "Because of a change in the law, Igor Stravinsky has been forced to place his manuscript collection, valued at $3.5 million, on the open market when prior to the change, he could have donated it to the Library and not been penalized financially." The last phrase indicates that the senator reads *The New York Review,* but he goes on to quote the Washington *Star:*

A few months ago Igor Stravinsky's original manuscripts and personal papers were put up for sale in the open market. The price tag was $3.5 million, and considering their importance, anyone buying them would be getting a bargain.

These days it costs $25 million per mile or more to build a super-highway. Are the thousands of items offered by Stravinsky, including the manuscripts of compositions which altered the entire history of twentieth-century music, worth less than one-fifth of a mile of concrete?

MARCH 14

I.S. is still super-swift, at times, in unmasking the villain in a film, play, or detective story, as he should be, considering how many of them he has read and seen. Thus, during a brief, sweeping landscape shot in an animal soap opera on TV today, he instantly spots and points to a hidden alligator that none of us has noticed. He is also hypersensitive to the weight, no less than to the texture, of clothes and bedding. When I first knew him, he was always shielded by layers of coats and sweaters, and it was the same when he was young: that awning-stripe blazer which he wears in so many old photographs, and which dates from Ustilug, concealed several thicknesses of clothing. But now he prefers to go about in shirtsleeves and to sleep under only one, not-tucked-in blanket (though a beret is also a part of his night garb at times). As with the Princess and the pea, a fold or wrinkle at the back of his pajamas is enough to keep him awake.

1971

MARCH 15

Talk by a visitor this noon about the Philharmonic's plans for a Liszt survey provokes us to listen to half a dozen of the tone poems tonight, but we make little enough headway with any of them. Several times I.S. actually giggles; at other, rarer times, he follows the score for a few moments with real interest and expectations always unfulfilled; but most of the time he is simply bored.

MARCH 18

Tikhon Khrennikov calls from Moscow this morning, but V. will not talk to him until I have looked up his patronymic in Grove. "Tikhon Nikolaitch," as she then greets him, invites the I.S.'s to spend the summer in the U.S.S.R., assuring V. that they will be treated like Czar and Czarina, which is exactly what she is afraid of.

But I.S. is unwell. His pulse is labile and his coughing spells are deep and prolonged. Dr. Lax diagnoses it as pulmonary edema, and within an hour I.S. is litter-borne and on the way not only to the hospital that was the scene of last year's crimes, but to the very same room (891). "What should I do? What should I do?" he asks V. again and again in the ambulance, but V., choking back her tears, can only say, trying to calm him, "You do nothing. Other people will do."

And do they ever! He is processed like a product on an assembly line, the chest clamped with cathodes, the trachea scoured by a vacuum cleaner, the nostrils invaded with plastic oxygen tubes, the right inner elbow embrocated to expose a vein that a Draculess then punctures to draw a remarkably copious "specimen." The left arm, meanwhile, is strangled by a sphygmomanometric pump, implanted with a tube for intravenous feeding (a rivulet of diuretics to flush the fluid from the lung), and bandaged to an ironing-board splint. Last and worst, he is catheterized, the deed done by the head of the Urology Department who, apologizing for the discomfort, says afterward, "Maestro, I hope we are still friends." But the maestro angrily demolishes any assumption that they ever were.

The gram on the cardiac monitor slopes like a *téléphérique,* then sags in a deep catenary, then drops out of sight, then stabilizes briefly in what looks like Persian script, the upper loops of which, recorded by a yellow light blinking on another part of the machine, plot the contractions of the heart. But at least some of this disjunct movement is caused by nervous agitation, for the patient is too clear, not sick enough to have been subjected to so suddenly shocking an experience. He refuses to eat, trapped in this maze of machinery and plastic lariats, but when R. reasons with him, he ignores the indignity, valiantly takes up his fork, and decides to go on.

Throughout the ordeal, the quality of the man most to the fore is his precision of language and the absence of confusion in switching from one to another according to the addressee. Thus, to V., he says, *"Ustal, ustal"* (Tired) and "Send them to the devil!" Then, turning to the doctor, he describes the characteristics of his pangs in German, and, to R., complains about something in French. As for my language, when I joke with him to the effect that he did not have to go to this length to avoid Liszt, he smiles.

The view from I.S.'s window is almost as depressing as the scene in the Intensive Care Unit: standing-room-only buildings, different in size but nearly uniform in ugliness, all with the same TV antennae, same window-sill air-conditioning boxes, same chimneys, skylights, water tanks, and, in the penthouses, same bits of shrubbery; even the narrow spire of a church, shoe-horned into the middle of this squeeze, is inhabited, a vase of forsythia and some books being visible beneath the half-drawn Venetian blind of a window near the base.

And the I.C.U. is at least brisk and businesslike—infectiously so, to judge by a clergyman who pops in to administer last rites and leaves soon after, as insouciant, if possible, as the doctors and nurses. In fact the gravest faces in the ward, so far as I can tell without peeking under oxygen masks, are those of three solicitors, come, I think, to witness a nuncupative will.

At one point, in reply to V.'s "Why do you call me every minute and rap on the bed railing with your rings when you *know* I am here?" I.S.

1971

403

says something marvelously, inimitably I.S.-ian: "But I want to be sure that *I* still exist."

MARCH 22

He has more edema today, as well as a moment of mental confusion, asking for "Katya." (His first wife. V. answers that "Katya is in Paris," afterward saying that "If he had asked *where* in Paris, I would have *had* to say, 'in the cemetery.'") But this revenant has been aroused, I think, by a nurse's question as to how many children he has. (He hears "had" for "has" and holds up four fingers.) Otherwise he refuses to talk, and we resort to panto-mime.

MARCH 29

Trying to induce him to drink water, R. explains, as a last resort, that he is dehydrated. "Well," he says accusingly, "no one told me," and he promptly swallows a quarter of a litre. He receives a transfusion in the afternoon and another in the evening.

I spend the afternoon with two European musicians, the three of us judging compositions for a prize. It is not rewarding work, partly because of the impossibility of giving enough time to it, partly because of incompa-rables of mediums and styles—how does one choose between an electronic Mass and a string quartet?—and very largely because of the unknowns, meaning the operas one has not seen, the multi-media pieces one cannot visualize, the scores whose notation is purely verbal, the scores not meant to sound the same way twice, and the complex works one cannot digest in a single read-through and without the aid of performance tapes.

How, furthermore, can three jurymen with radically different inclinations hold their natural prejudices in abeyance long enough to agree even on the stylistic area of the choice? Today's midway answer—for we do not bring down the gavel yet, lacking a really obvious winner—is that we begin to introduce such criteria as a composer's sensitivity to color and whether or not we can outguess him; and begin to veer toward established reputations, in the sense of giving them the benefits of our doubts.

1971

MARCH 30

At the ages of, respectively, seventy-nine and eighty-eight, but looking forward to a new life, V. and I.S. move to their new home, he coming directly from the hospital, she coming from the hotel and, following the Russian superstition, bringing bread and salt. Weak as he is, I.S. insists on two full tours of the apartment, which seems to please him, for he kisses V. again and again. But of all the new furnishings and accouterments, his greatest interest is in the new occupant of the birdcage, the canary Iago; which is not surprising in a man who once composed music for a "real" as well as a mechanical nightingale. When Iago, who can trill like Galli-Curci, repeats a note several times at near A-440, I.S. says that "He must be tuning up."[1]

Auden comes at seven, sniffs the fresh paint, observes (without overtaxing his acumen) that the apartment "needs to be lived in," embraces I.S. (saying to me, "You never know when it's the last time"), accompanies V. and myself to the Pavillon, where he orders a British dinner. Waiting for it, he shows his new book of clerihews, reciting a few yet to be included. Some are about composers, and when we reach the "B.'s," he asks V., "What made Igor stop being catty about Beethoven?"

He talks about his recent lecture tour, and expounds on what is "in" on the campuses. Lévi-Strauss still is, of course, "though he writes such bad prose." And Buckminster Fuller ("It was very unkind of the *Times* to publish that full-page 'poem' of his the other day"). The audience for his own Philadelphia Freud lecture "consisted entirely of analysts and hippies," he says, and he adds that "I read it from my own longhand, which made it seem even longer than it is." In Toronto, he found himself in a symposium with Marshall McLuhan, "a confrontation that, according to the press, I won. Voznesensky was there, too, and I read for him. And speaking of Canada, I now own tax-deductible Dominion oil stocks, an arrangement that looks a little *louche* to me, but my lawyer seems to know what the traffic will bear."

Recalling a symposium in Stockholm last year, he says that "The scientists were bigger prima donnas than artists ever are, and though they may know everything knowable about microbiology, they don't know their ass from a hole in the ground about human beings. Furthermore, when a speaker is asked to limit himself to twenty minutes, it is infuriating to have him take forty-five." All of this is said in a voice whose normally very substantial carrying power has been appreciably increased by the effects of two double vodka martinis and several glasses of champagne; which seems to be the reason that so many people at other tables are finding us more and more deserving of their undivided attention.

Switching to the subject of old age, he confesses to sleeping longer—"From nine to nine, in fact"—and is astonished to hear that I.S. rarely retires before eleven. (He is also incredulous that I.S. had two teeth extracted last month— that he *had* two teeth—and he mentions some recent work on his own "lowers" by Dr. Kallman, the father of the poet, "who, inci-dentally, charged only two hundred and fifty dollars, though in the case of a genius like Igor, it would certainly be more.") "I could never live in a siesta culture," he goes on. "If Mama had found me resting in the afternoon, she would have said, 'Are you ill?'" And the thought of his mother reminds him that he received a letter from her shortly after her death, in 1941, written just before. "I tore it up, of course. I simply could not bear to open and read it."

His intellectual enthusiasm of the moment is Oliver Sacks's book on

1. The bird died shortly after Stravinsky himself.

migraines, a review of which he expects to finish next week in Pisa. He confesses that he "turned down the Norton Lectures because I didn't have anything to say. Now I think that at least one requirement for a lecturer is that he should have something to say," which may or may not be one of his own immortal apothegms. He tells us that his adaptation of "*L.'s L.'s L.*" does not contain any anagrams. "They would have been too patent. Plays are for people who like that sort of thing, not operas. But this opera is more fun than the play, I think, in the sense that *Kiss Me Kate* is more fun than *The Taming of the Shrew.*"

But why Pisa? Are migraines related in some way to the architectural oddity there?

MARCH 31

Twenty-three years ago today I met the I.S.'s. We observe the date with a short musical banquet, the First "Rasumovsky" Quartet. I.S. is in good spirits and much amused by a remark that he read today, in a *TLS* review, on Herder's concept of *Kraft:* "a . . . hovering in status between an inanimate causal agency and a personified and intelligent agency."

APRIL 1

Happy as he is in the apartment, I.S. is greatly concerned whether he can afford it. *"Vraiment, tout ça appartient à moi?"* he asks, and it is hard to convince him that it does belong to him.

APRIL 2

I.S. is obliged to write a short note in Russian, which he does, but signs his name in Latin letters. V. asks him to do the signature over in Russian, whereupon he takes the pen, and, aware that she is watching him, writes not his name, but "Oh, how I love you!"

APRIL 3

Entering his room about midnight, I notice that he is sleeping too soundly on one side—he should move frequently—a foreboding that all is not well. Has the substitute nurse, unaccustomed to his restlessness, given too strong a sedative? V. is deeply asleep, too, however, and I do not disturb her.

APRIL 4

Palm Sunday. We can hardly wake I.S., and his breathing is very labored, in spite of which the nurse, another substitute, dresses him, and actually wheels him about the apartment. It is soon obvious, in fact, that he again has pulmonary edema. In mid-morning the nurse calls Lax, but apparently does not describe the condition as an emergency. Even worse, she does not call R., who would know enough to give Lassix or another diuretic immediately, along with dijoxin; which is what R. does do, happening by at about two-thirty, but by this time his pulse is dangerously rapid, and his breathing is like that of a fish out of water.

When at last the doctor arrives (after three o'clock), we reject his recommendation of the hospital—an unthinkable trauma for I.S. now, convenient as the removal would be for the medical functionaries—and insist that the intravenous apparatus be installed here and that an intern or doctor remain in attendance during the night. The I.V. equipment is delivered surprisingly quickly, but a weak vein is chosen, the needle slips out, and a full hour is lost before it is reinjected and the clysis begins to flow. Lax, meanwhile, trying to explain I.S.'s chances to V. and myself, seems oddly drawn to anecdotes about the last days of his one-time patient Béla Bartók. He quotes Bartók as saying that "'One of the most important things that I learned from Stravinsky was daring.'" But is Lax deliberately hinting to V., or, as I think, is he so disturbed himself that he cannot eject the memory of the other composer's death from his mind?

Two large green torpedoes of oxygen are trundled in, but the twin-pronged nostril-clamp feeder can be kept in place only by stretching a rubber band around the head. We cushion I.S. from the pull of the elastic by putting large tufts of cotton under it, on either cheek, where they remind me of Ibsen's sideburns (and bring to mind the great Norwegian's "To write is to judge one's self"; but surely a simpler use of writing, calling down no judgment if not exempt from it, is the writer's double-edged—partly cathartic—desire to remember?). I.S. is fearfully anxious, squeezing and kissing our hands, crossing himself and ourselves, but still and always panting like a stranded fish. And his body is *not* responding. The Lassix is *not* mobilizing the fluid, he does *not* pass any urine during the entire afternoon, and the lungs are no less audibly congested.

Worst of all, his pulse is wildly irregular and the signs of heart failure are alarming. At about 8 PM Dr. Lax and the night-watch intern decide that morphine must be given to slow the heartbeat, though it may perilously retard the other functions as well. Just before the injection, I talk to I.S., his big eyes studying my face as I promise that he shall have music tomorrow. He responds with a smile. "Do you want Beethoven?" I ask. But he does not answer. "Well, then, Stravinsky?" But at this he makes a sour face and firmly shakes his head to left and to right.

About an hour later, when he is still not reacting to the medications—would he have if he had received them five or six hours earlier?—R. disregards her nurse's uniform for the first time in two and a half years, and says, "Robert, you must hope that he dies now—for him. And I will tell you that already this afternoon *we* thought he would." But I do not want him to die—or, of course, want him to suffer; but if the choice were mine, it would be for more suffering, cruel and egoistical as that may be (or surely *is*), and I would take the responsibility for it on pain of perdition because I know there is more life in him still, and life of the most precious kind. At this point V. enters the room, seems not to comprehend the gravity of it, yet, after gazing at him a long time, says: "He is tired and would like to sleep 'forever,' but his mind is still making distinctions and he is afraid that 'forever' and 'death' are the same." We take turns moistening his open mouth and lips with lemon water—"Like Christ and the vinegar," she remarks.[1]

Then a little later, strangely, ominously, and for no reason except that the record is on the turntable—I had been listening to it only two days ago with I.S.—I start to play the *Symphonie pathétique*. Two days ago it delighted him; "Tchaikovsky's best music," he called it. But again I have no idea *why* we played it, for we have never listened to it together in all of our twenty-three years. Now, at the first sound of it, the last movement, V. runs from the room, begs me to turn it off, says that to Russians it predicts death.

APRIL 5

No change occurs during the night, the diuretics are having no effect, and no urine is passed. His breathing, too, is still like that of a runner after a race, and the sound of it is more and more like a death rattle. The intern, on his way out at 7 AM (after a reasonably good night's sleep on a pile of pillows near the bed), tells me that in his opinion nothing can be done, and that it cannot last more than an hour or two. But Dr. Lax, on his rounds, finds some accumulation of water in the bladder and he summons Dr. Slaughter (*sic*) to catheterize him and Dr. Brown to take blood for a B.U.N. Lax tells V. "It is not one hundred per cent hopeless. His strength is incredible and he is a man of surprises."

The catheterizing is accomplished without complications, but by about 1PM his life signs are failing; the pulse is weaker and even less regular, the lungs are still congested, and the catheter has drawn only 44 cc.'s of urine. At one point the blood pressure drops below 80, while the pulse climbs to 140 and the respiration continues steadily at 40. Nor can morphine or dijoxin be given again for at least two more hours. Three times when we are very briefly out of the room, R. calls us back to his bedside for what she apparently fears may be the end.

Then suddenly a great change comes over him. His *in*spirations sound less labored, and his lungs begin to clear. At the same time his blood pressure rises and his pulse falls (but only to 120). He responds to R.'s directions, too, turning from side to side when she explains how important it is for him to move—but fighting her like a wildcat when she attempts to insert a nasal suction tube. And whereas he was holding my hand loosely an hour ago, he clasps it now with a powerful grip and will not let go. Finally, in the late afternoon, when the B.U.N. report is not too unfavorable, it is clear that the outcome rests entirely with that mighty heart, which is so much more than a muscle in I.S.'s case, but which has already endured more than forty hours of almost superhuman strain.

He seems much improved in the evening, and Dr. Lax is noticeably less

1971

---

1. For weeks afterward V. was obsessed with the thought that he was in an agony of thirst which she could not quench because he was unable to swallow.

tense. Yet when I sit by his bed, he kisses my hand and holds it to his cheek as if he were saying good-bye; and when V. sits on the other side and he slowly strokes her cheek with the back of his left hand, which is bandaged to keep the I.V. needle in place, that is very obviously what he means. His eyes are aware of some new change, moreover, and he always was and still is ahead of everybody. But V., after dabbing his face and neck with eau de Cologne, goes to bed slightly relieved, or at any rate more hopeful than last night, and soon falls into an exhausted sleep. R., moreover, with whom, every few minutes, I have been lifting him to change his position (with *his* help, too, for he has great strength in his arms), actually returns to her room at the Essex House, "for some real sleep if I am to work well tomorrow," a disastrous decision, but evidence that she, who knows him best, believes in the rally and in his recovery.

APRIL 6

While the new intern and new nurse adjourn to the living room to play a few hands of cards (before turning in themselves), I pace the floor, looking in at him every two minutes, hoping and praying for a change in that terrible breathing. But it does not come. And an elderly relief nurse who remains in the room with him confirms my fears that it is, if anything, more labored. I go to the intern, but he tries to reassure me that the breathing will ease soon as a result of the last morphine injection. Unallayed, I go to my room, not so much to pray as to beg, then go back to him and find him looking weaker but perhaps more peaceful (Eliot's line, "His life is light, waiting for the death wind," comes into my mind), hold his hand awhile, and again return to my room. This time I doze off until awakened by L., who says he is sinking. I run to him in a half-stupor and see him die—a simple cessation, without struggle.

1971

The intern stethoscopes the chest, says he hears nothing, removes the intravenous tube (with all the feeling of a filling-station attendant removing a hose from an automobile tank), and remarks, "Gee, he went just like that." While he leaves the room to call Lax and certify the time of death as five-twenty, I wake V., but cannot directly tell her the truth: "He is very bad . . . dying . . . I think . . . No . . . he is dead." Then I go back to I.S. and hold his still-warm hands and kiss his still-feverish cheeks and forehead, during which I am certain that life is in his eyes for an instant and that in that instant he knows me. V. comes, kisses him, and leaves the room crying.

The brutal "Loved One" business begins immediately after the eyes have been closed and the sheet pulled over the head. First, the room is disinfected, by which time R. arrives from the Essex House and inserts his dentures, brushes his hair, replaces his wedding rings. We are then obliged to decide questions relating to the two funerals and burial, such as whether the casket is to be sealed for the New York service—which it should be, we agree, for V.'s sake, though contrary to the barbaric Russian Orthodox rule.[1] Fortunately R. takes over the macabre jobs of selecting burial clothes (it is especially painful to think of his Venetian-made shirts with "I.S." stitched on them to distinguish them from mine in the laundry) and of choosing the casket and flowers. His gold cross and silver medal go with him, but V. takes his sapphire ring[2] and gives me his wristwatch, which I can hardly bear to look at, remembering how he had to lift his sleeve halfway to the elbow to find it and tell us the time, his arm had become so thin.

In forty minutes the doctor arrives—if only he had been as quick on Sunday!—and soon after him, I.S.'s attorney, to advise V. of her financial and property rights and direct her to begin the inventory of the effects. Soon, too, attendants from the funeral home arrive for the "transferral of the decedent." Meanwhile, telegrams have gone off to I.S.'s children by his first marriage, and minutes later the news is on the "media," after which cables, telegrams, flowers, and hand-delivered messages arrive in overwhelming quantities while the telephones are so busy that one of our two lines breaks down and requires emergency repair (by a young man who says, "Stravinsky is my favorite composer"). But this worldwide response, instead of helping to confirm the reality, only makes it less believable.

The regular morning mail brings two supremely ill-timed letters, one from the lawyer of I.S.'s elder son proposing that a committee of custodians be formed to supervise I.S.'s affairs; the other, a ghost from the past, from lawyers representing the estate of Vaslav Nijinsky and claiming a share of the royalties from *Le Sacre du printemps* on the basis of a Société des Auteurs *"déclaration,"* signed by I.S., Nijinsky, and Roerich on June 9, 1913.

At 6 PM, in a daze, we go to the funeral home, where the flower-decked coffin seems unreal, a grotesquerie in no way related to I.S., and where a prayer service is held for the family (*i.e.,* V.) and a few friends (among them Lincoln Kirstein, weeping like a child, and Balanchine, very calm, who embraces and thanks me for "everything you did for him"). All of us are shaky, including the choir, and V. is able to stand for only a few minutes. But the service is long, and the room small and stifling, while Bishop Dmitri's extremely liberal dispensing of incense nearly asphyxiates us. Then a wondrous thing happens. An unseasonable snow has begun to fall just before the service, and the winds have begun to howl. And now, as the Bishop pronounces I.S.'s name, there are three great bursts of thunder, as if Nature herself were proclaiming the departure of a true natural force from the world.

It is terrible to read about it in the late newspapers, and to see and hear it reported on television, with the completed dates, 1882–1971, in the background. Worst of all are old film clips of him conducting. To us they seem like an attempt to make him remote, to say that he is no longer ours.

1. Orthodox ritual requires that a priest place an icon on the chest, cross the arms over it, and fasten a ribbon containing a printed prayer to the forehead.

2. She had given it to him in the 1920's, having purchased it with some money received as compensation in an automobile accident.

1971

410

We talk half the night, afraid of sleep, of forgetting in sleep and remembering again.

We *do* sleep, but at exactly five-twenty wake like bolts to the agony of memory. We don't want him to be with Bach and Mozart, as commentators and messages of condolence are saying he is. We want him in the next room, old, frail, and weak as he was, but more wonderfully alive than anyone in the world. And I want to hear his voice calling "Hello"; or, to give egoism its due (though I feel no "ego identification," no "guilt," and no other application of transference theory), "Where's Bob? Can we have some music?" ("What music, Maestro?" one of his nurses used to ask, and not wanting to say "Josquin des Prés" to her, he would say "Bob's music.") And I want to hold his hand, in which the pulse between the right thumb and forefinger throbbed almost nakedly. And laugh with him; and provoke one of his inimitable ripostes; and raise a glass to him, for he never failed to smile and raise his in return. And I want to look into his eyes, always so full of questions, though we always felt that he knew all of the answers, and at the moment of death knew it was that. I cannot believe and cannot accept that he is not and will never again be there.

V. is worse today, for her deeper reactions are always delayed. Yesterday she was simply numb, having gone to bed Monday partly believing he would be well in the morning, as he was so often before. But today, too, she is suddenly aware of the monstrously cruel joke of the "new apartment." For she has spent months in planning and preparing this new house for him, reconstructing his room after his old California studio, filling it with his music, icons, pictures, photographs, books. His piano is exactly as it was there, with the manuscript drawingboard over the keys, and, on top, the portraits of Monteverdi, Mozart, Beethoven, and Bach, whose *Well-Tempered Clavier,* Book I, is still open to the Prelude in E-flat minor, which he had been playing on Saturday. No wonder V. can hardly bring herself to pass the door of the room. And no wonder she says she cannot live in the "new home" now, even though the few happy days that he lived here bless the house as much as the death darkens it. Or so I argue. But she says, "It is as if he only came to pay a visit, for my sake."

And R. What must she feel, having washed his body almost every morning for two and a half years, and dressed him and brushed his hair, and read to him, and played cards with him, and pampered him, and wheeled him in the Park, and joked and fought with him?

Once again we sit around talking half the night, dreading to be alone and fearing to fall asleep, to wake again, to remember.

And again we wake at five-twenty, but do nothing all day except read some of the cables and letters from a thousand friends known and unknown. One

1971

of the latter says that "No other contemporary composer passes the test of a one-man concert, but Stravinsky survives about twenty of them." Another says: "He was keeping so much alive besides himself." And still another: "This is the first time since Guillaume de Machaut that the world is without a great composer." Claudio Arrau cables from London: "Now he joins the immortals where in any case he has already been for fifty years." But perhaps the most nearly perfect of them all, from Luciano Berio, simply says, *"Adieu père Igor et merci."*

V. is now obsessed with the thought that he knew he was dying, and that, caressing her cheek Monday night, he was already consoling her.

APRIL 9

It is Good Friday, the one day in the Church year that I.S. observed, keeping a strict fast, except for music (the Couperin and Tallis *Tenebrae,* the Schütz and Bach Passions—Bach's *St. John* being the last music he heard before being taken to the hospital on March 18); but he would not work (*i.e.,* compose) on that day, which is now the day of his funeral.

We fear for V. and the strain of the ceremony. She can hardly walk, and has been ordered by Lax to stay in bed and see and talk to no one. But I.S.'s children have arrived, and his elder son has asked to see her and will take her refusal in bad grace. "Why didn't they come to see him when he was *alive*?" V. asks. And, in truth, whereas she has not been away from him for more than two hours in two years, the children, except for the same son, have not been as much as two hours *with* him. His death has no doubt grieved them, but they were remote from him at the time, and for a long time; and their loss, at a distance, is simply not comparable to V.'s, who, moreover, after all the anguish, still has to face decisions relating to the Venetian funeral and interment. Which is why the children are able to spend two hours before the funeral talking with I.S.'s attorney and two attorneys of their own. In short,

> Some natural tears they drop'd
> But wip'd them soon . . .

A few minutes before three o'clock, we go to the funeral home at Eighty-first and Madison, where a crowd is gathered in front of the door and a line stretches around the block. We are ushered into a waiting room, then to the front row, right side of the chapel—the children are on the left—where we are given candles to hold throughout the service. The hardest moments are the sound of I.S.'s own *Pater Noster* at the beginning, and the sound of his first name, "Igor" (as if he were a little boy), in the mouth of the priest, near the end. (But how dare he mention I.S.'s "transgressions"? Has anyone left the world a richer legacy of love? For if music isn't a form of love, *what* is it?) It is also painful to hear the *"Gospodi pomilui"* (*"Kyrie*

1971

eleison"), which reminds me of the Russian services I used to attend with him in Hollywood two decades ago; and the three "Alleluias"

which, as he once acknowledged, were part of the inspiration for the *Symphony of Psalms*.[1]

After the service, V., more restless than I have ever seen her, says that she cannot return to the apartment. Accordingly, R., E., and I fly with her to Boca Raton and spend the night in the giddying glassed-in top of the Tower, a neighborless skyscraper that, even to a mild acrophobe, is like trying to sleep at the top of the Tour Eiffel.

APRIL 10

And again we wake at five-twenty and are still unable to comprehend, but at least manage for a time to talk about something else. I rent a car, drive it a short distance to an empty beach, skid while trying to turn around, bury it axle-deep in a dune. Walking far enough from the bogged vehicle—which looks as if it is sinking in quicksand—to rule out the suggestion of any link between it and my own circumstances, I attempt to hitchhike back to the hotel; but inspire no confidence and am obliged to walk all the way, which I blame on my Fellini-like apparel: red bedroom slippers, wet-through checkered pants, two large suitcases (from the trunk of the sand-swamped car). At the hotel, V., more restless than yesterday, is eager to return to New York, which we arrange to do tomorrow from Miami.

1971

APRIL 12-13

New York, Rome, Venice. V. has the 'flu, but insists on being in the airplane (a 747 flying auditorium, large enough for a memorial concert) with I.S.'s body. Also aboard is a man carrying I.S.'s passport, a Gogolian requirement of the Italian government. The landing at Rome is very late, and our connecting plane to Venice has to be recalled from the runway. A *motoscafo* meets us at Marco Polo Airport, and we cross the lagoon thinking of our last crossing with I.S., in 1962. (And of countless others, the most memorable being to Chioggia in 1951, three days after the *Rake* première, when he

1. The Slavonic "Alleluia," which adds, and stresses, a penultimate syllable

is possibly a source of a two-note motive endemic to Stravinsky's music. The word is written thus in the Slavonic prayer book which was at Stravinsky's bedside when he died, and which had belonged to his father:

а́ллилу́їа!

was applauded in the streets louder than the noise of the clogs that the women there still wore.)

We pass Murano, where he admired the floor mosaic of two cockerels carrying a Reynard trussed and slung on a pole; and San Michele, where he will be buried. But Venice is fog-wrapped and phantom-like today, and only the nearest and tallest towers—San Francesco della Vigna, the *pigna* of the Madonna dell'Orto—stand out in silhouette. We enter the great stone labyrinth beneath the Ponte Sepolcro, and, on a wall immediately inside, see one of the thousand *affiches:*

THE CITY OF VENICE HONORS THE GREAT MUSICIAN IGOR STRAVINSKY,
WHO WITH A GESTURE OF EXQUISITE FRIENDSHIP WANTED IN LIFE TO
BE BURIED IN THE CITY HE LOVED MORE THAN ANY OTHER.

And he did love it, if not more than, then in part because it reminded him of, St. Petersburg.

Carmen being on the stage at La Fenice tonight, we are obliged to rehearse in the foyer, where Bizet's most boisterous passions mingle profanely with our *Requiem.*

APRIL 14

The rehearsal this morning adds the RAI Chorus from Rome, but the singers are sight-reading and we still have no soloists.

This morning, too, a water-hearse moves the coffin, accompanied by two Orthodox priests, from the Campo San Tomà to Santi Giovanni e Paolo, pantheon of the doges, where it is placed in the Cappella del Rosario, and where people file around it for the rest of the day. We go to the chapel ourselves before the evening rehearsal, which seems to be more for the benefit of the television cameramen than of the musicians, but which confirms our apprehensions that the church is very reverberant (as well as very cold). The sight of the flower-decked bier is even more disturbing than in New York, if it is possible to measure such feelings.

1971

APRIL 15

And so the day of burial has come. At 11:30 AM a *motoscafo* takes us to, as it is written on old maps, S. Zuan e Polo. The Campo is thronged (five hundred, the *Gazzettino* says), and the Ponte Cavallo, and boats in the canal (the Rio dei Mendicanti), and windows and roofs of houses, and the great Gothic church itself (three thousand, the *Gazzettino* says), whose front doors are kept open so that the people outside may be a part of the ceremony. But the Campo is also crowded with memories, and as we cross it I see I.S. as he used to come in a blue water-ambulance to the Ospedale (Scuola di San Marco) for blood tests, and see him at the Caffè al Cavallo, to which he sometimes walked or was rowed in the evening for a *grappa*; by some coincidence, or premonition, he referred to the Cavallo itself (the Verrochio) in an interview only two months ago.

We enter the basilica through a lateral door and proceed to the left transept, where a row has been reserved for the *"famiglia"* (V. at one end, children and grandchildren at the other), facing the rose-covered bier. This rests on a black cloth ornamented with white Maltese crosses, while a huge taper, in large gold *candelabri del presbiterio,* burns at each corner. A young acolyte, in a black vestment with a pattern of white flowers and crosses, stands at the foot of the coffin, facing the altar and holding a tall processional cross (*croce astile*) to the floor; in a ceremony of more than three hours (here and on the island) he never fidgets, and his bearing is far more commanding than that of the attendant *carabinieri.* (It is a standing service—*kathistos*—not a sitting one—*kathisma*—and when V. sits for a moment, from fatigue, the archimandrite glances in her direction with noticeable lack of compassion.)

But the young cross-bearer cannot conceal his incredulity at the antics of the *paparazzi,* those nonstop camera-snappers who are all but on the verge of infiltrating the archimandrite's beard. (But without flapping him; not so me, for one of them follows me to the podium, no doubt sensing that a photo of me keeling over may be imminent: it is 6 AM for me biologically, besides which I have slept no more than minutes at a time in days, have conducted only once since I.S.'s illness two years ago, and am wholly unable to detach myself from the event; in fact, only by constantly thinking of what I.S. would say about every detail of the performance am I able to get through it.) The obsequies begin with Alessandro Scarlatti's *Requiem Missa Defunctorum,* added for bad measure by the chorus: it is featureless, dull, and in no way relates to I.S. (or even to Venice, being Neapolitan). The three organ pieces by Andrea Gabrieli played during the ritual would have pleased him, however; I remember walking with him from the Madonna dell'Orto to San Marco, tracing the route of the Lepanto victory procession, for which Andrea Gabrieli composed music. After the Scarlatti, the Mayor delivers an address, quoting encomia of Venice by I.S. and Ezra Pound; *il miglior fabbro* himself is present, and has been in the church since early morning, before the casket was moved from the chapel to the transept.

1971

The *Requiem Canticles* follow, faltering at first, the staccato accompaniment in the Prelude suffocating in the acoustical wool. The *Rex Tremendae* wobbles like *pasta,* and the *Libera me* sounds more like a mob scene than the background patter (*"bisbigliare"*) I.S. wanted. Worst of all, the celesta player volunteers to fill in part of one of the pauses in the Postlude, nearly ruining that explicit structure: the chord of Death, followed by silence, the tolling of bells, and again silence, all thrice repeated, then the three final chords of Death alone. (No wonder everything he composed after this was meant both to preserve it as his last work and to prevent it from becoming so too soon.)

At twelve-thirty, the archimandrite, Cheruvim Malissianos, gold cope and black hood (*klobook*) with veil trailing over the shoulders, parades down the center aisle to a vermilion throne at the entrance to the apse. He is followed by two acolytes, who stand on either side four steps below him, where together they hold the euchologion from which he reads one part of the service, and together or individually sing the antiphonal responses. The archimandrite is a young man with dark eyes, olive skin, black hair and beard, and the allure of a Byzantine Pantocrator. He is a dazzling performer, moreover, both to listen to and to watch, although his gestures are simple: whether raising his hand; or, fourth finger down, in the Orthodox way, touching his temples and heart (which is how I.S., too weak to trace the transverse, crossed himself the night before he died); or slowly swinging the thurible around the coffin, with extra and prolonged fumigations in the direction of the head. In fact, he is ostentatious only in the way he closes his eyes, but this has the effect of hushing the entire congregation and may even recommend it to pray.

What wonderful music it is, this remnant of Byzantium bedizened by corruptions from the Syrian, Hebrew, and Arabic Orient (though bastardized for want of a Rosetta Stone relating the different systems of notation)! And no wonder hymnographers were accorded positions of honor in Byzantine churches. How beautiful, too, are the Greek words: *"makarios"* and *"philanthropos"* and *"eleos"* and *"hosios,"* etcetera. The singing is an art of agogics, of the *kratema,* the *parakletike,* the *apodema;* and an art of ornaments, such as the *kylisma,* and whatever the names for that "break" of emotion in the voice and for the effect of trailing off to the last note, so that one is uncertain whether or not it has actually been sung. It is an art, above all, that would most have delighted and best been understood by the man who lies dead.

Alleluiatic antiphons begin the service, which celebrates the joyous passage from death to eternal life (and the Orthodox Church seems to emphasize the Resurrection as much as the Roman Church emphasizes the Crucifixion). Whereas the music is harmonic, syllabic, and tonal in the Russian service, here it is monodic, melismatic, and plagal—falling whole-tone cadences, exquisitely sung by the mellifluous Malissianos. *Psalm 118* follows (I.S. liked Josquin's setting of that), and the *Four Beatitudes* of John the Damascene, the Fourth Chapter of the First Epistle to the Thessalonians, and the *Song of Exodus.* Again the most painful moment comes with the sound of I.S.'s first name, art and ritual having helped, until then, to make this celebration of the mystery—not of death, of course, but of life—less personal.

At the end, the archimandrite summons V. to the coffin, to kneel before it and say good-bye. Then four gondoliers—black sashes, black armbands, black shirts showing at the neck beneath white blouses—wheel it slowly down the center aisle, V. walking behind, and out into the sunlight and azure and the Campo banked with flowers. Here it is transferred to the water-hearse, a gondola with gold lions of St. Mark on the sides (but, unlike Diaghilev's, no *Felze*), and a border of pink-and-white roses, like those on the bier; the gondoliers' oars are black-tipped and a black drape trails in the water. The archimandrite, seated, and his cross-bearer, standing, ride

416

in the first gondola, V. in the one behind the bier. As the bier passes, the people on the Fondamenta, in front of San Lazzaro dei Mendicanti, in windows and doorways, and in boats and on bridges—both of them packed to the parapets—bow their heads and cross themselves.

When the cortège sails under the Ponte dei Mendicanti and into the lagoon, the archimandrite rises behind the cross-bearer, his cope and *klobook* blowing in the breeze. But the faster boats of the TV men and the *paparazzi* cut in on the procession and confound the protocol. As a result, the heavy hearse-boat is the last to reach the island and to be unloaded. (When it has been, the thought occurs to me that I.S., who could not swim and was always nervous in gondolas, would be relieved.) We wait for it before the gateway, which is guarded in a Gothic pinnacle by the Archangel Michael, receiver of souls (scales in one hand) and sounder of the last trump (spear in the other), "When the dead shall be raised incorruptible, and we shall be changed."

Transubstantiation is not a consoling thought at this moment, I reflect, as the procession resumes and we enter the old Camaldolensian cloister. The flower displays are borne ahead now, President Saragat's first, and a large red one from the Soviet Union behind, along with those of many other countries, *not* including the U.S.A. The archimandrite follows, then the bier (again on wheels), and then ourselves with our own bouquets. But the gondolier pallbearers, not yet having found their terra-firma legs, are held up for an awkward minute or two by a small flight of stairs. Moving on, we cross a crunchy gravel path, by a wall of kennel-like mausoleums and through a field of small white crosses, each with a photograph of the deceased. The *"Rep. Greco,"* as it is designated over the portal, is a garden of laurels and cypresses and expired Orthodoxists, bordering the outermost wall of the island. We halt for a moment before a small chapel, at the end of the path, but long enough for me to decipher the name "Bakunin" from the Cyrillic of the third stone at the left.

The chapel is just large enough, lengthwise, for the coffin and some journalists—the *paparazzi* and the TV crews having set up on top of the vined wall above the grave—but room remains for us on the sides. The archimandrite and his acolytes disappear into the narrow, curtained-off prothesis, ostensibly to prepare for the final rites—he strips for a moment to his black cassock—but actually to stall while a telephone call is put through to the mayor for clearance to begin the service without him. It starts behind the curtain, Malissianos chanting now in a dolorous and weirdly "white" voice. One of the acolytes answers with three sepulchral *"Kyries,"* then the other begins to wail, and to precede the coffin outside to the grave, where he stands under a tree, wailing his unearthly music throughout the burial.

Before the actual interment begins, and while the scaffolding is being removed, Malissianos banters, Hamlet-like, but *sotto voce,* with two of the gravediggers, telling them in Venetian Vulgo to get it right because burial is a more or less permanent condition. But he does so without compromising his sacerdotal dignity (which may be inviolate, in any case, as I suspect at the end of the service when we are required to kiss his hand and see that it is impossible: *Noli me tangere*). Then—the most terrible moment—ropes lower the coffin, the archimandrite accompanies V. to throw the first handful of dirt, and "IGOR STRAVINSKY" on the steel nameplate gleams for a last instant in the sun.

APRIL 16

The clouds break suddenly, during our flight to Paris, just as we are over Evian, and we can make out the Hôtel Royale.

Suvchinsky, at dinner, encourages V. to write her memoirs, "the one really valuable book and the least postponable." And he wisely counsels her to "write it, or tell it to a tape recorder, in Russian, English, French, German, or a mixture of them all, but apart from necessary annotations, do not allow anyone to 'edit,' 'polish,' or 'rewrite' it."

He also airs a theory about *my* role. Which, he says, differs from the examples of I.S.'s earlier associates only in degree; and in that, being something of a conductor, I was a more broadly serviceable aide. At the beginning of the fifties, so the theory goes, I.S., lacking a sense of direction, supposedly found one in, or by reaction to, me. But I was not so much an "influence" as a catalyst, in the sense that I.S. reacted to me, not only "in his own ways," which would be obvious, but in ways that often ingeniously contradicted what I may have seemed to be espousing. Thus, if my advocacy of Schoenberg appeared to be uppermost, he would devote himself exclusively to Webern; and if I seemed to think that chromatic equality was a built-in tenet of serialism, he would opt for a diatonic species. (Which may or may not be true, *I* say, but all that anyone *else* can say, for certain, is that in my role as the Stravinsky housedog I was more Cerberus than spaniel.)

"The feelings of the children are plain enough," he goes on. "You took their place.[1] But never mind. It is more important to remember that a hero must be blameless. Which is the reason the U.S.S.R. will blame you because he was not buried there, even though everyone knew that his visit there in 1962 was possible only because of your—in this instance the word is correct—influence."

1971

APRIL 17

Paris. Eager as V. was to leave Venice, her decision to come to this even more memory-laden city was wrong. Her face streams with tears during a drive through the Bois de Boulogne. And on the return, lighting an Easter candle for I.S. in the rue Daru Church, she cries harder than at any time

---

1. No. None of them had performed the same role in their father's life that I did. Moreover, when I appeared on the scene, at twenty-three, they were, all three, married adults in their forties, leading lives independent of their father in every way except financially.

since his death. Nor is "the beauty of Paris" much balm. After the "coziness" of Venice—I.S.'s word and one of his reasons for living there—the Louvre merely looks pompous, and the "restored" place des Vosges, where we go for lunch, seems as new as a Disneyland replica. But Suvchinsky's conversation tonight is consoling.

APRIL 19

We fly to Marrakech to visit Ira Belline, I.S.'s niece and V.'s closest pre-1939 friend.[1] The two have not seen each other since then, Mademoiselle Belline having lived in Morocco since the war. Nor, for a nerve-wracking half-hour, is it at all certain that they will see each other now, our Royal Moroccan caravelle developing convulsions just as we are descending at Fez. The captain, with no respect for our imaginations, describes it as "motor trouble" and says that our course has to be shifted toward the larger runway at Casablanca. We drift down like a glider thereafter, and at a drastically reduced speed, and the runway, when we finally touch it, is flanked by ambulances and firetrucks with hoses at the ready. Two hours after an announcement about a short delay for repairs, when no noticeable step has been taken in that direction, we hire a taxi and complete the trip by car.

The cactus-and-adobe landscape could be New Mexican, if not the traffic: donkeys, whose passengers sit far back as if to keep the animals from tipping forward; camels, dark brown and shaggy except for a young, milk-white one tethered to a telephone pole; and women, in the same category as the donkeys except limited to freight, which they carry like canephoroi. Nor has Women's Lib made any inroads in other directions. Practically all females are veiled, and not only to the eyes but over them, which in the case of white with a white garment (*haik*) is distinctly djinnish. Women turn away at our approach, but the turbaned and jellabahed men turn *into* salesmen, holding up clutches of eggs, bouquets of wild flowers, and, near the muddy Oum er Rebia, catches of fish skewered on sticks. But these are the unchosen few who lack the gift of doing absolutely nothing, the majority being asleep or seated, legs akimbo, by the roadside. It is this inertness, in fact, which makes our driver's feat in capturing a wasp with his hands— actually tweaking its wings—seem the more remarkable.

But no sooner do we reach the palm oasis of Marrakech, with its kilometers of medieval walls, and settle in the brass-cuspidor hotel (a swimming pool, though, where Woman is displaying a lot more Lib) than we feel the emptiness at the center more acutely than ever. "I want to be near him," V. says, and she asks for airplane schedules and makes plans to return to Venice.

Ira comes at six. She is tall and sharp-featured and her family resemblance to I.S. is evident only in her quick brown eyes. She is a handsome woman,

1971

---

1. She died September 11, 1971. See the obituary by Cecil Beaton, *The Times* (London), September 30, 1971.

strikingly dressed in red turban, sweater, Spahi pants, gold Moorish brace-lets. But both she and V. are nervous, even tremulous, and the meeting is stiff. I go, meanwhile, for a walk in the gardens, but the gravel paths and the trees remind me of San Michele.

Averroes lived here, perhaps walked near these same ramparts. But all I can remember about him, and that vaguely, is his argument for the validity of alternative modes of access to truth; and his defense of the right to coexistence of conflicting truths. Which seems reasonable enough now, at least to one who believes in "permanent" musical and poetic truths, highly adjustable scientific truths, and modal philosophical working hypotheses; and who thinks, in the first place, that the answer to Jesting Pilate is a circumstantial formulation of a culture and an age. In other words, *not* "revealed" truth. But why not? That is also a cultural mode. Why am I intellectually intolerant of "revealed" religion as fact, for I have the feeling but lack the belief? And intolerant of dogma, though nonetheless dogmatic concerning what I don't know about it?

And for that matter, why these outpourings, why this soliloquy, why these particular questions? Because I have been more deeply shaken than ever before in my life, and because I am surprised—naïvely surprised, perhaps— to find that the arts, science, and philosophy are no succor at all, that the only help is to be found in other human beings. The change in me is that I am at least prepared to believe that other modes exist. V. has received word that Gerald Heard,[1] who for some time has been semi-paralyzed and mute, became very agitated the night of April 5-6, and about three hours before I.S. died began talking to him.

We eat in the hotel, where the headwaiter—whom I quickly recognize and greet, having an infallible memory for waiters, taxi drivers, and all "menials," and being infinitely less well-bred than V., who was taught to take no notice of her "surroundings"—is from the Royale in Evian. At sundown the sky turns indigo, the olive trees silver, the palms dark green, and the mountains (below the snow line) pure purple. The hum of nesting swallows now fills the jasmine-sweet air and, after a signal of distant cock crows, the night itself begins to snore in and out, like a concertina.

APRIL 20

We go to dinner at the Bellines. (Ira lives with her brother, Ganya, a man so startlingly "Russian" in appearance—Tolstoy nose, "Russian" goatee, old-fashioned silver-rimmed "Russian" spectacles—that he might have been made up for a part in Chekhov.) It is a twenty-minute trip from the Mamounia, in our one-camel-power taxi, not including a skirmish, on arrival, with the dogs. For the house is guarded by no fewer than ten of the world's

1. Died August 14, 1971.

420

most vociferous canines; they bark in concert throughout the evening, then suddenly fall silent when we leave, though not for that reason, surely, but because they are hoarse.

If the atmosphere of the house, which was once owned by a granddaughter of Tolstoy, is "Russian," that impression is not primarily owing to the Bellines themselves, or even to the many mementos of the Diaghilev Ballet. It is, rather, in a similarity between a way of life sustained by Arab fellaheen and one sustained by Russian peasants, the peasants of I.S.'s creations. (The principal *domestiques* in the Stravinsky household during I.S.'s own youth were Tartars, *i.e.,* Muslims.)

As if reading my thoughts, Ira tells a story remarkably akin to the world of *Les Noces*. It seems that when her Arab houseboy announced his forthcoming marriage, she unthinkingly asked a question about his betrothed, which obliged him to confess he had never seen her and that the wedding had been arranged by his mother. Ira's wedding present was a brass bedstead, which she found, at the ceremony, in the center of the one-room shack, with about twenty veiled women seated on the floor around it. The bride sat in a corner, swaddled in white from head to toe. . . . Then, when the marriage had been consummated, the sheet, proof of previous *hymen intactus,* was held up for the inspection of the twenty women. Ira says that the bride is fifteen now, has two children, and, in fact, prepared tonight's couscous, which I think has cauterized my tongue.

Ira lived in Ustilug during I.S.'s last summers there, but was too young to remember much about him. Her recollections of him in Morges in 1919, when her family reached Switzerland after a six-month trek fleeing the Bolsheviks, are more vivid. But she remembers him better as a worried investor in the Château Basque, her family's restaurant in Biarritz;[1] and best of all when he first met V.: "Your Russian friends called you 'Verinka,' then, but Uncle called you 'Verusha.'" I hardly listen, however, being distracted by a lizard on the wall devouring a moth, whose rescue I fail to attempt only partly out of respect for the ecological balance. (In truth, I conduct a careful search of my room later for other lacertilians, scorpions, millipedes, etc.)

Returning to the Mamounia—same one-camel-power taxi—V. is bursting to describe the evening to I.S. and missing him more than ever.

1971

---

1. July 25, 1971. Biarritz has changed virtually beyond V.'s recognition, the "bastard Tudor" Basque style of black-and-white timbering almost having disappeared in the mess of new buildings—though *not* the Basque language, which looks, on road signs, somewhat like IBM's "magnetic writing." The Russian Church, facing the Hôtel du Palais on the rue de Russie, is surprisingly large, and whatever the Russian population may have dwindled to now, it must have been considerable in the time of the grand dukes, and of I.S. When we enter the Palais—an unsuccessfully enlarged and updated relic of Eugénie—the *maître d'hôtel* informs V. that he "knew Monsieur Stravinsky and Monsieur Diaghilev in the twenties." Then when she walks away he whispers to me: *"Je crois que Monsieur et Madame n'étaient pas encore mariés en ce moment."* Which says something about the French memory.

421

A sandstorm blows over the oasis, followed by violent rains.

We eat Moroccan-style, beginning with *harira* (a soup), then a fish—succulent but viscous to touch, and *everything* here is eaten with the fingers—then a sugar-and-cinnamon pancake dunked in a bowl of orange juice and milk. The waiters wear tarbooshes and babouches, and white jackets and white *serwaks,* which are pleated, ankle-length bloomers. Their trays are covered with conical wicker lids, to keep the food warm in transit. And to keep us from smelling fishy, in *ditto,* perfume is squirted in our cupped hands at the end of the meal, from what look like silver syringes.

APRIL 22

The *souks* and the Jemaa el Fna are muddy from yesterday's rain; which reminds Ira of Ustilug, and me of I.S. talking about the mud there (with anything but *"nostalgie de la boue"*). Mere mud, however, does not interfere with the storytellers, the scriveners, the mullahs and holy men reading from the Koran, the barbecuers, teeth-pullers, water vendors, and snake charmers, all of whom live in the open air. Whether charmed or not, one of the snakes squirms very actively when suspended by the tail, but seems to suffer stage fright the moment it is set down.

The *souks* are mazes of narrow alleys roofed with rushes and dense with animals and people—on bicycles and motorcycles, as well as on foot. We visit carpet stalls and caftan stalls (silk, satin, nylon); wool dyers and leather tanners; a saddlery; metal embossers; spice and herb merchants (baskets of freshly picked mint); and fruit and vegetable *charrettes.* But "colorful" and "exotic" as it all is, one sight haunts me the rest of the day, that of a line of thirteen blind, ragged, barefoot, and no doubt diseased and consumptive beggars chanting "Allah is good," over and over, as they tap the ground with their white canes and hold out cups for alms. "Then let Allah give," a blasphemous boy jibes at them, himself a beggar, asking Ira for a groat, or a *dirham,* but being effectively shooed away by whatever she says to him in the demotic. Nor can I forget the sight of an old man displaying a few pieces of candy on a dirty handkerchief. *"On vend ce qu'on peut,"* Ira says, truly enough—though that is hardly the point.

1971

APRIL 23

The Evian waiter tells us that whereas the poor are still imprisoned for infractions of Ramadan, the King has a harem of one hundred and fifty—but my uppermost feeling about the latter part of the statement is more one of envy than of moral righteousness.

We drive to Ourika, in an Atlas pass, seeing several Berber casbahs on the way. The Berber women dress more colorfully than the women of

Marrakech, and are not veiled, but apparently still do all the work from swinging scythes to turning waterwheels.

Casablanca. A dirty city, and noisy, with radio music blaring in the streets from loudspeakers. The red fez is less popular here than the gray or black, and the turbans resemble bandages after skull surgery. Face-curtains are fewer, too, though we see girls on motorcycles wearing them. Are these veils exploited in the Venetian-masquerade sense, I wonder, as well as in the sense that probably many a disguise does not contain a blessing?

Casablanca to Rome. We leave for one of the two airports at 5 AM because of uncertainty as to which one handles our flight, and the fear that it will take a long time to go to the other. As it happens, the extra time is needed because of sheep and camels on the road, and because of the rigmarole of document stamping, taxpaying, customs declaring, and multiple inspecting of passports. Finally, we are airborne for about ten minutes, before landing— over a muddy, meandering river—at Rabat, where everyone is obliged to leave the plane with all baggage for another infinite wait, then hurry aboard again. (André Chénier's father, French Consul in the eighteenth century, described life here as a succession of inconveniences.) We fly on white clouds to the Mediterranean, like a sleigh ride.

Rome. We have come to ask Manzù to choose a stone and to carve the name and a cross that I.S. himself once drew for Giacometti.

Dinner at Passetto's with Berman, who reminisces about I.S. on a trip to Naples in 1959.

1971

The ride over the Apennines from Florence to Venice reminds us of an excursion with I.S. to Canossa, site of Ghibelline Henry's three barefoot nights in the snow (surely with chilblains, at least?). We were driving to Milan the day after a concert in Bologna (October 21, 1959), when I.S. expressed a desire to see the ruins; and accordingly we bumped up a steep mountain road for two hours before reaching the remains of the grim, fairy-story castle.

In Venice V. hears herself referred to for the first time, with a small jolt, as *"la vedova Stravinsky."* And the Royal Suite at the Gritti—beamed and coffered ceilings, baldachined and sparvered bed, canopied bath—reminds her sadly of I.S.'s return to Paris from his first American tour. "He cabled from the boat asking me to reserve the most luxurious suite in the Grand Hotel for a few days; which I did, but without seeing it. It was decorated in a *nouveau-riche* style which so shocked Diaghilev that he was upset for days wondering what could have happened to Stravinsky in America."

And so we go again to San Michele, past Santi Giovanni e Paolo, where the poster—*"La Città di Venezia . . . del Grande Musicista IGOR STRA-VINSKY"*—is still on the door; and past the Mendicanti, once renowned for its girl orchestra (admired by Goethe), but as neglected and impoverished now as the people—"Blessed are the poor"—it was meant to comfort. And again into the lagoon, silent and empty today. And again to the walled isle of cypresses and of the dead. Again, too, we pass beneath St. Michael's pointed arch, a wind now blowing his rusty iron balances—so much for weights and measures—this way and that. And again pass through the Convento, a solarium at this hour for a lazing tribe of cats. (I.S. would have spoken to them and picked one of them up by the scruff; when the *Gazzettino* published a photograph of him after the funeral, it was *not* one of him conducting in San Marco, but one showing him feeding cats.)

And again we follow the path to the Orthodox section, where lilacs and oleander are in bloom, and it is full springtime except for the man who created a spring of his own that of all mortally begotten versions will give Nature its longest run for everlasting joy. And again we walk to the chapel, the vined wall, and the iron gate, ajar today, framing a *veduta* of the lagoon.

The moment has come, too, when we must raise our eyes toward the mound of newly turned earth, which is exactly where we know it will be, of course, the most cruelly certain of all places in our memories. It is covered with flowers, like Rakewell's springtime grave; but the new earth is terrible to see, and terrible the bedlike form of the mound. V. weeps, laying her flowers on his head, and turns away. (Does she think of an afternoon long ago when, finding *her* fast asleep, he composed that most beautiful of all *berceuses* for her, Perséphone's *"Sur ce lit elle repose"*? And of that afternoon only a month ago when, instead of his name, he wrote "Oh, how I love you!") But three times, as she walks slowly toward the gate, she is stopped and asked if she knows the direction—for it is already venerated ground—"to Stravinsky's grave."

My turn to turn away comes when I notice the word "Strasvischi" scrawled beneath the "36" on the marker; for it is exactly what I.S., in one of his ironies, might have invented himself so short a time ago. In fact, it is impossible not to see and hear him saying it now, just as it is impossible to believe that the man whose immortal celebration of the resurrection of Nature, and all his other continuations of the highest humanizing art of man, lies beneath that mound of earth. Yet it is not *that* man we mourn, but the old, ill, frail, skin-and-bones one who was still so wonderfully alive. And it is that ill and frail *old* man I miss so much, miss more than I ever thought it was possible to miss anybody.

And again we leave. But will be back soon. And soon permanently, when my promise to him is fulfilled (if it should be V. first). And another promise, my own and unasked for, and I am somewhere nearby.

1971

Indexes

Index
of Stravinsky works
mentioned in the text

iii

General Index

A NOTE ON THE TYPE

The text of this book was set in a face called Times Roman, designed by Stanley Morison for *The Times* (London) and first introduced by that newspaper in 1932.

Among typographers and designers of the twentieth century, Stanley Morison has been a strong forming influence, as typographical adviser to the English Monotype Corporation, as a director of two distinguished English publishing houses, and as a writer of sensibility, erudition, and keen practical sense.

Composed by York Graphic Services, York, Pennsylvania. Printed and bound by The Haddon Craftsmen, Scranton, Pennsylvania.

Typography and binding design by CLINT ANGLIN.